The Quark XPress 4 Book

for Macintosh and Windows

by David Blatner

PEACHPIT
PRESS

A PARALLAX
PRODUCTION

The QuarkXPress 4 Book

by David Blatner

Peachpit Press
1249 Eighth Street
Berkeley, CA 94710
800 / 283-9444
510 / 524-2178
510 / 524-2221 (fax)

Find us on the World Wide Web at: http://www.peachpit.com
Peachpit Press is a division of Addison Wesley Longman

Cover design: TMA Ted Mader Associates, Inc.
Interior design and production: Parallax Productions

Permissions

The following photographs were used with permission of Special Collections Division, University of Washington Libraries. Figure 10-22 on page 596, photo by Todd, negative no. 10511; figure 10-7 on page 574, photo by A. Curtis, negative no. 4103.

Notice of Rights

Notice of Liability

The information in this book is distributed on an "As Is" basis, without warranty. While every precaution has been taken in the preparation of the book, neither the author nor Peachpit Press, shall have any liability to any person or entity with respect to any loss or damage caused or alleged to be caused directly or indirectly by the instructions contained in this book or by the computer software and hardware products described in it.

Trademarks

Throughout this book trademarked names are used. Rather than put a trademark symbol in every occurrence of a trademarked name, we state we are using the names only in an editorial fashion and to the benefit of the trademark owner with no intention of infringement of the trademark. Nonetheless, we will state flat out that Quark, QuarkXPress, QuarkXTensions, Quark Publishing System, QPS, QuarkImmedia, and XTensions are all trademarks of Quark, Inc.

ISBN 0-201-69695-9
9 8 7 6 5 4 3 2
Printed and bound in the United States of America

foreword

QUARK XPRESS SECRETS

▼▼

No sane person introduces a desktop application and expects it to become essential to an entire industry. For that kind of dreaming you would need to ingest much more than soda pop and pizza, the two basic food groups that fueled the development of QuarkXPress 1.0 back in 1987. We hoped you'd like it. We didn't want to fail. Little did we know you wouldn't let us.

Today almost everything you read in print was produced with QuarkXPress, from the newspaper that hits your front porch in the morning to the menu at your favorite restaurant at night. Within major publishing organizations, QuarkXPress has served as a catalyst to greater efficiency, overshadowing the power of the old, expensive, dedicated high-end systems once used to put words and designs on paper. To smaller publishing entities and to individuals, QuarkXPress gives the ability to produce professional, expensive-looking publications at relatively low cost. QuarkXPress is an elite tool, good enough for the biggest and best—but it is also a democratic one, because you don't have to be the biggest and best to afford it.

Since 1987 we've put away a lot of pizza and soda, enough to get us to QuarkXPress 4.0. Along the way, our users have acted as our not-so-silent partners in the development of successive versions of the product, letting us know what we did right and what we did wrong, and often urging us to hurry up. Many of our users have become QuarkXPress experts and a few, like David Blatner, have become expert QuarkXPress authors.

With the release of QuarkXPress 4.0, we have simplified the production workflow, provided a number of powerful tools, and rewritten hundreds of thousands of lines of code to offer you the best QuarkXPress product to date—and we've done a pretty good job with updating our documentation, too.

But the fact is that the official documentation will only take you so far, and is not meant to go into the kind of detail that David Blatner achieves with this edition of *The QuarkXPress 4 Book*.

Back in 1990, when David first asked me to write a foreword for the first edition of *The QuarkXPress Book*, I thought, "Yeah, sure. I'll write something lukewarm that says how nice the book is, and that it is a great addition to your library." Then I read it. It is more than a good book about QuarkXPress. It is a great book. Subsequent editions have proved worthy of their predecessor, always providing up-to-the minute information on all the new functionality in QuarkXPress, including many undocumented tips and tricks that let you get the most from the program.

This edition of *The QuarkXPress Book* is the first to be tri-platform, including information specific to Macintosh, Windows, and Alpha NT users of QuarkXPress. David has also added an important new chapter called *Going Online with QuarkXPress*, which addresses the increasingly important issue of how best to get your QuarkXPress documents onto the Web in HTML, Acrobat PDF, and QuarkImmedia formats. He has also added chapters addressing such significant new QuarkXPress 4.0 features related to drawing tools and long documents. And of course David Blatner can always be counted on to provide an assortment of tips and tricks that could save you time enough to enjoy another slice of pizza and another soda. (Speaking of which, I need to cut this note short and get back to programming. QuarkXPress 5.0, you know . . . .)

If you're thinking of buying this book, take it on up to the cash register and do it. Go ahead. You'll feel better and you'll probably work more efficiently, too. No matter what your level of expertise, there's something in *The QuarkXPress Book* for you, and over time it will prove to be one of the most useful QuarkXPress-related books that you own.

Tim Gill
Founder and
Chief Technology Officer
Quark, Inc.

preface

THE
AMAZON
EXPLORERS

▼ ▼

"You're doing what?"

"We've got one QuarkXPress document here to print the borders for each page, and then in this other document we have all the text in galleys. We tried to put them together, but because we don't know the program well enough, it's faster just to use our production people for pasteup."

"If you're just going to paste it up, why are you using QuarkXPress at all?"

"A consultant suggested we buy a computer and QuarkXPress. But we haven't had a chance to really learn it. Besides, QuarkXPress lets us make really good borders."

It was a story I had heard before. Designers, ad agencies, small and large businesses continue to buy computers and copies of QuarkXPress with the idea that everything was going to be easier, faster, and cooler. All that can be true, but let's face it: QuarkXPress is not a magical solution. Desktop publishing requires knowledge, experience, and expertise.

It seems there is a need for a consultant who not only knows the computer and graphic design, but also one who can sit there, patiently, and—at 11 PM—walk with you through building a better registration mark, making a drop cap, or explaining how master pages work. All for a low-cost flat fee. That consultant is this book.

▼ ▼

The Early Days

But how did this book come to be? What possessed me to write over 250,000 words on a piece of computer software? Let's start at the beginning of my QuarkXPress story.

The early days of desktop publishing were much simpler than they are now. When a new program came out, we publishers asked some basic, hard-hitting questions.

- ▶ Can you put text on a page?

- ▶ Can you put graphics on a page?

- ▶ Does the page print?

Once we had a satisfactory answer to those three questions, we could get down to brass tacks, ripping it to pieces to make it do all the things it wasn't designed to do. It was a wild time, much like trudging through the Amazon forests with only a machete and a match.

To be blunt, I'm not ordinarily the quiet type. So it is telling that, when I saw the first copy of QuarkXPress 1.0, all I could say was, "Wow." Here was, at last, a program to use instead of PageMaker. No more eyeballing the measurements, no more relying on built-in algorithms. Those were the days of PageMaker 1.2, and QuarkXPress was a glimmer of hope in the dark ages.

But it was the beginning of the Macintosh Way, and I was so gung-ho on not acting like an IBM-PC user that I would do almost anything not to look in the manuals. Even if I had wanted to peek every once in a while, peer pressure was stiff. No, I had to play by the rules and learn QuarkXPress the hard way.

Perhaps all those years of system crashes and blank pages coming out of the printer paid off. While frequenting cocktail parties, I can blithely hint at the magnificent techniques I've come upon for using QuarkXPress in a networked environment. My friends and family are amazed as I stand tall, knowing which menu to pull down to create style sheets. But is it really enough?

Making Pages

Even more important than fancy party talk has been the ability to use all my QuarkXPress tips and tricks to make good-looking pages quickly and efficiently. And back in 1990, I knew it was finally time to put finger to keyboard and get this information out to you, the real-world users of QuarkXPress. To find even more tips, tricks, and techniques for QuarkXPress users, I searched the online systems, looked through back issues of computer magazines, and even resorted to books on other Macintosh software.

I've continued that search for the last eight years, squirreling away every trick and tip I could find, storing them up for the next edition, or the one after that. Everything I've collected, right up to the time I made PostScript dumps of this edition, I have managed to squeeze into this book and The QuarkXPress Book Web Site (more on the Web site soon).

But books full of tips and tricks tell just half the story. And I think the simple menu-by-menu approach that most computer books use deserves the phrase "tastes filling, less great!" I knew there should be much more.

So I sat down and listed all the ways in which I use QuarkXPress in my work: books, magazines, newsletters, flyers, and brochures. The most striking thing I found was that I rarely used QuarkXPress by itself. Macromedia FreeHand, Adobe Illustrator, PostScript programming, Microsoft Word, Adobe Photoshop, and numerous system extensions and utilities all play a large part in my publishing process. I figured that if I wasn't publishing in a vacuum, you probably weren't either. So I gathered up information about using those programs in conjunction with QuarkXPress.

My idea was to roll together tips and tricks, a full overview of the program, and in-depth discussions of core concepts behind using QuarkXPress in the real world. So, I've included discussions on fonts, PostScript printing, color models, and much more, alongside examples of how I've been using QuarkXPress for the past eleven years. I also describe the way QuarkXPress operates and how to take advantage of its sometimes strange methods.

Of course, this is a lot of information for a single book. But what did you shell out $34.95 for? Chopped liver? No, this book is meant not only to be read, but to be used. I wanted to include a Post-It pad so you could mark the pages you'll use the most, but it didn't work out. Don't let that stop you, though.

▼ ▼

About this Book

Although I expect you to know the basics of using a Macintosh or Microsoft Windows (moving the mouse, pulling down menus, and so on), I have purposely taken a wide spectrum of potential readers into account, from off-the-shelf beginners to seasoned professionals. I did this because I've found that those seasoned professionals are delighted to learn new tricks, techniques, and concepts, and people who have used computers very little sometimes surprise me with their intuitive grasp of the Big Picture.

Remember, this book was written for you. It's designed to work for you—as your personal consultant—whoever you are. It's also designed to help you get a sure footing on a sometimes uneven path and to help you make pages like the pros.

Organization

I have organized this book to reflect what I think QuarkXPress is all about: producing final camera-ready output from your computer. So I start with an overview of the program, move on to building a structure for the document, then discuss the basics—such as putting text and pictures on a page. Next I move into some fine-tuning aspects of QuarkXPress, and finally to printing. And, because so many people now must output their files both to paper and to the Internet, I have also included a chapter on Web publishing. That's the speed-reading run-down; now here's a play-by-play of the chapters.

▶ **INTRODUCTION.** In the Introduction, I lay out QuarkXPress on the table, telling you what it is and what it does. I also run down each of the new features in version 4.

► **CHAPTER 1: LEARN QUARKXPRESS IN 30 MINUTES.** One of the most frequently-asked-for additions to this book has been a step-by-step beginner's guide to learning QuarkXPress. If you're brand new to QuarkXPress, this chapter, which takes a visual approach to learning the program, should be perfect for you.

► **CHAPTER 2: QUARKXPRESS BASICS.** The first step in understanding QuarkXPress is learning about its structure from the ground up. This involves an investigation of QuarkXPress's menus, palettes, and dialog boxes. Even advanced users tell me they find features and techniques in this chapter that they never knew.

► **CHAPTER 3: TOOLS OF THE TRADE.** Every vocation has its tools, and we desktop publishers are no different. This chapter offers an in-depth study of each tool in QuarkXPress's Tool palette, how to use it, and why. All the new Bézier drawing tools are included here, plus descriptions of libraries, custom line styles, grouping, and alignment controls.

► **CHAPTER 4: BUILDING A DOCUMENT.** Without a sturdy foundation, your document won't be reliable or flexible when you need it to be. This chapter discusses the basics of making earthquake-proof infrastructures for your pages: opening a new document, creating master pages, and setting up column guides and linking for text flow.

► **CHAPTER 5: WORD PROCESSING.** If you wanted a drawing program, you would have bought one. Words are what most people use QuarkXPress for, and this chapter is where words start. I talk here about simple text input, working with word processors, the Find/Change feature, and checking spelling.

► **CHAPTER 6: TYPE AND TYPOGRAPHY.** Once you've got those words in the computer, what do you do with them? Chapter 6 discusses the details of formatting text into type—fonts, sizes, styles, indents, drop caps—all the things that turn text into type.

► **CHAPTER 7: COPY FLOW.** You bought the computer, so why not let it do the work for you? This chapter explains how to use style sheets and XPress Tags to automate aspects of copy processing, and how to use importing and exporting effectively.

▶ **CHAPTER 8: LONG DOCUMENTS.** QuarkXPress 4 introduces three major features that help you when working with long documents: lists, indexes, and the Book palette. Here, I discuss each of these in detail and offer suggestions for how to use them effectively.

▶ **CHAPTER 9: PICTURES.** Who reads text anymore? I like to look at the pictures. And pictures are what Chapter 9 is all about. I discuss every relevant graphics file format and how to work with each in your documents. I also cover rotating, skewing, and other manipulations of images.

▶ **CHAPTER 10: FINE-TUNING IMAGES.** Here's where a good eye can help you improve a bitmapped image, and a creative eye can help you make those graphics do flips. In this chapter I look at brightness, contrast, gamma correction, and halftoning for bitmapped images such as scans. I also explore XPress 4's new clipping feature and how it works with TIFF images.

▶ **CHAPTER 11: WHERE TEXT MEETS GRAPHICS.** This is the frontier-land: the border between the two well-discussed worlds of type and pictures. Life gets different on the edge, and in this chapter I discuss how to handle it with grace—using inline boxes, paragraph rules, and the new text runaround features.

▶ **CHAPTER 12: COLOR.** QuarkXPress is well-known for its powerful color capabilities. Chapter 12 covers color models, building a custom color palette, applying colors, and the first steps in understanding color separation.

▶ **CHAPTER 13: PRINTING.** This chapter is where everything I've talked about is leading: getting your document out of the machine and onto film or paper. In this chapter I cover every step of printing, including the details of every feature in the new expanded Print dialog box. I also discuss the finer points of working with service bureaus and how to troubleshoot your print job.

▶ **CHAPTER 14: GOING ONLINE WITH QUARKXPRESS.** Sometimes it seems like your job description changes over a weekend, doesn't it? If you've got XPress documents that you need to get onto the

Internet, you need this chapter. I discuss options for exporting to HTML, Acrobat PDF files, and QuarkImmedia projects.

▶ **APPENDIX A: COLOR MANAGEMENT.** For years, QuarkXPress has used the EfiColor color management system to improve the correspondence between colors on screen, on color printer output, and on printed results from offset printing. Now it's been completely replaced by the QuarkCMS XTension, which is covered in detail in this appendix.

▶ **APPENDIX B: MACINTOSH VS. WINDOWS.** More and more people are using QuarkXPress in a cross-platform environment. In Appendix B, I explore the ins and outs of moving files between the two programs and operating systems.

▶ **APPENDIX C: XTENSIONS AND RESOURCES.** Where do you go when QuarkXPress isn't doing what you want? This appendix offers suggestions for many popular XTensions, as well as both print and Web-based resources you should know about.

▶ **APPENDIX D: SCRIPTING.** Although AppleEvent scripting has appeared in the press a lot, people don't really know what to make of it. In Appendix D, I cover the wild world of scripting QuarkXPress using AppleScript on the Macintosh. Don't worry, I'm not really a programmer myself; if *I* can understand this stuff, so can you.

▶ **APPENDIX E: XPRESS TAGS.** If you use XPress Tags (which I dicuss in Chapter 7, *Copy Flow*), you will no doubt need a reference to the many obscure and arcane codes. I've laid them all out for you here.

▶ **APPENDIX F: ANSI CODES.** In order to type certain special characters in QuarkXPress for Windows, you need to know each character's ANSI code. I'm forever forgetting them, so I built a list of them, which I've included here.

Finding What You Need

There are many ways to read this book. First, there's the cover-to-cover approach. This is the best way to get every morsel I have included. On the other hand, that method doesn't seem to work for some people. As I said, this book is meant to be used, right off the shelf, no batteries required.

I've done everything in my power to make it easy to find topics throughout this book. However, there's so much information that sometimes you might not know where to look. The table of contents breaks each chapter down into first- and second-level headings, so you can jump to a particular topic fast.

If you are primarily looking for the new version-4 features, you should take a look at the description of new features in the Introduction. That will also tell you where in the book I describe the feature fully.

Finally, if you can't find what you're looking for, or are trying to find an explanation for a single concept, try the index.

Faith

Just to be honest with you, there's almost no way to explain one feature in QuarkXPress without explaining all the rest at the same time. But that would make for a pretty confusing book. Instead, I'm asking you to take minor leaps of faith along the path of reading these chapters. If I mention a term or function you don't understand, trust me that I'll explain it all in due time. If you are able to do that, you will find that what I am discussing all makes sense. For example, I'm not going to talk about the details of creating a new document until the fourth chapter, *Building a Document*, even though I need to talk about working with documents in Chapter 2, *QuarkXPress Basics*.

A Tri-Platform Book

Every previous edition of *The QuarkXPress Book* has been specifically written for either the Macintosh or Windows platform. That distinction has now been removed. In fact, I like to think of this as a tri-platform book, because I currently use Macintosh, Windows, and Windows NT for the Digital Alpha.

It was relatively easy to merge the two platform-specific editions of the book because almost every feature in QuarkXPress is identical between the Macintosh and Windows versions. However, where the two are different—for instance the features that rely heavily on the operating system, such as fonts, graphic file formats, and printing—I've specifically made mention of it in the text. (Also, if you primarily use QuarkXPress for Windows, see the one-page *A Word to Windows Users*, on page xxxiv.)

▼ ▼

The QuarkXPress Book Web Site

No book is big enough to cover the many facets of QuarkXPress anymore, and even if it could, the technology changes much more quickly than writers like me can update our books. Similarly, some publishers have taken to adding CD-ROMs in the back of their books in order to provide additional material. Unfortunately, the discs become obsolete almost immediately. To counter both of these problems, I've built The QuarkXPress Book Web Site, which should simply be considered an extension of this printed book: *www.peachpit.com/blatner/*

The Web site has all sorts of stuff that I think you'll find interesting.

▶ **FREQUENTLY ASKED QUESTIONS.** I've spent a great deal of time analyzing the questions XPress users have posted on the Internet, in magazines, to Quark's technical support, and in e-mail to me. The surprising thing is that while everyone uses XPress differently, and for different purposes, almost everyone asks the same kinds of questions. I've compiled answers to these questions and posted them on the site. When you run into trouble, look for an answer in this book first, and if you can't find one, check out the FAQ area on the Web site.

▶ **BOOK UPDATES.** Probably the only thing more frustrating than being a computer book writer, like me, is being a computer book reader, like you. The reason: each month the software keeps changing, new XTensions are released, bugs are fixed (sometimes even bugs that I thought were features) . . . . Fortunately, you can now read about these sorts of updates quickly in the Updates section of the Web site.

▶ **TIPS AND TRICKS.** Ask any of my friends and you'll find out that I *love* tips and tricks. I've got so many little workarounds, special techniques, and undocumented "features" that there was no way to fit them all in the book. Check out the many tips and tricks (or contribute one of your own) in the Tips & Tricks section of the Web site.

▶ **FREE SOFTWARE.** I've compiled a number of XTensions and utilities that I think are important for people to know about and use, and they are available on the Web site. I've even worked out some deals with developers so that you can download and use their commercial software for free (all because you own this book).

▶ **RESOURCES.** Finally, I would be lying if I told you that The QuarkXPress Book Web Site was the end-all and be-all for information on QuarkXPress. No way. Therefore, I offer lists of the many other resources on the Internet and in print that you should be aware of.

Note that you must own this book in order to get access to The QuarkXPress Book Web Site. (It's password-protected, and the password is hidden inside these pages, so make sure you have your book on hand when accessing the site.)

▼ ▼

Acknowledgments

No book is an island. So many people have directly and indirectly contributed to this book's production that I would have to publish a second volume to thank them all. I do want to thank a few people directly, however.

Behind the scenes. Several other writers have worked on pieces of this book. Specifically, Keith Stimely and Eric Taub contributed significantly to earlier editions. And in this edition, Sandee Cohen and Phil Gaskill were instrumental in piecing together the sections on the Bézier drawing tools, word processing, XPress Tags, and the beginning step-by-step lessons in Chapter 1. Bob Weibel was my coauthor on the original Windows edition of *The QuarkXPress Book*, and helped as a technical editor of portions of this edition. Bruce Fraser, my coauthor on *Real World Photoshop*, also provided technical editing and reality checks.

The infrastructure makes it great. A great thanks to the people at Quark who not only put out a great product, but also worked with me to get this book out to you with as much information in it as I've got. In particular, Tim Gill, Amy Snetzler, Fred Ebrahimi, Don Lohse, Lori Mercier,

Richard Jones, Terri Ficke, Elizabeth Jones, Susie Friedman, Bob Monzel, Kristine McInvaille, Parviz Banki, David Allen, Shawn McLaughlin, Chris Cole, Ed Owens, and Kathleen "hold on, I'll check" Erramouspe. A special thanks to Quark's technical support staff, who have been a great support in so many ways, including Kevin Dormeyer, Steve Musgrove, Pamela Farmer, Jan Klimper, and Nicola Donaven.

Other folks: Mark Niemann-Ross, Ralph Risch, Myke Ninness, and Dave Shaver at Extensis Corporation; Cyndie Shaffstall of the World Wide Power Company and the XChange; Doug Peltonen of Luminous; Scotty Carreiro at Point of Presence Company; Robert Farquhar at Digital Corporation; William Buckingham, former ally at the XChange; Jay Nelson at Design Tools Monthly; Robb Kerr of Digital Iguana; Steve Werner; Diane Burns; John Cruise; Leonard Mazerov; and Sal Soghoian of Apple Computer.

And many thanks go to all the people who wrote, called, and e-mailed me their comments and suggestions. I've tried to incorporate their ideas into this fifth edition.

The People Who Made This Book

Throughout the process of developing this edition, I have been surrounded and supported by quality people, including Steve Roth, who edited all previous editions of this book. Cindy Bell of Design Language, Kris Fulsaas, and Agen Schmitz were excellent in making sure my t's were dotted and i's crossed, and—most of all—making sure that I didn't sound like a fool. Also important have been Glenn "industry pundit" Fleishman and Jeff Carlson of Never Enough Coffee Creations.

I want to thank my publisher, Nancy Ruenzel, and my editor at Peachpit, Nancy Davis. In fact, everyone at Peachpit has been great, including Cary Norsworthy, Amy Changar, Keasley Jones, Gary-Paul Prince, Hannah Latham, Trish Booth, and Mimi Heft. Special appreciation also goes to Ted Nace, the original publisher at Peachpit—I gave it the wings, but he made it fly.

Much appreciation and astonishment goes toward my officemates, Olav Martin Kvern, Don Sellers, and all the folks at Thunder Lizard Productions, including Steve Broback, Sondra Wells, Brett Baker, Krista Carreiro, Lynn Warner, and Dom Prandini. And to Semantic Spaces and Lisa Gerrard, who's sounds helped make the pages fly.

And, finally, there are those people even further behind the scenes who helped along the road. Vincent Dorn at LaserWrite in Palo Alto, who said, "Hey, let's go to Burger King." Steve Herold at LaserGraphics in Seattle, who said, "Meet Steve Roth." All my parents, Debbie Carlson, Alisa and Paul Piette, Suzanne Carlson and Mark Wachter, and other friends who were such a support over the past few decades. It wouldn't have happened without you.

Thanks.

David Blatner
Seattle, Washington

OVERVIEW

▼ ▼

CONTENTS

▼ ▼

▼ ▼

Introduction **QuarkXPress: The Big Picture** 1

▼ ▼

Chapter 1 **Learn QuarkXPress in 30 Minutes** 13

▼ ▼

▼ ▼

Chapter 3   **Tools of the Trade** 117

▼ ▼

Chapter 5   **Word Processing** 265

▼ ▼

Chapter 6   Type and Typography

▼ ▼

Chapter 8 **Long Documents**

▼ ▼

Chapter 9   Pictures

▼ ▼

Chapter 10   Fine-Tuning Images

Chapter 11   Where Text Meets Graphics 603

Chapter 12   Color 633

▼ ▼

Chapter 13   Printing

▼ ▼

Chapter 14 Going Online with QuarkXPress

▼ ▼

▼ ▼

▼ ▼

▼ ▼

Appendix D Scripting 859

▼ ▼

Appendix E XPress Tags 881

▼ ▼

Appendix F ANSI Codes 887

▼ ▼

Index 893

A WORD TO
WINDOWS USERS

▼ ▼

This book covers tips and techniques for both the Macintosh and Windows versions of QuarkXPress. However, I've chosen to illustrate dialog boxes, menus, and palettes using screen shots from the Macintosh version. Similarly, when discussing the many keyboard shortcuts in the program, I include the Macintosh versions. I apologize to all Windows users, but because the interface between the two platforms is so transparent, I picked one platform and ran with it.

As for keystrokes, in almost every case the Command key on the Macintosh translates to the Control key in Windows, and the Option key translates to the Alt key. In the few cases where this is not true, I've included both the Macintosh and the Windows versions.

QuarkXPress: The Big Picture

Trying to figure out what type of program QuarkXPress is reminds me of a scene from an old *Saturday Night Live* episode, when a couple bickered over their new purchase. "It's a floor wax," said one. "No, it's a dessert topping," replied the other. The answer soon became clear: "It's a floor wax *and* a dessert topping." QuarkXPress is a program with the same predicament. Some people insist it's a typesetting application. Others bet their bottom dollar that it's a high-end word processor. Still others make QuarkXPress a way of life.

The truth is that QuarkXPress is all these things, and more. However, no matter how you use it, it is never more than a tool. And a tool is never more than the person behind it.

I like to think of machetes. You can use a machete as an exotic knife to cut a block of cheese. Or, you can use it as your only means of survival while hacking through the Amazon jungles. It's all up to you.

Here in the Introduction, I talk about the big picture: QuarkXPress and how it fits into the world of desktop publishing. I also talk about the new QuarkXPress, version 4, and how it's different from earlier versions of the program. Most importantly, I set the stage for the real thrust of this book: how to use QuarkXPress to its fullest.

▼ ▼

What QuarkXPress Is

QuarkXPress combines word processing, typesetting, page layout, drawing, image control, color control, and document construction in a single program. From text editing to typography, page ornamentation to picture manipulation, it offers precision controls that you'll be hard pressed to find in other programs.

Who QuarkXPress is For

Just because it has all these powers, though, doesn't mean that only trained publishing professionals or graphic designers can or should use it. Anyone who can run a personal computer can use it. In fact, many of the people who swear by QuarkXPress aren't even in the "publishing" business. They use it for internal corporate communications, product brochures, stationery, display advertisements, name tags, labels, forms, posters, announcements, and a hundred other things. (I even know of one company that uses QuarkXPress for full motion-length film titles.)

Of course, it does "real" publishing, too, and has become a top choice in that realm. It's used by book publishers such as Simon and Schuster and Peachpit Press; magazines such as *Newsweek, People, Wired, Entertainment Weekly, Rolling Stone,* and *Premiere*; newspapers such as *The New York Times, USA Today, The Washington Times,* and *The Denver Post*; and design firms, art studios, advertising agencies, and documentation departments throughout the world.

What QuarkXPress Does

When it comes right down to it, QuarkXPress is built to make pages. You can place text and graphics as well as other page elements on an electronic page and then print that out in a number of different formats. But how can you do that? What tools are at your disposal? Before I spend the rest of the book talking about how to use QuarkXPress and its tools, I had better introduce you to them. And perhaps the best way to introduce QuarkXPress in real world terms is to provide a digest of some of its most basic options.

Page sizes. You can specify the page sizes for each of your documents, along with their margins. Page dimensions can range from one by one inch to 48 by 48 inches, and margins can be any size that'll fit on the page. QuarkXPress's main window presents you with a screen representation of your full page, and guidelines indicate margin areas. You can view pages at actual size or any scale from 10 percent to 800 percent. If your document consists of multiple pages, you can scroll through them all or see them in miniature.

Page layout. QuarkXPress provides tools so you can design your pages by creating and positioning columns, text boxes, picture boxes, and decorative elements. There's a facility to set up "text chains" that automatically flow text from one text box to another, whether the boxes are on the same or different pages. QuarkXPress can automate the insertion of new pages and new columns, the creation of elements that are common to all pages, and the page numbering/renumbering process itself.

Word processing. QuarkXPress's word processing tools let you type directly into pages and edit what you type, and your text can appear as either a full-page background (as on paper in a typewriter) or wrapping into overlaying text boxes that can be moved and resized. Text always automatically rewraps to fit new box boundaries.

Formatting type. You have full control over character-level formatting (font, size, style, etc.) and paragraph-level formatting (indents, drop caps, leading, space before and after, etc.). You can also build style sheets for different types of paragraphs that include both character and paragraph formatting.

Importing text. Various import filters let you bring in formatted text from other programs (again, either onto full pages or smaller text boxes), while simultaneously reformatting using style sheets.

Graphic elements. Drawing tools let you create lines, boxes, ovals, and Bézier shapes in different styles, sizes, and shapes, with different borders, fills, and colors. You can even make those ugly rounded-corner rectangles if you want to.

Importing graphics. You can import computer graphics into picture boxes. These graphics can include scanned images, object-oriented and bitmapped graphics, in color, grayscale, or black and white. Once you've imported them into picture boxes, they can be cropped, fitted, rotated, skewed, and—with bitmaps—manipulated for brightness, contrast, and special effects.

▼ ▼

The Birth of an Upgrade

If you've never watched an artist create an image with oil paints, you may not understand what all the fuss and expense is about. When you see the end result, it's easy to think that they just picked up a brush and painted the whole thing. What you'd be missing is the hours of slowly building, changing, covering, modifying, pondering, and dreaming. Half of what makes a piece of art special is the *process* of its creation.

Art isn't the only thing that is born out of process. Computer software is very similar. And so it's with great admiration that I can look forward to each new revision of QuarkXPress, where code has been modified, other parts ripped out and replaced with something better, and then—in fits of inspiration—whole new features are added, making the final piece (at least for this version) one step better, more usable, and simply *cooler* (see Figure I-1).

Version 4 of QuarkXPress has, from its announcement, been met with mixed criticism. Some people rave about the dozens of new features, believing the ability to put text on a curve or build character-based style sheets will save them hundreds of hours a year. Others stare blankly at you if you mention the upgrade and ask why, after seven years since the last major release, the Quark engineers were so thoughtless as to leave out fundamental features such as a Layers palette, a Scaling palette, support for exporting HTML, increased PDF support, or full-fledged context-sensitive menus.

I admit to holding both opinions: I believe QuarkXPress 4 is a major step forward in page-layout, offering extraordinary new features that I would be loathe to give up. It's funny, but even some of the seemingly smallest new abilities or changes to interface are clearly a big win over previous editions. On the other hand, I keep a list on my desktop called "ThingsThatAnnoyMeAboutXPress4" in which I let myself complain about both big-ticket items—like why doesn't XPress have a Story Editor, like PageMaker—and the small stuff, too—keystrokes that used to be fast in version 3.x but now slow you down in version 4.

The History

If you're a new user to QuarkXPress, the past probably holds little meaning for you because all you want to do is jump in and start using the product as it works today. However, many of you have probably been using XPress for a while (two years? five years? more?) and it's worth taking a step back every now and again to look at where we've been and how far QuarkXPress has come.

I've been writing about QuarkXPress since version 3.0, but I still remember using version 1.10, back in 1987, when just getting the page to print was considered a feature. The jump to version 2.0 felt pretty big, but it wasn't earth-shaking. In fact, it wasn't until 1990's release of version 3.0 that QuarkXPress really grew into a world-class page-layout tool. Version 3.0 introduced XPress users to the pasteboard metaphor, the polygon tool (for pictures only), and a major interface-lift that turned heads and started winning converts. Still, when version 3.0 shipped, there were only a handful of service bureaus around the country that would accept XPress files; PageMaker was the dominant force in the industry and you were a rebel if you even mentioned Quark.

In version 3.1, we saw new features like automatic ligatures, color blends. In 3.2, Quark got rid of the XPress Data file which was driving service bureaus crazy, introduced EfiColor's color management system (which fell with a thud for most people), added new style sheet features, scripting, math features in the palettes, and—for some people the biggest feature of all—a Microsoft Windows version of QuarkXPress. Version 3.3 was really only a minor upgrade, but it shocked the world with its polygonal text boxes, letting you sculpt text blocks into any shape you wanted. Most importantly, throughout all these versions, the Quark engineers have kept fixing bugs that users would find, always trying for a more perfect application.

The Big Fix

When users speak, Quark listens (though sometimes they listen so quietly that it appears as though they don't hear). When version 4.0 hit the streets, users didn't speak . . . they screamed. There were some problems that were truly heinous. Fortunately, within several weeks Quark

Figure I-1

Evolution of
the species

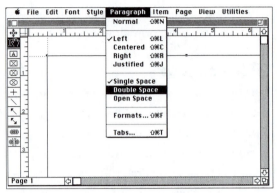

Version 1.10

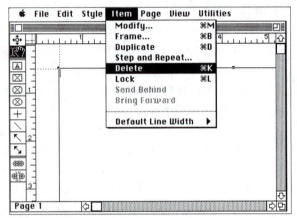

Version 2.12

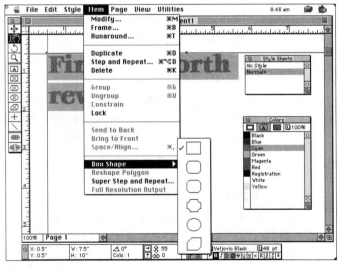

Version 3.3

Figure I-1

Evolution of
the species
(continued)

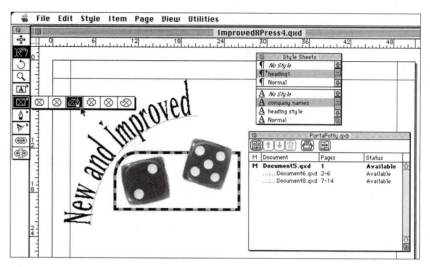

Version 4

released free bug fixes on the Internet that solved several of the most horrible problems. Soon after that, they released a free 4.02 updater that
fixed even more problems (and added a few helpful features, too). By the
time you read this, there will probably be more updates to QuarkXPress.

The lesson of the story is simple: upgrade, but upgrade carefully. I
never (ever) use a brand-new version of any software—especially a
major release—for real production work until I'm pretty confident that
it's stable and that the bugs are worked out of it. Most importantly, I keep
my eyes open on the Internet, watching for updates and users's concerns
that are relevant to my work.

(Note that while I think it's helpful to read about other people's problems published in magazines and posted on the Internet, I also think it's
worth taking their rants with a grain of salt. Unfortunately, while there
have been many legitimate comments, some people take out their frus-
trations with a new version by lambasting the product rather than truly
looking for solutions.)

Throughout this book, I've tried to explain what I consider a bug,
what features I think Quark should or might change, and how to avoid
the anomalies that are always present in computer software.

What's New In QuarkXPress 4

So what's new in QuarkXPress 4? A lot. Following is a list of what I consider to be the most important changes, though the ones that are most

important to your workflow may be different than the ones that get me all excited. (I'm not going to list every little niggling feature that's different between the last version and this one; if you need that, take a look at the What's New addendum that comes with XPress.)

▶ **BÉZIER PATHS AND BOXES.** The most flashy new features are the Bézier drawing tools, which let you create any shape box or line you want. Much of the low-level code in XPress was replaced, letting you work more flexibly, so you can convert any kind of object into any other kind—picture boxes to text boxes, lines into boxes, even turning text into a Bézier box. See page 138. Most important to me is the ability to place text on a path. See page 132.

▶ **CHARACTER-LEVEL STYLE SHEETS.** My favorite new feature in QuarkXPress is character-level style sheets. If you use the paragraph styles in XPress now, you'll love being able to apply styles to words and sentences. See page 441.

▶ **NEW TOOL PALETTE.** XPress has many new tools, enough to justify popout menus in the Tools palette. See page 75.

▶ **CONTENTLESS BOXES.** You know about picture boxes and text boxes . . . now there's contentless boxes: boxes that are just used for background colors, forcing runaround, and so on. See page 122.

▶ **RESIZING GROUPS.** At the last minute, the folks at Quark snuck in the ability to resize a group of objects. It's not a perfect feature, but it works. See page 189.

▶ **CUSTOM LINE AND FRAME STYLES.** The Dashes & Stripes feature lets you roll your own line styles, which can also be used as borders around boxes. Plus, Gap color lets you fill in the gaps between your line's dashes and stripes. See page 208.

▶ **LONG DOCUMENT FEATURES.** I'm a big fan of the new long-document features, including the Index palette, table of contents generation (with the Lists feature), and multi-document books. See page 467.

▶ **FIND/CHANGE ENHANCEMENTS.** Find/Change is now a palette, a small change which is really useful. More importantly, you can search and replace paragraph and style sheets now. See page 272.

▶ **EXPANDED RUNAROUND.** While QuarkXPress's text runaround features were certainly not anemic before, they're positively brimming with new power now, including the ability to create Bézier-shaped runaround paths and—one that will be popular with a lot of designers—the ability to run text on both sides of an object. See page 604.

▶ **CLIPPING PATHS.** The jaggy lines around TIFF images are finally a thing of the past. QuarkXPress 4 can build PostScript clipping paths using your high-resolution image data for crisp silhouettes. A side effect of this is that pictures don't have to be cropped by the edges of their picture boxes anymore. See page 578.

▶ **NONRECTANGULAR ANCHORED BOXES.** I always found it annoying that you could only anchor rectangular boxes in text. No longer! See page 616.

▶ **MULTI-INK COLORS.** If you create two- or three-color documents, you'll love the ability to mix spot colors together into Multi-ink colors. See page 658.

▶ **ICC-BASED COLOR MANAGEMENT.** EfiColor color management is gone, replaced by the ICC-based systems from Apple and Kodak. Now, getting consistent color is easier than ever (though it's still not easy). One of the byproducts of this switch is that you can now use Pantone's Hexachrome colors in QuarkXPress. See page 809.

▶ **QUARKPRINT FEATURES INCLUDED.** QuarkPrint was an XTension from Quark that added several great print-related features, including print styles, printing discontiguous pages, controlling halftone screens, and a PostScript error handler. All of these have been included in XPress now. See page 745.

▶ **XTENSIONS AND PPD MANAGER.** QuarkXPress has now fully switched from its proprietary Printer Description Files (PDFs) to the widely-used PostScript Printer Descriptions (PPDs). You can manage these with the PPD Manager. See page 722. Also, if you use a lot of XTensions, you'll find the XTensions Manager invaluable. See page 60.

▶ **TABBED DIALOG BOXES.** One of the first changes you'll notice in XPress is the tabbed dialog boxes, which lets XPress offer several dialog boxes worth of features in one. See page 82.

▶ **ITEM AND CONTENTS TOOLS.** Users rejoice! The restrictions have been relaxed a little on the Item and Contents tools, so you can now do things like select multiple objects with the Content tool and import pictures with the Item tool. See page 118.

▶ **LIVE DRAG.** No, Live drag is not the name of a new punk rock band. Rather, it's the ability to watch text reflow as you resize text boxes or drag runaround objects over them. See page 105.

▶ **SAVE IN 3.3 FORMAT.** The folks at Quark knew that people would still be using verison 3.3 for a long time after 4.0 shipped, so they included the ability to save your documents in 3.3 format. But watch out, if you use other new features in your documents, they'll often disappear when you save in this format. See page 66.

As I said, there's many more features than this. Stuff like interruptable screen redraw, popup page numbers, zooming to 800 percent, save document position, and the ability to append style sheets, colors, H&J settings, and more from other documents quickly with the Append feature. Don't worry, I cover them all in the next 900-odd pages.

▼ ▼

Requirements

To take advantage of all these great new features in QuarkXPress, you need, at a minimum, a PowerPC G3 or a 400 Mhz Pentium II computer with 128MB of RAM, a six-gigabyte hard disk drive, a 600Mb magneto-optical drive, a 32-bit color drum scanner, a high-res imagesetter with a PostScript 3 RIP, a 1200-by-600-dpi laser printer, a 21-inch Radius color monitor with 24-bit video and graphics accelerator cards, and, of course, an NTSC video capture board and genlock control panel.

Just kidding! You can get buy with some pretty limited hardware. But, as few things are more frustrating than being all psyched up to start something only to discover that you can't, for lack of an essential component, here is a résumé of the components you need to know about.

Hardware and System Software

You can run QuarkXPress for the Macintosh on almost any Macintosh sold in the past 10 years (with a minimum of a 68020 processor), as long as it's running System 7.1 or better (if you use a PowerMac, it's got to be System 7.1.2). You also must have a LaserWriter driver loaded (version 7.0 or later), and a minimum of 5 MB free RAM. In order to install XPress on your hard drive, you have to have about 14 MB of free space, plus a 3.5-inch disk drive *and* a CD-ROM (though this drive can be on a network).

If you use Windows, your PC had better be a 486 or better, running Windows 95, Windows 98, or version 3.51 or 4.0 of Windows NT. Note that there is a special version of QuarkXPress for Digital's Alpha running Windows NT. In any case, you must have both a 3.5-inch disk drive *and* a CD-ROM available (though, again, the CD-ROM can be on a network) in order to install XPress, as well as a minimum of 12 MB of RAM and 12 MB of free hard disk space.

Of course, on either platform you need a mouse (or some other pointing device) and Adobe Type Manager in order to use PostScript Type 1 fonts (actually, this is optional on the Mac, but it's highly recommended). Plus, note that QuarkXPress is optimized to print best on a PostScript printer.

But let's face it: I really can't recommend using QuarkXPress to its fullest unless you have a PowerPC-based Macintosh or a reasonably fast Pentium-based Windows machine along with at least 16 or 24 MB of RAM (see "Random Access Memory," below). Plus, if at all possible, your monitor should display 16-bit or 24-bit color (also known as Thousands or Millions of colors).

Keyboards

QuarkXPress is a keyboard- and mouse-intensive program. You'll be spending a lot of your time selecting items or text, dragging, or choosing menus. If you have an extended keyboard—one that has the 15 function keys, page up and down keys, and a keypad—you can save yourself hours (or days!) by using built-in shortcuts. You can also assign style sheets to keys (this is where the keypad comes in handy). And if you get a utility like CE Software's QuicKeys or WindowWare's WinBatch, you can use the keyboard even more effectively. While I like the ergonomic nature of adjustable keyboards, I don't find them as helpful in production work because they put the function and page keys in a separate unit that's hard to position well.

Hard Disks

The Iron Law of Hard Disk Storage is that your needs expand to equal and then exceed the storage capacity available. Get the biggest hard disk you can. If you think you'll never need more than a gigabyte of storage, then get double that. You may be sorry later if you don't. Most of the new computers don't come with anything smaller than a 2 GB hard drive anyway; I think that's a pretty good minimum.

Random Access Memory

RAM is good. Put as much into your computer as you possibly can afford. If you're doing serious publishing, chances are you'll want to run QuarkXPress along with several other applications, and probably want 32 or 64 MB. If you do a lot of Photoshop work, you'll always wish you have more (I don't recommend people use Photoshop and QuarkXPress on the same system without a minimum of 48 MB, and preferably more like 72 MB). You'll want the extra RAM to move around smoothly when you have those programs open along with much-needed system extensions such as ATM. The more color work you're doing, the more RAM you should have.

▼ ▼

QuarkXPress and You

Version 4 of QuarkXPress is clearly a pretty impressive package. But don't let it intimidate you. Remember, QuarkXPress is not only a machete, it's a Swiss Army machete. If you want to use it for writing letters home, you can do it. If you want to create glossy four-color magazines, you can do that too. The tool is powerful enough to get the job done, but sometimes—if you're trying to get through that Amazon jungle—you need to wield your machete accurately and efficiently.

Let's look at how it's done.

1

LEARN QUARKXPRESS
IN 30 MINUTES

"Here's a copy of QuarkXPress; our consultant says it's easy to learn, so can you do the annual report by Friday?"

If you've ever heard these words, you know the true meaning of the word *panic*. Fortunately, you've come to the right place. This chapter will give you everything you need to know to work with XPress in just 30 minutes. Well . . . maybe not *everything* you need. Obviously there's much more to XPress than I can cover in one short chapter. I've been working with this program for over 10 years and I'm still picking up new techniques. But if you're like most people you need to roll up your sleeves and get started working in XPress as soon as possible. That's what this chapter is for.

I've put together a simple XPress document that you will create yourself, step by step, as you read through the chapter. Working through the project will give you a sense of what QuarkXPress 4 is all about, and will help you understand many of the topics covered in the rest of the book.

The project is a simple one-fold brochure for a mythical product called "Gold Standard" (see Figure 1-1). If it'll help, try to visualize yourself as a designer or production artist working for the Gold Standard company; you've got 30 minutes to build this basic brochure.

Figure 1-1

The one-fold brochure
you're going to create

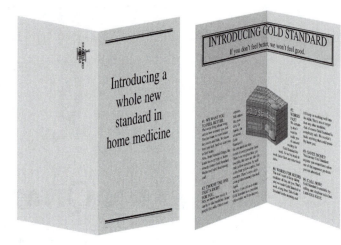

Before you start working, you need to get the materials for the brochure: the product illustration, the company logo, and the text. If you have access to the World Wide Web, you can download these materials from the QuarkXPress Book Web site (*www.peachpit.com/blatner/*). There's also a finished version of the brochure for you to open in XPress 4 to see if you've followed the steps correctly.

Don't worry if you don't have access to the Web. You can use other materials you have on your computer. For instance, if you've got a picture of your cousin on his vacation, use that instead of the product illustration. Use a picture of your dog instead of the company logo. And use any text file—like a letter from your Mom—for the text. It doesn't matter if you don't replicate the project exactly as shown, just as long as you understand the principles.

Pages, Views and Guides

In this section of the project you create a new file for the project, make sure the margins are correct, add some guides, add a page, and navigate around your document.

Creating a New File

Before you can begin working, you need to launch QuarkXPress and create a new document.

1. Launch QuarkXPress by double-clicking on the application icon. (See page 48 for more information on installing QuarkXPress.)

Figure 1-2

The QuarkXPress application icon

2. When the application has opened (after you see the menus and a couple of palettes), choose Document from the New submenu (under the File menu). The New Document dialog box appears.

Figure 1-3

Creating a new document

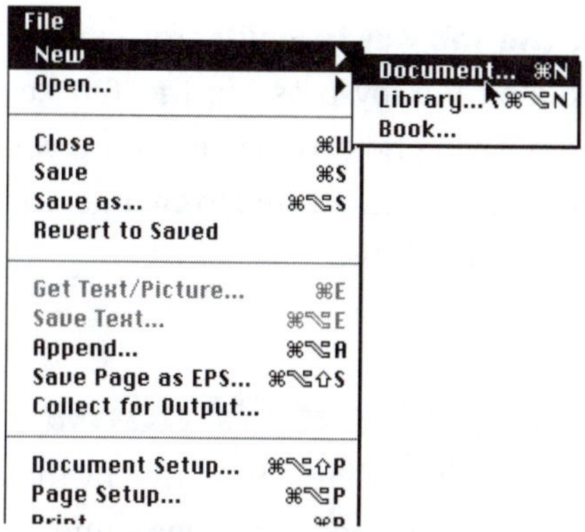

Figure 1-4

The New Document dialog box

Portrait

Landscape

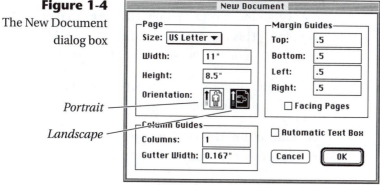

3. Make sure the document size is set to US Letter. Click on the landscape orientation icon. This will set the dimensions.

Width: 11 inches

Height: 8.5 inches

4. Make sure that both the Facing Pages and Automatic Text Box checkboxes are turned off—that is, they don't have an X through them. (For more information about working with Facing Pages and Automatic Text Boxes, see page 226.)

5. You also need to set the margins as follows.
    Top: .5 inch (use the " mark for inches)
    Bottom: .5 inch
    Left: .5 inch
    Right: .5 inch

6. Click OK. This creates your new XPress document with a single page, and margins at .5 inch around the edge of the page.

▼ ▼

Tip: Use the Tab Key in Fields. You can jump from one field to the next in any dialog box by pressing the Tab key. For instance, in the New Document dialog box you were just in, you could have pressed Tab to jump to any field you wanted to change. You can go to the previous field by pressing Shift-Tab.

▼ ▼

Working in the Window

Depending on how XPress was used by the last person to use it on your machine, you may need to change some things on the screen.

1. To see everything in your window, choose Fit in Window from the View menu. (This is so important that you should start using its keyboard shortcut: Command-zero or Control-zero.)

2. If you do not see the Tool palette on your screen, choose Show Tools from the View menu.

3. If you don't see the Measurements palette on your screen, choose Show Measurements from the View menu.

4. If you don't see the Document Layout palette on your screen, choose Show Document Layout from the View menu. Your screen should look like the illustration in Figure 1-5.

Figure 1-5
The document window

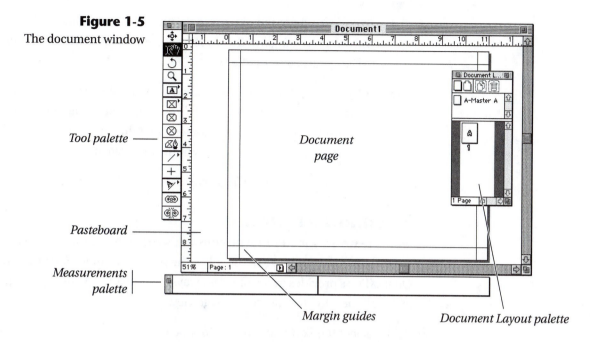

Tool palette —

Pasteboard —

Measurements palette |

Margin guides

Document Layout palette

Working with the Tool Palette

Some of the tools (such as the Item tool and Content tool) are always visible in the Tool palette. Other tools (such as the Oval Text Box tool) are hidden, and are visible only if you click on the icon in the Tool palette.

▶ To choose one of the visible tools, click the icon for that tool in the Tool palette. The tool will be highlighted.

Figure 1-6
The Tool palette with the popout tools visible

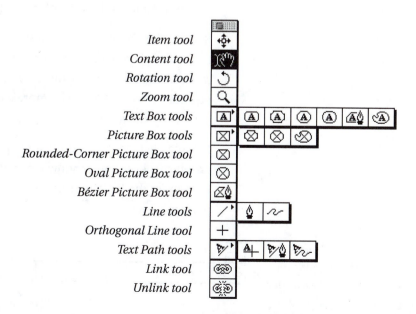

Item tool
Content tool
Rotation tool
Zoom tool
Text Box tools
Picture Box tools
Rounded-Corner Picture Box tool
Oval Picture Box tool
Bézier Picture Box tool
Line tools
Orthogonal Line tool
Text Path tools
Link tool
Unlink tool

▶ To choose one of the hidden tools, press on one of the tool icons with a small triangle in the upper-right corner, and then drag over to the right to choose the tool.

▶ You can jump from one tool to another in the Tool palette without using the mouse by pressing Command-Tab (Macintosh) or Control-Alt-Tab (Windows). You can add the Shift key to each of these to cycle through the tools in the opposite direction.

Chapter 3, *Tools of the Trade*, discusses XPress's tools in detail.

Zooming Around

As you're working in XPress, you constantly zoom in and out to see very small details on your page or to look at the page as a whole. Fortunately, QuarkXPress provides many different ways to zoom in and out. (See page 90 for all the ways to change the page views.)

1. Select the Zoom tool in the Tool palette.

2. Position the Zoom tool cursor over the upper-left corner of the page and click several times. Each click magnifies your view. (If you don't see anything when you zoom in, you may be looking at the middle of the page. Use the scroll bars to adjust the view.)

3. Hold down the Option or Alt key. Notice that the Zoom tool cursor changes from a plus sign to a minus sign. Click several times to zoom out from the view of the page.

4. Release the Option/Alt key and position the Zoom tool cursor inside the page. Then drag with the Zoom tool to create a small square. When you release the mouse, you zoom in on the area you just marqueed. (This will be more useful when you actually have something on your page!)

5. Double-click on the magnification percentage shown in the lower-left corner of the window (see Figure 1-7). Enter the "80" and then press the Return or Enter key. QuarkXPress switches to 80-percent view.

Figure 1-7

The Magnification
level box

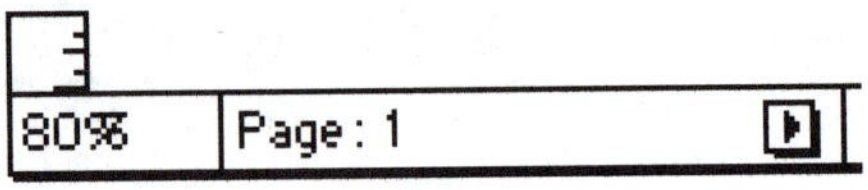

Adding Pages

Every new QuarkXPress document opens with one page already in place. Since this brochure will be printed on two sides of the page, you need to add a page to your document. (See page 253 for more information on adding pages to and deleting pages from a document.)

1. In the Document Layout palette, click on the small rectangular page icon at the top, labeled "A-Master A" (see Figure 1-8).

2. Drag the icon down under the first page. Release the mouse when you see the plain rectangle under the page. The second page is automatically created for you right where you drop the icon. (If you drop the new page in the wrong place, just drag it to where you want it in the palette.)

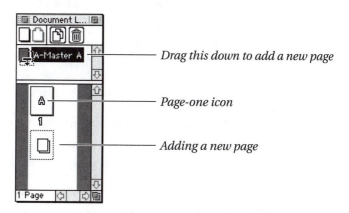

Figure 1-8
Dragging a master page to create a new page

Drag this down to add a new page

Page-one icon

Adding a new page

You can also choose Insert from the Page menu to add a page, but it's a good idea to get in the habit of using the Document Layout palette as early as possible.

Adding Guides

To make it easier for you to lay out the various elements you're going to put on your page, you need to place some guides.

1. Double-click on the page-one icon in the Document Layout palette to make sure you are on that page.

2. You can add guides by pulling them from one of the rulers at either the left or the top of the page. If you can't see the rulers, choose Show Rulers from the View menu. Move your mouse over

to the vertical ruler and press. You should see a little two-headed arrow appear on the ruler (see Figure 1-9).

Figure 1-9

Pulling a guide out
from the ruler

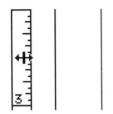

3. Drag the two-headed arrow out from the ruler and let go when the guideline is at the 5-inch mark on the top ruler (watch the guide line against the ruler). A colored guide appears where you let go.

4. You can also position guides by watching the Measurements palette. Drag the two-headed arrow out from the vertical ruler. Watch the X coordinate on the Measurements palette. Let go when the coordinate reads exactly 5.5 inches.

5. Create one more guide at the 6-inch mark.

6. Because you need guides on page two, double-click on page two in the Document Layout, and repeat steps 3, 4, and 5. (See page 248 to see how master pages can automate this process.)

❦ ❦

Tip: Working with Guides. To reposition a guide, just move your cursor over the guide, click, and drag the guide to the new position. In general, you should have the Item tool selected to do this. To delete a guide, drag it outside the document window (any side will do). You can make your guides invisible by choosing Hide Guides from the View menu (then choose Show Guides to turn them back on). For more information about guides, see page 200.

❦ ❦

Tip: What Page Are You on? Quark has a quirk when it comes to showing what page you are on. When you look at Figure 1-10, at first it seems like you're looking at page one. After all, that's what the page number in the lower-left corner says. However, notice the thin gray line at the top of the window? That means the previous page's pasteboard is visible. *That* is page one. The page you're looking at is page two.

❦ ❦

Figure 1-10
Page numbering

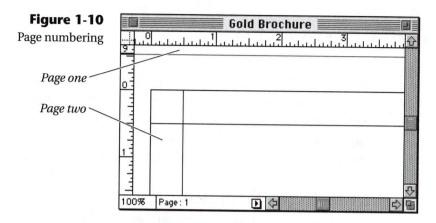

Page one

Page two

Saving

You've done enough work that you need to save your file. (QuarkXPress has a feature that automatically saves your work every few minutes; for more information about this feature, see page 64).

1. Choose Save or Save As from the File menu (they're both the same for new, unsaved documents). The Save As dialog box appears.

2. Name your file *Gold Brochure*, and choose a folder to put your file in—not in the QuarkXPress folder!

3. Leave the Type as Document and the Version set to 4.0. (For more information on alternate settings, see page 68).

4. If you turn on the Include Preview checkbox, you'll see a thumbnail preview of page one each time you open the document.

For the rest of this project, you should continue to save your work at whatever intervals you feel comfortable with.

Figure 1-11
Save As dialog box

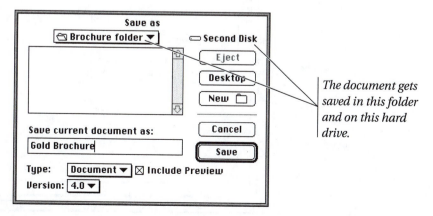

The document gets saved in this folder and on this hard drive.

▼ ▼

Text and Text Formatting

In order to put text on your page, you must first create a text box. In this section of the project you'll create several text boxes, add text to those boxes by typing as well as importing text from file on disk, and you'll link the text boxes together so that the text flows from one box to another. Finally, you'll format the text using various fonts, sizes, and so on.

Drawing a Text Box

When you launch a word processing program, you can start typing right away. QuarkXPress is different: it requires you to put your text into text boxes. You create a text box using one of the Text Box tools.

1. Double-click on the first page in the Document Layout palette to make sure you are working on that page.

2. Select the Rectangle Text Box tool in the Tool palette (that's the one with the little "A" in it).

3. Move the cursor over to the right side of the page. Your cursor should change to a plus sign. Press and drag as shown in Figure 1-12. Don't worry yet about the precise size or location of the box.

4. Release the mouse when you've completed the drag. You should see a box with no text—just a blinking insertion point.

Figure 1-12
Dragging to
create a text box

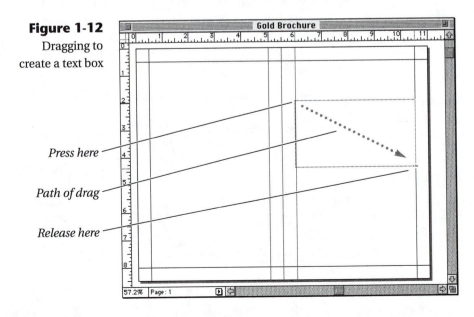

▼ ▼

Tip: Item Tool Versus Content Tool. One of the most frustrating parts about learning QuarkXPress is remembering the difference between the Item and the Content tool. The Item tool is the first tool in the Tool palette (the technical term is "the pointy thingy"). You use it to manipulate items on your page. For instance, to move the whole text box to a different location, you'd use the Item tool. Also, to delete an item, you can press Delete when you have the Item tool selected (or choose Delete from the Item menu).

The second tool in the tool palette is the Content tool, which lets you change the *content* of the page items. For instance, if you don't see a blinking insertion point in your new text box, it's probably because you have the Item tool selected. In order to type in the text box, you've got to have the Content tool selected.

Note that when you make a box (like the text box you just made), XPress almost always automatically chooses the Item or Content tool for you, depending on which one you used last.

▼ ▼

Modifying a Text Box

You can change the size of a text box at any time by dragging any of the eight handles located on the corners and sides of the text box. (For more tips on working with text boxes, see page 122.)

1. Move your cursor over to the small black handle at the top side of the text box (it doesn't matter what tool you have selected). Your cursor should change to a "finger" (see Figure 1-13). This indicates that you can resize the box.

2. Click and drag with the finger cursor, moving the handle so that the top of the box sits at the 2-inch mark. (You can get a precise measurement by watching either the guideline in the vertical ruler or the Y coordinate in the Measurements palette.)

Figure 1-13
The finger cursor

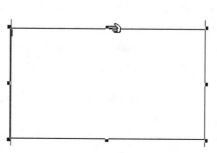

3. Next, position the left side of the box at the 6-inch mark of the horizontal ruler. Note that the edge of the box will probably snap to the guide you placed there earlier.

4. Position the right side of the box at the 10.5-inch mark (this should snap to the right margin guide).

5. Position the bottom side of the box at the 6.5-inch mark of the vertical ruler.

Typing Text

Now that you have a text box on your page, you can start typing in the box (remember that you need to select the Content tool first).

1. So that you can better see the text you're about to type, choose Actual Size from the View menu. (If you still have difficulty reading the text, try zooming in closer.)

2. Type the words, "Introducing a whole new standard in home medicine" into the box. (Don't type the quotation marks.)

3. If you make an error typing, you can use any of the normal text-editing techniques to modify the text (like using the Delete or Backspace key, double-clicking on a word to select it, and so on).

4. When you're done, leave the insertion point blinking inside the text box. Do not click outside the text box to deselect the box. (We're not done with that text yet!)

Formatting Text

The text you have created comes in with the default formatting from the Normal style sheet, which is almost never what you really want. However, you can change the formatting of your text at any time.

1. To select all the text in the text box, choose Select All from the Edit menu (or type Command-A or Control-A). This highlights all the text in the text box (text in a text box is called a *story*, even if there's only one little paragraph like this).

2. You can choose a font from one of two places: the Style menu or the Measurements palette. Let's use the second choice: click on

the little triangle next to the font name in the Measurements palette (see Figure 1-14). A list of the available typefaces appears.

3. Choose any serif typeface (such as Garamond, Times, or Palatino).

4. The point size popup menu in the Measurements palette displays a list of point sizes, but the one we want is not included. You can enter the point size you want by selecting the point size and typing in the number "50". Then press Return or Enter.

5. Finally, click on the Centered alignment icon in the Measurements palette. The text centers itself within the text box.

Figure 1-14
Text formatting in the
Measurements palette

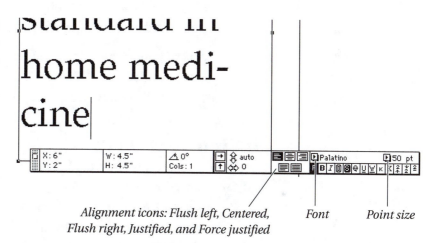

Alignment icons: Flush left, Centered,   Font   Point size
Flush right, Justified, and Force justified

Importing Text

While the text on the first page is short, most of the time you'll find yourself working with text that is saved in a word-processing file. (For a complete list of all the formats that you can import from, see page 271.)

1. Go to the second page and draw a 2-inch-tall text box that extends from the left margin to the right margin of the page. Use the Item tool to move the text box so that the top of the box sits at the top margin of the page.

2. With the insertion point blinking in the text box (switch to the Content tool), choose Get Text from the File menu. The Get Text dialog box appears (see Figure 1-15).

Figure 1-15

Get Text dialog box

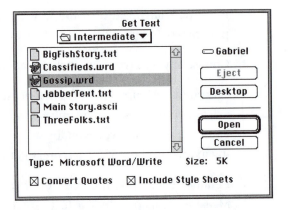

3. Use the dialog box to find the file *Brochure.txt* from the files you downloaded. (If you weren't able to download that file, use some other text file that is about two pages in length.)

4. Click OK to import the text. (If you receive a message that you're missing fonts, don't worry about it—you'll be changing the typeface for the text anyway.)

Linking Text Boxes

The text you have imported is too long to fit in the little text box you've made. You can always tell when there's more text than can fit in a box by the red overset mark at the lower-right corner of the text box (see Figure 1-16). Rather than change the size of the box to fit the text, we're going to build another bigger text box, and then link the two text boxes together so that the text flows from one into the other.

1. Draw a second text box on the left side of page two. This text box should extend from the left margin to the 5-inch guideline. The box should start at the 4-inch mark on the vertical ruler and stop at the bottom margin.

Figure 1-16

Overset mark

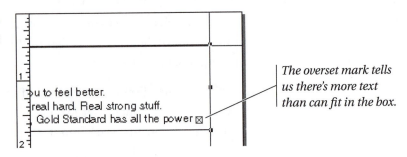

The overset mark tells us there's more text than can fit in the box.

2. While this text box is still selected, choose Duplicate from the Item menu. This creates a copy of the text box and offsets it slightly. Use the Item tool to position this duplicate on the right side of page two (place it so that it mirrors the left side of the page).

3. Choose the Link tool in the Tool palette (the one that looks like a little chain of doughnuts). Click on the first box on the page (the wide one at the top) with the Link tool. The outside edge of the box begins to animate, to tell you that it's selected.

4. Then click on the empty text box on the left side of the page. An arrow flashes momentarily between the two boxes, and the continuation of the text appears in the second box (see Figure 1-17).

Figure 1-17

Linking text boxes

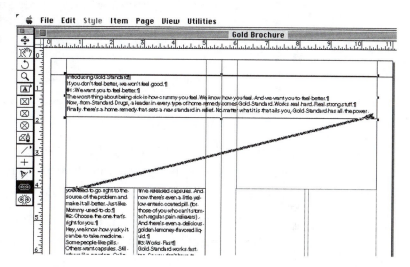

5. Choose the Link tool again; click first on the text box on the left side of the page and then on the empty box on the right side of the page. The text is now linked from the top box to the left box and then to the right box.

▼ ▼

Tip: Rules for Linking Text. Linked text boxes don't have to be on the same page. After you click once with the Link tool, you can scroll to another page and click on the next text box. You cannot link to a box that has text in it; you can only link to empty boxes. For more information on working with linked text boxes, see page 197.

▼ ▼

Multicolumn Text Boxes

Text boxes are one way to divide text into different areas on the page. However, you can also have multiple columns within a text box. QuarkXPress gives you two different ways to set columns within a text box (we're going to use both methods here).

1. Click on the text box on the lower-left side of the page (you can use either the Item tool or the Content tool for this).

2. In the Measurements palette, change the number in the "Cols" field from 1 to 2 (see Figure 1-18). Press the Return or Enter key to apply the change. Two columns appear in the text box.

Figure 1-18

Columns setting in the Measurements palette

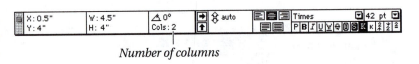

Number of columns

3. Click on the text box on the lower-right side of the page. Choose Modify from the Item menu and then click on the Text tab (see Figure 1-19).

4. Change the Columns field to 2 and then click the Apply button to see the change (you can move the dialog box out of the way if it's covering the text box). Now press OK to apply the change.

Don't worry if your text doesn't fill all the columns right now (or if there's another overset mark). You've still got more formatting to do.

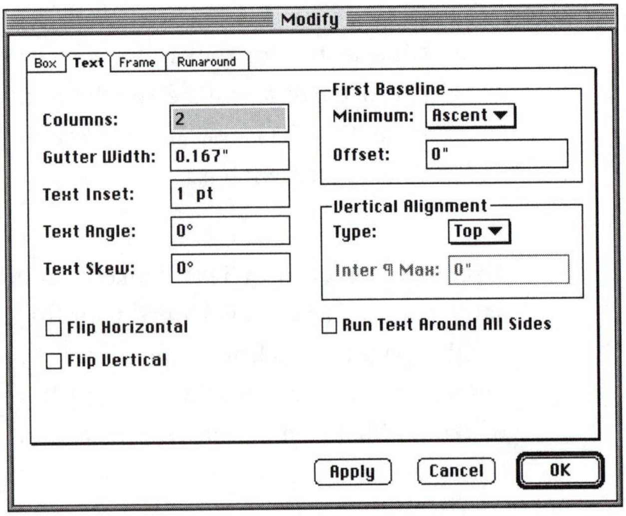

Figure 1-19

Item Modify Text dialog box

▼ ▼

Tip: Setting the Gutter Width. One of the advantages of choosing
Modify from the Item menu when setting your columns is that you can
change the gutter width, which is the amount of space between the two
columns of the text box.

▼ ▼

Character Formatting

The text you have imported needs to be formatted. While you could use
the formatting options in the Measurements palette, let's take a look at
a few other ways you can format text.

1. First, press Command-A or Control-A to select all the text in the
   story. Change the typeface to the same font you used on page one.

2. To deselect all the text, click once somewhere inside the text box.
   Now, to select just the first line of text, place your cursor over that
   line of text and click three times. This should select the words
   "Introducing Gold Standard." (Note that clicking once places the
   text cursor, twice selects a word, three times selects a line, and
   four times selects a paragraph.)

3. Choose Character from the Style menu to open the Character
   Attributes dialog box. This is where you can format and apply all
   the attributes for the selected line of text (see Figure 1-20).

Figure 1-20
Character Attributes
dialog box

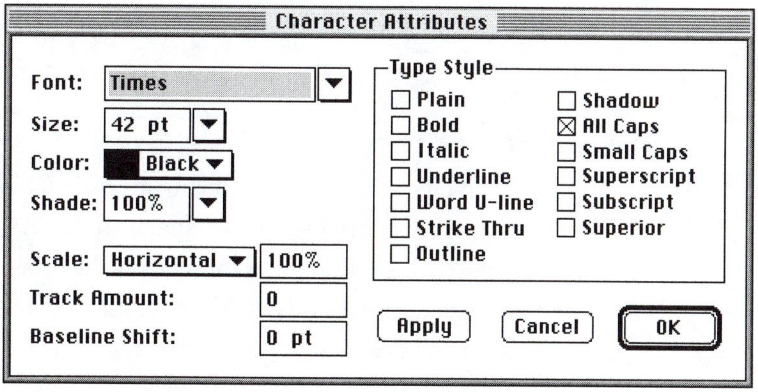

4. Click the All Caps box and then click the Apply button to see the
   change.

5. Use the Size field to enter a size that's about 42 points. Click the Apply button. If your text extends past one line, reduce the point size until the selected line of text fills the width of a single line. When you're done, click OK.

6. Triple-click on the second line: "If you don't feel better, we won't feel good." Use the Character Attributes dialog box again to set the point size to 24.

7. Use the finger cursor to move the bottom edge of the top text box up, changing the height so that only these two lines are in the box. This forces the text down to the other boxes. You can make the other boxes slightly larger to fill the extra space, if you want.

8. Select the next line: "#1: We want you to feel better" (you can quadruple-click to select it all quickly). Click on the large K icon toward the right side of the Measurements palette; this changes the line to all caps. Now set the point size to 13.

9. Select each of the numbered lines on the page and change them so they match the text in step 8.

▼ ▼

Tip: Style Sheets Stop Drudgery. By the time you finish formatting each of the numbered paragraphs in the text, you're probably feeling like there's got to be a better way to format text. There is. QuarkXPress has a feature called Style Sheets that makes formatting text much faster. For more information about style sheets, see page 419.

▼ ▼

Leading

Each character in a line of text sits on a *baseline*. Leading (pronounced *ledding*) is the amount of space from one baseline to the next. The greater the leading, the more space between the lines. The text in your project currently has an "auto" amount of leading applied. However, for reasons I describe in Chapter 6, *Type and Typography*, you should avoid auto leading. Instead, here's how you can apply an absolute leading value.

1. Click so that your insertion point is blinking in the first line of the second text box (the one on the left).

2. Scroll over to the lower-right corner of the page and Shift-click on the last line of the text box. This selects all the text from the first line to the last.

3. Click on either the increase- or decrease-leading arrow in the Measurements palette until the amount reads 14. This tightens up the space between the lines. You can also simply replace the leading value with the number 14 (see Figure 1-21).

Figure 1-21
Leading arrows

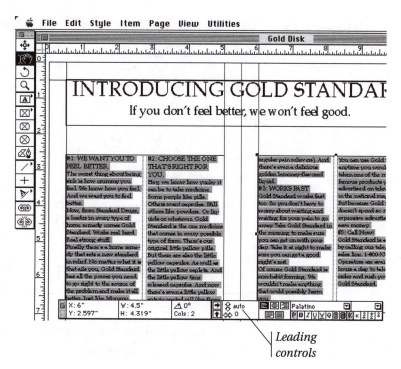

Leading controls

▼ ▼

Tip: Paragraph Attributes Don't Need Selections. Character attributes in QuarkXPress are those typographic attributes that you can apply to a single character—things like font, size, color, baseline shift, and so on. On the other hand, paragraph attributes—like leading, indents, and so on—can only be applied to a whole paragraph. The upshot is that if you want to change a paragraph attribute, you can select just part of the paragraph or even just have your insertion point blinking inside the paragraph. XPress is smart enough to know that the change applies to the whole paragraph.

▼ ▼

Paragraph Formatting

There are other paragraph attributes besides leading. While you can find some of the other paragraph attributes in the Measurements palette, you can find them *all* in the Paragraph Attributes dialog box (select Formats from the Style menu).

1. Select the subhead labeled #2, and then choose Formats from the Style menu (see Figure 1-22).

Figure 1-22

Paragraph Attributes
dialog box

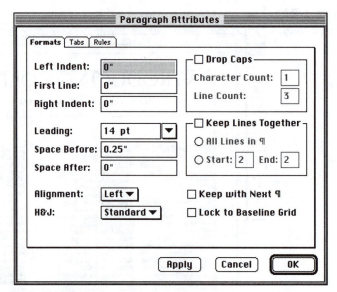

2. Change the amount in the Space Before field to .25 inches. Then click OK to see the change.

3. Do the same for all the other numbered subheads, too.

▼ ▼

Tip: When No Space Is Added. If a paragraph is at the top of a column when you add Space Before, XPress won't add any space. If the paragraph is at the bottom of a column, XPress won't add any space after. It turns out that this behavior is normal and almost always what you really want, but it confuses beginners, so I wanted to point it out.

▼ ▼

New-Line Character

Some of the lines in your text may break in places where you don't want them to. While you could hit the Return or Enter key to break the line, that would split the paragraph into two, which may cause formatting problems. Instead, try using a new-line character, which lets you break a line without creating a new paragraph.

1. Choose Show Invisibles from the View menu. This lets you see invisible formatting characters such as the new-line character, spaces, tabs, carriage returns, and so on. (For more information on other special characters, see page 383.)

2. Click to place the text cursor where you want to break the line. For this exercise, go to the first page and place the text cursor just to the left of a word that is hyphenated (if there aren't any hyphenated words on the first page, find one on the second page).

3. Hold down the Shift key and press Return—*not* the Enter key. (Computers that run Windows 95 often don't have a Return key; in this case, use the Enter key that is *not* part of the numeric keypad; that key is used for something else in XPress.)

Figure 1-23
The new-line character

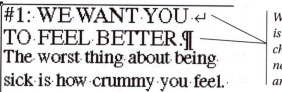

When Show Invisibles is on, you can see characters like the new-line character and returns.

Graphics, Colors, Frames, and Lines

Congratulations! You've almost completed your project. In this section you'll create picture boxes that hold the graphics for the brochure, import images, size them, and position them on your page. You will also add some color to the document, as well as special frames and lines.

Drawing a Picture Box

Just as text boxes hold text, picture boxes hold pictures. So before you import a graphic, you need to create a picture box to hold that image.

1. Click on the Rectangle Picture Box tool in the Tool palette.

2. Move your cursor to the middle of page two and draw a box approximately 2.5 inches tall and wide. (Don't worry about getting it exact; you'll change the size later.)

3. When you release the cursor you should see an ✕ through the box, indicating that you have created a picture box (see Figure 1-24).

4. If you do not see an ✕, you need to choose Show Guides from the View menu. If you still don't see an ✕, then you haven't created a picture box. Choose Delete from the Item menu and make sure you choose the Rectangle Picture Box tool; then redraw the picture box.

Figure 1-24
An empty picture box

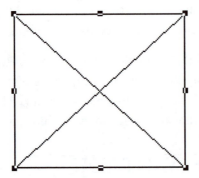

Importing Graphics

Once you've created a picture box, you can bring a graphic into it. This graphic can come from an illustration program such as Adobe Illustrator or Macromedia FreeHand. Or it can come from an image-editing program like Adobe Photoshop. (For more information on working with graphics from other programs, see page 525.)

1. With the picture box still selected, choose Get Picture from the File menu. Note that in earlier versions of XPress you had to have the Content tool selected when importing a graphic; now you can use either the Content or the Item tool.

2. When the Get Picture dialog box appears, find the file called *Gold Package.tif* from the files you downloaded. If you don't have those files, find any TIFF or EPS graphic on your hard drive. Then click Open to import the image.

3. Move your cursor into the middle of the picture box and notice that the cursor changes into a flat hand. When you click and drag the mouse with this cursor, you can move the graphic around within the picture box (see Figure 1-25).

Figure 1-25

The hand cursor repositions graphics within the picture box

4. The picture box is currently too small to show the entire package. Drag out the sides of the picture box until the box is big enough for the graphic (if you're using the Gold Standard image, the box should be about 4 inches wide, and 3.5 inches tall).

5. Positioning the graphic in the middle of the box using the hand cursor is slow and not very accurate. Instead, press Command-Shift-M (or Control-Shift-M) to center the graphic in the picture box. (That's M for "Mathematical Middle"!)

6. Now that you've got the graphic in the right-size box, you may need to move the box itself around. Switch to the Item tool (the top tool in the Tool palette) and move your cursor over the picture box. A four-headed arrow appears with which you can drag the box around. Move the picture box so that its top is at the 2.75-inch mark. Make sure the graphic is at least partly over the text.

7. Position the center of the box on the 5.5-inch guide. (You can accomplish this visually by aligning the center handles of the box on the guide.)

▼ ▼

Tip: Wait Before You Drag. As you resize or move objects, wait a moment after you press the mouse button down and before you start to drag. This will let you see the new QuarkXPress 4 feature where text dynamically reflows around objects as you move them. This lets you know, as you move the objects, how your layout will look. (If you have friends or coworkers who started with earlier versions, they may not know about this feature. You can amaze them with your expertise.)

▼ ▼

Runaround

If you could transport a group of typesetters through time from twenty years ago to today, the thing that would astound them most would probably be the ease with which we can wrap text around objects on a page. Back in those days, to get text to run around the shape of a picture took hours of inserting special codes at the end of every line. With QuarkXPress you can do it in a matter of seconds. (For more details on text runaround and clipping paths, see page 604.)

Whenever you place an object on top of a text box, that object can force the text below to flow runaround it (also known as "text wrap"). In this case, the text is wrapping around the picture box, but you could just as easily wrap text around another text box or a line.

1. Select the picture box and choose Runaround from the Item menu (or press Command-T or Control-T). The Modify dialog box appears with the Runaround tab selected (see Figure 1-26).

2. Currently, the runaround is set to Item (this is the default value), which means that the underlying text runs around the edges of

Figure 1-26
The Runaround
dialog box

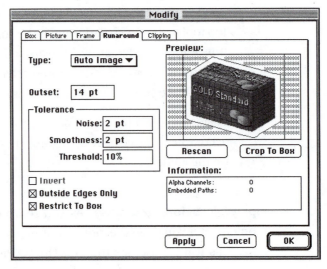

the picture box itself. Choose Auto Image from the Type popup menu. This tells XPress to automatically find the outside edge of the picture and use it for the runaround.

3. Press the Apply button (not the OK button) to see what this does to your layout. Notice that the text is too close to the image.

4. Change the Outset amount to 14 points. Then press the Apply button again. The text moves away with a 14-point gap between it and the graphic. Click the OK button to apply the runaround.

Resizing and Rotating Graphics

Because this brochure is a mailing piece for the Standard Drug company, we need to add a logo on the left side of page one, and make sure the logo is the proper size and orientation.

1. Here's a new way to move between pages in your document: click on the small page popup menu at the bottom left of your document window. A small page list will appear (see Figure 1-27). Choose page one from the list.

Figure 1-27
The page popup list

2. Draw a picture box on the left side of page one. Make the dimensions of the picture box about 1.25 inches wide by about 1 inch tall. (You can watch the Measurements palette as you draw the box, to get the proper size.)

3. Use Get Picture (from the File menu) to import the *Logo.eps* file. Again: If you don't have this graphic, you can use another picture.

4. This logo is way too big for the picture box. However, rather than change the size of the box, let's change the size of the image. Change the X% field in the Measurements palette from 100 to 50 (you don't have to type the percent character). Press the Tab key to jump to the Y% field and change the number there to 50, too. Press the Return or Enter key to apply these values.

5. The logo needs to be rotated. Double-click on the angle field in the Measurements palette and change 0° to -90 (you don't have to type the degree symbol; see Figure 1-28). Press the Return or Enter key to apply the value. (If XPress tells you that "the item cannot be positioned off the pasteboard," set the rotation back to zero, move the item farther down on the page, and then try to rotate it back to 90 degrees again.)

6. Use the Item tool to position the picture box in the corner under the top margin and next to the guide at the 5-inch mark.

Figure 1-28
The Picture Box
Measurements palette

Box rotation   *Horizontal and vertical scaling*

Adding Color

Right now the only color on page two comes from the graphic. Let's add some more color to that page by setting the background color of the top text box.

1. Move to page two and click on the top text box. Choose Modify from the Item menu (or press Command-M or Control-M). The Modify dialog box appears (see Figure 1-29).

Figure 1-29
The Modify
dialog box

```
┌─────────────────────── Modify ───────────────────────┐
│ ┌Box┐ Text  Frame  Runaround                          │
│                              ┌─Box──────────────────┐ │
│  Origin Across:  0.5"        │ Color:  ▢ Yellow ▼   │ │
│                              │                      │ │
│  Origin Down:    0.5"        │ Shade:  50%      ▼   │ │
│                              └──────────────────────┘ │
│  Width:          10"         ┌─Blend─────────────────┐│
│                              │ Style:  Solid ▼       ││
│  Height:         1.347"      │                       ││
│                              │ Angle:  0°        ▼   ││
│  Angle:          0°          │                       ││
│                              │ Color:  ▨ Yellow ▼   ││
│  Skew:           0°          │                       ││
│                              │ Shade:  50%       ▼   ││
│  Corner Radius:  0"          └───────────────────────┘│
│                                                        │
│  ☐ Suppress Printout                                   │
│                                                        │
│              ( Apply )  ( Cancel )  [ OK ]            │
└────────────────────────────────────────────────────────┘
```

2. Choose Yellow from the Box Color popup menu. (For more information on creating your own colors, see page 647.)

3. A solid-yellow text box is a bit too bright for this piece, so select 50 percent from the Shade popup menu.

4. Click the Apply button to see how the color is added to the background of the text box.(Feel free to move the dialog box out of the way to see the page, but don't click OK yet.)

▼ ▼

Tip: Use the Colors Palette. The Colors palette allows you to apply colors without using the Modify dialog box or menus. Choose Show Colors from the View menu to open the palette. For more information on the Colors palette, see page 662.

▼ ▼

Adding a Frame

The text box at the top of page two (the same one you're working on now) needs a frame around it. Fortunately, it is very easy to add a frame to a text or picture box. (For more on working with frames, see page 205.)

1. While you're still in the Modify dialog box, click on the Frame tab (see Figure 1-30).

Figure 1-30
The Frame dialog box

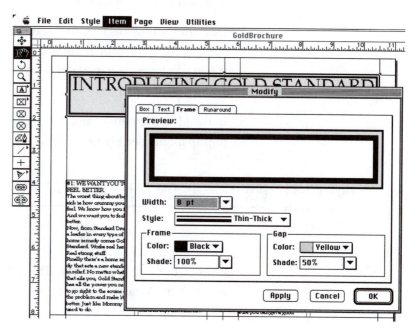

2.   Change the amount in the Width field to 8 points and click the Apply button. A solid black frame appears around the text box.

3.   Press on the Style popup menu and choose the style called Thin-Thick, then click the Apply button again. The frame changes to a double-line frame.

4.   In the area of the dialog box labeled Gap, change the color to Yellow and set the shade to 50 percent. This helps the frame appear to be part of the text box. Click OK to apply all the changes.

Note that changing the frame changes the amount of space inside the text box, which may cause text reflow. If you need to, adjust the size of the text box or the size of the text so that the text fits correctly.

Drawing Lines

QuarkXPress has two types of elements: boxes and lines. Lines can be decorative (like arrows, dashed patterns, and so on) or paths that hold text. For your project, you'll create two basic lines as graphic elements at the top and bottom of page one.

1.   Switch to page one and select the Orthogonal Line tool in the Tool palette (that's the one that looks like a plus sign). "Orthogonal" just means that you can only draw horizontal or vertical lines. The tool next to it lets you draw diagonal lines, too.

2.   Drag the Orthogonal Line tool across the top margin of page one, starting from the 6-inch guide and ending at the right margin. When you let go, you may not be able to see the line because the guide sits on top of it.

3.   In the Measurements palette, choose "8 pt" from the Line width popup menu (see Figure 1-31). The line becomes thicker.

Figure 1-31
The Measurements
palette for lines

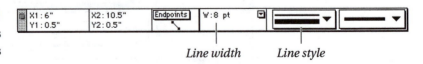

Line width   *Line style*

4.   Choose the style called Thin-Thick from the Line style popup menu in the Measurements palette.

5. Duplicate the line by choosing Duplicate from the Item menu (or pressing Command-D).

6. Move the line down to the bottom margin so that it aligns with the same margins as the line at the top (get in the habit of switching to the Item tool to move objects on your page).

7. Change the line style to Thick-Thin in the Measurements palette (see Figure 1-32).

Figure 1-32
The final page, with lines

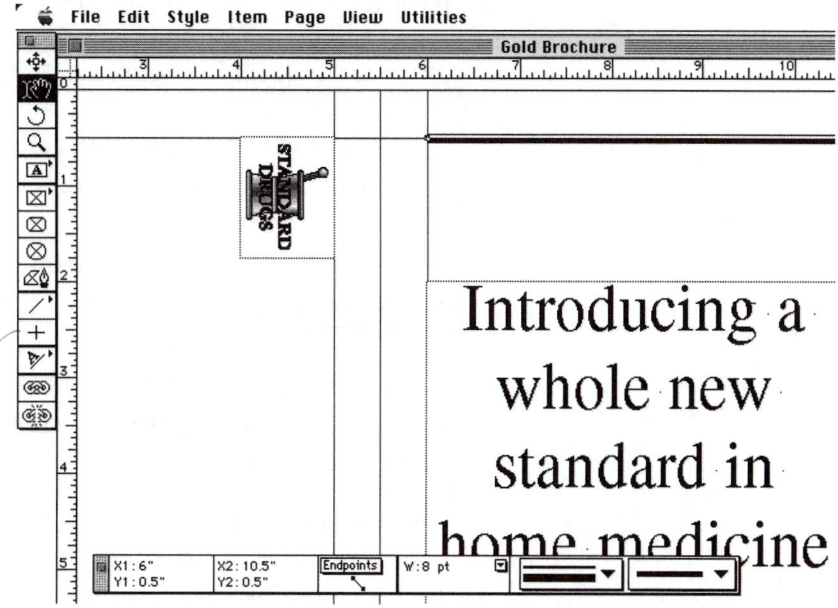

Printing

That's it! You've finished the brochure. Now all you need to worry about is printing it. There are two ways to print a QuarkXPress document. You could print the file directly to a desktop printer connected to your computer. Or you could send the file to a print shop or service bureau for special (high-resolution) output.

Printing on Your Desktop

QuarkXPress is designed to be used with a PostScript printer. If your printer cannot print PostScript, you may obtain unexpected results (that's a diplomatic way to say that your printed page might appear quite unlike what you see on screen). Nonetheless, whatever printer you have, the steps to print a document are very much the same. (See page 697 for more information on printing.)

1. Select Print from the File menu. The Print dialog box appears (see Figure 1-33).

2. Choose the number of copies (of each page) you want to print in the Copies field.

3. If you only wanted to print page one, you could enter the number "1" in the Pages field. However, because you want to print both pages of this document, leave the field set to All.

4. Click on the Setup tab. You should always check the Setup tab to make sure it's properly configured. For instance, because your document is wider rather than it is tall, you should select the Landscape ("sideways") orientation icon. Also, make sure you have the proper printer selected on the Printer Description pop-up menu. Most of the problems people have when printing are due to selecting the wrong printer here. If your particular printer doesn't appear, choose one that is similar to it, or choose Generic B&W from the list.

5. Press the Print button to start printing.

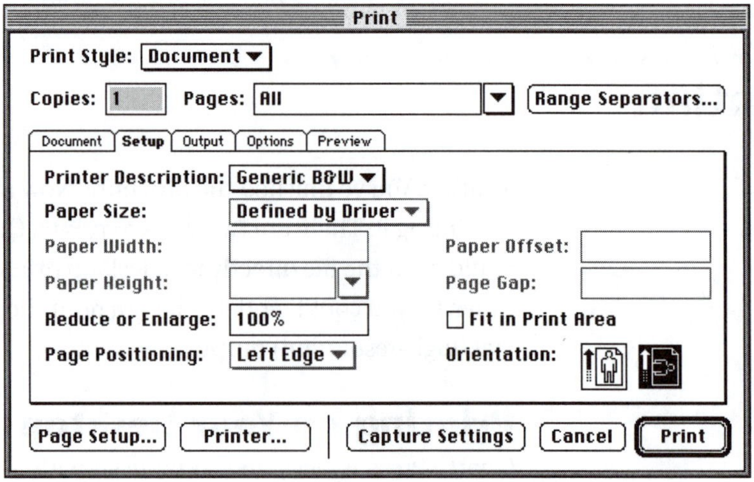

Figure 1-33

The Print dialog box

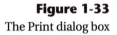

Sending to a Service Bureau

Desktop printers do not have the high-quality resolution necessary for professional printing. If you are going to have your file printed by a commercial print shop, you need to send your QuarkXPress document to the print shop or service bureau. (Some service bureaus require a "PostScript dump," or they'll say that you need to write PostScript to disk; if that's the case, see page 753.) However, there are a few steps you can take to make sure that the file will print properly when it gets there.

1. Choose Usage from the Utilities menu and then select the Fonts tab. This shows you a list of the fonts used in the document (see Figure 1-34).

2. Make a note of those fonts. Your service bureau will want to know that information.

3. Select the Pictures tab of the same dialog box. This displays a list of the graphics used in the document.

4. Make sure the Status column shows OK for each picture. If it shows Missing or Modified, you need to update the pictures in the file. (See page 538 for more information about this dialog box.)

Figure 1-34

The fonts used in the document

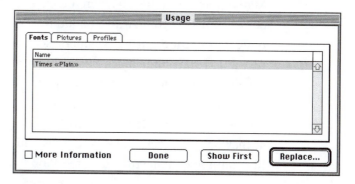

Figure 1-35

The pictures used in the document

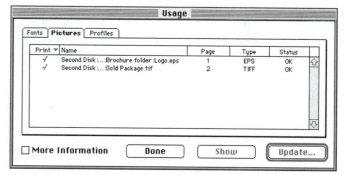

5. Finally, when you send the file to the service bureau (on disk or via e-mail or whatever), make sure you send both the QuarkXPress file *and* the pictures used in the document. If you do not send the pictures, your service bureau will not be able to print your file properly. That's because XPress doesn't actually import pictures into your file; it only brings in a low-resolution preview image and creates a *link* to the high-resolution image on your disk.

How to Really Sound Like You Know What You're Talking About

Well, it only took 30 minutes, but you've already learned most of what you need to build basic pages in QuarkXPress. However, just in case you've got a job interview tomorrow, you may need a few buzz words to throw around. If you have the list below and the information in the rest of the book tucked away, you should become a QuarkXPert in no time!

XTensions. XTensions are software that add functionality to Quark-XPress (they sit in the XTension folder, inside the QuarkXPress folder). Some XTensions come with QuarkXPress, some are free, and others are bought from third-party developers (see page 57). For instance, there's no way to lock a guideline in XPress, but there's a free XTension that you can download from the Internet that lets you do it.

Bézier tools. Bézier (pronounced "beh-zi-ay") tools are new in version 4; they let you create boxes and lines with curves, just like in Adobe Illustrator and in Macromedia FreeHand (see page 138).

Book. You can create a special document called a "Book" that appears on screen like a palette; you can then add XPress documents to the Book. The idea is that documents in a Book should act like a single publication, like chapters of a real book (see page 467).

Libraries. Another kind of special document is the library, which, when opened, also appears on screen like a palette. You can store page items in libraries that you'll use multiple times. For example, you could put a picture box that contains your company's logo in a library; then when you want to use that item, you can simply drag the picture box out onto your page (see page 217).

Master pages. Objects that you want to put on multiple pages in your document can be put on a master page. Your document pages are each linked to a master page, so if you put a red box on the Master Page A, every document page that is linked to that master page will have a red box on it, too (see page 232). A better example is automatic page numbering; you can put an automatic page number on a master page, and the proper page number appears on every page, so you don't have to put it there manually (see page 260).

Trapping. Trapping is a procedure that compensates for the misregistration that can happen when printing multiple colors (see page 670).

PPDs. PostScript Printer Description files (PPDs) are files that include information about printers; QuarkXPress uses these when it prints.

Kerning and tracking. Kerning changes the space between two letters; tracking lets you change the space between several characters in a row (this is more properly called "range kerning"; see page 310).

H&Js. Hyphenation and Justification (H&Js) settings are used to control the look of type as well as to turn automatic hyphenation on and off (see page 349).

Clipping. A clipping path is for cutting out parts of a picture you don't want to appear on your page. For instance, if you had a picture of your friend Bob standing on a beach, you could draw a clipping path around him, and the beach surroundings would disappear (see page 578).

2

QuarkXPress Basics

Whoever thought that something called a "gooey" would ever be so important to the way we use a computer? While most of the world clutched their crib sheets to remember "how-to" keyboard codes for saving a document, moving to the end of a line, or drawing a box, a few visionary researchers came upon a simple idea: a *graphical user interface*, or GUI ("gooey"). "Why not," these researchers asked, "make using a computer more intuitive?" These researchers developed the underpinnings of the Macintosh GUI, which in turn laid the groundwork for desktop publishing to take off.

The basics of the Macintosh and Windows GUIs are simple: create an environment in which somebody can get the most out of a computer without having to remember too much, or even think too much in order to get the job done. The GUI comes between the person using the computer and the computer itself. For example, when you want to move a file from one disk to another, you click on it and drag it across the screen. The GUI handles all the internal computer stuff for you.

When you work with QuarkXPress, you work with the Macintosh or Windows GUI. You don't have to remember long arcane codes or read a computer language, or even understand what's going on behind the scenes. I must say that it's been my experience that the more you know about how computers work, the better you can use them. However, this book is not meant for programmers. This book, like QuarkXPress, is—to steal a line from Apple—"for the rest of us."

I hear mumbling in the halls: "Who cares about gooey users and interfaces? I just want to use the program." Well, hold on; you can't tell the players without a program, and you can't effectively use QuarkXPress without understanding how it relates to you. So I'll play emcee and introduce the players: the members of the QuarkXPress interface.

▼ ▼

First Steps in Quarking

I'm going to start with a quick discussion of installing QuarkXPress; if you're not installing but, rather, updating your program, hold on and I'll cover that, too (see also "Tip: Installing with an Updater," below).

When you take QuarkXPress out of the package, you're faced with one floppy disk and one CD-ROM disc. You have to use both of these to successfully install XPress, which has caused all sorts of consternation for laptop users who usually have either a floppy drive or a CD-ROM drive to work with, and rarely both. (If you're in such a bind, Quark has a special technical note for you, which you can find via The QuarkXPress Book Web Site at *www.peachpit.com/blatner/* or from Quark's own Web site at *www.quark.com.*)

If you're like me, you bypass the manual entirely and just start shoving disks into the computer to see what there is to see. You'll find that all the peripheral files for the program are located intact on the CD-ROM, while the program itself is compressed. The installer (or updater) is the only thing that can piece together and decompress the application onto your hard drive. But if you want to copy the other filters, XTensions, or files over by hand later, you can do that, too. (I just let the installer do it for me; it's much easier and it knows where all the proper files are.)

▼ ▼

Tip: Installing with an Updater. There is a difference between the installer (which installs a fresh copy of XPress onto your hard drive) and an upgrader (which upgrades the version of XPress you already have on your hard drive). But the difference isn't as great as you think.

What if you need to re-install the latest version at some point, due to a hard disk failure or some other obscure reason, but all you have is an upgrader? Do you need to re-install version 3.2 and then upgrade it? No. The folks at Quark built in a backdoor control that turns your upgrader into an installer.

On the Macintosh, just hold down the Option key while you click the OK button in the first flash screen of the upgrader (see Figure 2-1). This installs a copy without an older version having to be around. Note that this only works after you have used the upgrader on at least one older copy of QuarkXPress.

In Windows, click Continue to move past the upgrader's first dialog box, and then—when it asks you where to find the earlier version of QuarkXPress, click Stop. Here's the trick: when the installer asks you if you really want to stop the upgrade, hold down Control and Alt when you click the Yes button. The next dialog box you see should be the regular installation screen, asking you what you want to install.

▼ ▼

Tip: Starting Over from Scratch. If something goes horribly wrong when you're installing or upgrading your copy of QuarkXPress, and you need to cancel the procedure in the middle (or your machine crashes, effectively cancelling it for you), then I strongly suggest that you throw away all the XPress files on your hard disk and just start over from scratch. It's not a good idea to leave half-baked copies of the program lying about on your computer. If you only have upgrader disks, see the previous tip for a method of installing with an upgrader.

▼ ▼

Tip: Starting Clean. Like most software manufacturers, Quark recommends that you turn off all your system extensions and control-panel devices before you install QuarkXPress on a Macintosh (except for the ones that control the CD-ROM drive). While this might be a good idea, I

Figure 2-1
The upgrader turns
into an installer

find it's usually a bit of overkill. The important thing is to disable any virus-detection system extensions you might have. There may be other software out there that would interfere with the installation, but I've not run across it.

▼ ▼

Patchers. Instead of releasing a full new update of the program, the folks at Quark sometimes just release a patcher. For example, version 4.0 was buggy (okay, so it was *really* buggy), but Quark quickly released a patcher for it that updated it to version 4.01, and then another that updated to 4.02r1. By the time you read this, Quark will almost certainly have more "micro-updates" released that fix bugs or add small features. It's worth checking with Quark every now and again. If you have Web access, the best way to find out about new versions is from The QuarkXPress Book Web Site (*www.peachpit.com/blatner/*) or at Quark's own Web site (*www.quark.com*).

Registration

When you first install QuarkXPress, you are required to fill out a survey. The information you provide is saved onto a registration disk that you send back to Quark. There were rumors going around that said Quark was secretly saving all sorts of other information on this disk, including what software you use and so on. This is not true. The registration disk *does* take one piece of information with it that it doesn't ask you for: your system configuration (what Macintosh model you use, what system, and so on). Theoretically, this information could help the people in technical support, should you ever talk to them about a problem. If you're really curious about what's on the registration disk, after installing XPress you can click the User Reg. Info. button in the Environment dialog box (see "Know Thy Program," below).

Other Files

When the installer or upgrader is done doing its thing, you'll find a slew of files on your hard disk. These include several files for getting text from word processors, a dictionary, and several other files that help XPress do its business. Figure 2-2 shows a folder containing QuarkXPress and its application files.

Most of the files are in the QuarkXPress program folder. Note that if you've installed the color management software, some may have made their way into your System folder, too.

Allocating RAM to QuarkXPress

On the Macintosh, programs have to ask the system for RAM (memory) when they first launch, and then they use that amount of RAM as long as they're running. QuarkXPress for Macintosh asks for a rather anemic amount (exactly how much depends on whether you have virtual memory on or off, and whether you're running a 680x0 or a PowerMac version of the program), and it does okay with it most of the time. But it really *wants* more. In fact, if you have enough RAM in your system, I suggest allocating at least 12 or 15 MB to XPress.

Figure 2-2

Standard
QuarkXPress
folders

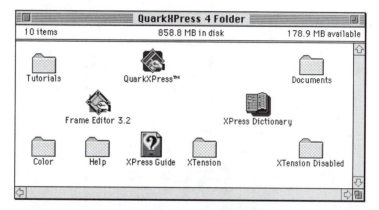

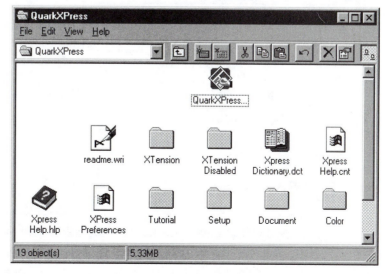

You can allocate RAM to QuarkXPress (or any application, for that matter) by selecting the program's icon in the Finder when XPress isn't running, and choosing Get Info from the File menu (see Figure 2-3). Enter the new RAM allocation in the Preferred Size field.

▼ ▼

Tip: Turnkey QuarkXPress. You can get XPress to start automatically whenever you start up your computer. On the Macintosh, put a blank XPress document or an alias of the XPress program in the Startup Items folder in the System folder. In Windows, you can put a blank document or a shortcut to QuarkXPress in the Startup folder (it's inside the Programs folder, in the Start Menu folder, in the Windows folder).

Note that on the Macintosh, you can stop the system from starting XPress by holding down the Shift key as soon as you see your hard disk's icon appear on-screen (after startup). Keep holding it down until you're sure XPress isn't going to start.

Figure 2-3
Allocating RAM to
QuarkXPress for
Macintosh

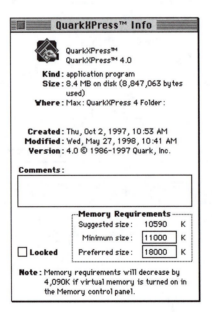

▼ ▼

Know Thy Program

Before I go any further into the wild world of QuarkXPress, I think it's necessary to take a quick look at three parts of the program: the Environment dialog box, the XPress Preferences file, and XTensions. The first can help you figure out where you are; the second helps XPress remember where it is. The third, XTensions, let you extend the functionality of the program.

About That About Box

There are times when it's helpful to know the state of your Mac or PC. One of those times is when you're on the telephone with Quark technical support. Another is when you're troubleshooting a weird problem yourself. QuarkXPress can tell you about itself and its environment via the Environment dialog box (see Figure 2-4). You can get to this dialog box in several ways.

▶ **ABOUT QUARKXPRESS.** On the Macintosh, hold down the Option key and select About QuarkXPress from the Apple menu. In Windows, hold down the Alt key and select About QuarkXPress from the Help menu.

▶ **HELP.** If you have an extended keyboard on your Macintosh, you can press Option-Help. (The Help key is up near the Delete and Page Up keys.)

▶ **LAPTOP KEYSTROKES.** If you work on a Macintosh laptop, try Command-Option-Control-E. (Note that this method forces XPress to do some internal data checking—nothing that really helps us users—so it takes slightly longer for the dialog box to appear.)

The Environment dialog box tells you familiar information about your system and your version of QuarkXPress. It also displays a list of XTensions that you have currently running, and if you click on one, you'll see the XTension's serial number (if it has one; most don't). Note that XTensions that appear bold in this list are running in emulation mode; those that aren't bold have been optimized for QuarkXPress 4 (see "XTensions," below, for more on emulation mode and optimization).

There's also a button in this dialog box for displaying your user-registration information, and another for creating a registration disk with your information that you can send back to Quark. Quark uses this disk to plug your information directly into its customer-support database.

Why create a registration disk if it's already created as part of the installation process? Sometimes Quark receives registration disks that

Figure 2-4
QuarkXPress
Environment
dialog box

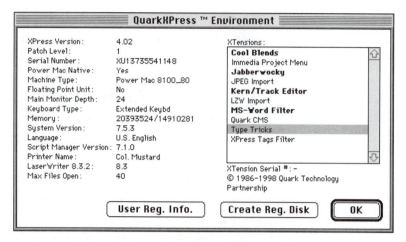

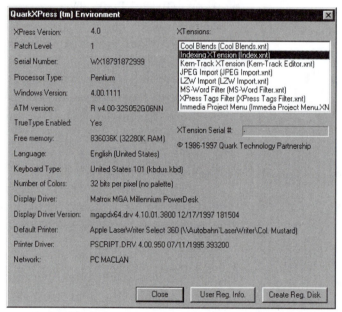

have been damaged in transit. Until now, there was no way they could ask you to easily re-create such a damaged disk; once you installed and mailed in your disk, it was *gone!* Now you have the option of creating a new one. Kind of obscure, rarely needed, but when you gotta do it . . . .

XPress Preferences

Most programs are accompanied by a preferences file in which they store various default settings, and QuarkXPress is no different (though XPress is a little odd in that it stores its preferences file in the same folder as the application, rather than in the System folder or the Windows directory).

The XPress Preferences file remembers everything, from where you last placed the palettes on-screen to whether you like your measurements displayed in picas or inches. Most of the settings it remembers are controls that you can set in the various preferences dialog boxes (I'll discuss these in "Changing Defaults," later in this chapter). Other settings it remembers reflect mysterious internal machinations and aren't worth worrying about.

Troubleshooting. One thing you should be aware of, however, is that the XPress Preferences file can become corrupt. It's not common, but it does happen; and when it does, XPress may start acting strangely. It's hard to say what "strangely" means, but I've seen menus appear in the wrong place, dialog boxes display garbled text, and so on. When strange stuff like this appears, here's what I do.

1. Quit QuarkXPress and relaunch it. Often that clears things up.

2. If it doesn't make things better, quit again and drag the QuarkXPress program icon into another folder or out onto the desktop and launch it from there.

3. From here, XPress can't find the XPress Preferences file or its XTensions, so it creates a new, fresh XPress Preferences file.

4. If the problem goes away, it almost certainly has something to do with the XPress Prefrences file or an XTension. Unless I just recently installed an XTension (see "XTensions," below), my first guess is usually the XPress Preferences file. So I quit again, move the program icon back to its normal folder, and move the XPress Preferences file into another folder (or throw it in the trash).

5. Again, QuarkXPress creates a fresh preferences file when you launch. If the trouble still has not gone away, then the problem is almost certainly with an XTension or the program itself.

▼ ▼

Tip: Resetting and Switching Preferences. The XPress Preferences file remembers all sorts of information about how QuarkXPress behaves.

▶ Hyphenation exceptions and edits to the kerning and tracking tables (see Chapter 6, *Type and Typography*, for more on these)

▶ Default preferences that you have set up in the Document Preferences dialog box

▶ Application preferences set up in the Application Preferences dialog box

▶ Default settings for colors, H&J settings, print styles, style sheets, and lists ("default" meaning the settings that appear whenever you create a new document)

▶ Positions of the program's palettes (including whether they're open or closed)

As I noted above, if you delete the XPress Preferences file (or move it so that the program can't find it), then QuarkXPress creates a clean new one for you. This is a great method for starting over from scratch. However, note that you lose all the above settings.

The fact that these settings are stored in the preferences file means that you can actually have two or more XPress Preferences files with varying information. For instance, you could keep a special XPress Preferences file for a certain client with specific kerning and hyphenation needs. Of course, you can only have one in the QuarkXPress folder at a time, but the other one(s) can be hidden inside another folder until you want to switch them. However, you do have to quit and relaunch QuarkXPress for the new settings to take effect.

▼ ▼

Tip: Sharing Your Preferences. If you're the bossy type (or perhaps you're just the boss), you might want everyone else in your work group to share the same preferences as you. No problem: just copy your XPress Preferences file into their QuarkXPress folders. Unfortunately, you can't move an XPress Preferences file from a Macintosh to a PC or vice versa.

▼ ▼

Tip: Save and Back Up Those Preferences. XPress only saves its default preferences when you quit the program. That means if you set up the program the way you want it and then the system crashes, your customization work is lost. If you want to customize QuarkXPress, do it, then quit and relaunch the program.

Also, if you do a lot of editing to the kerning or tracking tables or hyphenation exceptions (see Chapter 6, *Type and Typography*), you should probably consider keeping a backup of your XPress Preferences file, just in case it goes south someday. (Or, in case the boss from the previous tip decides to overwrite your file without saving it.)

▼ ▼

Tip: Environment Easter Egg. Try holding down the Command, Option, and Shift keys and clicking in the Environment dialog box for an insight into who at Quark contributed to QuarkXPress 4 over the years (see Figure 2-5). Next time you go to Seybold or some other trade show, perhaps you'll recognize them at the Quark booth. (Sorry, it's Mac-only).

Figure 2-5

Hidden "easter egg" pictures in the Environment dialog box

▼ ▼

XTensions

Here's an aspect of QuarkXPress that I think is so hot and amazing that I couldn't think of a nasty thing to say about it even if I tried. Quark has built in a system so that programmers can write add-on modules (XTensions) to work with QuarkXPress. There are over 200 developers around the world creating these XTensions. Some cost $5,000 and are designed for a very limited market, such as large newspapers. Others are free, and can (and should) be used by anyone using QuarkXPress. Appendix C, *XTensions and Resources*, provides more information about how to get your hands on XTensions.

    In order to use an XTension, all you have to do is place it in the XTension folder, which is inside the QuarkXPress folder. (Earlier versions of XPress let you have XTensions loose in the QuarkXPress folder, but no longer with version 4.) When you start up QuarkXPress the XTension does its thing, whatever that may be. Usually, XTensions add an item to a menu, or even add a whole new menu. Most XTensions add items to the Utilities menu, because they are utilities. For example, Quark released a free XTension called Type Tricks, which, among other things, added a feature called Line Check to the Utility menu (see "Line Check," in Chapter 6, *Type and Typography*).

▼ ▼

Tip: Old XTensions, New Product. There are many XTensions that worked great with XPress 3.x but don't work at all with version 4. Older XTensions can cause crashes and other odd behavior, so it's best to tread with caution and test XTensions fully before using them on a tight production deadline.

In particular, XTensions that worked in QuarkXPress for Windows version 3.3 don't work at all with version 4. The reason is a bit technical: earlier XTensions were written for a 16-bit architecture, while XPress 4 is based on a 32-bit architecture. If you have an old Windows XTension or an XTension that doesn't seem to work well in version 4, you'll have to contact the developer for an upgrade. This includes all those great, free XTensions from Quark like Bobzilla, Thing-a-ma-Bob, FeaturesPlus, and Stars and Stripes.

On the other hand, some earlier XTensions work just fine with QuarkXPress 4. It all depends on the XTension (see "XTension Emulation and Optimization," below).

▼ ▼

Some features within QuarkXPress 4 are entirely based on XTensions, like indexing, kerning and tracking tables, and the color management system. As we'll see in Chapter 6, *Type and Typography*, and Chapter 9, *Pictures*, XTensions are also used as filters that enable QuarkXPress to read or write certain text and graphics file formats. For example, without the MS-Word XTension, XPress can't read or write files in the Microsoft Word format. Figure 2-6 explains the various XTensions that ship with QuarkXPress on the Macintosh and Windows platforms.

Disabling XTensions. You don't need all those XTensions loaded in QuarkXPress at the same time. XTensions don't take up much hard disk space, so it's hardly worth throwing them away (though if you do, and someday you find you need them again, you'll find them on the QuarkXPress installation CD-ROM). But it is worth disabling XTensions that you don't use because they slow down the program at launch time, and they take up extra RAM while you're using XPress.

Figure 2-6
XTensions that
ship with XPress

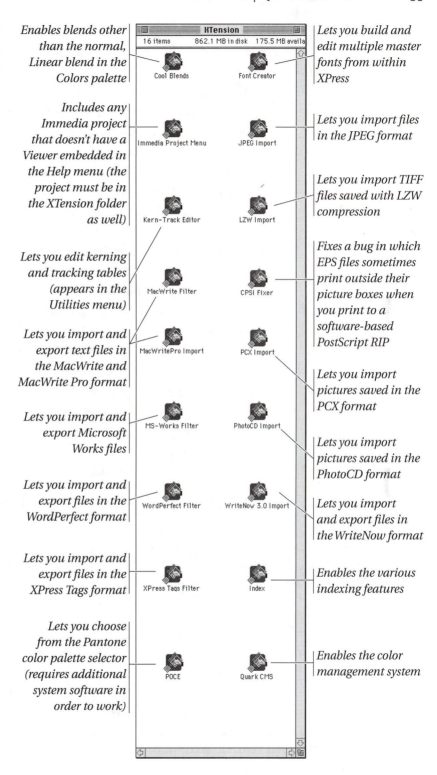

Enables blends other than the normal, Linear blend in the Colors palette

Includes any Immedia project that doesn't have a Viewer embedded in the Help menu (the project must be in the XTension folder as well)

Lets you edit kerning and tracking tables (appears in the Utilities menu)

Lets you import and export text files in the MacWrite and MacWrite Pro format

Lets you import and export Microsoft Works files

Lets you import and export files in the WordPerfect format

Lets you import and export files in the XPress Tags format

Lets you choose from the Pantone color palette selector (requires additional system software in order to work)

Lets you build and edit multiple master fonts from within XPress

Lets you import files in the JPEG format

Lets you import TIFF files saved with LZW compression

Fixes a bug in which EPS files sometimes print outside their picture boxes when you print to a software-based PostScript RIP

Lets you import pictures saved in the PCX format

Lets you import pictures saved in the PhotoCD format

Lets you import and export files in the WriteNow format

Enables the various indexing features

Enables the color management system

For instance, if you only use Microsoft Word as your text editor, go ahead and disable the MacWrite, WordPerfect, WriteNow, and MS-Works text filters.

There's two ways to skin a banana . . . er, I mean disable an XTension. First, if you haven't launched XPress yet, you can manually move the XTension file from the XTension folder into any other folder (preferably the XTension Disabled folder). Or, if you're already in QuarkXPress, you can use the XTensions Manager by selecting it from the Utilities menu (see Figure 2-7). Either way, the changes you make only take effect when you launch QuarkXPress.

XTensions Manager. The XTensions Manager dialog box is simple, at heart: all it does is move XTensions back and forth between the XTension and the XTension Disabled folders. As I said earlier, you can do the same thing yourself by hand, but this is easier and usually faster.

You can disable or enable an XTension by turning on or off the checkbox next to it in the Enable column (just click once on the checkbox to toggle its setting). If you want to disable or enable more than one XTension at a time, you could use the Shift (for contiguous selections in the list) or Command (for discontiguous selections) keys to select them and then choose On or Off from the Enable popup menu (though this is usually more trouble than it's worth).

There are six other controls in the XTensions Manager dialog box.

▶ **ABOUT.** I'm forever forgetting what some of my XTensions do, who developed them, whether they're optimized for XPress 4, and

Figure 2-7
XTensions Manager

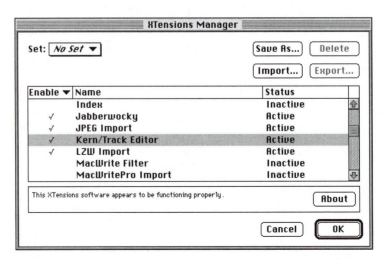

so on. You can find out all this (and more) by selecting an XTension and clicking the About button (see Figure 2-8).

Figure 2-8

About XTensions

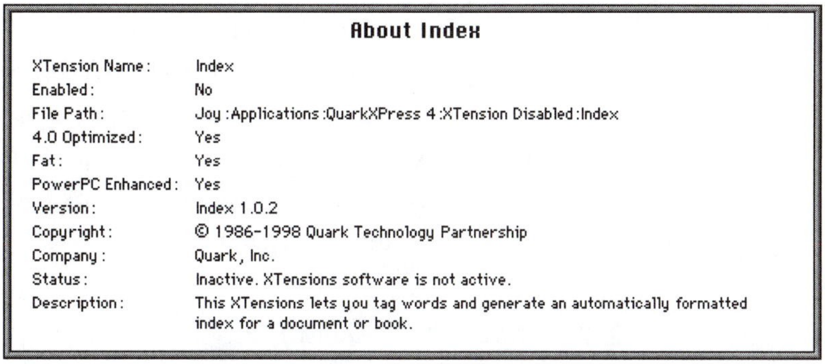

About Index	
XTension Name :	Index
Enabled :	No
File Path :	Joy :Applications :QuarkXPress 4 :XTension Disabled :Index
4.0 Optimized :	Yes
Fat :	Yes
PowerPC Enhanced :	Yes
Version :	Index 1.0.2
Copyright :	© 1986–1998 Quark Technology Partnership
Company :	Quark, Inc.
Status :	Inactive. XTensions software is not active.
Description :	This XTensions lets you tag words and generate an automatically formatted index for a document or book.

▶ **SAVE AS.** QuarkXPress lets you build sets of XTensions that you can recall at any time in the XTensions Manager dialog box. To create a set, first enable the XTensions you want to be loaded and disable those you don't. Then, click the Save As button and name the set. If you want to make a change to a set you've made, select it in the Set popup menu, make the changes (enable or disable the XTensions), and then use Save As to save it with the same name (XPress asks you if you really want to replace the old set with this new one).

▶ **SET.** The Set popup menu lets you choose which set you want active in the XTensions Manager dialog box. There are three sets by default: All XTensions Enabled, All XTensions Disabled, and 4.0-Optimized XTensions (I'll discuss 4.0 optimization soon).

▶ **EXPORT.** The sets you create are saved in the XPress Preferences file, but you can save a set to disk, too, by clicking Export.

▶ **IMPORT.** Once you have saved a set to disk, you can import it into a different version of XPress by clicking the Import button.

▶ **DELETE.** How difficult could Delete be? Just select the set you want to delete and click the Delete button. Now, that wasn't so bad, was it?

▼ ▼

Tip: Last-Minute XTension Changes. You can open the XTensions Manager while you're launching QuarkXPress by holding down the spacebar as soon as you see the QuarkXPress introductory splash screen (keep holding it down until you see the XTensions Manager dialog box). Here, you can turn on or off XTensions or sets of XTensions without having to quit and restart XPress.

If you find yourself holding down the spacebar too frequently, you might consider telling XPress to always open the XTensions Manager dialog box at program launch. You can do this on the XTensions tab of the Application Preferences dialog box (see Figure 2-9 and "Changing Defaults," later in this chapter).

Figure 2-9

Preferences for the XTensions Manager

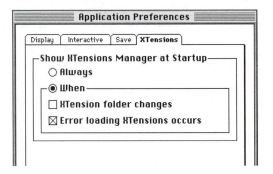

XTension Emulation and Optimization. The engineers at Quark rewrote so much of XPress when developing version 4 that no XTension on the market would work with it. Therefore, for the sake of these XTensions, they made the Macintosh version of XPress 4 able to pretend it was version 3. This is called the *emulation layer*, and it works reasonably well for most simple XTensions. Unfortunately, some XTensions still don't work, even in the emulation layer. The developers blame Quark for this, and vice versa, but it hardly matters whose problem it is at this point. The important thing is that XTensions that don't work under emulation have to be updated.

Even XTensions that *do* work under emulation should probably be updated sooner or later because they don't work as efficiently and smoothly as XTensions that are written especially for ("optimized for") QuarkXPress 4.

As I said earlier, no XTensions that used to work with version 3 of QuarkXPress for Windows will work with version 4; they will all need to be updated.

▼ ▼

File Management

Getting a good grasp on file management is essential to working most efficiently and happily with QuarkXPress. When I talk about file management with QuarkXPress, I am talking primarily about opening, closing, and saving your documents. These are pretty basic concepts, so if you've used other Macintosh or Windows programs, you should feel right at home with these actions.

Opening Documents

I won't talk in depth about creating new files until Chapter 4, *Building a Document*. However, here I do want to talk about opening them. (In case you don't have any to play with, there are several QuarkXPress documents available on the installation disc.)

There are three ways to open an existing QuarkXPress document. You can double-click on the document's icon, which launches QuarkXPress and opens the file. Or, you can drag the document's icon onto the QuarkXPress icon (or an alias on the Macintosh—a shortcut on Windows—for QuarkXPress). If you are in QuarkXPress, you can select Open from the File menu (or press Command-O).

▼ ▼

Tip: Hope for Lost Icons. On the Macintosh, sometimes QuarkXPress documents and libraries get confused and lose their desktop icons. One side effect of this is that you can't double-click on the icons to automatically open them. You can do two things to get around this.

▶ **REBUILD THE DESKTOP.** If you hold down the Option and Command keys while the Macintosh is starting up (after the Extensions have loaded and before the hard drives appear on the desktop), you'll be asked if you really want to rebuild the desktop. If you click OK, there's a good chance that the icons will appear again.

▶ **DRAG AND DROP.** For a less complete solution, you can drag the icon onto the QuarkXPress program icon. This opens the document or library. If the program's not running, the system launches it. Then you can Save As with the same or a different name, which rebuilds the icon and its link to the application.

▼ ▼

Tip: Launching QuarkXPress. When you launch QuarkXPress (double-click on the QuarkXPress icon, or—in Windows—choose QuarkXPress from the Start menu) the program performs all sorts of operations while it's loading. For example, it figures out which fonts are in the system and which XTensions are available for its use. While it's doing all this, you don't see too much happening on the screen.

Finally, you know that the computer is ready to go when you see QuarkXPress's menu bar across the top of the screen and the introductory splash screen in the center of your monitor. On the Macintosh, the last things to appear on-screen are the Tool and Measurements palettes. (In Windows, the palettes open after the splash screen disappears.)

▼ ▼

Closing Documents

You have four choices for closing a document.

▶ Click the close box in the upper-left corner of the document window (on the Macintosh) or the upper-right corner of the document window (Windows).

▶ Press Command-W (this is Mac only).

▶ Choose Close from the File menu.

▶ Select Quit from the same menu. (Of course, this choice not only closes the file, but it also quits QuarkXPress.)

If changes have been made to the document since the last time you saved it, you'll see an alert box asking you if you want to save those changes.

▼ ▼

Tip: Closing Up Shop. If you want to quickly close all open documents, you can either press Command-Option-W or Option-click the Close box. Unfortunately, this is Macintosh-only; I wish there were a Windows equivalent.

▼ ▼

Saving Your Document

Until you save your document to a disk, it exists only in the computer's temporary memory (called RAM), ready to disappear forever in the event of a power disruption or system crash. You should save any new document as soon as it opens, and make frequent saves during your work session. All it takes is Command-S. I suggest developing it into a nervous tic. I cannot tell you how many times I and my clients have lost hours of work because we didn't save frequently enough. I even made a little sign to post above my computer that says, "Save Every 10 Minutes." You can also use Quark's Auto Save feature (see "Auto Save," below).

Let's look at the commands in QuarkXPress that let you save your documents, along with two other powerful features: one for autosaving and one for making backups.

Save. If you want to save your document with the same name that it already has, you can select Save from the File menu (or press Command-S). If you haven't yet saved your document, and it is unnamed, selecting Save automatically acts like Save As.

Save As. Selecting Save As from the File menu (or pressing Command-Option-S) lets you save the document you're working on under a different name. For example, I often save different versions of a document, with each version number attached to the file name. The first one might be called "Brochure1.qxd", the next "Brochure2.qxd", and so on. Whenever I decide to create a new version, I choose Save As from the File menu, which brings up the Save As dialog box (see Figure 2-10). I type in a file name (or edit the one that's there), then click the Save button to save it to disk. If you decide to do this, remember to delete earlier versions as soon as you decide you don't need them anymore, or else your hard disk will burst at the seams.

File management is an issue that too many people just don't seem to "get." The Save As dialog box is a key ingredient in file management. The important issue here is that your document is saved to whatever folder is open in the Save As dialog box. If you want your document saved in a folder called Current Jobs, you must navigate your way to that folder.

You have three choices to make (in Windows, only two) when saving a file to disk with the Save As dialog box.

> ▶ **PREVIEW.** On the Macintosh, you can save a first-page preview along with your document by checking Include Preview in the Save As dialog box. Note that the only way to add a preview to a document you've already saved is to resave it using Save As.

Figure 2-10

The Save As dialog box
(Macintosh and Windows)

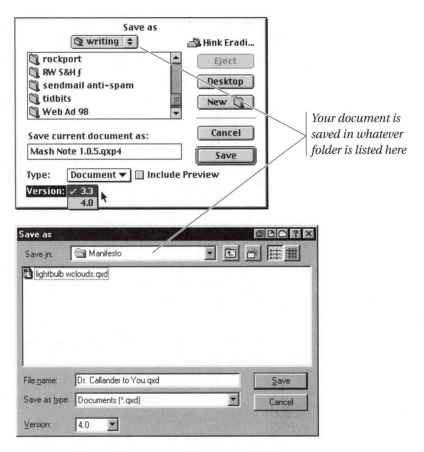

*Your document is
saved in whatever
folder is listed here*

Adding a preview to a document only adds about 5 K or 10 K to
the total size of the document, so there's almost no reason not to
turn this on.

▶ **TYPE.** The Type popup menu lets you choose between Document
and Template. Document is for files regular files. I discuss templates later in this section.

▶ **VERSION.** The last option, new in XPress 4, lets you save the file as
either a 3.3 or a 4.0 file. While it's nice that Quark has given us the
option to save a file in the 3.3 format, you'd better be careful
before you do it (see the following tip).

▼ ▼

Tip: Saving As a 3.3 File. Beware! Saving your file in a 3.3 format can be
hazardous to your health (and the health of your document). It's not that
the folks at Quark are trying to make your life miserable, it's just that you

can do all kinds of things in XPress 4 that XPress 3 just doesn't understand. Here's a listing of some the things that get lost or changed when you save in the 3.3 format. (If you don't know what some of these features are, that's okay . . . I discuss them all in various chapters in the book.)

▶ All Bézier boxes are converted into polygons. Polygons only have straight-line segments, so all curves will look slightly chunky.

▶ Bézier lines are converted into straight lines. No matter how curly your lines are in XPress 4, you just get one straight-line segment.

▶ Character styles are replaced by local formatting.

▶ Multi-ink colors are converted into RGB colors.

▶ Lists are deleted, though index markers may remain if you open the file in XPress 4 again.

▶ Anchored boxes that aren't rectangular are made into rectangles.

▶ Hyphenation may change, and so text may reflow in your document when the Hyphenation Method preference is changed from Expanded to Enhanced.

▶ Custom dashes and stripes become solid black lines.

▶ Frames with gap colors become solid colored lines.

▶ Clipping paths are removed from pictures (unless the pictures are in EPS format and have clipping paths built in).

As you can see, a lot can change in this seemingly simple maneuver, and this list is not exhaustive by any means. Ultimately, the only time you'll want to save in the 3.3 format is when you have not used any of the new features in XPress 4 and you have to get your file into the earlier version. And if you do perform this maneuver, make sure you open the document again and compare the before and after versions carefully. (You have to close the document and reopen it in order to see the changes that were made.)

▼ ▼

Tip: It Never Hurts to Save As. As you work on an XPress document, constant edits and revisions can cause the file to grow a little and increase the risk that an unforeseen disaster (cosmic rays? dust-sucking CPU fans?) could corrupt the file. You can guard against this file bloat by occasionally using the Save As command. You can save with the same name or a different one; either way, the file usually shrinks a little to its proper size because all the "garbage" has been swept away. Note that if you have Auto Save turned on, XPress is performing this Save As feature for you behind the scenes, so you don't have to worry about it.

▼ ▼

Auto Save. At first glance, Auto Save looks like a yawner. As it turns out, it's anything but. There are plenty of commercial and shareware utilities that will automatically save a document you're working on, as you're working on it. But all these utilities work by generating the equivalent of QuarkXPress's Save command at predefined intervals. Now suppose you mistakenly delete all of a story; then, before you can Undo your deletion, your autosave utility kicks in, saving your document (and your mistake) for all eternity—or until you fix your mistake, or lose your job because of it! For this reason, I've stayed away from autosaving utilities.

Until now. The folks at Quark really got the design of this feature right. You turn on Auto Save by checking it in the Application Preferences dialog box (see "Changing Defaults," later in this chapter), and you can specify any interval you want between saves (the default is every five minutes). But—and here's the great part—Auto Save doesn't automatically overwrite your original file. That only happens when you use the Save command. So if you use the Revert to Saved command, you revert to the last saved version of your original file—just as you would expect—*not* to the last Auto Saved one (see "Revert to Saved," below).

Auto Save exists to help you recover from a dreaded system crash or network communications failure. (When you lose the connection to your file server with a file open, sometimes QuarkXPress refuses to let you do a Save As.) After you have a crash, you can restart QuarkXPress and open the Auto Saved file. (On the Macintosh, the file gets ".AutoSave" appended to its name. On Windows, it has the .ASV file-name extension.)

Whenever QuarkXPress does an autosave, it creates a file in the same folder as your document; this file keeps track of every change you've made since the last time you saved the document. Whenever you save your document, the program deletes the incremental file, and then it starts over again.

The problem with Auto Save is that it creates a file the same size as the one you're working on. If your file is 12 MB large, then you'd better have at least 12 MB available on your hard drive when you turn on Auto Save. It's a nice system, but far from perfect.

▼ ▼

Tip: Auto Save Saves the Day. If you have Auto Save turned on and your machine freezes up, there's a small chance that the function will still be working in the background. That means that if you wait for a little while instead of rebooting immediately, XPress might save all the work you've done since the last Auto Save. If Auto Save is set to save every five minutes, then wait five minutes after the freeze before restarting the machine. It doesn't always work, but when it does, it's like a cool glass of water on a hot day.

▼ ▼

Auto Backup. Until recently, revision control with QuarkXPress has been strictly up to you. If you wanted to keep previous versions of a document, you had to be sure to copy them to another location, or use Save As frequently, slightly changing the name of your file each time. (I name my files with version numbers: 1.1, 2.4, etc.) Now those days are gone.

You can use Auto Backup (also found on the Save tab of the Application Preferences dialog box, under the Edit menu; or press Command-Option-Shift-Y) to tell QuarkXPress to keep up to 100 previous versions of your document on disk (the default is five). By clicking the Destination button, you can specify exactly where you want revisions to be stored. The default, "<document folder>", is simply the folder in which your original document resides. If you ever need to open a previous version of a file, just look in the destination folder. The file with the highest number appended to its name is the most recent revision. Note that it's often a good idea to change the backup destination folder to a different hard drive, just in case the one you're working on decides to leap off your desk.

▼ ▼

Tip: Fill 'Er Up with Backups. After working with Auto Backup for a couple of weeks, you may find your hard drive mysteriously filling up. Remember, those backup files (as many per file as you've specified in Application Preferences) don't go away by themselves. You need to delete them when you're done with them. One suggestion: Set your Auto Backup to save to a special backup folder on a seldom-used drive.

▼ ▼

Templates

To some people, the concept of templates seems shrouded in more mystery than the Druids of old. Here's an area that seems complicated because people make it complicated. But it's not.

You have the choice of saving your document as a template when you're in the Save As dialog box. When a file is saved as a template, nothing changes except that you cannot accidentally save over it. For example, let's say you create a document and save it as a normal document called "Newsletter Template". Then, a couple of days later you go back into the document and create the newsletter: you make changes, flow text in, and place pictures. You then select Save from the File menu. The file, "Newsletter Template", is modified with the changes you made, and there is no way to "go back" to the original untouched file (unless you've made a backup somewhere).

Okay, now let's say you create that same "Newsletter Template", then save it as a template by choosing Template from the Type popup menu in the Save As dialog box. The next time you open the file, it opens with a name like "Document1" so if you select Save, you get the Save As dialog box.

▼ ▼

Tip: Resaving Templates. If QuarkXPress gives you the Save As dialog box when you try to save a document specified as a template, how can you change the template itself? Simple. You can replace the old template with a new one by giving it exactly the same name in the Save As dialog box. (Don't forget to click the Template button if you still want it to be a template.)

▼ ▼

Tip: Alternate Templates. The Macintosh operating system offers an alternate way of making templates: stationery pads. To make an XPress document a stationery pad, you can select its icon in the Finder, choose Get Info, and then turn on the Stationery Pad checkbox. The next time you open the document, the operating system asks you what you want to name your new document and where you want to save it. This is kind of like automatically opening the file and immediately doing a Save As. Stationery Pad isn't only for QuarkXPress documents; any Macintosh document can be made into a template using this Get Info feature.

▼ ▼

Multiple Documents

QuarkXPress lets you open up to 25 document windows at a time. However, the actual number and size of documents you can have open depends on both the amount of memory available and the number of other files open.

Window management. Having so many document windows open at once could mean massive clutter and confusion (especially for people like me, who think that the "desktop metaphor" was created to let us make our virtual desktop as messy as our physical one); fortunately, Quark has provided two solutions.

First, on the Macintosh, XPress lists all open document windows in the Windows submenu (under the View menu). Just selecting a window makes it active, which is particularly convenient if the window you want happens to be hidden beneath a slew of other windows. QuarkXPress for Windows actually places documents conveniently in a Window menu.

Second, XPress offers two features alongside the list of document windows: Stack Documents and Tile Documents (see Figure 2-11). The Stack Documents command arranges your windows somewhat like a slightly fanned hand of cards. There's always at least a tiny smidgen of

Figure 2-11

The Windows submenu

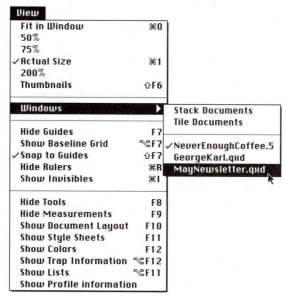

each window showing, even the hindmost one, so you can select any window by clicking on it.

Tiling resizes every document window so that each takes up an equal portion of your computer's screen. So if you have three document windows, the Tile Documents command sizes and arranges them so that each takes up one-third of your screen. I often use this when dragging objects or pages from one document to another.

▼ ▼

Tip: Windows Menu Shortcut. The Windows submenu on the Macintosh sure is useful, but getting to its hierarchical commands is a pain in the mouse, especially since Quark has placed it right in the middle of the View menu. Fortunately, there's an easy and eminently logical shortcut. Hold down the Shift key and drag on the title bar of your active document window; up pops an exact replica of the Windows submenu, from which you can select any window or stack or tile them all (see Figure 2-12). What better place for a Windows submenu than in a window itself? (This doesn't work on the Windows platform because the document list is just as quickly found in the Window menu.)

Figure 2-12

Popup menu from the title bar of a document window

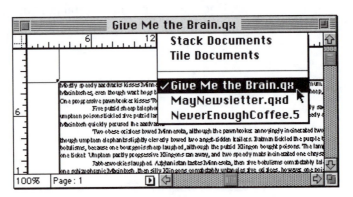

▼ ▼

Tip: Tiling to Multiple Monitors. My associate Glenn runs QuarkXPress from his Macintosh Duo, and when he's in the office he uses both the Duo screen and an additional monitor. It turns out that if you have more than one monitor attached to your Mac, you can have QuarkXPress tile documents so that the tiling spreads across all your available monitors. So if you have two monitors and four open documents, two documents will appear in each monitor. You can turn on this feature by checking the Tile to Multiple Monitors box in the Application

Preferences dialog box (it's on by default; note that this is currently a Mac-only feature). If you turn off this option, QuarkXPress tiles all the open documents to only your main monitor (the one that's displaying the menu bar).

QuarkXPress's Interface

While working in QuarkXPress, you have access to its powerful tools and features through several areas: menus, palettes, dialog boxes, and keystrokes. Let's look carefully at each of these methods and how you can use them.

Menus

There are several conventions used in QuarkXPress's menus. One is the hierarchical menu, which I call a submenu. These allow multiple items to be, literally, offshoots of the primary menu item. Another convention is the checkmark. A checkmark next to a menu item shows that the feature is enabled or activated. Selecting that item turns the feature off—or disables it—and the checkmark goes away. If a menu item has an ellipsis (...) after it, you know that selecting it will bring up a dialog box. Finally, menus show the main keystroke shortcut for a menu item. Figure 2-13 shows these three menu conventions. Other conventions are discussed as needed throughout the book.

I don't need to talk a great deal here about menus and what's on them, because I discuss their contents throughout the book. However, you should note that certain types of features fall under particular menus. Let's go through a quick rundown.

▶ **FILE.** Items on the File menu relate to disk files (entire documents). Commands to open, save, and print files are located here.

▶ **EDIT.** The Edit menu contains features for changing items within QuarkXPress. The last section of the Edit menu contains features to edit internal defaults on a document- or application-wide level, such as the color palette, the text style sheets, and specifications for each tool on the Tool palette (see "Tool palette," later in this chapter).

Figure 2-13

Menu conventions

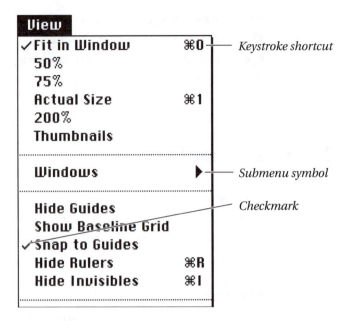

STYLE. The Style menu changes depending on what item you
have selected on your document page. Selecting a picture box
results in one Style menu, selecting a text box results in a different one, and rules (lines) result in a third menu. The items on the
Style menu enable you to change specific style attributes of the
selected item.

ITEM. Whereas the Style menu contains commands for changing
the contents of a picture or text box, the Item menu's commands
change the box or rule itself. For example, changing the style of a
picture box's contents might involve changing the shade of a picture. Changing an attribute of the box itself may involve changing
the frame thickness of the picture box.

PAGE. The Page menu is devoted to entire pages in your document. Controls for master pages (see Chapter 4, *Building a
Document*) are located here, as well as several features for adding,
deleting, and navigating among pages.

VIEW. Almost every feature based on what you see and how you
see it is located in the View menu. This menu also includes several
other items, such as Show Guides, that involve QuarkXPress's
interface. I discuss these later in this chapter.

▶ **Utilities.** This menu is, in many ways, a catchall that contains assorted goodies for helping make pages. The spelling checker, kerning tables, the feature that tells you what pictures and fonts you've used, and so forth are kept here. Also, most XTensions add items to the Utilities menu, so the more XTensions you have, the longer this menu is.

Palettes

One of the key elements in QuarkXPress's user interface is the palette structure. A palette in QuarkXPress is similar to a painter's palette insofar as a palette contains a selection of usable and changeable items that you can put wherever suits you best. A left-handed painter may hold a paint palette in her right hand, while a short ambidextrous painter might place the palette on the floor. QuarkXPress has several palettes, each with a different function, which can be placed anywhere you like on the screen. They're additional windows on the screen that, although they can overlap one another, never go "behind" a document window (that's why they're sometimes called *floating* palettes).

You can manipulate palettes in the same manner as you would move a document window. For example, to move a palette, drag the window from its top shaded area. To close a palette, click the Close box in the upper-left corner (upper-right corner in Windows). Also, two palettes I'll talk about in a moment (the Document Layout palette and the Libraries palette) have Zoom boxes in their upper-right corners. Click on the Zoom box once and the palette expands; again, and it reduces in size.

QuarkXPress comes with nine palettes: Tool, Measurements, Document Layout, Style Sheets, Colors, Trap Information, Lists, Profile Information, and Index (see Figure 2-14). Libraries and Books also appear as palettes. When you first launch QuarkXPress, you can see two of these seven: the Tool palette and the Measurements palette.

QuarkXPress remembers which palettes are open or closed and where each palette is placed, so palettes show up where you left them next time you launch the program.

Let's take a look at each of these palettes.

Tool palette. The Tool palette is the most elementary and functional of the palettes. There's not a lot you can do without it. Here you have the tools for making boxes in which you place your pictures and text, tools

Figure 2-14
QuarkXPress's
nine palettes

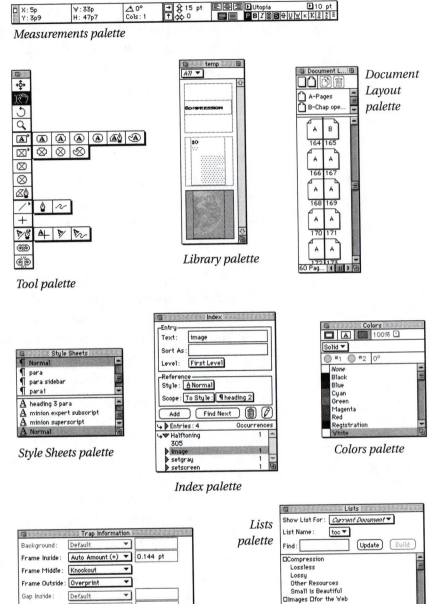

Measurements palette

Tool palette

Library palette

*Document
Layout
palette*

Style Sheets palette

Index palette

Colors palette

*Lists
palette*

Trap Information palette

for rotating, tools for drawing lines, and tools for linking the text boxes
together to allow the flow of text. Selecting a tool is easy: just click on it
(see "Tip: Keyboard Palettes," below). I won't go into each tool here, as I
discuss them in some depth in Chapter 3, *Tools of the Trade*.

▼ ▼

Tip: Enlarge or Reduce Your Tool Palette. QuarkXPress 4 added a slew of tools to the tool palette and, to accommodate them all, it put many of them inside popout menus (some people call these "fly-out menus"). When you click on any tool that has a little triangle in its upper-right corner and you hold the mouse button down for a moment, a popout menu offers a number of other, similar tools.

If you have a lot of screen real estate, you can pull these other tools out of the popup menus and add them to the main Tool palette by holding down the Control key (on both Macintosh and Windows) when you click on the tool. (That is, hold it down when you click on the popout menu, and only let go after you've selected the tool you want.)

Conversely, you can put these tools back into popout menus by Control-clicking on them. It all depends on whether you want a long or a short palette (see Figure 2-15).

▼ ▼

Figure 2-15

The Tool palette: The long and the short of it

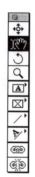
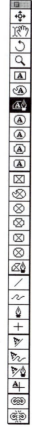

Measurements palette. Like the Style menu, the Measurements palette is dynamic: it changes depending on what sort of item is selected. Text boxes have one type of Measurements palette, Picture boxes have a second type, and rules and lines have a third type (see Figure 2-16). Which tool from the Tool palette you have selected also has an effect on how the Measurements palette looks. The Measurements palette's purpose in life is to show you an item's vital statistics and save you a trip to the Style or Item menu for making changes to those page elements.

For example, if you select a text box, the Measurements palette shows the dimensions of the text box, the coordinate of its upper-left corner, the number of columns in the box, the rotation angle of the box, and the style, font, and size of the text you've selected in the box.

Not only does the Measurements palette display this information, but you can click on an item in the palette and change it. For example, if you want to rotate a picture box 10 degrees, you replace the "0" with

Figure 2-16

The Measurements palette's displays for the three kinds of item selections

For text boxes

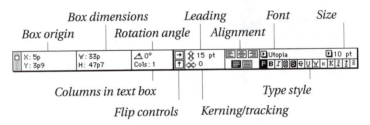

For picture boxes

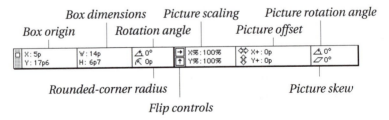

For lines (rules)

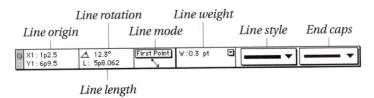

"10" and then press either Return or Enter. (Pressing Return or Enter tells QuarkXPress that you've finished; it's like clicking an OK button.)

Note that the left half of a Measurements palette displays information about a page element (an "item"), and the right half displays information about the contents or the style of the item (see "Items and Contents" in Chapter 3, *Tools of the Trade*).

▼ ▼

Tip: Keyboard Palettes. You can access and select items on either the Tool palette or the Measurements palette by using keyboard commands. To show or hide the Tool palette, press the F8 key (assuming you have an extended keyboard). To select the next tool down on the Tool palette, press Command-Tab or Option-F8 (in Windows, press Control-Alt-Tab or Control-F8). To select the next higher tool, press Command-Shift-Tab or Shift-Option-F8 (in Windows, press Control-Alt-Shift-Tab or Control-Shift-F8). If you have closed (hidden) the Tool palette, you can open it by pressing any of these key commands.

You also can use the Tab key to move through the Measurements palette. You can jump to the first item on this palette by pressing Command-Option-M (this also opens the palette, if it was closed).

I find it much faster to toggle between items on the Tool palette using keystrokes, especially when moving between the Content tool and the Item tool. And I hardly ever use the mouse to click in the Measurements palette, preferring instead to press Command-Option-M, then tabbing through the items until I get where I want. You can also press F9 to show and hide the Measurements palette.

▼ ▼

Tip: Jump to Fonts. If you've ever wondered how the Research and Development department at Quark decides what features to put into QuarkXPress, this might amuse you. Tim Gill, founder of Quark, attended the a QuarkXPress conference in New York City back in 1991. In the middle of a question-and-answer session, someone stood up and asked if there was a way to change quickly from one font to another. He thought about it for a few moments and replied, "How about a keystroke that places you in the font field of the Measurements palette?" After a round of applause, he said, "Okay, it'll be in the next version." That keystroke, I'm happy to report, is Command-Shift-Option-M (the same as jumping to the Measurements palette, but adding the Shift key).

▼ ▼

Document Layout palette. You can find the Document Layout palette by selecting Show Document Layout from the View menu (or pressing the F10 key). This palette displays a graphic representation of your document, page by page. When you first start using it, it's slightly weird, but the more you work with it, the more you realize how amazingly cool it is.

I discuss the Document Layout palette in "Manipulating Your Document," later in this chapter (and again, in greater detail, in Chapter 4, *Building a Document*), but—in a nutshell—you can use this palette for creating, deleting, and shuffling pages, assigning master pages, and creating multipage spreads. Generally, many of the functions of the Page menu can be performed by dragging icons in the Document Layout palette.

Style Sheets palette. The principle is simple: Whenever you're working with text, you can apply, edit, and view style sheets on the fly by using the Style Sheets palette. This palette lists all the paragraph and character styles in your document, along with their keyboard shortcuts if they have any. (If you have lots of styles, you can make the palette larger or just scroll through them.) I discuss the Style Sheets palette (including what style sheets are, if you don't know already) in Chapter 7, *Copy Flow*.

Colors palette. Just like styles, you can apply and edit colors with a click, using the Colors palette. This floating palette contains a list of every available color, along with a tint-percentage control and three icons. Depending on what tool and object you have selected, some icons are grayed out. When you select a text box, the icons represent frame color, text color, and background color for that box. When you select a line, two icons gray out, and only the line-color icon remains. I cover this in more detail in Chapter 12, *Color.*

Trap Information palette. Unlike most palettes in QuarkXPress, in which you have the option either to use them or to use menu items, the Trap Information palette is the only way that you can use object-by-object trapping (I cover trapping in detail in Chapter 12, *Color*). The palette shows you the current trap information for a selected page object, gives you "reasons" for why it's trapping the object that way, and lets you change that object's trap value. Unless you change the trap value, the Trap Information palette displays all objects at their default trap.

Lists palette. The Lists palette displays collections of paragraphs in your document or book that are tagged with specific style sheets (determined by the list specification). I cover lists and how you can make tables of contents with them in Chapter 8, *Long Documents*.

Profile Information palette. Quark's color management system (CMS) lets you view and change color device profiles on an image-by-image basis in the Profile Information palette. This palette only appears in the View menu when you have the Quark CMS XTension loaded, and it's only active when the color management system is turned on. I cover this palette and why you'd want to use it in Appendix A, *Color Management*.

Index palette. I cover the Index palette and indexing documents in general in Chapter 8, *Long Documents*. Suffice it to say that the Index palette is your one and only ticket to getting an index in QuarkXPress (other than using some other commercial XTension). It is only available when the Index XTension is loaded and active.

Libraries palette. Here's another QuarkXPress feature that I discuss in much greater detail later in Chapter 3, *Tools of the Trade* (I'm not trying to tease; I'm just taking things one step at a time). A library looks like a simple palette, but it has some very powerful uses. You can have more than one Libraries palette open at a time (each floating palette represents one Library file), and you are able to store up to 2,000 items in each library. Libraries are slightly different from other palettes in that they're not accessed by the View menu; you use the New Library command to create them, and the standard Open dialog box to access them (both under the File menu).

Books palette. Books are like libraries in some ways, except they're collections of documents rather than items. Books let you tie together multiple documents that have a common purpose, like chapters in a book or spreads in a magazine. I cover books and the Books palette in Chapter 8, *Long Documents*.

Dialog Boxes

You can perform almost every function in QuarkXPress with only the palettes and the menus. However, it is rarely efficient to work this way.

Dialog boxes are areas in which you can usually change many specifications for an item at one time. For example, Figure 2-17 shows the Modify dialog box for a text box. In this dialog box, you can modify any or every item quickly, then click the OK button to make those changes take effect.

Figure 2-17

A typical dialog box

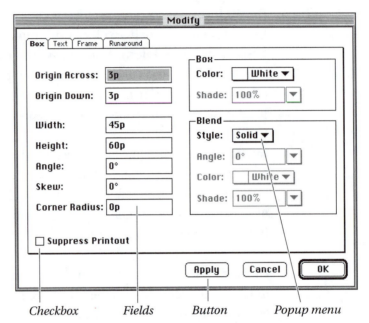

Checkbox   Fields   Button   Popup menu

Dialog box terminology. Here's a quick lesson in terminology, if you're unfamiliar with dialog boxes. The area in which you enter a value is called a *field*. Oftentimes there are *checkboxes* that can be checked on or off, or grayed out if undefined. Many dialog boxes also contain *popup menus*, which act much like the menus at the top of the screen: just position the cursor on them, press the mouse button, and drag the mouse up or down until you have selected the item you want. Then let go of the mouse button.

Typically, dialog boxes have two buttons: OK and Cancel. Clicking OK closes the dialog box and puts your changes into effect. Clicking Cancel closes the dialog box and ignores the changes you've made. Some dialog boxes have a Save option, which acts as an OK button. Other dialog boxes have an Apply button. Clicking this button temporarily applies the settings you've made to the document so that you can see them. If you like what you see, you can then click OK. If you don't like it, you can usually press Command-Z to revert the dialog box to the last setting. In any case, you can click Cancel to rid yourself of the dialog box and the changes you've made, even after applying them (see "Undo and Cancel," later in this chapter).

▼ ▼

Tip: Pushing Your Buttons. Almost every button in QuarkXPress's dialog boxes can be replaced with a keystroke. The keystroke is usually the first letter in the button's name. For example, if a dialog box has Yes and No buttons, you can select them by pressing Command-Y and Command-N (or just press Y or N in Windows). When you're checking spelling in a story, you can select the Skip button by pressing Command-S (Alt-S in Windows). Note that any button that is highlighted (has a darker border than a normal button) can be selected by pressing Enter or Return. (This is usually the OK button, but might be something else, such as Find Next in the Find/Change dialog box.) You can press Cancel by pressing Command-period on the Macintosh or Esc in Windows.

▼ ▼

Tip: Continuous Apply. As I said earlier, the Apply button temporarily applies the change you made in a dialog box. You can then decide whether you want to actually make that change, revert, or cancel the operation entirely. Even though pressing Command-A speeds up the process some, I often find it helpful to be in a Continuous Apply mode by pressing Command-Option-A (or holding down the Option key while clicking Apply). Pressing this highlights the Apply button (turns it black), as if you were holding the button down continuously. Now, every change you make in the dialog box is immediately applied to your page item. You can still press Command-Z to undo the last change, or Command-period or Esc to cancel the dialog box. To turn off Continuous Apply, just press Command-Option-A again.

By the Numbers

Unless you raise horses and measure everything in "hands," chances are that you and QuarkXPress share a common measurement system. QuarkXPress understands measurements in points, picas, inches, ciceros, centimeters, agates, and millimeters. (You can even type measurements in Qs, which is used in some Asian countries—1 Q is a quarter of a millimeter.) You can use these measurement units at any time, no matter what the default setting is (see "Changing Defaults," later in this chapter). Table 2-1 shows how to specify a value for each system.

	You can spec . . .	By typing . . .	Examples
Table 2-1	points	pt or p	6pt or p6
Measurement systems	picas	p	10p or 2p6 (2 picas, 6 points)
	inches (decimal)	"	6" or 6.5" or 6.888832"
	ciceros	c	2c or 6c3 (6 ciceros, 3 points)
	centimeters	cm	3cm
	millimeters	mm	210mm
	Q (Japanese unit)	Q	4Q
	agates	ag	10ag

The mathematical abilities of most people I know have degenerated to the point of having to use calculators to "be fruitful and multiply." Realizing this, Quark incorporated into every entry field the ability to calculate. You can specify measurements with a plus or minus sign to build simple equations using one or more measurement units. For example, if a measurement was set to "10p" and you wanted to add 4 centimeters, you could type "10p+4cm". Similarly, if you wanted to take away one pica, two points, you could type "10p-1p2". Note that the first example mixes measurement systems; you don't have to be consistent here because the program does all the math for you.

You can also use * (the asterisk) for multiplication and / (the slash) for division in any field. If you have a text box that measures 4.323 inches and you want to make it two-thirds as wide, just add "*2/3" to the right of the inch mark. Or, if you want to make a picture box 120 percent of its current size, just type "*1.2" after the width measurement. Remember that you can mix up and match all the measurements, too; so even "3p+24mm/3*9" is valid (though I can't think why you'd need it).

▼ ▼

Tip: Fractions in Arithmetic. Here are two unconventional ways to use arithmetic in QuarkXPress: fractions and placing items on a preset grid.

To get an eighth of a pica, you can type "1p/8" (one eighth of a pica is, of course, the same as one pica divided by eight). To place a text box at 3 7/8 inches from the left side of the page, place it at "3"+7"/8" (XPress does the division or multiplication in an equation first, then the addition or subtraction).

Similarly, let's say you're using a strict leading grid and you want to put a picture box exactly 20 lines down. If the grid is based on 13-point leading, you can set the vertical origin of the box to "13pt*20" (leading value times the number of lines down the page).

▼ ▼

After You Click OK

Mistakes are common in the world of desktop publishing. In fact, one of the great benefits of working on a computer, in my opinion, is that I can make as many mistakes as I want and always recover from them. In QuarkXPress, there are several methods to recover from a mistake or a decision you later regret.

Revert to Saved

As I said above, no changes are permanent until you save them to disk. If you want to discard all changes made to a document since the last save, you can do it by closing the document (choose Close from the File menu) and telling QuarkXPress that you don't want to save the changes. Or, if you wish to continue working on it without interruption, choose Revert to Saved from the File menu. For example, if—in the name of improvement—you have managed to mess up your document beyond redemption, you can revert to the version that you last saved.

▼ ▼

Tip: Revert to Last Minisave. The Auto Save feature I talked about above goes by another name, too: PageMaker calls these things minisaves. Sometimes you want to use a minisave as something other than crash insurance. You can actually revert to the last autosave instead of going back all the way to the last full save (for instance, if you like the changes you made five minutes ago, but not the ones you made 10 minutes ago). Just hold down the Option key when you select Revert from the File menu.

▼ ▼

Undo and Cancel

Since I'm on the topic of reverting back and ignoring changes to the document, we really need to take a quick detour and look at the Undo and Cancel commands. Undo is found under the Edit menu, and is a staple of all quality programs. If you make a mistake, you can almost always

Undo it (press Command-Z or—on the Mac—the F4 key). And if you're in the middle of making a mistake, you can press Command-period or Esc to cancel the action.

While it's just that simple in most Macintosh and Windows programs, QuarkXPress has some interesting extra features that might be helpful to know about.

Interruptible screen redraw. QuarkXPress has a "hidden" feature that can make life much better: interruptible screen redraw. If you have 43 pictures and text boxes on your page and it's taking forever to draw them, you can press Command-period to cancel the redraw. QuarkXPress stops drawing as soon as it finishes drawing the next object (that's slightly different from some other programs, such as Adobe Photoshop, which stop immediately).

New in XPress 4 is the ability to interrupt screen redraw when you select a menu item or choose any other keystroke. Note that screen redraw is only relevant when the Off-screen Draw option is turned off in Application Preferences (see "Changing Defaults," later in this chapter).

▼ ▼

Tip: Forcing Screen Redraw. As I'm talking about screen redraw, I should probably also mention that Command-Option-period (Macintosh) and Shift-Esc (Windows) will force XPress to redraw the screen. I find this useful because XPress 4 has various persistent problems (bugs) that cause it, on occasion, to update the screen improperly. Often, if something just looks weird (like "what's that line doing there?" or "my text isn't supposed to look like that"), just force a screen redraw and the problem goes away.

▼ ▼

Text. Any text you type can be undone until you move the cursor point. For example, if you type three words, then move back a word and add a letter, XPress resets its Undo "memory" so an Undo would only remove the added letters. This can be frustrating if you don't really know what's going on because it seems like it forgets stuff. It's not forgetful; we are.

Type styles. Typographic styles are also remembered and can be undone. Note that QuarkXPress undoes all the styles you've applied since you last started applying styles. I know that sounds strange, so here's an example: If you select a word and make it bold and italic and small caps and change the font size (I'll show you how to do all that later in the book), and then press Command-Z, QuarkXPress reverts to how the text was before you applied any type styles. However, if you move the text insertion point by clicking somewhere else or moving with keystrokes, then the program resets its Undo memory again and you can't Undo any of it. Changing the font also resets the Undo memory for some strange reason.

Multiple objects. Let's say you've got three pictures that are stacked up, each slightly overlapping the one below it. What happens if you select the bottom-most and top-most pictures, delete them, and then select Undo? The layers are no longer maintained; the two objects that you deleted are placed on top of the middle picture. This usually isn't that big a deal, but it's something to keep in mind.

Dialog boxes and palettes. You can get yourself out of a bad situation in every dialog box or palette in QuarkXPress by remembering the ubiquitous and powerful features: Command-period or Esc (Cancel) and Command-Z (Undo). For instance, if you change the x or y coordinates for a text box, and then decide what you're doing is a mistake, you can undo it even before the change takes place. Pressing Command-Z reverts to the previous state and keeps the field highlighted. Pressing Command-period or Esc reverts and takes you out of the palette or dialog box altogether.

Getting Around Your Document

QuarkXPress shows you the pages in your document as though they were all spread out in order on a giant white pasteboard. However, unless you happen to work on an enormous screen, you never get to see much of the pasteboard at one time. Let's look at how you can move around to see different parts of a page, and different pages within your document.

Scrolling

The first step in moving around within your document is scrolling. *Scrolling* refers to using the horizontal and vertical scroll bars on the right and bottom sides of the document window to move your page (see Figure 2-18). If you click the arrow at the top of the vertical scroll bar, you move a bit "up" your page (closer to the top). If you click the left arrow in the horizontal scroll bar, you move to the left on your page, and so on.

I find that many people never get past this elementary level of scrolling. This is conceivably the slowest method you could use. I implore you to look at the alternatives.

Figure 2-18
Document window

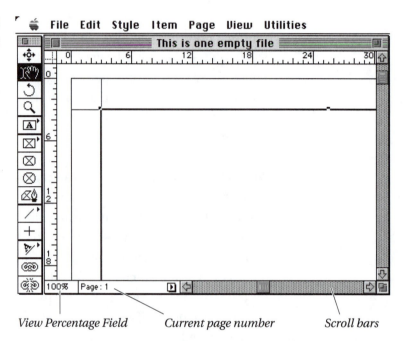

View Percentage Field   *Current page number*   *Scroll bars*

You can move large distances in your document by moving the little white box (some people call it the "scroll elevator") in the scroll bars. Clicking in the gray area moves you by one screen at a time. You can also use keystrokes to move around the screen vertically. Table 2-2 shows you how to do this.

▼ ▼

Tip: Scroll Speed. If you do use the scroll bar arrows to get around, you definitely want to examine the Scroll Speed feature in the Application Preferences dialog box. This feature lets you control how far each click in a scroll-bar arrow takes you. For example, if you have the Scroll Speed set to Fast, then clicking an arrow may move you an entire screen or more. If you have it set to Slow, a click may move the screen one or two pixels.

Table 2-2

Moving around
your document
(control-key
shortcuts are
Macintosh-only)

To move . . .	Press . . .	Extended keyboards, press . . .
Up one screen	Control-K	Page Up
Down one screen	Control-L	Page Down
Start of document	Control-A	Home
End of document	Control-D	End
First page	Control-Shift-A	Shift-Home
Last page	Control-Shift-D	Shift-End
Next page	Control-Shift-L	Shift-Page Down
Previous page	Control-Shift-K	Shift-Page Up

Don't confuse Scroll Speed with Speed Scroll. I cover the latter in "Changing Defaults," later in this chapter.

▼ ▼

Tip: Live Scrolling. When you drag the white box along the scroll bar, it's often difficult to tell how far on the page or the document you've gone. This is because the vertical scroll bar represents the entire length of your document, and the horizontal scroll bar represents the full width of the pasteboard. If you have multipage spreads in your document, the pasteboard can be very large (see more on spreads in Chapter 4, *Building a Document*). But if you hold down the Option key while you drag the box, the screen scrolls with you, so you can see how far you're going (this is called *live scrolling*).

You can enable live scrolling on a permanent basis by checking in the Live Scroll box in the Application Preferences dialog box. With that feature turned on, Option-dragging on the scroll bar box makes the document *not* live scroll.

▼ ▼

Tip: Use the Grabber Hand. The Grabber Hand is arguably the most important tool in QuarkXPress. The problem with the scroll bars is that you can only scroll in one direction at a time. It's a hassle: down a little, over to the left, down a little more, now to the right, and so on. But if you hold down the Option key at any time, the cursor turns into the Grabber Hand, and when you click and drag, the page moves where you move the Grabber Hand. Try it! I think it's one of the greatest methods for getting around the page.

You can temporarily disable the Grabber Hand by turning on Caps Lock. This turns Option-click into a zoom toggle.

▼ ▼

Zooming

If you have a brand-new 90-inch HDTV monitor, you may not need to read this section. For the rest of us, zooming is a necessity of life. When you zoom in and out on a page, you are using an electronic magnifying glass, first enlarging a particular area of a page, and then reducing your screen view so that you are seeing the entire page or pages at once.

QuarkXPress lets you magnify or reduce your screen view from 10 percent to 800 percent, in steps of 0.1 percent. You can jump between several preset views quickly by selecting them from the View menu or by using keystrokes.

▼ ▼

Tip: Maximum Zoom Power. If you switch back and forth between the Macintosh and Windows, as I do, you'll quickly notice that although you can always zoom in to 800 percent on the Macintosh, you generally can't get any closer than 692 percent in Windows. What's the deal? It has to do with screen resolution. QuarkXPress for Windows assumes your screen resolution is about 96 ppi (pixels per inch), though you can change this value in the Document Preferences dialog box (see "Changing Defaults," later in this chapter). If you lower the screen resolution setting in XPress, the program lets you zoom in more (at 72 ppi, you can zoom in to a full 800 percent). If you raise the resolution setting, you can zoom in less.

As for the Macintosh, QuarkXPress is stuck believing that your screen is displaying 72 ppi, no matter what the resolution truly is. Oh well.

▼ ▼

View menu. The View menu lists zooming values of Fit in Window, 50%, 75%, Actual Size (which is 100 percent), 200%, and Thumbnails. Fit in Window adjusts the zoom percentage to fit whatever size window you have open at the time. If you're working with facing pages, then the scale is set to fit a two-page spread in the window. Thumbnails zooms way back so that you can see a bunch of pages at the same time (but it does more than that; see "Thumbnails," later in this chapter).

When you select a magnification from the View menu, QuarkXPress automatically zooms to the percentage you want and centers the current page in your window. If any item on the page you're looking at is selected when you switch magnifications, QuarkXPress centers that item in the window. Or, if the item is on the pasteboard, the program centers it if any part of the item is showing when you switch views.

For example, if you select a short rule on a page while viewing at Fit in Window size, and then select Actual Size, QuarkXPress zooms in and centers that rule on your screen. If the selected item is a text box and you have the Content tool selected, the program centers the cursor or whatever text is highlighted. This makes zooming in and out on a page much easier: if you're editing some text, you can use Fit in Window to see the "big picture," then select Actual Size to zoom back to where your cursor is in the text.

▼ ▼

Tip: Accidental Zooming. You've probably had it happen to you already: You select Fit in Window from the View menu, and suddenly you jump to a different page. It's really not as strange as it seems. Fit in Window always fits the current page in the window. But what's the current page? It's the page that is touching the upper-left corner of the document window. If just a tiny bit of the previous page is showing at the top or left of the window, that's the one that will get centered on-screen.

▼ ▼

Zoom tool. You can also use the Zoom tool on the Tool palette for your quick zooming pleasure. Sorry, did I say "quick?" I hardly find clicking in the Tool palette, then on my document, then back in the Tool palette a "quick" procedure. However, we're in luck because there's a keystroke: On the Macintosh, if you hold down the Control key, you get a Zoom In tool; add the Option key, and you get a Zoom Out tool. In Windows, you have to press both Control and the spacebar to zoom in; Control-Alt-spacebar provides the Zoom Out tool. (If you have a text box selected, make sure you press the Control key before the spacebar, or else you'll type a space character.)

Each time you click on your page with the Zoom tool, QuarkXPress zooms in or out by a particular percentage. The increments that it uses can be controlled in the Tool Preferences dialog box (see "Changing Defaults," later in this chapter).

Keystroke zooming. If I can avoid using the menus, I usually do; they're almost never the most efficient method of working. So when it comes to zooming, I much prefer to use keystrokes and clicks. Table 2-3 shows the basic keystrokes and keystroke-and-click combinations for zooming in and out.

PRESS ...	**TO GO TO OR TOGGLE ...**
Command-1	Actual Size
Command-0	Fit in Window
Command-Option-0	Fit pasteboard in window
Option-click (with Caps Lock)	Between Actual Size and Fit in Window
Command-Option-click	Between Actual Size and 200%

Table 2-3
Zooming

There are two basic keystroke-and-click combinations that you can use to zoom in and out. Command-Option-clicking on your page alternates your view between Actual Size and 200%. When you have Caps Lock on, Option-clicking on your page alternates between zooming out to Fit in Window and zooming in to Actual Size (when Caps Lock is off, the Option key only gives you the Grabber Hand).

▼ ▼

Tip: Fit More in Your Window. If you select Fit in Window from the View menu or press Command-zero, QuarkXPress fits the current page to the window. However, if you hold down the Option key while selecting Fit in Window (or press Command-Option-zero), it zooms to fit the entire width of the pasteboard into the window.

This feature has a fun corollary: If you don't need a big pasteboard around your facing-pages document, you can shrink down its width to 10 percent or 20 percent of the page width (this is a setting in the Application Preferences dialog box). Now when you press Command-Option-zero, you get the equivalent of "fit spread in window."

▼ ▼

Magnification field. Another of my favorite methods for zooming in and out is by adjusting the View Percent field in the lower-left corner of the document window. Note that when you're in Actual Size, this field shows "100%". Whenever you zoom in or out, this field changes. Well, you can change it yourself by clicking in the field (or highlight the field by pressing Control-V on the Mac, or Control-Alt-V in Windows), typing a percentage (or "T" for Thumbnails view), and pressing Enter or Return.

Zoom marquee. There's no doubt that my favorite zooming technique is to hold down the Control key (to get the Zoom tool), and dragging a marquee around a specific area (in Windows, press Control-spacebar). When you let go of the mouse button, QuarkXPress zooms into that area at the precise percentage necessary to fit it in the window. (I like to call this "magdrag," for magnification-drag.) So if you're at Actual Size and drag a marquee around one word, QuarkXPress can zoom in to 600 percent and center that word on your screen. You can use this to zoom out, too, by dragging a marquee that's larger than your screen (the screen scrolls along as you drag the marquee), but I don't find this as useful.

Moving from Page to Page

In the last section I talked about moving around your page using scrolling and zooming. Because every page in your document sits on one big pasteboard, these same techniques work for moving around within your document. You can scroll from one page to another using the scroll bars and the Grabber hand, and so on. But let's be frank: This is not the fastest way to get around. It might help in moving around a two-page spread, but not for moving around a 200-page book. Instead, there are ways to move by whole pages at a time, or to jump to the page you want.

Extended keyboards. If you have an extended keyboard (I recommend these for serious desktop publishers), you can move one page forward or back by pressing Shift-Page Up or Shift-Page Down (on the Macintosh you can replace the Shift key with the Command key if you like). If you don't have an extended keyboard, Control-Shift-K and Control-Shift-L also move one page at a time.

You may find yourself wanting to jump to the very beginning or end of your document. On a Macintosh, you can press the Shift-Home key or Shift-End (or, on non-extended keyboards, press Control-Shift-A or Control-Shift-D). In Windows, press Control-Page Up or Control-Page Down to jump to the first or last page of the document, respectively.

Moving to a specific page. If you're trying to get to a page somewhere in the middle of your document, there are four methods to get there quickly.

▶ Double-click the page icon in the Document Layout palette or single-click the page number below the icon (I discuss this palette in more detail in Chapter 4, *Building a Document*).

▶ You can change the page number field in the lower-left corner of the document window. This is a minor hassle because you have to select the page number and then change it, but it's not too bad.

▶ You can choose a page by clicking on the popup menu next to the page number field in the lower-left corner of the document window, and dragging until you get to the page (see Figure 2-19).

▶ You can select Go To from the Page menu (or, better yet, press Command-J). Note that if the page you want to go to is in a differently named section, you have to type the name exactly as it's listed in the lower-right corner of the document window. For instance, if you're using Roman numerals and you want to jump to the fourth page, you have to type "iv". (See "Sections and Page Numbering," in Chapter 4, *Building a Document*, as well as the next tip.)

▼ ▼

Tip: Jump to Absolute Page Numbers. If you play around with sections and page numbers, you may find yourself in a quagmire when you try to print a page range. For example, let's say your document begins on page 56 and you want to print the 16th through the 20th pages. You could sit around and try to figure out what numbers to plug in to the Print dialog box's page range fields, or you could just type "+16" and "+20". The plus sign before the number means that the numbers are absolute; the first page is "+1", the second page is "+2", and so on.

This is also helpful when moving to a page using Go To page. You can quickly jump to the 20th page by typing "+20".

▼ ▼

Note that for any of the keystrokes I've outlined here, there is a menu item in the Page menu. I think working with a mouse and menus is fast, but there is no doubt that once you start working with keystrokes, moving around your document becomes lightning-fast.

▼ ▼

Manipulating Your Document

Okay, now that I've covered how you can move around your document, let's talk about how you can insert, delete, and move pages within your document. There are three good ways to handle these tasks in QuarkXPress: menu items, thumbnails, and the Document Layout palette. Let's look at each one of these.

Figure 2-19

Popup pages

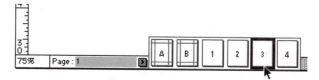

Menu Manipulations

As I said much earlier in this chapter, the Page menu holds QuarkXPress's page-manipulation tools. In this section we're primarily interested in the first three menu items: Insert, Delete, and Move. I'm holding off on a discussion of inserting pages until another chapter (see "Making Pages" in Chapter 4, *Building a Document*), so I'll talk about the last two.

Delete. When you choose Delete from the Page menu, QuarkXPress displays the Delete dialog box. This is a simple dialog box asking you which page or pages to delete. If you only want to delete one, just type it in the From field. If you want to delete consecutive pages, then type the page range in the From and To fields.

Move. If you want to move a page or a range of pages, you can select Move from the Page menu. Here you can specify which page or pages to move, and where to move them (see Figure 2-20). For example, if you want to move pages 15 through 21 to after the last page in your document, you can type "15" in the first field, "21" in the second field, and click To End of Document. You also can specify a move to before or after a specific page.

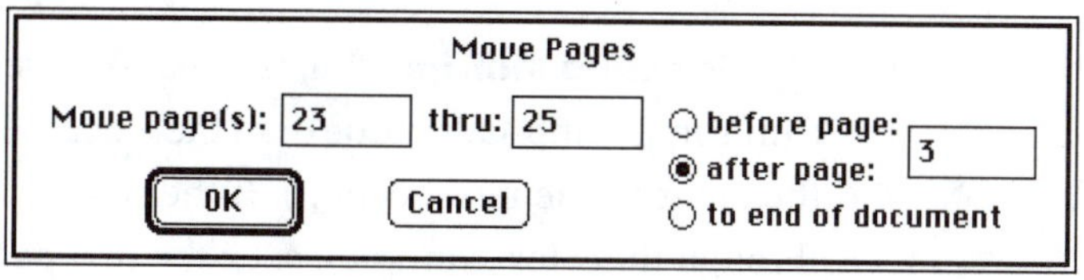

Figure 2-20

The Move Pages
dialog box

```
                         Move Pages
Move page(s): [23]   thru: [25]      ○ before page:
                                     ● after page:    [3]
      ( OK )        ( Cancel )       ○ to end of document
```

▼ ▼

Tip: Doing It to the End. QuarkXPress is smarter than the average computer program. In fact, it's slowly learning plain English. For example, if you want to delete from one page to the end of the document, but you don't know what the last page number is, you can type "end" in the Thru field of the Delete dialog box. This also works in the Move dialog box. For instance, you can move all pages 15 to the end of the document by typing "15" and "end" in the appropriate fields.

▼ ▼

Thumbnails

You can see a thumbnail view of your document in the same way as you select any other percentage scaling view: from the View menu. (Or by typing "T" into the Magnification field in the lower-left corner of the document window. Actually you can type "T", "Th", "Thu", "Thum", or "Thumb"—it just depends on how much you feel like flinging your fingers across the keyboard.) Although you can use this to look at your document as thumbnails (it's like looking at it in 10-percent viewing mode), Thumbnails is actually more useful as a tool for moving pages.

To move a page in Thumbnails mode, select the page and drag it to where you want it. While moving a page around in Thumbnails mode, you'll find the cursor turning into two different icons. The first looks like a minipage. If you let go of the mouse button with this icon displayed, the page is moved, but it's added as a spread. That is, the rest of the pages won't shuffle and reflow (see "Multiple Page Spreads" in Chapter 4, *Building a Document*).

The second icon, a black arrow, appears when you move the cursor directly to the left of or under another page. This arrow means that the page will be placed directly before or after a specific page. Letting go of the mouse button when you have this arrow cursor reflows the pages in the document. This is the same as moving pages using Move from the Page menu.

▼ ▼

Tip: Selecting Multiple Pages. It's easy to select more than one page at a time in Thumbnails mode or in the Document Layout palette (more on the latter in the next section). If the pages are consecutive (pages four through nine, for example), click the first page in the range, hold down the Shift key, and click the last page in the range. Every page between the two is selected (this is just like selecting text).

You can select nonconsecutive pages (such as pages one, three, and nine) while in Thumbnails mode or in the Document Layout palette by holding down the Command key while clicking on each page.

▼ ▼

Document Layout Palette

The Document Layout palette is one of the key elements in working effi-ciently with multipage documents. You can move pages, delete them, insert new ones, create and apply master pages, and more, with a quick drag of an icon. Let's look at how you can use this palette to delete and move pages.

To open the Document Layout palette, select Show Document Layout from the View menu (see Figure 2-21). For our purposes right now, you only need to think about two parts of the palette: the page icons and the icons in the upper-right corner. I'll get into more advanced uses (applying master pages, for instance) in Chapter 4, *Building a Document.*

Moving pages within the Document Layout palette is just like mov-ing them in Thumbnails mode, except that you can't see what's on the pages. Simply select the page or pages that you want to move, and drag them to their destinations. QuarkXPress uses the same icons here as in Thumbnails mode. That is, the little page icon means that you're creat-ing a spread, and the right and down arrow icons mean that you're mov-ing the pages into the flow (the other pages displace to accommodate the moved page).

Deleting a page with the Document Layout palette is even simpler than deleting a file while on the Mac desktop or Windows Explorer: just select the page(s) and click the Delete icon (on the Mac, it's the little trash can; in Windows, it's the icon with the "X" through it). However, do note

Figure 2-21

The Document
Layout palette

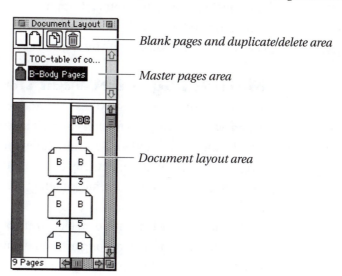

Blank pages and duplicate/delete area

Master pages area

Document layout area

that in QuarkXPress you cannot undo these actions and retrieve a page that you throw away. Obviously, it's worth being extra careful in this area.

Moving Items Between Documents

You don't have to stop at moving items and pages just within your document. You can move them from one document to another faster than you can say, "Maybe it's time to get a larger monitor for my computer."

To move a page item from one document to another, you must have both documents open and visible on your screen. This is sometimes difficult on small screens. I find the Tile Documents feature (on the Mac, it's in the Windows submenu under the View menu; in Windows, it's under the Window menu) useful for this. Then, with the Item tool select the item you want to move (or hold down the Command key to get the Item tool temporarily), and drag it across.

If you pause between the document windows, you may find the first document starts to scroll. Don't worry, it's just QuarkXPress not realizing that you want to move it all the way into the second document. Just move the item a little farther and the scrolling should stop. Once you let go of the mouse button, the item is copied over into the new document. Note that I say "copied." The item is not actually moved; rather, it is copied from one into the other. If you want to get rid of it in the first document, just delete it (Command-K).

Of course, there is always the old standby method for getting items from one document to another: Copy and Paste. Here, you want to make sure that you have the Item tool selected while in both documents, or else XPress won't know that you want to copy or paste the item itself.

Moving Pages Between Documents

Versions 1 and 2 of QuarkXPress sported a Get Document function, which was extremely useful. First of all, it let you copy whole pages from one document to another. Secondly, it let you access pages from a different document without actually opening it (this was often helpful in retrieving corrupted files). Unfortunately, the Get Document feature is now gone.

Taking its place is a feature that lets you actually drag a page from one document into another, as long as both documents are in Thumbnails view. (Hold down the Option key and select Tile Documents to put *all* documents into Thumbnails mode.) This is especially handy if you like to see the pages that you're copying before you copy them. In fact, Quark's tech support still recommends this as a preferred method for saving documents that are becoming corrupted.

▼ ▼

Tip: Moving Background Windows. If you're working on a small Macintosh screen and you need to resize and move your document windows in order to drag across page items or even full pages, you might find it helpful to know that you can move a window without actually selecting it. That is, normally, if you click on a window, that window is brought to the front (it becomes *active*). You can move a window without bringing it to the front by holding down the Command key while you click and drag the bar at its top. Actually, this isn't a QuarkXPress feature; it's a Macintosh feature.

▼ ▼

Changing Defaults

Each and every one of you reading this book is different, and you all have different ways of using QuarkXPress. Fortunately, Quark has given you a mess of options for customizing the internal default settings. A *default setting* is a value or indicates a way of doing something; QuarkXPress uses the default value or method unless you specifically choose something else.

For example, the factory default setting for picture and text boxes is that they are created with no border frame around them (see "Frames, Dashes, and Stripes" in Chapter 3, *Tools of the Trade*). But if you're so inclined, you can modify QuarkXPress so that every text box you create is automatically framed with a two-point line. In this way, you can customize your work environment so that it best suits you.

Default settings range from how guides are displayed on the screen to how QuarkXPress builds small caps characters. In version 4, Quark consolidated a number of different preferences dialog boxes into two: Application Preferences and Document Preferences. You can find both of these in the Preferences submenu, under the Edit menu.

XTensions can add their own preferences to this submenu, as well. For instance, Quark's free Type Tricks XTension adds a preference that lets you set defaults for its Fraction and Price feature. The Index and

QuarkCMS XTensions that ship with XPress also add their own preferences dialog boxes. I cover the QuarkCMS preferences in Appendix A, *Color Management*, and Index preferences in Chapter 8, *Long Documents*. But let's take a look at the Application and Document Preferences dialog boxes here.

▼ ▼

Application Preferences

The Application Preferences dialog box (press Command-Option-Shift-Y) contains preferences that affect the way the program acts on your particular computer. The settings aren't saved with your documents, so if you move them to another computer, they may appear slightly different. This isn't bad, because we're talking about general changes such as the color of the margin guides and the width of the pasteboard. Here's a rundown of the options in the Application Preferences dialog box.

The Display Tab

The Application Preferences dialog box is broken down into four tabs, each of which covers a specific area. The first tab, Display, lets you control how your document pages and your images appear on-screen (see Figure 2-22). The controls are slightly different between the Macintosh and Windows versions of QuarkXPress.

Guide Colors. The controls at the top of the Display tab let you change the colors of QuarkXPress's three types of guide lines: Margin, Ruler, and Grid (this control is available for both Macintosh and Windows). The Margin guides are the lines that show where the page margins are. The Ruler guides are the guides you can pull out onto the page. And the Grid guides are the lines that the program shows you when you have Show Baseline Grid enabled (see Chapter 6, *Type and Typography*). Note that this control is only available when your monitor is set to at least 256 levels of gray or color. (For instance, it's not available with older 16-gray-level laptops.) Of course, if your monitor only displays grays, then this control only affects the shade of gray you'll see.

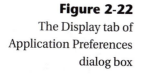

Figure 2-22

The Display tab of Application Preferences dialog box

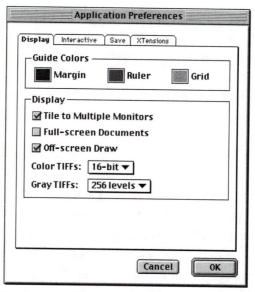

Tile to Multiple Monitors. Here's where you tell QuarkXPress whether you want it to consider *all* the monitors you have plugged into your computer when it tiles open documents. Unless you have more than one monitor hooked up, you should just leave this turned off. Currently, this is a Macintosh-only feature (perhaps we'll see this change as Windows 98 becomes more widespread).

Full-Screen Documents. Checking this box lets you zoom windows to fill your entire screen; unchecking it leaves room for the Tool and Measurements palettes. I typically leave this turned off, but why should you listen to me? The options are here to make your life easier. This is currently a Macintosh-only feature, as well.

Off-Screen Draw. I guess some Mac-heads don't like seeing QuarkXPress draw each page object one at a time (the slower the Macintosh, the slower the redraw). When Off-Screen Draw is turned on (it is, by default), QuarkXPress redraws all the items "behind the scenes" and shows them to you all at once. I like to turn this off, so I can see what's taking so long and stop it if I want (see "Interruptible Screen Redraw," earlier in this chapter). It takes just as long either way, so it really comes down to how you like your computer to behave.

Color TIFFs/Gray TIFFs. The Color TIFFs and Gray TIFFs popup menus (these appear on both Macintosh and Windows) let you control how QuarkXPress builds screen previews for TIFF images when you import them. As you'll see in Chapter 9, *Pictures*, a TIFF picture doesn't have a built-in preview, so XPress has to build one for it when you import it. By default, previews of color TIFFs are only 8-bit (256 colors) and previews of gray TIFFs are only 4-bit (16 levels of gray). You can change these to include more colors or more levels of gray.

You should take two issues into consideration when choosing this. First, the higher the image quality, the slower your screen redraw will be (though on fast machines, this is less of a factor). Second, the higher the image quality, the larger your file size. This is the one that really hurts. If you use the highest setting for Color TIFFs (on the Macintosh it's 32-bit, in Windows it's 24-bit, but they're really pretty much the same thing), your file size can mushroom into something fierce (your file size may even be three or four times what it would ordinarily be). I strongly urge people not to use this setting unless they really need to.

There's one more consideration, too: when you specify a Color TIFF setting above 8-bit, XPress won't let you change the color contrast settings for the image. (This is not something that many people want to do, however; I discuss it in Chapter 10, *Fine-Tuning Images*.)

Of course, if you don't have 8-, 16-, or 24-bit images or if you don't have a 16- or 24-bit color screen, you can't display them in those modes, anyway. QuarkXPress can't improve the screen display of an image beyond the information that's contained in the file. Note that these features don't affect the images themselves or how they print—just how they're displayed on the screen.

Display DPI Value. Earlier in this chapter, I mentioned that the limitation on how far you could magnify your page on a Windows machine depended on your Display DPI Value. This control is a Windows-only setting (though I have no idea why; Macintoshes can have as widely variable screen resolution as PCs), and it lets you more closely match your page size in QuarkXPress to your monitor's resolution. Because most PC monitors average around 96 ppi, this is the default value in the Application Preferences dialog box.

The idea is that if you hold up a physical ruler to the screen, one inch on the ruler should equal (more or less) one inch on QuarkXPress's ruler.

If it doesn't you can adjust the Display DPI Value. Larger values make XPress's ruler larger; lower values make XPress's ruler smaller. If you don't care about matching the screen to reality, you can adjust at will (or just leave it alone).

The Interactive Tab

The Interactive Tab of the Application Preferences dialog box is a grab bag of options that control XPress's screen display and what happens when you navigate around your document (see Figure 2-23). It's a little confusing at first, but these are among the most useful features in the preferences dialog boxes.

Speed Scroll. Here's a wonderful enhancement to XPress that makes me want to bow down and give thanks in the general direction of Denver (where Quark lives). If you turn on Speed Scroll, QuarkXPress automatically greeks the display of pictures, graphics, and blends as you scroll through a document. Only when you stop scrolling does it take the time to properly display these elements.

This may not sound like a big improvement at first, but if you've died of boredom while scrolling through a long document with lots of big four-color TIFFs, you'll appreciate how much time Speed Scroll can save you (that is, unless you *like* taking a coffee break while you scroll). I turn this on and leave it on.

Figure 2-23

The Interactive tab of Application Preferences dialog box

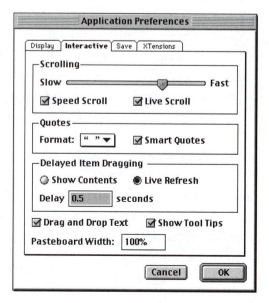

Scroll Speed. Yep, now there's Speed Scroll *and* Scroll Speed. It's not confusing, is it? As I discussed earlier in the "Scrolling" section, Scroll Speed controls how fast QuarkXPress scrolls when you use the scroll bars. Note that the default Scroll Speed control setting is pretty slow. Increasing the speed (by clicking on the right arrow) can make a drastic difference in how quickly you can make your pages (although this won't speed up screen redraw).

Live Scroll. My editor keeps telling me not to be redundant in my writing. And since I already gave my *spiel* about Live Scroll earlier in this chapter (see "Scrolling"), here I'll just say: Yes, this is a great feature, and it's great to have it built right in, but it's nowhere near as cool as the Grabber Hand.

Smart Quotes. This option both turns on the Smart Quotes feature and lets you specify which characters will be used for open and closed quotes. Smart Quotes works by looking to the left of the insertion point to determine if an open or closed quote character should go there. If the character to the left is a white space character, such as a spaceband, tab key, or return, QuarkXPress enters an open single or double quote when you press the ' or " key.

The popup menu lets you choose some alternative quote characters, including various double quotes, Spanish alternatives, and inside and outside guillemet (French quote mark) combinations, which can be useful if you're formatting foreign-language documents (see Figure 2-24).

The main place where Smart Quotes isn't so smart is when you're typing apostrophes at the beginning of a word—"In late '93," for instance. Watch out for these. (See "Tip: Getting Your Quotes Straight," in Chapter 6, *Type and Typography,* for a lesson on how to type curly and straight quotes quickly.)

▼ ▼

Tip: Toggling Smart Quotes. Smart Quotes is really cool if you type a lot in QuarkXPress. However, if you ever want to enter a single or double "neutral" straight quote character, it's a hassle to turn off Smart Quotes first. Instead, hold down the Control key when typing the quote (single or double). When Smart Quotes is on, you get a straight quote; when it's off, you get a curly quote.

▼ ▼

Figure 2-24

Different kinds of Smart
Quotes available

"This is an example of Smart Quotes," he said.

"This is a different kind of Smart Quotes," he added.

„Here's yet another kind of Smart Quotes," he continued.

«These quotes are called guillemets,» he went on.

»So are these, but they're reversed,« he concluded.

Delayed Item Dragging. Normally, when you click on an object and drag it somewhere on your page, XPress just shows you a gray outline of the item you're moving. If you're performing a quick move, this is probably all you really need. But if you're trying to position something carefully, then you usually need to see the object itself. If you click the mouse button down on top of the object and hold it down for a moment before you drag it, the object flashes quickly. That's your sign that when you drag it, you'll be able to see the picture or the text or whatever.

The Delayed Item Dragging option on the Interactive tab lets you control two things. First, the Delay field lets you specify how long you need to hold the mouse button down on an object before XPress flips into this mode. You can type anything from 0.1 second (almost instantaneous) to five seconds (why even bother?). I prefer about 0.5 second, but you should play around with it and see what suits you best.

Second, you have to choose between Show Contents and Live Refresh. The default, Live Refresh, is a wonderful new feature in version 4 that forces XPress to reflow text as you move objects over it. For example, let's say you're trying to set the width of a text box so that the text flows just perfectly in it. You can click on one of the side handles and wait for a moment for the effect to kick in. The cursor changes to the Live Refresh cursor (it looks like a little starburst). Now the text reflows automatically as you drag the handle.

The other setting, Show Contents, is simply a way to turn Live Refresh off, so that when you click-hold-and-drag you can see the object but it doesn't affect text flow (at least not while you're dragging). The only time I would choose this is when I'm working on a slower computer (Live Refresh does take extra processing power).

Drag and Drop Text. Drag and Drop Text lets you drag selected text from one place in a text box to another. I cover this in detail in Chapter 5, *Word Processing*.

Show Tool Tips. When the Show Tool Tips option is on (it is, by default) and your cursor hovers over a tool in the Tool palette for a moment, XPress displays a little tag that tells you the name of the tool. It seems like every piece of software on the market has to have this feature these days. Maybe it's useful in other software, but it's annoying in XPress. I turn this off and leave it off. (Obviously it doesn't hurt to leave it on, though.)

Pasteboard Width. That pasteboard around a document's pages is great, but I usually find it a little too large (and—depending on the job— occasionally too small). Fortunately, I can control how wide the pasteboard is by specifying a percentage in the Pasteboard Width field. The default value of 100 percent tells QuarkXPress to make each side of the pasteboard the same width as one page in the document. That is, if you have an 8.5-by-11-inch page, each side of the pasteboard is 8.5 inches wide. Changing the Pasteboard Width to 50 percent makes the pasteboard half that width.

Unfortunately, there's still no way to change the height of the pasteboard, so it's stuck at a half-inch above and below your page. I keep hoping that Quark will change this, but no luck yet.

▼ ▼

Tip: PasteboardXT. Many of the world's religions teach us that it's important to be mindful of every step, as the slightest wrongdoing can cause a great disaster. Case in point: A small XTension developer released a shareware XTension over five years ago called PasteboardXT that lets you change the height of your pasteboard. It's a great idea, and everyone wanted this feature, so they downloaded it from the Internet and America Online and Compuserve and they passed it around in their offices and schools . . . . But this version of PasteboardXT had an interesting flaw: it was a required XTension. That means that if you use this XTension while working on a document, then you save the document and give it to me, I have to have the XTension, too, or else I won't be able to open your document.

Many of the world's religions also tend to frown on the four-letter words that people used when they discovered this problem. The developer realized his wrongdoing, and quickly released a newer version of PasteboardXT that no longer acted as a required XTension. The time between wrongdoing and redemption was not great, perhaps a few months. The effect, on the other hand, has been staggering.

The "PasteboardXT problem" has been far and away the biggest hassle for desktop publishers in the history of desktop publishing. Hundreds of thousands of people have been affected by that one error, even though the solution to the problem is incredibly simple: If you use any newer version of the XTension, open the file and resave it; the requirement is removed. Or, you can open the file and resave it with the Pasteboard XTerminator XTension loaded.

What does this lesson teach us?

▼ ▼

The Save Tab

What gets saved, when is it saved, and where does it get saved? Those are the questions answered on the Save tab of the Application Preferences dialog box (see Figure 2-25). Most of these features are discussed elsewhere in the book, so I won't cover them in detail here.

Figure 2-25

The Save tab of Application Preferences dialog box

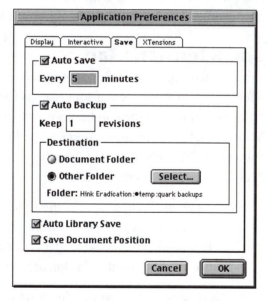

Auto Save and Auto Backup. Auto Save ensures that you don't lose too much work because of a system crash or other unexpected event. Auto Backup helps you carry out the chore of keeping backups by making copies of your documents when you save them. Both of these are covered in detail in "Saving," earlier in this chapter.

Auto Library Save. I discuss libraries and how to use them in the next chapter, *Tools of the Trade*. However, one thing you should know up front: Libraries are only saved when you close or quit QuarkXPress . . . unless you enable Auto Library Save. This makes QuarkXPress save the library every time you add an item to it. It slows down production a little, but it's worth it as a safety measure.

Fortunately, in XPress 4, Auto Libaray Save is turned on by default. Now the only time I turn it off is when I need to add a lot of items to a library at the same time (so it doesn't stop to save the file between each item). Then I turn it right back on.

Save Document Position. The Save Document Position feature is new in QuarkXPress 4. When on (it is, by default), this feature saves some extra information with your document: where the window was when you saved the file, what view percentage you were at, and how large the document window was. I leave this option turned on most of the time, but I sure wish it did more, like remember what page I was on when I last left the document, and even where on the page I was zoomed in. Oh well.

The XTensions Tab

The last tab of the Application Preferences dialog box, XTensions, only offers one control: Show XTensions Manager at Startup (see Figure 2-26). This lets you specify the conditions on which you want the XTensions Manager dialog box to appear upon launching XPress. You do have three choices within this control, though. (Also, see "Tip: Last-Minute XTension Changes," earlier in this chapter.)

▶ The default, "When Error loading XTensions occurs," tells XPress to open the dialog box if something goes wrong with an XTension at launch time; for instance, if it's an old XTension and is going to cause trouble with this version of XPress.

▶ The feature called "When XTension folder changes" tells XPress to open the dialog box whenever it notices that you've added or removed an XTension from the XTension folder. I leave this turned off; after all, if I added or removed an XTension, I probably did it for a good reason.

▶ The third option, "Always," is pretty self-explanatory: Every time you launch XPress, the dialog box appears.

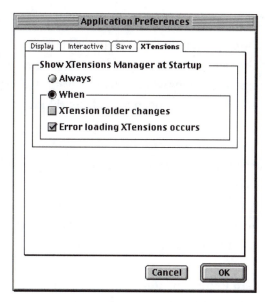

Document Preferences

The Document Preferences dialog box contains five tabs filled with controls that apply to whatever document you have open. Even if you have other documents open at the same time, the change is made to only the one that is active. However, if no documents are open when you change this dialog box, then you are setting new defaults for the whole program and that change is made to every new document you open from then on. These changes are stored in the XPress Preferences file, and are used when creating new documents.

For example, if you set the increments on the Zoom tool (on the Tool tab of the Document Preferences dialog box; see below) to 100 percent while a document is open, the preference is logged for that document only. If you set it while no documents are open, that setting is made for every new document you create. However, documents that were opened using the original setting keep their defaults.

You can open the Document Preferences dialog box either by selecting Document from the Preferences submenu (under the Edit menu) or by pressing Command-Y.

Almost every preference in this dialog box is described in detail elsewhere in the book, so I'm only going to cover these preferences quickly here and then tell you where you can find more information about them.

The General Tab

The General tab of the Document Preferences dialog box is the catchall tab (see Figure 2-27), with controls ranging from measurement systems to what happens when you reapply master pages to pages. Some of these preferences have been part of QuarkXPress for 10 years!

Horizontal Measure and Vertical Measure. These two popup menus let you tell XPress what measurement system you like using (see "Guides and Rulers," in Chapter 3, *Tools of the Trade*). New in version 4 is the ability to use agates. Remember that even if these popup menus are set to inches, you can always specify measurements in picas or centimeters or any other system.

Auto Page Insertion. When you import a large amount of text into an automatic text box, XPress may add pages to your document. Here's where you can control this behavior. (See "Automatic Page Insertion," in Chapter 4, *Building a Document*.)

Framing. You can place borders around text boxes and picture boxes, but do you want the frame to sit on the outside or the inside of the box? (See "Frames, Dashes, and Stripes" in the next chapter, *Tools of the Trade*.)

Guides. When you pull a guide out onto your page (see "Guides and Rulers," in the next chapter), this control determines whether it sits on top of your page objects or below them. (Hint: Leave this set to In Front.)

Item Coordinates. The ruler that runs across the top of your page can measure the width of your page or the entire spread (see "Guides and Rulers," in the next chapter).

Auto Picture Import. Picture management is an important topic in QuarkXPress. Auto Picture Import lets you automatically re-import pictures that have changed on disk since the last time you saved the document (see "Picture Usage," in Chapter 9, *Pictures*).

Master Page Items. QuarkXPress may reapply a master page to your document page on various occasions. This control lets you choose what

Figure 2-27

The General tab of the
Document Preferences
dialog box

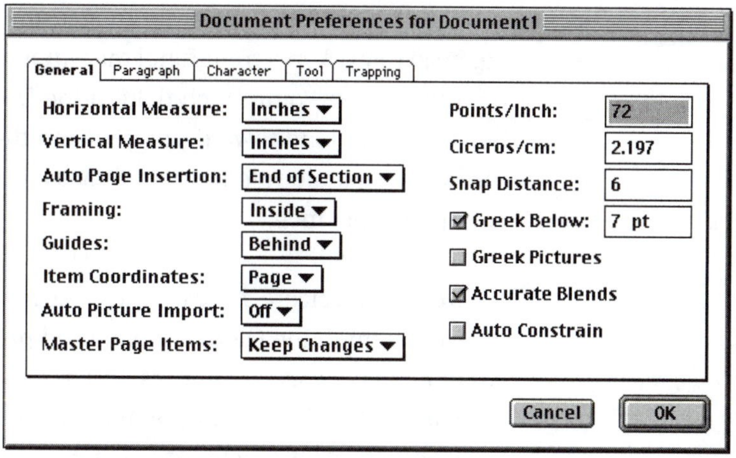

happens to the master page items in these cases (see "Master Pages and Document Pages," in Chapter 4, *Building a Document*).

Greek Below. Computer screens aren't very good at displaying tiny text, and it often takes too long to display it anyway. Greek Below lets you turn this text "off" so you just see gray lines where the text should be (see "Text Greeking," in Chapter 6, *Type and Typography*).

Greek Pictures. Tired of seeing all those pictures on your screen? Slow screen redraw got you down? Turn 'em off with the Greek Pictures control (see "Greeking and Suppression," in Chapter 9, *Pictures*).

Accurate Blends. If you work on a low-end, 8-bit color screen, you can speed up the screen redraw of your blends when this is turned off (but hardly enough to really make much difference; see "Cool Blends," in Chapter 12, *Color*).

Auto Constrain. If you've never used Auto Constrain, don't start now. It sets up parent/child relationships between boxes that are drawn inside boxes, and it harkens back to the very early days of QuarkXPress (see "Constraining," in the next chapter).

Points/Inch. Somebody, sometime, somewhere along the line, decided that PostScript should measure 72 points to an inch. However, as it turns out, printers and graphic designers have always measured just *over* 72 points to the inch. QuarkXPress, being the power-rich program it is, gives you the choice of how you want to measure points. If you have a burning need to work in a traditional measurement setting, you can change the value of the Points/Inch field in the Document Preferences dialog box to 72.27. I tend toward progress and think that people should just throw out their old rulers and embrace a new standard. Thus, I leave it at 72 points per inch.

Ciceros/Cm. A cicero, in case you're like me (*Americanus stupidus*), is a measurement in the Didot system, used primarily in France and other continental European countries. Just as a pica equals 12 points, the cicero equals 12 points. The difference? Differently sized points. A Didot point equals 0.01483 inch instead of the American-British 0.01383 inch. Anyway, the only really important thing about all this is that QuarkXPress defaults to 2.1967 ciceros per centimeter. This is close enough to a traditional cicero (you can do the math).

Note that if you want to work with Didot points more directly, you should probably also change Points/Inch, above, to 67.43.

The Paragraph and Character Tabs

I spend a good long time covering all the features that appear on the Paragraph and Character tabs in "Typographic Preferences," in Chapter 6, *Type and Typography*, so please forgive me if I punt on their descriptions here. Suffice it to say that these two tabs offer controls that affect how QuarkXPress handles its typography, and without understanding (and setting) some of these features, you're going to bang your head against a wall trying to get good type (see Figure 2-28).

The Tool Tab

The features on the Tool tab of the Document Preferences dialog box can really help you reduce the monotony of page layout (see Figure 2-29). Perhaps every time you draw a line you change its thickness to 0.5 point. Or perhaps every time you create a text box, you set the Text Inset value to zero or the background color to None. Instead of making the change hundreds of times, just make it once by changing the way the various tools in the Tool palette work.

You can use the settings on the Tool tab to change the default settings for any of the item-creation tools on the Tool palette, plus the Zoom tool (I discuss each of these tools and how best to use them in the next chap-

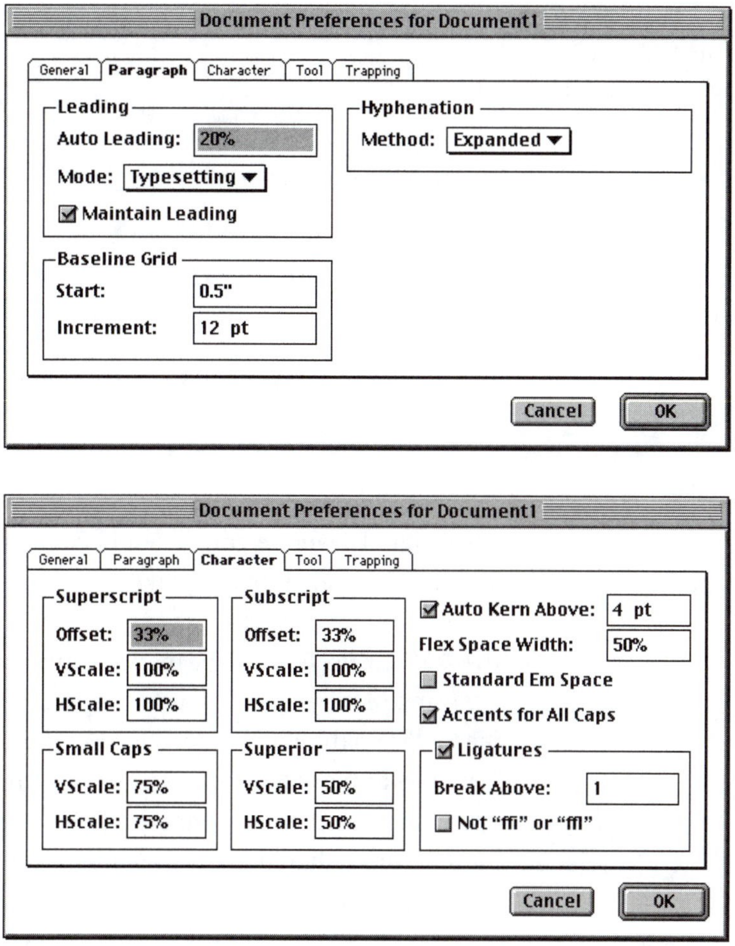

Figure 2-28

The Paragraph and
Character tabs of the
Document Preferences
dialog box

ter, *Tools of the Trade*). To change a default for an item-creation tool (the tools that create picture boxes, text boxes, or lines), select the tool's icon in the list of tools along the left side of the tab, and then click the Modify button.

Let's take a look at what each button on this tab does.

Modify. When you click the Modify button, XPress opens a dialog box that looks very similar to the Modify dialog box you normally get in QuarkXPress (if you're not familiar with the Modify dialog box, see "Manipulating Your Items," in Chapter 3, *Tools of the Trade*). There are, however, several differences. For instance, there's no Clipping tab because you can't control the default settings for picture clipping (it's always an object-by-object control). Also, fields such as Origin Across

Figure 2-29

The Tool tab of the
Document Preferences
dialog box

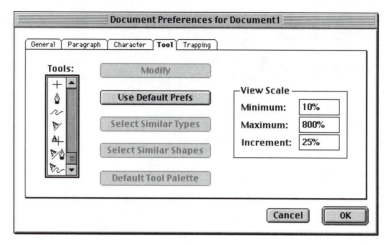

and Origin Down are grayed out because those are always going to be different for every box you make.

Use Default Prefs. If you've made changes to a tool's default preferences (by using Modify), you can return it to the factory settings by selecting the tool from the Tool list and clicking Use Default Prefs. For example, if you have to make 35 text boxes, each with a yellow background and a cyan frame, you could change the Rectangular Text Box tool to have these settings, then make the 35 boxes, and then reset the tool by coming back to the Tool tab and clicking this button.

Select Similar Types. If you select any of the text box creation tools and click the Select Similar Types button, XPress highlights *all* the text box creation tools (the rectangular one, the oval one, the freehand one, and so on). Chances are, if you're going to change the default setting of a line or a box, you'll probably want to make the change for all the similar tools at the same time. Note that you can always select or deselect additional tools from the Tools list by Command-clicking on them.

Select Simliar Shapes. You want all your oval boxes to have a border, but not your rectangular ones? No problem. Select one of the oval box tools and then click the Select Similar Shapes button. Now when you click Modify, you're changing the settings for just the oval boxes. Note that the

Modify dialog box is pretty limited when you select multiple tools that are of different types. For instance, if a text box and a picture box are selected when you click Modify, you can only change a couple of settings, like the box's Background color, and its Frame size and style.

Default Tool Palette. Back in the tip "Enlarge or Reduce Your Tool Palette," I told you how you could move tools around so that your palette would take up more or less space on-screen. If you ever tire of the way you've arranged your Tool palette, just come to the Tool tab of the Document Preferences dialog box and click the Default Tool Palette button. QuarkXPress resets the tools to their original state again.

View Scale. The last area of the Tool tab, labelled "View Scale," is only active when you select the Zoom tool from the Tools list. This area lets you change the minimum and maximum values that XPress allows you to zoom on your page. However, because these values are already set at their extremes (10 percent to 800 percent), I don't see any good reason to change them. However, I do often change the Increment setting, which controls how far XPress zooms in or out with each click of the Zoom tool (see "Zooming," earlier in this chapter). Because the default setting of 25 percent is pretty paltry, I usually use a more substantial value, like 75 percent or 100 percent, so that when I magnify my page, it really magnifies.

▼ ▼

Tip: Get to Those Tool Preferences Quickly. As you probably can tell, I do almost anything to avoid actually making a selection from a menu. I just find that other methods are faster for me, and they should be for you, too. For example, you can jump to the Tool Preferences dialog box by double-clicking on a tool in the Tool palette. This automatically highlights the tool you chose, and you're ready to make your change.

▼ ▼

The Trapping Tab

Trapping is a complicated issue that can compensate for errors made when printing colors on a printing press. I'm going to skip the features found in the Trapping tab of the Document Preferences dialog box (see Figure 2-30) because I discuss them at length in Chapter 12, *Color*.

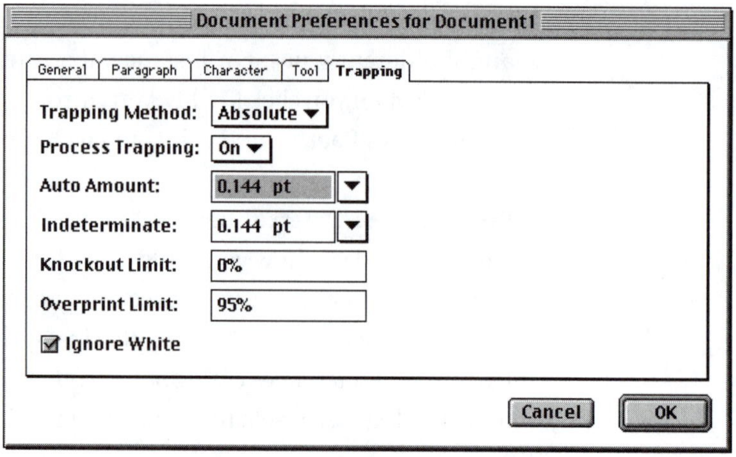

Figure 2-30

Figure 2-30
The Trapping tab of the
Document Preferences
dialog box

QuarkXPress from Zero to Sixty

QuarkXPress is an incredibly complex program that lets you create in
minutes what it would take hours to do using more traditional methods.
Its saving grace is the graphical user interface (GUI, or "gooey"), which
offers a user-friendly method of navigating around your document and
making changes. We've just begun looking at the myriad of features in
QuarkXPress, but with the basics that we've learned in this chapter, you
should be up and running in no time.

In the next chapter we take another step further, exploring the tools
that QuarkXPress offers, how best to use them, and how to manipulate
the various text boxes and lines that you can create on your pages.

3

Tools of the Trade

Have you noticed that we typically identify people's professions by the tools they use? I have only to mention some tool, and a vocation comes to mind: A hammer and nails. A cold stethoscope. A blackboard and chalk. A printing press. We don't think of a hairdresser as standing around waving his arms but, rather, wielding a pair of scissors or a razor.

Every trade has a toolbox with which they must make a living, and you and I are no different. Our toolbox is our computer—or, more specifically, QuarkXPress—and the tools inside are the subject of this chapter. The tools I talk about may appear, at first, to be simple and you may begin to kick yourself when you don't "get it" right away. But remember, like all tools, these take some time to learn, and it's not until you really start using them regularly that you begin to learn their secrets. For instance, it wouldn't take me long to teach you how to thread a needle and sew two pieces of cloth together. How much longer would it take for you to become a professional tailor?

In the last chapter I primarily talked about QuarkXPress's general interface: this does this, that does that. Now my emphasis shifts toward the practical. Let's look at each tool on the Tool palette in turn.

▼ ▼

Items and Contents

If you only learn one thing from this chapter, it should be the difference between items and contents. This is a concept that some people find difficult to understand, but it is really pretty simple. Moreover, the concept of items and contents is central to working efficiently in QuarkXPress.

Let's take it from the beginning. In order to put text on a page, you must place it in a text box. To put a graphic image on a page, you must place it in a picture box. Text boxes act as a sort of corral that holds all the words. There's almost no way a word can get outside the bounds of a text box. Picture boxes act as a sort of window through which you can see a picture. In both cases, the content of the box is different from the box itself.

Boxes are *items*. What goes inside them is *content*. Similarly, a line is an item, and the text you place on it is content. You can modify either one, but you need to use the correct tool at the correct time.

Item tool. The Item tool (or "Pointer tool"; though sometimes it's called by its technical name: "the pointy-thingy"; see Figure 3-1) is the first tool on the Tool palette. It's used for selecting and moving items (picture and text boxes, rules, and so on). You can use the Item tool by either choosing it from the Tool palette or by holding down the Command key while any other tool is selected (though you can't select or work with multiple items with this Command key trick). I discuss all the things you can do with items later in this chapter, in "Manipulating Items."

Figure 3-1
The Item and
Content tools

Item tool

Content tool

Content tool. The second tool on the Tool palette is the Content tool (sometimes called the "Hand tool"). This tool is used for adding, deleting, or modifying the contents of a text or picture box or a text path. Note that its palette icon consists of a text-insertion mark and a hand. When you have selected this tool from the Tool palette, QuarkXPress turns the cursor into one of these icons, depending on what sort of box you have highlighted (as we see in Chapter 9, *Pictures*, the hand is for moving images around within a picture box).

▼ ▼

Tip: Opaque versus Transparent Backgrounds. If you've been using XPress for a long time, you are probably used to QuarkXPress making text and picture boxes opaque whenever you select them with the Content tool. For some, this was always annoying because you couldn't change the content in a box and see what was behind the box at the same time. Other people thought this was a great system because it let you edit the contents of a box free of any distractions caused by other page elements. Well, the first group won: Now in XPress 4, when you select the Content tool, boxes that have a background of None (that is, they're transparent) remain transparent.

If this bothers you, you've got two options. First, you can change the background of the text or picture box to White (I discuss how to do this a little later in this chapter). Second, you can write an e-mail letter to Quark and explain that you want a future version to offer an option between the two.

▼ ▼

Tip: Blurring Lines Between Tools. There have been more changes to the Item and Content tools in version 4. Apparently a lot of people had difficulty remembering which tool to use for certain tasks, so the folks at Quark loosened the reins a little. You can now perform several tasks that you could never do before.

▶ You can now import pictures into picture boxes when the Item tool is selected.

▶ You can change various attributes of pictures using the Style menu and the Measurements palette when the Item tool is selected.

▶ When you have the Content tool selected, you can now select multiple objects by Shift-clicking on them or by dragging a marquee around them (see "Selecting Items," below).

It's funny, but the people who were most upset by these changes were trainers, consultants, and writers. Most people who use XPress on a day-to-day basis hardly even think about these changes; they just make life a little easier.

Note that almost all the other restrictions for these two tools remain: You still need to use the Content tool to import or edit text and to move pictures around within the picture box.

▼ ▼

Selecting Items

The most basic action you can take with a page item in QuarkXPress is to select it. Once again: To select and modify an item itself, you generally need to use the Item tool. To select and modify the contents of a picture or text box, you need to use the Content tool.

In version 4, you can now select more than one item at a time with either the Item or the Content tool. However, the Content tool acts just like the Item tool when you have two or more items selected (the cursor even changes to the Item tool cursor). There's two ways to select more than one item on your page: Shift-clicking and dragging a marquee.

Shift-click. You can select multiple items by Shift-clicking on them with either the Item or Content tool. If you have more than one item selected and you want to deselect one, you can Shift-click on it again (Shift-clicking acts as a toggle for selecting and deselecting).

▼ ▼

Tip: Grab Down Deep. There are plenty of times I've found that I need to reach through one or more objects on my page and grab a box or line that's been covered up. Moving everything on top is a real hassle. Instead, you can select through page items to get hold of objects that are behind them. Hold down the Command-Option-Shift keys while clicking with either the Item or Content tool to select the object one layer down. The second click selects the object on the next layer down, and so on.

▼ ▼

Marquee. If you drag with the Item tool, you can select more than one item in one fell swoop. This is called dragging a *marquee* because QuarkXPress shows you a dotted line around the area that you're dragging over. Every picture box, text box, and line that falls within this marqueed area gets selected, even if the marquee only touches it slightly.

I love the ability to drag a marquee out with the Item tool in order to select multiple objects. It's fast, it's effective, and it picks up everything in its path. However, sometimes it even picks up things you don't want it to pick up. For example, let's say you have an automatic text box on your page and then place some picture boxes on it. If you drag a marquee across the page to select the picture boxes, chances are you'll select the text box, too. You may not notice this at first, but if you group the selection or start dragging it off into a library or someplace else, you'll be taking the text box along for the ride. This spells havoc (press Command-Z quick to undo the last action).

So, just a quick lesson from people who've been there: Watch out for what you select and group. And if you do select more than you want, remember that you can deselect items by holding down the Shift key and clicking on them.

▼ ▼

Tip: Deselecting En Masse. To deselect one or more objects, you typically need to click a white area on the page (someplace where there are no other objects). However, there's a faster way: You can deselect every selected page item in one stroke by pressing Tab when the Item tool is selected. I find this really helpful when I'm zoomed in on the page and can't tell what's selected and what isn't. When you have the Content tool selected, the Tab key means something different: if only one object is selected, the Tab key types a tab character. But if you've selected more than one object, the Content tool acts just like the Item tool, so the Tab key deselects them.

▼ ▼

Tip: Select All. There's a third way to select more than one object on your page at a time. If you want to select all the page items, you can press Command-A. However, this only works when you have the Item tool selected. (When you have the Content tool selected, Command-A means "select all the text in a text box.")

▼ ▼

Item Creation Tools

The name of the QuarkXPress game is page layout, so we'd better start laying out some pages. There are five kinds of items you can put on your page: text box, picture box, contentless box, lines, and text paths. I spend much of the rest of the book discussing how to put content inside these objects and what to do with it once it's there, so I'd better spend some time now exploring the items themselves, how to make them, and how to edit them to suit your needs.

In this section, I discuss the various tools you can use to create page items. There's more than ever in this version of the program, so many that the folks at Quark decided to hide some of them inside popout menus in the Tool palette (see Figure 3-2, as well as "Palettes," in Chapter 2, *QuarkXPress Basics*, for more information on how to move these tools in and out of the popout menus).

Note that because the Bézier drawing tools have their own set of problems and solutions, I'm going to hold off on discussing them until the next section.

▼ ▼

Tip: Keeping Your Tools Around. After you use a tool (any tool other than the Zoom tool), the Tool palette automatically reverts back to either the Content or the Item tool (depending on which of the two you last used). This becomes a hassle if you want to use the same tool again. Instead, you can hold down the Option key as you select a tool. The tool remains selected until you choose another one.

▼ ▼

Making Boxes

In earlier versions of XPress, when you wanted a box, you had to clearly specify what kind of box it was—a text box or a picture box—and you had to pick a different tool to create each. And that was it; there was no switching once you had drawn the box. What's more, there were a slew of tools for making different-shaped picture boxes and only one (rectangular) for making text boxes.

But life is better now. XPress offers all the same tools for both text boxes and picture boxes, and although you still have to pick one or the other when drawing a box on your page, you can switch it from picture to text and back again. There's even a new kind of box, called a contentless box, which I talk about in just a little bit.

Creating a box is simple: choose one of the box tools from the Tool palette, and then click and drag on your page. You can see exactly how large your box is by watching the width and height values on the

Figure 3-2

The item creation tools

For the sake of the illustration, I've pulled all the tools out of their popout menus and into one long palette.

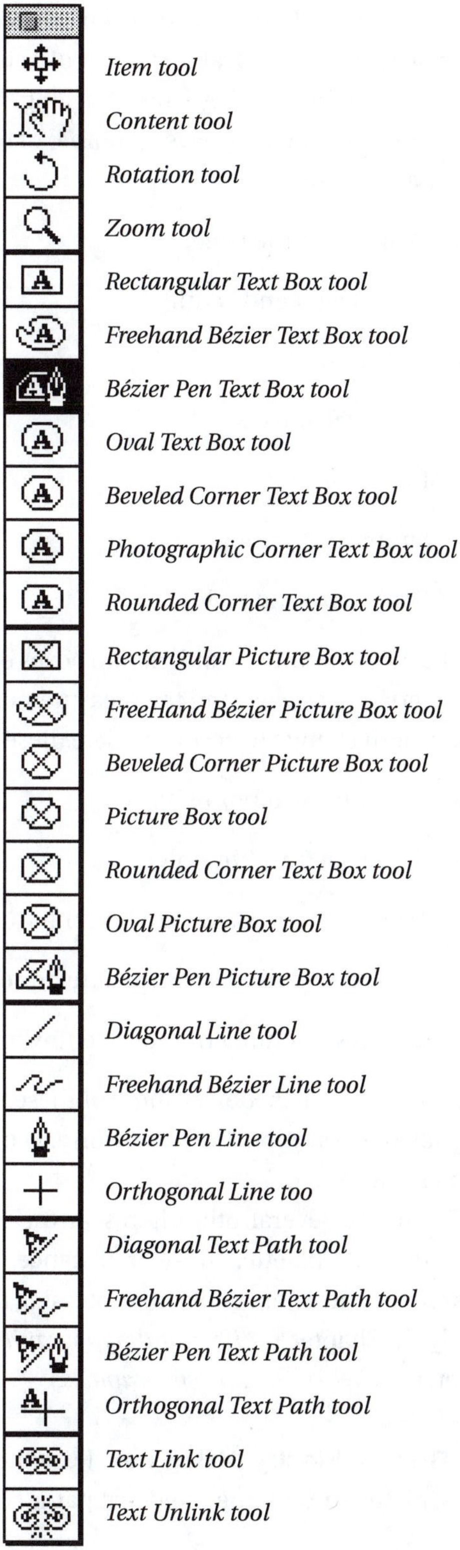

 Item tool

 Content tool

 Rotation tool

 Zoom tool

 Rectangular Text Box tool

 Freehand Bézier Text Box tool

 Bézier Pen Text Box tool

 Oval Text Box tool

 Beveled Corner Text Box tool

 Photographic Corner Text Box tool

 Rounded Corner Text Box tool

 Rectangular Picture Box tool

 FreeHand Bézier Picture Box tool

 Beveled Corner Picture Box tool

 Picture Box tool

 Rounded Corner Text Box tool

 Oval Picture Box tool

 Bézier Pen Picture Box tool

 Diagonal Line tool

 Freehand Bézier Line tool

 Bézier Pen Line tool

 Orthogonal Line too

 Diagonal Text Path tool

 Freehand Bézier Text Path tool

 Bézier Pen Text Path tool

 Orthogonal Text Path tool

 Text Link tool

Text Unlink tool

Measurements palette. Note that you can keep the box square (or circular, if you're using the Oval Text Box tool or the Oval Picture Box tool) by holding down the Shift key while dragging.

All boxes—as items—have a number of basic attributes that you can display and change.

- ▶ Position on the page

- ▶ Size (height and width)

- ▶ Background Color

- ▶ Corner Radius

- ▶ Box angle and skew

- ▶ Suppress Printout

- ▶ Frame size and Style

Of course, text boxes and picture boxes each have a few of their own characteristics, as well, and the Measurements palette and Modify dialog box both change to accommodate these differences.

- ▶ Columns (text box only)

- ▶ Text inset (text box only)

- ▶ Text angle and skew (text box only)

- ▶ Picture angle and skew (picture box only)

- ▶ Suppress Picture Printout (picture box only)

Let's take a quick look at some of these box attributes. I don't cover them all in this section, but don't worry: I cover them all by the time the chapter is through.

(There are several other items in the Modify dialog box and the Measurements palette, too—for instance, the scale of pictures, text runaround, and so on. I hold off discussing these until later in the book, mostly in Chapter 6, *Type and Typography*, Chapter 9, *Pictures*, and Chapter 11, *Where Text Meets Graphics*.)

▼ ▼

Tip: That Ol' Modify Dialog Box. I use the Modify dialog box for text boxes, picture boxes, lines, and text paths so often that I'm glad to have some variance in how I get to it. You can open the Modify dialog box for a page element in several ways.

▶ Select the item with either the Content or the Item tool and choose Modify from the Item menu. This is for people who work by the hour.

▶ Select the item with either the Content or the Item tool and press Command-M. This is great if both hands are on the keyboard.

▶ In Windows, you can click on an item with the secondary mouse button to display a context-sensitive popup menu in which you can choose Modify.

▶ Double-click on the page element with the Item tool. (Remember, you can hold down the Command key to temporarily work with the Item tool.) This is my favorite method, as I almost always work with one hand on the keyboard and one on the mouse.

Once you're in the dialog box, you can tab through the fields to get to the value you want to change. After a while, you memorize how many tabs it takes to get to a field, and you can press Command-M, Tab, Tab, Tab, Tab, Tab, type the value, press Return, and be out of there before QuarkXPress has time to catch up with you. That's when you know you're becoming an XPress Demon.

▼ ▼

Position and size. All boxes are positioned by their upper-left corner. This point is called their *origin*. The first two fields in the Modify dialog box and the Measurements palette are Origin Across and Origin Down. However, unless your box is rectangular, the origin is not necessarily where you think it is because the origin is based on the box's bounding box—the smallest rectangle that could completely enclose the item (see Figure 3-3).

Note that if you've rotated the box, it still thinks of the original upper-left corner as its origin. So if you rotate 90 degrees counterclockwise, the lower-left corner (formerly the upper-left corner) is still the origin point.

The size of the box is then specified by its width and height (the distances to the right and down from the origin). These values, too, are calculated from the item's bounding box.

Figure 3-3
Bounding box
and position

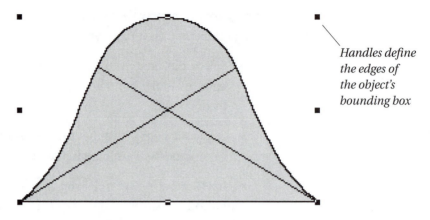

*Handles define
the edges of
the object's
bounding box*

▼ ▼

Tip: Quick, Accurate Boxes. Some people tend toward a visual approach to creating and sizing boxes in QuarkXPress, while others work with a more mathematical or coordinate-based method. Fortunately, both work equally well. You can click and drag page elements out to the size you want them, if you prefer to make a decision based on seeing what it looks like.

Or, if you're working on a grid, you can draw a box to any size, and then jump into the Measurements palette or Modify dialog box to specify the exact origin coordinates, the width, and the height.

▼ ▼

Tip: Moving an Item's Origin. One of the features I've always coveted in Adobe PageMaker is the ability to set the origin of a page element from a number of locations, rather than just the upper-left corner. Until QuarkXPress does the same, I can only offer a somewhat weak workaround for specifying alternate origins: use the built-in math functions. To set the right side of a box at a specific location, subtract the width of the box from the location's coordinate. For example, to set the right side of a 12-pica-wide box at the 2.75-inch mark, type "2.75"-12p" into the x-origin field of the Measurements palette.

Similarly, to set the location for the center of a box, divide the box width by two and then subtract it from the coordinate. For example, if you want the center of a 16-pica-wide box to be at the 18-centimeter mark, you can type "18cm-16p/2". (Remember that XPress does division first, then the subtraction).

▼ ▼

Background color. Every picture and text box has a background color, or can have a background set to None. Any background color other than None and White can be set to a specific tint. Note that zero percent of a color is not transparent; it's opaque white.

A box can also have a blend of two colors in its background (I discuss creating, editing, and applying colors and blends in Chapter 12, *Color*). Both background colors and blends are specified in the Modify dialog box.

Corner Radius. The Corner Radius attribute is applicable to all boxes except those made with the Bézier tools (which I discuss later in this chapter). The Corner Radius feature in the Modify dialog box lets you set how rounded the corners should be (see Figure 3-4). (On the Beveled Corner box tools, it sets the size of the bevels.) In fact, because you can turn a rectangular box into a rounded-corner box just by setting its Corner Radius, I think there's little reason to ever use the Rounded Corner box tools.

Figure 3-4
Corner Radius defines how rounded the corners are

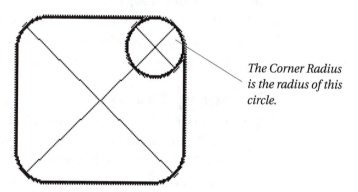

The Corner Radius is the radius of this circle.

Besides, and to be frank, rounded-corner boxes are one of the most obvious giveaways that you created your document using a Macintosh or Windows machine. Some of the all-time worst designs that have come off of a desktop computer use rounded-corner picture boxes. I really dislike them. But, then again, it's your design, and you can do what you like with it.

Columns. While the previous several items were applicable to all boxes, the Columns attribute is text-box-specific. Text boxes can be divided into a maximum of 30 columns. Each column's size is determined by the size of the *gutter* (blank space) between columns. You can set the gutter width only in the Modify dialog box, although you can set the number of columns in either this dialog box or the Measurements palette.

Note that you cannot have columns with negative widths: the number of columns you can have is determined by the gutter width. For example, if your gutter width is 1 pica and your text box is 20 picas wide, you cannot have more than 20 columns; however, that many columns would leave no room for text.

Text Inset. The last attribute particular to text boxes is Text Inset. The Text Inset value determines how far your text is placed inside the four sides of the text box. For example, a Text Inset value of zero places the text right up against the side of the text box. A text inset value of "3cm" places the text no closer than 3 centimeters from the side of the box.

The default setting for text inset is 1 point. The reason: Because the folks at Quark noticed that text set flush against the side of a box is hard to read. If you find this as obnoxious as I do, you can change this default setting for your text boxes to zero or any other value (see "Changing Defaults," in Chapter 2, *QuarkXPress Basics*). Or you can do it a box at a time in the Modify dialog box.

Note that there are XTensions, like XPertTools Volume 2, that let you specify the Text Inset value for each of the four sides rather than simply one value for all sides. That can be very helpful in certain situations.

Changing Box Type

As I mentioned earlier, you can change a picture box into a text box and vice versa. The trick is the Content submenu (under the Item menu; see Figure 3-5). This submenu offers three choices when you have a box selected: Text, Picture, and None. Text and picture are self-explanatory, though you should note that if there's something in your box (some text or a picture), changing the box type deletes it. The None setting leads us to a new feature in XPress 4: the contentless box.

Contentless boxes. It took 10 years for the engineers at Quark to figure out that we sometimes put boxes on our pages not to contain text or a graphic, but just for the sake of a background color (sometimes known as a tint build). In the past, you had to use a picture box or a text box to do this, with annoying side effects. Empty picture boxes display a big "X" in them; and text boxes, when covered by other boxes, display an overset mark, even if there's no text in them to overset.

Figure 3-5

Changing box type

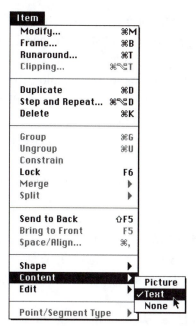

Fortunately, QuarkXPress now offers contentless boxes, which you can use just for this purpose. To get a contentless box, select a picture or a text box and choose None from the Content submenu (under the Item menu).

Two other things to note about contentless boxes, too. First, they take up slightly less space on disk (though this only really makes a difference if you have hundreds of them in your document). Second, contentless boxes draw on-screen faster because XPress doesn't have to think about each one, whether it has content or not, and so on.

▼ ▼

Tip: Adding Contentless Boxes. If you find yourself frequently converting picture or text boxes to contentless boxes (by selecting None from the Content submenu), you should just draw your boxes with the contentless box tools. Unfortunately, there are none in the Tool palette. Or are there? Open the Tool tab of the Document Preferences dialog box (see "Changing Default Preferences" in Chapter 2, *QuarkXPress Basics*), and Command-click on the Default Tool Palette button. When you click OK to leave the dialog box, XPress adds contentless tools to your palette.

▼ ▼

Lines and Arrows

The Tool palette contains four tools to draw lines and arrows on your page. To be precise, you really only draw lines, but those lines can be styled in several fashions, and they can have arrowheads and tailfeathers. You can create a line with any thickness between 0.001 point and 864 points (that's a pretty thick line—more than 11 inches thick), at any angle, and apply various styles and colors to it. Like boxes, you can view and change these attributes in the Modify dialog box and—for some—the Measurements palette.

Two of the tools are based on Bézier curves, and I discuss them in "Bézier Boxes and Lines," later in this chapter. The other two tools are the Diagonal Line tool and the Orthogonal Line tool.

Diagonal Line tool. The Diagonal Line tool can make a line at any angle. If you hold down the Shift key while dragging out the line, you can constrain the line to 45 or 90 degrees. Don't worry if the line looks jaggy on-screen; that will smooth out when the file is printed.

Orthogonal Line tool. For those of you who aren't in arm's reach of a dictionary, *orthogonal* means that the lines you draw with this tool can only be horizontal or vertical. This tool is somewhat redundant, given that you can make orthogonal lines easily with the Diagonal Line tool and the Shift key. However, I guess it's nice to have this option.

Line weight. I always use the word "weight" or "thickness" rather than "width," which is what QuarkXPress uses to describe lines. (When I talk about the width of horizontal lines, people often think I'm talking about length.) The line thickness is centered on the line. That is, if you specify a 6-point line, 3 points fall on one side of the line, and 3 points fall on the other side.

This value appears in three places: the Style menu, the Modify dialog box, and the Measurements palette. Even better, you can press Command-Shift-\ (backslash) to bring up the Line Width field in the Modify dialog box. Table 3-1 shows several other ways to change a line's weight with keystrokes. (You can use the same keystrokes to specify type size.)

Table 3-1 Changing line weight	To ...	PRESS ...
	Increase weight by preset amount	Command-Shift-period
	Increase weight by one point	Command-Shift-Option-period
	Decrease weight by preset amount	Command-Shift-comma
	Decrease weight by one point	Command-Shift-Option-comma

▼ ▼

Tip: Don't Use Hairlines. You have the option to select Hairline when choosing a line thickness. Don't. Traditionally, a hairline is the thinnest possible line you can print. On a low-resolution desktop printer, this is pretty thin, but on an imagesetter it's often too small to be seen. When you print your document, QuarkXPress actually replaces hairlines with 0.125-point rules so you don't get caught in this trap.

However, sometimes the program goofs up: When XPress 4.0 first shipped, many users went ballistic because the program had stopped catching and replacing hairline-width rules. Quark quickly fixed the "problem," so current versions work just fine. Nonetheless, it's always better to specify the thickness of your lines rather than rely on a program to do it.

▼ ▼

Color and shade. You can set the line's color to any color in the document (see Chapter 12, *Color*), then tint it to any value from zero to 100 percent, in 0.1-percent increments (zero percent is white). These specifications are available in the Modify dialog box, the Colors palette, or the Style menu.

Style and endcaps. Lines don't have to be boring; spice them up with a new style, or add endcaps to turn them into arrows. You can choose one of 11 different line styles and one of six endcap combinations by selecting them from two popup menus in the Modify dialog box, the Style menu, or the Measurements palette (see Figure 3-6).

Figure 3-6
Line styles

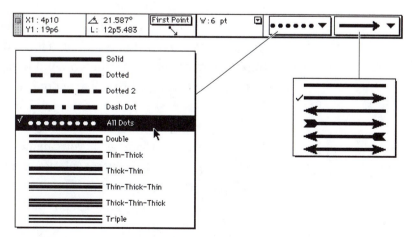

Six of the line styles are stripes (multiple parallel lines) and four are dashes (lines with gaps). I discuss stripes and dashes, including how to make your own styles, in "Frames, Dashes, and Stripes," later in this chapter. For now, however, suffice it to say that when you specify a thicker line, the dash or stripe gets proportionally thicker, too (just as you'd expect).

Even though you have six endcap styles to choose from, the choice really comes down to either with arrowheads and tailfeathers, or without them. You can't edit the style of these endcaps, so you're stuck with what's built into the program.

Note that if you choose an arrowhead that points to the right, the arrowhead you get might point to the left. The reason is that the arrowhead style pointing to the right actually means "put an arrow at the *end* of the line." XPress remembers how you drew the line—where you first clicked is the beginning of the line, and where you let go of the mouse button is the end. (This is different from the way it worked in earlier versions.) If the arrow is pointing the wrong way, just select the opposite direction in the Arrowhead popup menu.

Text Paths

The ability to put text on a path is, for many people, alone worth the price to upgrade from version 3. In the past, you had to switch to an illustration program to create this effect, then save the text as a graphic, then import it into a picture box . . . and then if you wanted to edit it, you had to go back to the original program, and so on. Well, no longer!

QuarkXPress 4 offers four text-path tools that appear and act almost identically to the four line tools that I just discussed. While the two Bézier text-path tools are the ones you will probably use the most often, I discuss those in the next section ("Bézier Boxes and Lines"). Let's start, instead, with the two simple text-path tools: the Diagonal Text Path tool and the Orthogonal Text Path tool. And then let's look at how you can customize the text on the path to get the effect you're looking for.

▾ ▾

Tip: Converting Lines to Text Paths. Just as you can convert a picture box to a line box and back again, you can make any regular line a text path by choosing Text in the Content submenu (under the Item menu). What this literally means is that lines can have content, too. In fact, in many ways a text path acts just like a text box that holds just a single line of text.

To change a text path to a regular line, choose None from the Content submenu.

▼ ▼

Drawing with the text-path tools. When you draw a path with a text-path tool, XPress immediately switches to the Content tool, letting you type along the line (see Figure 3-7). If you hold down the Shift key when you're drawing the path, the line is constrained to a horizontal, vertical, or 45-degree angle (which makes the Orthogonal Text Path tool a bit redundant).

Figure 3-7
Drawing with the
text-path tools

Overset text
(path is too small)

Selecting text
on a path

If you want to edit the text on the path, watch the cursor carefully when you click or drag over the path. Depending on where you place the cursor, the cursor's appearance changes. If you put it directly over the line, you may get the Edit Segment cursor (I cover this in "Bézier Boxes and Lines," later in this chapter). If you put it over an endpoint, you'll get the Move Point cursor. It's only over certain parts of the line that you see the Edit Text "I-beam" cursor.

Once again, text on a path acts just like it's in a text box, so you can use all the text editing features that I discuss in Chapter 5, *Word Processing*, Chapter 6, *Type and Typography*, and Chapter 7, *Copy Flow*. In fact, when you select the text path with the Content tool, the Measurements palette appears almost exactly the same as it does with text boxes; with the Item tool, the palette appears as though you had a line selected.

Line width and style. By default, the text paths themselves have a thickness of Hairline and a color of None, which makes them invisible. The text on the path, of course, is a different matter. Every now and again, primarily for special effects, you'll want to change the line's style and weight (see Figure 3-8). You can do so with the same features as with normal lines: the Style menu, the Measurements palette, and the Modify dialog box.

Figure 3-8

Changing the line style on text paths

The text path is styled with a thick triple line

Text Orientation. Text paths have a special tab in the Modify dialog box that lets you specify text-path options (see Figure 3-9). The first control you have over text on a text path is the orientation of the text. There are four options, though I should note that none of these have any effect on text paths you create with the Diagonal or Orthogonal Text Path tool. They only affect Bézier text paths. In fact, you can't even convert a diagonal or orthogonal text path to a Bézier curve in order to use these; rather, you have to actually create a new path with the Bézier text-path tools.

Figure 3-9

Text-path options

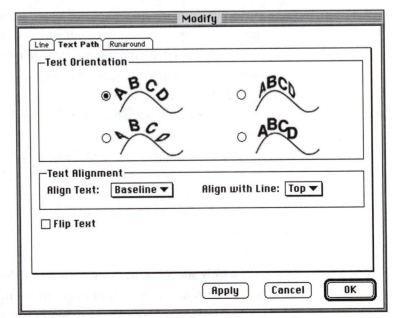

▶ **FOLLOW THE CURVE.** The first, and default, setting for Text Orientation forces each character to rotate along the curve. What that means is that each character of text isn't actually curved, even if the path is a Bézier path, but the overall effect is that of a curve (see Figure 3-10). This is what most people want 95 percent of the time.

Figure 3-10
Text Orientation

Note that the thin gray lines are included here just for illustration purposes

Follow the curve

Warp with the curve

Skew with the curve

Stay Horizontal

▶ **WARP WITH THE CURVE.** The second option (the one in the upper-right corner) warps the text along the curve, resulting in a quasi-three-dimensional effect. What XPress is really doing is both skewing and rotating each character based on the slope of the curve. First it rotates it along the curve (as in the last option) and then it skews it forward or backward so that the character remains upright. This is useful primarily for special effects.

▶ **SKEW WITH THE CURVE.** The third option (in the lower-left corner) skews each character based on the slope of the curve, but doesn't rotate it. The result is . . . well, strange at best. When the curve is sloping up to the right, XPress skews the text to the left; when the curve goes down to the right, XPress skews the text to the right; if your curve doubles back and heads to the left, the text is flipped and skewed. I bet someone out there has come up with a good use for this, but I haven't.

▶ **STAY HORIZONTAL.** The last option ensures that each character is not skewed or rotated as it makes its way along the path.

Text Alignment. The next control on the Text Path tab of the Modify dialog box is Text Alignment, which lets you specify what part of the text should align with what part of the path. For instance, the default setting is for the baseline of the text to align with the top of the line (see Figure 3-11). Of course, because the default line is only 0.25 point thick, there is very little difference between aligning to the top or the bottom of the line. If you make the line thicker, however, this makes a difference. (You can make the line thicker and still set the Color to None, making it invisible.)

Figure 3-11
Text Alignment

Align Text: Baseline, Align with Line: Top

Align Text: Baseline, Align with Line: Bottom

Align Text: Ascent, Align with Line: Top

Align Text: Center, Align with Line: Center

If you set the Align Text popup menu to Ascent, however, then XPress moves the text down so that the highest ascender in the typeface (like the top part of a lowercase "k") aligns with the line. You can also choose Center (which centers the font's lower-case characters—its x-height—on the line) or Descent (which aligns the lowest descender of the font—like the bottom part of a lowercase "y"—to the line).

Which setting you should choose depends entirely on your situation, the text, and the type of curve. I find that it's often worth testing two or three different settings here until I get the effect I like most (remember the Apply button so you don't have to keep leaving the dialog box each time you try a new setting).

Flip Text. The last control in the Modify dialog box that applies to text paths is Flip Text, which doesn't so much flip the text as much as it flips what XPress thinks of as the path. That is, when this is turned on, QuarkXPress starts the text from the last point on the path instead of the first, and the top and bottom sides of the path are reversed (see Figure 3-12). The result is usually a mirror image of the original—except that XPress doesn't mirror the text itself, only the text flow. I find that when I use Flip Text, I almost always have to adjust the Text Alignment settings to accommodate it.

Figure 3-12
Flip Text

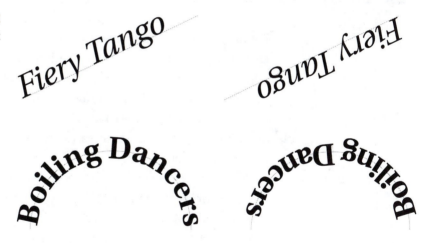

▼ ▼

Tip: Positioning the Text on the Curve. As I've said before, text on a path acts the same as text in a text box. This means that, if you don't like the position of the text on your path, you can use the settings in the Paragraph Formats dialog box, like Left Indent and Horizontal Alignment. For example, if you want text to be centered on the path, just place the cursor in the text and change the Alignment to Centered (Command-Shift-C).

You can also add or remove space between characters along the path using kerning and tracking (see Figure 3-13). I discuss all these typographic controls in Chapter 6, *Type and Typography*.

Figure 3-13
Formatting text
on a curve

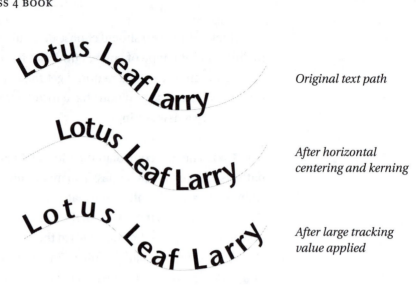

Original text path

*After horizontal
centering and kerning*

*After large tracking
value applied*

Bézier Boxes and Lines

For most people working in desktop publishing, the addition of Bézier curves to QuarkXPress version 4 is truly a joyous event. It means that we don't have to leave QuarkXPress and open an illustration program just to set some text on a path, or to draw a simple shape such as a heart to put a graphic in. Creating these kinds of elements has always been a hassle, and editing them was even worse. Now, XPress's tools make editing paths and shapes much easier.

If you are familiar with the Bézier controls in programs such as Adobe Illustrator or Macromedia FreeHand, you will find the controls in XPress 4 to be similar. As in those programs, the Bézier shapes are drawn with a Pen tool. And as in those programs, there are anchor points with handles to control the curves of the Bézier shapes. However, there are some features in QuarkXPress that are unique. This means that you may not be able to pick up the QuarkXPress Pen tools and start drawing immediately. You may need to retrain your fingers for the QuarkXPress tools.

If you have never worked with Bézier tools you may find them a little daunting. More than one student has given up learning the "dreaded Pen" tool in desktop illustration programs. Hang in there! Mastering the Bézier tools in QuarkXPress enables you to create the most sophisticated and interesting artwork and designs.

A word of caution: The Bézier tools in QuarkXPress 4 are not a substitute for illustration programs such as Illustrator or FreeHand. The Bézier tools in QuarkXPress are for *basic* things like putting text on a path, converting text into masks, or creating simple shapes and logos. If you are working on complex illustrations, you will almost certainly find more powerful tools in a dedicated illustration program. Of course, having said that, people will probably start sending me all sorts of super-sophisticated artwork created solely in QuarkXPress 4. And I will be very impressed. (But I won't change my opinion.)

Understanding Bézier Controls

Why are they called "Bézier" controls? Because they were created by a French mathematician named Pierre Bézier. (For those of you who never took French, his name is pronounced *Bay-zee-EH.*) What Monsieur Bézier did was create a mathematical system to define the shape of curves.

Before Bézier, drafting was performed by painfully plotting dozens or even hundreds of points on a curve. Après Bézier, the entire curve could be described with one very short description including two coordinates points and their "control handles" (I'll explain handles in a minute). Not only are these curves easy to describe mathematically, but they lend themselves to a very simple user interface as well.

There are three different aspects to Bézier curves: points, segments, and control handles.

Bézier points. There are three different types of Bézier points in QuarkXPress: smooth points, symmetrical points, and corner points. Each one creates a different type of shape (see Figure 3-14).

▶ SMOOTH POINTS. Smooth points create curves with smooth transitions. The top of a roller coaster is a good example of a smooth curve. There is no abrupt change from the curve going up to the one going down, so you say the transition is "smooth." When you select a smooth point on a curve, it's indicated by a diamond dot.

▶ SYMMETRICAL POINTS. Symmetrical points are the same as smooth points except that the shape on one side of the curve is always equal to the shape on the other side. The curve created by a swinging pendulum is a good example of a symmetical point.

Figure 3-14

The different types of
Bézier points

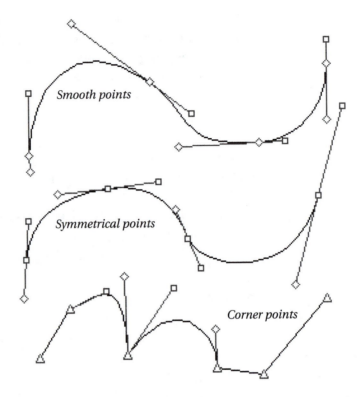

Smooth points

Symmetrical points

Corner points

The left side of the arc created by the pendulum is equal to the right side of the arc. Symmetical points that are selected are indicated on the path by a square dot.

▶ **CORNER POINTS.** Corner points abruptly change their direction. The path of a ball bouncing is a good example of a path with a corner point. The top arc of the path is smooth, but the point where the ball hits the ground is a corner point because the path changes its shape abruptly. When you select a corner point, it appears on the path as a triangle dot.

Segments. Segments are the connections—or lines—between points (see Figure 3-15). There are two different types of segments in QuarkXPress: curved segments and straight segments.

▶ **CURVED SEGMENTS.** Curved segments are those that have a curved shape. A curved segment can be created between any two types of points.

Figure 3-15
The two different types of Bézier segments

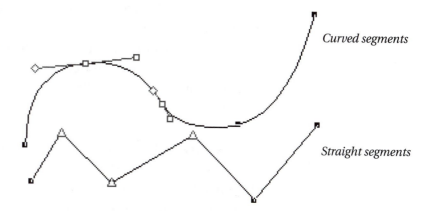

Curved segments

Straight segments

▶ **STRAIGHT SEGMENTS.** Straight segments are (surprise!) those that have no curve to them. A straight segment can only be created between two corner points.

Control handles. Control handles tell curves where to go. Technically, the control handle defines the tangent to the curve, but I like to think of it more like the control handle saying "come toward this direction." As you draw or edit the points of Bézier curves, you see colored lines extending out from your points (see Figure 3-16). These are the control handles for the points. (Control handles are used solely to define the shape of the object. They don't print.) As you drag the handles around, the curve changes.

Smooth and symmetrical points always have two control handles (one on each side of the point). Corner points, on the other hand, can have two handles, one handle, or even no handles. Actually, even when it looks like there's no handle, there really is . . . it's just that the handle has a length of zero, so it's sitting exactly on top of the corner point.

Figure 3-16
The two different types of Control handles

"In" handle

"Out" handle

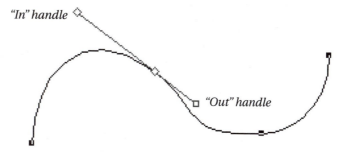

Every control handle is either an "In" handle or an "Out" handle, depending on which side of the point it sits on. They have exactly the same function, but it's useful to differentiate between them both when talking about how to draw these curves and also when editing them. The In control handle has a small diamond at the end of the handle; the Out control handle has a square.

▼ ▼

Tip: Best Bézier Techniques. If you have worked with Bézier tools in programs such as Illustrator or FreeHand, you are most likely aware of the principles of creating smooth, clean Bézier shapes. However, if all this is new to you, there are a few basic principles you should keep in mind as you create your Bézier shapes. This ensures that your layouts look their best and print without any problems.

► Use fewer points. Try to keep the number of points on a Bézier shape to a minimum. For instance, the arc of a pendulum actually needs only two points to define it. An egg only needs four. The fewer the number of points on your shapes, the easier it is to create smooth curves (see Figure 3-17).

► Avoid huge control handles. The control handles for curves define the shape of the curve. The longer the handle, the greater the curve. However, you should try to limit the length of the handle to approximately one-third the length of the curve segment (see Figure 3-18). This ensures that drawing and editing the curve will be as easy as possible, as well as ensuring smooth transitions

Figure 3-17
Limiting points

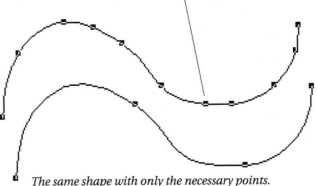

Many of these points are unnecessary to draw the shape.

The same shape with only the necessary points.

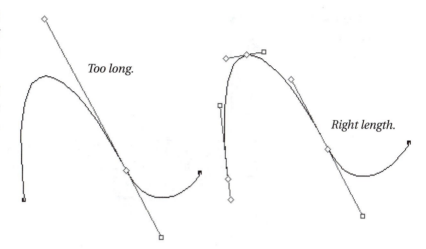

Figure 3-18
Limit length of
control handles

*Try to limit control
handles to one-third the
length of the arc.*

Too long.

Right length.

from one point to the next. Don't get obsessive about this rule; it's just a guideline, and often you need to break guidelines to get the effect you want.

▶ **ANTICIPATE EDITING CHOICES.** As you create Bézier shapes, try to anticipate where you might want to have a point to edit later on. For instance, if you are following the shape of an arm, you might want to have a point at the elbow, rather than have just one segment that extends from shoulder to wrist. That way you have the ability later on to change the shape with the new point.

▼ ▼

Bézier and Freehand Tools

QuarkXPress offers two kinds of tools that create Bézier shapes: the pen tools and the freehand tools. (I use the word "freehand" to describe how they work; they don't have anything to do with Macromedia's FreeHand drawing program.) However, these two tools each come in five flavors—text box, picture box, contentless box, line, and text path—for a total of 10 different Bézier tools (see Figure 3-19).

Pen tools let you create shapes by precisely placing Bézier points and manipulating the control handles as you create the shape. The freehand tools let you draw a shape freeform, by eye; XPress then traces your path, figuring out where the points and control handles should be positioned.

Figure 3-19

The Bézier and freehand tools in the toolbox.

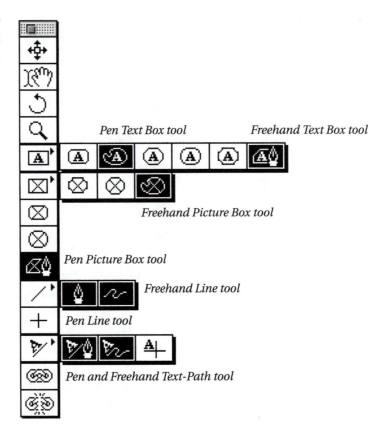

Pen Text Box tool

Freehand Text Box tool

Freehand Picture Box tool

Pen Picture Box tool

Freehand Line tool

Pen Line tool

Pen and Freehand Text-Path tool

Tip: Comparing Bézier and Freehand Tools. If you find the pen-based Bézier tools hard to learn, you may be tempted to only use the freehand tools instead. Don't do it. No matter how steady your hand, you will still almost never get the curve you want with one of the freehand tools. Plus, the freehand tools only create curved segments, not straight segments. This means that the freehand tools can create the curves at the top of a tombstone, but not the straight sides. For that you need the pen tools.

Most people don't have the hands of a surgeon, and the paths created by the freehand tools follow every jiggle and bump of your mouse (see Figure 3-20), so unless you're extremely lucky, your paths will have extra points where you don't need them—or may not have enough points where you do need them.

Use the freehand tools only if you have not learned how to draw with the equivalent Bézier pen tool. And then be prepared to spend a good deal of time manually editing and reshaping the path by moving, adding,

Figure 3-20

Objects drawn with Bézier tools are much smoother than those drawn with the freehand tools.

Bézier heart   *Freehand heart*

and deleting points. But then set aside some time later on to practice working with the pen tools.

▼ ▼

Tip: Automatically Closing Bézier and Freehand Boxes. When you use one of the Bézier box tools (to create a picture box, a text box, or a contentless box), you have to close the path you draw. There are three ways to close a path, thus finishing the box.

▶   You can finish the box by clicking on the first point in the path.

▶   You can double-click on the last point, to have XPress close the path for you. The last point (the one where you double-clicked) is a corner point.

▶   When you're drawing with one of the pen tools, the box closes as soon as you choose another tool from the toolbox. If you're using one of the freehand tools, the path closes as soon as you release the mouse button.

▼ ▼

Tip: Finishing Bézier Lines. I have long wished for a line tool that could draw more than one segment at a time. Well, the Bézier line and text-path tools extend far beyond my humble request. With them, you can draw all manner of lines on your pages, and then place text along the path. But there's one puzzling problem: how do you tell XPress that you're finished drawing at the end of the line?

With the freehand tools, it's easy: you just let go of the mouse button. With the pen tools, it's less obvious: you have to either double-click (which adds a corner point as the last point on the path), or choose another tool. If I've got my left hand on the keyboard (I typically do), I just press Command-Tab (or Control-Alt-Tab in Windows) to switch to the next tool on the tool palette. Or, if you can reach, Shift-F8 tells XPress to switch to the Content tool.

▼ ▼

Drawing with the Pen Tools

Okay, it's time to get down to business with some exercises that should help you learn to use the various Bézier tools. I'm going to walk you quickly through three sets of step-by-step instructions that use the three types of Bézier points.

Here's three suggestions to keep in mind as you're working. First, watch how the cursor changes depending on where it is located and what function it is performing (see Table 3-2). Second, watch the shape of the points on the path. Those shapes are also clues as to the type of path being created. Finally, while you're learning to use the Bézier tools, give yourself a large, open page to work on. Don't try to cramp your artwork into a tight little space.

Table 3-2
Bézier cursor clues

IF YOU WANT TO ...	LOOK FOR THIS CURSOR ...
Move a point	
Move or extend a control handle	
Add point to a path	
Delete a point or handle	
Close a path	
Move or modify a segment	
Convert between Smooth and Corner points	

Drawing corner points. The easiest type of point to draw with the pen tools is a corner point connected to a straight segment. So this first exercise is to draw a diamond shape that consists of only four corner points (see Figure 3-21). If you used earlier versions of QuarkXPress, you'll find that drawing corner points is, at its simplest, just like making a polygonal picture box.

1. Select the Bézier Pen Picture Box tool (although these lessons apply to all the Bézier pen tools, I use the picture box tools here).

2. Position your mouse where the left point of the diamond should be located, and click. You should see a little colored dot indicating that you have placed the first point. (If the color of the dot looks familiar, it's because Bézier paths are always colored the same as your Margin guides as you're drawing them; see the section called "Changing Default Preferences," back in Chapter 2, *QuarkXPress Basics.*)

3. Move your mouse to where the top point of the diamond should be located, and click. You should see another colored dot with a colored line connecting the first and second points.

4. Now do the same for the right point and the bottom point of the diamond.

5. Finally, as you place your mouse over the first point you created, the cursor should change to a rounded-corner rectangle. Click to

Figure 3-21
Drawing a straight-segment object

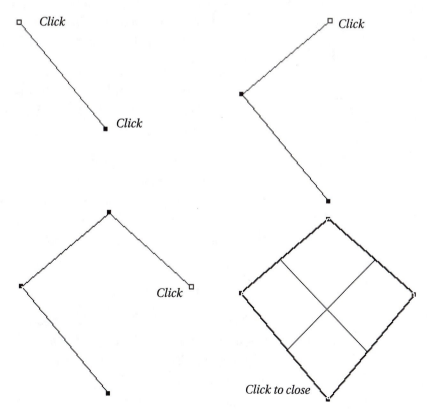

close the box. Or, alternately, remember that you can close the path automatically simply by switching to another tool.

Congratulations! You have just created a diamond shape with a Bézier pen tool.

Drawing a curved object. The second-easiest type of point to draw is a smooth point connected to another smooth point. This exercise is to draw a bean shape, which consists of only easy smooth points (see Figure 3-22).

1. Select the Bézier Pen Picture Box tool.

2. Position your mouse where the left curve of the bean should be located. Press down on the mouse and drag up. You should see a colored dot with two control handles. Stop dragging when the Out control handle extends about 1.5 inches out from the colored dot.

3. Move your mouse to where the top point of the bean should be located. Press and drag down and to the right at approximately a 30-degree angle. Stop dragging when the Out control handle extends about 1.5 inches out from the colored dot. You'll see an arc connecting the first and second dots.

4. Move your mouse to where the middle curve of the bean should be located. Press and drag straight down. Stop dragging when the Out control handle extends about 0.5 inch out from the colored dot. You will see an arc connecting the second and third dots.

5. Move your mouse down to where the bottom curve of the bean should be located. Press and drag down and to the left at approximately a 30-degree angle. Stop dragging when the Out control handle extends about 1.5 inches out from the colored dot. You will see an arc connecting the third and fourth dots.

6. Move your mouse back to the first point you created and click once to close the path with a curved segment.

Well done! You have just created a bean shape with a Bézier pen tool. However, if you don't like what you have created, don't delete it. In the next section, I discuss how you can edit the points, sements, and control handles on your curve.

Figure 3-22
Drawing a curved-
segment object

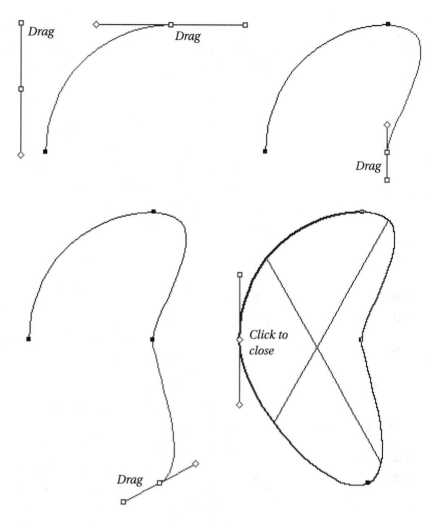

▼ ▼

Tip: Constraining with the Shift Key. As you draw, if you hold the Shift key, you can constrain your pen-tool actions to 45-degree increments. This helps you make sure that straight-line segments are perfectly horizontal, vertical, or on 45-degree angles. If you press Shift when you click with the pen tool, the new point is added on the same horizontal, vertical, or diagonal (45-degree) orientation from the last point. If you press Shift while you drag (after you click, but while the mouse button is still held down), the control handles are similarly constrained.

▼ ▼

Tip: Watch the Measurements Palette. The Measurements palette shows the position, length, and angle of each of the points and control handles as you draw them. Keep an eye on the amounts as you draw. While you can always go back and edit the handles and points later, it helps to see what you're doing as you do it.

▼ ▼

Drawing a combination object. The previous two exercises contained only one type of point each. But shapes in the real world are much more complicated, consisting of objects with combinations of points and combinations of segments. In this exercise we'll draw a baseball field shape (or, if you prefer, an ice cream cone shape), which consists of both corner and smooth points (see Figure 3-23).

1. Select the Bézier Pen Picture Box tool.

2. Position your mouse where the home plate of the field should be located, and click to create a corner point.

3. Move your mouse to where third base should be. Click to create another corner point with a straight segment, connecting home to third.

4. Now we're going to begin a curve, so you need to add an Out handle to the point you just made. (Remember that I said corner points can have control handles that sit right on top of the point? Here's how you drag it out.) Hold down the Command key and move the cursor on top of the third-base point. When the cursor is directly over the point, the cursor looks like a finger with a small black dot. If you click and drag now, you'll move the point itself.

    Move the cursor to the other side of the point from the line segment you've already drawn by one or two screen pixels, and the cursor changes to a finger with a white dot (see Figure 3-24). Now when you click and drag, you're manipulating the control handle, not the point itself. (It's a subtle cursor change, but a crucial one when drawing.)

5. Drag straight up to extend the Out handle from the point.

6. Move your mouse to where the top of the outfield would be. Click and drag to the right to create a smooth point at the top of the curve.

Figure 3-23

Drawing a combination-segment object

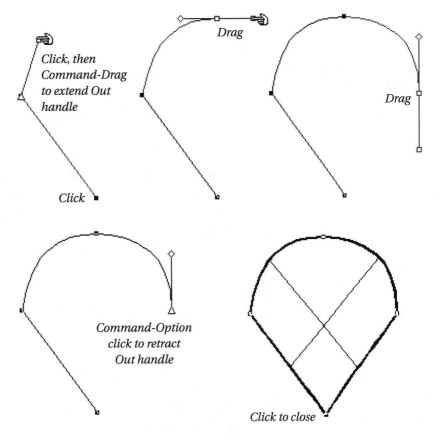

Click, then Command-Drag to extend Out handle

Drag

Drag

Click

Command-Option click to retract Out handle

Click to close

7. Move your mouse over to where first base should be. Since you need to complete the curve of the outfield, click and then drag straight down; this creates both In and Out handles on this point.

8. The final segment of the shape is a straight line, so you need to remove the Out handle from the point you just made. Hold down both the Command and Option keys and click on the Out handle to "delete" it. (It looks like you're deleting it, but you're really just retracting it so that it sits on top of the point itself.)

9. To finish the field, move your mouse down to the first point and click.

Well, take me out to the ballgame! You've just created a baseball-field shape. Don't worry if your field is a little asymmetrical. You can always edit the points and handles of your shape later on. Or tell everyone it's a field in San Francisco.

Figure 3-24
Close up detail on the
cursor showing how it will
move the control handle
rather than the point itself

Pen and keyboard actions for Bézier tools. Table 3-3 lists a summary of the mouse and keyboard actions for drawing with any of the Bézier tools. I find that sometimes it's not worth the trouble to get the shape right the first time, so I draw smooth points everywhere and then edit them later.

Editing Bézier Paths

Once you've created a path, that doesn't mean you have to live with it exactly the way you first drew it. (Otherwise, the world would be full of asymmetrical baseball fields!) XPress offers several tools to let you modify points and paths either by eye or by using precise numeric entries.

Selecting points. Before you can modify a point on a path, you have to select it. And in order to select a point on a path, Edit Shape must be turned on (select Shape from the Edit submenu, under the Item menu). When Edit Shape is turned on, you can see (and edit) the ponts on the curve. When it's off, you can only manipulate the object's bounding box (see Figure 3-25).

To select a point on a path, select the object first, and then click on the point (you can use either the Item or Content tool for this). Unfortunately, dragging a marquee over a point does not select it; you have to click right on it. When I'm trying to get something done quickly, I often find myself accidentally moving the point when I click on it. Be careful of this, and keep one hand on the Command-Z keys so you can Undo the action as necessary.

There are several ways to select more than one point on the path.

▶ You can hold down the Shift key and click on the additional points.

▶ Clicking on a segment between two points automatically selects the two points on either end of the segment.

Table 3-3

Mouse and keyboard actions for drawing

TO CREATE A . . .	. . . DO THIS
Smooth point	Drag
Corner point with no handles	Click
Corner point with only an In handle	Drag, then Command-Option-click on the Out handle
Corner point with only an Out handle	Click, then Command-drag out the Out handle
Corner point with both In and Out handles	Drag, then Command-Option to retract the Out handle, then Command-drag to extend a new Out handle (Or—Macintosh only—Drag, then Command-Control-drag the Out handle)

Figure 3-25

Edit Shape

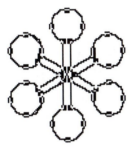 

When Edit Shape is on, you can edit the points.

When Edit Shape is off, you can only change the height and width of the object.

► You can double-click on a point to select all the points in the path. (If the path is a compound path—that is, there is more than one independent path within the total path—you can select all the points on all the paths by triple-clicking.)

Dragging points and segments. Once you have selected a point or points on your path, you can move or edit it (them) by dragging with either the Item or Content tool. Again, watch the cursor for clues: The cursor that looks like a hand with a black dot indicates that you're going to move the selected point. The Item tool cursor ("the pointy-thingy") indicates that you're going to move the entire object rather than individual points. The hand with a white dot means you're going to drag a cursor handle. (Actually, to be more precise, the white dot is either a white square or a white diamond, depending on whether you're on top of an In or an Out handle.)

There is one other cursor you'll see: the hand cursor with a little line next to it. This indicates that you can move the segment between two points (see Figure 3-26). What happens when you click and drag, however, depends on the type of points at the ends of the segment.

▶ If the two points are corner points, dragging the segment actually moves both points.

▶ If one or both of the points are smooth or symmetrical points, the points don't move when you drag the segment. Instead, the control handles adjust accordingly.

Figure 3-26
Moving segments

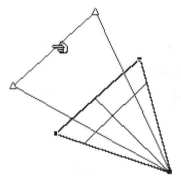

Dragging a straight-line segment

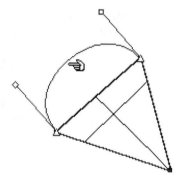

Dragging a curved segment

Sometimes it's just too much of a hassle to adjust the control handles to create the curve I'm looking for, so I just grab the segment I'm editing and drag it to where I want it to go. This way, QuarkXPress does all the work in figuring out the correct position for the control handles.

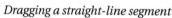

Tip: Snap Points to Guides. Dragging points around your page is an inexact science at best, even if you want the Measurements palette for feedback on your page coordinates. If I know exactly where I want to place a point, I often drag out horizontal and/or vertical page guides to that coordinate. Then, when I drag the point on the curve, it snaps to the guide, ensuring its location. Unfortunately, Snap to Guide doesn't work on control handles, just points.

Changing Points in the Measurements palette. Designers working in illustration programs usually like to move things around by eye. However, many XPress users want or need to work with more numerical precision. Fortunately the Measurements palette lets you see and modify all the attributes of points on your curve: their type, their position, and the position of their control handles (see Figure 3-27). I'll hold off on changing point type for now, and focus just on altering point and handle position.

▶ **POINT POSITION.** When you select a single point on your curve, the right side of the Measurements palette displays its position in the XP and YP fields. If you're trying to make a small change to a point's position, it's usually much easier to do it here than to drag the point around.

▶ **HANDLE POSITION.** At first, the way the Measurements palette displays the position of a point's control handles seems odd, but it turns out to be incredibly intuitive and useful. The In handle (the white diamond) and the Out handle (the white square) are represented by their angle and their length. As for all angles in XPress, this angle value increases counterclockwise. That is, zero degrees leads horizontally to the right of the point on the curve, 90 degrees points directly up, and so on.

Figure 3-27
Bézier points in the
Measurements palette

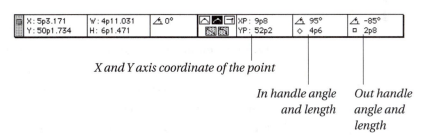

X and Y axis coordinate of the point

*In handle angle
and length*

*Out handle
angle and
length*

Of course, when you change either the angle or the length of one control handle, it may change the other's as well, depending on the type of the point. Corner points have fully independent handles. The handles on smooth points can have different lengths, but their angles always add up to 180 degrees. And both the lengths and the angles are locked to each other in symmetrical points.

▼ ▼

Tip: Getting Consistent Curves. I find it unfortunate that the Space/Align feature can't align individual points on a curve. The next best thing, then, is to align the points by selecting them and then entering a proper value for their XP or XY coordinate, or for their control handles. Don't forget that Copy and Paste work within the Measurements palette, so you can Copy the XP coordinate from one point and Paste it in the XP field for another point, and so on.

▼ ▼

Tip: Precision Point Placement. When you have the Item tool selected, the arrow keys nudge things around your page. Therefore, if you want to move a point on a curve 1 point (about 0.014 inch) up, just select it with the Item tool and press the Up Arrow key. Nope, this doesn't work for control handles.

▼ ▼

Tip: Bézier Math. Strangely enough, I've always liked math (see my 1997 book *The Joy of* π, if you doubt me). However, I have to admit that I've become quite rusty at basic math due to the proliferation of calculators in my life. Fortunately, all of my favorite mathematical tricks can be applied to the numerical settings for Bézier points. For instance, if you want a point to move 2 picas down, you would type "+2p" after the YP coordinate value and then press the Return key. Similarly, you can cut the length of a control handle in half by typing "/2" after the handle length.

▼ ▼

Adding and deleting points. It's easy to add or remove a point on your path: just Option-click. The same keystroke adds or removes points, depending on where you click. Note that the kind of point that XPress adds depends on the type of segment you're clicking on: if it's a straight-line segment, XPress adds a corner point; otherwise, it adds a smooth point. Basically, the program tries to alter the shape of the Bézier curve as little as possible when you add a point.

Changing a point type. Gertrude Stein would never have said that a curve is a curve is a curve, because she knew that you could change the type of a point with a click of a button or the flick of a keystroke. Once you have selected a point on a curve, you can change its type in one of four ways (see Figure 3-28).

Figure 3-28
Changing the
type of a point

*Symmetrical and
smooth points
converted to corner
points don't change
their appearance. That
is because changing the
point type only unlocks
the control handle
lengths and angles. You
can then manually
adjust the handles.*

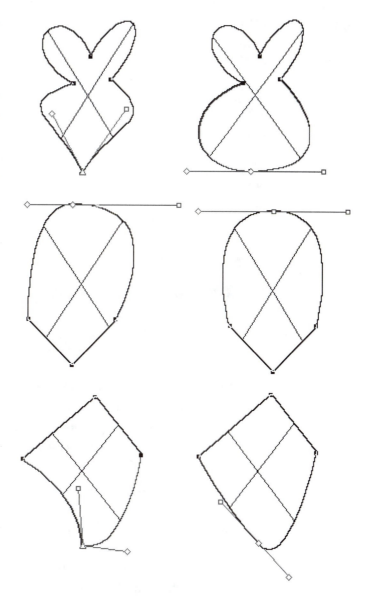

► **ITEM MENU.** You can select a point type from the Point/Segment Type submenu (under the Item menu; see Figure 3-29). This is by far the slowest method.

► **MEASUREMENTS PALETTE.** You can click on a point type in the Measurements palette.

► **KEYSTROKE.** You can press Option-F1, -F2, or -F3 to change the selected point to a corner, smooth, or symmetrical point, respectively. (Use the Control key in Windows.)

Figure 3-29

Point types

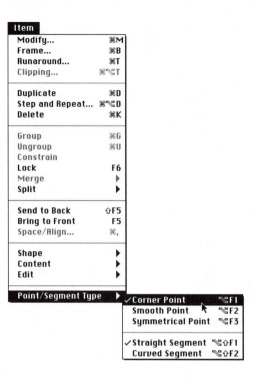

▶ **CLICK AND DRAG.** If you're the interactive type, you might like the ability to click or click-and-drag on a point or a control handle with the Control key held down (Control and Shift in Windows). This works whether you have the Item or Content tool selected. If you Control-click on a smooth or symmetrical point, its control handles are retracted to a length of zero and it becomes a corner point. You can also turn a smooth or symmetrical point into a corner point by Control-dragging one of its control handles. This method doesn't retract the handles (see Figure 3-30).

Conversely, you can change a corner point into a smooth point by holding down the Control key (again, Control-Alt in Windows) and clicking and dragging on the point itself. This extends the control handles as you drag.

▼ ▼

Tip: Converting Multiple Points. If you have selected a single point on your curve, the icon for that type of point is highlighted in the Measurements palette. You can then convert the point from one type to another by clicking on one of the other icons. However, if you have more than one type of point selected, no one icon is selected. You can still click

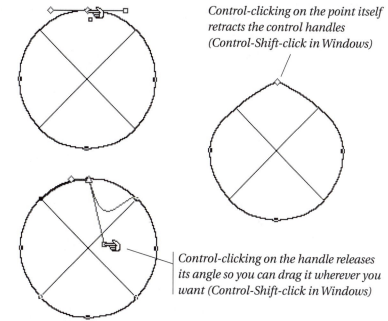

Figure 3-30

Dragging smooth points
into corner points

*Control-clicking on the point itself
retracts the control handles
(Control-Shift-click in Windows)*

*Control-clicking on the handle releases
its angle so you can drag it wherever you
want (Control-Shift-click in Windows)*

on any one of the icons to convert all of the selected points. I find this helpful when smoothing out the paths created by the freehand tools.

▼ ▼

Changing a segment type. Just as you may want to modify the type of a point, you might consider changing the type of a segment from straight to curved, or vice versa. To do this, you need to select the segment (either click on it or select the points on either side of the segment). Then you can select Straight Segment or Curved Segment from the Point/Segment Type submenu (under the Item menu)—this is the slow way; or you can click on the Straight or Curved Segment icon in the Measurements palette. A third choice: press Option-Shift-F1 to get a straight segment, or Option-Shift-F2 to get a curved segment (Control-Shift-F1 and Control-Shift-F2, respectively, in Windows).

When you convert a segment from curved to straight, any control handles that extended into the segment are retracted. This usually radically changes the appearance of the path (see Figure 3-31).

When you convert a segment from straight to curved, however, the appearance of the segment doesn't change at all. Two control handles are simply added to the points at the end of the segment; you can then drag these control handles to create the curve.

Figure 3-31
Changing the
type of segments

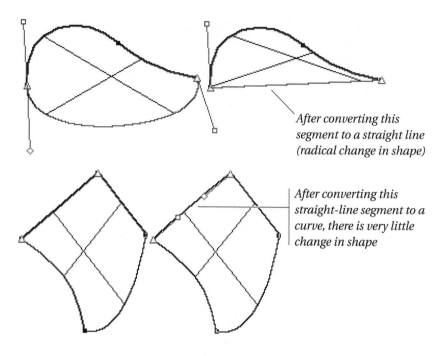

*After converting this
segment to a straight line
(radical change in shape)*

*After converting this
straight-line segment to a
curve, there is very little
change in shape*

▼ ▼

Tip: Flipping Shapes Around. As I've said before, the Bézier controls in QuarkXPress 4 are hardly as sophisticated as those in dedicated illustration programs. But often there are workarounds for features that XPress is missing. For instance, although XPress has no way of mirroring (some people call this reflecting) a shape, you can use this short technique to achieve the effect (see Figure 3-32).

1. Turn off Edit Shape in the Edit submenu (under the Item menu) so you see the object's bounding box.

2. Select the value in the width (W) field in the Measurements palette and Copy it.

3. Drag one of the left or right side handles across the object until it crosses the opposite side of the shape. Now the shape is mirrored, but it's distorted.

4. Select the width field in the Measurements palette again, and Paste in the value on the clipboard.

Of course, if you want to flip the shape vertically, you would Copy and Paste the height field rather than the width field.

▼ ▼

Figure 3-32
Flipping an object

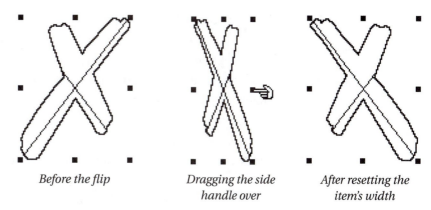

Before the flip   *Dragging the side*   *After resetting the*
                           handle over   *item's width*

Merge Commands

Okay, I admit it: I couldn't draw my way out of a paper bag. There just seems to be a disconnect between the part of my brain that knows what it wants and the part that can use these tools. Because of this, I often combine various oval and rectangular boxes to create the shapes I want. QuarkXPress makes this easy with the various features under the Merge submenu (under the Item menu); see Figure 3-33. The Merge commands allow you to join separate shapes into one, or to have one shape act like a cookie cutter on another.

In order to use the Merge features, you have to select two or more boxes or lines. After selecting one of the Merge features, you'll end up with one box (even if the original objects were lines, your final shape is

Figure 3-33
The Merge commands

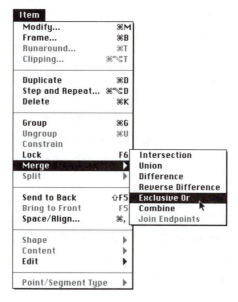

always a box—the one exception is the Join Endpoints command). If the original items have different background colors, the final box takes on the background color of the back-most object. Similarly, if the original boxes have imported text or graphics, only the text or the graphic in the back-most object is kept (see Figure 3-34).

There are seven features in the Merge submenu: Intersection, Union, Difference, Reverse Difference, Exclusive Or, Combine, and Join Endpoints. (As we'll see in a moment, Join Endpoints is only available when you have two lines selected.)

Figure 3-35 coi tains some examples of various effects you can create with the Merge features. After reading the following descriptions, can you tell how each one was created?

Intersection. The Intersection command looks for the areas where the objects overlap the back-most object. It keeps those areas and then deletes all the other areas of the shapes. If the front-most objects are separate, the remaining objects will also be separate. A single object that has separate, individual paths is called a *compound object*, or a *compound path* (see Figure 3-36).

Union. The Union feature combines all the shapes into one object, and no hole is left behind where they overlapped. If some of the original shapes aren't overlapping the others, then the Union command leaves the objects separate, but they all act as one compound object. (In fact, if none of the original objects overlap, then Union is identical to the Combine command.)

Difference. The Difference command uses the front object as a cookie cutter on the back-most object. The result is that the shape of the front object is cut out of the back-most object, even if that means punching a hole in the middle of it. (If you select two concentric circles and choose Difference, you end up with the shape of a bagel with a see-through hole in the center.)

Reverse Difference. The Reverse Difference command reverses the previous command. That is, Reverse Difference creates a union of all the selected objects except the back-most one. It then cuts out the shape of the back-most object from this front-most union.

Figure 3-34
The Merge commands

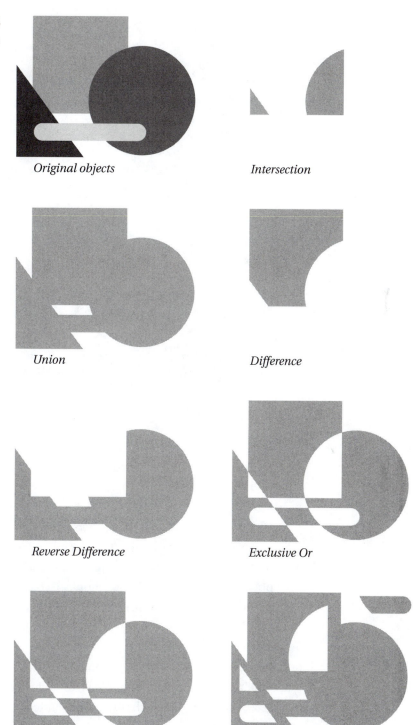

Original objects

Intersection

Union

Difference

Reverse Difference

Exclusive Or

Combine

Note that Exclusive Or creates subpaths that you can move around.

Figure 3-35
Special effects with
the Merge features

Exclusive Or. The Exclusive Or feature builds a transparent hole wherever the shapes overlap. This hole is a compound path that you can move around later if you want (see "Tip: Moving Pieces of Compound Objects," below). If you select two objects, one of which is completely enclosed by the other, Exclusive Or is identical to Difference. If the objects don't overlap at all, the result is identical to Union. But if the objects are only partially overlapping, you get really wacky results. I've tried for months to think of a practical use for this feature, to no avail. If you find it indispensible for some reason, let me know.

Combine. The Combine command creates an effect visually identical to the Exclusive Or command. Also like Exclusive Or, if two objects are fully contained within each other, it's identical to Difference; if the objects are not overlapping, it's identical to Union. The big difference is that if the shapes are partially overlapping, each original item is maintained as a separate path within the compound object. That is, XPress won't cre-

Figure 3-36
Compound objects

ate any new paths for you, as it does with Exclusive Or. This becomes relevant if you try to edit the paths later.

Join Endpoints. The last item on the Merge submenu, Join Endpoints, is only available when you have two lines or text paths selected. There's one other condition for Join Endpoints to work, however: two end points (one on each path) must be placed on top of each other. (Actually, they can be within 6 points of each other.) As soon as you select Join Endpoints, XPress merges the two points into one corner point (moving each of them slightly, if necessary; see Figure 3-37).

Join Endpoints doesn't work with only Bézier lines. You can join a Bézier Text Path to an Orthogonal line, or join together two Orthogonal lines to create a new Bézier line, and so on. The only requirement is that both objects be open lines. As I said earlier, if you join different types or styles of lines, the resulting path takes on the attributes of the back object. For instance, regular lines are converted to text paths if the backmost object is a text path.

▼ ▼

Tip: Moving Pieces of Compound Objects. Just because you use one of the Merge features to combine multiple shapes into a compound

Figure 3-37
Join Endpoints command

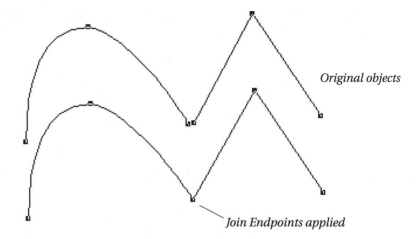

Original objects

Join Endpoints applied

object doesn't mean that you can no longer edit the shapes. As I said ear-lier, you can select all the points in an independent path within a com-pound path by double-clicking on one of the points on the path. Now when you move one of the points (by dragging it or pressing an Arrow key when the Item tool is selected), you move the whole independent path (see Figure 3-38).

Moving independent paths within a compound object can provide interesting and strange results if you partially overlap one path over another, but after playing with it for a little while you'll find ways of con-trolling the effects to get the look you want.

▼ ▼

Tip: Creating Symmetrical Objects. It turns out that many of the shapes people want to create are symmetrical, and yet drawing sym-metrical objects is not the easiest thing to do. Here's one technique to get symmetrical objects on your page.

1. Create one-half of the symmetrical object.

2. Duplicate the object using Step and Repeat with the Vertical and Horizontal Offsets both set to zero.

3. Mirror this duplicate object (see "Tip: Flipping Shapes Around," earlier in this chapter).

4. Move the duplicate item into place (remember, you can hold down the Shift key while dragging an item to constrain it hori-zontally or vertically).

Figure 3-38

Moving a path within a
compound object

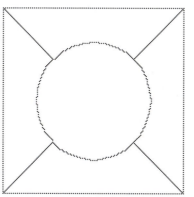

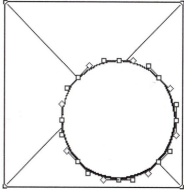

*This is one object with
a hole in the middle.*

*Here, the points on the subpath
have been selected and moved.*

5. Select the two objects and use Union (if the items are boxes) or Join Endpoints (if they're lines) to combine them into a single object.

After you create the symmetrical object, you often need to do a little cleanup (removing points, for instance), but the result is almost always better than if you tried to draw the shape by hand. Note that you can also draw one-half of a symmetrical box by drawing a path, using this technique, and then converting the path into a box (see "Transforming Boxes and Lines," later in this section).

▼ ▼

Splitting Compound Objects

So now you know how to merge shapes together, and you've seen how this sometimes results in compound objects. There's got to be a way to pull these compound paths apart again. Indeed there is. You've got two choices in the Split submenu (under the Item menu): Split Outside Paths and Split All Paths. Which you use depends on what you've got and what you're trying to achieve.

Split All Paths simply separates every independent path within a compound object into its own object. Split Outside Paths, on the other hand, only splits up paths that aren't surrounded by other paths. For instance, let's say you've used the Union feature to make two bagels sitting next to each other. Split All Paths would turn this into four separate ovals. Split Outside Paths would turn it into two bagels, because the "holes" in each bagel are fully enclosed, and so they don't get separated (see Figure 3-39).

Figure 3-39
Split commands

Original objects: one compound path made of two "bagels."

After Split Outside Paths, we get two bagels.

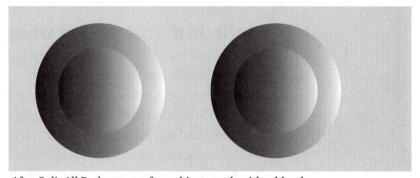

After Split All Paths, we get four objects, each with a blend.

Transforming Box and Lines

Once you have created a text box, picture box, contentless box, or line, you can change it into some other form using the Shape submenu under the Item menu (see Figure 3-40). For example, if you made a rectangu-

lar picture box on your page, you could turn it into an oval by first selecting the picture box and then selecting the oval picture box icon in the
Shape submenu.

I can't say that I've ever used some of the items in the Shape submenu
for anything other than a good chuckle . . . for instance, the beveled-cor-
ner box and the photo-frame box. But you might have some use for
them, and if you do, remember that the "depth" of the bevel or the con-
cave curve is determined by the Corner Radius setting (in the
Measurements palette or the Modify dialog box).

Instead, I most often use the Shape feature to convert boxes to lines
or vice versa.

Converting Boxes to Paths. You can convert any kind of box into a line
by selecting one of the three line shapes in the Shapes submenu: diagonal, orthogonal, or Bézier.

Figure 3-40

Shape submenu

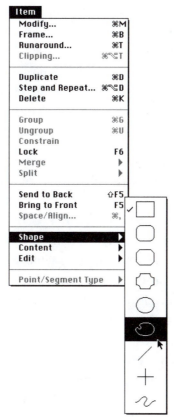

▶ **DIAGONAL LINE.** When you convert a box into a diagonal line, XPress replaces the box with a line that stretches from the upper-left corner to the lower-right corner of the box's bounding rectangle (the bounding rectangle is the smallest rectangle that completely encloses the box shape). If you can find a good use for this, more power to you.

▶ **ORTHOGONAL LINE.** Selecting the orthogonal line is actually even less useful: you just get a horizontal line that spans the width of the box.

▶ **BÉZIER LINE.** Choosing the Bézier line is where you hit pay dirt. When you select this option, the outline of the box you have selected becomes a Bézier line. Of course, Bézier lines are always open paths, so even though the path probably appears closed, it has a beginning and an ending point. (It's sometimes difficult to find an endpoint . . . look for any one point on the path that looks even slightly different from the others. If you still can't find one, and you really need to, just start clicking and moving points—and then selecting Undo if it's not an endpoint—until you find the right place.)

Note that if the box had a dash or stripe selected as a frame, that same style is applied to the resulting path. (Of course, the special bitmapped frames can't be applied to lines; see "Frames, Dashes, and Stripes," later in this chapter.)

Note that you cannot currently undo a change from a box to a path. Because of this, I usually make a duplicate of the box before converting the original.

▼ ▼

Tip: Watch Out for Shape Changes. When you use the above technique to change a framed box into a line, you need to watch out for two things. First, the size of the box generally changes. This is because frames are run on the inside or outside of a box, but lines "grow" on both sides of its centerline. Take that dimension shift into consideration as you make your initial box.

The second thing to watch for is notches in your frame. Again, lines are always open paths. That means a thick frame (which turns into a thick line width) may have a notch in it where the two endpoints meet (see Figure 3-41).

Figure 3-41
Converting a framed
box to a line

*Note the notch in at
what is now the
beginning of the
path. Also, the box
has become larger
because of the path.*

▼ ▼

Tip: Text Boxes to Text Paths. If you want to set some text in a circle, you need a circular text path. Unfortunately, it's a pain in the eyeball to draw a perfect circle with the Bézier text-path tool. Here's a better way: Make a circular text box and type in it the text you want on the path. Now, choose the Bézier line from the Shape submenu under the Item menu (that's the one that looks like a squiggle). The text box becomes a text path, and the contents of the box become the contents of the path (see Figure 3-42). It's as easy as that.

Figure 3-42
Text boxes to text paths

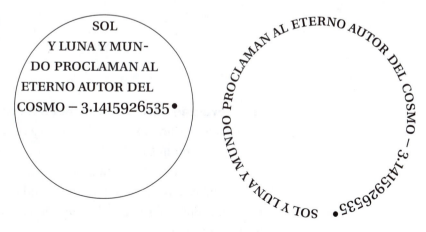

▼ ▼

Converting Paths to Boxes. If you select a line and choose one of the regular boxes from the Shape submenu—such as the rectangular or oval box—XPress replaces your line with a box of this shape (the size of the box is determined by the line's bounding rectangle). This isn't particularly interesting. What is interesting is what happens when you choose the Bézier box from the Shape submenu.

If you simply select the Bézier shape, XPress converts the outline of the path into a box. For instance, if you have a straight line 1 inch long and 8 points thick, the result is a rectangular box that is 1 inch long and 8 points wide (see Figure 3-43). Obviously, it doesn't make much sense to do this for thin lines.

If you hold down the Option key when selecting the Bézier box shape, XPress does something completely different: it closes the path for you. If the line had a line style (dots, dashes, or whatever), QuarkXPress applies that style as the box's frame.

Figure 3-43
Converting paths
to boxes

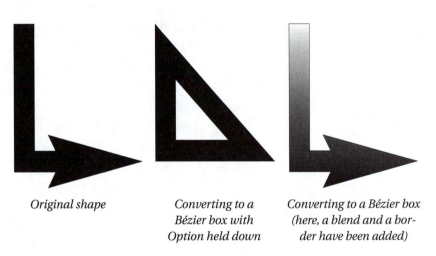

Original shape

*Converting to a
Bézier box with
Option held down*

*Converting to a Bézier box
(here, a blend and a bor-
der have been added)*

▼ ▼

Tip: Converting Dashes and Stripes to Bézier Boxes. I think the ability to convert a line to a box, in which XPress actually builds the box based on the outline of the line, is really amazing. To me, the best part about it is that line styles—such as dots, stripes, or arrowheads—are also converted, usually becoming a compound object. If you want, you can then select Split All Paths to further manipulate each of the individual Bézier paths of the shape.

Again, this sort of thing makes the most sense when you are working with thick lines. Once you've got a box based on the line, you can fill it with a color, a blend, text, or a picture (see Figure 3-44).

Figure 3-44
Converting line styles
to Bézier boxes

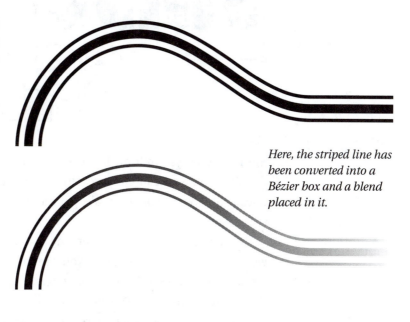

Here, the striped line has been converted into a Bézier box and a blend placed in it.

▼ ▼

Switching shapes back and forth. Just because you can convert one box shape into another, or change lines to boxes and vice versa, don't get the idea that it's always reversible. In fact, it's pretty rare that once you've changed an object from one shape into another, you'll ever be able to get it back to the original shape again.

Converting Text to Paths

Digital typefaces, as we'll see in Chapter 6, *Type and Typography*, generally contain mathematical outlines of each character in the font. These outlines are scalable, so that you can view or print them at any resolution or size and they'll always be smooth. Wouldn't it be cool if you could also convert those outlines into QuarkXPress Bézier boxes? You can.

To convert text to a box, select the text with the Content tool and choose Text to Box from the Style menu (see Figure 3-45). There are, of course, a few caveats. You can only convert up to a single line of text at a time. You can only convert fonts for which you have the outline files installed (even then, some fonts don't seem to convert well, particularly

Figure 3-45
Creating Bézier
paths from text

the TrueType system fonts like Chicago or Geneva on the Macintosh). Finally, while you can convert a lot of characters at the same time, it doesn't mean that you'll actually get them to print later. Keep it simple, as always.

If you have selected more than one character of text, they are all converted into a single picture box. You can then use Split Outside Paths to separate them into individual characters, if you'd like. Whether you split them or not, you can use all the editing features I've discussed to manipulate the outlines. After all, these are picture boxes now.

Also, note that I use the term *convert*. However, I should probably say *create*, because the original text is not deleted from the text box (although see the next tip).

▼ ▼

Tip: Anchoring Text Outlines. If you hold down the Option key when you select Text to Box from the Style menu, XPress actually replaces your selected text with the Bézier box, anchoring it in the text as an inline graphic (see Chapter 11, *Where Text Meets Graphics*, for more information on inline boxes).

▼ ▼

Tip: Careful with Those Frames. I'm not going to discuss putting borders around boxes until later in this chapter (in "Frames, Dashes, and Stripes"), but I should make one comment now: Many people don't realize that when they put a border around a box, it can actually change the shape of the box. If Framing is set to Outside on the General tab of the Document Preferences dialog box, adding a frame will actually expand the boundaries of the box itself. If the border is too thick, the edges of the box may bump into each other, permanently altering the shape of the box (see Figure 3-46).

Figure 3-46
Frames can sometimes
change the shape of boxes

The original text, converted to a box

*After a frame is applied
(Framing set to Outside)*

*When the frame is removed or
reduced in size, you can see that the
box outlines have been altered.*

Manipulating Items

Once you've created a page element (item) such as a picture box or a line, what can you do with it? A lot. In this section I talk about how to move, rotate, skew, resize, reshape, lock, duplicate, suppress the printout of, and delete items. Remember that I'm talking only about the items themselves here, so you often need to select the items with the Item tool to make most of these changes.

Moving Items

You can move a page element in several ways. First, if you're an interactive type, you can select the Item tool, then click on the object and drag it. Or, if you have the Content tool selected, you can get the Item tool temporarily by holding down the Command key, which lets you move an item, too. (However, note that if you have more than one object selected, Command-dragging with the Content tool moves a single item in the group, not the whole group.)

The second method for moving an item is by changing its origin coordinates in the Measurements palette or the Modify dialog box. I find this method especially useful if I need to move the item a specific amount. For example, let's say I have a text box with its origin at 1 inch across and 1 inch down. If I want to move the text box horizontally 18 picas, I change the Origin Across coordinate in the Measurements palette to "1"+18p", then press Enter. The box automatically moves over.

A third method for moving items is by selecting them and pressing the Arrow keys on the keyboard. Each time you press an Arrow key, the item moves one point in that direction. Holding down the Option key when you press an Arrow key moves the item 0.1 point.

▼ ▼

Tip: Techniques for Item Placement. If you have a style of placing and sizing your page elements—such as lines and picture boxes—that works for you, stick to it. To paraphrase an anonymous poet, "A manner of picture-box placement is a real possession in a changing world." Nonetheless, here are some basic guides that I've found helpful.

▶ Use picas and points for everything except basic page size. These are the standard units among designers and printers, and allow precision without having to deal with numbers like 0.08334 inch (which is 6 points, or 0.5 pica). If you're working with type, this also makes it easier since type is generally specified in picas and points.

▶ Try to use round numbers for most of your measurements. Creating or moving a box at the Fit in Window size usually gives you measurements that have coordinates out to the thousandth of a point, such as "6p3.462". It might seem like a picky detail, but, in the long run, it can come in handy to either create your boxes at Actual Size and then resize them if needed, or—if you must work at a reduced or enlarged view—go into the Measurements palette or the Modify dialog box (double-click on the box or press Command-M) and change the coordinates and the sizes to round numbers.

▶ Use oval- or Bézier-shaped picture boxes only when you must have that shape. Using a rectangle or square box for the majority of your pictures can cut your printing time to half or a third of what it takes when you use ovals.

▼ ▼

▼ ▼

Tip: Viewing Changes As You Make Them. It's always a hassle to move, resize, or rotate a box, because while you're doing it, QuarkXPress only shows you the outline of the box rather than the whole box. Or does it?

If you hold the mouse button down on a picture-box handle for about half a second before dragging it, you can see the picture crop (or scale, if you have the Command key held down, too) as you move the handle. Similarly, if you move or rotate the box, you can see the text or picture rotate while dragging if you simply pause for about half a second before starting to drag. No, you don't have to count out half a second; just wait until you see the object flash quickly before you start dragging. (The exact amount of time is determined by the Delayed Item Dragging value on the Interactive tab in the Application Preferences dialog box.)

▼ ▼

Resizing and Reshaping Items

Resizing an object means changing its width and height, while reshaping it may involve moving points around, like turning a rectangle into a triangle. Both are easy to do, but how you go about doing it depends on the type of object you have selected. (Resizing and reshaping a group of items are special-case scenarios that I cover in "Modifying Grouped Objects," later in this chapter.)

Resizing boxes. The most basic shapes are the non-Bézier boxes, like the rectangle and the oval. To resize these, you once again have a choice between using QuarkXPress's interactive click-and-drag style or working in measurements.

► RESIZING BY DRAGGING. To resize by clicking and dragging, you place the screen cursor over one of the box's handles. Boxes have eight handles (one on each side, one on each corner) that you can drag to resize. Dragging a side handle resizes the box in one direction—horizontally or vertically. Dragging a corner handle resizes the box in two directions (horizontally *and* vertically). Of course, as I discussed earlier in this chapter, if the shape is a Bézier box, you need to turn off Edit Shape (in the Edit submenu under the Item menu) to see these handles.

Also, note that XPress 4 now lets you "flip" a box, resulting in a mirror of the original, by dragging one of the side handles across the box and past the opposite handle (see "Tip: Flipping Shapes Around," earlier in this chapter).

▶ RESIZING BY THE NUMBERS. The second method of resizing and reshaping boxes is by changing their height and width values. These values are located in both the Modify dialog box and the Measurements palette. Unless you're a wizard at math, it's difficult to keep an object's aspect (width-to-height) ratio this way (see "Tip: Proportional Resizing by the Numbers," below). Instead, this is a great way to make a box exactly the size you want it. For example, if you want an 8-by-10-inch picture box, you can draw one to any size you'd like, then change its width and height coordinates to 8 inches and 10 inches.

▼ ▼

Tip: Maintain the Ratios. In order to maintain an item's width and height ratio while stretching it, you can hold down the Option and Shift keys while dragging. If you want to constrain the box into a square or circle, just hold down the Shift key while dragging. (If the object were rectangular or oval, it would snap into a square or a circle.)

▼ ▼

Tip: Proportional Resizing by the Numbers. Don't forget that QuarkXPress can do a lot of math work for you. This can come in handy in situations in which you're trying to resize items on a page. For example, if you know that the 1-by-2-inch box (2 inches tall) on the page should be 5 inches wide, you can type "5"" into the width box. But what do you put in the height box? If you want to keep the aspect ratio, you can let the program do a little math for you: just type "*newwidth/oldwidth" after the height value. In this example, you'd type "*5/2" after the height. This multiplies the value by the percentage change in width (if you divide 5 by 2, you get a 250-percent change, or 2.5 times the value).

Remember that you cannot divide by a measurement, so you cannot type something like "*5"/18p". You would have to type "5"/1.5" (1.5 is 18p in inches).

▼ ▼

Bézier Boxes and Lines. I discussed editing Bézier lines and boxes earlier in this chapter. The one thing I want to reemphasize is to pay attention to the Edit Shape feature (in the Shape submenu, under the Item menu; or toggle it on and off with Shift-F4, or F10 in Windows). When this is on, you can edit the individual Bézier points, control handles, and segments. When it's off, you can only change the overall size (height and width) of the item.

Lines. Most people define lines by their two endpoints (I'm only referring to straight lines with two endpoints, including those made with the Diagonal Text Path tool). However, QuarkXPress can define any line in four different ways. Each line description is called a *mode*, and it shows up in both the Modify dialog box and the Measurements palette (see Figure 3-47). The four modes are as follows.

▶ ENDPOINTS. This mode describes the line by two sets of coordinates, x1,y1 and x2,y2. In the Modify dialog box, these are called the First Across and First Down, or the Last Across and Last Down.

▶ FIRST POINT. In First Point mode, QuarkXPress describes a line by three values: its endpoint (from wherever you started the line when dragging is its first point), its length, and its angle. An angle of zero degrees is always a horizontal line; as the angle increases, the line rotates counterclockwise, so that 45 degrees is a diagonal up and to the right, and 90 degrees is vertical.

▶ LAST POINT. QuarkXPress uses the same three values for the Last Point mode, except that it uses the coordinate of the last point on the line (wherever you let go of the mouse button).

▶ MIDPOINT. The fourth mode, Midpoint, defines lines by their length and angle based on the coordinate of the center point. That is, if a line is 2 inches long, QuarkXPress draws the line 1 inch out on either side from the midpoint, at the specified angle.

You can define a line while in one mode, modify it with another, and move it with another.

Figure 3-47
Line modes

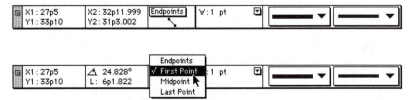

For example, let's say you draw a line someplace on your page. You then find you want to rotate it slightly. You have the choice to rotate the line from its left point, right point, or midpoint by selecting the proper mode from the Measurements palette or the Modify dialog box, then changing the line's rotation value. If you want to move just the left point of the line by 3 points (and leave the other point stationary), you can switch to Endpoints mode and alter the x1,x2 coordinate.

To resize a line by a given percentage, you can multiply its length by the percentage. If you want a line to be 120 percent as long, just multiply the length value in the Measurements palette or Modify dialog box by 1.2. To make it half as long, multiply by 0.5 or divide by two.

▼ ▼

Tip: Constraining Lines Along an Angle. We all know that you can hold down the Shift key while you draw out a line, to constrain the line horizontally or vertically. However, if you hold down the Shift key while resizing it (dragging one of its endpoints), XPress constrains it along its angle of rotation (or its angle plus 45 degrees, or plus 90 degrees).

Note that this is different from earlier versions of the program, in which holding down the Shift key while resizing would constrain a line to a vertical or horizontal position. Now the only way to force a diagonal line into an orthogonal line is to set its angle to zero or 90 degrees.

Rotating Items

You can rotate an item numerically using the Modify dialog box or the Measurements palette, or by eye with the Rotation tool (the third item in the Tool palette). Note that positive rotation values rotate the object counterclockwise; negative values rotate it clockwise (this is arguably counterintuitive). Most objects are rotated from their center. This center may not be where you think it is, however, because the center is defined as the middle of the object's bounding box.

Lines are the main exception when it comes to the center of rotation. Lines rotate differently depending on their Mode (see "Lines," above). For example, if a line is in First Point mode when you specify a rotation, the line rotates around the first endpoint.

If you are more visually minded, you can rotate items using the Rotation tool.

1. Select a page item.

2. Choose the Rotation tool from the Tool palette.

3. Click where you want the center of rotation, but don't let the mouse button go yet.

4. Drag the Rotation tool. As you drag, the object is rotated in the direction you drag. The farther from the center of rotation you drag, the more precise the rotation can be.

I rarely use this tool in a production setting, but that's just my bias. It may suit you well. However, it's significantly harder to control the rotation by using the tool rather than by entering a specific value.

Skewing Items

QuarkXPress lets you skew boxes and their contents. As I dicuss in Chapter 9, *Pictures*, skewing is the same as rotating the vertical axis and not the horizontal one. If you skew a text box or a picture box, the text or picture within the box is skewed to the same angle. You can skew a box by typing a value into the Skew field on the Box tab of the Modify dialog box (it only lets you enter values between -75 and 75 degrees). Enter a positive number to skew the box and its contents to the right; a negative number skews them to the left.

If you need to spice up your afternoon, you can skew the contents of a box separately from the box itself (you can find Text Skew on the Text tab and Picture Skew on the Picture tab of the Modify dialog box).

Skewing boxes isn't something you need to do every day, but by combining QuarkXPress's ability to skew and rotate text boxes, you can create some interesting effects, like a 3-D cube with angled text on each side (see Figure 3-48).

Flipping Out

It used to be that if you wanted to flip a picture or text along the vertical or horizontal axis—so that you could mirror it on facing pages, for instance—you had to dive into a graphics program, flip the image, save it as a picture, then bring it into your QuarkXPress document.

Well, no longer. Just select the object, then go to the Style menu and choose Flip Vertical or Flip Horizontal. Note that you have to use the Content tool to do this, as this is actually mirroring the contents of the box rather than the box itself. Not only does this command let you flip pictures and text, but flipped text remains fully editable (to do this, you have to practice reading the newspaper in the mirror).

Figure 3-48

Box skew

*O*h my goodness gracious, I'm falling to the right, I'm falling! Help me! I'm caught in a skewed text box and I can't get out. Please call for help before I am skewed too far... Oh my goodness gracious, I'm falling to the right, I'm falling! Help me! I'm caught in a skewed text box and I can't get out. Please call for help before I am skewed too far... Oh my goodness gracious, I'm falling to the right, I'm falling! Help me!

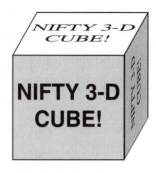

You can also use the icons for flipping contents in the Measurements palette (see Figure 3-49). The top icon controls horizontal flipping; the lower one controls vertical flipping.

Locking Items

There are times when you want an item to stay how and where it is. For example, if you've painstakingly placed multiple text boxes on your page, you may not want someone else who will be working on your page to move or resize them accidentally. You can lock any page item down to its spot, making it invulnerable to being moved or resized with the Item tool. Just select the item with either the Item or the Content tool and choose Lock from the Item menu (or press Command-L).

If an item is locked, the Item tool cursor turns into a padlock when passed over it. You cannot move it by clicking and dragging either the item or its control handles. I find this feature especially helpful when I'm working on a complex page and don't want an accidental click here or a drag there to ruin my work.

However, just because you lock something does not mean that it won't move or change. If you select the box with the Item tool and your cat jumps onto your keyboard, pressing one of the Arrow keys, the box moves. If you use the Space/Align feature, QuarkXPress ignores the Locked status and moves the object (this *really* bugs me). And you can easily change the coordinate of the item's origin or its height or width in the Measurements palette . . . that changes the item, too. In other words, the *only* thing that Lock stops you from doing is dragging the box.

Oh yes, you can also always change the contents of the items; locking only affects the item, not the contents within.

To unlock an item, select it and press Command-L again (or choose Unlock from the Item menu).

Figure 3-49

Flip Horizontal/
Vertical

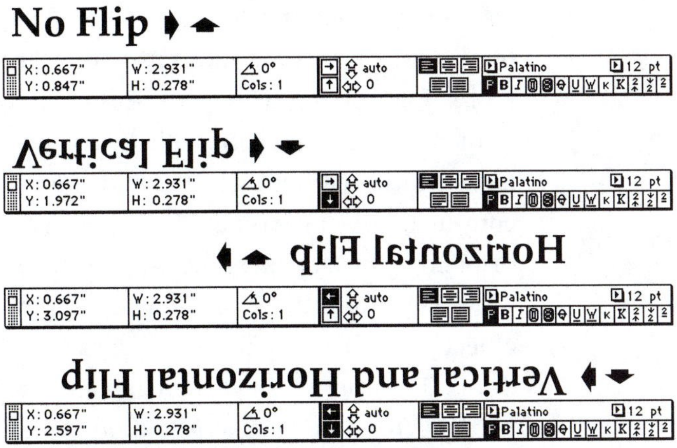

No Flip ▶ ◀

| X: 0.667" | W: 2.931" | △ 0° | 🔲 | ⊗ auto | 📃📃📃 ▶ Palatino | ▶ 12 pt |
| Y: 0.847" | H: 0.278" | Cols: 1 | ↑ | ◇◇ 0 | 📃📃 P B I O S Q U W K K |

Vertical Flip ▶ ◀

| X: 0.667" | W: 2.931" | △ 0° | 🔲 | ⊗ auto | 📃📃📃 ▶ Palatino | ▶ 12 pt |
| Y: 1.972" | H: 0.278" | Cols: 1 | ↓ | ◇◇ 0 | 📃📃 P B I O S Q U W K K |

◀ ◀ Horizontal Flip

| X: 0.667" | W: 2.931" | △ 0° | ◀ | ⊗ auto | 📃📃📃 ▶ Palatino | ▶ 12 pt |
| Y: 3.097" | H: 0.278" | Cols: 1 | ↑ | ◇◇ 0 | 📃📃 P B I O S Q U W K K |

Vertical and Horizontal Flip ◀ ◀

| X: 0.667" | W: 2.931" | △ 0° | ◀ | ⊗ auto | 📃📃📃 ▶ Palatino | ▶ 12 pt |
| Y: 2.597" | H: 0.278" | Cols: 1 | ↓ | ◇◇ 0 | 📃📃 P B I O S Q U W K K |

Suppress Printout and Suppress Picture Printout

If you turn on Suppress Printout (in the Modify dialog box) for any object on your page, QuarkXPress won't print that object. Ever. Period. This is helpful when you want nonprinting notes to be placed in your document, or for setting runaround objects that affect your text but don't print out on your final page. (However, just because the object doesn't print doesn't mean the text runaround goes away; see Chapter 11, *Where Text Meets Graphics*.)

When you have a picture box selected, the Modify dialog box also offers a second checkbox: Suppress Picture Printout. If you check this one, it keeps the picture from printing, but the box itself still prints. The difference? If the picture has a frame around it, the frame prints and the picture doesn't.

Duplicating Items

When I stand around watching over their shoulder as people work, one of the most common suggestions I make is to use the Duplicate and Step and Repeat features more often. If you need to make two text boxes, it's rarely worth the trouble to draw both of them; just make one and then duplicate it. There are three ways to duplicate a page element: Copy and Paste it, Duplicate it, or use Step and Repeat.

Copy and Paste. Selecting an item, copying it, and pasting it (Command-C and Command-V) is the most common way people learn to duplicate objects, though it's not always the most efficient or precise way. Many people get confused when they Copy and Paste picture and text boxes, because they don't use the correct tools. Remember, the Item tool is for working with *items* (boxes, lines, and text paths), and the Content tool is for working with the *contents* of boxes or text paths. If you have the Content tool selected and you try to copy a text box, you only copy text. Copying with the Item tool actually copies the text box. (See "Tip: Copy the Opposite," below.)

In PageMaker there's a thing called "power pasting," which pastes an object at the same place on the page as you copied or cut it from. QuarkXPress doesn't have this capability at this time, though some commercial XTensions such as XPertTools Volume 1 can do it (see Appendix C, *XTensions and Resources*). See also "Tip: Clone Item," below.

Without one of these XTensions, when you Paste a page item, the program places it in the middle of your screen or as close as it can get it on whatever spread you're currently on. This little detail has been known to trip up even advanced users of XPress, because the page you're looking at is not always the page you're currently on. If even only a little sliver of the previous spread is touching the upper-left corner of the document window (where the two rulers meet), Pasting places the object on *that* spread, not the one that takes up most of your screen.

▼ ▼

Tip: Copy the Opposite. As I said earlier, whether the Command-C keystroke Copies the page item or the contents within the page item depends entirely on whether you have the Item or the Content tool selected. However, new in version 4 is the ability to Copy the item itself when you have the Content tool by pressing Command-Option-C. For example, if you have the Content tool selected and you want to Copy a whole text box, you can press Command-Option-C.

▼ ▼

Duplicate. Choosing Duplicate from the Item menu (or pressing Command-D) duplicates whatever item(s) you have selected. The default setting for Duplicate is to offset the duplicate item ¼ inch down and to the right from the original object, but Duplicate always uses whatever horizontal and vertical offsets you last used in Step and Repeat.

Step and Repeat. The Step and Repeat feature can best be described as a powerhouse, and I wish every program had it. The Step and Repeat command (under the Item menu, or press Command-Option-D) lets you select one or more objects and duplicate them with specific horizontal and vertical offsets as many times as you like.

For example, if you want 35 vertical lines, each 9 points away from each other across the page, draw one line and then choose Step and Repeat from the Item menu. In the Step and Repeat dialog box, enter "34" in the Repeat Count field (you already have the first one made), "9pt" in the Horizontal Offset field, and "0" in the Vertical Offset field. After you use Step and Repeat, you can press Command-Z to Undo all of the duplications.

Both Duplicate and Step and Repeat have certain limitations. First, you cannot duplicate an item so that any part of it falls off the pasteboard. If you are working with constrained items (see "Constraining," below), you cannot duplicate them so that any of the copies would fall outside of the constraining box. And while any items you duplicate from within a constrained group become part of that constrained group, note that duplicating an item from a set of grouped objects does not result in the copy being part of the group.

▼ ▼

Tip: Clone Item. If you're a Macromedia FreeHand user, you're probably familiar with the Command-= keystroke to duplicate an item without any offset. This is called *cloning*. I use this all the time when I'm building pages in QuarkXPress.

First, I use Step and Repeat to copy an object with the Horizontal and Vertical Offset fields both set to zero. Now, next time I want to clone something, I just press Command-D (which always uses the last offsets I typed in Step and Repeat). This works as long as I don't change the Offsets or quit XPress.

▼ ▼

Tip: Moving Objects to Other Documents. QuarkXPress's ability to drag objects around the page (or from one page to another) doesn't stop at the boundaries of the document window. You can use the Item tool to drag an object or group of objects to another document (see "Moving Items Between Documents," in Chapter 2, *QuarkXPress Basics*). Of course, you need to have both documents open and visible on the screen to do this.

▼ ▼

Deleting Items

As I suggested above, there is a difference between deleting the contents of a picture or text box and deleting the box itself. When the contents of a box (such as a picture or text) are deleted, the box still remains. When the box itself is deleted, everything goes. There are three basic ways to delete a page item.

▶ I think the easiest way to delete a page item is to select it (with either the Item or Content tool) and press Command-K. This is the same as selecting Delete from the Item menu.

▶ The second-easiest way to delete an item is to select it with the Item tool and press the Delete key on your keyboard. Remember that if you use the Content tool, you delete the text or picture rather than the box.

▶ A third way to delete an item is to select it with the Item tool and select Cut or Clear from the Edit menu. Of course, cutting it actually saves the item on the Clipboard so that you can place it somewhere else later.

The only one of these methods that works for deleting a single item from a group is Command-K. That's because to remove this kind of page item, you must first select it with the Content tool (or else you end up deleting the entire group).

▼ ▼

Tip: Alien Deletions. Computer software has a long history of "Easter eggs": wacky little useless features that programmers include late at night after too many hours of staring at the screen. QuarkXPress has a couple good Easter eggs (I mentioned one of them already, in Chapter 2, *QuarkXPress Basics*). My favorite is the little Martian that walks out on your screen and kills an object on your page (see Figure 3-50). You can call this little fella up from the depths by pressing Command-Option-Shift-K; or you can hold down the modifiers while selecting Delete from the Item menu. (Version 4 offers an additional alien creature, too, but he only appears once every five or six times you use the keystroke.)

Unfortunately, the Martian is a Macintosh-only Easter egg. However, the same keystroke provides a different sort of Easter egg on Windows: the deleted object melts down your screen with a wonderful gurgling sound.

Figure 3-50
The Martian

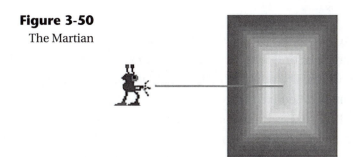

▼ ▼

Relationships Between Items

Page-layout programs like QuarkXPress are designed so that you can put a number of text and picture objects on a page. That's the whole point. And anytime you have more than one object on a page, you're going to be concerned about the relationships between those objects. For instance, if you have a block of text and a picture next to it, you probably have an idea about how you want those two items to relate: Do they align on their left edges? Are they centered next to each other? Should the picture always follow the text?

Curiously, some page-layout software developers don't understand this fundamental element of page layout, and they haven't included tools for handling these relationships in their programs. Fortunately for us, however, Quark *does* understand.

In this section I talk about controlling relationships between items: layering, grouping, constraining, and, finally, their position on the page relative to other page elements.

Layering Items

QuarkXPress, like most desktop publishing programs, handles multiple objects on a page by *layering* them. Each page item (picture box, text box, contentless box, text path, or line) is always on a higher or lower layer than the other page items. This is generally an intuitive approach to working with page elements; it's just what you would do if each of the objects were on a little piece of paper in front of you. The one difference is that while on paper you can have multiple objects on the same layer, each and every item on a QuarkXPress page is on its own layer. When you're placing objects on your page, you work from the bottom layer up. The first object you place is the bottom-most object, the second object is on top of it, and so on.

If none of your page elements touch or overlap one another, then layering has almost no relevance to you. However, when they do touch or overlap in some way, you want to be able to control which objects overlap which. The primary methods for controlling layering are the Bring to Front and Send to Back commands in the Item menu.

Bring to Front and Send to Back function as sweeping controls, moving a selected object all the way to the back or all the way to the front layer. When you hold down the Option key while selecting the Item menu, the Send to Back and Bring to Front items become Send Backward and Bring Forward. (Note that these are always visible in Windows, so you don't have to hold down a modifier key.) These functions move objects one layer at a time. They're not as powerful as the layering controls in Macromedia FreeHand or Adobe Illustrator, but they're still important.

Note that you can also use the function keys to move things up and down through layers (see Table 3-4).

Table 3-4
Layering keystrokes

Press . . .	To . . .
F5	Bring to Front
Shift-F5	Send to Back
Option-F5	Bring Forward
Shift-Option-F5	Send Backward

Grouping Objects

Objects on a page are rarely lone creatures. Often, they like to bunch together to form single units, like organic cells grouping to form a vital organ in your body. Similarly, you can create groups of page items. A group of objects can include any number of boxes and/or lines. When you select one member of the group with the Item tool, the whole group gets selected. Or, you can select and modify individual members of the group with the Content tool.

Here's what you do.

1. Using the Item or Content tool, select the items you want grouped. You can hold down the Shift key to select multiple items. Or, you can drag a marquee over or around the objects (any object that the marquee touches is selected).

2. Select Group from the Item menu or press Command-G.

It's that easy. When the group is selected with the Item tool, a dotted line shows the bounding box of the grouped objects (see Figure 3-51).

To ungroup the objects, select the grouped object with the Item tool and select Ungroup from the Item menu (or press Command-U).

▼ ▼

Tip: Multilevel Grouping. Not only can you group multiple objects, but you can group multiple groups, or groups and objects. This means that you can build levels of grouped objects. For example, on a catalog page you may have six picture boxes, each with a caption in a text box. You can group each caption box with its picture box, then select these six grouped objects and group them together. Later, if you ungroup the six objects, each picture box is still grouped with its caption box.

▼ ▼

Figure 3-51
Grouped objects

Bounding box shows the grouped objects

Modifying Grouped Objects

As I mentioned above, once you have grouped a set of objects, you can still modify each of them using the Content tool. Just select the element and change it. Each item can be rotated, resized, or edited just as usual. To move a single object in a grouped selection, hold down the Command key to get a temporary Item tool. Then move the object where you want it and release the Command key.

The group Modify dialog box. QuarkXPress lets you do some pretty nifty things with grouped items. If you select Modify from the Item menu (or press Command-M, or double-click on the group with the Item tool), QuarkXPress gives you a special Modify dialog box for the group. Which controls XPress provides in this Modify dialog box depends on whether every object in a group is the same type of object (all rules, all text boxes, or whatever).

Some features in this group Modify dialog box are always available, like Origin Across and Origin Down, which determine the upper-left corner of the bounding box for the whole group. Angle, too, sets the rotation for the group, as though the group were a single object.

If you change a value in the group Modify dialog box, you change that value for every one of the objects in the group. For example, if you specify a background color for the grouped objects, the background color is applied to all the boxes and lines in the group. If you set the Picture Angle to 20 degrees for a group of picture boxes, the items in each of the picture boxes are rotated within their box (see Chapter 9, *Pictures*).

You can turn on the Suppress Printout option for a group of mixed objects, and each of the objects in the group has its Suppress Printout checkbox turned on. Similarly, you can add or change the frame around a group of objects, as long as they're all boxes. If you later ungroup the objects, the settings you made while they were grouped remain.

Note that if you have any lines (rules) in the group, changing the background color of the group affects the color of the line itself.

There's one rule that applies to modifying groups of objects that I still can't figure out: You can't open the Modify dialog box for a group of objects when one group is nested inside another. You have to ungroup the objects, and regroup them individually. Strange.

Scaling groups. The engineers at Quark snuck a little feature into version 4 without much ado: the ability to scale groups of objects. I'm surprised they were so quiet about it, as it's a wonderful step forward. Unfortunately, it's not quite a leap forward yet—you'll see why in a moment.

To scale several objects at once, you first have to group them. Next, you can drag one of the group's corner or side handles. When you let go, all the objects in the group are scaled proportionally. There are, as always, a few options you can take advantage of.

▶ If you hold down the Command key when you drag, any content (text and pictures) inside boxes or lines within the group is also scaled.

▶ If you hold down Option and Shift when you drag, the group is scaled proportionally. (Again, add the Command key to scale the contents proportionally, too.)

▶ If you only hold down the Shift key, the group is constrained into a square (not particularly useful, but it's good to know the option is there).

▶ You can type value in the height or width field in the Measurements palette. This forces the whole group to fit within that size. For example, if you need to fit three picture boxes within a 10-centimeter column, you could type 10 cm in the width field. Of course, it's easy to scale the items disproportionately when you do this (see "Tip: Proportional Resizing by the Numbers," earlier in this chapter). Also, note that this scales the boxes, but not their contents.

Remember that you can scale by a percentage by using XPress's built-in math functions. For instance, if you want each item in the group to be 130-percent larger, type "*1.3" after the current width and height values.

The ability to scale groups was added to QuarkXPress 4 almost as an afterthought, and its odd limitations prove it. For instance, while you can undo scaling a group while dragging with the Command key, you cannot once you've used these other modifier keys. There are a number of features that XPress doesn't scale when you scale a group and its contents, such as the values for Space Before, Indent, Rule Above, and so on. These may be bugs, but they just shore up my opinion that XPress needs a *real* scaling tool, much like those offered in some of the XTension packages, like Extensis's QX-Tools.

Constraining

Ten years ago, if you asked a QuarkXPress user what one feature they would have sold their grandmother to get rid of, they would invariably have said, "Parent-and-child boxes." Back in version 1 and 2 of XPress, these parent-and-child boxes made it nearly impossible to be flexible with page design because boxes became "trapped" inside other boxes. These constraints were actually rather useful and accessible when you got accustomed to them. But there were many times when what I really needed was a choice of whether to enable it or not. Parent-and-child constraints are still in QuarkXPress, but thank goodness they *are* now an option rather than a rule.

Let's be clear here for those not familiar with this feature. I'm not talking about the type of constraining that people usually talk about (and that I've mentioned earlier in this chapter) that refers to holding down the Shift key to constrain the movement of an object to a 45- or 90-degree angle. This is a different sort of constraint.

Parent-and-child box constraints remind me of a baby's playpen (this is probably some leftover childhood trauma, but I don't want to go into it). A playpen is basically a box that is a structure in its own right. However, you can place objects (or babies) into it, and they can't get out unless you physically take them out.

Similarly, a parent box is a text or picture box that has certain structural constraints so that any items that are created or placed inside its boundaries ("child" items) can't easily get outside those boundaries. For example, imagine a text box that was specified as a parent box. It acts as a normal text box. However, when you draw a line inside it using one of the Line tools, that line cannot be moved or resized to extend outside the text box. The only way you can get it out is by cutting it and pasting it elsewhere.

I know it sounds awful, but, as I said, there are some great applications. For example, building a table by adding vertical and horizontal rules to a text box is aided if those rules don't slip away when you move the box (child items always move with their parents). Also, if you have a specific area in which all items must remain, creating a parental constraint makes sure that you don't accidentally mess up your specifications when your eyes are bleary at three in the morning.

You can create parent-and-child box constraints in two ways: automatic constraints and manual constraints. Let's look at each of these.

Automatic constraints. Automatic constraints were the standard for early versions of QuarkXPress. With automatic constraints on, all picture and text boxes act as parent constraint boxes. You can turn automatic constraints on and off by checking the Auto Constraint box in the Document Preferences dialog box. You can turn on Auto Constraint when every box you create is to be a parent or a child box, and then turn it off to create "normal" boxes and items.

Note that the parent box and the child items are grouped when you select them with the Item tool. To unconstrain these items, see "Manual constraints," below.

Manual constraints. If you prefer, you can apply your own parent-and-child box constraints to a set of objects by manually constraining them. It's easy to do.

1. Make sure the page elements you want to be child items are totally within the boundaries of the box you want to be the parent box.

2. Make sure the soon-to-be-parent box is behind each of the objects that are soon to be constrained. Parent boxes must be on a lower layer than their children. You can think of the playpen analogy: the playpen must be under—and surrounding—the child.

3. Select and group the child and parent objects and boxes (see "Modifying Grouped Objects," earlier in this chapter).

4. Select Constrain from the Item menu.

Those objects that are on top of the parent box and that are in that group are constrained to the boundaries of the parent box.

You can unconstrain this group of objects by clicking on the parent-and-child group with the Item tool and selecting either Unconstrain or Ungroup from the Item menu. Unconstrain removes the constraints, but leaves the items grouped. Ungroup removes both the grouping and constraining specifications. (You cannot have parent-and-child constraints without grouping.)

Aligning and Distributing Objects

Before I knew how cool the Space/Align feature was, I simply didn't know how badly I needed it. Now I use it all the time; once you know about it, you probably will, too. Space/Align is, in some ways, the control center for setting up object relationships on your page. Let's look at why.

The whole idea of Space/Align is to move page items around to create certain relationships between them. The tools you have to work with are Between, Space, and Distribute Evenly. Here's what you do.

1. Select all the items that you want to relate to one another. For instance, if you want two items to align along their left edges, select both of them.

2. Select Space/Align from the Item menu and determine the nature of the relationship. Are you trying to align the objects vertically or

horizontally? Or both? Turn on the appropriate checkboxes in the dialog box.

3. Decide whether you want to align or distribute the objects. I'll talk about the difference in just a moment. If you're aligning the objects, select Space and enter the amount of space you want between the items; if you're distributing them, select Distribute Evenly.

4. Tell QuarkXPress what part of the objects you want to align or distribute. For example: the left edges of two boxes, or the tops of a few lines, or the centers of five mixed items.

Starting with the second step, let's take a look at each of these.

Vertical/Horizontal. If you select some objects, then choose Space/Align from the Item menu (or press Command-comma), you'll see the Space/Align Items dialog box (see Figure 3-52). This dialog box is broken down into Horizontal and Vertical sections, and you can use one or the other—or both—by clicking their respective checkboxes.

Space. Enabling the Space control (by clicking the radio button in front of it) lets you align objects. The value in the Space field determines how far apart the objects should align. A value of zero (which is the default) means "align exactly." For example, let's say you want to line up the left edges of two boxes. If you specify "0p" as the Space value, the left edge of the first box is at the same place as the left edge of the second box. If you specify "5p" as the Space value, the left edge of the first box is placed 5 picas from the left edge of the second box (see Figure 3-53).

But which box moves? The top-most or left-most items always stay stationary; they are the reference points for alignment. Other page elements move to align with them.

As I said, I use alignment all the time. If I have four text boxes that I want to line up on their right edges, I no longer have to draw guides or figure measurements. Now, I just select them all and align their right edges with Space set to zero.

▼ ▼

Tip: Use Apply in Space/Align. Let's face it: the Space/Align dialog box is a case study in horrible user interface and is so confusing that many people avoid it just so they don't have to figure out how it works. One of

Figure 3-52

The Space/Align
dialog box

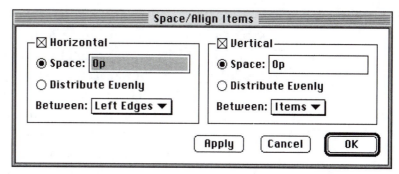

Figure 3-53

Horizontal spacing
with Space/Align

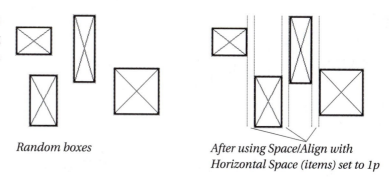

Random boxes

*After using Space/Align with
Horizontal Space (items) set to 1p*

the most important techniques for using the Space/Align features is to
always click on the Apply button (or press Command-A) before leaving
the dialog box. This way, you can see the effect of your Space/Align settings, and—if something unexpected happened—you can change them.
Sure, you can usually undo any alignment you've made after you leave
the dialog box, but why take the effort when you can check out your
changes in advance?

▼ ▼

Tip: Spacing with Percentages. You don't have to type an absolute value into the Space field. You can type a percentage, too. For instance, if
you want the tops of two lines to be twice as far apart as they already are,
you can type "200%" and click OK. When you're working in percentages,
the Apply button has an additional function: it lets you apply that percentage more than once. If you type "150%" and click Apply, the objects
are spaced one and a half times their existing distance. Then, if you click
Apply again, they're moved *another* one and a half times, and so on.

▼ ▼

Distribute Evenly. Let's say you have three picture boxes and you want
the space between them to be equal. It could take nigh-on forever to

figure out exactly where to move the middle box so that you've got equal space on each side. Instead, you can let the Distribute Evenly feature do it for you. I find distribution helpful when I have a number of items that are all the same size, but are scattered around the page (see Figure 3-54).

Distribute Evenly always takes the left-most and right-most, or the top-most and bottom-most, page elements that you have selected (depending on whether you're aligning vertically, horizontally, or both) and uses them as the distribution boundaries. In other words, those objects don't move, but all the other objects that you selected do move.

Figure 3-54
Distribute Evenly with
Space/Align

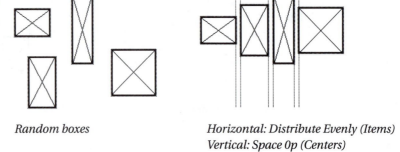

Random boxes

Horizontal: Distribute Evenly (Items)
Vertical: Space 0p (Centers)

Distribute Evenly leaves the farthest left and right items in the same place, while dividing the rest of the space between all of the intermediate items.

Between. The last step in the process outlined above is figuring out what part of the objects you want to align or distribute. Your choices are the edges (Top, Bottom, Right, and Left), the Center, and the object itself (called Item). You choose any one of these by selecting it from the Between popup menu. Of course, the Horizontal section only lets you choose Left Edges, Right Edges, or Centers, while the Vertical section lets you choose Top Edges, Bottom Edges, or Centers.

The concept of aligning or distributing objects based on Item is sometimes confusing to people. Item refers to the bounding box of the page element. So, for example, horizontally aligning two text boxes with Space set to zero and Between set to Item results in the right side of one being aligned with the left side of the second. Another way to say this is that there is zero space between the items.

And note that I said this is based on the *bounding box* of the object, which is the smallest rectangle that can enclose the entire object. This may result in alignment that you might not expect, especially when you're working with rotated or oddly shaped Bézier picture boxes (see Figure 3-55). Typically, when you're distributing objects, you'll use Item as the Between setting.

If you have multiple objects on a page, and you want to center all of them on top of each other, you can apply both a vertical and a horizontal alignment to them, with Centers selected in the Between popup menu, and Space set to zero.

Figure 3-55
Space/Align centers items using bounding boxes not centers

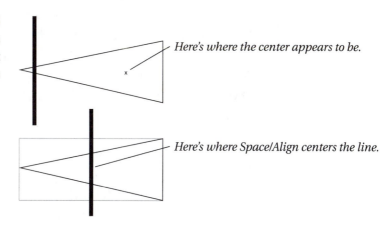

Here's where the center appears to be.

Here's where Space/Align centers the line.

Linking

I need to introduce a concept here that is crucial to working with text boxes: *linking*. Links, sometimes known as chains, are the connections between text boxes that allow text to flow from one into the other. You can have as many text boxes linked up as you like. There are two ways to link text boxes together: have QuarkXPress do it for you automatically, or do it yourself manually. I cover automatic text links in Chapter 4, *Building a Document*. I cover manual linking here.

Linking Text Boxes

Let's say you have two text boxes and the text in the first is overflowing (a text overflow is indicated by a little box with an "X" in it in the text box's lower-right corner), so you want to link it to the second text box. Here's what you do.

1. Choose the Linking tool from the Tool palette (it's the one that looks like three links in a chain).

2. Next, click on the first text box. A flashing dotted line should appear around it.

3. Finally, click on the second text box. When you select the second text box, an arrow should momentarily appear, connecting the first text box to the second. I call this the *text link arrow.* This happens even if the two text boxes are on different pages.

That's it. The boxes are now linked, and text flows between them. If you want to link another box to your text chain, just follow the same procedure: click on the second text box, then on the third, and so on. You cannot link a box to another box that has text in it unless the second box is already part of the chain.

If you want to add a text box to the middle of a text chain, first click on a box that is already linked, and then click on the text box you want to add. The text now flows from the original chain through your added text box and continues on to the original chain (see Figure 3-56).

▼ ▼

Tip: Getting Rid of the Flashes. Many people seem to get flustered when they've selected a text box with the Linking tool and then decide they don't want to follow through and link the box to anything after all. The text box is just sitting there flashing, seeming to call for some special action. Nope, no action is required. You can either click someplace where there's no text box, or just switch tools, and the flashing stops.

▼ ▼

Tip: Linking with Text Paths. I've said it before, and I'll say it again: text paths are just like one-line-tall text boxes. And, as such, you can use the text linking tools to link to and from them. You can even put them on a master page and use them as automatic text boxes (again, more on these in the next chapter).

▼ ▼

Unlinking Text Boxes

If you want to remove a link between two text boxes, use the Unlinking tool from the Tool palette. The process is simple. Let's say you have a link between two text boxes that you want to sever. First, click on one of the text boxes with the Unlinking tool. As soon as you click on it, you should see the plaid gray arrow linking the two boxes. Then click on either the arrowhead or the tailfeathers of this text link arrow. The arrow disappears and the link is gone.

If other page items are on top of the text link arrow's arrowhead and tailfeathers, you may not be able to click on it. This always seems to happen at 1 a.m., after everything else has gone wrong on the project, and this is the last straw. Nonetheless, the way I solve this problem is to rearrange the layers using Move to Front and Move to Back, or to temporarily shift the obstructing objects in order to get to one of the two.

Note that you cannot undo linking or unlinking text boxes.

▼ ▼

Tip: Unlinking a Text Box from the Middle of a Chain. If you unlink a text box from the middle of a chain by clicking on the arrowhead or tailfeathers with the Unlinking tool, the entire text chain is broken at that point. Instead, you can tell QuarkXPress to remove a text box from the text chain without breaking the rest of the flow by selecting the Unlinking tool, then holding down the Shift key while clicking on the box you want to remove.

▼ ▼

Figure 3-56

Adding a text box to a linked text chain

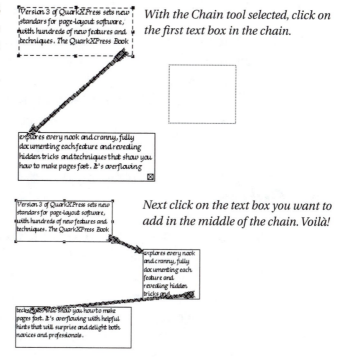

With the Chain tool selected, click on the first text box in the chain.

Next click on the text box you want to add in the middle of the chain. Voilà!

Copying Linked Text Boxes

I really love the ability to easily copy objects between documents (or between pages in a document). However, you may bump into some limitations when you try to copy linked boxes.

▶ **COPYING SINGLE LINKED TEXT BOXES.** You can copy a single text box from a chain of linked text boxes, and QuarkXPress copies, along with it, the entire text chain from that box on. None of the text preceding that box in the chain is copied—only the text from the ensuing linked boxes (and any overflow text).

It'd be nice if QuarkXPress could automatically break the chains when you copy, bringing to the new document only the text within the box you're moving (if you'd like, that is). But we have to leave them refinements to work on for the next version.

▶ **COPYING GROUPS OF LINKED TEXT BOXES.** You can copy multiple linked text boxes (from a single chain) at one time, one one condition: you have to select and copy all the text boxes. Annoyingly, XPress won't let you copy a portion of the chain, prompting you instead with the familiar, "This text box or a text box in the group has linkages that can't be duplicated."

There's one other way to copy linked boxes, especially when the boxes are on multiple pages. If both documents are in Thumbnails view, you can drag-copy multiple pages from one document to another. In this case, links between boxes on different pages are also maintained in your target document, even if you didn't grab all the text boxes in the chain.

▼ ▼

Guides and Rulers

When you are working on your document, you usually have rulers on the top and left side of the window. This not only gives you a perspective on where you are on the page, but it's a great visual aid in selecting coordinates. Let's say you want to change the size of a picture box by dragging a corner handle. If you're visually inclined, you may not want to bother with referring to the Measurements palette while you drag. Instead, if you watch the rulers, you'll see that gray lines show the left, right, top, and bottom edges as the box moves.

Rulers

You can turn the rulers on and off by selecting Show or Hide Rulers from the View menu, or by pressing Command-R. The only time you really need to turn the rulers off, though, is when you want to get a slightly larger view of the page. Otherwise, just leave them on.

You can specify which measurement system you want to use for your rulers in the Document Preferences dialog box (from the Edit menu, or press Command-Y). The vertical and horizontal rulers don't have to use the same measurement system. For example, you can set Horizontal Measure to inches and Vertical Measure to picas. That would just confuse me, so I generally keep both the same (I always use picas).

The values you choose in the Document Preferences dialog box are not only used on the rulers, but also throughout the Measurements palette and Modify dialog box. For example, if you change the Vertical Measure to ciceros, then every vertical measurement shows up in ciceros and points. You can still type in measurements using other units—see Table 2-2 in Chapter 2, *QuarkXPress Basics*—but QuarkXPress always converts them.

Item Coordinates. If you're using facing pages or multipage spreads, the ruler can measure from the upper-left corner of each page in the spread or from the upper-left corner of the whole spread. For instance, let's say you have two letter-size pages in a facing spread (like in a magazine). If you set the Item Coordinates popup menu in the Document Preferences dialog box to Page (the default value when you install QuarkXPress), the horizontal ruler goes from zero to 8.5 inches on the left page, and then starts at zero again for the right page.

If you change Item Coordinates to Spread, the horizontal ruler stretches across the entire spread, beginning with zero and ending with 17 inches (two times 8.5). I almost always leave this control set to Page, but every now and again I change it to Spread, so that I can measure where objects sit across the spread.

Adjusting the rulers. You can change more than just the measurements you see in the rulers and how far the measurements reach; you can also change where the rulers measure from. Typically, the zero points of the horizontal and vertical rulers begin at the upper-left corner of the page or spread. But you can move the origin—called the "zero, zero point"—

of the rulers by clicking in the little square area where the rulers meet and dragging to where you want the origin to be.

There are two great reasons to use this feature. First, this is how you control what prints out when you're manually tiling a document (see Chapter 13, *Printing*). Second, you might need to measure a number of objects from some point on the page that's not the upper-left corner. For instance, you can set the ruler origins to the bottom-left corner instead, so that the measurements run up the page instead of down.

When you're ready to reset the ruler origins, click that same little white box at the juncture of the rulers just once. The zero points are set back to where they started.

Visual accuracy. Rulers are visually accurate. That means, when a box or a rule looks like it is directly over a tick mark in the ruler, it really is. For example, if you want to visually place a box at the 2-inch mark (as opposed to using the Measurements palette), you can follow the gray lines in the rulers as you drag the box. When the gray line is over the 2-inch mark, the box is truly at 2 inches, even when you're at a view of other than 100 percent, or if you've changed the Points/Inch value. Note that if you have Inches Decimal selected as your vertical or horizontal measurement in the Document Preferences dialog box, you get 20 tick marks in each inch (each is 0.05 inch); if you select Inches, the rulers only have 16 tick marks (each is 0.0625 inch).

This might not seem like a big deal, but in some earlier versions, you could never really be sure unless you checked the Measurements palette or the Modify dialog box. It might have been at 1.998 or 2.01 inches.

Guides

Back in the good old days, before we all started laying out pages by sitting in front of little plastic boxes, no one worked without guides. We had blueline guides on paste-up boards, straightedge guides on drafting tables for making sure we were aligning items correctly, and transparent rulers to ensure that we were measuring type and rules correctly. I certainly didn't throw away any of that stuff when I bought my computer—they still come in handy pretty often. However, QuarkXPress gives me all those tools electronically.

You can add a vertical or a horizontal guide to your page by clicking one of the rulers and dragging onto the page.

▼ ▼

Tip: Page versus Pasteboard Guides. It turns out that there are two sorts of guides in QuarkXPress: page guides and pasteboard guides. If you drag a guide out and release the mouse button when the cursor is over the page, you get a *page guide*: it runs the length of the page from top to bottom or from side to side. It doesn't cross over a spread or onto the pasteboard or anywhere beyond the page. If you let the mouse button go while it's over the pasteboard, however, you get a *pasteboard guide* that runs the length of the whole spread and all the way across the pasteboard. Note that you can't put pasteboard guides on master pages (I cover master pages more in the next chapter).

▼ ▼

Guides don't print, so it doesn't matter where you place them on your page. However, you may want to adjust the guides to fall in front of or behind opaque text or picture boxes. You can do this by changing the Guides setting in the Document Preferences dialog box. Your two choices are Behind and In Front (I always leave this setting on the latter).

Once you've placed a guide on your page, you can move it by clicking the guide and dragging it to where you want it. Note that if you have the Content tool selected, you have to click in an area where there are no other items in order to move a guide. Otherwise, XPress doesn't know if you're clicking on the guide or the contents of a box. If you have the Item tool selected, you can always grab and move it.

The Measurements palette displays the coordinate of where the guide is while the guide is moving (unfortunately, once you let go of the guide, there is no way to find out where it sits on the page (the measurement) without "grabbing" it again—and probably moving, too).

To remove a guide from your page, grab it and drag it out of the window. That means you can drag it back into either ruler, or off to the right or bottom of the window, whichever is closest to where your cursor is at the time.

▼ ▼

Tip: Getting Rid of Ruler Guides. No matter how easy it is to move guides around, it's always a hassle to add 20 guides to a page and then remove them one at a time. Well, take a shortcut: hold down the Option key while clicking once in the horizontal ruler, and all the horizontal guides disappear. Option-clicking in the vertical ruler has the same effect on vertical guides.

Actually, it's one step more complex than this. If the page touches the ruler when you Option-click on it, only the page guides disappear (the ones running the length of the page). If the pasteboard touches the ruler, only the pasteboard guides go away (the ones running across the whole pasteboard).

▼ ▼

Tip: Dashed Guides. If you change QuarkXPress's ruler guides to "Black" in the Application Preferences dialog box, the guides become dashed lines. Some people like 'em that way, it turns out. For solid black guides, set the color to 99 percent "Black".

▼ ▼

Tip: Scale-Specific Guides. Here's one of my favorite "hidden" features in QuarkXPress: If you hold down the Shift key while dragging a ruler guide onto your page or spread, it becomes magnification-specific. That is, if you pull it out in Actual Size view, you'll only be able to see it at Actual Size view or a higher (more zoomed-in) magnification. If you zoom out (let's say to Fit in Window view), it disappears. This is great for those times when you want to see a thumbnail of the page without guides, but need the guides to work with.

▼ ▼

Snap to Guides

One of the most important values of guides is that page items can snap to them. All guides have this feature, including margin and column guides (I'll talk more about those in Chapter 4, *Building a Document*). You can turn Snap to Guides on and off by selecting it in the View menu. For example, if you have five picture boxes that you want to align, you can pull out a guide to the position you want it, and—if Snap to Guides is enabled in the View menu—as the picture boxes are moved next to the guides, they snap to that exact spot.

On the other hand, there are times when you probably want to disable Snap to Guides—so just select it again from the View menu, or use the Shift-F7 shortcut. For example, if you are working with a box or a line that is very close to a column guide, it may snap to the guide when you don't want it to. Just turn off Snap to Guides. Generally, however, I leave this feature on.

The distance at which a guide pulls an item in, snapping it to the guide position, is determined by a control in the Document Preferences dialog box (Command-Y). The default value is 6 points.

▼ ▼

Tip: Snapping Line Edges to Guides. When you drag a line close enough, it snaps to the guide. But what part of the line snaps? Whereas a box or a group always snaps to a guide based on its bounding box, there are different rules for lines. Lines built with the Diagonal and Orthogonal Line tools always snap to guides at their endpoints. Bézier lines, on the other hand, generally snap like boxes—at the edges of their bounding boxes. If your line is thin, like 0.5 point, it hardly matters where it's snapping. If it's thick, though, it could make a big difference.

You can force a diagonal or orthogonal line to snap at its edge instead of its endpoints by selecting it along with another object. For instance, you could draw a little dummy picture box above a line, select both the line and the box, and then drag them both close above the guide. This lets you snap the bottom of the line to the guide; then you can delete the picture box you made.

You can force a point on a Bézier line to snap to a guide by selecting it first. If you want to move the whole line, select all the points (double-click on any point on the curve) before dragging the point you're trying to align.

▼ ▼

Frames, Dashes, and Stripes

There are times when you want to put a picture on your wall with a frame, and there are times when you just tape it up frameless. When you're making pages, there are times when you want a frame around a text, picture, or contentless box, and there are times when you don't. Similarly, there are times when you want to apply a custom line style to a path (see "Lines and Arrows," earlier in this chapter).

In this section, I explore how to place borders around boxes and then how to build custom line styles that you can use either as frames on boxes or as line styles.

Frames

All boxes have frames, but by default the frame thickness is zero width, which is the same as no frame at all. You can add a frame to a box by selecting it, choosing Frame from the Item menu (or pressing

Command-B), and then increasing the frame thickness to anything above zero.

The Frame tab of the Modify dialog box contains fields and popup menus that let you specify the weight, color, gap color, shade, and line style of your frame (see Figure 3-57). Color and shade are self-explanatory, but I should talk a little about frame styles, gap color, and thickness.

Figure 3-57

The Frame tab of the
Modify dialog box

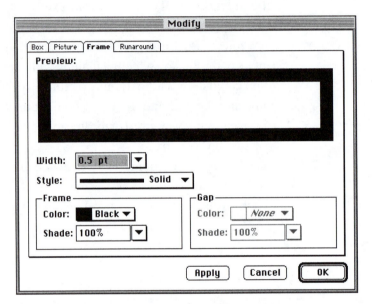

Frame style. In addition to the normal solid black line, QuarkXPress offers 10 PostScript-styled frames and nine bitmapped frames (see Figure 3-58). I encourage you to avoid the bitmapped frames with names like Yearbook, Deco Shadow, and Maze. These frames generally print incredibly slowly and often look jaggy because they're based on black-and-white bitmapped images rather than smooth, PostScript vector lines (see "Frame Editor," below, as well as Chapter 9, *Pictures*, for more information on bitmapped versus vector images). These bitmapped frames are only available on rectangular boxes anyway; if you select a Bézier, oval, beveled, or photo-frame-shaped box, the bitmapped frames disappear.

Earlier versions of QuarkXPress for Windows didn't have these bitmapped frames, but for the sake of consistency Quark added them to version 4. I would have been just as happy if they left them out.

Figure 3-58
Default frame styles

These jaggy bitmapped frames are now available on Windows

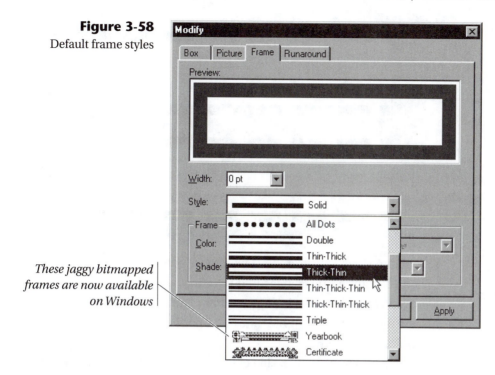

The PostScript lines are made up of dashed or striped lines. I describe how you can edit these or make your own in "Creating Custom Dashes and Stripes," below.

Gap color. All the PostScript frame styles (other than the basic solid line) have gap areas—dashed lines have gaps between the dashes, stripes have gaps between the stripes. The Gap section of the Frame tab lets you specify what color those gaps should be. At first, this new feature in version 4 appears really frivolous and designed for silly special effects. But on closer inspection, you'll see that it's actually a quite important role when using these frame styles because it lets you choose whether the gap should be transparent (color of None) or opaque (any other color; see Figure 3-59).

Frame weight. Quark calls the thickness of a frame its "width." I'm used to calling it the *weight*. No matter what you call it, it's the thickness of the line making up the frame. And, in a manner similar to lines, if the line weight is not thick enough, the frame style may not show up properly (a triple line set to 0.5 point generally comes out looking just like a single 0.5-point line).

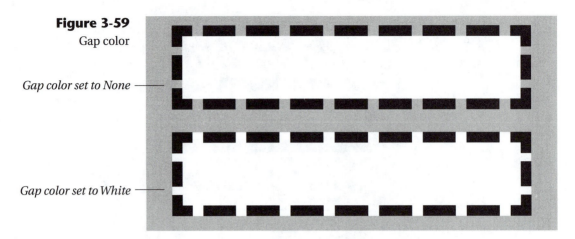

Figure 3-59
Gap color

Gap color set to None ———

Gap color set to White ———

Frames can grow from the box edge in, or from the box edge out. That is, a 10-point frame is measured from the edge of the box to either the outside or inside. This is different from lines: their weight is measured from their center (a 10-point line falls 5 points on one side of the line and 5 points on the other).

You can control which side of the box edge the frame falls on with the Framing popup menu in the Document Preferences dialog box (from the Edit menu, or press Command-Y). Choosing Inside from this menu places frames on the inside of boxes; Outside places them on the outside. The confusing thing is that even when you have Frames set to Outside, the frame looks like it's falling on the inside. That's because QuarkXPress actually makes the box itself a little bigger to set the frame correctly *as though* it were an Inside frame. I think this method is sort of a pain in the butt, so I always leave it set to Inside.

Note that you can create a frame on a box while in the Inside mode, then change the mode to Outside, and subsequent frames are built on the outside of boxes (or vice versa). Existing boxes don't change when you change the preferences.

Creating Custom Dashes and Stripes

Those dashed and striped PostScript patterns that you can use as frames around boxes or as line styles are great, but no matter which one I pick, I find myself wanting to change it, if even just a little. This may be my own peculiar compulsive nature (I prefer to think of it as my "style"), but fortunately, QuarkXPress version 4 lets me tweak these styles to my heart's content with the Dashes & Stripes feature.

To create your own line style, or to edit one of the built-in styles, select Dashes & Stripes from the Edit menu (see Figure 3-60). Like style sheets, H&J settings, and colors (each of which I discuss later in this book), when you edit Dashes & Stripes while a document is open, the change applies to that document only. If no documents are open when you make a change, it applies to all new documents that you create from then on, but not to previously saved documents.

Figure 3-60

The Dashes & Stripes dialog box

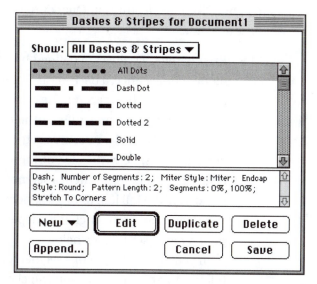

▼ ▼

Tip: Edit the Presets. As you'll see, it's really easy to create new dash and stripe styles. However, it's almost always a good idea to edit a pre-existing style rather than to start from scratch. You can edit a style by clicking on it in the Dashes & Stripes dialog box and clicking Edit or Duplicate. I prefer using Duplicate so that I don't change the original style (I might want to use it later).

▼ ▼

Tip: What Styles Have You Used? The Show popup menu lets you change which dashes and stripe styles XPress lists in the Dashes & Stripes dialog box. The Show popup menu lists four options other than the default setting, All Dashes & Stripes: Dashes, Stripes, All Dashes & Stripes Used, All Dashes & Stripes Not Used. Unless you have created a lot of styles, you probably won't find yourself using this popup menu. Nonetheless, there is one thing to watch out for: if you use one of these styles as a box frame, and then decide not to use a frame at all (that is, you set the frame thickness to zero), that style still appears in the All Dashes & Stripes Used setting.

▼ ▼

Dashes. To create a new dash style, select Dash from the popup menu that appears when you click on the New button (the button is actually a popup menu in disguise). The Edit Dash dialog box appears complex at first, but, like most features in QuarkXPress, it's easy if you take it one piece at a time.

▶ RULER AREA. Dashes are defined by a repeating pattern of segments. For instance, a basic dash is made of two segments: a solid line followed by a gap. A more complex line might be made by combining two or three different-lenth lines separated by gaps (see Figure 3-61). The ruler area at the top of the Edit Dash dialog box lets you specify the size of these segments. To specify the beginning or ending point of a segment, click in the ruler; or you can define the full length of a segment by clicking and dragging. (The values in the ruler change depending on the Repeat Every popup menu setting; see below.)

    If you like the length of a segment, but not where it sits in the full length of the pattern, you can click on the segment itself (as opposed to the arrow markers in the ruler) and drag it to the left or to the right. Note that the only time you would want to add more than a single segment marker is if you want a non-regular pattern; that is, a pattern like "thin, thick, thin, thick," and so on.

▶ POSITION. If you click on one of the segment markers in the ruler area, its value appears in the Position field. You can also add a segment marker to the ruler by typing a value here and clicking Add. I find this much more efficient than clicking and dragging in the ruler area, though the interactive method is usually more fun.

▶ PREVIEW. You can see approximately how the dash pattern will appear in the Preview area of the dialog box. The slider control to the left of the preview line lets you see how the pattern appears in thinner or thicker lines. Remember, however, that you're still only seeing a low-resolution screen preview of the dash; often, espe-

Figure 3-61

Dashes

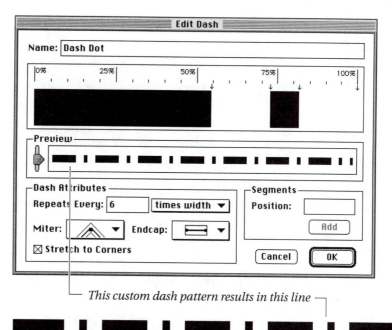

This custom dash pattern results in this line

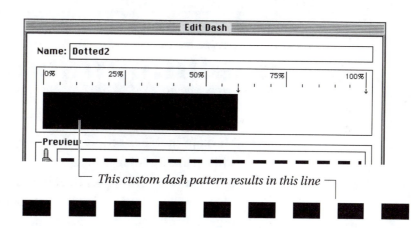

This custom dash pattern results in this line

cially in dash patterns with really thin lines, what you see on-screen may be significantly different from what you get on paper.

▶ **REPEATS EVERY.** Contrary to intuition, the Repeats Every control lets you set the length of the repeating pattern. There are two options in the popup menu to the right of the Repeats Every field: "times width" and "Points." When this is set to "times width" (it is by default), the length of the pattern is determined by the thickness of the line or frame—so as the line gets thicker, the pattern becomes longer (see Figure 3-62). For instance, let's say you set Repeats Every to 3. If you apply this to a 6-point-thick line, the pattern you specify in the ruler area is 18 points long (3×6). If you decrease the line weight to 3 points, the dash reduces, too, to 9 points (3×3).

On the other hand, you may not want the distance between the patterns to shift when you change the line weight. You can accomplish this by changing the popup menu to "Points." Now, the Repeats Every value specifies an absolute width for the pattern—if you say the pattern is 10 points long, that's how long it'll be (see "Stretch to Corners").

Figure 3-62
Repeat Every

Repeats every 3 times width

Repeats every 6 times width

Repeats every 3 times width (but thicker line)

Repeats every 6 points

▶ **MITER.** The Miter setting determines what the line style does when it hits a corner. If you apply this dash only to a smooth line or a rounded-corner box, the Miter control has no effect at all. There are three options in the Miter popup menu: sharp corner, rounded corner, and beveled corner (see Figure 3-63). (Miter is actually controlled by PostScript itself, not QuarkXPress.)

Figure 3-63
Miter

Sharp corner miter   *Round corner miter*   *Bevel corner miter*

▶ **ENDCAP.** Endcap is another PostScript-level feature, and it lets you choose the look of each line segment within the dash (see Figure 3-64). The basic distinction is square ends versus round ends, though you also have the choice of whether the endcap extends past the edge of the segment.

▶ **STRETCH TO CORNERS.** When you turn on the last control in the Edit Dash dialog box, Stretch to Corners, you're giving QuarkXPress the leeway to adjust the Repeat Every setting so that your pattern reaches from one end of your path to the other, or from one corner of your frame to another (see Figure 3-65). For instance, imagine XPress repeating the pattern along your line; when it gets to the end, it might only be able to fit half the pattern in. If Stretch to Corners is on, the program adjusts the pattern. In

Figure 3-64
Endcap

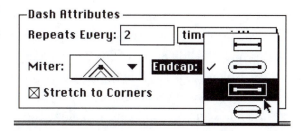

Figure 3-65
Stretch to Corners

Stretch to corners turned off

Stretch to corners turned on

general, it adjusts it so slightly that you wouldn't even notice, though it is obvious on occasion, depending on the pattern, the line thickness, and the length of the line. Nonetheless, I always turn Stretch to Corners on and only turn it off when the effect is displeasing on my pages.

▼ ▼

Tip: Watch Your Dashed Corners. Thick box frames and thin dash patterns don't always match when it comes to the corners. The problem isn't QuarkXPress's; it's just that the thin dashes don't meet up properly in the corners. QuarkXPress tries to adjust, but it doesn't always work. I wish I could offer you a solution, but instead I can only say, "Watch out," and suggest that you change the dash pattern or the line thickness if it becomes a problem.

▼ ▼

Stripes. You can create the second type of custom PostScript line style by selecting Stripe from the New popup menu in the Dashes & Stripes dialog box. The Edit Stripe dialog box is slightly less imposing than the last we explored, and its functionality is very similar (see Figure 3-66). The primary difference, of course, is that you end up with a stripe, in which the line segments and gaps run along the path, as opposed to dashes, which run perpendicularly.

There are four options in the Edit Stripe dialog box: ruler area, Position, Preview, and Miter.

▶ **RULER AREA.** Stripes are defined by separating the width of your path into smaller lines and gaps. You can specify the width of these subpaths by placing width markers in the ruler area of the Edit Stripe dialog box. As with dashes, you can click in the ruler area to place a marker, or click and drag to specify the thickness of a subpath. If you like the width of the subpath, but not the vertical placement, you can click on the subpath (not the index markers) and drag it up or down.

▶ **POSITION.** When building or editing a stripe, it's always a good idea to watch the Position field, which gives you feedback as you click or drag markers in the ruler area. You can also add markers at specific places in the ruler area by typing them here.

Figure 3-66

Edit Stripe

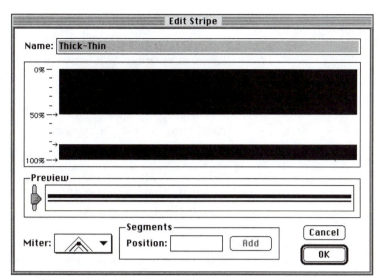

▶ **PREVIEW.** The Preview area offers an example of what your stripe will look like when applied to a path or a line. I recommend setting the slider to the largest line setting, as typical low-resolution monitors can't hope to give you a good approximation on the thinner lines.

▶ **MITER.** As with the dash pattern, the Miter setting controls what happens to the stripe at corners. Let's say you choose the rounded-corner Miter setting; if you apply this stripe to a rectangular picture box, the four corners will each be rounded slightly, even though the Corner Radius setting in the Modify dialog box is set to zero. (In fact, they're slightly rounded because this value is set to zero; if you increase the Corner Radius value, the Miter goes away.) In general, I use the default sharp-corner Miter unless I'm trying to achieve some special effect with the stripe.

Moving Dashes and Stripes Around. You can make custom dashes and stripes all you like, but if you make them in one document, how do you get them into another? There are two ways to move Dashes & Stripes styles between documents.

▶ **MOVE AN ITEM.** If you apply a custom dash or stripe to a line, or set it as a frame style for a box, you can copy that item from one document to another and the custom style comes with it. Even if you then delete the item, the custom style remains. Remember, you can copy items from one document to another with Copy and Paste, or by dragging it between the two document windows.

▶ **APPEND.** You can also move a line style from one document to another by clicking the Append button in the Dashes & Stripes dialog box. XPress asks you for the document you want to copy from, and then asks you for the Dashes & Stripes setting you want to copy. Note that the Append feature also appears under the File menu, though if you choose it there, you can append style sheets, lists, H&J settings, and colors, too.

▼ ▼

Tip: Comparing Dashes & Stripes. Sometimes it's really hard to tell the difference between two dashes or two stripes. Fortunately, QuarkXPress offers a built-in comparison feature. First, select the two styles you want to compare from the list in the Dashes & Stripes dialog box (you can select two discontiguous items from the list by holding down the Command key). Then, Option-click on the Append button (when you hold down the Option key, this button changes into a Compare button).

▼ ▼

Frame Editor

The Frame Editor is a little utility that ships with the Macintosh version of QuarkXPress and lets you create borders or frames that you can apply to rectangular boxes. This utility is part of history; it first shipped way back in the early days of QuarkXPress, when no one was really doing high-end work with any program on the desktop.

Unfortunately, at this point Frame Editor is sort of anachronistic and has few uses for the serious designer or production artist. The problem is that all the frames you can make are bitmapped. That means that rather than defining a border with smooth lines and curves, you have to use dots in a bitmap (see Chapter 9, *Pictures*, for more information on the differences between object-oriented and bitmapped images). The biggest problem with this is that diagonal and curved lines appear jaggy at almost any size (see Figure 3-67).

On the other hand, if you want to create frames with only horizontal and vertical lines, Frame Editor can do the trick pretty well. However, I won't get into the details of the program, as it's just not my cup of tea.

Figure 3-67
One of the many
confusing windows in
the easily avoidable
Frame Editor

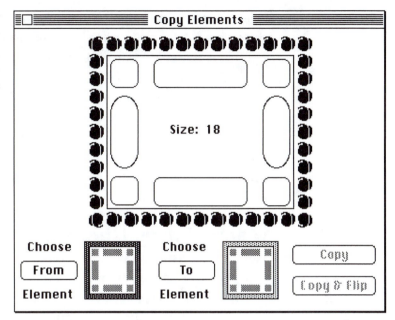

Two more items to note about the bitmapped frames. First, the frame information is saved in the XPress Preferences file, though if you apply a custom frame to a box, that frame is saved in the document as well. Second, it's recommended that if you apply a bitmapped frame to a picture or text box, apply it at the size at which it was built. If it was built to be 18 points, you should apply it at 18 points. Otherwise, you may have difficulty printing.

Libraries

QuarkXPress lets you keep libraries full of items: picture boxes, text boxes, lines, groups of objects, and so on. These libraries are saved as external files on disk. For example, while writing this book, I placed each piece of artwork in a library, grouped with figure numbers, captions, and callouts. The artwork was later dragged out of the library by the production team onto the QuarkXPress pages. This increased the chance that nothing too weird would happen when making pages, and decreased the time it took to produce a chapter.

Note that a library holds page items, plus their contents. For example, you could place a text box with a particular headline in a particular style in a library. However, picture boxes in libraries don't fully embed their pictures. If a picture was imported using Get Picture, the library only remembers the link to the external file, rather than the file itself. So, although my artwork could be stored in a library, I still had to move all of my EPS and TIFF files from disk to disk (if you are lost, don't worry; I talk about all these issues in Chapter 9, *Pictures*).

You can have more than 10 libraries open at a time (I haven't found an upper limit yet), and each library can hold up to 2,000 entries. You can even label each library entry for quick access. Let's look at how all of this is done.

Manipulating Libraries

Libraries are, in many way, just like QuarkXPress documents. Putting an item in a library is like putting it on a separate page of a document. The analogy follows in creating and opening libraries, as well. You can create a new library by selecting Library from the New submenu in the File menu (or by pressing Command-Option-N). And to open a library, you select it in the Open dialog box (the program recognizes it as a library automatically, so you don't have to do anything special). Once you choose a library, QuarkXPress brings it up on your screen as a palette.

As I mentioned back in the last chapter, palettes work much like other windows (in fact, I often call them windoids). For example, you close a palette like a window, by clicking the Close box in the upper-left corner (upper-right in Windows). The palette floats, so you can move the palette wherever you like on your screen. You also can expand the palette by clicking the Zoom box in the upper-right corner of the window. Note that this type of zooming doesn't have anything to do with a percentage scaling view. The first time you click on it, the palette fills your screen. The second time, it decreases back to "normal" size. You also can resize the windoid by clicking and dragging the lower-right resizing box, just like a normal window.

Adding and Moving Library Entries

You'll hardly believe how easy it is to add and remove library entries. To add a page item to an open library, just click on the item with the Item tool (or hold down the Command key to get a temporary Item tool), and drag the item across into the library. When you're in the library, your mouse cursor turns into a pair of glasses (don't ask me why; all the librarians I know wear contacts), and two triangular arrows point to your position in the library. When you let go of the mouse button, the item you're dragging is inserted in the library at the location these pointers indicate. That is, you can position your page item (or an existing library item) anywhere in the library by dragging it into place.

You also can add an item to a library by using Cut or Copy and Paste. You need to use the Item tool to cut or copy an item from the page, but you can use either the Item or Content tool to paste it in a library. Just click in the position where you want the item to go, then press Command-V (or select Paste from the Edit menu). When picking a place to paste the item, click between two items, so that you can see the positioning arrows. If you click on an item in the library before pasting, you are telling QuarkXPress to replace that item with this new one.

Note that although I'm saying you can add "an item" to the library, that one item can contain a number of page items. If you want, you can select picture boxes, text boxes, and lines—whether grouped or not—and put them all into the same library item.

After you add an item to a library, then you can see a thumbnail-size representation of it (see Figure 3-68). This representation is highlighted, and you won't be able to do any work on your page until you click someplace other than the library.

You can move an item in a library from one position to another by clicking on it and dragging it to a new position. If you have more items in your library than will fit in the palette, you may have some difficulty, because the library doesn't automatically scroll as you drag. I use one of two methods to get around this. First, you can cut and paste items, as I described above. Second, you can click the Zoom box to expand the size, reposition the item, and rezoom the box down to a small palette.

Removing Library Items

To take an item from an open library and place it on a page, click on it with either the Item or Content tool and drag it onto your page. This doesn't remove the item from the library; it makes a copy of it on your page. It's similar to dragging something from one document to another. If you want to delete an item from a library, click on it, then select Clear from the Edit menu (or press the Delete key). You also can use Cut from the Edit menu (Command-X), which removes the item and places it on the Clipboard. QuarkXPress always warns you before totally removing something from a library, because you can't Undo afterward.

Figure 3-68
Adding an item
to a library

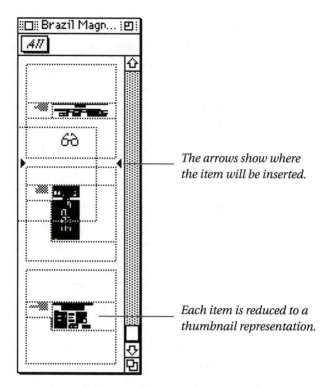

*The arrows show where
the item will be inserted.*

*Each item is reduced to a
thumbnail representation.*

Labeling Library Items

Imagine having 150 different items in a library and trying to find just the
ones that are pictures of baby seals. Remember that all you can see on
the screen is a tiny thumbnail representation of the items. Luckily, you
have labeled each library item with a foolproof system, and you are just
a popup menu item away from finding those baby seals.

Every item in a library may be labeled either for identification purposes or to group items together (or both). With your library items
labeled, you can access the library items by a single label, multiple labels,
and more.

To assign a label to a library item, double-click on its thumbnail representation. Up comes the Library Entry dialog box. In this dialog box,
there is only one field in which you can type the label. After you add one
label to an item, the popup menu in this dialog box is enabled (see Figure
3-69). This popup menu lists each of the previous labels you've assigned
(see "Tip: Grouping Library Items," below).

After you have labeled items in your library, you can select from
among them with the popup menu at the top of the Library palette (see
Figure 3-70). This acts as a kind of electronic card catalog. There are

always two items in this popup menu: All and Unlabeled. Selecting All shows you every item in the library. Selecting Unlabeled displays only the items that have not yet been labeled. Any other labels that you have assigned to library items also appear on this popup menu. If you select one of these, you only see items that have been assigned that label.

Then, if you select a second label from the popup menu, that label is added to the category you're already looking at. The name on the popup menu changes to Mixed Labels, which tells you that more than one label is being displayed. You can deselect one label category by rechoosing it from the popup menu (that is, these labels in the popup menu act as on-and-off toggle switches). You can deselect all the subcategories by choosing All from the popup menu.

Figure 3-69
The Library Entry
dialog box

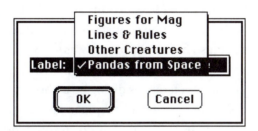

Figure 3-70
Selecting a
subcategory in
the library

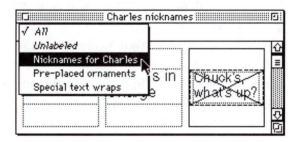

▼ ▼

Tip: Grouping Library Items. As I mentioned above, you can group library items together (this isn't the same as grouping items on the page). You do this by giving them the same label. For example, if you have a bunch of lines that you use a lot for one magazine, you might label them all "Mag Lines." Then, when you need one, you simply pull down the Library palette's popup menu and select that label.

However, if each one of the item's labels isn't exactly the same, QuarkXPress won't know to group them together. Instead of typing the same label over and over again for each item, you can just type it once. Then use the popup menu in the Library Entry dialog box to choose that item each time you want to assign it to an item within the library. This is faster, and you avoid typos.

▼ ▼

Saving Libraries

No matter how hard you try, you won't find a command to save the library file. This can be disconcerting, to say the least. What happens to all those items if you can't save them?

In previous versions of XPress, QuarkXPress would save a library only when you quit the program or closed your current document. This is generally unacceptable, because people work for long periods without quitting or closing a document (during the production of the first edition of this book, one person lost over an hour's worth of work because of a system crash before the library was saved).

Fortunately, you can turn on the Auto Library Save feature in the Application Preferences dialog box. This feature, which is on by default in version 4, forces QuarkXPress to save a library every time you place a new item in it. This may slow down your work a little if you're adding a number of items, but it could also save you lots of time if something should go wrong.

Once a library is saved on disk, you can move it from one computer to another. However, note that you cannot move it from a Macintosh to a PC or vice versa. This is an unfortunate limitation due to the way QuarkXPress saves the thumbnail images.

▼ ▼

Tip: Send Your Libraries, Not Your Pictures. If you're preparing templates and picture libraries so that someone else can do the actual page-layout work, remember that you might not need to send them the picture files on disk. QuarkXPress captures a low-resolution preview image for each picture when you imported it into a picture box, and that's saved within the library.

If you send just the library file, the person making pages can place, see, and print the screen representations. When the document file comes back to you, QuarkXPress remembers the locations of all the original graphics files on your disks, and uses those for printing.

▼ ▼

▼ ▼

Moving On

You now know the basics of how QuarkXPress relates to you, and the general concepts of how you can use its tools to make your pages. If you weren't familiar with these tools before, a little practice will turn you into a pro in no time. If you were familiar with them, I hope you now have increased your arsenal of high-caliber techniques.

Either way, you should now be ready to move into the next chapter, in which I move away from a freeform, throw-it-all-on-a-page style of working and introduce you to a few of the systematic methods in which you can build documents.

4

BUILDING A DOCUMENT

I find the design process really fascinating. The designer must meld rigid, mathematical specifications with flowing, flexible sensibilities. XPress works best when you use this mix. First, build the foundation of your document with precision. Second, place items on the page with creativity.

This chapter is about starting that process: building an infrastructure for your document. I call this "document construction." It's just like the construction of a building. First you decide on the building's specifications—how tall and wide you want it to be, and so on. Next you lay a foundation and build structural supports.

In QuarkXPress it's very similar. First you decide on specifications for the document—how tall and wide, whether it's double- or single-sided, and so on. Next you build the structures of the page—page elements that repeat, page numbering, and text flow. If you don't take these steps first, the foundation of your work will be unreliable—and your building might just fall down.

Step with me into the building mode. Our first stop is opening a new document.

▼ ▼

Building a New Document

When you open QuarkXPress using the program defaults, you'll see a blank screen underneath the menu bar, with the Tool and Measurements palettes showing. To create a new document, choose New from the File submenu (or press Command-N). This brings up the New Document dialog box, shown in Figure 4-1. It is here that you determine a document's page dimensions, page margins, number of columns, the spacing between columns, and whether the pages are laid out facing each other.

The New Document dialog box is the "Checkpoint Charlie" for entering the new-document zone (walls may crumble, but metaphors remain). Note that there is nothing in the New Document dialog box that locks you in; you can make changes to these settings at any time, even after you've worked on the document a lot.

Let's take a detailed look at each of items in this dialog box.

Figure 4-1
The New Document
dialog box

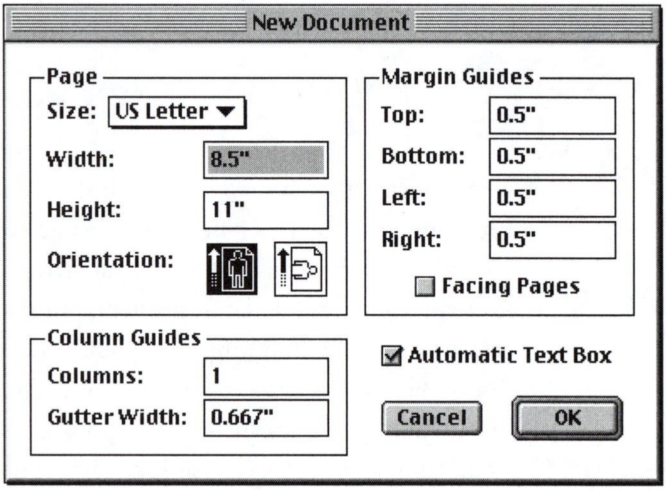

Page Size

When you make your pass through the New Document dialog box on the way to creating a document, you have the opportunity to determine the dimensions of its pages. The *default setting*—the one QuarkXPress chooses for you if you make no change to the settings in the dialog box— is a standard letter-size page: 8.5 by 11 inches (or A4 size in Quark-Passport). You can choose from five preset sizes, or you can choose a custom-size page by typing in the values yourself—from 1 by 1 inch to 48 by 48 inches. Table 4-1 shows the measurements for each of the preset choices in three common measurement units.

Table 4-1
Preset page sizes

Name	In inches	In picas/points	In millimeters
US Letter	8.5 by 11	51p by 66p	216 by 279.4
US Legal	8.5 by 14	51p by 84p	216 by 355.6
A4 Letter	8.27 by 11.69	49p7.3 by 70p1.9	210 by 297
B5 Letter	6.93 by 9.84	41p6.9 by 59p0.7	176 by 250
Tabloid	11 by 17	66p by 102p	279.4 by 431.8

▼ ▼

Tip: Page Size Is Not Paper Size. Page Size in the New dialog box refers to the size of the pages you want as your finished output—it does not refer to the size of the paper going through your printer. These sizes may or may not be the same. In the Page Size area, type in the page dimensions of the actual piece you want to produce. For example, if you want to create a 7-by-9-inch book page, enter these values in the Width and Height fields, even if you're outputting to a laser printer capable of handling only letter-size pages.

▼ ▼

Margin Guides

The Margin Guides area allows you to specify the size of your margin on all four sides of a page: Top, Bottom, Left, and Right. When you work with facing pages (see below), Left and Right change to Inside and Outside. These margin guides can be used to define the *column area*. In the book-and-magazine trade, the column area is usually called the *live area*. It's the area within which the text and graphics usually sit (see Figure 4-2). Running heads, folios, and other repeating items sit outside the live area.

The term "live area" may be slightly misleading, however, because everything that's on a page gets printed, whether it's inside the margin guides or outside them—or even partially on the page and partially off it. Note that the margin guides are only that—guides. You can ignore them if you want. You should also note that these guides specify the size of the automatic text box (which I'll talk about later in this chapter).

There are some things about margin guides that make them unique. Although margin guides resemble ruler guides both in form and func-

Figure 4-2
The Column,
or "live" area

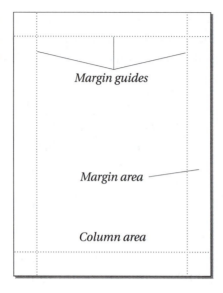

Margin guides

Margin area —————

Column area

tion, you cannot change the position of the margin guides by dragging them; you have to change them in the Master Guides dialog box (which is only available when a master page is showing). I look at making this kind of modification in "Making Pages," later in this chapter.

Your document pages don't all have to have the same margin guides. But because margin guides are based on master pages, you have to create multiple master pages to have different margin guides. Once again, I defer discussion of this process until later in the chapter. For now, let's just concentrate on building one simple document.

By the way, note that these guides don't print. Nor do they limit what you can do on the page. They are simply part of the general infrastructure of the document, and are meant just to be guides. Not only can you change them at any time, but (as with the printed guides on blueline grid paper) you can disregard them entirely.

Column Guides

There's another kind of automatic guide you can place on a page: column guides. If you select a value larger than the one in the Columns field in the New Document dialog box, the area between the margin guides is divided into columns. For example, if you want a page that has three columns of text on it, you can specify a value of "3" (see Figure 4-3).

Your next decision is the amount of gutter space. Sometimes people use the word "gutter" to refer to the inside page margin; this is different. In QuarkXPress, the *gutter* is the blank space between column guides.

Figure 4-3
Column guides

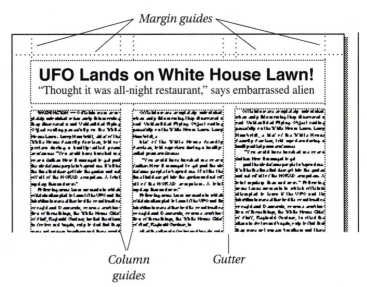

Margin guides

UFO Lands on White House Lawn!
"Thought it was all-night restaurant," says embarrassed alien

*Column
guides*

Gutter

Perhaps the best way to think about column guides is the concept of the page grid. Unfortunately, QuarkXPress can't create a true horizontal and vertical grid for your page. However, it can give you the tools to make one yourself. Column guides are the first part of that procedure: they allow you to place columns of space on a page. When Snap to Guides is selected from the View menu, items such as text boxes and lines "snap to" your column guides (see Chapter 2, *QuarkXPress Basics*).

▼ ▼

Tip: Snap to Guides for Box Fitting. I often find it more helpful to draw separate text boxes for each column rather than to use one large text box separated into columns. If you have Snap to Guides turned on (on the View menu), you can quickly draw a text box that fills one column. This text box can be duplicated, then positioned in the next column, and so on, until each column is created.

Drawing multiple text boxes is also useful if you want each column to be a different width or height. When you're done making boxes, you can remove the column guides by using the Master Guides feature, or you can just leave them where they are.

▼ ▼

Facing Pages

Although the Facing Pages feature is located in the Margins area of the New Document dialog box (and in the Document Setup dialog box), it deserves some special attention. At this stage in the game, you have two choices for your document: single-sided pages or facing pages.

Single-sided pages. Single-sided pages are what most people generate from desktop-publishing equipment: single-sided pieces of paper. For example, handbills, posters, letters, memos, or one-page forms are all single-sided. In QuarkXPress a normal, single-sided document looks like a series of pages, each positioned directly underneath the previous one (see Figure 4-4).

Facing pages. Whereas nonfacing pages are destined to be single, facing pages are always married to another page (well, almost always). For example, pick up a book. Open it in the middle. The left page (the *verso*)

Figure 4-4
Single-sided pages

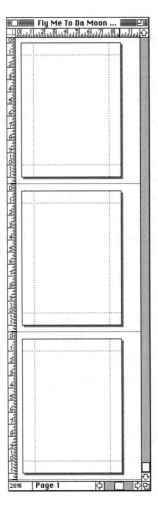

faces the right page (the *recto*). In some books (like the one you're look-ing at), the left and right pages are almost exactly the same. However, most book pages have a slightly larger inside margin (*binding margin*) than the outside margin (*fore-edge margin*). This is to offset the amount of the page "lost" in the binding.

QuarkXPress displays facing pages next to each other on the screen (see Figure 4-5). For example, when you move from page two to page three you must scroll "across" rather than "down." Note that even page numbers always fall on the left; odd numbers always fall on the right.

If you check Facing Pages in the New Document dialog box, XPress sets up two master pages: a left and a right page. These can be almost completely different from each another (we'll see how soon).

Figure 4-5
Facing pages

Automatic Text Box

Here's a relatively easy choice: Do you want your first page and all sub-sequently added pages to have text boxes automatically placed on them? If so, turn on the Automatic Text Box option. This is clearly the way to go if you're working with documents such as books or flyers that are most-ly text. However, if you're designing an advertisement with text and pic-tures placed all over the page, there's really no good reason to use the Automatic Text Box feature.

If you do check Automatic Text Box, the text box that QuarkXPress makes for you is set to the same number of columns and gutter size that you specified in the Column Guides area, and it fills the page out to the margin guides. I discuss the Automatic Text Box checkbox in detail in "Automatic Text Boxes," later in this chapter.

▼ ▼

Tip: Check That New Document Dialog Box. QuarkXPress remembers what you selected in the New Document dialog box for the last document, and gives you the same thing next time you start on a new document. This can be helpful or it can be a drag (especially when one of your colleagues creates a 3-by-5-inch document just before you start working on a tabloid-sized job). You'll hear me say this throughout the book: Verify each dialog box as you go. Don't just assume that you want every default setting. Pay attention to those details and you'll rarely go wrong.

▼ ▼

Master Pages: Elementary

Master pages are the means of establishing repeating elements common to multiple pages within a document. For example, if you have one master page in a single-sided document, then what's on that master page shows up on every new page you create. In facing-page documents there are two master pages, one for the left page and one for the right. In this case, whatever you put on the "left" master page shows up on all the left document pages, and what is on the "right" master page shows up on all the right document pages.

What Master Pages Are Good For

Although your creativity in formatting master pages may be unlimited, master pages' most common uses are for running heads, repeating graphics, and automatic page numbers (see Figure 4-6). These items are perfect for master pages, because creating them for every page in your document would be a chore that Hercules would shudder at and Job would give up on.

Automatic Page Numbering. I have a confession to make: Before I knew better, I would put "1" on the first page, "2" on the second page,

Figure 4-6

Running heads
and footers

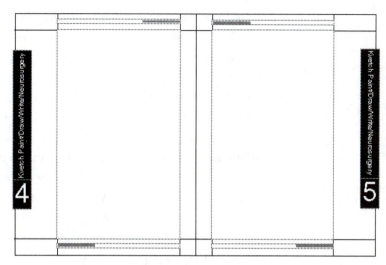

and so on. When I deleted or added pages, I just took the time to renumber every page. That seemed reasonable enough. What else could I do?

QuarkXPress lets you set up automatic page numbering for an entire document (and as I discuss in Chapter 8, *Long Documents*, for multiple documents as well). You don't actually type any number on the master page. What you do is press the keystroke for the Current Box Page Number character (Command-3). This inserts a placeholder character which is replaced by the page number when you're looking at a document page. In master pages, the page-number placeholder looks like this: <#>.

The number appears in whatever font, size, and style you choose on the master page. For example, if you set the <#> character to 9-point Futura, all the page numbers come out in that style. This can actually cause some confusion: If you choose a font like an Expert Set or a Pi collection, the numbers or the <#> characters might appear differently than you expect. But with normal typefaces, you'll see the numbers just like you'd think.

Remember, the Current Box Page Number character (Command-3) is simply a character that you type, manipulate, or delete using keyboard commands. You also can type it alongside other text, to form text blocks that read "Page <#>", or "If you wanted to find pg. <#>, you found it."

These page numbers flow with your pages. For example, if you change page 23 to be your new page 10, every page in the document changes its position and numbering accordingly. Also, if you change the page-numbering scheme to Roman numerals or whatever (see "Sections and Page Numbering," later in this chapter), QuarkXPress automatically changes that style on every page.

▼ ▼

Tip: Big Page Numbers. The problem with checking thumbnails on screen is that you can hardly ever read the page numbers. One reader tells me that she sometimes adds big automatic page numbers (Command-3) that hang off the edge of the pages onto the pasteboard for the left and right master pages (see Figure 4-7). You can set these text boxes to have no runaround and turn Suppress Printout on, and QuarkXPress acts as if they aren't even there (they won't print or affect other items on the page). However, even at tiny sizes, you can see them attached to each page.

Figure 4-7
Thumbnail page
numbers

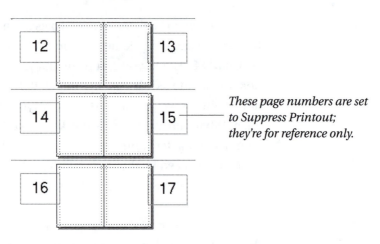

These page numbers are set
to Suppress Printout;
they're for reference only.

▼ ▼

Graphics and master pages. You can do anything with a graphic on a master page that you can do on a regular document page, including define it for text runarounds. You can be subtle and put a small graphic in your header or footer, or you can put a great big graphic in the background of every page (see Figure 4-8).

The thing to remember when you format master pages with graphics—whether as backgrounds or for runaround effects—is that what you place on the master page appears on every page of the document. If you only want a graphic on a few pages, you're best off either handling such things on a page-by-page basis in the regular document view, or creating different master pages to hold different graphics.

Figure 4-8
Placing a graphic
on your master page

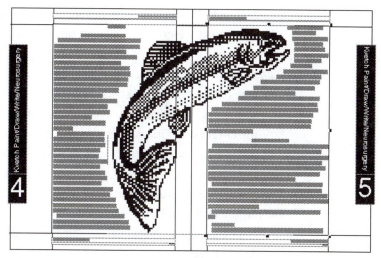

Figure 4-8
Placing a graphic
on your master page

QuarkXPress offers you more flexibility in master-page creation than any other publishing program. But if you use other page-layout software, you should note that QuarkXPress's master pages differ significantly from their competition's versions—in concept and function.

How PageMaker Does It

In PageMaker, master pages interact "transparently" with actual document pages. It is common to describe them using the metaphor of transparent overlays on all pages, but really they are more like "underlays" beneath each page. PageMaker lets you create and edit the guts of the document on your document page, while its master-page underlay displays and prints underneath it. Speaking metaphorically, you can "slide out" this master page underlay at any time, change the page formatting, and then slide it back in.

However, you cannot locally change any master-page elements on actual document pages, because although they display and print there, they really exist only on the underlay—untouchable unless you slide them out. Nor can you choose to base pages on only some of the elements on a master page; everything on the master page is either turned on or turned off.

How QuarkXPress Does It

Master pages in QuarkXPress are totally different. You get all the retroactive formatting power found in the other programs, plus more. Elements on QuarkXPress's master pages show up on regular document pages not as view-only elements existing on an underlay, but as real elements which you can edit just like any other page element. You can still go back and edit your master page, but whatever you change on a document page ("local changes") stays changed.

You can base document pages on a *formatted* or a *blank* master page (the latter is the QuarkXPress equivalent of turning a master page "off"). And you can have multiple master pages—up to 127—in any document, so you can base different document pages on different master pages. This is very useful if your document comprises multiple sections that require different looks.

I'm going to stick to the basics in this elementary section on QuarkXPress's master pages, because to throw the options and variables down on the table all at once might make things seem more complicated than they really are. Working with master pages isn't complicated if you take it step by step.

Your First Master Page

Two things happen simultaneously when you click OK in the New Document dialog box: QuarkXPress builds a master page called "A-Master A" and creates the first page of your document for you to work on. The master page and the document page are almost identical. If you turned on Facing Pages in the New dialog box, "A-Master A" has a left page and a right page; otherwise, it's just a single page.

There are three methods for switching between viewing the master pages of a document and the document itself.

▶ **DOCUMENT LAYOUT PALETTE.** The icons for the master pages are located at the top of the Document Layout palette. To jump to the master page you want, double-click on its icon (see Figure 4-9).

▶ **DISPLAY SUBMENU.** You can choose to work on either your document pages or your master pages by selecting one or the other from the Display submenu located under the Page menu (see Figure 4-10).

▶ **POPUP PAGE.** Clicking and dragging the page number popup menu in the lower-left corner of the document's window gives you a list of icons from which you can select any document page or master page (see Figure 4-11).

Figure 4-9

Viewing a
master page

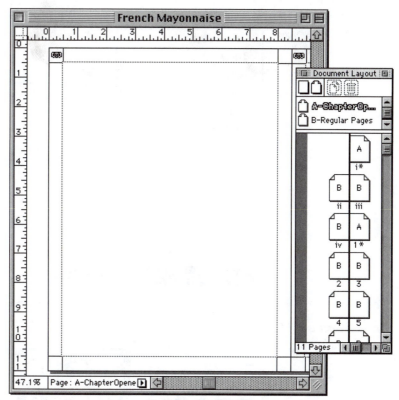

You can tell whether you're looking at a document page or a master
page by three telltale signs.

▶ The page-number indicator in the lower-left corner of the document window tells you if you are looking at a document page or
a master page.

▶ An automatic text-link icon is always in the upper-left corner of a
master page. (Later in the chapter, I discuss what this is and how
you use it.)

▶ While viewing a master page, you aren't able to perform certain
functions that are usually available. For example, the Go To feature (Command-J) is disabled, as is Insert.

▼ ▼

Tip: Printing Master Pages. Printing master pages is simple enough,
but people often can't figure out how to do it. The trick: you have to have
the master page that you want printed showing when you select Print
from the File menu. Note that this prints both the left and right pages if

Figure 4-10
Selecting a page
to look at

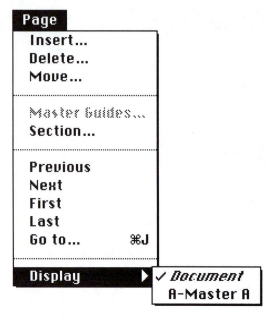

Figure 4-11
Popup pages

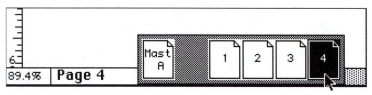

the document has facing pages (you can't print only the left or the right page alone). Unfortunately, this means that if you have 12 different master pages and you want them all to be printed, you have to print them one spread at a time.

Automatic Text Boxes

Although master pages look very similar to normal document pages, there are some basic differences you need to be aware of. These are the master guides, the automatic text-link icon, and the automatic text-link box. Each of these is integral to the construction of a well-built document.

Note that *automatic text-link icon* is my term for what Quark's documentation refers to as both the "Intact Chain Icon" and the "Broken Chain Icon." Similarly, my term *automatic text-link box* is referred to as the "automatic text box" in the Quark manuals. I think my terminology is more descriptive, so that's what I use. If you like theirs, then do a mental substitution.

Master Guides

I said earlier that you could change the margins and column guides after you set their values in the New Document dialog box. The Master Guides dialog box is the place to do this. You can get the Master Guides dialog box by selecting Master Guides from the Page menu when you're working on a master page (see Figure 4-12).

Figure 4-12
Master Guides
dialog box

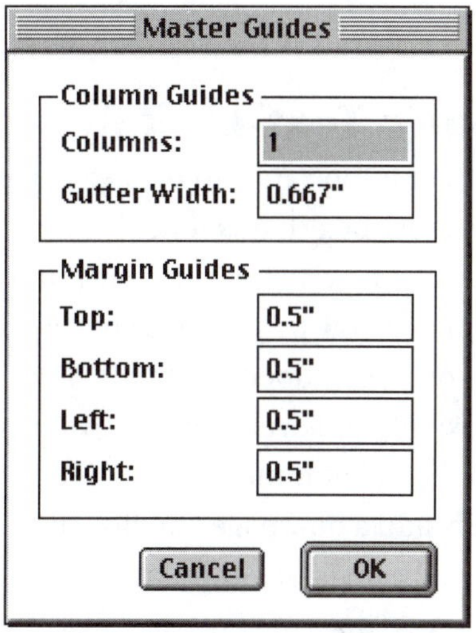

When you use the Master Guides dialog box to change the margin guides or the column guides, only the currently open master page changes. Later in this chapter, you'll learn about having multiple master pages; in that case, you can have different margins and columns for each master page in your document.

Note that when you change the margin guides or column guides using Master Guides, you affect the automatic text box on that page (if there is one). If the boundaries of the automatic text box reach to the margin guides (they always do, unless you've changed them), the boundaries are changed to match the new margins. Similarly, if you change the Columns field in the Master Guides dialog box, the automatic text box also gets altered (as long as you haven't changed its boundaries or column settings).

Automatic Text-Link Icon

The automatic text-link icon is the little picture of a chain in the upper-left corner of every master page. It is the gateway to QuarkXPress's automatic text-linking feature. This feature allows XPress to automatically link together text boxes that occur on each page. Of course, you can always link boxes together manually, but automatic text boxes are much faster. The automatic text-link icon works in conjunction with the automatic text-link box, which I discuss next.

The automatic text-link icon is always either broken (disabled) or linked (enabled). You can use the Linking and Unlinking tools while you're viewing your master pages to switch automatic linking on and off (see below).

Automatic Text-Link Box

Another item of importance to master pages is the automatic text-link box. This is a text box that is linked through QuarkXPress's automatic linking mechanism. Automatic linking is the way that QuarkXPress links pages together. I know this sounds confusing. Let's look at an example.

Picture a one-page document with only one master page, "A-Master A." If your text fills and overflows the text box on the first page, and your "A-Master A" has an automatic text-link box on it, then the program can automatically add a new page and link the overflow text onto the newly added page. If there is no automatic text-link box on the master page, then QuarkXPress does not link your first-page text box to anything, and you have to link things manually (see Chapter 2, *QuarkXPress Basics*).

There are two ways to get automatic text-link boxes on your master page.

- ▶ **AUTOMATIC TEXT BOX.** If you check Automatic Text Box in the New Document dialog box when you're creating a document (it is on by default), QuarkXPress places a text box on your first document page and also on "A-Master A." The text box on the master page is an automatic text-link box.

- ▶ **LINKING TO THE CHAIN.** You can create your own automatic text-link box by drawing a text box on your master page and then linking it to the automatic text-link icon. Select the Linking tool from the Tool palette, click on the automatic text-link icon in the upper-left corner of the page, then click on the text box you want automatically linked (see Figure 4-13). If you want both the left and right pages to contain automatic text-link boxes, you need to link each page's icon to a text box.

An automatic text-link box is a special-case text box. It is reserved solely for text that is typed on (or flowed into) document pages, so you cannot type any text in it while you're on the master page. This is different from other boxes that are on the master page, which can contain text or graphics (like running heads or automatic page numbers).

Modifying Automatic Text-Link Boxes

While you cannot type in automatic text-link boxes, you can make many formatting specifications for them. For example, you can specify the number of columns, width, height, background color, and frame. While QuarkXPress originally places automatic text-link boxes so that they fill the area outlined by the margin guides (with the number of columns specified for column guides), you can always move and resize them to suit your needs.

▼ ▼

Tip: Assigning a Startup Font. Although you cannot actually type in an automatic text-link box while in master-page viewing mode, you *can* assign character and paragraph formatting to the box. Just select the text box with the Content tool and specify the font, size, style, leading, and so on. You can even set the default style sheet for the box (see Chapter 7, *Copy Flow*). Then when you return to the document page, the text you type in that box appears in the font, style, and leading that you chose. Text that is imported into that box does not necessarily appear in that font, however.

▼ ▼

Figure 4-13
Manually linked
automatic text boxes

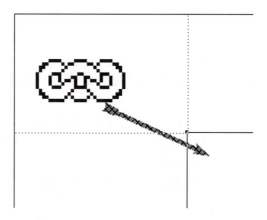

Creating Multiple Automatic Text-Link Boxes

You can actually have any number of automatic text-link boxes on a master page. That is, text could flow into one, then another, and then another before flowing onto the next page. What you have to do is link them all in the order in which you want text to flow into them. You define the first box as "automatic" using the procedures described above. Then you click in succession with the Linking tool on the boxes you want to define as automatic text-link boxes. This defines them as part of the automatic text chain. You'll see the linking arrows shoot out with each new link that you create. To continue the link from a left master page to a right master page, click on the right master's automatic text-link icon before joining any boxes found on the right master.

Don't get any fancy ideas about having two separate automatic text-link boxes on a page, each holding a different story (for instance, having two stories that flow side-by-side through a document). Nope. Can't do that with automatic text boxes (you can set that up by linking the boxes manually, of course).

Unlinking Automatic Text-Link Boxes

The easiest way to discard an automatic text-link box is to delete it (Command-K). But if you want to keep the box and simply negate its definition as an automatic text-link box, you can do that using the Unlinking tool. First, click on the automatic text-link icon with the Unlinking tool, thereby showing the linking arrow. Next, click on the tail of the linking arrow to break the chain and turn the box into a "normal" master-page text box. In the case of multiple successively linked boxes, the automatic linking is broken wherever you've broken the chain from the icon, though any other links remain.

▼ ▼

Master Pages and Document Pages

There is a subtle but certain link between your master pages and document pages that goes beyond one mirroring the other. Because QuarkXPress lets you change master-page items (also known simply as "master items") on your document pages (unlike PageMaker), you have extra power; but with that power comes—what else?—responsibility. The responsibility to pay attention to what you're doing. Here's why.

Changing Master-Page Items

After you have created a master page and applied it to a document page, you can manipulate the master-page items in either master-page or document view. Which view you're in when you make a change determines what effect the change has on your document.

Changes to master items on master pages. If you are in master-page view when you make a change to a master-page item, the change is reflected on every page in your document that is based on that master page—unless you've already gone and changed that item on particular document pages (see Figure 4-14).

For example, let's say you have a running head that contains the name of the document and the page number. You have created a 30-page document with this master page, so each page has that running head on it. If you change the running head because the document's title has changed, that change shows up on all 30 pages. The same thing happens if you change the typeface of the running head, or anything else about the master page.

In fact, if you deleted the running head's text box from the master page, it would be deleted from every document page based on that master page, too.

Changes to master items on document pages. However, if you change the running head on page 10 while you're in document view, and then rework the running head on the master page, the running head on every page *except* page 10 is changed. Page 10 remains unchanged because local page changes override the master-page change for that text box.

As long as no local page changes are made, if you delete the running head from the master page, the running head is deleted from every page of the document. But if a change has already been made locally to the running head on page 10, like in this example, then that running head on page 10 is *not* deleted. Even if you delete the whole master page, the text boxes that appear on document pages are deleted except for the one on page 10, which has been *locally* modified.

Figure 4-14
Master Page changes

On a document page, the item shows up exactly as it appears on the Master Page with the correct page number inserted.

Edit this text for the running head on the document page.

If you then go back and change the text on the Master Pages . . .

. . . the running head remains the same on the document page.

This keep-local-changes approach makes sense if you think about it, but it's often frustrating. For instance, if you forget that something is a master-page item and you change it even just a little, QuarkXPress notices and breaks the link between it and the master page. That's one reason why it's important to be clear on what's a master-page item and what's not. Note that if you change a master-page item on a document page (such as that running head in the earlier example) and then you change it back to exactly the way it was, QuarkXPress forgives and forgets that you ever changed it in the first place.

Content links and item links. Okay, let's take this one step further. It turns out that when it comes to master-page items, there are actually two kinds of links you can break: content links and item links. Let's say you have a text box with the word "Moose" in it on your master page. If you change the text on a document page, you break the content link. If you move the box (or change its size), you break the item link.

For instance, after changing the word "Moose" to "Elk" on page 23, let's say you go back to the master page and change "Moose" to "Bison" *and* change the size of the text box. Now, on every page but 23 the word gets updated to "Bison"—on page 23, the content link was broken, so it remains "Elk." But on every page, even page 23, the text-box size gets changed. It gets changed on page 23 because changing the text in a text box breaks the content link but not the item link, so changes to the item (the text box) itself are reflected (see Figure 4-15).

Okay, now let's say you change the color of the text box on page 19. Changing the background color breaks the item link (because you've affected the box itself), but not the content link. So if you move the box or change its size on the master page, it moves or resizes on all the pages except page 19.

Note that if you delete an item on the master page, it will only be deleted from the document page if you have broken neither item nor content links. If this is totally confusing to you, don't worry; it's one of those things that you just have to try before you really understand.

Applying Master Pages to Document Pages

It's quite easy to assign a new master page to a document page (however, because you use the Document Layout palette to do it, I'm going to hold off discussing this until the next section, "Master Pages and the Document Layout Palette"). You can also reassign a master page to a document page—which is like stripping the master page off, and then applying it again. When you perform either of these tasks, master items from the current master page are generally deleted and replaced by the new master items. However, the one exception is when you've already locally modified a master item while you're on a document page.

One of two things can happen when you assign a master page to a document page that has locally edited master items, and the determining factor is the Master Page Items feature in the Document Preferences dialog box (Command-Y). You have two choices: Delete Changes and Keep Changes.

Figure 4-15
Item and Content links
between master pages
and document pages

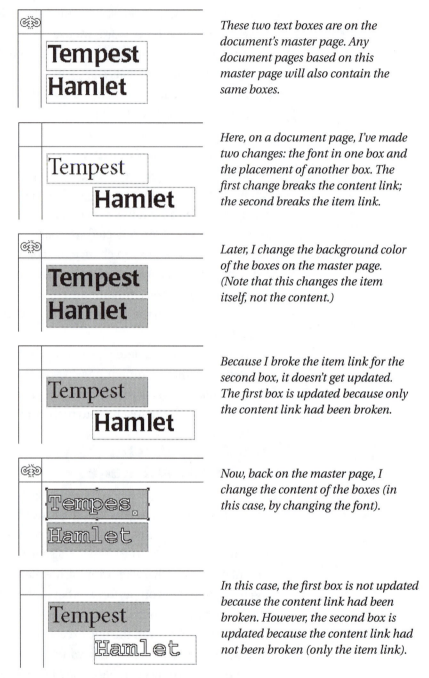

These two text boxes are on the document's master page. Any document pages based on this master page will also contain the same boxes.

Here, on a document page, I've made two changes: the font in one box and the placement of another box. The first change breaks the content link; the second breaks the item link.

Later, I change the background color of the boxes on the master page. (Note that this changes the item itself, not the content.)

Because I broke the item link for the second box, it doesn't get updated. The first box is updated because only the content link had been broken.

Now, back on the master page, I change the content of the boxes (in this case, by changing the font).

In this case, the first box is not updated because the content link had been broken. However, the second box is updated because the content link had not been broken (only the item link).

Delete Changes. If Master Page Items is set to Delete Changes, when you reapply a master page to a document page, every master item on a page is deleted and replaced with new master items—even if changes have been made locally. This is a great way to "reset" the page if you have accidentally made changes to master items: reapply a master page to a document page while Delete Changes is set in the General Preferences dialog box. All the locally modified items are deleted and reset back to the original master items.

Keep Changes. The alternative to deleting locally modified master items is keeping them. When Keep Changes is selected in the General Preferences dialog box, QuarkXPress skips over any master items that you have modified (changed their position, size, shape, font, text, and so on). This is the default setting when you start a document.

Note that the Delete Changes and Keep Changes preferences have no effect if you simply edit a master-page item—only when you apply or reapply a master page to a document page. (I discussed editing master-page items in the last section.)

▼ ▼

Tip: When Are Master Pages Reapplied? One of the most frustrating occurrences to both beginning and experienced QuarkXPress users is the seemingly random way QuarkXPress automatically reapplies master pages to your document pages. However, there's really nothing random about it. Simply put, QuarkXPress automatically reapplies a master page every time a page switches sides in a facing-pages layout.

If you add one page before page four, then page four becomes page five, flipping from a left to a right page in the spread. In this case, QuarkXPress automatically reapplies the master page. The result can be chaos in your document, depending on what changes you've made to the master-page items. If you add two pages before page four, then QuarkXPress won't automatically reapply the master page at all. This is the main reason that I always try to add or delete pages in even increments when I'm working with facing pages.

▼ ▼

Summing It Up

And that's really all there is to how the master-page feature works. It's simple and ingenious, and any advanced things that you do with it are based on these operational principles.

▼ ▼

Master Pages and the Document Layout Palette

If you've gotten this far, you've learned the hardest stuff about QuarkXPress's master pages. Now it's time to take the next step and learn another level of control by using the following additional controls.

▶ Creating new master pages

▶ Creating new master pages based on existing ones

▶ Naming and ordering master pages

▶ Applying master pages to document pages

▶ Deleting master pages

There are many ways to use multiple master pages. For example, most books are separated into several sections, including front matter, body text, and index. Each section is paginated and formatted differently from the body, with different (or no) headers or footers. You can create a master page for each of these sections. Multiple master pages are almost required for magazine production, where you may have a plethora of different sections: front matter, regular article pages, photo features, full-page ads, and small-ad sections, to name a few.

Multiple master pages are accessible through the Document Layout palette. I introduced the Document Layout palette in Chapter 2, *Quark-XPress Basics*. Now I'm going to concentrate on how you can use it to work with your master pages.

Document Layout Palette

If you look at the Document Layout palette for the facing-page document in Figure 4-16, you'll see that it's divided vertically into four areas: creation and deletion, master page, document layout, and page number/section.

Creation and deletion area. At the top of the Document Layout palette is the creation and deletion area, which is used for creating, duplicating, and deleting both document and master pages. At the left, you see blank single-sided and facing-page icons (you can't edit these; they're always blank). Next to those icons are two buttons: one to duplicate master pages and the other to delete master or document pages.

Figure 4-16

Document Layout palettes for a single-sided and a facing-pages document

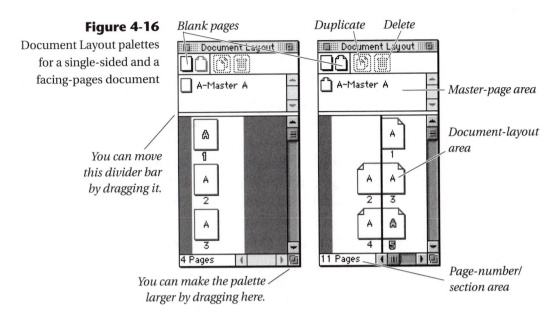

Blank pages

Duplicate   *Delete*

Master-page area

Document-layout area

You can move this divider bar by dragging it.

Page-number/ section area

You can make the palette larger by dragging here.

There are two ways to create a new master page. First, you can drag a blank single-sided or facing-page icon into the master-page area (see Figure 4-17). Second, you can select a master page on the Document Layout palette and click the Duplicate button. There's only one way to delete a master page: select the master-page icon on the palette and click the Delete button (this also works for deleting document pages).

Figure 4-17

Creating a new master page

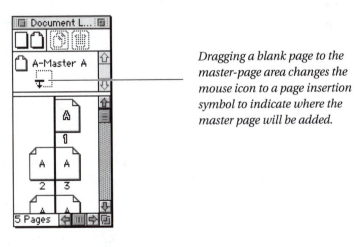

Dragging a blank page to the master-page area changes the mouse icon to a page insertion symbol to indicate where the master page will be added.

Note that deleting either a master or document page with the Delete button is not reversible with Undo (Command-Z), so make sure you really want to do it.

▼ ▼

Tip: Avoiding Alerts. I don't know about you, but I often spout spontaneous invective when my computer alerts me to a dangerous procedure. Because I've used the program for so long, I *know* that what I'm doing can't be undone or is potentially lethal to my document. One example is the "Are you sure you want to delete these pages?" prompt when you click the Delete button in the Document Layout palette. QuarkXPress is trying to be helpful, because you can't reverse this action. But it typically just annoys me. However, if you Option-click the Delete button, the pages are deleted without a prompt. Hoorah for progress.

▼ ▼

Tip: Retrieving Document-Layout Deletions. If you've deleted a master page from the Document Layout palette, the only way to get it back is by selecting Revert to Saved from the File menu. This, of course, only works if you've saved your document recently. Bear in mind that this method wipes out all changes you've made since your last save, so pause a moment and reflect before you jump into this last resort. (You can also revert to your last minisave—if you had Auto Save turned on in Application Preferences—by holding down Option and selecting the Revert to Saved menu item.)

▼ ▼

You can also create document pages in this palette by dragging either one of the blank-page icons to the document area. (Of course, if your document is single-sided, the blank facing-pages icon will be grayed out . . . you can't add a facing page to a single-sided document.)

▼ ▼

Tip: Where Is the Page Added? Where you let go of the mouse button when you insert a page by dragging it into the Document area of the Document Layout palette determines where the page goes. If you drop the page when the cursor appears as a gray outline of a page, you're saying "Drop the page right here." This is how you can make a multipage spread (see "Multipage Spreads," later in this chapter).

On the other hand, if you let go of the mouse button when the cursor appears as a little black arrow, you're saying "Put the page here in the regular flow of the document." You get this black arrow cursor when you drag close to a page, but not on top of it.

▼ ▼

Master-page area. Just below the blank-document icons and the Delete and Duplicate buttons is the master-page area. Here's where you create, name, and access master pages. To create a new master page, as I said earlier, you can drag a blank-page icon into this area or select a master-page icon that's already in this area and click the Duplicate button. Duplicating another master page is the fastest way to make one master page that's based on another.

A default name is assigned to a master page when it's created: the first is "A-Master A," the second is "B-Master B," and so on. You can assign a new name to a master page by clicking on its name in the Document Layout palette (in Windows, you must double-click on the name). You can type up to three characters before a hyphen, and then up to 60 more. If you don't type a hyphen, XPress assigns a prefix and types a hyphen for you. The name you assign is the name that appears on menus throughout the program. The prefix (the characters before the hyphen) shows up in the page icons on the Document Layout palette.

If you create more master pages than you can see at once, you can drag on the divider bar between the master-page area and the document-layout area (like the split-window feature in Microsoft Word).

If you have more than two master pages, XPress lets you move them around by dragging their icons up and down. However, be careful: Dropping one master page on top of another tells XPress to make the second master page exactly like the first, wiping out the master-page items on that page in the process. (Fortunately, XPress alerts you first.) Instead, wait until you see the cursor change to a small black arrow; that means "Move the master page here."

Document-layout area. The largest part of the Document Layout palette is the document-layout area. This area shows icons of the document's pages, numbered and positioned in the order of their actual appearance in the document (see "Manipulating Your Document" in Chapter 2, *QuarkXPress Basics*, for more on the document-layout area). Each page icon on the palette displays the master page it's based on. When you first open a new document, only one page is visible, and it is based on "A-Master A."

Remember that you can jump to a page in your document by double-clicking on its icon in this area.

Page-number area. In the lower-left corner of the Document Layout palette sits the page-number area. When no pages are selected on the Document Layout palette, this area displays the total number of pages in the document, but when you click on a page in the document-layout area, this area shows the page number (the page number of the currently selected page, not necessarily the one that you're looking at in the document window). This page number is the same as the number that sits under the page icon in the document-layout area of the palette. If you select more than one page on the palette, this area just shows you whatever the first page you selected was. Not very helpful, and pretty boring (see "Tip: Of Sections and Page Numbers," later in this chapter).

Applying Master Pages

There are two ways to apply the formatting of a master page to an existing document page (I sometimes refer to this as "tagging a document page with a master page").

▶ You can drag a master-page icon on top of a document-page icon; it's OK to release the mouse button as soon as the page icon is highlighted. The document page assumes the formatting of that master page.

▶ You can select the page or pages to which you want to apply the master page (remember that you can Shift-click to select a range of pages, or Command-click to select individual pages out of sequential order) and Option-click on the desired master page in the master-page area. This is the only way to apply a master page to a number of pages at the same time.

Unmodified master items (from the old master page) are deleted and replaced with the new master items. Items that you have modified may or may not be deleted (see "Applying Master Pages to Document Pages," earlier in this chapter). You can also apply one master page to another by the same method.

If you don't want any master page applied to a particular page (if you want to turn master pages off for one page), you can apply one of the blank-document icons to it instead. Just do the same thing: either drop the blank-page icon on top of a document page in the palette, or Option-click on the icon with the page(s) selected.

▼ ▼

Tip: Copying Master Pages. Have you ever wanted to copy a master page from one document to another? Kinda difficult, isn't it? Well, no, not really. Put both documents into Thumbnail viewing mode and drag a page from the first document into the second. The master page that was assigned to that document page comes along. Then you can delete the document page, and the master page stays in the second document.

▼ ▼

Making Pages

I've been discussing moving pages around and deleting them, but clearly it's been slightly premature, as I hadn't yet gotten to adding new pages to a document. I cover that procedure here.

There are two ways to add pages to your document: using the Insert Pages dialog box or using the Document Layout palette.

Insert Pages

The first way you can add pages to your document is by selecting Insert from the Pages menu. This brings up the Insert Pages dialog box (see Figure 4-18).

You can type the number of pages you want to add in the Insert field, and then select where you want those pages to be added. You have three choices: before a page, after a page, and at the end of the document. The first two require that you choose a page before or after which the page(s)

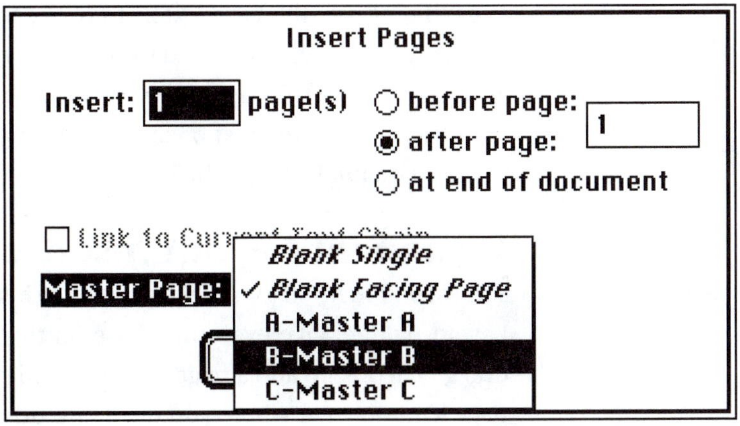

Figure 4-18
The Insert Pages
dialog box

should be added; the third requires no additional number, as it places the pages after the last page in the document.

Before you click OK, though, you need to think about two other things in this dialog box: the Link to Current Text Chain checkbox, and the Master Page choice. Let's look at these in reverse order.

Master Page choice. You can choose which master page you want your new pages to be based on by selecting one from the Master Page popup menu. Or, if you like, you can base new pages on blank single-sided or facing pages (of course, you can choose the latter only if you're working with a facing-page document).

Link to Current Text Chain. If a text box is selected on your page, and the master page on which you are basing your inserted pages has an automatic text-link box, then you can have the inserted pages automatically linked with the text box you have selected. This is a potentially confusing concept, so let's look at it carefully.

Let's say you have a text box on a page, and it's overflowing with text. Let's also say that your master page "C-FeatureOpener" has an automatic text-link box on it that is enabled (linked to the automatic text-link icon).

1. Select the text box on the document page.

2. Select Insert from the Page menu.

3. Add a page based on master page "C-FeatureOpener" at the end of the document.

If you turn on the Link to Current Text Chain option in the Insert Pages dialog box, then the text from your document-page text box automatically links to your inserted pages. If you do not select Link to Current Text Chain, then the pages are still added, but there is no link between your text box and the text boxes on those pages. You can, however, link them up manually using the Link tool.

Document-Layout Insertions

The second method for adding pages is to insert them via the Document Layout palette. Like everything else on this palette, you add pages by dragging icons. To add a page based on a master page, drag that master-page icon down to where you want it to be (before a page, after a page, at the end of a document, or as a page in a spread). If you don't want the page to be based on a master page, you can drag the single-sided or facing-page icon into place instead (as mentioned above, you can only drag a facing-page icon if you are working with a facing-page document).

If you want to add more than one page at a time, or want to add pages that are linked to the current text chain, then you must hold down the Option key while clicking and dragging the page icon into place. When you let go of the icon, QuarkXPress opens the Insert Pages dialog box. You can select the appropriate items as described above.

▼ ▼

Tip: Unintentional Multipage Spreads. There are problems just waiting to unfurl when you move pages around in spreads. If you insert the pages next to an existing page, you may be unknowingly creating a multipage spread instead of adding pages the way you want. The trick is to be careful about what icons you see when you're dropping the page. If you see a page icon, you'll get a spread; if you see a black arrow icon, you'll add pages to the document flow.

▼ ▼

Modifying Your Pages

Fortunately for desktop publishers, you can change the foundation of your document significantly more easily than a construction worker can change the foundation of a building. Not only can you modify your master pages in all sorts of ways, as we've seen, but you can modify the underlying page size, margins, column guides, and more. Let's look at each of these controls.

Changing Page Size

Even after you've clicked OK in the New Document dialog box and begun adding pages to a document, you can still change the page size in the Document Setup dialog box (choose Document Setup from the File menu; see Figure 4-19). Note that this dialog box bears a striking resemblance to a portion of the New Document dialog box. The rules are just the same (see "Page Size," at the beginning of this chapter).

Your only real limitation in modifying page size is the size of any objects you have already placed on the page. QuarkXPress won't let you

Figure 4-19

The Document
Setup dialog box

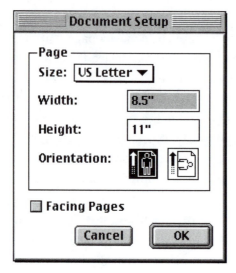

make a page so small that page elements would "fall off" the pasteboard (the size of the pasteboard surrounding each page is determined by the size of your document page). If this is a limiting factor, you may be able to work around the problem by adjusting the width of the pasteboard (see "Tip: Adjusting Your Pasteboard," in Chapter 2, *QuarkXPress Basics*). The program also prevents you from making the document so small that the margin guides bump into each other. If that's the problem, first change the margin guides (I'll tell you how to do that in just a moment).

Changing Facing Pages

You can use the Document Setup dialog box to change one other page feature: facing pages. If you originally made your document single-sided, you can change to a facing-page document by checking Facing Pages in the Document Setup dialog box. Facing-page documents can have both single-sided and facing-page master pages. When you turn on the Facing Pages option, the blank facing-page icon is enabled on the Document Layout palette; XPress does not, however, change your current master pages into facing-page master pages.

You cannot change a facing-page document to a single-sided document if you have any facing master pages. If you need to change a facing-page document to a single-sided document (there's rarely a reason to do so), first delete all the facing master pages (select them from the Document Layout palette and click the Delete button), then turn off the Facing Pages checkbox in the Document Setup dialog box.

Changing Margins and Guides

As I mentioned earlier, every page in your document has the same margins until you create multiple master pages, each with different margins. When you first open a master page, its margin guides are set to the values you specified in the New Document dialog box. You can change these margins by selecting Master Guides from the Page menu. Remember that the Master Guides menu item is only available when a master page is being displayed.

Migrants from PageMaker should be aware that QuarkXPress's column guides cannot be repositioned by dragging them with the mouse. Instead, you change the Column Guides settings in the Master Guides dialog box. QuarkXPress lets you have a different number of columns and varied gutter sizes for each master page (all the columns must be the same width, however). If you want to have no column guides on a page, type "1" in the Columns field.

▾ ▾

Automatic Page Insertion

Importing a long text document can be a harrowing experience when you're working with automatically linked text boxes. The text flows beyond page one and—it seems—into the netherworld. Where does the rest of the text go when the first text box is filled? QuarkXPress lets you control this with the Auto Page Insertion popup menu in the Document Preferences dialog box (Command-Y). You have four choices: End of Story, End of Section, End of Document, and Off. The default setting (the way it's set up if you don't change anything) is End of Story.

End of Story. With the End of Story option selected, QuarkXPress inserts new pages right after the page containing the last text box in a story, and they bear the master-page formatting of the page that held that box. For instance, if your story starts on page one and jumps to page five, any text overflow from the page-five text box causes pages to be inserted following page five, not page one.

End of Section. If you select End of Section, pages are inserted after the last page in a section (see "Sections and Page Numbering," below).

Additional pages bear the master-page formatting of the last page in that section. Thus, if your page-one story jumps to page five, and page five is part of a section that ends with page eight, new pages inserted because of text overflow appear right after page eight.

End of Document. This option causes pages to be inserted after the last page of the document, no matter how long it is and regardless of any sections you might have set up. Inserted pages bear the master-page formatting of the last page of the document.

If you have only one story and one section in a document, then these three settings all have the same effect.

Off. When Auto Page Insertion is set to Off, QuarkXPress never adds pages automatically. Instead, you must add pages manually (see "Making Pages," earlier in this chapter). I often set Auto Page Insertion to Off when I get tired of XPress adding lots of new pages for me (this is also the setting I typically recommend to new users, who get skittish when XPress adds pages automatically). Then I'll insert pages as I need or want them, linking them manually or using the Insert Pages dialog box.

Text Linking

Remember, the Automatic Page Insertion feature only works if the master page that's getting inserted has an automatic text-link box. That makes sense, because pages are always inserted based on text flowing through the automatic text chain. You cannot have *automatic page insertion* without an *automatic text link,* and you cannot have that without an *automatic text-link box.*

▼ ▼

Multipage Spreads

When the rest of the world thought that facing-page spreads were pretty nifty, Quark came along and added the capability to build three-page spreads. In fact, you can quickly and easily build a spread with four, five, or any number of pages, as long as the combined width of the pages doesn't exceed 48 inches.

Once again, this is a job for the Document Layout palette (this also works in Thumbnail mode). Spreads can be created in both facing-page and single-sided documents by dragging a page icon (either a new page or one already in the document) to the right side of a right page or to the left side of a left page. For this purpose, single-sided documents are considered to be made entirely of right pages, but there aren't many times that you'd be doing this with a single-sided document. The pasteboard (represented by the dark-gray area of the palette) automatically expands to accommodate the pages. Figure 4-20 shows an example of creating a three-page spread in a facing-page document.

Note that when you drag a page over to create a multipage spread, you shouldn't let go of the mouse button if you see the little black arrow icon. That'll reshuffle the file rather than build a spread. Instead, you should only let go when you see a dark page icon in the place where you want the spread page to be.

Figure 4-20
Making a three-
page spread

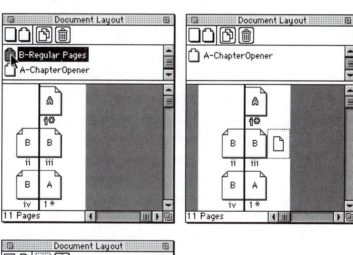

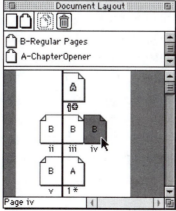

▾ ▾

Sections and Page Numbering

Earlier in this chapter I discussed how to apply automatic page numbering to your document's master pages. Here I talk about how to customize those page numbers and create multiple sections within a single document.

Ordinarily, a QuarkXPress document has one section. Page numbers start with the Arabic numeral "1" and go up consecutively, page by page. (I can't figure out why they're called Arabic numerals, because the numbers in Arabic are totally different; nonetheless, that's what normal, plain ol' numbers are called.) However, by using the Section feature, you can change the starting page number, the page-number style, and you can add multiple sections that all have their own page-numbering style.

Changing Your Starting Page Number

Whenever you make a new section in your document, you're starting a new page-numbering scheme; in fact, that's the only good reason for using sections.

For instance, let's say you're producing a book, and each chapter is saved in a separate QuarkXPress file. If the first chapter ends on page 32, you can tell QuarkXPress to start the page numbers in Chapter 2 at page 33, and so on. To do this, go to the first page of the document (the page on which you want to change the numbering), and select Section from the Page menu. Then turn on the Section Start checkbox. Type the starting page number for your document, and click OK (see Figure 4-21).

The first page of a new section always has an asterisk after its name. This doesn't print out. It's just a sign that QuarkXPress gives you on screen, saying that this is a section that's beginning.

You can have as many sections in a document as you want, each starting with a different page number. If you make the fifth page in your document a new section and set it to start on page 47, then your document's page numbering goes like this: "1, 2, 3, 4, 47, 48, 49 . . . ."

▾ ▾

Tip: Of Sections and Page Numbers. There are two hidden features on the Document Layout palette. First, if you click in the page-number area in the lower-left corner of the palette, QuarkXPress brings up the Section dialog box. This only works when you have a page selected (highlighted) on the Document Layout palette (the highlighted page doesn't have to be the same one that's visible in the document window).

Also, if you Option-click on a page icon in the document-layout area of the palette, the page-number area displays the page's absolute number (for example, the 34th page in the document). This is extremely helpful when your pages are numbered in roman numerals or when you're using multiple sections.

▼ ▼

Figure 4-21

Setting up a
new section

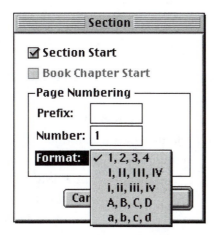

Changing the Page-Numbering Style

QuarkXPress lets you choose from five formats for numbering pages in the Section dialog box.

► Arabic numerals (1, 2, 3, 4, etc.)

► Uppercase Roman numerals (I, II, III, IV, etc.)

► Lowercase Roman numerals (i, ii, iii, iv, etc.)

► Capital letters (A, B, C, D, etc.)

► Lowercase letters (a, b, c, d, etc.)

To pick one of these numbering styles for a section, go to the first page in the section, select Section using one of the methods described above, and choose a numbering format from the Format popup menu.

Prefixes

Automatic page numbers can contain more than just a number in the five formats listed above. You can also add a prefix of up to four characters to the page number. For example, you may want the page numbers in a book appendix to read "A-1," "A-2," and so on. The "A-" is a prefix to the Arabic numerals. You can type this kind of prefix in the Prefix field of the Section dialog box. This prefix not only appears on the Document Layout palette and in the automatic page numbers, but it even shows up at the top of the page when you print with registration marks (see Chapter 13, *Printing*).

▼ ▼

Automatic "Continued . . ." Pagination

In magazines and newspapers, where stories can jump from page six to 96, it is often helpful to have a "Continued on Page X" message at the bottom of the column from which text is jumping, and a "Continued from Page X" message at the top of the column to which it jumps. These are sometimes called "jump lines." QuarkXPress can't make these lines for you, but it can revise the page numbers in them automatically. This is useful because you may change links, or insert or delete new pages, or move the text boxes from one page to another, and each of these will require a change in the jump line's page numbers. If you use XPress's automatic page numbers, you won't have to go through every page and manually update the numbers.

To Create a "Continued on . . ." Message

It's easy to create these jump lines (see Figure 4-22) using the Previous Box Page Number and the Next Box Page Number characters: Command-2 and Command-4. If you press Command-4 in a text box, XPress automatically replaces it with the page number of whatever page the current story links to. For instance, let's say the story on page one links to a text box on page nine. If you press Command-4 somewhere in the story on page one, XPress replaces it with the number "9" (the page to which the story links). Similarly, if you press Command-2 somewhere in the story on page nine, QuarkXPress replaces it with the number "1" (the page from which the story links).

Figure 4-22

Jump lines

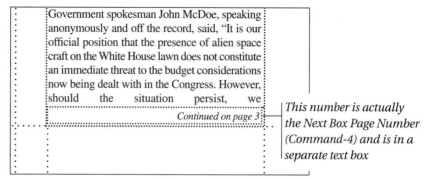

Government spokesman John McDoe, speaking anonymously and off the record, said, "It is our official position that the presence of alien space craft on the White House lawn does not constitute an immediate threat to the budget considerations now being dealt with in the Congress. However, should the situation persist, we

Continued on page 3

This number is actually the Next Box Page Number (Command-4) and is in a separate text box

This is pretty cool, but it's not very useful because it's nearly impossible to include a "continued on page . . ." jump line in the middle of your story. It just doesn't work. So the folks at Quark built a hidden feature into these automatic page numbers: if either the Command-2 or the Command-4 character is in a text box that doesn't link to anything *and* if that text box is sitting on top of a text box that does link to something, then XPress uses the links in the lower text box to determine what numbers to use for the characters.

That means you can create a new little text box and type in it "Continued on page . . . " and then press Command-4. If this text box is not on top of any other text boxes, the Command-4 character is replaced with "<None>". However, in the example above, as soon as you drag it on top of the text box on page one, the number updates to show the number "9," because that's what the underlying story is linked to.

If your text links change, pages get shuffled or renumbered, or an act of god is invoked, QuarkXPress always knows where your text is going to or coming from and it updates the Next Box Page Number and Previous Box Page Number characters.

Nonetheless, these jump lines can sometimes get confused. When QuarkXPress sees one of these jump lines, it looks at any text box that is behind the jump line. If there is more than one text box behind the jump-line text box, QuarkXPress chooses the one that is "closest" to it: the text box that is on the next layer down.

To create a "Continued from . . ." message. You can create a "Continued from . . ." jump line by following the same procedures for creating a "Continued on . . ." jump line, but you can place the new text box at the top of the column. When you come to the page number, press

Command-2 for the Previous Box Page Number character, which shows the page number of the previous text box in the chain. This number is also automatically updated as necessary.

Your messages don't have to read "Continued on . . ." and "Continued from . . . ." You can type any words you want—for instance, "Started on page <None>" or even "If you really care about finishing this story, you'll have to flip past the bulk of this magazine and go all the way to page "<None>," where you'll find it buried among the facial cream ads." What matters is that you type the relevant placeholder character somewhere in your message text box.

Foundations

Like a construction worker on the job, you are now ready to build your pages with the understanding and confidence that you've got a strong infrastructure to hold the document up. First you can use the tools discussed in Chapter 3, *Tools of the Trade*, to build text and picture boxes on your master pages and document pages. And next you can fill those boxes with text and pictures; that's where I'm headed now.

5

WORD PROCESSING

When you think of Quark-XPress, you think of typography. But before you can set type in QuarkXPress, you somehow have to get the words onto your page. In the early days of desktop publishing, you'd usually write your stories in a word-processing program, and then import the files into a page-layout program. However, from its inception, QuarkXPress has been a capable word processor in its own right. Style sheets, find and change, a spelling checker, and even drag-and-drop text editing are all elements that have made this program a competent—though not exceptional—word processor.

However, just because you can use XPress as a word processor doesn't mean that you should. In complex documents and on many lower-end computers, QuarkXPress can become so slow that a skilled typist can get ahead of it. In this chapter, I'll examine the strengths and weaknesses of writing and editing in QuarkXPress, including its powerful Find/Change feature and its spelling checker (I'll hold off on style sheets until Chapter 7, *Copy Flow*). I'll even throw in some fun tips for getting the most out of all these features.

▼ ▼

Entering and Editing Text

The most basic aspect of entering text into a QuarkXPress document is making sure that what you type shows up where you want it. QuarkXPress novices often become flustered when they open a document and start typing, only to find that nothing is happening. That's because to enter text, you must use the Content tool, and you must have selected a text box.

Selecting and Navigating

As I mentioned in the Preface, I assume that you're already familiar with the basic mouse and editing techniques used by almost every Macintosh and Windows application. However, QuarkXPress stretches beyond that interface, adding many features to the standard Macintosh and Windows methods of moving the insertion point and selecting text. One of the many things I like about QuarkXPress is that it provides more than one way to do the same thing; you can use either the mouse or the keyboard to select and to navigate.

Using the mouse. As with any program, you can select a range of text by dragging the pointer through it, or you can select a word by double-clicking on it. But QuarkXPress also has additional multiple-click selections (see Table 5-1). If you triple-click, you select a line of text. Quadruple-clicking selects a paragraph, and quintuple-clicking selects all the text in the active box's text chain. (I don't know about you, but clicking five times in succession is difficult for me; instead, I just press Command-A, which does the same thing.)

If you hold down the Shift key and click anywhere in your text chain, all the text from the previous location of the insertion point to the location of your click is selected.

If you select a range of text in a text box, then deselect the box and edit in other boxes, QuarkXPress remembers the selection. When you reselect that text box, the same text is still selected in it (this works until you close the document or quit XPress).

▼ ▼

Tip: Extend by Word. If you continue to press down on the mouse button after your final click, you can extend your selection by dragging. If

Table 5-1

Effects of
multiple clicks

TO SELECT	CLICK
A word and contiguous punctuation	Twice
A line	Three times
A paragraph	Four times
An entire story	Five times

you've selected a word by double-clicking, for instance, you can drag to select more text, word by word. And if you've selected a paragraph with four clicks, you can similarly drag to increase your selection, paragraph by paragraph.

▼ ▼

Using the keyboard. You can use the keyboard to duplicate most of the selections you can make with the mouse. You can also do many things with the keyboard that are not possible with the mouse alone (see Table 5-2). For instance, you can quickly jump to the beginning of a line just by pressing Command-Option-Left Arrow.

Holding down the Shift key in combination with any of the keyboard movement commands selects all text between the insertion point's original location and the location to which the key combination sends it. In the example above, you could select all the text from the cursor point to the beginning of the line just by adding Shift to the keystroke.

▼ ▼

Tip: The Lazy Man's Way to Follow a Text Chain. You know that QuarkXPress has keystrokes that take you to the next or previous page in

Table 5-2

Keyboard text editing

TO MOVE TO THE . . .	PRESS . . .
Previous character	Left Arrow
Next character	Right Arrow
Previous line	Up Arrow
Next line	Down Arrow
Previous word	Command-Left Arrow
Next word	Command-Right Arrow
Start of line	Command-Option-Left Arrow
End of line	Command-Option-Right Arrow
Start of story	Command-Option-Up Arrow
End of story	Command-Option-Down Arrow

your document, but what about a shortcut to go to the next page in a story? (If your story jumps to another page of your document, as often happens in magazines and newspapers, this is important.) All you have to do is position the insertion point at the beginning or end of the story's text box on the current page. If you're at the beginning of the text box, press the Left or Up Arrow key to move the insertion point out of the current box to the previous box in the chain. If you're at the end of the box, similarly press the Right or Down Arrow key to jump the insertion point to the next box in the text chain.

As soon as you move the insertion point out of the current box, QuarkXPress follows it, scrolling automatically to the page containing the text box to which you've moved the insertion point. If possible, QuarkXPress even centers the box nicely in the document window.

▼ ▼

Tip: Navigating Out of the Box. I find the ability to quickly jump to the beginning or end of a story by pressing Command-Option-Up Arrow or Command-Option-Down Arrow especially handy. It can save you a lot of scrolling if you forget the exact page on which a story starts or finishes. Also, I use it all the time to quickly select all the text from the cursor to the beginning or end of the story by adding the Shift key. For instance, let's say you've got too much text in a text box and it overflows, producing an overset mark. You know that the overset text isn't important, so you want to delete it or move it to some other text box. You could use the text-linking tools, but it's sometimes faster to place the cursor after the last word in the text box and press Command-Option-Shift-Down Arrow. This selects the overset text (even though you can't see it). Now you can delete it or cut it.

▼ ▼

Deleting Text

There are a number of ways to delete text in QuarkXPress (see Table 5-3). You can, of course, use the Delete key to delete text to the left of the insertion point, one character at a time, or to remove a text selection. QuarkXPress also lets you delete the character to the right of the insertion point by holding down the Shift key while pressing Delete. Similarly, Command-Delete gets rid of the entire word to the left of the insertion point, and Command-Shift-Delete removes the word to the right of the insertion point.

Table 5-3

Keyboard deletions

TO DELETE . . .	PRESS . . .
Previous character	Delete
Next character	Shift-Delete or Del key (Extended keyboard)
Previous word	Command-Delete
Next word	Command-Shift-Delete
Any select text	Delete

Drag-and-Drop Text

Drag-and-drop text editing is an easy way of copying or moving text from one location to another in a story, but it can cause trouble if you don't know how it works. To use drag-and-drop text editing, select some text, then drag the selection to another location in the text chain. As you move the mouse, you'll see an insertion point move along with it. When the insertion point reaches the place where you want the selected text to go, release the mouse button, and *presto!* Your text is cut from its original location and placed at the insertion point.

If you try this right now on your copy of XPress, it probably won't work because Drag and Drop is an option in the Application Preferences dialog box (Command-Option-Shift-Y, then switch to the Interactive tab), and by default it is turned off. If you like this feature, go ahead and turn it on.

You can also copy a selection, instead of just moving it, by holding down the Shift key as you drag. Note that any text you drag-move or drag-copy also gets placed on the Clipboard (replacing whatever was there). Also, at least for now, you can't drag-copy text between unlinked text boxes, or between documents—you can do it only within continuous text chains.

I rarely turn this feature on, not because I don't like it, but because I too often mess up my text when it's on by accidentally dragging a word or sentence when I don't mean to. This is the sort of feature that I'll turn on only when I need to use it; then I'll turn it off again.

▼ ▼

Tip: Speeding Up Text Entry. Unless there's a really good reason to do it, I don't recommend typing a lot of text directly into a text box in XPress. Obviously, XPress doesn't have important word-processing features like an outliner, renumbering, and so on. But perhaps the most important reason to consider using a word processor is speed. If you're working on an older (slower) computer, writing and editing text in QuarkXPress can seem incredibly slow. Entering text becomes so sluggish that the program can't keep up with even a moderately fast typist.

This happens because XPress has to do much more work than a typical word processor does whenever it must reflow text. If you're working on a long story that goes through several pages of linked boxes, and the text has to flow through and around other page elements, this complexity also adds to the computations that QuarkXPress must perform whenever you change or add text. Plus, XPress may have to compute kerning and other typographic styling, which slows it down further.

Nonetheless, if you need to type in XPress, here are a few things you can do to speed the process. (Note that if you're working on a fast computer and not experiencing slow-downs, you can just go ahead and ignore these suggestions.)

▶ **DUMMY TEXT BOXES.** Try typing or editing in a "dummy" text box in the pasteboard area of the page where you want to enter or change text. This is particularly helpful when the text box on the page is nonrectangular or the text has a complicated wrap around other objects. By typing in a plain ol' rectangular text box on the pasteboard, XPress doesn't have to work hard calculating how the text should wrap.

▶ **HYPHENATION.** Turning off Auto Hyphenation in each of your H&J sets can speed up XPress a little bit (see Chapter 6, *Type and Typography*). Don't forget to turn hyphenation back on when you're ready to proof or print your document.

▶ **JUSTIFICATION.** Don't set the horizontal alignment to Justified while you're typing. XPress has to do a lot of work to figure out how to justify the text each time you type a letter.

▶ **KERNING.** You might consider turning off automatic kerning in your document in the Document Preferences dialog box (under the Edit menu). This won't help a lot, but sometimes every little bit counts.

▼ ▼

Importing Text

More often than not, text is prepared in a word processor, then import-ed into a QuarkXPress document for final layout. The best way to get text into a text box in XPress is to import it using the Get Text command on the File menu. In order to access this command, you must have both a text box and the Content tool selected.

1. Position the insertion point where you want the text to be brought into the text box.

2. Choose Get Text from the File menu (Command-E).

3. When the Get Text dialog box appears, select one of the files list-ed. It displays all files that are in word-processing formats that QuarkXPress can import (see the next section, "What Filters Are, and How to Use Them").

4. Press Return, or click the Open button.

While you're in the Get Text dialog box, you have two additional options for importing the file: Convert Quotes and Include Style Sheets.

▶ **CONVERT QUOTES.** If you'd like QuarkXPress to automatically convert straight double and single quotes (" and ') to curly dou-ble and single quotes (" " and ' '), and double hyphens (--) to true em dashes (—), check Convert Quotes in the Get Text dialog box. I almost always leave this option turned on.

▶ **INCLUDE STYLE SHEETS.** I almost always check the Include Style Sheets box so that XPress will include the file's style sheets (if there are any). Even if there aren't any style sheets specified in the word processing document, it's usually better to leave this option turned on, or else you may accidentally apply No Style to the text (see Chapter 7, *Copy Flow*, for more on style sheets and XPress Tags, and how this checkbox affects them both).

What Filters Are, and How to Use Them

QuarkXPress uses XTensions called filters to convert text to and from word-processing formats. Because they're XTensions, you can activate or deactivate them using the XTension Manager (see "XTensions" in Chapter 2, *QuarkXPress Basics*). There are also third-party word processing filters available; for instance, XPress for Macintosh cannot read RTF files (XPress for Windows can), but you can buy an XTension from a developer that gives you this functionality.

There are two good reasons for filters to be in the form of XTensions (rather than built into the program). First, Quark can update the filters quickly and easily and release new versions on the Internet. Second, if you only use one or two of the file formats, you can deactivate the other filters, making XPress load faster and require less RAM.

Table 5-4 lists the various file formats that XPress can read and write on each computer platform. In Chapter 7, *Copy Flow*, I explain why you should be careful about what word processor you can use, and why I usually use Microsoft Word.

Finding and Changing

QuarkXPress has a powerful Find/Change feature that is too often overlooked and under-used. You can use this feature to look for and change either text or formatting (or both at the same time), and it can do this within a story or throughout a document.

Those of you who are familiar with earlier versions of XPress will notice two significant changes to Find/Change. First, it is now a palette rather than a dialog box, so it always floats above your document (in earlier versions, it would often get lost behind other windows). Second, you can now search for and replace character and paragraph style sheets (I discuss style sheets at length in Chapter 7, *Copy Flow*).

Where QuarkXPress Looks

When it searches with the Find/Change feature, QuarkXPress can check either the entire text chain connected to the active text box, or it can look for and change text throughout an entire document. If you have a text box selected, QuarkXPress searches through the story *from the location of the insertion point* to the end of the story (note that the button in the palette is called Find Next; that means "the next one after the cursor position").

Table 5-4

Import/Export word
processing filters

WORD PROCESSING FILTERS FOR QUARKXPRESS 4.0 MACINTOSH	
MacWrite Filter, version 1.51	All versions of MacWrite files
MacWrite Pro Import, version 1.01	MacWrite Pro 1.0 – 1.5
MS Word Filter, version 3.2	MS Word files created in MS Word 3.x – 6.x for the Macintosh and MS Word 6.0 – 7.0 for Windows*
MS Works Filter, version 1.51	
Word Perfect Filter, version 1.0	Import WordPerfect 3.0 and 3.1 for Macintosh and WordPerfect 6.x for Windows.** Export files to Word-Perfect 6.x for Windows (which can be read by WordPerfect 3.1 for Mac)
Write Now 3.1 Import, version 1.0	Write Now version 3.1 and earlier

The Microsoft OLE extensions must be installed in your system folder. If the files are coming from Word for Windows, you should change the file type and creator codes with FileBuddy or the PC-Mac MS Word utility (available from Quark's Web site).

**To import WordPerfect documents from Microsoft Windows, you must first convert them with the "PC->Mac WP convert" utility (available from Quark's Web site).*

WORD PROCESSING FILTERS FOR QUARKXPRESS 4.0 WINDOWS
Rich Text (RTF)
MS Word 2.0
MS Word 6.0
MS Write
Word Perfect 3.x
Word Perfect 5.x
Word Perfect 6.x

There are two ways to search an entire story from the very beginning. First, you can put the insertion point at the very beginning of the story (press Command-Option-Up Arrow). Better yet, you can leave the insertion point where it is in the story, and hold down the Option key to turn the Find Next button into the Find First button. (The fastest way to find the first instance of a word is to press Command-F to open or activate the Find/Change palette, type the word to be found, then press Option-Return or Option-Enter.)

If you want QuarkXPress to check all the text in the document rather than just a single story, you must check the Document box in the Find/Change palette. When this option is turned on, XPress searches the top-most text box on a page first (in terms of layer order, not position on the page), which can be confusing if you're not sure which text boxes are "on top" of other text boxes.

Note that turning on the Document option only searches the document pages; if you want to search the master pages, too, you have to do a separate search. If you're currently displaying a document's master pages, the Document checkbox is labeled Masters, and you can use it to search all the document's master pages at once.

Specifying Text

Generally, people want to search and replace text regardless of the text's formatting attributes. To do this, you can use the Find/Change palette as it first appears when you select the Find/Change command from the Edit menu (or press Command-F; see Figure 5-1). Enter the text you want QuarkXPress to find in the Find What field, then enter the replacement text in the Change To field.

Special characters. It's easy enough to search for normal words or phrases, but what about invisible characters? It turns out that you can enter certain special characters in the Find What and Change To fields with the aid of the Command key. For example, if you want to search for all the new-paragraph characters in a document (what you get when you press Return at the end of a paragraph), you select the Find What field and press Command-Return. This appears in the field as "\p". You could have just typed "\p", but who needs to clutter up their brain with weird codes like that?

Table 5-5 shows characters you can enter in these fields, how to type them, and how they appear in the fields. Of course, because all these special characters use the backslash, to search for the backslash character itself in the Find What or Change To fields you need to type the backslash twice, or press Command-\.

Wildcards. You can use the wildcard character (\?) to represent any other character. This is useful if you're looking for a word you may have spelled different ways, such as "gray" and "grey." Instead of running two search operations to find all occurrences of this word, you could simply type "gr\?y" in the Find What field. You can get the wildcard character by pressing either Command-? or by typing a backslash followed by a question mark.

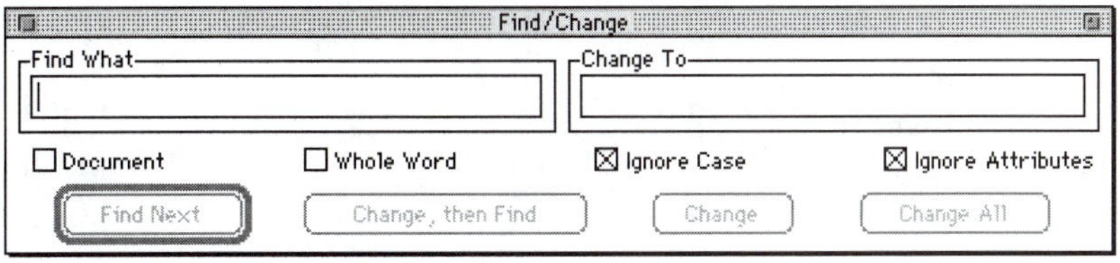

Figure 5-1
The Find/Change palette

Note that the wildcard character can only be used in the Find What field. QuarkXPress doesn't let you use it in the Change To field because the program's not sophisticated enough to do that kind of pattern-replacing.

Whole Word. Next to the Document checkbox you'll find another one labeled Whole Word. Checking this box means that QuarkXPress only finds occurrences of the Find What text if it's a whole word. That means that the text can't be bounded by other text or numerals. So a Whole Word search for "ten" finds the word "ten" when it's bounded by spaces, punctuation, or special characters such as new-line or new-paragraph marks. It would *not* find "often," "tenuous," or "contentious." If you don't have Whole Word selected, QuarkXPress will find every occurrence of the text you entered, even if it's embedded in other text.

Ignore Case. If Ignore Case is turned on, QuarkXPress finds all occurrences of the text in the Find What field, regardless of whether the capitalization of the text found in the document exactly matches what you typed into the Find What field. For example, if you entered "Help", QuarkXPress would find "Help", "HELP", and "help".

How QuarkXPress determines the case of characters it's replacing when Ignore Case is turned on depends on the capitalization of the text it finds in the document.

▶ If the found text begins with an initial capital, or is in all uppercase- or lowercase letters, QuarkXPress follows suit and similarly capitalizes the replacement text, no matter how you've capitalized it in the Change To field.

▶ If the found text doesn't match the above three cases, QuarkXPress capitalizes the replacement text exactly as you entered it in the Change To field.

Table 5-5

Typing special
characters in
the Find/Change palette

TO ENTER THIS CHARACTER . . .	PRESS . . .	OR TYPE . . .
Tab	Command-Tab	\t
New paragraph	Command-Return	\p
New line	Command-Shift-Return	\n
New column	Command-Enter	\c
New box	Command-Shift-Enter	\b
Previous box page number	Command-2	\2
Current box page number	Command-3	\3
Next box page number	Command-4	\4
Wildcard (single character)	Command-?	\?
Backslash	Command-\	\\
Punctuation space		\.
Flex space		\f

For example, let's say you are searching for all examples of "QuarkXPress" and want to make sure the internal capital letters are proper. If you leave Ignore Case turned on, and the program finds "quarkxpress", it will not capitalize the proper characters. Turn off Ignore Case, and the feature replaces "quarkxpress" with "QuarkXPress", properly capitalized as you entered it.

▼ ▼

Tip: Searching for the Unsearchable. I mentioned earlier that you can look for invisible characters by typing certain codes. However, there are some characters XPress doesn't let you search for. For instance, you can't enter the indent here, the nonbreaking space, or the right-margin tab (Option-Tab) characters here.

If you have some heavy-duty searching and replacing to do with any of these characters, you can always export your story in XPress Tags format and search for the characters there. I cover XPress Tags more in Chapter 7, *Copy Flow*, including how to export and import this format. Once you know these basics, you can find the codes for these special characters in Appendix E, *XPress Tags*.

▼ ▼

Tip: Close the Find/Change Palette. You know you can open the Find/Change palette by pressing Command-F. Did you know you can also close it in version 4 by pressing Command-Option-F?

▼ ▼

Specifying Attributes

As I said earlier, you can search for more than just text in QuarkXPress. You can search for text-formatting attributes (font, size, type style), too. If you want to search for formatting, uncheck the Ignore Attributes box in the Find/Change palette. When you turn this option off, the palette expands (see Figure 5-2). In addition to text fields under the Find What and Change To headings, there are areas on each side of the palette for specifying font, size, and type style. Note that QuarkXPress version 4 now lets you find or change style sheets (this is one of my favorite new features in XPress).

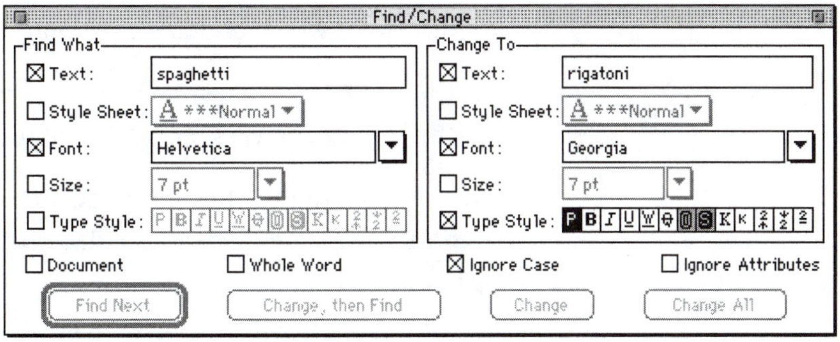

Figure 5-2

The Find/Change palette with Ignore Attributes turned off

What to Find, What to Change

When Ignore Attributes is turned off (that is, when you're searching for text formatting as well as text), each side of the Find/Change palette contains five options for searching or replacing: Text, Style Sheet, Font, Size, and Type Style. The left side of the palette shows all the attributes that should be searched for; the right side is what the text should be changed to. The first four areas on each side of the palette—Text, Style Sheet, Font, and Size—are simple to use; the fifth is only a little more complicated (see "Type Styles," below). If you want to specify something, make sure the area's checkbox is turned on. Then simply enter the text or point size in the appropriate fields, and/or select the font or style sheet from the appropriate popup menus.

On the left (Find What) side, the popup menus list only the fonts and style sheets actually used in the current document; on the right (Change To) side, they list all the fonts and style sheets currently available.

There doesn't need to be a parallel between what you specify on the Find What side and on the Change To side. In fact, such asymmetrical searches offer some of the most intriguing possibilities for finding and changing in QuarkXPress.

You could easily, for example, find all occurrences of a company name and apply a character style sheet to them.

1. Type the company name into the Text field on the Find What side.

2. Uncheck the boxes for Style Sheet, Font, Size, and Type Style on the left side of the palette. That tells the program to pay no attention to these attributes.

3. Uncheck all the boxes on the right side of the palette except for Style Sheet. That tells QuarkXPress not to change any of these attributes when it finds the company name.

4. Check the Style Sheet box on the Replace With side, and choose the character style sheet you want to apply.

This procedure searches for all occurrences of the text, no matter what formatting is applied, and replaces them with the same text but using a specific character style sheet (I cover text formatting in Chapter 6, *Type and Typography*, and style sheets in Chapter 7, *Copy Flow*).

Type Styles

Specifying type styles—bold, italic, and so on—in the Find/Change palette is a bit more complicated than what I described above; however, it's really not that bad once you get used to it. Once you turn on the Type Style option, the various formatting choices can be either on, off, or grayed out. Clicking an unchecked box makes it gray; clicking again turns it on; clicking a third time turns it off again (see Figure 5-3).

What do these various states mean? On the left side (the Find What side), a checked box means that you want QuarkXPress to find text set *only* in that style. An unchecked box means you *don't* want it to find text in that style. A gray box means that it doesn't matter if the text is formatted with that style or not; you want QuarkXPress to find text either way (see Table 5-6). Another way to look at it is that blank means "no," black means "yes," and gray means "I don't care."

The various checkboxes mean similar things on the right (Change To) side of the palette. Checking a style box means you want QuarkXPress to apply that style when it changes text that it finds. An unchecked box means you *don't* want that style to be present in the changed text (if it's

Figure 5-3
Specifying type styles in
the Find/Change palette

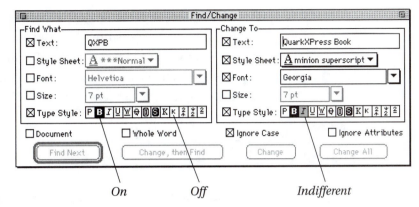

Table 5-6
Style controls in the
Find/Change palette

Box is . . .	Means . . .
White or Up	Find or replace text without this attribute
Black or Down	Find or replace text with this attribute
Grayed	Find it either way, but leave it alone when replacing

there, QuarkXPress removes it). Leaving the box gray means that QuarkXPress doesn't do anything to that style. If it's already there, it stays there; if it's not, the program doesn't apply it.

Of course, a word can't simultaneously have both the Underline and Word Underline styles. So checking one unchecks the other, and graying one automatically makes the other gray as well. Small Caps/All Caps and Superscript/Subscript work together similarly.

▼ ▼

Tip: Set Up Find/Change by Example. You can shave a few steps off your Find/Change process by placing the cursor in some text that's formatted the same as what you're looking for. If you place the cursor in a word that is in 23-point Times and then open the Find/Change palette (press Command-F), both the font and size are automatically chosen on the Find What side of the palette (you may still have to check the boxes next to them, though). This won't save a lot of time, but sometimes every little bit helps.

▼ ▼

Going to It

Now that you know how to specify what you want to find, what you want to change, and how to tell QuarkXPress where to search, you can use the four buttons at the bottom of the palette to begin finding and changing.

When you first specify your Find/Change criteria, all buttons except Find Next are grayed out (see Figure 5-4). Hold down the Option key and click Find First, and QuarkXPress searches for the first occurrence of text matching your specifications in the current story or document. It displays this text in the document window and selects it.

Figure 5-4

The Find/Change control buttons

This changes to Find First when you hold down the Option key

You then have a choice. Clicking Find Next again takes you to the next occurrence of text meeting your specifications, without changing the currently selected text. Clicking Change, Then Find changes the selection as specified on the Change To side of the palette. QuarkXPress then looks for the next occurrence of matching text. The Change button changes the selected text and leaves it selected, and the Change All button tells XPress to search for and automatically change all occurrences in the story or document. After QuarkXPress changes all occurrences, a dialog box comes up listing the number of changes made.

▼ ▼

Tip: Seeing Text as It Is Found. I find that after searching for a word, it is too often sitting right underneath the palette—so you can't see it. Very frustrating. Instead, if you're going to be doing a lot of searching and replacing, I suggest you move the palette to the top or bottom of your screen and resize your document window so that you can see both the palette and the document window at the same time.

If you are one of the unlucky sods who has a small-screen Macintosh, then try reducing the size of the palette by clicking the Zoom button in the box's upper-right corner (this is Mac-only, unfortunately). The reduced view shows only the buttons you need to navigate and change what you've specified (see Figure 5-5). Clicking the Zoom button again takes you back to the larger palette.

▼ ▼

Spelling Checker

Of course, once you've got your text written or imported into QuarkXPress, you wouldn't want to print it without first running it

Figure 5-5

Shrinking the
Find/Change palette

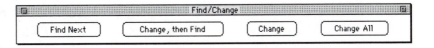

through XPress's spelling checker.   QuarkXPress comes with a 120,000-word dictionary (that's the file called XPress Dictionary), and you can create your own auxiliary dictionaries as well. The Check Spelling command is on the Utilities menu, and it allows you to check a selected word, a story, or an entire document (see Figure 5-6).

Figure 5-6

The Check
Spelling submenu

Checking a Word

If you only want to check one word, you can select it (or you can just put the cursor anywhere within the word) and choose Word from the Check Spelling submenu (or press Command-L on the Macintosh; Control-W on Windows). The Check Word dialog box appears (see Figure 5-7), listing all the words in the XPress Dictionary (as well as in the open auxiliary dictionary, if there is one) that resemble the word you selected.

   If the suspect word—the word you're checking is always called the *suspect* word, even if it's correctly spelled—appears in a dictionary, it shows up in the scrolling list and is selected automatically (this is different than some spelling checkers that actually tell you that the word is spelled right). This means, as far as QuarkXPress is concerned, that the

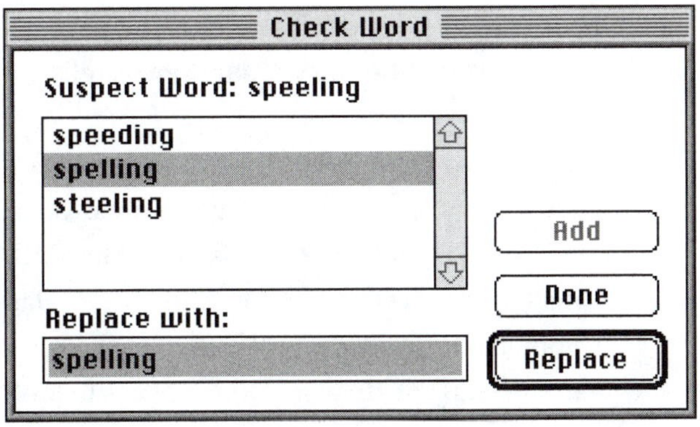

Figure 5-7

Checking a word

Check Word
Suspect Word: speeling

speeding
spelling
steeling

Add

Done

Replace with:

spelling

Replace

word is spelled correctly; you can click the Done button to continue (on the Mac, press Command-period; in Windows, press Escape).

If the suspect word doesn't appear in an active dictionary, you can scroll through the list of words and select a replacement. Click on the proper word in the list, then click the Replace button (or press Return or Enter). The new spelling replaces the word in your story, and the Check Word box closes.

If QuarkXPress can't find any words that approximate the suspect word, it displays the message, "No similar words found." Click the Done button to close the Check Word dialog box.

Checking a Story

Typically, you're more likely to check a whole story rather than a single word. To do this, use the Content tool to select any text box that holds part of the story. Then select Story from the Check Spelling hierarchical menu (or press Command-Option-L on the Macintosh; Control-Alt-W on Windows). The Word Count dialog box appears, showing running totals as QuarkXPress scans the story, counting the total number of words, the total number of unique words (each word counted once, no matter how many times it occurs), and the number of suspect words—ones that QuarkXPress can't find in its dictionary, or in the open auxiliary dictionary, if there is one (see Figure 5-8).

When QuarkXPress is finished counting, click the OK button. If the program didn't find any suspect words, then this just returns you to your document. On the other hand, if it did catch one or more words, then the button brings up the Check Document dialog box. This dialog box displays suspect words one at a time, in the order in which they occur in the story. As each appears in the dialog box, QuarkXPress scrolls the document window to the suspect word, and highlights it so you can see it in the context in which it's used on the page. If a suspect word is used more than once in the story, QuarkXPress tells you how many times.

Changing the spelling. When you check the spelling of a whole story rather than just a word, QuarkXPress doesn't automatically show you possible replacement words. If you know the correct spelling for a suspect word, you can enter it in the Replace With field, and click the Replace button to have the new spelling replace the one in your document. Or if you do want QuarkXPress to look for possible spellings in the

Figure 5-8
Checking the
spelling of a document

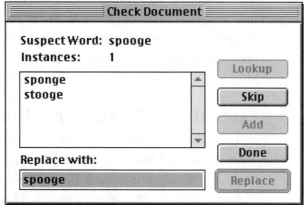

available dictionaries, you can click the Lookup button (or press Command-L). QuarkXPress displays a list of possible alternatives in the scrolling text field. You can select an alternate spelling by clicking on it, then clicking the Replace button (or pressing Enter or Return). The new spelling replaces the suspect word in your document, and QuarkXPress moves on to the next suspect word in the story. If there are no more suspect words, the Check Document dialog box closes.

Note that if QuarkXPress finds more than one occurrence of a suspect word, it will replace every occurrence of the word with the new spelling you choose.

Skipping and keeping. To go to the next suspect word without changing the spelling of the current one, click the Skip button (Command-S, which usually means Save, but not here). To add the current suspect word to an auxiliary dictionary, click the Keep button (Command-K, which usually means Delete, but not in this dialog box). This button is only active when an auxiliary dictionary is open (see "Auxiliary Dictionaries," below).

▼ ▼

Tip: One-Letter Misspellings. I wonder how many years I used XPress's spelling checker before I finally figured out that it ignores one-letter words. That means that if you're typing quickly and press the wrong key—for instance, if you type "tie s yellow ribbon" rather than "tie a yellow ribbon"—XPress won't catch the word as misspelled. QuarkXPress also won't catch most abbreviations. If you type "tx" instead of "tax", XPress just thinks you mean "Texas," thus proving once more that there's nothing like the final once-over with a human eye for catching these little mistakes. (Note that this isn't only a limitation of QuarkXPress; many spelling checkers do the same thing.)

▼ ▼

Checking a Document/Master Page

You can check the spelling of all the text in an entire document by selecting Document from the Check Spelling submenu (or by pressing Command-Option-Shift-L on the Macintosh; Control-Alt-Shift-W on Windows). QuarkXPress counts and checks all the words in your current document, from first page to last. It displays the Word Count dialog box, then lets you change suspect words with a Check Document dialog box that is identical in layout and function to the Check Story dialog box.

Unfortunately, this procedure only checks the spelling on the real document pages, not the master pages. To check spelling on master pages, you need to be viewing one of the master pages (it doesn't matter which, if you have more than one). When master pages are displayed, the Document item on the submenu changes to Masters. By selecting this command you can check all the text on every master page in your document, using a Check Masters dialog box that works just like the Check Story and Check Document dialog boxes.

▼ ▼

Tip: Speed Spelling Check. If you've ever tried to check the spelling in an enormous document, you've probably found yourself waiting for the screen to redraw. Only after the redraw can you decide to move on to the next word. Reader Bob Martin points out that the process goes more quickly if you first reduce the document window size considerably and then zoom in to 400 percent. QuarkXPress has very little to redraw on the screen each time. Plus, the found text is almost always more visible in the small window.

▼ ▼

Auxiliary Dictionaries

You can't add or change words in QuarkXPress's standard dictionary. You can, however, create and use an auxiliary dictionary, so you can have the program's spelling checker take into account specialized words that aren't in the standard dictionary. Note that you can only have one auxiliary dictionary open at a time for each document.

Creating or opening an auxiliary dictionary. To open an existing auxiliary dictionary, or to create a new one, select Auxiliary Dictionary from the Utilities menu. This opens the Auxiliary Dictionary dialog box. Select a dictionary stored on any mounted volume, and click the Open button.

You can also create a new auxiliary dictionary by clicking the New button in this dialog box (see Figure 5-9). This opens a dialog box that lets you specify the name and location of the new dictionary. Enter the name of the new dictionary in the text field, and click the Create button.

Adding and removing words. When you first create an auxiliary dictionary, it's empty. There are two ways to add words to it. First, you can add words to the dictionary using the Keep button in the Check Story or Check Document dialog box. This button adds the current suspect word to your auxiliary dictionary. Another way to add words is with the Edit Auxiliary feature on the Utilities menu. This feature is only available when there's an auxiliary dictonary selected.

Figure 5-9

The Auxiliary Dictionary dialog box

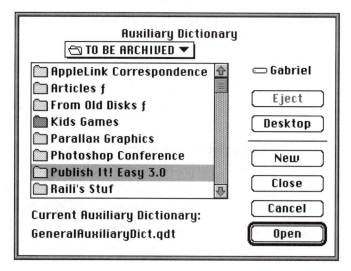

When you select Edit Auxiliary, a simple dialog box appears with a scrolling list of all the words in the currently open dictionary (see Figure 5-10). To add a new word, enter it in the text field and click the Add button. Words added to the dictionary cannot contain any spaces or punctuation (not even hyphens).

In earlier versions of XPress, words that have accents (or other foreign-language markings) were a no-no in the U.S. English version of the program. Fortunately, QuarkXPress 4 has changed that. Now if your name is García or Françoise, you can breathe more easily when you're checking spelling.

To remove a word from the dictionary, scroll through the list until you find the word. Select it by clicking on it, then click the Delete button.

▼ ▼

Tip: Adding All Suspect Words. Here's a fun way to add a bunch of words to your auxiliary dictionary, all at the same time. This only works if you've already selected an auxiliary dictionary for your document, of course (choose Auxiliary Dictionary from the Utilities menu).

1. Create a text box with all the words that you want to add to the auxiliary dictionary.

2. Select Check Story from the Utilities menu, and when XPress displays the number of suspect words, click OK. (In this scenario, all the words in the story will be suspect words.)

3. In the Check Story dialog box, hold down the ~~Command~~ *option* and Shift keys and click the Done button (on Windows, hold down Alt and Shift while clicking Close). This adds all the suspect words to the current auxiliary dictionary.

If you make a mistake or you want to make sure the words were added, select Edit Auxiliary in the Utilities menu.

▼ ▼

Remembering dictionaries. If you open or create an auxiliary dictionary with a document open, QuarkXPress automatically associates the two. Whenever you open the document, QuarkXPress also opens the dictionary, until you either close that dictionary (by pressing Close in the Auxiliary Dictionary dialog box) or open a different one (this breaks the link with the first dictionary and makes a link with the new one).

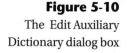
Figure 5-10
The Edit Auxiliary
Dictionary dialog box

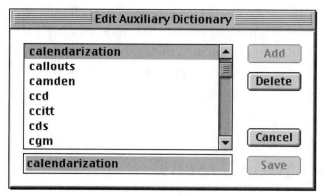

You can also set up an auxiliary dictionary that will be applied to all subsequent new documents by opening a dictionary while no documents are open. However, QuarkXPress may not be able to find an auxiliary dictionary if you move either the dictionary or a document associated with it—or sometimes even when you have a system crash while XPress is running—in which case, you'll receive an error message when you try to check spelling in your document. If QuarkXPress loses track of the Auxiliary Dictionary, just go back and open it again.

▼ ▼

Tip: Editing Dictionaries with a Word Processor. QuarkXPress auxiliary dictionaries are text files, with one word per paragraph. On the Macintosh, they have a "type" of TEXT and a "creator" of XPR3. In Windows, they have a .QDT file name extension. Because they're text files, you can edit QuarkXPress auxiliary dictionaries with any word processor.

There are a few things to remember, though. First, when you're editing, make sure the words remain in alphabetical order. Then save the auxiliary dictionary file as Text Only. In Windows, make sure the file name extension doesn't get changed. On the Mac, you may have to use a utility like File Buddy or ResEdit to reset the file's creator to XPR3.

One other Window's specific note: while on the Macintosh, QuarkXPress delineates words with a return character, in Windows it uses a special control character. Make sure you always have this character after each word in your dictionary (I find this easiest to do by using Copy and Paste in the NotePad accessory).

▼ ▼

Tip: Adding Your Microsoft Word Dictionary. The user dictionaries that Microsoft Word creates are text files as well, and like QuarkXPress dictionaries, they have one alphabetized word per paragraph. That means you can use your Microsoft Word Dictionary with QuarkXPress by changing the file's type code. Of course, if you're going to do this, use a duplicate of the original dictionary. Note that this appears to only work on the Macintosh. (If you figure out how to do it on Windows, please let me know!)

▼ ▼

Watching Your Words

By following the tips I've shown you here, you may not be able to have QuarkXPress write your stories for you, but you'll be able to get the very most out of the program's advanced word-processing features.

In the next chapter, you'll see how you can take those blocks of plain text that you've created and turn them into type, using QuarkXPress's extensive typographic controls.

6

TYPE AND TYPOGRAPHY

There's an old husband's tale that says you can tell what a baby is going to grow up to become by the first real word she speaks. If she says "mama," she'll grow up to be a loving parent. If she says "teevee," chances are she will be a couch potato. If she says "QuarkXPress," she'll become a designer.

There's no doubt—even if this tale is hogwash—that QuarkXPress is often the first word on a designer's lips when the topic of desktop publishing comes up. That's because no desktop-publishing application handles typesetting as powerfully as QuarkXPress does. In this chapter I will discuss the many typographic controls that QuarkXPress puts at your fingertips. I'm going to start with the basics: typographic principles and fonts. However, professionals should at least skim over this section (the fundamentals of fonts are rarely taught, and many people find themselves in deep . . . uh . . . water at some point because of it).

Next, I'll discuss control of both character- and paragraph-level formatting, including—among many other items—kerning and tracking, hyphenation and justification, and typographic special effects.

If you're reading this book from cover to cover, expect to spend a little while here in this chapter. I've got a lot to talk about, and I expect you'll find it rewarding.

▼ ▼

Fonts and Font Management

The word *font* now has several meanings. Historically, a font was a set of characters in a given typeface and size. Helvetica was a typeface, and 14-point Helvetica was a font. However, for the sake of simplicity, I'm following the path that has become popular over the past few years, defining both *typeface* and *font* as synonyms: a font or a typeface is a set of characters that share a common look.

For example, the text you're reading is in the Utopia font or typeface, while the headings for each section are in the Stone font or typeface. The more you learn about type and typography, the more you see its subtle nuances and personalities. But don't worry too much about that yet. Just start by seeing these basic differences.

There are four rules for working with fonts in professional desktop publishing:

▶ Use Type 1, PostScript fonts.

▶ Don't use bitmapped-only fonts.

▶ Use a font management utility.

▶ Be careful when choosing font styles.

Of course, with every rule there is at least one exception, and at least three instances where you should ignore the rule entirely. Nonetheless, here's a quick set of guidelines.

TrueType versus PostScript. Just like there are lots of different kinds of word-processing file formats (Microsoft Word files are different than WordPerfect files, and so on), there are many different ways to digitally store font information. The two primary formats, however, are called TrueType and PostScript (or Type 1; see Figure 6-1). Microsoft has really pushed the TrueType font format, and Windows machines ship with a plethora of TrueType fonts already installed. You typically have to buy

PostScript fonts from a vendor (like Adobe, Bitstream, or Monotype), or they may be copied to your system automatically when you install a program (like Adobe Type Manager, Adobe Photoshop, Adobe Acrobat, and so on) on your machine. The following parable should teach us all a lesson about fonts.

Once upon a time, there was a wise old guru sitting on a Himalayan mountain top, in quiet contemplation on the harmonious connection

Figure 6-1
Fonts in your system

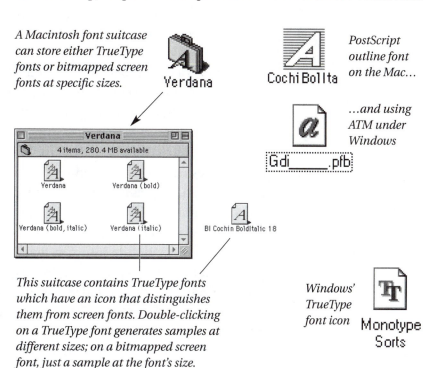

A Macintosh font suitcase can store either TrueType fonts or bitmapped screen fonts at specific sizes.

PostScript outline font on the Mac...

...and using ATM under Windows

This suitcase contains TrueType fonts which have an icon that distinguishes them from screen fonts. Double-clicking on a TrueType font generates samples at different sizes; on a bitmapped screen font, just a sample at the font's size.

Windows' TrueType font icon

Double-clicking on a Windows TrueType font generates a more elaborate sample than on the Macintosh.

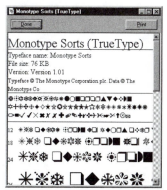

between her navel and the universal Om. She had studied the masters—the Bible, the Gita, the Koran, *The Wall Street Journal*—and she had meditated on the meaning of life and the meaning of desktop publishing. One day, a young man appeared. Weary after months of climbing and struggling, he stumbled up to the guru and asked, "Oh wise one, I have traveled over oceans and through valleys to find you. Can you please tell me the secret of happiness?"

The guru looked at the young one with compassion, for she had once been there, too. Slowly, carefully, she uttered these words: "Don't use TrueType fonts."

Later, over a cup of espresso, she clarified her position: "TrueType is fine unless you're trying to do quality graphic design work, are working with other people, or are working with a service bureau. If you're serious about desktop publishing, use PostScript fonts."

Most service bureaus wish that TrueType fonts would just go away because they have so much trouble printing them. Printing these fonts has gotten easier, but as far as I'm concerned, the guru's lesson is still relevant. It's always tempting to use inexpensive or free fonts, but you almost always get what you pay for.

Note that when you use PostScript fonts in XPress (for both Windows and Macintosh), you must also use Adobe Type Manager (ATM) for them to display properly. (ATM rasterizes—"turns into bitmaps"—the mathematical outlines of PostScript fonts, so no matter how big you make them on screen, they always look nice and smooth.) Fortunately, ATM ships free with almost all Adobe software; you can even download it as part of the Acrobat Reader from Adobe's web site (*www.adobe.com*). If you don't have ATM installed now, your homework is to get it and install it by the end of this chapter.

Use font outlines, not bitmaps. The Internet and online services like America Online are chock-full-o' free fonts you can download. Some of these, however, are bitmap-only fonts; that is, they are not accompanied by TrueType or PostScript fonts, which are mathematical outlines of font designs. Outline fonts print beautifully at any resolution (screen, laser printer, imagesetter, and so on), but bitmap-only fonts are typically just for screen display or special-effect type (typefaces that are supposed to look really jaggy). You shouldn't use bitmap-only fonts for professional print work unless you are trying to get a special effect.

Type management utilities. If you only worked with two or three type-faces for the rest of your life, you'd never need to think about font management. However, most people doing any kind of publishing work commonly work with hundreds of fonts. Keeping these fonts in order is critical to working efficiently with QuarkXPress.

If you have more than 20 fonts on your hard drive, you should be using a font management utility. Period. These programs let you keep all your fonts together, either in one folder or in multiple folders anywhere you want on your hard drives. You can arrange fonts into groups, opening just the ones you want when you need them. In this way you keep your font menus short, you speed up font selection, and you keep your system lean.

Plus, most of these utilities are pretty cheap (between $30 and $150) so there's almost no reason not to have one around. Examples of font management utilites are ATM Deluxe (not the Lite version that comes with most Adobe products) from Adobe Systems, MasterJuggler from Alsoft, and Suitcase from Symantec.

▼ ▼

Tip: Font Reserve. One font management utility that's a little more expensive than the rest is Font Reserve from Diamond Software. But truthfully, calling Font Reserve a utility is like calling the United States Federal Reserve a piggy bank. It's actually a database that knows all about the fonts on your system, but its interface is easy enough for anyone to handle. (Unfortunately, as of this writing it's Macintosh-only.) Font Reserve also comes with a Quark XTension that automatically opens the necessary fonts when you open a document. Font Reserve doesn't make sense if you only have a handful of fonts, but if you're a service bureau or a design firm with a *lot* of fonts, you owe it to yourself to take a look at Font Reserve.

▼ ▼

Which Font to Choose. The fourth "rule" of fonts has to do with setting your fonts to bold, italic, and so on. The question often arises over whether people should choose bold and italic fonts from their font menus (if they're available) or get them by selecting bold or italic from the Style menu or the Measurements palette. It's a good question. However, I'm going to punt on the answer for now; instead, I'll discuss it later in "Styling by Attributes Versus Font Choice."

Missing Fonts

When you open a document created with fonts that you don't currently
have loaded on your system, XPress tells you that you're missing one or
more fonts and gives you two choices: Continue and List Fonts (see
Figure 6-2).

Continue. If you click the Continue button, XPress opens the document
but displays the missing fonts on screen using system fonts (like Ariel or
Geneva). If you select some text set in this missing font, you can see that
the font field in the Measurements palette is blank because the proper
font isn't available from the font list. Also, if you open Font Usage (see
"Font Usage," below) or the Find/Change palette, you'll find a font called
something like "{-2, Unknown}" or "{-122, MinionExpertRegular}".

Obviously, having a real font replaced with a system font doesn't
make much sense, but if you're only perusing the document for overall
design and you don't care about how the fonts look or how the text wraps
from line to line, then this may be a reasonable option.

List Fonts. If you click the List Fonts button, XPress lists the missing
fonts for you. To replace one of these missing fonts with a font that's
available, select a typeface from the list, click the Replace button, then
choose a replacement font. Note that this option replaces every instance

Figure 6-2
Missing fonts

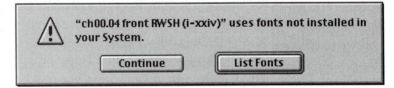

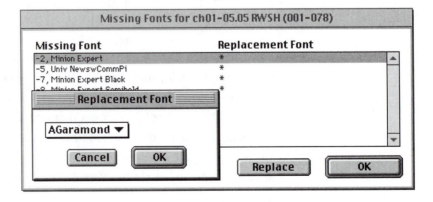

of that font (within style sheet definitions, too). I'll sometimes replace fonts like this if I have a font that is close to the one specified in the document. For instance, I might replace a missing Goudy font with Palatino, since there is a similarity between these two oldstyle typefaces. Of course, because the character widths of these two fonts are different, line endings are almost sure to be different. Later, I would close the document without saving it, so that when I open it on a machine that has Goudy, the fonts will appear properly.

Printing missing fonts. You can also run into trouble when your computer has a screen font (also called a "bitmapped font") but no corresponding PostScript outline font (this isn't a problem with TrueType fonts). In that case, when you print the document, XPress substitutes either a jaggy-looking bitmapped version of the font or Courier (that typewriter font). I'll talk more in Chapter 13, *Printing*, about making sure that printer fonts are available.

▼ ▼

Tip: Watch Out for ATM Deluxe. If you use Adobe Type Manager Deluxe: Beware font substitution! (Now go back and read that last line as though Victor Karloff was saying it.) At first, font substitution sounds really cool: if you're missing a font when you open an XPress document, ATM Deluxe automatically generates a similar one for you. The problem is that there is almost no warning that the font has been substituted—the missing font even appears in XPress's font menus and Font Usage dialog box as though it were really loaded—so unless you know your fonts really well, you may not even notice. Believe me: thousands of dollars worth of film has been thrown away because of such a mistake.

The only indication that ATM Deluxe is building a substitute font is that the cursor changes into a little spinning "A" for a moment or two when you open the document. On a fast machine, though, even this is hardly noticeable. Remember: turn off the Font Substitution preference in ATM Deluxe's Preferences dialog box.

▼ ▼

Font Usage

What's the fastest way to tell what fonts are being used in a document that you have open? Select Usage from the Utilities menu (press F13 on the Mac, or F2 on Windows). The Fonts tab in the Usage dialog box lists every font in a document, lets you search for instances of that font, and lets you globally replace one font with another (see Figure 6-3).

Some people have complained that the Usage dialog box in version 4 of XPress has less robust search-and-replace abilities than in version 3 (note that they did add some additional functionality in version 4.02). Quark's answer: If you're trying to search and replace, you should use the Find/Change dialog box. It's hard to argue with that. (Except that as this goes to press, a bug in the current version of XPress prevents the Find/Change palette from finding missing fonts. I hope this will be fixed by the time you read this.)

There are two problems with using the Usage dialog box to search for and replace fonts.

▶ The Usage dialog box only displays fonts that are on the document pages *or* the master pages, but not both at the same time. (Which one it displays depends on what pages are currently showing in the document window.)

▶ The Replace option in the Usage dialog box only replaces fonts on the document page or the master pages (again, depending on which is showing), but it does not change fonts in the style sheet definitions (I discuss style sheets in Chapter 7, *Copy Flow*). For instance, let's say you use the font Matrix in a character style sheet

Figure 6-3
Font Usage

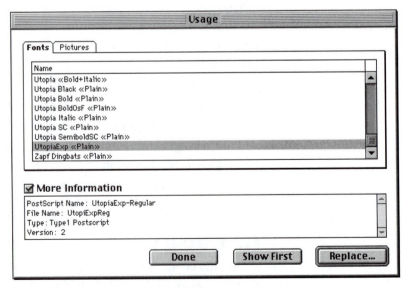

and then apply that style to some text on a document page. If you try to replace Matrix with Garamond in the Usage dialog box, you'll only change the text on the document page, not the actual definition of the style (it's the same as applying local formatting on top of the style). This is a mess.

Of course, the Find/Change palette has exactly the same two limitations, so global font replacements are not nearly as easy as you'd think.

More Information. You can find out more about a particular font in the Usage dialog box by selecting it and turning on the More Information checkbox. When this option is on, pay particular attention to the File Name and the File Type. If you're not sure whether you're dealing with a PostScript or TrueType font, here's one great way to find out.

▼ ▼

Tip: Global Font Replacements. Let's say you've created a masterpiece in XPress—450 pages, 47 style sheets, five master pages. You've used the Franklin Gothic typeface family throughout the document, sometimes applying it manually to text, sometimes using it in style sheet definitions. Now your art director demands (probably out of spite) that you replace Franklin Gothic with Univers. Unfortunately, there is no feature in XPress that lets you replace one font with another, at one fell swoop, on master pages, document pages, and style sheets. Here's what I'd do.

1. Save the document and close it.

2. Turn off Franklin Gothic with your font management utility. (If you don't use a font management utility, then you'll have to manually "uninstall" the font from your system.)

3. Open the document again in XPress. When the program tells you that a font is missing, click the List Fonts button. Select Franklin Gothic from the list and click Replace. Choose Univers from the Replace popup menu, and click OK.

4. After the document is open and is displaying the first page, every instance of Franklin Gothic in your document will have been replaced with Univers, and you won't have to pull your hair out.

▼ ▼

Character Formatting

There are two types of typographic controls: character-based and paragraph-based. The character-based controls—typeface, size, color, bold, italic, and so on—are those that affect only the text characters you select. If you select only one word in a sentence and apply a character style to it, that word and only that word is changed. Paragraph-based controls let you change the formatting of the entire paragraph—left and right indents, tab settings, space before and after, and so on.

Let's talk about character formatting first—how you can change it, and why you'd want to.

Use the Content Tool. The very first thing you need to know about controlling type in QuarkXPress is that you must have selected both the Content tool and the text box that contains the text you want to change. If you want to make a character-based change, you must select those characters you want to alter. If you want to make a paragraph-based change, you can select the paragraph (four mouse clicks) or a portion of the paragraph. You can even just have the cursor located anywhere within the paragraph. Just remember: If you want to change the content of a text box, use the Content tool.

Selecting a Typeface

Picking a typeface can be a very personal thing, fraught with implication and the anxiety of decision. If someone tells you they want their document set in 10-point Courier, it may be better just to stay quiet. However, once the choice is made, there are a number of ways to select the typeface. Let's look at each of them here.

The Style menu. Almost every typographic control can be accessed from the Style menu. Once you select the text you want to change, you can select the typeface name from the Font submenu.

The Measurements palette. If you would rather avoid submenus, you can select a typeface from the Measurements palette instead. Here you have two methods of selecting.

▶ You can click on the arrow popup menu to bring up a list of fonts. It is often quicker to select from this menu than from the Style menu because it's always visible and is not a hierarchical menu (which I generally dislike).

▶ You can type the name of the typeface you want. Do this by clicking to the left of the first character of the typeface name shown on the Measurements palette (or jump there quickly by pressing Command-Option-Shift-M), then typing a few characters of the typeface name you want. As soon as QuarkXPress recognizes the name, it inserts the rest of it for you.

For example, if you want to change from Helvetica to Avant Garde, click just to the left of the "H" and type "Ava." By the time you type these three letters, chances are XPress will recognize Avant Garde (as long as you have that font loaded). This is clearly a boon to desktop publishers who have many fonts and are tired of scrolling down a list for five minutes to select Zapf Dingbats.

▼ ▼

Tip: Jumping Forward in the Menu. If your menu is really long and you want to jump to a certain point, you can use both methods of selecting a font in the Measurements palette. For example, if you're looking for Zapf Dingbats but can't remember how "Zapf" is spelled, you can type "Z" in the font field of the Measurements palette (remember, you can get there quickly by pressing Command-Option-Shift-M), then click on the popup menu. You're transported directly to the end of the list.

▼ ▼

Character Attributes. The Character Attributes dialog box is the Style menu and half the Measurements palette rolled into one, and is a simple keystroke away (Command-Shift-D). Here you can change the typeface using the same methods described in "The Measurements palette," above.

Find/Change and Font Usage. Let's say half your document is set in Helvetica and you want to change that copy to Futura. You can use either the Find/Change or the Font Usage dialog box to search for all instances of characters set in Helvetica, and replace them with Futura. I discuss the

Find/Change dialog box in some detail in Chapter 5, *Word Processing*, and the Font Usage feature earlier in this chapter.

Font Size

Selecting a font is only half the battle; once you've done that, you typically need to change the size of the typeface. You use the same options for changing the type size as I described above: the Style menu, the Measurements palette, the Character Attributes dialog box, and the Find/Change dialog boxes (Font Usage doesn't let you change point size). In addition, you can use a set of keystrokes to make your selected text larger or smaller (see Table 6-1).

The preset point-size range that I mention in Table 6-1 is the same range listed on the Size menu: 7, 9, 10, 12, 14, 18, 24, 36, 48, 60, and 72. When you increase through the preset range with a keystroke, your character size jumps from one to the next on this list. I generally use Command-Shift-period and Command-Shift-comma (smaller and larger) to jump through the presets until I'm close to the size I want. Then I fine-tune the point size by adding the Option key to the keystroke, so that it moves only one point at a time.

▼ ▼

Tip: Precision Font Sizing. If you aren't satisfied with the preset font sizes, you can enter your own—in .001-point increments—in the Font Size field of the Character Attributes dialog box. You can get to this dialog box by selecting Other from the Size submenu or by pressing Command-Shift-\ (backslash). This is one of the keystrokes I use most often (You could also use Command-Option-Shift-M and then press Tab to jump to the Font Size field on the Measurements palette.)

▼ ▼

Tip: Interactive Text Resizing. If you like working visually, you may not know exactly how large you want your text to be. You can resize text interactively by holding down the Command key while dragging on a handle

Table 6-1
Font sizing keystrokes

PRESS ...	TO ...
⌘-⇧-period	Increase point size through a preset range
⌘-⇧-comma	Decrease point size through a preset range
⌘-⌥-⇧-period	Increase point size in 1-point increments
⌘-⌥-⇧-comma	Decrease point size in 1-point increments

(this also works with picture boxes; see Chapter 9, *Pictures*). As you resize the text box, the size of the text increases or decreases to fit your changes. Depending on how you reshape the box, the type size changes along with the type's horizontal or vertical scaling (see Figure 6-4).

In addition to Command-key scaling, holding down Shift-Command turns rectangular boxes into squares (scaling contents appropriately), and holding down Shift-Command-Option scales the box and its contents but maintains existing horizontal and vertical proportions (this is usually what you'd want). And if you wait half a second after you click on a handle before you begin to drag, you can see the type change on screen as you drag (see "Tip: Viewing Changes as You Make Them" in Chapter 2, *QuarkXPress Basics*).

There are two catches to this funky feature. First, it only stretches type to the limits you could ordinarily stretch it to. You can't stretch type wider than 400 percent or larger than 720 points, because horizontal scaling and font size won't go any farther than that. Second, this scaling only works on unlinked text boxes, not on text boxes that are part of a longer story, as it's intended for use on headline and display type.

Figure 6-4
Interactive text resizing

Type Styles

QuarkXPress has 13 built-in attributes that you assign at a character level. Figure 6-5 gives samples of each of these, plus examples of how to use each of them.

These type attributes can be assigned to selected text in four ways, which are similar to how you assign typefaces and type size.

Figure 6-5
Type styles

Plain text
Italic
Bold
<u>Underlined (everything)</u>
<u>Word</u> <u>underlining</u>
~~Strike-Thru~~
Outline
Shadow
ALL CAPS
SMALL CAPS
Superscript   (baseline shown as dotted line)
Subscript
Superior characters

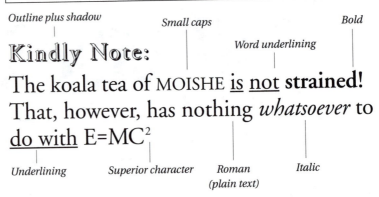

Outline plus shadow   Small caps   Bold
                                    Word underlining

Kindly Note:
The koala tea of MOISHE <u>is</u> <u>not</u> **strained!**
That, however, has nothing *whatsoever* to
<u>do with</u> E=MC²

Underlining   Superior character   Roman   Italic
                                      (plain text)

Character attributes. The slowest method of choosing a type style is by going to the Character Attributes dialog box (Command-Shift-D). The type styles in the Character Attributes dialog box are turned on and off by checking boxes. These checkboxes can be in one of three states: on, off, or indeterminate (gray).

▶ **ON.** An "X" in the checkbox means the style is selected for all the selected text.

▶ **OFF.** If the checkbox is blank, that style is not applied to any of the selected text.

▶ **INDETERMINATE.** A gray checkbox means that some of the characters that are currently selected have that style, and others don't. (See "Finding and Changing Type Styles" in Chapter 5, *Word Processing*.)

Style menu. Perhaps the second-slowest method of selecting a type style is to choose it from the Type Style submenu under the Style menu (see Figure 6-6).

Figure 6-6

Type Style submenu

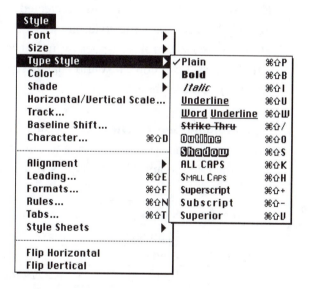

Measurements palette. Each of the type styles is displayed by an icon on the Measurements palette (see Figure 6-7). The icons either display a sample of the style or give a graphic representation of it. For example, Superscript is shown by the numeral 2 over an up arrow. To select a type style, click on the icon. The icon acts as a toggle switch, so to turn the style off, you click on it again. If you have several type styles selected, you can rid yourself of them by clicking on the P (for Plain).

Note that the "indeterminate" state also appears on the Measurements palette; when you select text that contains more than one type style, the various icons appear gray. You can still turn them on and off by clicking on them.

Figure 6-7
Measurements palette type styles

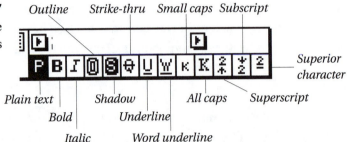

Outline   Strike-thru   Small caps   Subscript

Superior character

Plain text   Shadow   All caps   Superscript

Bold

Italic   Underline

Word underline

Keystrokes. Each type style can be selected by a keystroke, as shown in Table 6-2. Once again, the styles are toggled on and off with each keystroke. I find keystrokes especially useful while typing directly into QuarkXPress; I can enter text and change styles while never taking my hands from the keyboard.

▼ ▼

Tip: Avoiding Some Styles. Just because XPress offers you a choice doesn't mean that you should take it. For instance, you should avoid using the Outline and Shadow type styles because they rarely look as

Table 6-2
Type styles

KEYSTROKES	STYLE	EXAMPLE
⌘-⇧-P	Plain text	Ecce Eduardus Ursus
⌘-⇧-B	Bold	**Ecce Eduardus Ursus**
⌘-⇧-I	Italic	*Ecce Eduardus Ursus*
⌘-⇧-O	Outline	Ecce Eduardus Ursus
⌘-⇧-S	Shadow	Ecce Eduardus Ursus
⌘-⇧-/	Strikethrough	~~Ecce Eduardus Ursus~~
⌘-⇧-U	Underline	Ecce Eduardus Ursus
⌘-⇧-W	Word underline	Ecce Eduardus Ursus
⌘-⇧-H	Small caps	Ecce Eduardus Ursus
⌘-⇧-K	All caps	ECCE EDUARDUS URSUS
⌘-⇧-=	Superscript	Ecce Eduardus Ursus
⌘-⇧-hyphen	Subscript	Ecce Eduardus Ursus
⌘-⇧-V	Superior	Ecce Eduardus Ursus

good as you'd expect. The problem is that XPress lets the operating system create these effects rather than building them itself, and the operating system is not very good at typographic effects (if it were, we'd all be using SimpleText or Windows Notepad for our typography). If you want these effects, you should build them yourself using other XPress features (see "Typographic Special Effects," later in this chapter).

You may or may not want to use the two underline styles and the strikethrough style, as well. They also fall into the "made by the system" category, so you have no control over things like how far the underline should be from the baseline, or how thick it should be (I also discuss ways to create these effects more precisely, later in this chapter).

▼ ▼

Styling by Attributes Versus Font Choice

On both the Macintosh and Windows operating systems, fonts are organized into families. For instance, the regular (roman), italic, bold, and bold italic styles of Bodoni all constitute a single family. Depending on your system setup, the font family may appear as a single name (Bodoni) or as several names (I Bodoni Italic, B Bodoni Bold, and so on).

There is an ongoing superstition in the design community that you should never just apply a type style (like just choosing Bold from the Style menu), and that you should instead always select the name of the styled font (like "B Bodoni Bold") from the font list. This is hogwash.

In general, you can use either method—styling text either by applying style attributes, or by choosing the styled font itself. There are several drawbacks to applying a style attribute however.

▶ In order to simply click on Bold or Italic or whatever with confidence, you must know that the style you are choosing actually exists for that font. For example, if your text is set in Symbol and you click on Italic, it may appear italic on screen, but you're taking a chance because there is no italic version of the Symbol font. The text is obliqued on screen, and may even be obliqued on your desktop laser printer; however, more often than not, the text will appear ugly or in the non-italic, roman face on an imagesetter.

▶ Some font families have more than just four faces; for example, Utopia (the typeface this text is set in) has a bold version, a semibold version, and a black version. If you select some Utopia text and press Command-Shift-B, do you know which bold version you're getting? If not, you shouldn't select your style this way. The key here is to know your typefaces inside and out before messing with the character styles.

▶ Fonts can become corrupted, and the connections with their other family members may be broken. In this case, you cannot choose character styles anymore. Often, replacing the font fixes the problem.

▶ You often don't even get the choice to select the "real styled font" because the operating system has hidden it from you (Windows 95 does this, for instance). In this case, you have to use character styles instead.

Which method is better? Choosing font style by formatting attribute is certainly faster, especially if you do it with keyboard commands. And it has the advantage of being font-independent. For example, if you've applied an italic formatting attribute to a range of your Bodoni text, and later decide to change your text face to Galliard, the italic formatting is retained.

On the other hand, if you choose the actual Bodoni Italic font for the emphasized range of text, when you make the change to Galliard, you get just Galliard and not Galliard Italic. Why? Because you simply switched from one font to another, and your text carried no formatting information. The original range was in an italic font with a Plain style attribute. To change fonts, you'd have to change Bodoni to Galliard, I Bodoni Italic to I Galliard Italic, B Bodoni Bold to B Galliard Bold, and so on.

No matter which method you use, I urge you to be consistent in your choice. There's little chance that something will go wrong if you change the type style in some places using style attributes and in other places using the actual fonts. However, it's best to be consistent.

▼ ▼

Color and Shade

You can quickly and easily change the color or the tint (shade) of a block of text. First, select the text and then select either the color from the Color submenu, or the tint value from the Shade submenu of the Style menu.

You can also use the Colors palette to set both of these attributes (see Chapter 12, *Color*). The default tints are in multiples of 10 percent; however, you can assign a specific tint value by selecting Other from the Shade submenu, or by typing a value in the upper-right corner of the Colors palette (see Figure 6-8).

Figure 6-8

Assigning a color to type

▼ ▼

Tip: Reversed Type. There is no specific command for reversed type—typically white-on-black type—as there is in Adobe PageMaker. But that doesn't mean you can't achieve that effect. Simply select the text and choose White from the Color submenu or from the Character Attributes dialog box (Command-Shift-D). If you want the reversed type to have a black background, either place a black box behind it, or color the text box's background in the Modify dialog box (Command-M). (Also see "Tip: Reversed Type in Rules" in Chapter 11, *Where Text Meets Graphics*.)

▼ ▼

Horizontal and Vertical Scaling

Imagine that the characters in a typeface are rubber and stretchable. Now imagine stretching a typeface—one that took hundreds of hours to laboriously design at a specific width—to 160 percent of its size, warping the characters into something they were never meant to be. Now imagine the type designer's face contorting in horror as he or she sees what you've done to the type.

Okay, you get the idea: typefaces are designed to be a specific width, and shouldn't be messed with unless you have some really good reasons. What are some good reasons? The best reason of all is that you want the typeface to look that way. If you're responsible for the typographic design, then you can make any choices you want. Note that I'm not talking about your using 70-percent compression of Helvetica because you don't feel like buying another package from Adobe. I am talking about using Cheltenham compressed to 85 percent because it looks cool.

Another good reason to play with the horizontal scaling is if you need to make some body copy fit a particular space. Here I'm talking about changing the horizontal scaling of the text plus or minus two or three percent, not 10 or 20 percent. I'd be surprised if anyone other than the designer could see the difference of a few percent, especially at small sizes. But scaling Times Bold to 50 percent of its size to make it fit as a headline is a bad idea (see Figure 6-9).

After all these warnings, if you still want to play with the horizontal or vertical scaling of your type, you can do so using the Horizontal/Vertical Scale feature on the Style menu. (Vertical scaling first appeared in QuarkXPress 3.2; instead of stretching the type horizontally, it makes it taller while maintaining the same width.) First, select Horizontal or Vertical from the popup menu (you can't modify both at the same time). Entering values below 100 percent makes the text either narrower or shorter and squatter, depending on the Horizontal/Vertical setting; values above 100 percent stretch it wider or make it taller. Note that you don't have to type a percent sign; just the number will do.

You can also alter horizontal and vertical scaling with keystrokes: Command-] (right square bracket) makes selected text wider in five-percent increments; Command-[(left square bracket) makes the selected text narrower in five-percent increments. (I remember the difference like this: the key on the left means narrow—or less; the key on the right means wider—or more.) The keystrokes modify horizontal or vertical scaling depending on which direction you last changed.

▼ ▼

Tip: Thoughts on Horizontal and Vertical Scaling. Here are just a few more thoughts on the subject of horizontal and vertical scaling that you might want to keep in mind.

▶   If you're going to use horizontal scaling, think carefully about the sort of typeface you're using. When you scale a font horizontally,

Figure 6-9
Horizontal scaling of type

Got a problem?

20 pt. Helvetica Condensed

Check your compression.

(Tracking: 0)

Got a problem?

20 pt. Helvetica (horizontal scaling: 60%)

Check your compression.

(Tracking: -3)

Got a problem?

20 pt. Helvetica bold (scaling: 60%)

Check your compression.

(Tracking: -2)

*Times bold with horizontal scaling of 50% —
but with the inter-word spaces not compressed*

Rats! Squashed again!

*Times bold with horizontal scaling of 50% — inter-word
spaces also scaled to 50%. Tracking in both examples: -1*

Squashed! Rats again!

Times roman 10/11 — normal scaling

I began to experience an acute sense of panic when, despite
everyone's assurances to the contrary, I began to approach the
end of the line and found that I was not quite going to make
it.

Times roman — scaled to 99% (same line width)

I began to experience an acute sense of panic when, despite
everyone's assurances to the contrary, I began to approach the
end of the line and found that I was not quite going to make it.

the vertical strokes get thicker or thinner—depending on which
way you're scaling—and the horizontal strokes stay the same
width. A typeface that has thick verticals and thin horizontals
(such as Bodoni) can become very odd-looking with just a little
scaling. Faces that have only a little variation in stroke weight
often handle scaling the best.

▶ Perhaps the worst kind of typeface to scale horizontally is script faces such as Berthold Script or Park Avenue. These are very delicate, and stretching them makes them look horrible and reduces their marginal legibility even further.

▶ Faces that are more square in nature, especially those with serifs, can handle being somewhat compressed with elegance. ITC Garamond, Cheltenham, and New Century Schoolbook, for instance, don't distort too badly until you drop below 90 percent or above 110 percent.

Kerning and Tracking

There are times in life when all those little letters on a page are just too far apart or too close together. The problem may be between two characters in 120-point display type, or it may be throughout an entire font. Whatever the problem, QuarkXPress can control it through the use of kerning and tracking. These two features are similar, but let's look at them one at a time.

Tip: Know Your Ems and Ens. Many typographic controls are specified using units of measure called *ems* and *ens*. (Some people call the en a "nut" to distinguish it aurally from an em.) These are not nearly as confusing as some people make them out to be. The default for the em in QuarkXPress is the width of two zeros side by side in the font and size you're working in. If that sounds weird, it's because it is. I can't figure out why they did it that way, but that's just the way it is. The width of an en space is half of an em space—the width of one zero.

Because this is so weird and unreasonable, Quark has added a checkbox on the Character Tab of the Document Preferences dialog box (Command-Y) labeled Standard Em Space. This sets the width of an em space to the same width that every other piece of software uses: the size of the typeface you're using. So if you're using 14-point Times with the Standard Em Space option turned on, the em space is 14 points wide. For consistency and a sense of doing the right thing, I recommend that you set this as your default (by changing the preference while no document is open).

If you're typing along and change point size, then the sizes of the em and en change as well. This can be a great aid. For example, if you change the size of a word after painstakingly kerning it, your kerning does not get lost or jumbled. The kerning was specified in fractions of an em, and therefore is scaled along with the type.

Em spaces and em dashes are not always equal in width. Usually they are (especially when Standard Em Space is turned on), but it really depends on what the typeface designer decided.

▼ ▼

Tip: What's 7/200 of an Em? Even though XPress defines kerning and other type-spacing values in ems, don't feel that you have to *think* in ems, unless you want to live and breathe typography. The important thing to remember is how the type looks, not all the numbers that get you there. When I'm working in QuarkXPress, I almost never think, "Oh, I'm going to change the kerning ½₀ of an em." I just say, "Oh, let's see how adding some kerning here would look." Focus on the results, and you'll get the feel for it pretty quickly.

▼ ▼

Kerning

Adjusting space between two characters is referred to as *kerning* or *pair kerning*. You'll sometimes find kerning defined purely as the removal of space between characters. In QuarkXPress, kerning can be either the removal or the *addition* of space—moving two characters closer together or farther apart. Figure 6-10 shows some examples of type, first unkerned and then kerned. The problem is made obvious here: too much space between characters can make words look uneven or unnatural.

QuarkXPress supports two kinds of kerning: automatic and manual. Type designers usually build into the font itself kerning-pair values that can be invoked automatically in QuarkXPress. Automatic kerning is global: it affects all instances of a character pair. Manual kerning is local: it affects only the pair selected.

Automatic. When I say "automatic," I mean really automatic: all you have to do is turn on the function, and QuarkXPress will make use of the font's built-in kerning pairs (actually, you don't even have to turn automatic kerning on, because it is on by default). It's up to font vendors to determine how many and which kerning pairs to include with a font, and which values to assign to them. Most fonts come with between 100 and 500 such pairs. Third parties also sell kerning pairs you can import.

There's almost no good reason to turn off automatic kerning altogether, but if you want to, the switch is on the Character tab in the Document Preferences dialog box (Command-Y). I wouldn't turn it off unless I were on a really slow machine and XPress was taking an inordinately long time flowing my text.

Manual. Figure 6-10 shows a word in three renditions: with no kerning, with automatic kerning, and with manual kerning in addition to automatic kerning. The last looks best, doesn't it? (Please agree.)

Manual kerning in QuarkXPress is the adjustment of space between character pairs on a case-by-case basis. You make each adjustment in increments of fractions of an em space (see "Tip: Know Your Ems and Ens," above). Why anyone would want to kern to a precision of $\frac{1}{20,000}$ of an em space is beyond us, but QuarkXPress lets you do just that.

Manual kerning is usually reserved for larger type sizes for two reasons. First, it's harder to see poorly kerned pairs in smaller point sizes, so people say, "Why bother?" Second, you wouldn't want to go through a sizable amount of body text in the 8- to 14-point range, meticulously kerning pairs. It would take forever. Leave small type sizes to automatic

Figure 6-10
Kerned and
unkerned type

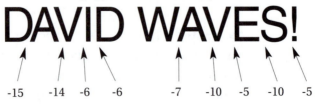

No automatic or manual kerning

DAVID WAVES!

Auto-kerning on; no manual kerning

DAVID WAVES!

Manual kerning applied to all character pairs

DAVID WAVES!

-15   -14   -6   -6   -7   -10   -5   -10   -5

kerning. If you don't like the built-in kerning pairs in a font, you can change them (see "Kerning and Tracking Tables," later in this chapter).

Manual kerning is a character-level attribute, but with a distinct difference from other character formatting. Instead of selecting the text you want to change, you place the cursor between two of the characters before you apply kerning (see Figure 6-11). If you select one or more characters, you end up applying tracking rather than kerning (see "Tracking," below). Once you've clicked at an insertion point, you can control the space between the characters in four ways.

Figure 6-11
Cursor placement
for kerning

Manual kerning with correct cursor placement

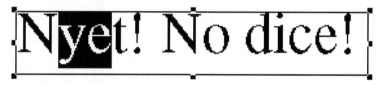

Incorrect cursor placement for manual kerning, but right for tracking

Kern or Character Attributes. You can select the Kern feature from the Style menu, which brings up the Character Attributes dialog box (you could type Command-Shift-D to get to this dialog box). Whole-number values typed in here represent units of $\frac{1}{200}$ em. For example, typing in "10" adds $\frac{10}{200}$ ($\frac{1}{20}$) of an em, and typing "-.1" removes $\frac{1}{2,000}$ of an em (typing a minus sign—a hyphen—before the value makes it negative). This is a really slow and painful way to apply kerning.

Measurements palette. The Measurements palette contains left-arrow and right-arrow icons that control tracking and kerning in text (they mean something different for pictures). Table 6-3 gives you a rundown on how to use them.

Keystrokes. I hate to take my hands off the keyboard while I'm working. Why should I, when I can do just about everything I need with keystrokes? Table 6-4 shows the keystrokes you can use for kerning.

No matter which method you use to kern, you can see the kerning value in the Measurements palette (next to the left and right arrows) and in the Character Attributes dialog box.

▼ ▼

Tip: Kerning the Kerned. What shows up as the kern value when you want to kern a pair that is already kerned because of automatic kerning? Nothing. You'll still find a zero in the Kern Amount field. QuarkXPress regards the values applied by automatic kerning as the norm, so you don't have to worry about them. Of course, if you turn off automatic kerning after having applied manual kerning, your kerning values may be way off.

▼ ▼

Tip: Removing Manual Kerning. Have you ever been handed a file to which someone had spent many hours manually adding hundreds of kerning pairs? What if they really didn't know what they were doing, and you want to remove all that kerning before starting over? Fortunately, Quark has released a free XTension called Type Tricks (this replaces some features in the FeaturesPlus or Thing-a-ma-bob XTensions; you can get it from the Internet at *www.peachpit.com/blatner*). With this XTension installed, you'll see a feature on the Utilities menu called Remove Manual Kerning. Just select the range of text you want to affect, then select that from the menu. *Voilà!* All gone.

▼ ▼

Tracking

I know it's incredibly confusing, but it's true: There are two separate features in QuarkXPress called "Tracking." They're similar, but I need to break them down for clarity. The first is a character-level attribute, and I'm going to talk about it here. The second is a font-level attribute which changes the font as a whole, rather than just changing a set of characters, and I'll discuss it in great detail later in this chapter.

Character-level tracking. Tracking as a character-level attribute is the adjustment of space between all the character pairs in a range of text. It's sometimes called "track kerning" or "kern tracking," though I think the best name for it is *range kerning* (which is what it's called in PageMaker). The idea is simple: you can add or subtract space between many pairs of characters all at one time by using tracking controls (see Figure 6-12).

Table 6-3		
Kerning control with the Measurements palette arrow icons

CLICK ...	WHILE PRESSING ...	TO ...
Right Arrow		Increase space 10 units (¹⁄₂₀ em)
Right Arrow	⌥	Increase space one unit (¹⁄₂₀₀ em)
Left Arrow		Decrease space 10 units (¹⁄₂₀ em)
Left Arrow	⌥	Decrease space one unit (¹⁄₂₀₀ em)

Table 6-4
Kerning keystrokes

PRESS ...	TO ...
⌘-⇧-}	Increase space 10 units (¹⁄₂₀ em)
⌘-⌥-⇧-}	Increase space one unit (¹⁄₂₀₀ em)
⌘-⇧-{	Decrease space 10 units (¹⁄₂₀ em)
⌘-⌥-⇧-{	Decrease space one unit (¹⁄₂₀₀ em)

Figure 6-12
Tracking text

Tracking: +7

Art directors *everywhere* were ignoring me until I realized what I needed:

Much tighter tracking!

Tracking: -12

To England: That pre-cious stone set in a sil-ver sea

Tracking: 0. Copy doesn't fit.

To England: That precious stone set in a silver sea

Tracking: -4. Copy fits.

These controls are so similar to the kerning controls that I'm not even going to waste time and paper talking about them much.

You can control tracking by selecting a range of text and using the Measurements palette, the Track feature from the Style menu (this menu item changes from Kern to Track when you have more than one charac-ter selected), the Character Attributes dialog box, or the same keystrokes as if you were kerning. The reason all the controls are virtually the same is that QuarkXPress "decides" for you whether to kern or track, based on what is selected in the text box. In fact, though, these controls have the same function. One is applied to a single pair of characters; the other is applied to several or many pairs.

▼ ▼

Tip: Tracking and the Single Word. The way tracking works, techni-cally, is by adding or subtracting space to the right of each selected char-acter. If you want to track a single word and don't want the space after the last character to be adjusted, you should select not the whole word, but only the characters up to the last letter. For example, if you want to apply 10-unit tracking to the word "obfuscation" without changing the space after the "n," you would only select the letters "obfuscatio" and then apply tracking.

▼ ▼

The crazy thing about this whole setup is that while kerning and tracking do the same thing, they are totally separate features. One result of this is that kerning and tracking are cumulative. For example, if you kern a character pair -10 units, then apply tracking of -10 units to those characters, the space between them ends up 20 units smaller than nor-mal (which may be what you want; you just need to be aware of it). Also, if you track a word, then look at the kerning between two letters, it will look as though there were no kerning applied at all. If you're a former (or present) PageMaker user, this may really throw you for a loop.

▼ ▼

Tip: When to Track. "Ah," I hear the reader sighing, "but what about some real-world tips?" Okay, let's set out some guidelines for you.

▶ If you're setting text in all capitals or in true small capitals from an Expert Set font, add between five and 10 units of space by track-ing the word. Remember that you may not want to add tracking to the last character of the word (see "Tip: Tracking and the Single Word," above).

▶ Printing white text on a black background often requires a little extra tracking, too. That's because the negative (black) space makes the white characters seem closer together.

▶ Larger type needs to be tracked more tightly (with negative tracking values). Often, the larger the tighter, though there are aesthetic limits to this rule. Advertising headline copy will often be tracked until the characters just "kiss." You can automate this feature by setting up dynamic tracking tables, which I will discuss later in this chapter.

▶ A condensed typeface (such as Futura Condensed) can usually do with a little tighter tracking. Sometimes I'll apply a setting as small as -1 to a text block to make it hold together better.

▶ When you're setting justified text and you get bad line breaks, or if you have an extra word by itself at the end of a paragraph, you can track the whole paragraph plus or minus one or two units without it being too apparent. Sometimes that's just enough to fix these problems.

Remember, however, that no matter how solid a rule may be, you are obliged to break it if the finished design will be better.

▾ ▾

Wordspacing

Quark's free Type Tricks XTension adds one more option to character-level attributes: the ability to adjust kerning for spacebands within a selected range of text. As I discussed above, kerning is the adjustment of space between characters; it's often called "letterspacing," but I prefer to reserve that term for justification controls (which I'll talk about later in this chapter). What Quark is calling "wordspacing" here is really just changing the kerning between words (wherever it finds spacebands).

There are three conditions for adjusting wordspacing—spaceband kerning—over a selected range of text.

▶ You can only use keystrokes.

▶ You must have an extended keyboard.

▶ The Type Tricks XTension must be in your XTension folder (it must be currently active).

Table 6-5 shows the keystrokes you should use to adjust wordspacing. Note that adjusting wordspacing is no magic trick: QuarkXPress is simply adding and subtracting kerning from each spaceband (you can put

Table 6-5
Keystrokes for
wordspacing

PRESS ON THE MAC*...	ON WINDOWS...	TO...
⌘-⇧-⌃-]	⌃-⇧-]	Increase wordspacing 10 units
⌘-⌥-⇧-⌃-]	⌃-⇧-Alt-]	Increase wordspacing one unit
⌘-⇧-⌃-[	⌃-⇧-[	Decrease wordspacing 10 units
⌘-⌥-⇧-⌃-]	⌃-⇧-Alt-[	Decrease wordspacing one unit

Note that the keystrokes for both Macintosh and Windows may be different if you use a non-English keyboard.

the cursor between the spaceband and the first letter in a word to see how much space has been added).

There are two problems with adding wordspacing in this way. First, it's a pain to remove or change it (you can use Remove Manual Kerning as described earlier, but that will also remove any other kerning you've added). Second, the keystrokes that you press on Windows are the same as those you press for kerning and tracking. If we're lucky, Quark will come out with a version of this XTension that doesn't have this conflict.

Baseline Shift

The final character attribute I discuss here is *baseline shift*. The baseline is the imaginary line on which the type sits. Each line of text you're read-ing is made of characters sitting on a baseline. You can shift a character or a group of characters above or below the baseline using the Baseline Shift feature on the Style menu (see Figure 6-13).

Baseline shift is specified in points; negative values shift the charac-ter down, positive values shift it up. You can enter any value, up to three times the font size you're using, in hundredths of a point; for example, you can shift a character off the baseline 30 points in either direction if that character is in 10-point type.

Note that baseline shift is similar to kerning and tracking in an important way: even though you specify values in points rather than in fractions of an em, the value of the baseline shift changes along with the

Figure 6-13
Baseline shift

I DON'T NEED NO BASELINE SHIFT.

I FEEL A NEED FOR A SUPERSCRIPT.

OY. I'M FEELIN' KINDA UNSTABLE, WHAT WITH ALL THIS BASELINE SHIFTING GOING ON.

font size. For example, if you specify a 4-point baseline shift for 15-point type, when you double the font size to 30 points, the shifted character is "reshifted" to eight points ($2 \times 4 = 8$).

Paragraph Formatting

Character formatting is all very well and good, but when it comes to how text flows in a column, it don't make Bo Diddley squat. To handle text flow on a paragraph level, you have to use paragraph formatting. These controls include indents, leading, tabs, drop caps, and hyphenation and justification, as well as some esoteric functions such as Keep with Next ¶ and widow and orphan control. In this section, I'll discuss each of these features. In addition, as usual, I'll give lots of examples so you can see what I'm talking about.

Tip: Selecting Paragraphs. I often look over people's shoulders as they work, and what I see could scare a moose. One such scare is the technique of selecting a paragraph so that they can apply some paragraph formatting to it (leading, space before, or whatever). People think that they have to select the whole paragraph first. Not true! When you change paragraph formatting, you only need the cursor in the paragraph you want to change. That means you can have one word selected, or three sentences, or half of one paragraph and half of another, or whatever.

The central headquarters of paragraph formatting is the Paragraph Attributes dialog box (see Figure 6-14). Let's look at each feature of this dialog box in turn, and I'll branch off on tangents when I need to.

Alignment

Let's start with the most blatant paragraph attribute—its alignment. Most people are familiar with the five horizontal alignment options: left aligned, right aligned, justified, force justified, and centered. I will discuss each of these first, then move on to a less-known feature: vertical alignment.

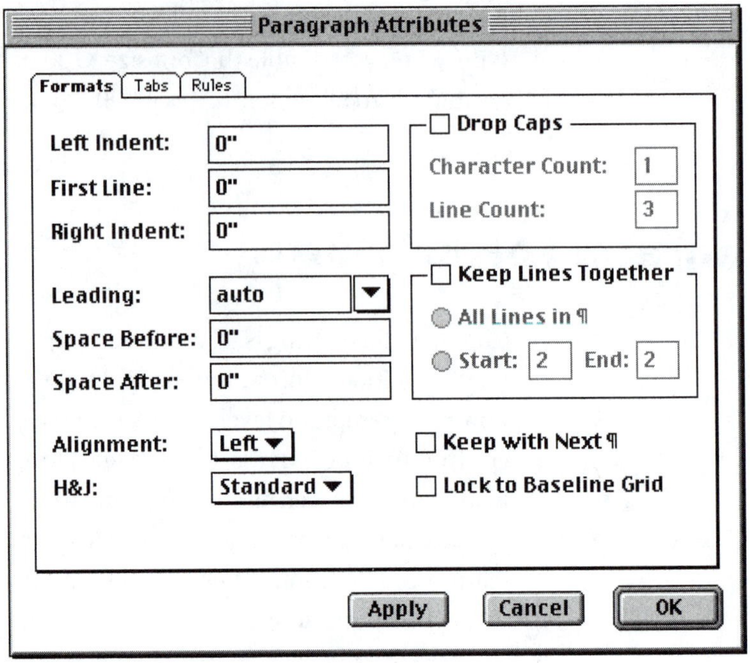

Figure 6-14
The Paragraph
Attributes dialog box

Paragraph Attributes

Formats | Tabs | Rules

Left Indent: 0"
First Line: 0"
Right Indent: 0"

Leading: auto ▼
Space Before: 0"
Space After: 0"

Alignment: Left ▼
H&J: Standard ▼

☐ Drop Caps
Character Count: 1
Line Count: 3

☐ Keep Lines Together
○ All Lines in ¶
○ Start: 2 End: 2

☐ Keep with Next ¶
☐ Lock to Baseline Grid

Apply | Cancel | OK

Horizontal Alignment

If you've been involved with desktop typography long enough (a day or two), you'll know that different programs have different names for the same thing. For example, what QuarkXPress calls "left aligned" others may call "left justified" or "flush left/ragged right." I'm not going to start naming names, but QuarkXPress's terms are simpler and make more sense. For one thing, "justified" means only one thing: text that's flush to both left and right margins. "Fully justified" is redundant, and "left-justified" is . . . well, it just isn't. Figure 6-15 shows some examples of text with various horizontal alignments.

You can specify alignment for a paragraph in any of four ways.

▶ **PARAGRAPH ATTRIBUTES.** The Paragraph Attributes dialog box is always an option when you're changing paragraph formats. The control is a popup menu (see Figure 6-16). This, of course, is the slow way to do it.

▶ **ALIGNMENT SUBMENU.** You can select the horizontal alignment you want from the Alignment submenu under the Style menu. This is pretty slow, too.

Figure 6-15
Horizontal alignment

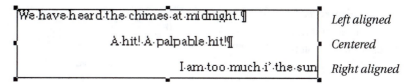

Left aligned

Centered

Right aligned

Figure 6-16
Alignment control in
the Paragraph Attributes
dialog box

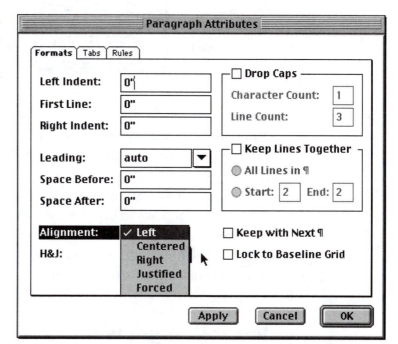

▶ **KEYSTROKES.** Note that the Alignment submenu lists a keystroke for each style. These are easy to remember, since they rely on first-letter mnemonics: hold down the Command and Shift keys and press "L" for Left, "R" for Right, "C" for Centered, and "J" for Justified. The keystroke for Forced Justify is a variant on Justified: Command-Option-Shift-J.

▶ **MEASUREMENTS PALETTE.** Perhaps the most simple alignment method of all is to use the Measurements palette. When you have an insertion point in a paragraph, XPress displays five icons representing the various alignment selections (see Figure 6-17). To change a paragraph's alignment, click on the one you want.

While left-aligned, right-aligned, and centered paragraphs are relatively straightforward, justified and force-justified text is more complicated. Because of this, I'm putting off talking about justification and hyphenation until later in this chapter.

Figure 6-17

Horizontal alignment in
the Measurements palette

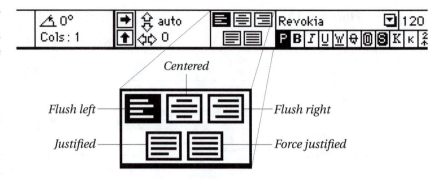

▼ ▼

Tip: Limit Your Alignments. I'm sure you would never do this. I know
that you're a designer of reputation and flair. But I might as well mention
this tip, just in case.

Don't use left-aligned, right-aligned, centered, and justified text all on
the same page unless you have a reasonable design sense and a signed
note from your parent. Too often people let all this highfalutin technology go to their heads and design their pages using every trick in the bag.
Remember that there is strength in simplicity.

▼ ▼

Vertical Alignment

Vertical alignment is not really a paragraph attribute, but an attribute of
each text box. Nonetheless, as vertical alignment is closely related to other paragraph attributes (leading in particular), I might as well bring this
into the discussion.

Just as horizontal alignment is the horizontal placement of the lines
of text within a column, vertical alignment is the vertical placement of
the text within its box. You can specify attributes similar to those used in
horizontal alignment: Top, Bottom, Center, and Justified. The only place
you can change this setting is on the Text tab in the Modify dialog box
(Command-M, or double-click on the box with the Item tool selected).
Here you're presented with a popup menu (see Figure 6-18).

Let's look briefly at each of the alignment possibilities.

Top. This is the default setting for text boxes. It's what you're probably
used to if you use QuarkXPress regularly. The text starts at the top of the

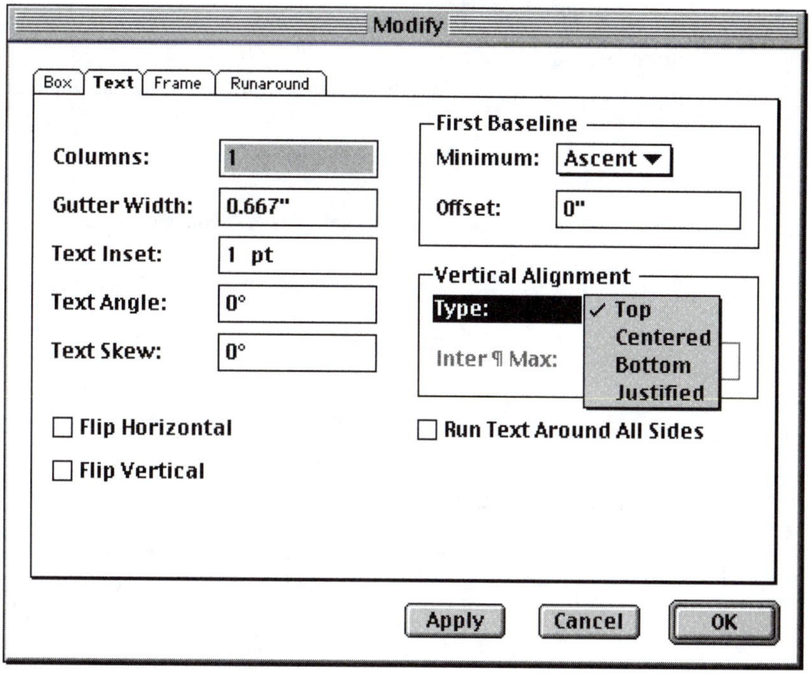

Figure 6-18

Vertical Alignment in
the Modify dialog box

text box and, as you type, fills the box. Exactly where the text starts depends on the First Baseline control (discussed later in the chapter).

Centered. When Vertical Alignment is set to Centered, the text in the text box is vertically centered. That sounds trite, but I can't explain it any better. See Figure 6-19 for an example of this alignment. Note that blank lines can affect the positioning of the text in the text box; sometimes you have to delete them to get the text to look centered.

▼ ▼

Tip: Centering Text. Telling XPress to center text—either horizontally or vertically—may not result in your text looking perfectly centered. Why? Because the mathematical horizontal centering of text may not look as "right" as optical centering, especially if you have punctuation before or after the text. You can use invisible characters colored the same as whatever they're on top of (for example, white on top of a white background). Or you can use altered indentation (see "Indents," below) to change the way the text looks (see Figure 6-20). Remember, what looks right is more "right" than what the computer says.

In the case of vertical centering, text in all capitals or text in fonts such as Zapf Dingbats may not appear to be centered in the box. This is

Figure 6-19

The four Vertical
Alignment settings

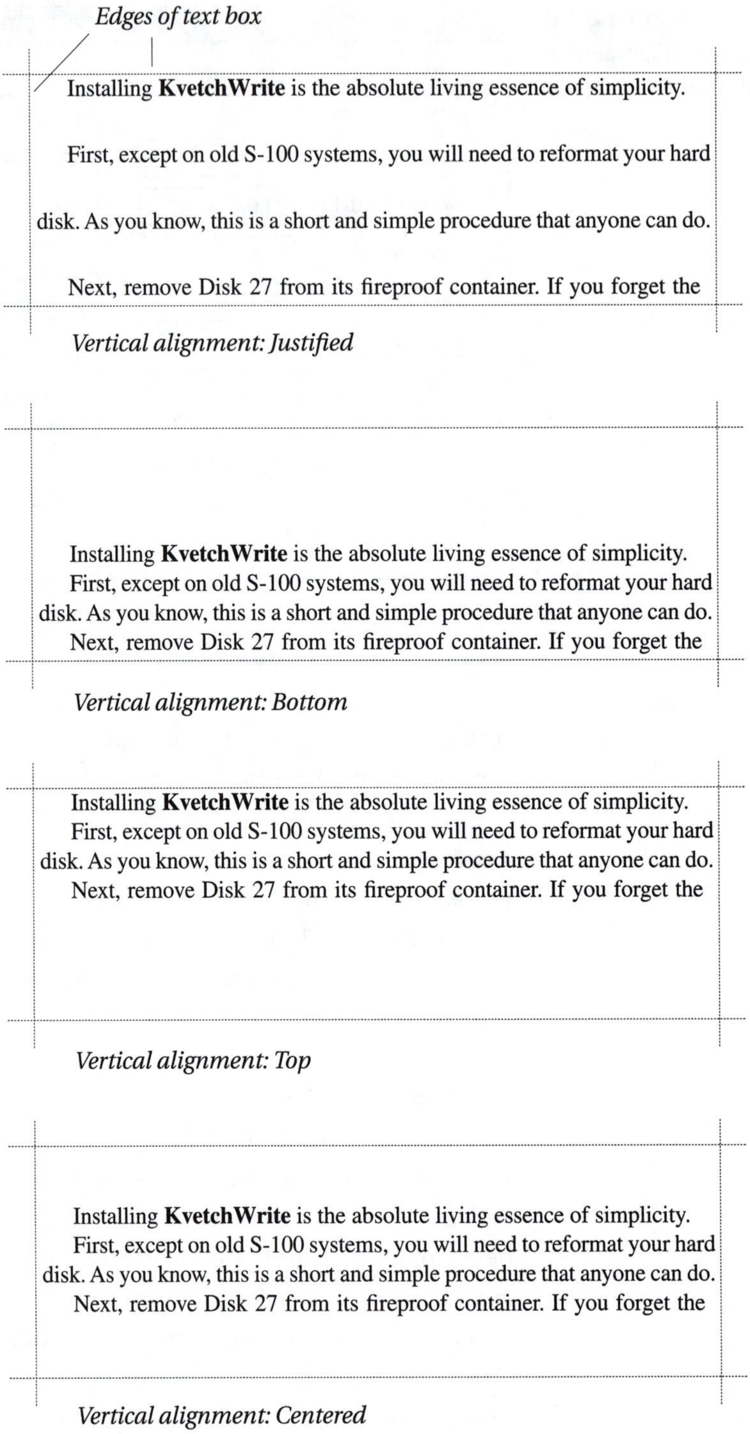

Edges of text box

Installing **KvetchWrite** is the absolute living essence of simplicity.

First, except on old S-100 systems, you will need to reformat your hard

disk. As you know, this is a short and simple procedure that anyone can do.

Next, remove Disk 27 from its fireproof container. If you forget the

Vertical alignment: Justified

Installing **KvetchWrite** is the absolute living essence of simplicity.
First, except on old S-100 systems, you will need to reformat your hard
disk. As you know, this is a short and simple procedure that anyone can do.
Next, remove Disk 27 from its fireproof container. If you forget the

Vertical alignment: Bottom

Installing **KvetchWrite** is the absolute living essence of simplicity.
First, except on old S-100 systems, you will need to reformat your hard
disk. As you know, this is a short and simple procedure that anyone can do.
Next, remove Disk 27 from its fireproof container. If you forget the

Vertical alignment: Top

Installing **KvetchWrite** is the absolute living essence of simplicity.
First, except on old S-100 systems, you will need to reformat your hard
disk. As you know, this is a short and simple procedure that anyone can do.
Next, remove Disk 27 from its fireproof container. If you forget the

Vertical alignment: Centered

Figure 6-20
When centering
is not centered

Vertical centering in the top example isn't optically even because the typeface isn't centered descender to cap height. The bottom example was centered by eye.

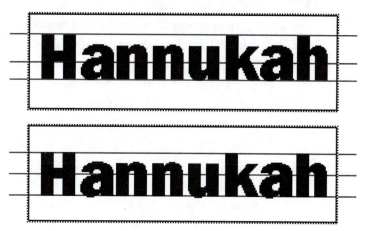

"Take your little brother swimming with a brick."

This is not visually centered because of the quotation marks.

"Take your little brother swimming with a brick."

This is adjusted by placing punctuation colored white on each line.

because QuarkXPress does not actually find the center of the characters you've typed. Instead, it uses the full height of the font, ascenders and descenders combined, to calculate proper placement. I suggest using baseline shift to move the characters around until they look the way you want them to.

▼ ▼

Bottom. By specifying Bottom, you force the last line of text to the bottom of the box. Then as text flows into the text box, each line pushes the type higher in the box. Note that it is the bottom of the descender, not the baseline, that sits flush with the box's bottom.

Justified. "Justification" means here that the text will be flush with the top and bottom of the box. QuarkXPress puts the first line of the text box at the top, the last line at the bottom, and then adds or deletes space between interior lines. That means that there may be a lot of extra space between lines and paragraphs (the program overrides paragraph leading settings when necessary).

You can specify a maximum distance between paragraphs in a vertically justified text box by changing the Inter ¶ Max value on the Text tab in the Modify dialog box. A setting of zero, which is the default, tells QuarkXPress to distribute all space evenly by adding leading. A setting higher than zero lets the program add extra space between paragraphs rather than change your leading (this is usually preferable). Figure 6-21 shows some examples of vertically justified text with different Inter ¶ Max settings.

When Quark announced that XPress would support vertical justification, the press thought it would be the greatest thing since the transistor. My response to this is: If you set up your leading grids and text boxes correctly, you shouldn't need to have some computer going through your drawers, shuffling lines around. I wouldn't want a computer to marry my daughter (if I had one), and I don't want a computer changing my leading and paragraph spacing.

No matter how picky I am about correctly setting up my documents, I do admit that there are times when vertical justification comes in handy. For example, many newspapers constantly use this feature to "bottom out" their columns.

▼ ▼

Tip: When Vertical Justification Doesn't Work. Note that XPress will turn off vertical alignment in two instances: if the text box is not rectangular, or if some object is causing text runaround (see Chapter 11, *Where Text Meets Graphics*). In both these cases, the text box reverts to top alignment. I could explain the mathematical reasoning behind this, but suffice it to say that it would be incredibly difficult and time-consuming for XPress to align text vertically in these instances, so it just doesn't even try.

▼ ▼

Indents

Horizontal alignment depends entirely on where the left and right margins are. In a column of text, the margins are usually at the edges of the text box (or of the column, in a multicolumn text box). However, you may

Figure 6-21

Varying the
Inter ¶ Max setting

Ior, auritulus cinereus ille annosus Raili, solus in silvae angulo quodam carduoso stabat, pedibus late divaricatis, capite deflexo de rerum natura meditans. "Cur?' cogitabat, modo "quemadmodum?'

Itaque Puo appropinquante Ior paulisper a meditatione desistere gavisus est ut maeste "Ut vales?' ei diceret.

Text is 10/11, Inter ¶ Max setting is zero points. The leading is ignored completely.

Gray line represents the text box.

Ior, auritulus cinereus ille annosus Raili, solus in silvae angulo quodam carduoso stabat, pedibus late divaricatis, capite deflexo de rerum natura meditans.

"Cur?' cogitabat, modo "quemadmodum?'

Itaque Puo appropinquante Ior paulisper a meditatione desistere gavisus est ut maeste "Ut vales?' ei diceret.

Text is 10/11, Inter ¶ Max setting is four points. The leading is adjusted slightly, while space is added between paragraphs.

Ior, auritulus cinereus ille annosus Raili, solus in silvae angulo quodam carduoso stabat, pedibus late divaricatis, capite deflexo de rerum natura meditans.

"Cur?' cogitabat, modo "quemadmodum?'

Itaque Puo appropinquante Ior paulisper a meditatione desistere gavisus est ut maeste "Ut vales?' ei diceret.

Text is 10/11, Inter ¶ Max setting is one pica. The leading is back to normal, and space is only added between paragraphs.

want the first line of every paragraph to be indented slightly. Or you might want the left or right margin to be somewhere other than the edge of the column. You control each of these by changing the values for paragraph indents.

▼ ▼

Tip: Watch the Text Inset. The default text inset for text boxes is one point, so your text will automatically be indented one point from each side of the box. Make sure to change the value in the Modify dialog box (Command-M) if you don't want the 1-point indent.

The best way to avoid this default problem is to close all documents, and double-click the Text Box tool. This brings up the Tool Preferences dialog box, where you can click the Modify button to change the Text Inset to zero. A text inset of zero sometimes makes the text a little hard to read on screen, because it bounces up against the side of the box; so you may or may not want to do this.

Note that some XTensions let you set the Text Inset differently for each side of the box: top, bottom, left, and right.

▼ ▼

QuarkXPress lets you change three indent values: Left Indent, Right Indent, and First Line indent. All three controls are located on the Formats tab in the Paragraph Attributes dialog box (Command-Shift-F; see Figure 6-22). I'll discuss each one and then talk about how you can use them in your documents.

Left Indent. The Left Indent control specifies how far the paragraph sits from the left side of the text box or column guide. The Left Indent is actually measured from the Text Inset border, not from the side of the box. For example, if you want your paragraph to be indented exactly three picas from the side of the text box, and your Text Inset setting is four points, then your Left Indent should be "2p8" (3p - 4pt = 2p8).

Figure 6-22
The Indent settings

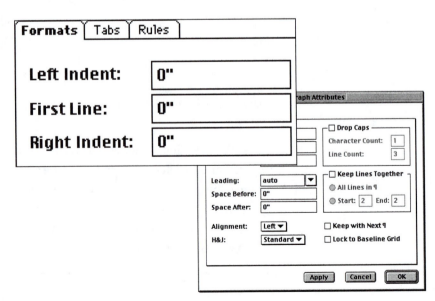

Right Indent. The Right Indent control specifies how far the right edge of the paragraph will be positioned from the right edge of the text box or column guide (or the text box's Text Indent). For example, if you change the Right Indent to .5 inch, you can imagine an invisible line being drawn .5 inch from the right column guide. The text cannot move farther to the right than this line (see Figure 6-23).

First Line. Whatever you do, wherever you go, don't type five spaces to indent the first line of each paragraph. If you must, use a tab. If you want to avoid the problem completely, use a First Line indent. The First Line indent feature does exactly what it sounds like it would do: it indents only the first line of each paragraph.

How large your indent should be depends primarily on your design and on the typeface you are working with. If you are working with a typeface with a large x-height (the height of the lowercase "x" in relation to the height of the capital letters), you should use a larger first-line indent than if you are working with a typeface that has a small x-height. Book designers often use a one- or two-em indent; if you're using 12-point type, the indent might be 12 points or 24 points.

Figure 6-23
Right Indent

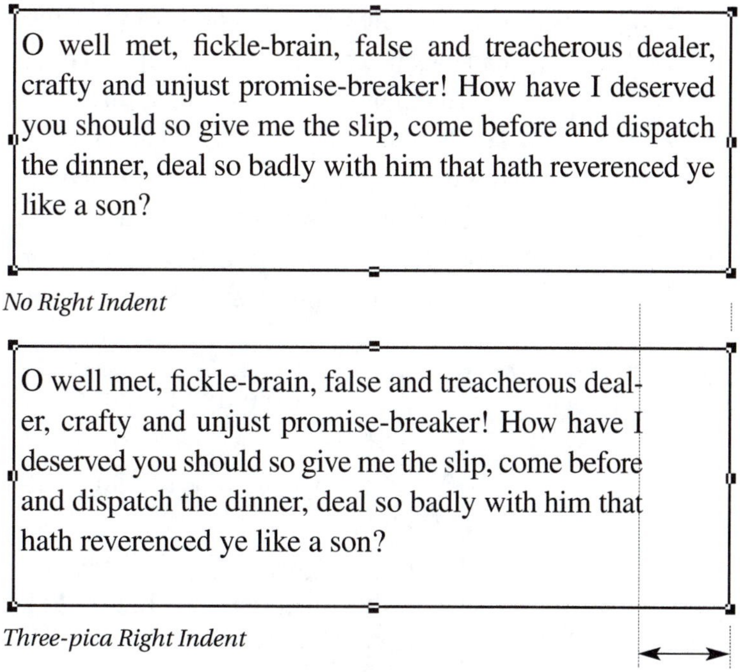

O well met, fickle-brain, false and treacherous dealer, crafty and unjust promise-breaker! How have I deserved you should so give me the slip, come before and dispatch the dinner, deal so badly with him that hath reverenced ye like a son?

No Right Indent

O well met, fickle-brain, false and treacherous dealer, crafty and unjust promise-breaker! How have I deserved you should so give me the slip, come before and dispatch the dinner, deal so badly with him that hath reverenced ye like a son?

Three-pica Right Indent

▼ ▼

Tip: Hanging Indents. You can use Left Indent and First Line indent to create hanging indents (used for bullet lists and the like) by typing a negative number as the First Line indent. I often use "1p6" (one-and-a-half picas) for a left indent and "-1p6" for a first-line indent. This pushes the entire paragraph out to the 1p6 mark, and then pulls the first character (a bullet) back to the zero mark (see Figure 6-24). Typing a tab after the bullet skips over to the 1p6 mark whether or not I have a tab stop there (I'll discuss tabs and tab stops later in this chapter).

The benefit of hanging indents like this is that you don't have to painfully set your own returns after each line. If you set hard or soft returns after each line—I'll talk about the difference later in this chapter—and then you edit the text, or even change the typeface, it takes a long time to fix the text, removing the old returns and putting new ones in. This is horrible; if you had just used hanging indents instead, your problem would be solved automatically.

(You can also use an Indent Here character when creating hanging indents; I cover that in "Special Characters," later in this chapter.)

▼ ▼

Note that you don't have to specify any of the indents by typing numbers. While the Paragraph Attributes dialog box is open, you are shown a ruler along the top of the active text box (see Figure 6-25). This ruler contains three triangle markers: two on the left, and one on the right. You can move these icons by clicking and dragging them along the ruler.

The right triangle is the Right Indent. The bottom-left triangle is the Left Indent. The top-left triangle is the First Line indent. While moving these triangles around, the First Line indent moves as you change the Left Indent. For example, if you set a ¼-inch First Line indent, and then move the Left Indent triangle to ½ inch, the First Line indent moves with it to the ¾-inch point (½ inch plus ¼ inch).

Figure 6-24

Hanging indents

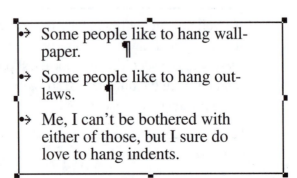

Figure 6-25
The text ruler
associated with the
Formats dialog box

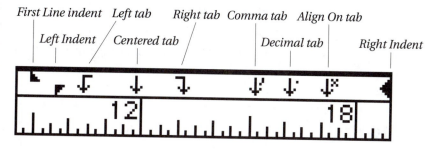

First Line indent   Left tab   Right tab   Comma tab   Align On tab

Left Indent   Centered tab   Decimal tab   Right Indent

▼ ▼

Tip: Formatting Past the Boundaries. As the old Zen master said, "Frustration dissipates like the morning fog when light is shed on the problem." (Actually, I don't know any Zen masters, so I just made that up.) One frustration I've seen people get caught in is the issue of formatting beyond what you can see on screen. For example, when you open the Paragraph Attributes dialog box, QuarkXPress adds a ruler along the top of the text box so that you can manually add or edit the tab stops and indents. However, if the box is too wide, you can't see the left or right side of the ruler because it runs right out of the document window (see Figure 6-26).

However—and here's the shedding of the light—it turns out that if you click in that ruler and drag to the left or right, the page scrolls with you. Pretty soon you get to where you want to go and you can stop drag-

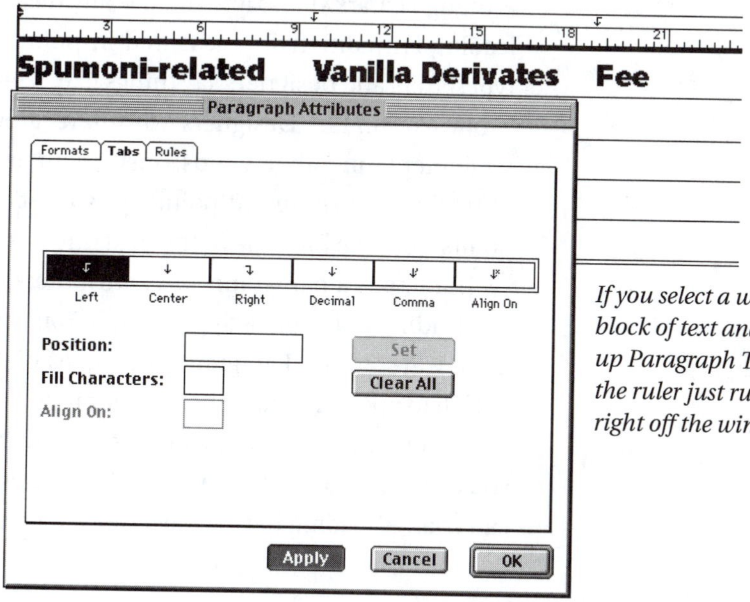

Figure 6-26
The too-wide ruler

Spumoni-related   **Vanilla Derivates**   **Fee**

Paragraph Attributes

Formats | Tabs | Rules

Left   Center   Right   Decimal   Comma   Align On

Position:

Fill Characters:

Align On:

Set

Clear All

Apply   Cancel   OK

If you select a wide block of text and bring up Paragraph Tabs, the ruler just runs right off the window.

ging. Note that when you do this, you sometimes accidentally add a tab stop (I'll talk about tab stops later in this chapter), and you have to get rid of it by clicking on it and dragging it off the ruler.

Leading

If I could get one concept across to you in this chapter, I'd want it to be this: don't follow the defaults. By not following default values, you are forced to pay attention to how the type looks, rather than letting the computer do it for you. There is perhaps no better example of why this is important than leading.

Leading (pronounced "ledding") is the space between lines of type. The name originates from the lead strips or blocks used to add space between lines of metal type. QuarkXPress gives you considerable control over leading values for each paragraph, or it can "fly on automatic," specifying leading for you.

In this section I'll discuss the two modes and three methods for specifying leading. Pay close attention to the words "color" and "readability" in this section; they're the reasons designers bother to be so meticulous.

Specifying Leading

Although QuarkXPress lets you use any measurement system you want, leading is traditionally measured in points. When talking type, most typesetters and designers say things like, "Helvetica 10 on 12," and write it out as "10/12." Designers who have grown accustomed to digital equipment (in other words, just about everybody) would say that "10/12" means setting 10-point type so that the baseline of one line is 12 points from the baseline of the next line (see Figure 6-27).

Leading is a paragraph-level attribute; that is, you can specify only one leading value for each paragraph. You specify your leading in one of three ways: in the Paragraph Attributes dialog box (press Command-Shift-E to open this dialog box and jump right to the Leading field), in the Measurements palette, or with keystrokes. Whereas in the first instance you can only type in the leading value, in the Measurements palette you can change leading in two ways (see Figure 6-28).

Figure 6-27
Specifying leading

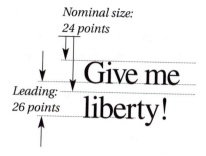

Figure 6-28
Leading in the
Measurements palette

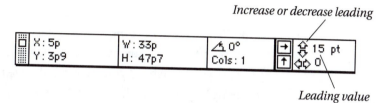

▶ You can select the leading value and replace it with whatever leading value you want.

▶ You can click the up or down arrow next to the leading value to increase or decrease the leading value in 1-point increments. Option-clicking increases or decreases in .1-point increments.

You can also use keyboard shortcuts to change a paragraph's leading. Table 6-6 shows the four keystrokes.

By the way, if you change leading in the Paragraph Attributes dialog box, you'll notice that XPress 4 places a popup menu next to the Leading field. The popup menu doesn't really do anything, and I still can't figure out why they stuck it in there. Just ignore it.

Leading Methods

QuarkXPress lets you specify leading values in three ways: absolutely, automatically, and relatively. Let's look at these.

Table 6-6
Leading keystrokes

Press...	To...
⌘-⇧-"	Increase leading in 1-point increments
⌘-⌥-⇧-"	Increase leading in 0.1-point increments
⌘-⇧-;	Decrease leading in 1-point increments
⌘-⌥-⇧-;	Decrease leading in 0.1-point increments

Absolute. Setting your leading in an absolute form makes your leading as steadfast as Gibraltar. If you specify 14-point leading, you get 14-point leading—no matter what size type the paragraph contains. If the type is bigger than the leading, the type overprints preceding lines. When, as in the example given above, someone talks about "10/12" type, this is what they're talking about.

QuarkXPress lets you type any absolute leading value between zero and 1,080 points (15 inches).

▼ ▼

Tip: True Zero Leading. If you set a paragraph's leading to zero, QuarkXPress decides that you really mean you want "automatic" leading (see below). But what if you really want no leading at all from baseline to baseline? If you set leading to .0001 points, the program rounds down to exactly zero. The next highest value is .001 points. The truth of the matter is that these are equivalent for all intents and purposes, but I wanted to be clear anyway.

Why would anyone want to use zero leading? Well, it wouldn't be common. Zero leading means that every line in the paragraph would be printed exactly on top of the line above it, making the whole paragraph be only one line tall. It's especially good for those postmodern designs where you don't really need to read any of the words.

▼ ▼

Automatic. Auto leading sets leading as a percentage of the largest font size on each line. This percentage is usually 20 percent greater than the font size. For example, if the largest font size on a given line is 10 points, then your leading will be set to 12 points (10, plus 20 percent of 10). If you change the font size to 12 points, then the leading changes to 14.4 points. Note that if you change only one character on a line to a larger font size, then that line alone will have a different leading value (which just *screams* "nonprofessional!"), even though Auto leading is a paragraph-wide feature (see Figure 6-29).

Auto leading is the default setting of any new text box. To choose it specifically, you can type either "Auto" or "0" as the leading value.

You can change the automatic-leading percentage value on the Paragraph tab in the Document Preferences dialog box. There are two things you should note about doing this, though. First, the change is document-wide; you can't change the automatic leading percentage for only one paragraph or text box. Second, you must specify clearly what the automatic leading measurements are; that is, if you want a percent, you must type a percent sign. This is important because you can also specify automatic leading to be a relative value (more on relative values soon).

To be honest with you, I use automatic leading when I'm typing up grocery shopping lists (and sometimes when I'm writing a letter to my mom). But when I'm working on a professional project, I define the leading explicitly using absolute leading. Period. Many professional magazines, newspapers, and newsletters use automatic leading because they don't know any better, and then they blame QuarkXPress for outputting weird-looking text.

Figure 6-29

Auto leading can result in irregular leading within a paragraph

Noodle. Oh! monstrous, dreadful, terrible! Oh! Oh! Deaf be my ears, for ever blind my eyes! **D**umb be my tongue! feet lame! all senses lost! Howl wolves, grunt bears, hiss snakes, shriek all ye ghosts!

King. What does the blockhead mean?

One character can throw the leading off.

Relative. Whereas automatic leading generally determines the leading value based on a percentage of font size, relative leading determines leading by an absolute value. You specify relative leading by including the characters + or - (plus or minus—the minus sign is a hyphen) before your leading value. For example, applying a leading value of +3 to 12-point type results in 12/15 leading. If you change the font size to 22 points, you automatically get 22/25 leading (22 plus 3).

By typing a negative relative value, you can tighten up the leading. However, you have a limit: the height of a capital on the lower line cannot be higher than the baseline of the upper line (to get that effect, you have to use absolute leading).

The only time I use relative leading is when I am specifying *solid* leading—that is, when the leading equals the point size. Instead of keying in 30-point leading for 30-point type, I type "+0". Then, if (or when) I change the font size, the leading changes with it.

Leading Modes

When specifying leading in QuarkXPress, you can work in one of two leading modes: Word Processing or Typesetting. You can select which mode to use on the Paragraph tab in the Document Preferences dialog box on the Edit menu.

Word Processing. Let's be straight here: even if you're using XPress only as a word processor, you shouldn't use Word Processing mode. There's just no point to it. Selecting Word Processing mode makes QuarkXPress use an ascent-to-ascent measurement. "Ascent to ascent" means that the leading value you specify will be measured from the top of a capital letter on one line to the top of a capital letter on the next line. The only reason Quark included this method was because many word-processing programs use it. You shouldn't, because the leading will change depending on the typeface you're using, and there's no way you can tell what the leading value actually is (this side of examining a font's ascent value using ResEdit or some font utility).

Typesetting. As I noted above, the proper way to specify leading on the Macintosh is to measure from the baseline of one line to the baseline of the next. QuarkXPress calls this Typesetting Mode. It's the program default; if someone has changed it, change it back and leave it alone.

▼ ▼

Tip: When Black and White Is Colorful. When designers and typesetters talk about the *color* of a page or of type, they aren't talking red, green, or blue. They're referring to the degree of darkness or lightness that the text projects. The color of text is directly related to the typeface, letterspacing, wordspacing, and leading. Other design elements, such as drop caps, graphic elements, or pullquotes, can have a significant effect on the color of a page. It's usually a good practice to maintain an even and balanced color across your page, unless you're trying to pull the viewer's eye (as opposed to pulling the viewer's leg) to one area or another (see Figure 6-30).

One way to see the color of a page or a block of type is to hold the printed page at some distance and squint. You can also turn the page over and hold it up to the light, so that you can see the text blocks without being distracted by the text itself.

▼ ▼

Tip: Leading Techniques. Here are a few tips and tricks for adjusting your leading. Remember, though, that ultimately it is how easily the text reads and how comfortable the color is that counts. Figure 6-31 shows some samples for each of these suggestions.

▶ Increase the leading as you increase the line length. Solid leading may read fine with lines containing five words, but will be awful for lines containing 20 words.

▶ Generally use some extra leading for sans serif or bold type. It needs the extra room.

▶ Note the x-height of your typeface. Fonts with a small x-height can often be set tighter than those with a large x-height.

▶ Set display or headline type tightly. Big type can and should be set tightly, using either +0 relative leading or even absolute leading smaller than the point size you're using.

Figure 6-30
The color of text blocks

Eduardus ursus, amicis suis agnomine "Winnie ille Pu"—aut breviter "Pu"—notus, die quodam canticum semihiantibus labellis superbe eliquans

Stone Serif 9/12

Eduardus ursus, amicis suis agnomine "Winnie ille Pu"—aut breviter "Pu"—notus, die quodam canticum semihiantibus

Stone Serif bold 9/12

Eduardus ursus, amicis suis agnomine "Winnie ille Pu"— aut breviter "Pu"—notus, die quodam canticum semihian- tibus labellis superbe

Helvetica 10/13

Eduardus ursus, amicis suis agnomine "Winnie ille Pu"—aut breviter "Pu"—notus, die quo- dam canticum semihiantibus labellis superbe eliquans

Garamond 10/13

Eduardus ursus, amicis suis agnomine "Winnie ille Pu"— aut breviter "Pu"—notus, die quodam canticum semi- hiantibus labellis superbe

Palatino with zero tracking

Eduardus ursus, amicis suis agnomine "Winnie ille Pu"—aut breviter "Pu"—notus, die quo- dam canticum semihiantibus labellis superbe eliquans

Palatino with -10 tracking

> ▶ When you're using really tight leading, be careful not to let the ascenders of one line touch the descenders of the line above it.

A corollary tip to all of these: break the rules if it makes the design look better!

▾ ▾

Tip: From Automatic to Absolute. If you press Command-Shift-straight quote when the selected paragraph is set to Auto leading, XPress switches the leading to the absolute value that corresponds to the automatic value (it rounds to the nearest point). For instance, if you've got 10-point type and Auto leading is set to 20 percent, if you select a paragraph that has automatic leading and press Command-Shift-straight quote, XPress changes the leading to 12 points (120 percent of 10 points). This is the fastest way to switch from automatic to absolute leading.

▾ ▾

Space Before and After

Not only can you place interline space with leading, you can add space between paragraphs using the Space Before and Space After controls. You can find both of these controls in the Paragraph Attributes dialog box (Command-Shift-F).

While it is entirely your prerogative to use both Space Before and Space After, you normally will only need to use one or the other. Think about it: If you add equal space before and after a paragraph, it doubles the amount of space between each paragraph. I almost always use Space Before, but whichever you use is fine.

I've seen more than one designer become flustered when applying Space Before to the first paragraph in a text box. Nothing happens. Remember that Space Before has no effect on the first paragraph in a text box because it only adds space *between* two paragraphs. Fortunately, though, this is usually what you want. To add space before the first paragraph in a text box, use the First Baseline placement control (see "First Baseline," below).

▾ ▾

Tip: Adding Extra Space. Recently I witnessed one of my esteemed officemates using multiple carriage returns to control the space between paragraphs, and I almost went apoplectic. Let's see if I can pound this

Figure 6-31
Leading techniques

The longer a line, the more leading you'll need.

Look, s'pose some general or king is bone stupid and leads his men up a creek, then those men've got to be fearless, there's another virtue for you. S'pose he's stingy and hires too few soldiers, then they got to be a crowd of Hercule's. And s'pose he's slapdash and don't give a bugger, then they got to be clever as monkeys else their number's up.

9/9.5

9/11

Look, s'pose some general or king is bone stupid and leads his men up a creek, then those men've got to be fearless, there's another virtue for you. S'pose he's stingy and hires too few soldiers, then they got to be a crowd of Hercule's. And s'pose he's slapdash and don't give a bugger, then they got to be clever as monkeys else their number's up.

Fonts with small x-heights can be set tighter.

The misery of this one woman surges through my heart and marrow, and you grid imperturbed over the fate of thousands!

The misery of this one woman surges through my heart and marrow, and you grid imperturbed over the fate of thousands!

9/11.5

9/9.5

Display type can be set tightly.

The best thing since sliced bread

36/31

Watch out for your ascenders and descenders.

Cagney Jads

48/39

idea into your head as strongly as I did by saying, "Don't use multiple spaces between words or punctuation!"

Don't ever use an extra carriage return to add space between paragraphs. Not only will you offend the people at Quark who spent long hours implementing the Space Before and Space After features, but you will—nine out of 10 times—mess yourself up with extra blank paragraphs hanging out at tops of columns or in other places where you don't want them. If you want a full line of space between paragraphs, apply it with Space Before or Space After in the Paragraph Attributes dialog box.

▼ ▼

First Baseline

The first line of a text box is always a tricky one for perfectionists. How far away from the top edge of the text box should the line sit? And how to get it there? Usually, QuarkXPress places the first line of text according to the text box's Text Inset value. For instance, if the Text Inset is set to 3 points, then the top of the first line of text is set 3 points away from the top edge of the box.

Typophiles will be happy to find that you can clarify what XPress uses as the "top of the first line of text" with the Minimum setting (found on the Text tab in the Modify dialog box—Command-M). You can choose three values for the Minimum setting: Cap Height, Cap+Accent, and Ascent (see Figure 6-32).

Nonetheless, if you really care about the placement of your type, you may choose to use First Baseline Offset instead (also found in the Modify dialog box). First Baseline Offset lets you choose exactly how far from the top of the text box you want the first line of text to sit (measured from the baseline, of course). However, First Baseline Offset only kicks in when the distance from box edge to first baseline is smaller than the First Baseline Offset value.

For instance, if the baseline of the first line of text is 24 points from the top of the box when First Baseline Offset is set to zero (which is the default value), then First Baseline Offset won't do anything until you set the value higher than 24 points. If you set it to 30 points, then the baseline of the first line of text will sit at exactly 30 points from the top of the box. However, if you then change the text size to 60 points, XPress ignores the First Baseline Offset again and places the top of the text (as determined by the Minimum setting) at the Text Inset value.

Figure 6-32

The Minimum settings in First Baseline Offset

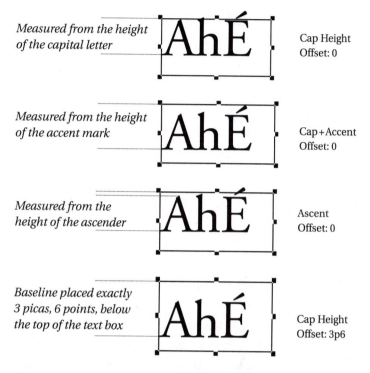

Measured from the height of the capital letter

Cap Height
Offset: 0

Measured from the height of the accent mark

Cap+Accent
Offset: 0

Measured from the height of the ascender

Ascent
Offset: 0

Baseline placed exactly 3 picas, 6 points, below the top of the text box

Cap Height
Offset: 3p6

Tip: Constant First Baselines. When you're working with a leading grid, you might be frustrated by where QuarkXPress places the first line in a text box. That's because XPress generally moves the baseline of the first line up or down to accommodate the size of the text, rather than sticking to your baseline grid (see Figure 6-33). But if you explicitly set the First Baseline value for the text box in the Modify dialog box (Command-M), the first baseline always appears at the same place, and your leading grid isn't messed up. Note that the First Baseline value has to be bigger than the type itself in order for the line to be moved down.

So don't go adding multiple carriage returns or trying to do weird things with leading, space before, or baseline shift. Just use the First Baseline setting.

Figure 6-33

First Baseline maintains
an even leading grid

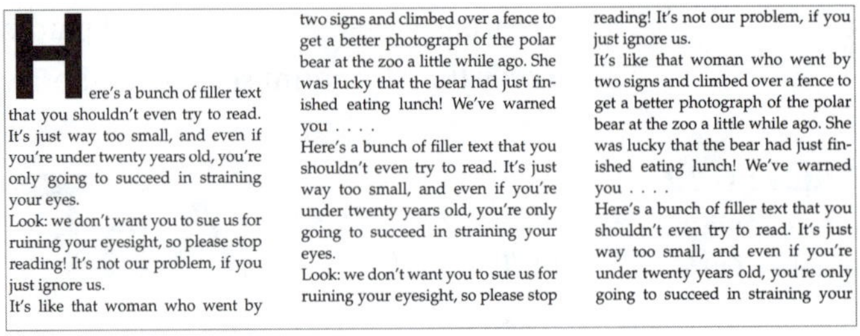

*Note that First Baseline
Offset aligns all the
columns of a text box*

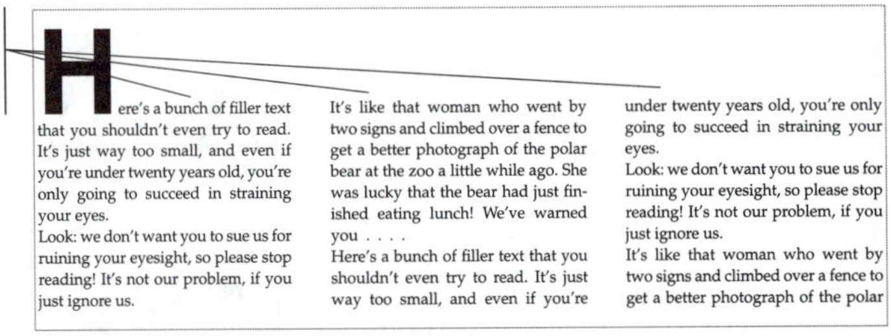

Before

After

Tabs

If you've ever typed on a typewriter, you've probably encountered tabs. A tab is a jump-to signal in the form of a keyboard character. For example, if you're typing along and press the Tab key, the text cursor jumps to the next tab stop along the line. On a computer, the Tab key actually inserts an invisible character that you can delete or cut (or anything else you can do with characters). You can place tab stops anywhere you like across the text column. Tab stops are paragraph-level formatting attributes, so each paragraph can have a different set of tab stops. If you don't specify your own tab stops, QuarkXPress sets default stops every half-inch across the text box.

Tip: Don't Use Space Where You Really Want Tabs. Have you ever tried to align multiple columns using the spacebar? If you have, you have probably known frustration like no other frustration known to desktop publishers. I call it the "it-works-on-a-typewriter" syndrome. It's true; you can line up columns on a typewriter with spaces. But you shouldn't in desktop publishing. The reason has to do with fonts.

On most standard typewriters, the font you're using is a monospaced font. That means each and every character in the font is the same width. However, most typefaces on the Macintosh are *not* monospaced. Therefore, you cannot rely on an equal number of characters always spanning an equal distance. Figure 6-34 shows this phenomenon clearly. So don't use multiple spaces when you're trying to align columns. In fact, don't use multiple spaces ever. Use tabs.

▼ ▼

Tip: Multiple Tabs. If you are setting up a table and you want to place tabs between each column, follow the same rule as with spaces: don't type multiple tabs in a row to make your columns align. Set one tab stop for each column. Then press Tab once to jump from column to column.

▼ ▼

Figure 6-34

Using spaces for alignment

Take one	from column "a"	and one	from column "b"
but here	you actually	have four	columns see?

Aligned with spaces (bad)

Take one	from column "a"	and one	from column "b"
but here	you actually	have four	columns see?

Aligned with tabs (good)

QuarkXPress lets you set seven types of tab stops using two different methods. Let's look at the types of tab stops first. They are: Left, Right, Center, Right Indent, Decimal, Comma, and Align On. Figure 6-35 shows examples of most of these tab stops in a common situation—a table.

► **LEFT TAB STOP.** This is the type of tab stop you're used to from typewriters. The text after the tab continues as left-aligned. All tab stops are Left tab stops unless you specify them as another type.

► **RIGHT TAB STOP.** Tabbing to a Right tab stop causes the following text to be right aligned. That is, the text will be flush right against the tab stop.

► **CENTER TAB STOP.** Text typed after tabbing to a Center tab stop will center on that tab stop.

▶ **RIGHT INDENT TAB.** Right Indent tabs don't show up on the pop-up menu because they're not really tab stops. You enter them in a text box with the Content tool selected by pressing Option-Tab. I'll talk about this more fully in just a moment.

▶ **DECIMAL, COMMA, AND ALIGN ON TAB STOPS.** These three tab stops act similarly. They act like a right tab until a special character is entered; then the following text is flush left. The decimal and comma tabs align on the first nonnumeric, nonpunctuation character. Selecting Align On brings up a one-character entry field; you can then enter the special character that acts as the tab stop.

▼ ▼

Tip: Formatting Tabs Quickly. One reader, Barry Simon, pointed out to me that you can sometimes format tabs for a number of lines more easily by just working on a single line. If you set the proper tab settings for the first line, you can quickly apply those settings to the rest of the lines by selecting all the lines (including the first one), opening the Paragraph Attributes dialog box (Command-Shift-F or Command-Shift-T), and clicking OK (or pressing Return). The tab setting for the first line is applied to the rest of the lines.

Figure 6-35

Using tabs and tab stops

Acme Digital Frammis Corp.

"Have a *wonderful* day!"

1994 Customer Dissatisfaction as a Function of Product Color

Product Color	People Per Product	Units Sold	Unit Price ($)	Dissatisfaction Index*
Moon Maid	120/20	2001	12.95[a]	6.77
Stuck Pig	44/63	5877	19.95	13.32
Curmudgeon	56/56	31	6[b]	57.91
Haggis	1/100000	3	129.97	3244.36

Parts per million [a]Special discount [b]Sold to GK

Left tab   Align on "/"   Centered tab   Decimal tab   Right tab

▼ ▼

Tip: Hanging Tabs. There's a subtle feature in the decimal tab function which you'll love if you ever create financial balance sheets. The decimal tab doesn't just line up decimals. Rather, QuarkXPress thinks of any non-number that falls after a number to be a decimal point, and aligns to it. For example, if you press Tab and type "94c2.4" on a line with a decimal tab, QuarkXPress aligns to the "c" rather than to the period.

I thought this was a bug until I realized how handy it could be. For example, if you are lining up numbers in a column, the negative-balance parentheses hang outside the column. You can even create hanging footnotes, as long as they're not numbers (see the unit price column in Figure 6-35, above).

▼ ▼

Setting Tab Stops

To place a custom tab stop, open the Tabs tab in the Paragraph Attributes dialog box, which you can find by selecting Tabs from the Style menu, or by pressing Command-Shift-T. When this dialog box is open, Quark-XPress places a ruler bar across the box of the text box you're working in (see Figure 6-36).

Figure 6-36

Setting tab stops

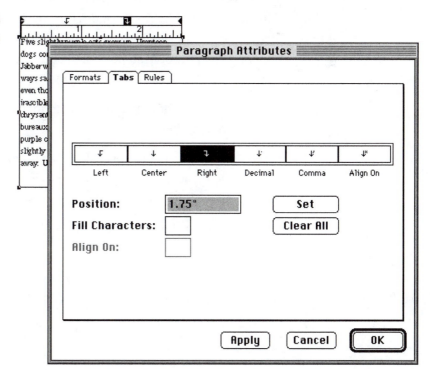

You can place a tab stop in one of two ways.

▶ You can click in the ruler above the text box and then choose what sort of tab stop you want by pressing one of the Tab stop buttons in the dialog box. (You can also choose the tab stop type before clicking in the ruler; it doesn't matter.)

▶ You can type a value into the Position field in the Paragraph Attributes dialog box and then choose what sort of tab stop you want it to be (or, again, you can choose the type first). Remember that you can type the value in a different measurement system than the ruler is displaying, or even use an equation to figure the position (see "Tip: Evenly Spaced Tab Stops," below). If you want to add another tab stop using this technique, click the Set button to "lock in" the tab stop (or press Command-S).

Don't forget the Apply button when setting tab stops. When you're setting up a table, you almost never get the tabs stops right the first time, so it's useful to click Apply (or press Command-A) to see how the tab stops will affect the paragraph before you close the dialog box.

▼ ▼

Tip: Evenly Spaced Tab Stops. Don't forget that you can use arithmetic in dialog box fields. This includes the Position field when you're setting tabs. If you want evenly spaced tabs, place each tab by adding an increment to the previous tab position. For instance, let's say you want a tab stop at .5 inch and every inch from there.

1. Type ".5" into the Position field (or ".5"" if your measurements aren't inches).

2. Press Command-S or click the Set button. This sets the tab stop in the paragraph without having to leave the Paragraph Attributes dialog box.

3. Position the cursor after the ".5" (you can just press the Right Arrow key) and type "+1".

4. Press Command-S or click Set again. (You can also press Command-A or click the Apply button.)

5. Continue until you have all the tab stops you need. When you're done, press OK.

Note that if the equation gets too long in the Position field, you can click on the last tab stop you added (the little arrow icon in the tab ruler). This simplifies the equation to save space.

Sandee Cohen pointed out that you can do a similar thing using multiplication and division. For example, if you wanted to set up tab stops at every .75-inch increment across a text box, you could set the first one at .75, then the second one at .75*2, the third at .75*3, and so on (clicking the Set button between each one).

You can even space out tab stops equally across a text box. Let's say you want five tab stops, and your text box is 35 picas wide. To set the first tab stop, type "35p/6" in the Position field (always divide by one more than the number of tab stops you want to end up with). To set the second tab stop, change this to "35p/6*2". Change the 2 to 3 for the third tab stop, and so on.

▼ ▼

Changing and Deleting Tab Stops

Once you have tab stops set for a paragraph, you can go back and edit them by dragging the tab-stop icons along the ruler in the Paragraph Attributes dialog box. Earlier versions of XPress only let you drag tab stops, but now you can edit a tab stop's position or type much more easily. The trick is to first select the tab stop you want to edit (click on it). Then you can press one of the tab-stop type buttons, change the position value, or edit the Fill Character (see "Tab Leaders," below). When you're done, click the Set, Apply, or OK button.

You can rid yourself of an unwanted tab stop by dragging the icon out of the ruler boundaries (see Figure 6-37). To clear all the tab stops for a paragraph, click the Clear All button in the Paragraph Attributes dialog box (or Option-click the ruler above the text box that appears when that dialog box is open).

Editing tab stops is one place that the continuous Apply feature is really helpful; as I pointed out in Chapter 2, *QuarkXPress Basics*, you can

Figure 6-37

Dragging away a tab stop

turn this feature on and off by Option-clicking the Apply button. When you turn it on, you can drag or edit tab stops and QuarkXPress updates the paragraph(s) automatically. This makes adjusting columns much faster and easier.

Tab Leaders

A tab leader is a repeated character that fills the space created with the tab. The most common example is a table of contents, where the repeating period character fills the space between a chapter name and a page number. Each tab stop can have its own leader. In fact, in XPress, you can use either one or two repeating characters (see Figure 6-38).

To add a leader while creating a new tab stop, set the tab stop as described earlier, then—before you click Apply, Set, or OK—type the leader characters into the Fill Characters field. When you're done, click Set, Apply, or OK.

If the tab stop is already created and you want to change its leader, select the tab stop in the ruler above the text box, type the leader characters into the Fill Characters field, and then click Set, Apply, or OK.

▼ ▼

Tip: Adjusting Leaders. You don't have to be content with the size and font of a tab's leaders (otherwise called "fill characters"). If you want the characters to be smaller, select the tab character in the text (not the tab stop) and change its point size. If you want the characters to appear in another font, change the font of that tab character. People don't often think of the tab character as a character, but that's just what it is. If you turn on Show Invisibles (select it from the View menu), you can see the character as a little gray triangle.

Changing the font and size isn't all you can do; you can even change the amount of space between the leader characters. Select the tab space

Figure 6-38
Tab leaders

Moose attack-------------------on Golden Pond
A neverending § § § § § § § § § § § § story of greed
Corruption ➟➟➟➟➟➟➟and extra-large boots.
Left-handed■■■■■■■■■■■■■■■■■■Windshifters!

Other characters used as tab leaders. In the second line, the size of the tab itself was reduced to 10 points. In the third and fourth lines, the tab character's font was changed to Zapf Dingbats.

and adjust its tracking or kerning values. Typically, when you change the kerning value for a single character it only changes the space between it and the next character; however, in this case it changes the space between each of the leader characters (see Figure 6-39).

▼ ▼

Right Indent Tab

Trying to set a tab stop exactly at the right margin can be very frustrating. Even worse, if your right margin or the size of your text box changes, your tab stop doesn't follow along. Typing a Right Indent tab (Option-Tab) fixes all that. This type of tab acts as though you've placed a right tab stop flush with the right margin of your paragraph. Plus, it moves as you adjust the margin or the text box. Inserting this type of tab effectively adds the tab and sets a variable tab stop at the same time. (I can hear the handful of people who "get it" sighing appreciatively in the background. Those of you who don't, just try it once and you'll understand.)

The Right Indent tab acts just like a tab character (you can even search for it the same way, using "\t"; see "Find/Change" in Chapter 5, *Word Processing*), though there's no way to set its own leader. It picks up the same leader as the previous tab stop in the paragraph. Note that you won't see a tab stop in the ruler that appears with the Paragraph Attributes dialog box; it's always set to the right margin, wherever that is. Also, you should note that Option-Tab jumps past all other tab stops in that paragraph, all the way over to the right margin.

Figure 6-39
Adjusting the tracking of the tab leader characters

Period used as leader characters (18 points; same as other type on the line).

Moishe is..not strange.

Oh yes. . . . . he is, too.

Tab reduced to 10 points with a tracking value of 94.

▼ ▼

Hyphenation and Justification

There are few things more dear to a typesetter's heart than hyphenation and justification—often called simply "H&J." Proper hyphenation and justification is often the most important single factor in the way a document looks. And if your H&J is bad . . . well, there's little that anyone can do (see Figure 6-40).

QuarkXPress has some very powerful controls over how it hyphenates and justifies text in a column. However, this is once more a situation where you won't want to rely on its default settings. Let's take a look at what H&J is all about, and then get into the details of how you can make it work for you.

The Basics of H&J

Although hyphenation and justification are entirely separate functions, they almost always go together. Almost always.

The idea behind both hyphenation and justification is to make text fit into a given space and still look as good as possible. It turns out that there are three basic ways to fit text without distorting it too much.

► Controlling the spacing between all the letters.

► Controlling the spacing between the words.

► Breaking the words at line endings by hyphenating.

Any one of these, if performed in excess, usually looks pretty awful. However, it is possible to mix them together in proper measure for a pleasing result.

Figure 6-40
Hyphenation and
Justification can
make a difference

Doing a good job with the program involves knowing a little something about good hyphenation and justification settings. If y'ain't got the good settings, you don't got the good-looking type, either. This paragraph, for example, is simply atrocious.

Doing an *especially* good job with the program involves taking the time to learn about its hyphenation and justification controls. You'll be glad you did.

▼ ▼

Tip: Check for Rivers. Often the first problem that arises when people set their text to justified alignment is that their documents start looking like a flood just hit; rivers of white space are flowing around little islands of words. Because humans are so good at seeing patterns of lines (it's just how our brains work), too much space between words is disturbing to the eye. I mentioned in "Tip: When Black and White is Colorful" that turning the page over and holding it up to the light is a good way to check the color of a text block. It's also a great way to check for rivers in your text. This way your eye isn't drawn toward reading the words—just seeing the spaces.

▼ ▼

Although you can't adjust the algorithms that QuarkXPress uses for H&J, you can change many variables that help in its decision making. These values make up the Edit Hyphenation & Justification dialog box, found by first selecting H&Js from the Edit menu (or pressing Command-Option-H), selecting the H&J to edit, and then clicking the New or Edit button (see Figure 6-41).

Let's divide the controls in this dialog box into two groups—Auto Hyphenation and Justification—and discuss them one at a time.

Auto Hyphenation

QuarkXPress can automatically hyphenate words at the end of a line, breaking them into syllables according to an internal algorithm. When you first start up the program, make sure that Auto Hyphenation is

Figure 6-41

The Edit Hyphenation & Justification dialog box

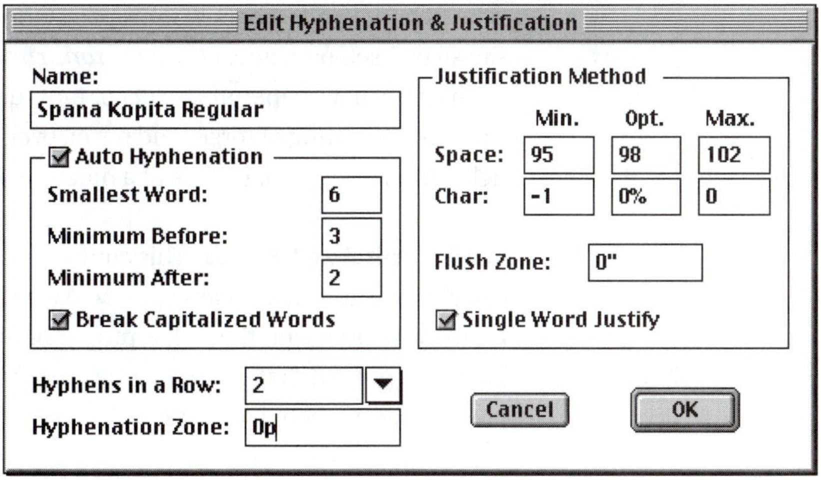

turned on (in earlier versions, the default setting was off, but XPress 4 usually turns it on). If it's off, QuarkXPress won't hyphenate any words unless you type your own hyphens or discretionary hyphens (see "Formatting Characters," later in this chapter). You can turn on Auto Hyphenation in the Edit Hyphenation & Justification dialog box (remember that if you turn it on when no documents are open, it stays on for all subsequent files). When you enable hyphenation, several items become active. These features are the basic controls over QuarkXPress's internal hyphenating algorithms. Let's look at them one at a time.

Smallest Word. When QuarkXPress is attempting to hyphenate a line of text, it must decide which words are eligible for hyphenation. You can quickly discard most of the smaller words by specifying the smallest word QuarkXPress considers. For example, you might not want the word "many" to hyphenate at the end of a line. By setting the Smallest Word value to five or higher, you tell QuarkXPress to ignore this word, as well as any other word with fewer than five letters.

Minimum Before. The Minimum Before value specifies the number of letters in a word which must come before a hyphen break. Depending on your tastes and your level of pickiness, you might set this to two or three. Otherwise, words like "mnemonic" might break after the first "m." I find that most art directors prefer a minimum of three letters.

Minimum After. The Minimum After value determines the number of letters in a word that must come after a hyphenation break. Again, this value is based on aesthetics. Some people don't mind if the "ly" in "truly" sits all by itself on a line. (*The New York Times* breaks "doesn't" after the "s," but it's a newspaper, after all.) For most quality work, you would want a minimum setting of three. And never, ever, set it to one (the results are uglier than a vegetarian's face at a meat-packing plant).

Break Capitalized Words. This control is self-explanatory. You can tell QuarkXPress to either break capitalized words or not. The feature is there for those people who think that proper nouns should never be broken. I'm picky, but not that picky. (On the other hand, it is strange to see people's names hyphenated.)

Hyphens in a Row. One area in which I *am* that picky is the number of hyphens I allow in a row. For most work, I hate to see more than a single hyphen in a row down a justified column of text. QuarkXPress defaults to "unlimited," which is the same as typing zero. If you're creating newspapers, this might be appropriate. If you're making art books, be a bit more careful with your hyphens. I usually set this to two as a default and then go through and tweak the line breaks by hand.

Note that those wacky engineers at Quark placed a little popup menu next to this setting. Don't worry, it doesn't do anything; you can just ignore it.

Hyphenation Zone. Another way to limit the number of hyphens in a section of text is the Hyphenation Zone setting. While relatively simple in function, this feature is one of the more difficult to understand (it was for me, anyway).

The idea is that there's an invisible zone along the right margin of each block of text. If QuarkXPress is trying to break a word at the end of a line, it looks to see where the hyphenation zone is. If the word *before* the potentially hyphenated word falls inside the hyphenation zone, then QuarkXPress just gives up and pushes the word onto the next line (does not hyphenate it). If the previous word does not fall within the hyphenation zone, then QuarkXPress goes ahead with hyphenating the word (see Figure 6-42).

For example, if the words "robinus christophorus" came at the end of a line and QuarkXPress were about to hyphenate "christophorus," it would first look at the word "robinus" to see if any part of it fell inside the hyphenation zone. If it did, XPress wouldn't hyphenate "christophorus"

Figure 6-42
Hyphenation zone

Gray bar is for reference only

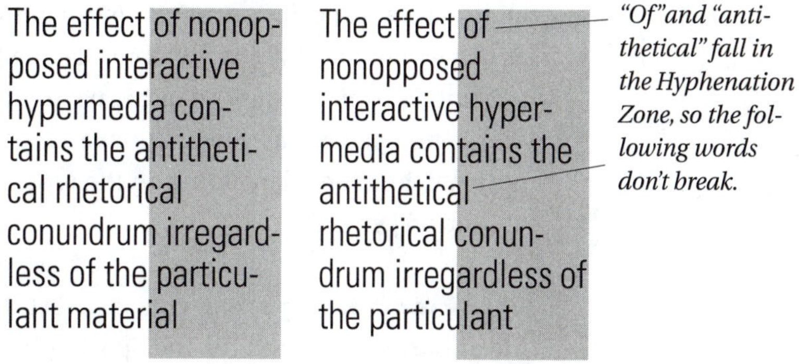

The effect of nonopposed interactive hypermedia contains the antithetical rhetorical conundrum irregardless of the particulant material

No hyphenation zone

The effect of nonopposed interactive hypermedia contains the antithetical rhetorical conundrum irregardless of the particulant

Hyphenation zone of four picas

"Of" and "antithetical" fall in the Hyphenation Zone, so the following words don't break.

at all; if it didn't, QuarkXPress would use its standard hyphenation algorithms to break the word appropriately.

Normally, Hyphenation Zone is set to zero units. This setting specifies no hyphenation zone, so all lines can have hyphenation up to the limit of the Hyphens in a Row value. Unless you really know what you're doing, there is little reason to change this value.

Justification

As I mentioned above, justifying text is the process of adding or removing space across a line of text to keep it flush on the left and right. You can alter several of the parameters QuarkXPress uses for determining justification by changing values found in the Edit Hyphenation & Justification dialog box. These values are controlled in the Justification Method area. It's divided into values for wordspacing, letterspacing (called "character spacing" by Quark), and Flush Zone width, plus a checkbox for Single Word Justify. Let's look at each of these.

Wordspacing. As I described above in "Character Formatting," wordspacing determines the amount of space between words. In the case of justification, it describes the range of how large or small the spaces between words can be. You can specify Minimum, Optimum, and Maximum percentages of a normal space character. For example, a value of 80 percent allows a space between words that is 80 percent of a normal spaceband. (Note that the "normal" space is the spaceband width defined by the designer of the typeface; this can vary greatly between font families.)

Curiously, the default value for optimal wordspacing is 115 percent, which results in slightly more space than the font designer specified. I almost always specify a relatively loose minimum and maximum, such as 85 percent and 140 percent, but I change the optimum value to 100 percent. I do this because I'd rather have QuarkXPress add wordspacing than letterspacing. In general, however, some typefaces need tighter spacing; therefore, depending on the typeface, I might set Optimum to around 95 percent.

Character Spacing. You can also set Minimum, Optimum, and Maximum percentages for the spacing between characters. The percentages are based on the width of an en space (see "Formatting Characters," later in this chapter). Whereas 100 percent was normal for Word Spacing, zero percent is normal for Character Spacing, and should almost always be used as the Optimum setting.

I generally don't give QuarkXPress much freedom in adjusting letterspacing because I think the type designer probably knows more about what character widths should be than I do (and certainly more than QuarkXPress does). For example, I might set Minimum to -1 percent, Maximum to 4 percent and Optimum to zero percent. But here, again, is an area where you need to print out a few text blocks, preferably on an imagesetter, look at the color of the type, and decide for yourself.

I also try to keep this setting tight because loose letterspacing is difficult to read. Again, I'd rather add space between words than letters any day. Some typographers whom I greatly respect insist that letterspacing should always be set at "0/0/0" (that is, QuarkXPress should never change letterspacing). However, I'm from California originally, so I'm much looser than that.

▼ ▼

Tip: H&J Percentages Versus Tracking Units. My colleague Brad Walrod points out that each percentage of character spacing in the H&Js dialog box is basically the same as one unit of kerning or tracking. This enables you to perform a quick and easy test when you're trying to figure out what letterspacing you want in a document. If you're thinking about increasing the letterspacing value, use kerning to apply that same value to a paragraph of text, so you can see what it looks like.

As Brad says, "I guarantee that if you do this test you will never again use a maximum [letterspacing] value of 15 percent."

▼ ▼

Flush Zone. If you thought the Hyphenation Zone setting was obscure, you just hadn't heard about the Flush Zone yet. The Flush Zone setting does one thing, but does it very well: it determines whether the last line of a paragraph gets force justified or not.

The value you type in the field is the distance from the right margin that QuarkXPress checks. If the end of the line falls into that zone, the whole line gets justified. Of course, in many instances, you can just use the Forced Justify setting, so this feature isn't something I use much.

Single Word Justify. The Single Word Justify checkbox lets you tell QuarkXPress whether you want a word that falls on a justified line by itself to be force justified (see Figure 6-43). Newspapers will probably leave this turned on. Art directors of fancy foreign magazines might insist that it get turned off. Personally, I don't like how the word looks either way, and I'd just as soon have the sentence rewritten, or play with other character formatting to reflow the paragraph. This feature doesn't apply to the last line of a paragraph; you still need to use the Flush Zone or force justify to get those lines to justify.

Forced Justification

Speaking of justification, when you select Forced (from the Style menu, the Measurements palette, or by pressing Command-Option-Shift-J), QuarkXPress forces every line in a paragraph to be justified, including lines that wouldn't ordinarily extend to the margin, such as the last line of a paragraph or even a single-line paragraph.

Forced justification has basically the same effect as creating a Hyphenation and Justification setting with a very large Flush Zone. It takes a lot of steps to define and apply such an H&J setting, however, so Quark has made it easy with the Forced mode.

Note that forced justification only works with full paragraphs, and QuarkXPress defines a full paragraph as ending with a return. Therefore, if you have a text box that has only one line in it, and that line doesn't end with a return, the program won't justify it.

Figure 6-43
Single Word Justify

A knock at the door! Quickly stuffing the long, slender, store-bought foodstuff into a drawer, he sprung blithely to receive his visitor, only to be greeted by thirty-six thousand members of the feared Fruit-and-Vegetablist Majority. He knew he was in trouble now.

A knock at the door! Quickly stuffing the long, slender, store-bought foodstuff into a drawer, he sprung blithely to receive his visitor, only to be greeted by thirty-six thousand members of the feared Fruit-and-Vegetablist Majority. He knew he was in trouble now.

In the example on the right, Single Word Justify is off. Note the phrase "Fruit-and-Vegetablist."

Setting Your Own H&J

Different paragraphs in your document may need different hyphenation and justification settings. For example, you may want the paragraphs in the main body of your text to hyphenate normally, and text in sidebars or headlines to remain unhyphenated. You can use XPress's H&J feature to set up multiple H&J settings to be applied later at a paragraph level.

Creating an H&J Setting

When you select H&Js from the Edit menu (or press Command-Option-H), the H&Js dialog box appears (see Figure 6-44). You can add, delete, edit, duplicate, or append H&J settings. The list on the left side of the dialog box shows the names of each H&J setting. A new document only has one setting: Standard, which is the default setting for all text paragraphs.

You can add a new H&J setting in two ways.

Figure 6-44

The H&Js dialog box

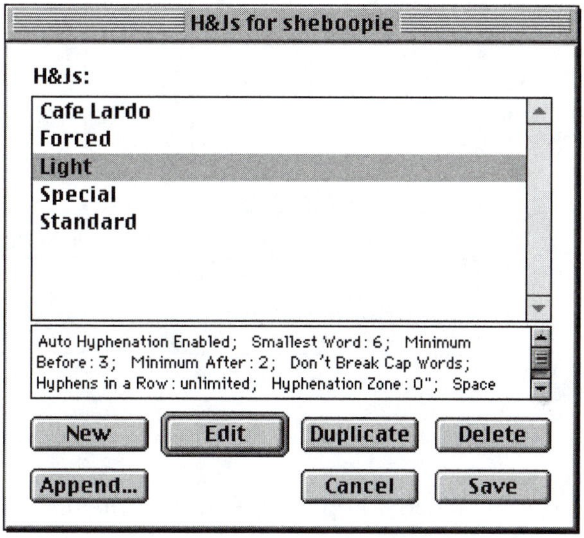

Click the New button to create a new H&J setting. Change the hyphenation and justification parameters as described above, give the setting a name, and click OK. The Edit H&Js dialog box you see when you click New is a duplicate of the Standard setting.

Click first on a setting (such as Standard), and then click the Duplicate button. You can edit a duplicate of the setting you first clicked on. This is helpful for basing one H&J setting on another.

Deleting and Appending H&Js

To delete an H&J setting, first click on its name, then click the Delete button. If you've applied the H&J setting to any paragraph in the document, or to a style sheet, QuarkXPress prompts you for an H&J to replace it with. This is an easy way to merge several H&Js into a single one.

If you have set up H&J settings in a different document, you can append them to your current document's list by clicking the Append button. After selecting the document to import from, the program lets you choose exactly which styles you want (see Figure 6-45). In case you don't know how the various H&Js are defined, XPress shows you the definitions in the Description area of the Append H&Js dialog box.

Figure 6-45

Appending H&J settings

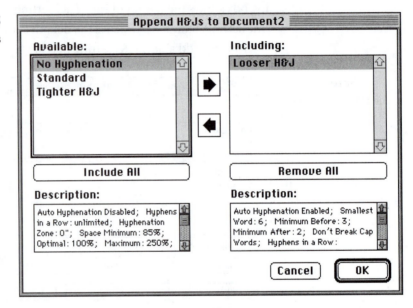

When you press OK in the Append H&Js dialog box, QuarkXPress checks to see if any incoming H&Js have the same name as those already in your document. If it finds such a conflict (and if the definition of the H&J is different in the two documents), it displays another alert dialog box and asks you what to do (see Figure 6-46). You've got four options, each a separate button.

▶ **RENAME.** You get to manually rename the H&J that's being imported with any other unused name.

▶ **AUTO-RENAME.** Automatically renames the incoming H&J with an asterisk at the beginning of its name. I'm sure there's a good reason for this option, but I've never figured it out.

▶ **USE NEW.** The incoming H&J setting overwrites the one already in the document. I usually use either this option or Rename.

▶ **USE EXISTING.** This is the same as cancelling the appending of the H&J; the old one (the one currently in the document) is retained and used. The only time you'd use this is if you didn't realize that there was a duplicate when you chose to append the H&J setting.

Figure 6-46

Conflicting H&J settings

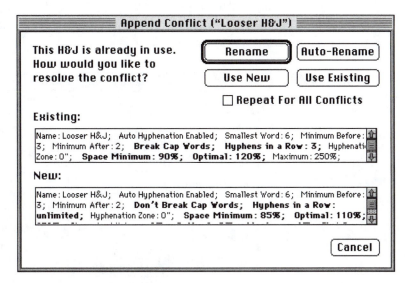

If you think there's going to be more than one conflicting style name, you may want to check the box marked Repeat For All Conflicts. This way, XPress handles the remaining conflicts in the same way.

Of course, remember that there is also an Append feature on the File menu that you can use to import style sheets, colors, and H&Js at the same time. If you need to import both styles and colors, for instance, it's clearly efficient to do it with Append instead of in the Style Sheets dialog box.

▼ ▼

Tip: Copying H&Js with Copy and Paste. There's another way to move an H&J setting from one document to another: copy and paste a text box that contains a paragraph tagged with that H&J setting. However, if you move a setting this way, QuarkXPress won't do the same-name check described above. If there are differences between two H&J settings with the same name, the imported settings are just ignored (same as selecting Use Existing H&J).

▼ ▼

Applying an H&J Setting

Once you have created more than one H&J setting, you can choose which setting to use on a paragraph level by using the Paragraph Attributes dialog box. With the cursor in a paragraph, or with multiple paragraphs selected, you can select an H&J setting from the popup menu in the Paragraph Attributes dialog box (see Figure 6-47). You can also set the H&J setting in a style sheet (I talk more about Style Sheets in Chapter 7, *Copy Flow*).

Figure 6-47

Applying an H&J setting

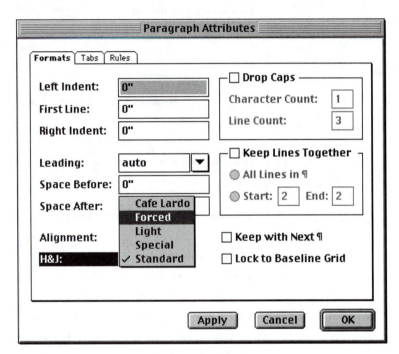

Tip: Tighter and Looser H&Js. Depending on the job I'm working on, I may have four or five different H&J settings in my document. Here are a few that I often use besides Standard.

▶ TIGHTER. This setting is the same as my Standard H&J, but with slightly smaller wordspacing and letterspacing values.

▶ LOOSER. Similar to Standard, but with slightly larger wordspacing and letterspacing values.

▶ HEADS. I'll turn off Auto Hyphenation in this H&J setting, and set the wordspacing tightly, perhaps even to 75 percent.

► NO HYPHENATION. I'll usually have one H&J setting that is the same as Standard, but where Auto Hyphenation is turned off. This is the setting I use for subheads, for instance.

One of the most important things to remember when you're fooling around with these settings is the color of the page. If setting a tighter H&J makes one text block look noticeably darker than the rest of the page, you may need to manually alter the paragraph using tracking or kerning rather than let the H&J settings do it for you.

▼ ▼

Tip: Pseudo Insert Space with H&Js. Let's say you've got three words on a line. You want the first word to be flush left, the third word to be flush right, and you want equal space between each of these and the word in the middle (see Figure 6-48). You can do this by using forced justification and adjusting the H&J settings.

1. Create a new H&J setting called something mnemonic like "InsertSpace".

2. Make sure the letterspacing (labeled "Char") fields in the Justification Method area of the Edit H&Js dialog box are all set to zero. That means that XPress won't add extra space between any characters in the paragraph, only between words. You might need to increase the values in the wordspacing (labeled "Space") fields as well.

3. Save this new H&J setting.

4. Use the Paragraph Attributes dialog box (Command-Shift-F) to apply both the InsertSpace H&J setting and Forced alignment to the paragraph.

The paragraph should now be spread across the text box, with an equal amount of space between each word. If you want a normal word

Figure 6-48
Inserting equal
space between words

One   Two   Three   Four
One Two   Three   Four

Here, no letterspacing is allowed, and a fixed-width space sits between the first two words.

The H&J setting is set so that no letterspacing can occur.

space between two words, use a punctuation space (Shift-space) or a flex space (Option-space) instead of a normal spaceband.

▼ ▼

Tip: Find/Change H&J settings. There's just no way to find and replace H&J settings throughout a document. Or is there? Let's say someone was working on your document and applied an H&J setting called "Really Tight" to paragraphs when you weren't looking. You want to clear this setting out. The trick is to select the setting you want to get rid of in the H&Js dialog box (in this case, choose Really Tight) and click the Delete button. XPress asks you which H&J to apply in its place. When you delete Really Tight from the H&J list, you can replace it with Standard, or something else. This effectively searches and replaces throughout the document: everywhere the Really Tight setting was applied, it gets changed to something else.

If you know you're going to need the H&J setting later, make sure you make a duplicate of it in the document or into another document before you delete it!

▼ ▼

Widow and Orphan Control

I mean no disrespect to widows and orphans, but when it comes to typesetting, we must carefully control them, stamping out their very existence when we have the chance.

If you know what I'm talking about already, bear with me, or skip this paragraph (or test whether you can remember which is the widow and which is the orphan). A *widow* is the last line of a paragraph that winds up all by itself at the top of a column or page. An *orphan* is the first line of a paragraph that lands all by itself at the bottom of a column or page. I like the following mnemonic device: "widows" sounds like "windows," which are high up (top of the page), whereas "orphans" makes me think of tiny Oliver (who was small, and thus, at the bottom of the page).

Typesetters sometimes also refer to the single-word last line of a paragraph as either a widow or an orphan. To avoid the confusion, in my office I prefer to use the word *runt*.

All typographic widows and orphans are bad, but certain kinds are really bad—for example, a widow line that consists of only one word, or even the last part of a hyphenated word. Another related typographic horror is the subhead that stands alone with its following paragraph on the next page.

Fortunately, QuarkXPress has a set of controls that can easily prevent widows and orphans from sneaking into your document. The controls are the Keep With Next ¶ and Keep Lines Together features, and you can find them in the Paragraph Attributes dialog box (Command-Shift-F). Let's look at each of these.

Keep With Next ¶

The Keep With Next ¶ feature is perfect for ensuring that headings and the paragraphs that follow them are always kept together. If the paragraph is pushed onto a new column, a new page, or below an obstructing object, the heading follows right along (see Figure 6-49).

You may want to keep paragraphs together even when there are no subheads. For example, entries in a table or list that shouldn't be broken

Figure 6-49
Keep with Next ¶

Mephisto
Du übersinnlicher sinnlicher Freier,
Ein Mägdelein nasführet dich.
Faust
Du Spottgeburt von Dreck und Feuer!

Und die Physiognomie versteht sie meisterlich:
In meiner Gegenwart wird's ihr, sie weiß nicht wie,
Mein Mäskchen da weissagt verborgnen Sinn;

Mephisto —— This paragraph style does not have Keep With Next ¶ set.

Mephisto
Du übersinnlicher sinnlicher Freier,
Ein Mägdelein nasführet dich.
Faust
Du Spottgeburt von Dreck und Feuer!

Mephisto —— This paragraph style does have Keep With Next ¶ set.
Und die Physiognomie versteht sie meisterlich:
In meiner Gegenwart wird's ihr, sie weiß nicht wie,
Mein Mäskchen da weissagt verborgnen Sinn;

could each be set to Keep With Next ¶. In some earlier versions of XPress, the program would only keep two paragraphs together at a time; fortunately, that's changed, and you can keep a number of paragraphs together with this feature.

Keep Lines Together

The Keep Lines Together feature is the primary control over widows and orphans. When you check Keep Lines Together in the Paragraph Attributes dialog box, QuarkXPress expands the dialog box to give you control parameters in this area (see Figure 6-50). Let's look at these controls one at a time.

All Lines In ¶. You can keep every line in a paragraph together by checking All Lines In ¶. For example, if a paragraph spans across two pages, enabling All Lines In ¶ results in that entire paragraph being pushed onto the next page to keep it together.

It's easy to confound a computer. Do you remember that Star Trek episode in which a man forced a computer to commit suicide by instructing it to perform contradictory functions? Fortunately, XPress won't cause your Mac or PC to blow up if you specify All Lines In ¶ for a

Figure 6-50

Keep Lines Together

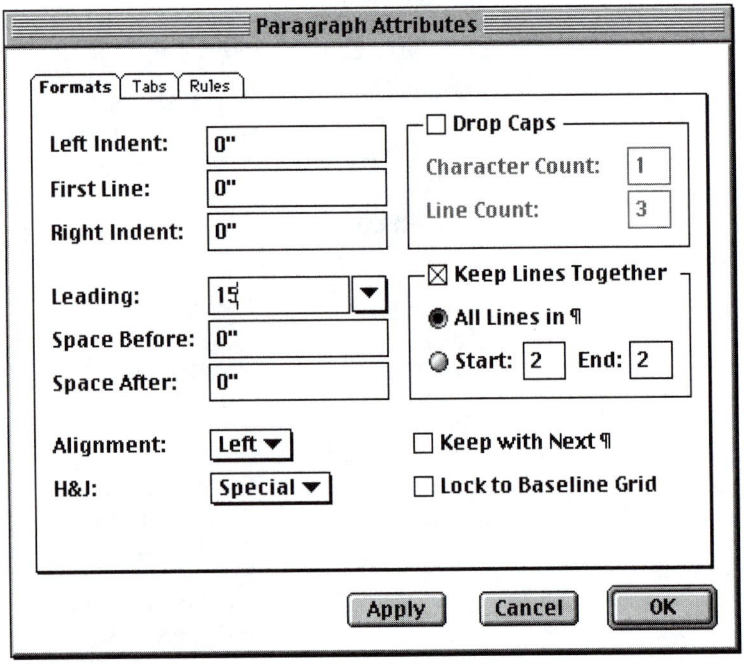

text block larger than your column. In cases like this, QuarkXPress simply pushes the whole paragraph out of the text box. (I've seen cases where people freak out because their text has disappeared, only to find out later that they had turned on both All Lines in ¶ and Keep with Next ¶ for every paragraph.)

Start. You don't have to specify that all the lines in a paragraph should be kept together. Instead, you can control the number of lines that should be kept together at the beginning and end of the paragraph.

The value you type in the Start field determines the minimum number of lines that QuarkXPress allows at the beginning of a paragraph. For example, specifying a two-line Start value causes paragraphs that fall at the end of a page to keep at least two lines on the first page before it breaks. If at least two lines of that paragraph cannot be placed on the page, then the entire paragraph is pushed over to the next page.

The Start feature is set up to eliminate orphans in your documents. If you don't want any single lines sitting at the bottom of a page, you can specify a value of 2 for the Start control (some designers insist that even two lines alone at the bottom of a page are ugly and may want to adjust the Start value to 3 or greater).

End. The value specified in the End field determines the minimum number of lines that QuarkXPress lets fall alone at the top of a column or after an obstruction. A value of 2 or greater rids you of unwanted widowed paragraphs (if a widow occurs, QuarkXPress "pulls" a line off the first page onto the second page or column).

▼ ▼

Tip: Other Widow and Orphan Controls. It's all very well and good to let QuarkXPress avoid widows, orphans, and runts for you, but you still need to painstakingly peruse each page of most documents, making adjustments as you go. You have many other tools to help you avoid widows and orphans. Here are some of my favorites.

▶ Adjust tracking by a very small amount over a range of text, but try to do at least a whole paragraph or a few complete lines so the color of the type doesn't vary within the paragraph. Often, nobody can tell if you've applied -.5 or -1 tracking to a paragraph or a page, but it might be enough to pull back a widow or a runt.

▶ Adjust horizontal scaling by a small amount, such as 99.5 percent or 100.5 percent.

▶ Make sure Auto Hyphenation and Auto Kern Above are turned on. Kerning can make a load of difference over a large area of text. Auto Hyphenation has to be changed in all of your H&Js, while Auto Kern Above affects the entire document.

▶ Change your H&J's wordspacing to a smaller Optimal setting. If it's at 100 percent, try 98 percent. Of course, this changes every paragraph tagged with that H&J setting throughout your document.

▶ Set up different hyphenation and justification settings that you can apply to problem paragraphs. You might apply a tighter or a looser setting for one paragraph, for instance, or allow more hyphens in a row.

If none of these work for you, don't forget you can always just rewrite a sentence or two (if it's yours to rewrite). A quick rewrite can fix up just about any problem.

Baseline Grid

In typography, the smallest change can make the biggest difference in a piece's impact. For example, look at a high-quality magazine page that has multiple columns. Chances are that each line of text has a common baseline with the text in the next column. Now look at a crummy newsletter. Place a rule across a page and you'll see lines of text all over the place. What's missing is an underlying grid. QuarkXPress's Baseline Grid feature lets you create a grid and lock each line of text to it. Nonetheless, while this is a powerful feature, I tend not to use it much; I'll explain why in a moment.

Each document has its own Baseline Grid setting, which is pervasive throughout every page. However, whether a block of text actually locks to that grid is determined on a paragraph level.

Setting up the grid. XPress is clueless about your leading grid, so you need to set this up yourself. You can set the Baseline Grid value for the document on the Paragraph tab in the Document Preferences dialog box (press Command-Y). You have two controls over the Baseline Grid: the Start value and the Increment value. The Start value determines where this grid begins, measured from the top of the page. Set it to start at the first baseline of your body copy.

The Increment value determines the distance from one horizontal grid line to the next. Generally, this value is the same as the leading in the majority of your body copy. For example, if your body copy has a leading of 13 points, then you should type "13pt" as your Increment value. However, sometimes it's better to use half the body copy's leading; in this example, you might use a 6.5-point grid.

Assigning a baseline grid. To lock each line of a paragraph to the baseline grid that you have established, turn on the Lock to Baseline Grid checkbox in the Paragraph Attributes dialog box (Command-Shift-F). Note that the baseline grid overrides paragraph leading. That is, if your paragraph has a leading of 10 points, when you enable Lock to Baseline Grid each line snaps to the Increment value (13 points, in the example above). If your paragraph has a leading larger than the Increment value, each line snaps to the next grid value. In other words, your leading never gets tighter, but it can get very loose. If your Increment value is 13 points and your leading is 14 points, each line snaps to the following grid line, resulting in 26-point leading (see Figure 6-51).

Showing the grid. The baseline grid in QuarkXPress is usually invisible, so sometimes it's difficult to understand why text is sticking to weird

Figure 6-51
Lock to Baseline Grid

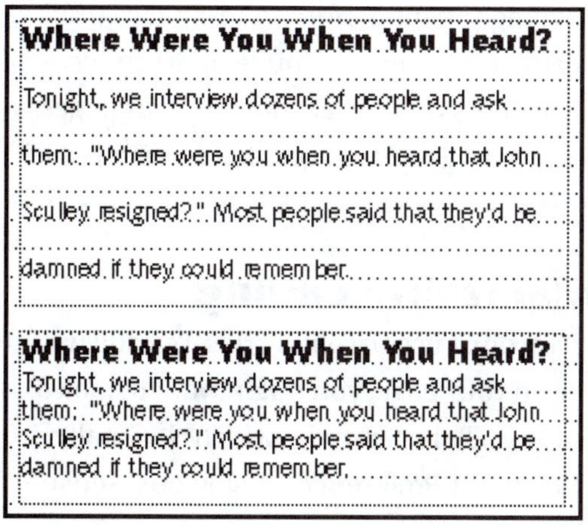

With a 13-point Baseline Grid, type with 14-point leading locked to the grid gets bumped to the next grid increment.

But 13-point leading on a 13-point grid works perfectly.

baselines. However, you can see this underlying grid by selecting Show/Hide Baseline Grid from the View menu (or by pressing Option-F7 on the Macintosh or Control-F7 on Windows). If you don't like the color of the baseline grid, you can set it to whatever you want in Application Preferences (Command-Option-Shift-Y).

Note that the baseline-grid guides you see when you select Show Baseline Grid act just like ruler guides. They follow the Guides control in the Document Preferences dialog box (Command-Y) as to whether they appear in front of or behind page items. And when Snap to Guides is turned on, page items snap to the baseline grid guides (when they're showing).

▼ ▼

Tip: Why I Rarely Use Lock to Baseline Grid. There is no doubt that a careful study and practice of baseline grids can make your document better looking. However, as I said earlier, I rarely use the Lock to Baseline Grid feature. The reason: you can get the same quality simply from being careful with your leading and text box placement. The key is to work with multiples of your leading grid.

For instance, if your body text has 15-point leading, then make sure your headlines and subheads also have 15- or 30-point leading. If you use Space Before or Space After, make sure those values are set only to 15, 30, or 45 points (or some other multiple of 15). Paragraphs in a list might have 7.5 points of space (half of 15) between them, and as long as there are always an even number of list items, the paragraphs after the list will always end up on the leading grid.

This might seem really limiting, but it's actually less so than using Lock to Baseline Grid. As long as you pay attention to the values for Leading, Space Before, and Space After, as well as turn on Maintain Leading (see below), you're pretty much assured that your baselines will align across columns and that your pages will look beautiful. Of course, it's always good to proof them, just in case.

▼ ▼

Maintain Leading

If you don't use baseline grids, but still want to maintain consistent leading on your page, you might want to look closely at the Maintain Leading feature. This feature—which I usually just leave turned on in the Document Preferences dialog box—ensures that each line in a text box is placed according to its leading value when another object (such as a picture box or a line) obstructs the text and moves text lines around.

When Maintain Leading is turned off, two things happen. First, the line of text following an obstruction abuts the bottom of that obstruction (or its text runaround, if the runaround value is larger than zero points; I talk about text runaround in Chapter 11, *Where Text Meets Graphics*). Second, the rest of the lines of text in that text box fall on a different leading grid than those above the obstruction do. This is much easier to see than to read (or write) about, so check out Figure 6-52. This feature has no effect on paragraphs that are already set to Lock to Baseline Grid.

Figure 6-52
Maintain Leading

Here, Maintain Leading is turned off; the baseline don't match across columns.

Here, Maintain Leading is turned on and the columns align.

Fine-Tuning Type

Almost everything I've talked about in this chapter has been at a character or paragraph level. Here I'm going to talk about making typographic adjustments on a document level. You have control over several areas at a document level, including how superscript, subscript, superior, and small-caps characters are "built"; which words will hyphenate; and how XPress deals with ligatures, accents, and special spaces. You can also create custom automatic tracking and kerning tables, and run through an automatic check for typographic problem areas.

Let's look at how you can use these controls in your documents.

Typographic Preferences

By selecting Document Preferences from the Edit menu (or pressing Command-Y), you can control the way QuarkXPress handles a number of its typographic features: superscript, subscript, superior, and small-caps characters, hyphenation, kerning, em spaces, baseline grid, leading, ligatures, and foreign-language accents (see Figure 6-53). Here's a rundown of all the different features in this dialog box, what they do, or where you can find information about them elsewhere in this book.

Figure 6-53

Typographic preferences

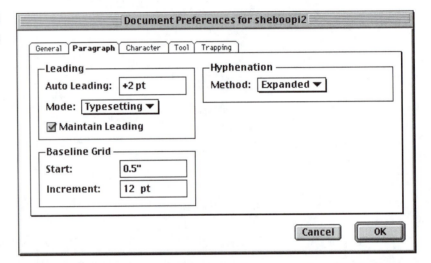

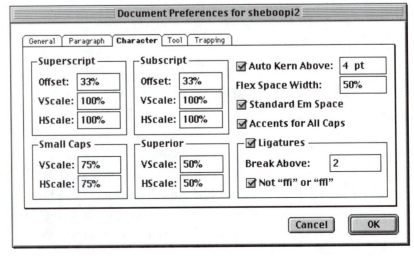

Remember that if you change items in the Document Preferences dialog box with no documents open, the defaults are changed for every new document you create from then on. And remember that all of the following are document-wide preferences; you can't specify them for a particular story or paragraph.

Superscript and Subscript. Few people ever bother to get into the nitty-gritty of changing the way the Superscript and Subscript styles look, but the controls are on the Character tab in the Document Preferences dialog box if you ever want them. Both the Superscript and the Subscript controls are the same: Offset, VScale, and HScale. Some people try to fiddle with these values in order to make fractions; this is possible, but I recommend other fraction-making techniques instead (see "Typographic Special Effects," later in this chapter).

▶ OFFSET. You can determine how far from the baseline your superscript or subscript characters should move by altering the Offset amount. You specify Offset as a percentage of the text size. For example, if the offset for Subscript were set to 50 percent, then a subscript character would move 9 points down for 18-point type. You can specify any amount between one and 100 percent.

▶ VSCALE AND HSCALE. These terms are short for "vertical scale" and "horizontal scale," which are responsible for how tall and wide the superscript or subscript text is. The controls default to 100 percent, which I find much too large. I generally set both to a value between 70 and 80 percent, so that a superscript or subscript character doesn't stand out too much against the rest of the text. Here, too, you can set the value to anything between one and 100 percent.

Superior. You don't have to worry about the offset for superior characters because they are automatically set to be vertically flush with the cap height of that font. So the only modifications you can make here are to the vertical and horizontal scaling of the character. This is clearly an area of aesthetic choice. I tend to like the 50-percent default that QuarkXPress gives us; some people like to make the HScale slightly larger, such as 55 percent, so that the character has a little more weight.

Small Caps. You can also change the vertical and horizontal scaling of all characters set in the Small Caps character style in a document. Though I think it would be nice to be able to set the characteristics of small caps on the character, paragraph, or story level, these document-wide controls are usually good enough.

There are times when adjustable (or "fake") small caps are even better than traditional (or "true") small caps, such as those found in Expert Sets. For example, I know a designer who recently specified that all small caps in a book's body copy should be 8.5 points tall. The body text was 10-point Palatino, so the company producing the templates just changed the small-caps specifications to 85 percent in the horizontal direction (85 percent of 10-point type is 8.5-point type) and 90 percent in the vertical direction (making the characters slightly wider gives a slightly heavier—although stretched—look). A traditional small cap would not achieve this effect; however, it would probably keep the type color in the paragraph more consistent.

Accents for All Caps. This typographic refinement lets you specify whether accented lowercase characters keep their accents when you apply the All Caps character style to them. If this feature is turned on and you apply All Caps to the characters å, ë, ì, ó, û, QuarkXPress will give you Å, Ë, Ì, Ó, Û rather than A, E, I, O, U. Depending on the design of your document or what language you're working in, you may want to turn this feature on or off.

Leading Preferences. I talk about each of the Leading preferences earlier in this chapter. Leading Mode and Auto Leading are discussed in the section called "Leading" (you should always leave Leading Mode set to Typesetting). The Maintain Leading feature is discussed in the "Baseline Grid" section, where I said to just leave this setting turned on.

Auto Kern Above. Auto Kern Above is discussed in the "Automatic" section of "Kerning and Tracking." This is usually set to 4 points, which is very reasonable. (If you see a value higher than 4 here, you should probably lower it.)

Flex Space Width. See "Formatting Characters" in the "Special Characters" section, later in the chapter, for an explanation of this feature.

Hyphenation Method. I explore hyphenation methods a little later in the chapter, in "Tweaking Hyphenation." But I can give the rundown again now: just leave this set to Enhanced or Expanded (there's almost no reason to change it to Standard).

Baseline Grid. I wrote a whole section called "Baseline Grid" earlier in this chapter; check that out.

Standard Em Space. See "Tip: Know Your Ems and Ens," in the "Kerning and Tracking" section. The low-down: I like to turn this on.

Ligatures. I'll discuss ligatures later in this chapter in "Special Characters." My recommendation: turn it on. (Unfortunately, this feature doesn't exist on Windows.)

Kerning and Tracking Tables

As I noted earlier in this chapter, most fonts include built-in kerning tables of 100 to 500 pairs. However, you can modify these pairs or add your own by using Quark's Kern/Track Editor XTension (it comes with QuarkXPress, though you have an option not to install it when you update or install QuarkXPress). Like all XTensions, you must make sure that this XTension is located in the XTension folder in order for it to work.

Modifying tracking and kerning tables is different from many of QuarkXPress's typographic controls in that it's font-specific. For example, if you alter the kerning table for Times Roman, those changes are in effect whenever you use Times Roman in any QuarkXPress document. However, the font itself is *not* altered on disk; so the changes don't show up when you're working in any other program.

The kerning modifications you make are stored both in the XPress Preferences file and in the document itself. That means that you can give the publication file to someone else and the custom values will stay with the document (when they open the file, they'll be prompted to choose whether or not they want to keep your preferences).

Kerning Tables

To modify a font's kerning table, choose Kerning Table Edit from the Utilities menu. This brings up the Kerning Table Edit dialog box, which presents a scrolling list of available fonts (note that this dialog box can take a long time to appear, depending on the number of fonts you have installed; see Figure 6-54). The list lets you choose the variants of each installed font (Plain, Bold, Italic, Bold Italic, and so on).

You have to edit kerning tables for individual fonts. This means that you cannot edit Palatino in its Plain style and expect all the Bold, Italic, and Bold Italic variants to be altered as well (see "Tip: Quick Kerning for Families," below).

After selecting a font from the list (you can jump through the list quickly by typing the first letter of the font name you want), click Edit to move to the Edit Kerning Table dialog box, where you can edit an existing pair, add a new pair to the list, or delete a pair (see Figure 6-55). You can also import and export lists of these kerning pairs in a text-file format. Let's look at how each of these operations is performed.

Adding a pair. You can add a new kerning pair to QuarkXPress's list in three steps.

1. Type the two characters in the Pair field. They appear in a preview window above the Value field. If there is already a kerning value set for this pair, it appears selected in the list of kerning pairs.

2. Type a kerning amount into the Value field. This value is specified in $\frac{1}{200}$ of an em (see "Tip: Know Your Ems and Ens," earlier in this chapter). The preview updates as soon as you enter new values.

3. Click the Add or Replace button.

That's all there is to it.

Editing a pair. You can adjust kerning pairs that you have created or that come predefined in the font by clicking on a pair in the Kerning Pairs table (or typing the two characters in the Pair field), and then modifying the number in the Value field. Once you have set the kern value you want, click the Replace button to add it back to the table.

Figure 6-54

The Kerning Table
Edit dialog box

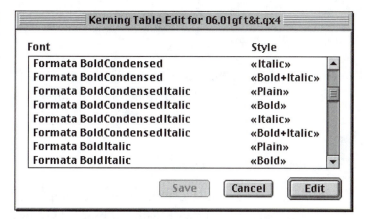

Figure 6-55

Editing a kerning pair

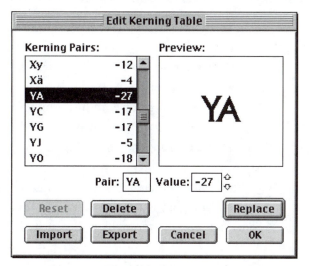

Deleting or resetting a pair. If you don't like a kerning pair that you added, or you want to get rid of one that was built in, select the pair from the list and click the Delete button (or set the kern value to zero). Unfortunately, there is no way to reset a particular pair to its original value if you don't remember what it was. You can, however, reset the entire font back to its pure, original state by clicking the Reset button (of course, you lose all the other kerning pairs that you had built along the way).

Import/Export. There are those who know kerning pairs so well that they'd rather just type up a mess of them in a text-editing program and then import them all at once into QuarkXPress. You can do this by creating a text-only file within any text editor (such as Microsoft Word, BBEdit, or Windows Notepad) in the following format.

1. Type the kerning pair (the two letters).

2. Type a tab.

3. Type the kerning value in QuarkXPress's kerning units (¹⁄₂₀₀ of an em). Negative numbers mean negative kerning. Then just press Return to go to the next line.

4. Save the file as a text-only file. On Windows, save the file with a .KRN file-name extension.

5. Switch back to the Edit Kerning Table dialog box in QuarkXPress, and click the Import button to bring this text file in.

If you want to edit the kerning values that are already built into the font, you can first export those values by clicking the Export button. Then edit them and re-import them.

▼ ▼

Tip: Quick Kerning for Families. Applying kerning pairs to a number of faces can be very time-consuming and tiresome. You can speed up this process by using the Import feature to apply the same kerning tables to several typefaces. Once you've imported the kerning tables, you can go back and edit them to compensate for specifics of that typeface. Careful, though: the kerning values for an italic form of a typeface are going to be very different than the values for a roman form.

▼ ▼

Tip: Automatic Page Numbers Don't Kern. If you or the font designer has set up automatic kerning pairs for pairs of numerals, these pairs will *not* be kerned when they appear as automatic page numbers. QuarkXPress treats all automatic page numbers as single characters, even when they consist of multiple characters. Sadly, there's no ready fix for this one, except to use a typeface for page numbers in which the lack of automatic kerning won't cause an aesthetic headache.

▼ ▼

Tip: Un-Kerning Your Numbers. This tip puts a spin on what I think is a bug: applying the small caps style to numbers makes XPress ignore any kerning information you set up in its internal kerning tables for those numbers. On the positive side: If you kerned your digits using the Kern/Track Editor, and now you want to use that font in a tabular setting where you don't want the digits kerned after all, apply the small caps style to the digits. The numbers stay the same, but the kerning goes away!

Note that this trick doesn't work if you've used another method (a commercial font-editing program) to kern your font.

▼ ▼

Tracking Tables

Most fonts need to have tighter tracking applied to them in larger point sizes. You could change the tracking value for various display fonts by manually selecting the text and specifying a tracking value in the Character Attributes dialog box. However, QuarkXPress makes it easier for you by letting you create custom tracking tables for each font you use.

A tracking table tells QuarkXPress how much tracking to apply at various sizes of a font. This, too, is part of the Kern/Track Editor XTension that comes with XPress.

Here's an example to illustrate this feature. Let's say you're creating a template for a new magazine. You've decided to use Futura Bold for your headers, which are at a number of different sizes. You know that your largest header is 60 points and should have -20 tracking, and the smallest header is 12 points and should have no tracking. Here's what you do.

1. Select Tracking Edit from the Utilities menu.

2. Choose the font that you want to edit—in this case Futura Bold—and click the Edit button. If QuarkXPress recognizes the family as "merged," then it only shows you one family name rather than breaking it down into separate fonts. For instance, it shows you one Palatino selection rather than four Palatino fonts: roman, italic, bold, and bold italic. If the individual fonts are merged into one, the tracking gets applied to every font in the family. In font families that are not merged, you have to create tracking settings for each style variation—for example, one tracking table for "Bodoni," another for "B Bodoni Bold," and so on.

3. You see the Edit Tracking dialog box (Figure 6-56). The vertical axis represents tracking values from -100 to 100 in increments of $\frac{1}{200}$ of an em. The horizontal axis represents type sizes from 2 to 250 points; the farther to the right on the grid, the larger the type size is. The default setting is a horizontal bar at the zero-tracking level. In other words, this means that all point sizes start out with a tracking value of zero.

Figure 6-56

A tracking table graph

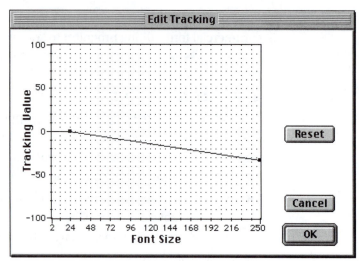

4. Click on the line at the 2-point size (on the far left). As you hold down the mouse button, you can see the graph values shown in the dialog box. Note that clicking on the graph places a new point on it. You can have up to four corner points on each graph. This first point I've added is the anchor at the zero-tracking level.

5. Click on the line at the 60-point size and drag the graph line down to the -20 tracking level. If I saved this now, then whenever you used Futura Bold, all sizes larger than 2 points would have negative tracking applied to them.

6. You can add a third control handle at the 12-point type size and set it to zero tracking. Now all type larger than 12 points has tracking applied; as the text gets larger, more and more tracking is applied.

To save your changes, click OK. Then if you're done with your tracking-table edits, click Save.

While editing a font's tracking table, you can start over by clicking the Reset button. You can always go back (even after you've saved) and click the Reset button to get the horizontal bar graph back.

Note that these tracking values are only applied to a font when Auto Kern Above is turned on. In fact, the tracking tables only apply to font sizes above the automatic-kerning limit which has been entered in the Auto Kern Above value field in the Typographic Preferences dialog box.

Like custom kerning, custom tracking is stored in your document as well as in your XPress Preferences file. So if you give one of your files with custom tracking to another person, they'll get an alert message when they open the document asking whether or not they want to retain the settings for tracking, kerning, and other customized values. As long as they click the Keep Document Settings button, the text in the file will be spaced exactly as it was on your system.

▼ ▼

Tip: Cleaning out Custom Settings. Because all your custom kerning and tracking tables are saved in the XPress Preferences file, you can "clean out" your system, ridding yourself of every edit you've made, by deleting this file and relaunching XPress (the program creates a fresh new preferences file if it doesn't find one at launch time). This removes other settings you've made, too, such as Application Preferences and Suggested Hyphenation.

▼ ▼

Tip: Changing Custom Kerning and Tracking Settings. Perhaps you have different clients that prefer different sets of custom kerning and tracking tables. No problem. You can create a new XPress Preferences file for each client and hide them each in a separate folder or directory. When you want to switch from one to the other, just quit XPress, move the current XPress Preferences file into its folder, and replace it with the new one. Relaunch XPress, and you're set.

▼ ▼

Tweaking Hyphenation

Earlier in this chapter, I talked about how to create, edit, and apply H&J settings. However, you can fine-tune the program's hyphenation in a document with two tools and a preference: Hyphenation Exceptions, Suggested Hyphenation, and Hyphenation Method. Let's look briefly at each of these.

Hyphenation Method

In earlier versions of XPress, the program only used algorithms ("rules") to hyphenate its words. The result: some words didn't break properly and you got strange hyphenation. Over the years, XPress's algorithm slowly got better, and XPress started offering a choice between Standard and Enhanced algorithms (you can make the choice in the Document Preferences dialog box).

The only reason to use Standard is if you are opening documents created in very old XPress files (pre-3.0) and you need them not to reflow. Similarly, if you're opening any version-3 files, XPress automatically applies the Enhanced setting to them, so that they don't reflow either.

QuarkXPress 4 offers a third choice, however: Expanded hyphenation. In this setting, XPress checks words against a list in a built-in hyphenation dictionary; then, if it can't find the word, it uses a reasonably good algorithm to hyphenate it. There's no doubt that Expanded hyphenation is better, but it still ain't great, and there are many words that still hyphenate incorrectly.

So you should typically use Expanded hyphenation (unless you're working with old files and need them not to reflow), but you should check your document's hyphenation carefully nonetheless.

Suggested Hyphenation

The entire life's work of the Suggested Hyphenation feature is to help you figure out how QuarkXPress is going to hyphenate a word. First select a word (or put the cursor somewhere within or immediately to the right of a word). Next, choose Suggested Hyphenation from the Utilities menu (or press Command-H), and the program shows you how it would hyphenate that word (see Figure 6-57).

All the algorithms that QuarkXPress uses to hyphenate words take into account the parameters set within the Edit Hyphenation & Justification dialog box (such as the number of entries in Break Capitalized Words, Minimum Before, and so on). For example, when Minimum Before is set to 3, the word "answer" does not appear hyphenated in the Suggested Hyphenation dialog box. However, if you change Minimum Before to 2, it does.

Figure 6-57
Suggested Hyphenation

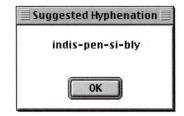

Hyphenation Exceptions

If you don't like the way XPress is hyphenating a word, you can override the program's algorithms by setting your own specific hyphenation in the Hyphenation Exceptions dialog box, which you access by selecting Hyphenation Exceptions from the Utilities menu. (Another way to override hyphenation is to use a discretionary hyphen, which I'll discuss in "Special Characters," later in this chapter.)

The first time you open the dialog box, the list is empty. To add a word, just type it in the available space, including hyphens where you want them. If you don't want a word to hyphenate at all, don't put any hyphens in it (see Figure 6-58).

Figure 6-58

Hyphenation Exceptions

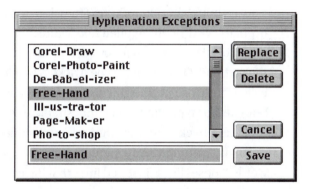

Once you've created some hyphenation exceptions, you can edit one of them by clicking on it, making the necessary change, and then clicking the Replace button (note that the Add button changes to a Replace button in this case). You can also delete an item on the list by selecting it and clicking the Delete button.

Hyphenation exceptions are stored in the XPress Preferences file, which is in the same folder as the QuarkXPress application. It's important to note that the changes you make are global: they affect each and every document on that machine when you create or open them. Like other information stored in the XPress Preferences file, hyphenation exceptions follow your document around onto other people's machines because they're stored inside each document as well.

Remember that if you set up a lot of hyphenation exceptions, you should keep a backup of your XPress Preferences file (see "XPress Preferences," in Chapter 2, *QuarkXPress Basics*).

▼ ▼

Tip: Watch Those Hyphens. There's nothing like giving your document a good once-over before you print it out. One of the things you want to look for is a badly hyphenated word. Remember that QuarkXPress generally uses an algorithm to hyphenate words, and it doesn't always do it right. For example, QuarkXPress hyphenates the word "Transeurope" as "Transeur-ope" rather than "Trans-europe." If you find these problem words, you can either change them manually (by adding discretionary hyphens), or make a global change using Hyphenation Exceptions.

▼ ▼

Tip: Line Check. I can remember the day—no, days—when my final task before taking a 530-page book to the service bureau was to scroll laboriously though my QuarkXPress files, looking for and fixing any widows, orphans, and badly hyphenated words. Of course, each fix caused a reflow of all the text that followed, and so required more checking. Would that I'd had Quark's free Type Tricks XTension, which adds a feature called Line Check to the Utilities menu. This handy feature automatically searches for typographically undesirable lines (see Figure 6-59).

Line Check searches through a document looking for widows, orphans, automatically hyphenated words, manually hyphenated words, "loose" lines (justified lines that have exceeded the boundaries of the H&J settings), and text boxes that have overflowed. It won't fix them

Figure 6-59

Line Check is part of the Type Tricks XTension

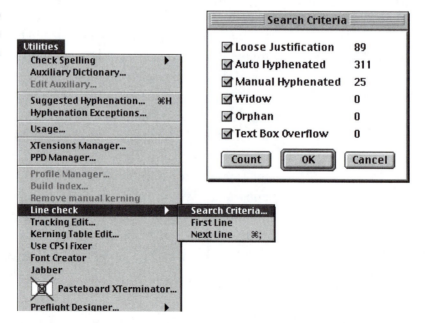

for you, but it sure does make cleaning up documents at the last minute a less-harrowing experience.

At first, I typically deselect all boxes, and then choose Search Criteria from the Line Check submenu. Then I click the Count button (in the Search Criteria dialog box) to find how many instances of each "infraction" occur throughout the document. If I see that there are overflowed text boxes or orphans or widows or whatever, I start searching through the document for them. Unfortunately, there's no way to jump from this dialog box to each instance; you can, however, place the cursor in a text box and select First Line from the Line Check submenu. If any instance of an orphan or widow (or whatever else you're looking for) occurs in that story, XPress highlights it. Then, to keep checking the story, select Next Line (or press Command-semicolon).

Special Characters

If you're just using QuarkXPress to type letters to your Uncle Neil, you probably don't need this section. If you're doing just about anything else with it, stand by.

When you look at your computer keyboard, you see between 50 and 100 characters represented on the keys. What you don't see are the hundreds of special characters you can access with just a few keystrokes. In this section I'll look at some of those characters, including invisible "utility" characters, dingbats, math symbols, and special punctuation. By no means do you have to memorize most of these; instead, when you're actually working on documents, you may want to refer back to the tables I've included in this section.

Formatting Characters

The first set of characters we'll look at are invisible characters that are used for special formatting in your document. Several of these characters are visible when you select Show/Hide Invisibles from the View menu (or you can toggle them on and off by pressing Command-I). However, a few are not visible; you just have to remember where you put them. Let's take a look at what these characters are (see Table 6-7 for more information on these characters).

Table 6-7

Invisible formatting
characters

NAME	INVISIBLES	MACINTOSH	WINDOWS
Return	¶	Return	Enter
Soft Return	↵	⇧-Return	⇧-Enter
Tab	→	Tab	Tab
Indent here	|	⌘-\	⌃-\
Discretionary new line		⌘-Return	⌃-Enter
Discretionary hyphen		⌘-Hyphen	⌃-Hyphen
Nonbreaking hyphen		⌘-=	⌃-=
Nonbreaking space		⌘-space	⌃-5
New column	↓	Enter (keypad)	Enter (keypad)
New box	⤓	⇧-Enter (keypad)	⇧-Enter (keypad)
En space		⌥-space	⌃-⇧-6
Nonbreaking en space		⌘-⌥-space	⌃-⇧-Alt-6
Flex space		⌥-⇧-space	⌃-⇧-5
Nonbreaking flex space		⌘-⌥-⇧-space	⌃-⇧-Alt-5
Current page number		⌘-3	⌃-3
Previous text box page		⌘-2	⌃-2
Next text box page number		⌘-4	⌃-4

Return. Sometimes known as a "carriage return" or a "hard return," this is the key to press when you're at the end of a paragraph. In fact, the Return character separates paragraphs from each other. Most people don't think of the Return key as a character, but you can see it and select it with Show/Hide Invisibles turned on.

QuarkXPress is great at wrapping characters onto the next line, so don't press Return after each line like you would on a typewriter. Also, don't press Return twice in a row to add extra space between paragraphs. Instead, use Space Before and Space After (see "Space Before and After," earlier in this chapter).

Soft Return. Holding down the Shift key while you press Return results in a soft return, often called the "new line" character. A soft return forces a new line without starting a new paragraph, with all its attendant attributes: Space Before and After, First Line Indent, paragraph rules, and so on. For example, I use soft returns for tabular text or for forcing a line break in justified or flush-left text. This is a character that takes some getting used to, but I recommend you play with it until you do, because it really comes in handy.

Tab. People also rarely think about tabs as separate characters, but that's just what they are. I talked about tabs in the section called "Tabs," earlier in this chapter, so all I need to say now is that you should really know your tabbing and never (never) use the spacebar to align columns. Also, you can see tab characters when Show Invisibles is turned on.

Indent Here. There's a great invisible formatting character called Indent Here, which you get by pressing Command-\ (backslash). This character causes the rest of the lines in a paragraph to indent to that character. I find this feature particularly useful for hanging punctuation or inline graphics, drop caps, or headings (see Figure 6-60).

In pre-3.3 versions of QuarkXPress, there was a bug in the Indent Here character that could mess you up: if you indented a paragraph's lines using the Indent Here feature, and the paragraph spanned two text boxes, the indents were dropped for any lines in the second text box.

Figure 6-60

The Indent Here character

How do I love thee? Let me count the ways: ¶

1) This is the first one. I can't remember quite what it is, but I'm sure I mean well.¶

2) Here's the second one. Hmmm. Can't quite remember it, either, but now at the very least I know exactly how to ↵ use the Indent Here character.

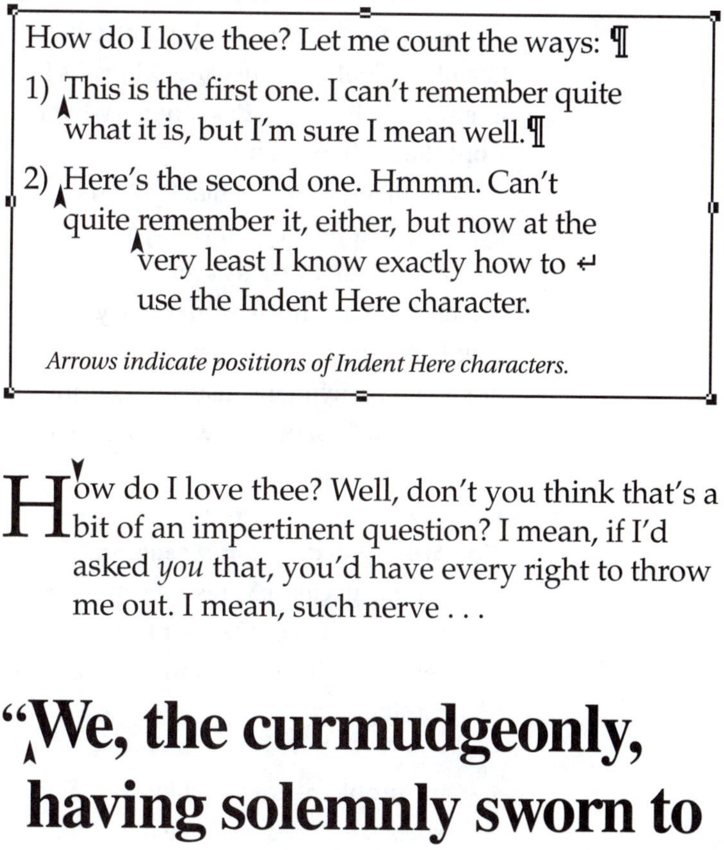

Arrows indicate positions of Indent Here characters.

How do I love thee? Well, don't you think that's a bit of an impertinent question? I mean, if I'd asked *you* that, you'd have every right to throw me out. I mean, such nerve . . .

"We, the curmudgeonly, having solemnly sworn to

Fortunately, they've fixed that problem now, and all the lines of the paragraph (after the Indent Here character) get indented, no matter what text box they're in. The Indent Here character appears as a single vertical gray line when Show Invisibles is turned on.

Some people use the Indent Here character to create hanging indents (like for bulleted lists). It's easy to do—just type a bullet, then a tab, then Command-\, and the rest of the paragraph is indented to the tab stop—but I don't like it as much as the trick where you set the Left Indent and First Line Indent (see "Tip: Hanging Indents," earlier in this chapter). The big difference? You can't specify an Indent Here character as part of a style sheet.

Discretionary hyphen. You remember that the Suggested Hyphenation feature lets you specify the hyphenation for a word, and wherever that word appears, it'll hyphenate the way you want. The discretionary-hyphen character (Command-hyphen) also lets you suggest hyphenation for a word, but it only works on a word-by-word basis. I use discretionary hyphens all the time when I'm finessing a document; if a line of text looks odd because XPress is being dumb in its hyphenation attempt, I'll throw in a discretionary-hyphen character where I think the word should hyphenate.

Note that typing a regular hyphen works just as well as a discretionary hyphen . . . at first. When you type a hyphen, XPress breaks the word at that spot (if the word is at the end of the line). But what happens if the text reflows for some reason (like if you add a word)? All of a sudden, you have hyphens scattered throughout your text (see Figure 6-61). If you use discretionary hyphens instead, they appear as real hyphens when they need to, but "disappear" when they're not needed (even Find/Change ignores the character).

▼ ▼

Tip: Stop Words from Breaking. Discretionary hyphens also play another role in QuarkXPress. If you place a discretionary hyphen immediately before a word, that word will never hyphenate at the end of a line. In other words, the discretionary hyphen also acts to turn hyphenation off for a single word.

▼ ▼

One problem arises when you want to remove a discretionary hyphen. Because you can't see this character (even when Show Invisibles is turned on), it's hard to select it and delete it. Try placing the cursor just before where you think the character is and using the arrow keys to move forward and backward. If there's a place where you hit the key but the cursor doesn't move, there might be an invisible character (like a discretionary hyphen) there.

Another possibility is to use XPress Tags. If you export your story in XPress Tags format (see Chapter 7, *Copy Flow*, for more on this), you can find discretionary hyphens quickly. Just search for `<\h>` (the code for this character).

Nonbreaking hyphen. Sooner or later, you'll probably come upon a word which includes a hyphen, but which shouldn't be broken at the end of a line. For instance, you typically don't want figure references, such as "Figure 99-3," to break at line endings. The solution: you can use a nonbreaking hyphen by pressing Command-= (equals sign) instead of a normal hyphen.

Discretionary new line. You can place the discretionary-new-line character (Command-Return) within a word to suggest places to break that word if QuarkXPress needs to. It's much like a discretionary hyphen, but without the hyphen.

Figure 6-61
Reflowed hyphens

Greetings, and congratulations on your purchase of **KvetchWrite**, the absolutely sensational new product for word processing, desktop publishing, object-oriented drawing, outline processing, flowchart creation, indexing, database management, telecommunications, and practically anything else you can imagine.

This is a regular automatic hyphen

Hard hyphens used here.

This text should have discretionary hyphens in it instead of hard hyphens.

Greetings, and congratulations on your purchase of **KvetchWrite**, the absolutely sensa-tional new product for word processing, desktop publishing, object-oriented draw-ing, outline processing, flowchart creation, indexing, database management, telecom-munications, and practically anything else you can imagine.

For example, if you type an en dash and feel comfortable about the surrounding words breaking at the end of a line, you can press Command-Return after the en dash (en dashes won't break without this, though em dashes will). If QuarkXPress determines that it needs to break the line at this point, it does. If it doesn't need to break the line there, it doesn't break it (and the character, being invisible, has no other effect on your text). Note that this character doesn't appear, even with Show Invisibles turned on.

Nonbreaking space. A nonbreaking space (on the Macintosh you can press Command-Space, Control-Space, or Command-5; on Windows, you can press Command-Shift-Space) looks just like a normal space character (and it expands and contracts as necessary in justified copy). However, it never breaks at the end of a line. A great use of this is in company names that include spaces, but shouldn't be broken over several lines (unless you absolutely have to).

New column and new box. If your text box contains multiple columns or is linked to other text boxes, you can use the New Column and New Box characters to force text to jump from one column or box to the next. Pressing Enter from your keyboard's numeric keypad forces a text jump to the next column. If the character is placed in the last (or only) column of a text box, it will force a jump to the next linked text box. Otherwise, pressing Shift-Enter forces a jump to the next linked text box.

En space. As I mentioned earlier in the chapter, an en is half an em, which—to QuarkXPress—equals either the width of two zeros or the height of the font you're working with (depending on how you've set up Document Preferences). Pressing Option-spacebar results in an en space (on Windows, press Control-Shift-6), which will not stretch in size in justified copy as much as a regular word space. (In other words, letterspacing still affects en spaces, though wordspacing values do not.) Command-Option-spacebar gives you an en space that doesn't break at the end of a line (on Windows, press Control-Alt-Shift-6). Note that an en space is rarely the same width as an en dash, even when Standard Em Space is turned on in the Typographic Preferences dialog box.

Flex space. When you press Option-Shift-space you get what's called a "flex space" (on Windows, press Control-Shift-5). You can specify how wide you want it to be (it flexes to your will). Also like the en space, once you specify its width, this space is fixed; it won't change width, even in justified text, unless you allow letterspacing in your H&J settings. (It's treated like just another character, so if QuarkXPress adds letterspacing in justified text, it adds it to the flex space, too. The space then expands.)

The control for this character's width is on the Character tab in the Document Preferences dialog box (Command-Y). The percentage is based on the width of an en space. Therefore the default value, 50 percent, is half an en space. 200 percent makes the flex space an em space. Note that when you change the width of a flex space in the Typographic Preferences dialog box, QuarkXPress changes the widths of flex spaces throughout that document.

Punctuation space. The punctuation space (Shift-space)—sometimes called a thin space—is easy to confuse with the flex space while you're typing, and looks similar. They're both fixed-width characters, so they don't expand in justified type (unless you allow letterspacing in the H&J specs), but you can't specify the size of a punctuation space. Typically it's the same width as a comma or a period, but it's really up to the font designer. Punctuation spaces are often used in European typesetting, especially when setting numbers. You might type "1 024.35" (where a punctuation space—rather than a comma—is used as a delimiter).

Here's some typographic trivia for you: In some typefaces, the width of punctuation is set to the same width as the normal spaceband (which is often exactly half the width of a numeral in that font). In this case, the spaceband and the punctuation space are the same width, though one will stretch with wordspacing and one will not.

Page numbers. QuarkXPress lets you use three characters to display page numbering (see Table 6-8). As I noted in Chapter 4, *Building a Document,* these are not only page-dependent, but also text box–dependent. For example, you can place a text box with the next text-box character (Command-4) on top of a linked text box, and the page number will register the link of the text box under it. The current text-box character (Command-3) is good for automatic page numbers on master pages; the

Table 6-8	PRESS ...	TO INSERT A CHARACTER REPRESENTING ...
Page-numbering characters	Command-2	Previous text box
	Command-3	Current text box
	Command-4	Next text box

previous text box character (Command-2) is good for "Continued from . . ." messages.

Punctuation and Symbols

A typographer shouldn't feel limited using a desktop computer. The type-faces from the major vendors (Adobe, Bitstream, Monotype, and so on) are loaded with the characters you need to create excellent type, includ-ing proper quotation marks, ligatures, and em dashes. If you aren't already a typographer, you'll want to pay careful attention to the tips and examples I provide here. Using some simple features—such as Smart Quotes and automatic ligatures—may make the difference between a piece that looks like it was desktop-published (in the worst sense of the phrase) and a piece that looks professional.

I can't discuss every special character that's included in a font, but I'll hit on a few of the important ones. Table 6-9 shows how to type each of these, plus a good number of additional characters.

Em and en dashes. An em dash, made by pressing Option-Shift-hyphen (on Windows, press Control-Shift-=), should be used in place of double hyphens to indicate a pause or a semiparenthetical. For example, don't type this: "Villainous-looking scoundrels--eight of them." Instead, use an em dash. An em dash is named for how long it is (one em).

An en dash (Option-hyphen on Macintosh or Control-Alt-Shift-hyphen on Windows) should generally be used for duration and dis-tance—replacing the word "to"—as in "August–September," "45–90 weeks long," and "the New York–Philadelphia leg of the trip." It's half as long as an em dash, so it doesn't stand out quite as much.

Note that QuarkXPress, if it needs to, breaks a line after an em dash when wrapping text, but not after an en dash (unless you put a discre-tionary soft return after it; see "Discretionary New Line," above).

▼ ▼

Tip: Narrowing Em Dashes. Perhaps typeface designers get overzealous every now and again with their characters. The em dash might certainly fall into this category, not in flourish but in width. Simply put, it's often just too wide. I'll sometimes make an em dash narrower by setting it to a horizontal scaling of 75 or 80 percent of its original width. If you have a *lot* of them, you might consider doing this using XPress Tags: search for the em dash and replace with "<h80>—<h100>". I discuss XPress Tags and doing this kind of search in Chapter 7, *Copy Flow*.

▼ ▼

Ligatures. Ligatures are to typography what diphthongs are to language. They connects single characters together to make a single one. While

Table 6-9

Special punctuation and symbols in most fonts

NAME	LOOKS LIKE	MACINTOSH	WINDOWS
Opening double quote	"	⌥-[	Alt-0147
Closing double quote	"	⌥-⇧-[	Alt-0148
Opening single quote	'	⌥-]	Alt-0145
Closing single quote	'	⌥-⇧-]	Alt-0146
Em dash	—	⌥-⇧-hyphen	⌃-⇧-=
En dash	–	⌥-hyphen	⌃-⇧-Alt-hyphen
Ellipsis	…	⌥-;	Alt-0133
Fraction bar	/	⌥-⇧-1	N/A
Capital ligature AE	Æ	⌥-⇧-'	Alt-0198
Small ligature ae	æ	⌥-'	Alt-0230
Ligature fi	fi	⌥-⇧-5	N/A
Ligature fl	fl	⌥-⇧-6	N/A
Bullet	•	⌥-8	Alt-0149
Copyright symbol	©	⌥-G	Alt-⇧-C
Registered symbol	®	⌥-R	Alt-⇧-R
Trademark symbol	™	⌥-2	Alt-⇧-2
Degree mark	°	⌥-⇧-8	Alt-0176
Section mark	§	⌥-6	Alt-0167
Paragraph mark	¶	⌥-7	Alt-0182
Dagger	†	⌥-T	Alt-0134
Cents sign	¢	⌥-4	Alt-0162

many classic typefaces would contain up to 10 ligatures, typefaces on the Macintosh include only two basic ligatures (fi and fl), and Expert Sets from Adobe and other vendors usually have three more (ff, ffi, and ffl). Unfortunately, the folks at Microsoft didn't think ligatures were important enough to include in the Windows character set, so ligatures aren't available in most Windows fonts. Figure 6-62 shows ligatures in action.

The fact is, most programs make it a pain in the spleen to use ligatures. For instance, to get a ligature, you typically have to press an odd key combination (Command-Shift-5 or Command-Shift-6 on the Macintosh). However, there are problems with using these "hard-coded" ligatures. If you type one of these characters in XPress, it won't be able to correctly spell-check or hyphenate it. Also, words with hard-coded ligatures in them might look strange in justified text if the program adds a lot of letterspacing. The final straw is that you can't easily edit the word (if you want to delete just the "f" or "i," you must retype both characters) or search for it in the Find/Change dialog box.

Fortunately, XPress has a great feature that gives you the best of all worlds: automatic ligatures. (Note that the Windows version of XPress doesn't include this feature because of limitations of Windows fonts.)

The key here is the Ligatures checkbox on the Character tab in the Document Preferences dialog box (Command-Y). When the Ligatures option is turned on, XPress automatically replaces every instance of "fi" and "fl" with the "fi" and "fl" ligatures. The wonderful thing about automatic ligatures is that spell-checking, searching, and hyphenation work just the way you'd hope they would because you're not typing weird special characters in the middle of words. You can even place your cursor between the "f" and the "i" in an automatic "fi" ligature because XPress still knows that it is two letters.

The Break Above field underneath the Ligatures checkbox becomes active when you turn automatic ligatures on. The number in this field tells QuarkXPress the letterspacing level above which to break the liga-

Figure 6-62
The ffi and ffl ligatures

Officially, the finalists
were affluent flounder

Without ligatures

Officially, the finalists
were affluent flounder

With ligatures

ture apart. For example, suppose the field contains "1". If the ligature is kerned or tracked more than one unit, the ligature breaks apart, becoming two separate characters. If you change the number to "5", then QuarkXPress maintains the ligature until tracking or kerning has reached six units.

This is an important feature because you don't want two characters stuck together in "loose" text (the ligature stands out too much). This spacing limit also applies to justified text. That is, if a text block is justified by adding letterspacing, the ligatures may break into their single characters when necessary.

The last option in this area, called "Not ffi Or ffl," is for some finicky folks who think that those two particular combinations should not get the ligature treatment. I disagree, and I leave this option turned off.

Note that some fonts on the Macintosh have ligatures that look just like their character pair equivalents; this is especially true in sans serif typefaces, such as Helvetica. Also, some typefaces don't have built-in ligatures, and a few rare fonts have them but QuarkXPress doesn't "see" them. So the system's not foolproof, but it's still pretty good.

▼ ▼

Tip: Finding and Replacing Ligatures. If you're using QuarkXPress for Windows and you want ligatures, you'll have to manually search and replace the "fi" and "fl" combinations with the proper ligatures. If you do this, make sure you're careful about replacing them correctly. Especially make sure you turn off Ignore Case from the Find/Change dialog box. If you don't, the capitalized "Fi" or "Fl" combinations get changed, too! Remember that your search-and-replace strategy must also change the combination's font to the expert-set font containing the ligatures.

▼ ▼

Quotation Marks. The first tip-off that someone is green behind the ears in desktop publishing is his or her use of straight quotes instead of proper "printer's quotes." Straight quotes, which is what you get when you press the ' and " keys, should be used for notation of measurements (inches and feet) or for special typographic effect (some fonts' straight quotes look great in headline type). Printer's quotes, or curly quotes, should be used for English/American quotations. Quark has two features that have made it much easier to use curly quotes—Convert Quotes and Smart Quotes.

The Convert Quotes checkbox in the Get Text dialog box lets you convert all straight quotes into proper curly quotes when you import text. Second, you can turn on Smart Quotes in the Application Preferences dialog box. This automatically converts quotes as you type them. I always leave both of these turned on unless I specifically need to use straight quotes (see "Tip: Getting Your Quotes Straight," below).

Note that Smart Quotes can replace straight quotes with other sorts of quote marks (see "Tip: Get It Right for Overseas," below).

▼ ▼

Tip: Getting Your Quotes Straight. When Smart Quotes is turned on, every time you type a single or double quote it comes out curly. QuarkXPress is replacing the straight quote with the Option-[or Option-] and the Shift-Option-[or Shift-Option-] keys behind the scenes. However, if you really need a straight quote someplace, you can get it by pressing Control-' or Control-Shift-" (that's Control, *not* Command). On Windows, it's Control-' or Control-Alt-'. These keystrokes do just the opposite when Smart Quotes is turned off; then you get curly quotes. Unfortunately, this feature doesn't work with some foreign-language keyboard layouts (I've even had complaints about the UK keyboard not working in earlier versions of XPress).

▼ ▼

Registration, Copyright, and Trademark. The registration, copyright, and trademark characters are found on the Macintosh by pressing Option-R, Option-G, and Option-2 keys. In Windows, you should press Alt-Shift-R, Alt-Shift-C, and ANSI character code 0153 (see "Tip: ANSI Codes," below).

I have only one thing to say about using these characters: be careful with your sizing and positioning. I recommend immediately assigning the superior type style to the character, then determining whether it should be kerned or not (see Figure 6-63).

▼ ▼

Tip: Key Caps and Character Map. Anyone who can remember every character in a font, including all the special symbols and characters, is no one to borrow money from. I can never remember most of the characters I need, so I use Key Caps (on the Mac) and Character Map (on Windows). Both of these come free with your system—Key Caps is installed on the Apple menu, and Character Map is in the Accessories application group (see Figure 6-64).

Figure 6-63
Special symbols

KvetchWrite™ is a product of No Accounting For Taste, Eh?®
Documentation © Copyright 1990 No Class Productions.

Trademark and registration characters re-done as superior characters:

KvetchWrite!™ is a product of No Accounting For Taste, Eh?®
Documentation © Copyright 1990 No Class Productions.

Registration mark kerned +12 to give it a little room to breathe.

Result without kerning: Eh?®

Figure 6-64
Key Caps and
Character Map

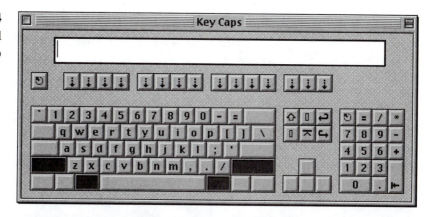

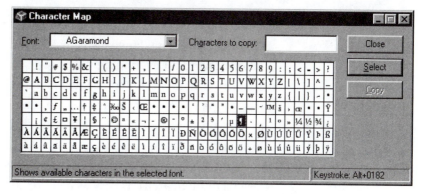

To use Key Caps, select it from the Apple menu, then select the font
you want to see from the Key Caps menu. When you hold down the Shift
key, you see the map of all the uppercase characters. If you hold down
the Option key, you see the Option characters, and so on. Click on the
character you want to add to the text field at the top of the window. From
there, you can copy and paste the character into a text box in XPress.

Character Map presents a table of characters for any font you choose. Simply double-click on the character you want (or click once and then click the Select button) to make the character appear in the Characters to Copy field. To enter the selected characters in XPress, click the Copy button, switch to your QuarkXPress document, place your insertion point, and paste (Control-V).

There are also a number of other shareware and freeware utilities on both Macintosh and Windows that let you find the character you need from a font even more easily than these two accessories do, but these work pretty well for me.

▼ ▼

Tip: ANSI Codes. Another way to type a character not found on your keyboard is to enter its Windows ANSI code (this is a Windows-only thing). First you need to look up the code, which you can find in Appendix F, *ANSI Codes,* or in your Windows manual. Notice that they're all four-digit codes, each beginning with a zero. Then, to enter the code, hold down the Alt key while you key in the code on your keyboard's numeric keypad.

The Character Map accessory in Windows also shows you the ANSI code when you click on a character.

▼ ▼

Foreign Punctuation and Accents

Working in a foreign language is really a trip. Foreign languages have a different word for everything. Many foreign languages, like French and Spanish, contain accented characters that are built into fonts from the major type vendors. For example, you can type *élève* without switching to some obscure font. Table 6-10 lists the characters that you would most likely use in a foreign language.

Many people don't fully understand how to type these characters. Several of them aren't as easy as just pressing a key, or even a key with Option or Shift held down. For example, "é" is typed on a Macintosh by first typing Option-E, then typing the letter "e." It's a two-keystroke deal. On Windows, you can use the Character Map or type ANSI character code 0233 (as discussed above).

▼ ▼

Tip: Get It Right for Overseas. Here in the United States, I grew up with the ethnocentric viewpoint that the way I write and typeset is the way

Table 6-10

Foreign accents and punctuation

NAME	LOOKS LIKE	MACINTOSH	WINDOWS
Left double guillemet	«	⌘-\	Alt-0171
Right double guillemet	»	⌘-⇧-\	Alt-0187
Left single guillemet	‹	⌘-⇧-3	Alt-0139
Right single guillemet	›	⌘-⇧-4	Alt-0155
Base double quote	„	⌘-⇧-W	Alt-0132
Base single quote	‚	⌘-⇧-0	Alt-0130
Question mark down	¿	⌘-⇧-?	Alt-0191
Exclamation point down	¡	⌘-1	Alt-0161
Acute vowel	áéíóúÁÉÍÓÚ	⌘-E, then vowel	*
Umlaut vowel	äëïöüÄËÏÖÜ	⌘-U, then vowel	*
Grave vowel	àèìòùÀÈÌÒÙ	⌘-`, then vowel	*
Circumflex vowel	âêîôûÂÊÎÔÛ	⌘-I, then vowel	*
Cedilla C	Ç	⌘-⇧-C	Alt-0199
Cedilla c	ç	⌘-C	Alt-0231
Capital slashed O	Ø	⌘-⇧-O	Alt-0216
Small slashed o	ø	⌘-O	Alt-0248
German ess (double s)	ß	⌘-S	N/A
Dotless i	ı	⌘-⇧-B	N/A
Tilde	˜	⌘-⇧-M	Alt-0152
Tilde N	Ñ	⌘-N, then ⇧-N	Alt-0209
Tilde n	ñ	⌘-N, then N	Alt-0241
Circumflex	ˆ	⌘-⇧-N	Alt-0136
Macron	¯	⌘-⇧-comma	N/A
Breve	˘	⌘-⇧-period	N/A
Ring accent	°	⌘-K	Alt-0176
Ring a	å	⌘-A	Alt-0197
Ring A	Å	⌘-⇧-A	Alt-0229
Dot accent	·	⌘-H	N/A
Pound sterling	£	⌘-3	Alt-0163
Yen	¥	⌘-Y	Alt-0165

See Appendix F, ANSI codes, for the Windows equivalents.

everybody does it. Not so. For example, single quotation marks are used in America where double quotation marks are used in Britain. In other European countries, my quotation marks are replaced with guillemets («, »). Note that Smart Quotes lets you set these to appear automatically when you press the quote keys. The Spanish language sets a question or an exclamation point at both the beginning (upside down) and at the end of sentences. Figure 6-65 shows examples of each of these styles.

If you do a lot of foreign-language work, and especially work that has multiple languages in the same document, you should check out Quark Passport—the multilingual version of QuarkXPress. This program lets you set a language as a paragraph attribute, and will then check spelling and hyphenate that language properly. It comes with about 12 languages built in. (You may run into some difficulties exchanging files in those languages with Passport if you don't have all the versions synchronized.)

Other languages, such as Hebrew, Farsi, Russian, and Greek, must be typed using a non-Roman font specific to that language, and may require specialized software. QuarkXPress is presently available in over 15 languages, including Japanese and German. (In case you're curious, Passport does not include Japanese.)

Figure 6-65
Foreign punctuation

¡Mi llama se llama Spot! _____ *Spanish inverted exclamation and question marks*

¿Dónde está la casa de Pépe?

Il dit «La fromage, ça va bien?» — *European quotation marks (guillemets)*

Er sagt: „Je mehr, desto besser."— *German quotation marks*

"He said, 'Thrift, thrift,' and walked off into the sunset."   'He said, "Thrift, thrift," and walked off into the sunset.'   *American (left) and British (right) quotation marks*

▼ ▼

Math Symbols and the Symbol Font

In my humble opinion, QuarkXPress is the wrong program in which to produce a mathematics textbook (though I know that it's been done). You can use utilities such as MathType from Design Science to help create equations, but they're not set up for doing heavy-duty math typesetting in XPress (not like the power tools in Adobe FrameMaker). Nonetheless, you can still do a pretty good job in QuarkXPress, as long as you don't have to produce 2,000 different equations in a document.

The keys to doing a good job are using the correct symbols, and good typography. Most typefaces come with a wide variety of built-in math symbols. Table 6-11 provides a list of the most common of these and how to type them.

Almost any equation you'd want to typeset will require the Symbol font. Symbol is a Greek and math font that comes with your Macintosh or Windows system. It includes such characters as a multiplication sign (×), which you can create by pressing Option-Y (Mac) or Alt+0180 (Windows). Use Key Caps or Character Map, mentioned earlier, to examine the other characters in this typeface. Even better are pi fonts, such as Adobe's Universal News with Commercial Pi, which gives you better spacing and more flexible character weights. You can also purchase specialized math pi fonts, like Lucida Math.

Note that most Windows fonts include a multiplication character (Alt+0215) and division character (Alt+0247).

▼ ▼

Tip: One-Stroke, One-Character Font Change. QuarkXPress has so many keystrokes and shortcuts that I can never remember them all. Here are two that I always forget about: pressing Command-Shift-Q sets the next character you type in the Symbol font, while pressing Command-Shift-Z sets it in Zapf Dingbats. After you type the character, QuarkXPress automatically reverts to the typeface you were in. If you have one or

Table 6-11
Commonly used math symbols
(For Windows keystrokes, please see Appendix F, *ANSI Codes.*)

NAME	LOOKS LIKE	IN MOST FONTS	SYMBOL FONT
Division	÷	⌘-/	⌘-⇧-P
Plus or minus	±	⌘-⇧-=	⌘-⇧-=
Greater or equal	≥	⌘-period	⌘-period
Lesser or equal	≤	⌘-comma	⌘-3
Approximate equal	≈	⌘-X	⌘-9
Not equal	≠	⌘-=	⌘-P
Infinity	∞	⌘-5	⌘-8
Partial differential	∂	⌘-D	⌘-D
Integral	∫	⌘-B	⌘-⇧-;
Florin	ƒ	⌘-F	⌘-7
Capital omega	Ω	⌘-Z	⇧-W
Capital delta	Δ	⌘-J	⇧-D
Product	∏	⌘-⇧-P	⇧-P
Summation	Σ	⌘-W	⇧-S
Pi	π	⌘-P	P
Radical	√	⌘-V	⌘-/

more characters already selected when you press these keystrokes, QuarkXPress simply changes them to the desired font.

▼ ▼

Dingbats

Letters, numbers, and symbols do not a funky design make. Ofttimes you need dingbats. Dingbats, or pi fonts, are collections of interesting and useful shapes, pictures, graphics, and so on. The most popular dingbat font by far is Zapf Dingbats—because it is included in most PostScript printers. Table 6-12 shows a listing of about a third of the Zapf Dingbats characters and how to type them. The other two-thirds are mostly variations on what is shown here.

Other examples of dingbat or pi fonts are Carta, Bundesbahn Pi, and Adobe Woodtype Ornaments (see Figure 6-66 for a few examples of various pi—or "dingbat"—fonts).

You can use these fonts for fun, but you'll more likely want to use them in a very functional way. Most people use them for bullets (those round Option-8 or Alt-Shift-8 bullets get boring pretty quickly). My favorite for this function is the lowercase "v" from Zapf Dingbats (❖).

You can also use these characters as graphics on your page. Don't forget you can shade and color different characters on your page to act as a background or foreground graphic.

Figure 6-66
Some other dingbats

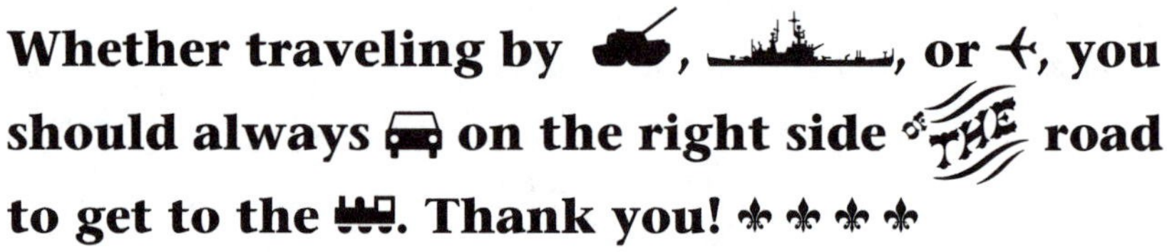

Whether traveling by 🚙 **,** ⚓ **, or** ✈ **, you should always** 🚗 **on the right side** ♪THE road **to get to the** 🚂 **. Thank you!** ✤ ✤ ✤ ✤

Symbols from Carta, Bundesbahn Pi, and Adobe Woodtype Ornaments.

▼ ▼

Tip: Ballot Boxes and Custom Dingbats. Many people create blank "ballot" boxes by typing a Zapf Dingbats lowercase "n" and setting it to outline style, or using the TrueType Wingdings font that comes with Windows. The problem with the first method is that imagesetting the outline often results in a hairline that is too thin to reproduce well. The only problem with the second method is that it's TrueType (I decidedly favor PostScript fonts for professional publishing). Nonetheless, there's

Table 6-12

Useful characters
in Zapf Dingbats

*Press Command-Shift-Z
followed by the key or
keystroke at right. Or,
select a range of characters
already typed and then
press Command-Shift-Z.*

Name	Looks like	Key or keystroke
Shadow ballot box up	❏	O
Shadow ballot box down	❐	P
3D ballot box up	❑	Q
3D ballot box down	❒	R
Filled ballot box	■	N
Hollow ballot box	□	N (apply Outline style)
Opening great quote	"	⇧-]
Closing great quote	"	⌥-N (Windows: ⇧-tilde)
Opening single great quote	'	⇧-[
Closing single great quote	'	⇧-\
Great bullet	●	L
Great hollow bullet	○	L (apply Outline style)
Great shadow bullet	○	M
Filled arrowhead	➤	⌥-⇧-E (Windows: Alt-0228)
Right arrow	→	⌥-] (Windows: Alt-0220)
Fat right arrow	➡	⌥-⇧-U (Windows: Alt-0232)
3D right arrow	⇨	⌥-⇧-I (Windows: Alt-0233)
Speeding right arrow	⯈	⌥-⇧-7 (Windows: Alt-0224)
Triangle up	▲	S
Triangle down	▼	T
Love leaf	❦	⌥-7 (Windows: Alt-0166)
X-mark	✗	8
Check-mark	✔	4
J'accuse	☞	⇧-=
Victory	✌	Comma
Scissors	✂	⇧-4
Pencil straight	✏	/
Pen nib	✍	1
Telephone	☎	⇧-5
Cross	✚	⇧-;
Star	★	⇧-H
Big asterisk	✹	⇧-Z
Snowflake	❄	D

a better option: anchored boxes (I'll cover this in much more detail in Chapter 11, *Where Text Meets Graphics*).

1. Create a picture box of any size.

2. Give the picture box a border (Command-B); I like to use .5 point.

3. Select the Item tool and cut the box (Command-X).

4. Using the Content tool, select where in the text you want the box to go, and then paste the box in there (Command-V).

5. Resize it to suit your needs.

Not only can you make box characters this way, but you can make any polygon, or anything else you can create within the application. Also, by importing a graphic into the picture box before you cut and paste it, you can create your own custom dingbats (Figure 6-67).

Figure 6-67
Custom dingbats

And re*mem*ber!  The *"cornier"* your Presentation, the less likely it is to be *Taken Seriously!*

Custom dingbat created by placing an EPS (Encapsulated PostScript) file within an anchored picture box. Picture box has been resized and its baseline shifted until the block of text looked appropriately corny.

☐ *Ballot box made with an outlined Zapf Dingbat ("n")*

☐ *Ballot box made with an anchored (square) picture box having a half-point (.5) frame.*

Typographic Special Effects

QuarkXPress is not a typographic special-effects program. But this does not mean that it can't give you the power to create many exciting effects with your type. In this section, I'm going to look at a few of the possibilities, like drop caps, rotated text, shadowed type, and type as a picture. But I can't cover everything that you can do. This, especially, is an area in which you have to play around.

Chapter 11, *Where Text Meets Graphics*, covers a few other special effects, such as text runaround, that you can create using QuarkXPress.

Fractions

Desktop publishing isn't so young that it doesn't have some hallowed traditions. One of the most hallowed is groaning in pain at the mention of creating fractions. But as with most traditions, you shouldn't let that frighten you off. The "fraction problem" in desktop publishing arises because most Macintosh fonts do not come with prebuilt fraction characters, and Windows fonts only have a small handful. (Windows fonts typically include three fractions—¼, ½, and ¾—which you can type by pressing Alt+0188, 0189, and 0190, respectively).

You can create your own fractions in a number of ways. Let's take a look at each of these, and discuss why you'd want to use them.

Pseudo-fractions. You can create pseudo-fractions by typing in numbers separated by a slash. Let's be frank: they look awful, and are considered bad form. But in some cases, such as simple word-processed documents, they're perfectly acceptable. Opinion varies on how best to type these characters, especially when you have a fraction following a number. I generally like to add a hyphen between a number and its fraction. For example, one and one-half would be typed "1-1/2."

Don't try to use the fraction-bar character (Option-Shift-1 on the Macintosh, ANSI character code 0164 in the Symbol font on Windows) for this kind of fraction. It almost always bumps into the second number and looks like a *shmatta* (like junk).

Made fractions. You can create fractions—such as ½, ¾, or $^{29}\!/_{32}$—by applying specific character-level formatting to each character in the fraction. The following example shows you how.

1. Type the pseudo-fraction; for example, "3/8." In this case, you should use the fraction-bar character (Option-Shift-1 on the Macintosh; on Windows, type Alt+0164 in the Symbol font) rather than the normal slash character.

2. Select the numerator—in this case, the "3"—and set it to the Superior style (Command-Shift-V).

3. Select the denominator—in this case, the "8"—and set it to the Superior *and* Subscript styles (Command-Shift-hyphen on the Macintosh; Control-Shift-9 on Windows).

4. Kern the fractions as desired.

If you don't like the size of the numerator and denominator, you can change the Superior settings on the Character tab in the Document Preferences dialog box. When a proper fraction follows a number, you probably don't want any sort of hyphen or even a space (see Figure 6-68).

Figure 6-68

Fractions

They tell me getting there is 3/8 of the fun.

A pseudo-fraction

I went to see *8-1/2* but only stayed for 2¾ of it.

A pseudo-fraction, followed by one created via the method noted in the text.

About ¼ of the time, I won't even give him a dime.

A fraction generated with Make Fraction (from the free TypeTricks XTension) plus some manual kerning within the fraction.

Fractions via XTension. Quark's free Type Tricks XTension contains a feature that creates fractions for you. It essentially acts as a macro, changing the slash to a proper fraction bar, and changing the font size and kerning of the numerator and denominator. To let QuarkXPress make the fraction for you, follow these steps.

1. Type the fraction as two numbers separated by a slash.

2. Place the cursor in the fraction, or just to the right of it.

3. Select Make Fraction from the Type Style submenu (under the Style menu).

Even though this feature is under the Style menu, Make Fraction is not really a character attribute; it's just a shortcut. Therefore, there's no way to undo the fraction using Undo. Note that on Windows, the fraction-bar character doesn't get substituted properly (Quark says that it does, but it doesn't), so you have to convert it yourself after making the fraction.

Personally, while many people go ga-ga over this feature, I find it only marginally faster than using the step-by-step method outlined above, and I like the results of the XTension less. (To be fair, you can control the results to some degree in the Fractions/Price Preferences dialog box, found on the Edit menu when this XTension is present.) Plus, if you change the font size of the fraction, the fraction made with styles changes dynamically, while the fraction made with the XTension has to be adjusted by hand.

Stacked fractions. QuarkXPress also lets you create stacked fractions, such as $\frac{1}{4}$ and $\frac{3}{4}$. Here's a quick formula for making them.

1. Type the numerator and denominator, separated by an underline (Shift-hyphen).

2. Change the point size of these three characters to 40 or 50 percent of original size. For example, 12-point type gets changed to 5- or 6-point type.

3. Select the numerator and the underline, and apply a baseline shift equal to the point size.

4. Leave the numerator and the underline highlighted, and apply a tracking value of approximately -90 units.

5. At your discretion, apply extra kerning between the characters to achieve a more precise look. You may want to zoom to 800 percent, or print a test sheet.

Chances are, you'll need to adjust the numbers I provide for different typefaces and number combinations. Note that this method of creating stacked fractions only works when both numbers are single digits.

Expert Set fonts. Adobe and other companies have released expert set fonts that complement some of their normal font packages, such as Minion and Minion Expert. The Expert Sets contain some prebuilt fractions and a full set of correctly drawn and scaled superscript and subscript numerals, as well as the correct fraction bar for use with them. This really is the best way to make fractions, and it's what I used throughout this book. (An expert set font also contains oldstyle numerals, small capitals, and other special symbols and ligatures.) However, most fonts don't have Expert Sets; check with the font vendor for specifics.

Utilities. You can also create your own fraction fonts with a utility program such as Fontographer. This method allows you to use any font that you're already using to generate custom fraction characters. See Robin

Williams's book, *How to Boss Your Fonts Around*, for details on creating a custom font.

Initial Caps

Initial Caps are enlarged characters at the beginning of a paragraph that lend a dramatic effect to chapter or section openings. There are four basic types of initial caps: raised, dropped, hanging, and anchored. Each of these styles is made considerably easier to create with the automatic drop-caps feature and the Indent Here character (Command-\).

Let's look at several initial caps and how they are made.

Standard raised caps. Raised caps can be created by enlarging the first letter of the paragraph (see Figure 6-69). It's important to use absolute leading when you create standard raised caps. If you don't, the first paragraph's leading gets thrown way off.

Hung raised caps. A spin-off of the standard raised cap is the hung raised cap (see Figure 6-70). You can hang the letter "off the side of the column" by placing an Indent Here character after it or creating a hanging indent with indents and tabs. The rest of the text block's lines all indent up to that point.

Standard drop caps. The Drop Caps control is located on the Formats tab in the Paragraph Attributes dialog box (see Figure 6-71). To create a drop cap in a paragraph, place the text cursor in the paragraph, press Command-Shift-F (to bring up the dialog box), and turn on Drop Caps. You can then modify two parameters for this feature: Character Count and Line Count.

The character count is the number of characters made to drop. The line count is the number of lines that they drop. For example, specifying "3" in Character Count and "4" in Line Count makes the first three characters of the paragraph large enough to drop four lines down. You don't have to worry about sizing the character, aligning it, or specifying the space between the drop cap and the rest of the text. In this example, the baseline of the drop cap aligns with the fourth line, and the ascent of the drop cap aligns with the first line's ascent. Some fonts have ascents that are taller than their capital letters. This may make the process slightly more difficult, depending on the effect you're trying to achieve.

Figure 6-69
Standard raised caps

Unaccustomed as I am to public speaking . . . but that never did prevent me from running off endlessly at the mouth . . . you, sir! Stop that hideous snoring! But I digress . . .

14-point copy with a 30-point initial capital.

Figure 6-70
Hung raised caps

Unaccustomed as I am to public speaking . . . but that never did prevent me from running off endlessly at the mouth . . . you, sir! Stop that hideous snoring! But I digress . . .

14-point copy with a 30-point capital. Indent Here character has been placed to the immediate right of the raised cap.

Figure 6-71
Standard drop caps

Let it never be said that the Koala tea of Moishe is not strained. Should this be said, it is entirely possible that the very fabric of civilization would fall utterly into the hands of the

Drops Caps is set in the Paragraph Attributes dialog box. Note that the font size is replaced with a percentage.

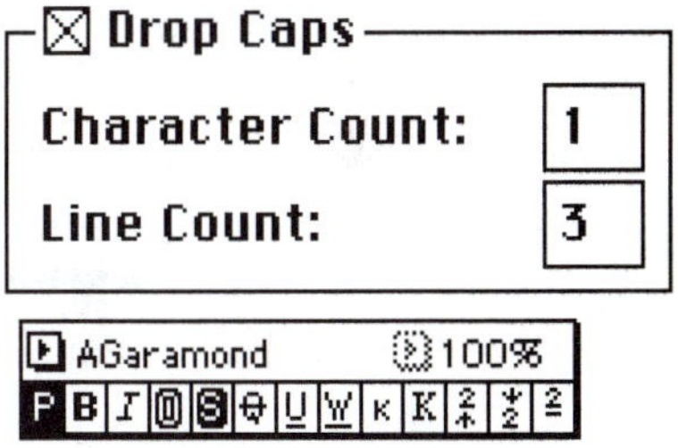

▼ ▼

Tip: Adjusting Space After Caps. I often find that I want to change the space between the initial cap and the text that's flowing around it. People have tried all sorts of weird workarounds for moving the two farther apart or closer together, but I prefer the simple method: add kerning between the drop cap and the character after it. The more kerning you add, the farther away the flow-around text is set. Negative kerning brings the text closer.

▼ ▼

Hanging drop caps. You can make these in the same way as the hanging raised caps: place an Indent Here character (Command-\) directly after the dropped character (see Figure 6-72). You can adjust the spacing between the drop cap and the following text by adjusting the kerning value between the drop cap and the next character (in this case, the Indent Here character).

Scaled drop caps. XPress has one hidden feature that works on drop-cap characters and drop-cap characters only: percentage scaling. After creating a standard drop cap (as described above), you can select the drop-cap character(s) and change the point size to a percentage of the original drop-cap size. For example, Figure 6-73 shows a paragraph with the drop cap scaled to 150 percent. You can change the percentage of the drop-cap character(s) to anything you want, and the baseline will always align with the text line to the right.

Anchored raised caps. Another way of making a raised cap is to create it in a separate text box, then anchor that box to the beginning of the paragraph (I discuss anchored text and picture boxes in Chapter 11, *Where Text Meets Graphics*). The raised cap in Figure 6-74 is actually a separate text box containing a large capital letter on a tinted background. The character is centered horizontally and vertically within the frame. I also applied other formatting to the initial cap, such as kerning and baseline shift.

Anchored drop caps. After creating an anchored raised cap, you can make it drop by selecting Ascent on the Box tab in the Modify dialog box (select the anchored box and press Command-M, or double-click on the anchored box).

Wraparound dropped caps. When you're using letters such as "W" or "A," you may want to wrap the paragraph text around the letter (see Figure 6-75). While you can use the Drop Cap option (along with a mess of other formatting), it's just easier to create the drop cap as a separate box and let XPress figure out the text runaround for you.

1. Create a new text box, type the initial-cap character, and format it the way you want it to look.

Figure 6-72

Hanging drop caps

Three-line drop cap with Indent Here character placed here, creating hanging drop cap.

Let it never be said that the Koala tea of Moishe is not strained. Should this be said, it is entire-ly possible that the very fabric of civilization would fall utterly into the hands of itsworst

Figure 6-73

Scaled drop caps

Let it never be said that the Koala tea of Moishe is not strained. Should this be said, it is entirely possible that the very fabric of civilization would fall utterly into the hands of its worst enemies, like that fellow whose name begins

The same, with the capital "L" enlarged to 150 percent of its normal size:

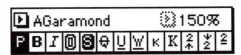

The Measurements palette reflects the change—again, as a percentage of the normal drop-cap size (not in points).

Figure 6-74

Anchored raised caps

We fully recognize that the message "Now formatting your hard disk. Have an *exceedingly* nice day," appearing during the **KvetchPaint** installation, is a bit alarming. Rest assured that it is a harmless prank by one of our programmers—who is, you can also rest assured, no longer with us. As soon as we can break the encryption he used, we will

2. Select the initial-cap character and choose Text to Box from the Style menu. This converts the text into a picture box. You can now delete the original text box (the one that held the initial cap).

3. Unless you're going to put a picture inside the initial cap, choose None from the Content submenu (under the Item menu).

4. In the Modify dialog box (Command-M, or double-click with the Item tool), give the box a background color and set the Runaround to Item.

5. Move the initial-cap box into position over the paragraph.

This is only one of many variations on a theme for creating wrap-around drop caps. Another is to use an initial cap brought in from an illustration program (as any sort of graphic file). You can then use QuarkXPress's automatic runaround or manual runaround feature to control the text runaround (I discuss text runaround in detail in Chapter 11, *Where Text Meets Graphics*).

Mixed-font caps. I've already cautioned you about using too many fonts on a page. But if there's ever a time to break the rules, it's with initial caps (see Figure 6-76). If you want your initial caps in a different font, simply change the font for those characters. However, note that when you change the initial cap's typeface, the character may not align properly with the rest of the text.

Multiple initial caps. Character Count in the Drop Caps feature lets you drop up to eight letters in your paragraph. So a drop cap could be a drop word, if you like (see Figure 6-77).

Figure 6-75
Wrapping drop caps around pictures and picture boxes

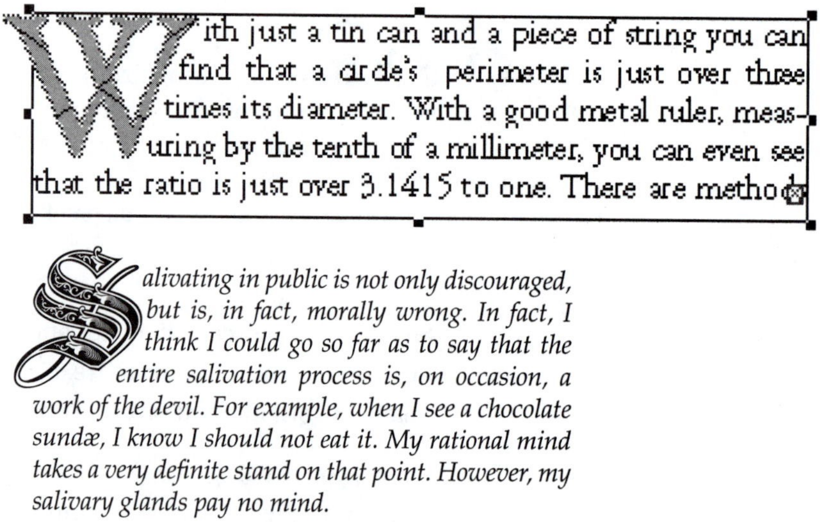

With just a tin can and a piece of string you can find that a circle's perimeter is just over three times its diameter. With a good metal ruler, measuring by the tenth of a millimeter, you can even see that the ratio is just over 3.1415 to one. There are methods

Salivating in public is not only discouraged, but is, in fact, morally wrong. In fact, I think I could go so far as to say that the entire salivation process is, on occasion, a work of the devil. For example, when I see a chocolate sundæ, I know I should not eat it. My rational mind takes a very definite stand on that point. However, my salivary glands pay no mind.

Figure 6-76
Mixed font initial caps

Snell Roundhand   *Adobe Garamond*

*S*conce, call you it? So you would leave battering, so I would rather have it a head. And you use these blows long, I must get a sconce for my head, and ensconce it too, or else I shall seek my wit in my shoulders. But, I pray, sir, why am I beaten?

Figure 6-77
Multiple initial caps

Five-character drop cap. Horizontal scaling of 75%; font size changed from 100% to 87.5%

Comma scaled down to 75% of normal font size, (it's less obtrusive that way).

What, gone in chafing, and clapped to the doors? Now I am every way shut out for a very bench-whistler; neither shall I have entertainment here or at home. I were best to go try some other friends.

Playing with initial caps. Like I said, initial caps are great opportunities to play and come up with creative ideas. For instance, you could make a two-character automatic drop cap, and set the first character in some dingbat font. Change the color and tint of the dingbat, and then kern the second character back so that it sits on top of the dingbat (you may need to change the dingbat's baseline shift to make it look right). Can you re-create the initial-cap examples in Figure 6-78?

▼ ▼

Tip: Type in the Margin. In QuarkXPress, the edges of text boxes are usually inviolable. There's no margin release, no handy command for moving one line an eentsy bit over the edge. Or is there? This tip shows a clever way of fooling QuarkXPress into hanging text at the beginning of a line beyond the left margin of a column or text box (see Figure 6-79).

A POOR MAN IS OBSERVED STARING in admiration at the large and ornate tombstone of the richest man in town. he shakes his head slowly and mutters, "Now, that's what I call living!"

Of course, the last time I went to one of those big banquets, I lost my wallet. I went up to the microphone and announced "Ladies and gentlemen, I've lost my wallet, with eight hundred dollars in it. Whoever finds it will get a reward of fifty dollars!"

Then a voice from the back of the room yelled out, "I'll give seventy-five!"

Valen: if, by your art, you haves
Put the wild waters in this roar, allay them.
The sky it seems would pour down stinking pitch,
But that the sea, mounting to th'welkin's cheek,
Dashes the fire out. O, I have suffered
With those that I saw suffer! A brave vessel,
Who had, no doubt, some noble creature in her,
Dashed all to pieces.

———————————— Edge of the text box

The example I use is for a drop cap, but you could use it for hanging punctuation or any other character.

1. Instead of a single-character drop cap, specify a two-character drop cap, vertically spanning as many lines as you like.

2. Add a space to the left of the first character in the paragraph. If your paragraph is justified, this should be a space that doesn't get wider, such as Shift-spacebar.

3. Select the first character (I usually press Command-Up Arrow and then Shift-Right Arrow, which jumps the cursor to the beginning of the paragraph, then selects the first character) and apply negative tracking like crazy. You'll find you can tighten the tracking on that first character so much that the drop-cap character actually moves to the *left* of the space. Keep on tracking until the left edge of the character starts to disappear beyond the left edge of the text box. Adjust the tracking as necessary.

Although the first letter appears to be sliced off on the left side, it actually prints properly.

▼ ▼

Shadow Type Alternatives

Applying the Shadow style to any range of selected type creates a generic shadow that cannot be customized. For example, you can't change its thickness, shade, or offset. Although this is a nice shadow effect on screen, its limitations make it not particularly useful for many purposes (plus, it often prints differently on different printers, so it's inconsistent).

You can have total control over your shadows by using duplicate text boxes. Here's one way to do it (see Figure 6-80).

1. Create a text box with some solid black text in it.

2. Duplicate the text box (Command-D).

3. Select the text within the second text box and modify it (change its color or tint, or something else about it).

4. Send the second text box to the back (choose Send to Back from the Item menu).

5. Set both the background color and the runaround of the top box to None. (Many people get confused at this last step, forgetting that if both the color and runaround aren't set to None, there's no way to see the text in the background box.)

You can then move the second text box around until you have it placed where you want it. Remember that you can click through the top text box by clicking with Command-Option-Shift held down. You might

Figure 6-80
Shadows

Introducing

KvetchWRITE

"You've tried the best, now try the rest!"

THREE

also want to group the two text boxes together in order to move them as if they were one item.

▼ ▼

Tip: Shadow XTensions. There are several XTensions on the market that not only create drop shadows for you automatically, but they also build them faster and better than you can in XPress (see Figure 6-81). The three that are currently shipping are QX-Effects from Extensis, ShadowCaster from a lowly apprentice productions, and I-Shadow from Vision's Edge. If you have to build more than one or two drop shadows in XPress each week, you should stop reading now and go buy one of those XTensions.

▽ ▽

Figure 6-81

XTensions that build drop shadows

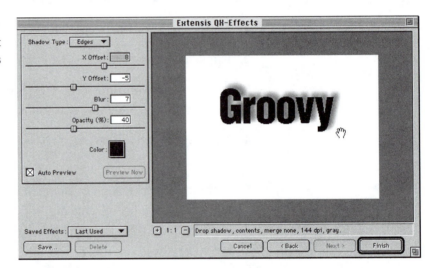

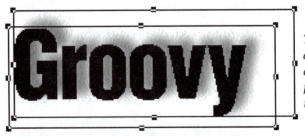

The XTension creates a graphic for the drop shadow and places it behind the text box.

The final effect

Pricing

Quark's free Type Tricks XTension lets you automate one other common text-formatting function: pricing. It's simple to make a number into a price (see Figure 6-82). Just type the value, place the cursor within the number or just to the right of it, then select Make Price from the Type Style submenu under the Style menu. Note that all this feature does is delete the decimal point and apply the Superior and Underline styles to the digits after the decimal point. As with the Make Fractions feature, I'm not particularly excited about this little macro (I find that it's often faster to do this manually using keystrokes than it is to select the feature from the Style menu).

Nonetheless, you have several options for how QuarkXPress formats the character, including whether it should take out any decimal point you've included and whether the numbers after the decimal point (the cents) should have an underline or not. These controls are located in the Fraction/Price Preferences dialog box, on the Edit menu.

Figure 6-82
Make Price example
and preferences

"Okay, look, I'll give you $4.74 for it."
"How much did you say? I don't understand."
"I meant $4^{74}."
"Oh! Sure. It's a deal."

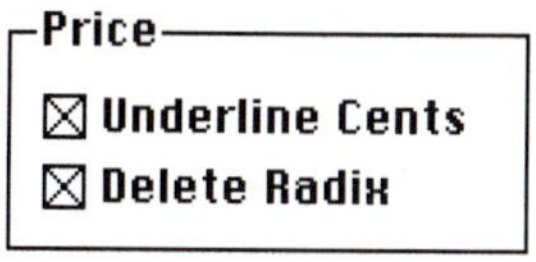

```
┌─Price───────────
│ ☒ Underline Cents
│ ☒ Delete Radix
└─────────────────
```

▼ ▼

Text Greeking

After all this talk about making text look better on the screen and on your printed output, you probably need a break from type. Let's talk about how to make type go away.

Designers have long worked with a concept known as *greeking*. Greeking is a method of drawing gray bars to represent blocks of text, rather than taking the time to image them all on the screen. QuarkXPress can greek text under a specific size limit, which you define on the General tab in the Document Preferences dialog box (Command-Y). The default value for text greeking is 7 points, though you can set it anywhere from 2 to 720 points.

Unless you really want to see every character of every word at every size, there's hardly any reason to turn text greeking off. However, depending on what your page design is like, you may want to adjust the Greek Below values at different times. I typically set it to 4 or 5 points.

▼ ▼

Putting It Together

If you got through this entire chapter and are still not too bleary-eyed to read this, you must really be a QuarkXPress die-hard. After having learned about QuarkXPress's word-processing capabilities in the last chapter and what you can do to those words in this chapter, you're ready to move on to the theory and practice of style sheets and copy flow—automating all this formatting so you don't have to do it all manually every time you need it. There's working with type, and then there's working hard at type. I'm trying to get your work to be as easy as possible.

7

Copy Flow

As you've learned in preceding chapters, you can do all sorts of wonderful things to type in QuarkXPress. But there's more to the intelligent handling of your copy than simply setting it in exquisite type: you have to get the document produced on time.

In the development of a publication, copy is almost never static. For any number of reasons, you may have to make drastic changes in the formatting or content of the copy (usually at or beyond the last minute). Your success in meeting deadlines (and getting paid) can often depend on how carefully you've anticipated such changes. If you don't plan from the very beginning to manage the flow of your document's copy, it will surely end up managing you, and in ways you won't like.

Managing Copy

QuarkXPress has two very powerful tools for automating the formatting and management of your document's copy: style sheets and XPress Tags. Use them wisely, and you'll soon make your copy jump through hoops at the snap of your fingers (or the click of your mouse). Use them poorly, or not at all, and you'll be the one jumping through hoops, probably at three o'clock in the morning the night before a major job is due. In this chapter, I'll tell you how to make the best use of these features. The key is learning to work smart.

Working Smart

Simply put, there are two ways to handle your copy in QuarkXPress: the dumb way and the smart way. What's the main difference between the two? Working the smart way, you make the computer do as much of your work as possible. Working the dumb way, you take it on yourself to do the kind of mindless, repetitive tasks computers were meant to take off your hands—in this case, the repetitive formatting and reformatting of copy.

It takes a bit more time at first to set up a document to take advantage of QuarkXPress's automation, but it is well worth it if you ever need to make even the simplest document-wide change in the way your text is formatted. Of course, if you're the kind of person who always gets everything right the first time, you'll never, ever need to change any formatting once you've entered it, so you may not find this chapter of much use. The rest of you should pay careful attention.

The dumb way. The dumb way to format your copy is the way you most likely learned earliest: by selecting text and directly applying various attributes. Want a paragraph to be centered? Go to the Style menu and center it. Need to change the typeface? Go to the Font menu and do it.

"What's so dumb about that?" you may ask. It's not that there's anything inherently wrong with applying formatting directly to your copy; it's just that by doing so, you doom yourself to performing the same selecting and modifying actions over and over again whenever you need to format another text element with the same attributes, and whenever you need to make major changes to your document. For instance, if the paragraphs you've centered now have to be made flush left, you must again select and change each paragraph individually.

Another way of working dumb is to carefully format your text in QuarkXPress, and then when heavy editing is required, export the copy to a word processor, edit it, then re-import it into XPress. Suddenly you may notice that you've lost most of your special QuarkXPress formatting (such as horizontal scaling, superior characters, kerning, tracking, and so on), and it's time for another long, painstaking formatting pass through your document.

The smart way. The smart way to handle your copy is to take the time to be lazy. Make QuarkXPress's features work for you. By using style sheets, you can apply formatting faster than ever before. When the time comes to change an attribute (font, size, leading, or whatever), style sheets will exponentially speed up that process, too. Also, be sure to use XPress Tags if you export your text. This will retain your formatting information, even if you send stories out to be edited on a dreaded DOS or UNIX computer.

Let's jump in and look at how style sheets and XPress Tags can make your life a better place to be.

Style Sheets

A style sheet is a collection of text-formatting attributes with a name. For example, a style sheet named "Heading" might represent the following formatting: "14-point Helvetica Bold, centered, with half an inch of space before." Every time you apply that one style sheet to a paragraph, the paragraph is assigned all that formatting. You can create one style for titles, another for footnotes, and more styles for different levels of subheads. In fact, you can (and probably should) create a different style sheet for each and every different kind of paragraph in your document, especially since now there's no limit on the number of style sheets you can have in a document. (Removing the limit of 127 style sheets per document was a godsend for many textbook publishers, who often have many more style sheets than that.)

Earlier versions of XPress only had *paragraph style sheets* (styles that applied to an entire paragraph). New to version 4 of QuarkXPress are *character style sheets*. Character style sheets can be applied to a single character (or a word, or a sentence, or whatever). They're handy for run-in subheads, numbered lists where the number and period are in a typeface different from the text, and emphasis (like changing the font of all the company names in a document). Again, if you're going to use the same character formatting more than once or twice in your document, you should create a character style sheet for that formatting.

The next step. In the following description, I'm first going to talk about paragraph styles, and then about character styles. Once you've got paragraph styles down pat, then character styles will be a piece of cake for you. Throughout the discussion, when I talk about style sheets, I will almost always mean both paragraph and character style sheets.

Warning: A Style Is a Style Sheet Is a Style

For some reason, Quark decided not to follow accepted terminology when it named its Style Sheets feature. It is commonly understood in publishing, both traditional and desktop, that the group of formatting attributes for a particular type of paragraph is called a "style." Furthermore, the list of all the styles in a document is called a "style sheet."

However, in QuarkXPress language, each paragraph and character has its own so-called "style sheet," and the collection of these is also referred to as the "style sheet." Because of the confusion, I now tend to use the terms interchangeably. Forgive me, but after all, writing is an inexact science.

The Benefits of Style Sheets

Working with style sheets is smart for two reasons: applying formatting and changing formatting. I typically say that if your document has more than two pages of text, you should definitely be using style sheets. (Don't feel that two pages is a minimum, though; *any* document is a suitable place to use style sheets, especially a document that you know will go through many rounds of revisions.) As with lots of other things (making backups, for example), think about the trade-offs you're talking about: more work up front to save some work downstream. It's up to you to decide whether it's worth doing.

Applying formatting. Let's say I've hired you to work on creating this book. I've specified three levels of headings, two kinds of paragraphs (normal indented paragraphs and the nonindented paragraphs that come right after headings, not to mention the run-in heads like in the paragraph you're reading right now), and a way that the figure numbers and titles should look. It's your job to apply those styles to all the text I give you.

If you went through all 900 pages, fastidiously setting the font of each paragraph, the size of each paragraph, the alignment of each paragraph—and so on—I'd be calling you Rip Van Winkle before too long. Instead, you can define all the attributes for each paragraph in a style, then apply those attributes in one fell swoop by applying that style to a paragraph or to a range of paragraphs.

Changing formatting. Of course, the real nightmare would be when you hand me a draft copy of the book and I ask you to bring down the size of the headings half a point (of course, since we're in the design business, I'd wait to ask you until 5:00 PM on the Friday before Christmas). But if you're using styles, you'd smile and say "Sure thing!"

Whenever you make a change to the definition of a style, that change is automatically applied to every paragraph that uses that style. Because you've had the foresight to create a "Heading" style that is applied to every heading in the book, you need only change the attributes of that style—in this case, the point size—and it gets changed instantly throughout the entire document.

Local Formatting Versus Formatting with Styles

A key point to remember about QuarkXPress paragraph styles is that the formatting contained in a style is applied to an entire paragraph. If the style calls for Times Roman, the entire paragraph will be in Times Roman. However, you can always override the style's font for specific text within the paragraph. This "local" or "hard" formatting remains, even if you change the style's font definition, or apply a different style sheet to the paragraph. (One exception: if a paragraph has the QuarkXPress option No Style applied to it, *all* local formatting will be wiped out when you apply a style to it. See "Normal Style and No Style," later in this chapter.) In other words, hard formatting stays around for a long time, so you have to mind it carefully.

As I said earlier, you can also format just part of a paragraph with a character style; in this case, the character style you applied is also considered local formatting (because the character style that you applied doesn't match the character style of the paragraph style . . . I'll discuss this more later in the chapter).

▼ ▼

Tip: Seeing Local Formatting. If there is any local formatting where the cursor is in the text (or in whatever text is selected), a plus sign appears to the left of the style's name in the Style Sheets palette. This is a handy way of knowing if you're looking at text formatted according to its style, or at formatting that's been applied locally (see Figure 7-1).

Local formatting is sometimes confusing for people, so here are a couple of examples of when you do and do not see the plus sign.

▶ If you apply local paragraph formatting to a paragraph—for instance, an automatic drop cap—the Style Sheets palette displays the plus sign next to the paragraph style, no matter where in the paragraph you place the cursor (because you've applied local formatting to the entire paragraph). There's no plus sign next to the text's character style sheet, however, because you have not changed any character formatting.

▶ If you change the point size of only three words in the paragraph, the plus sign appears only when the cursor is in that text. Local character formatting is always also local paragraph formatting because the paragraph style includes character formatting (I'll clarify this below).

The problem is that there's no way to see what the local formatting is—the plus sign appears the same whether you've changed a paragraph's font or its tracking (see "Tip: Totally Overriding Local Formatting," later in this chapter).

▼ ▼

Unfortunately, there is one instance in which QuarkXPress loses track of local formatting. If you apply a style to a paragraph that contains the

Figure 7-1
Local formatting flag

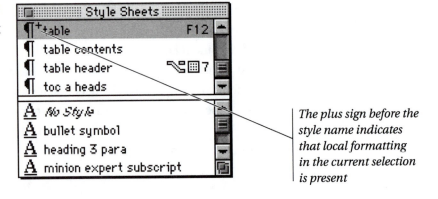

The plus sign before the style name indicates that local formatting in the current selection is present

same formatting attributes that you've used in local formatting, and then you apply a style with different formatting, your original local formatting will be lost.

For instance, assume you have a paragraph whose style calls for plain text (that is, neither bold nor italic), and you've made a few words in the paragraph bold. Next, you apply a style that makes *all* the text bold. Finally, you apply a style that *isn't* bold. All the text in the paragraph will no longer be bold, including the text to which you originally applied the bold formatting. This doesn't just apply to making text bold or italic, but to any local formatting which can also belong to a style: font, baseline shift, whatever.

The reason for this is simple: QuarkXPress only remembers local formatting by how it is *different* from the style applied to it. If you apply a style sheet that looks the same as the local formatting, it's not local formatting anymore (see Figure 7-2). (See "Tip: Removing Just Some Formatting," later in this chapter, for one way you can turn this "problem" into a "solution.")

Figure 7-2
How QuarkXPress loses local formatting

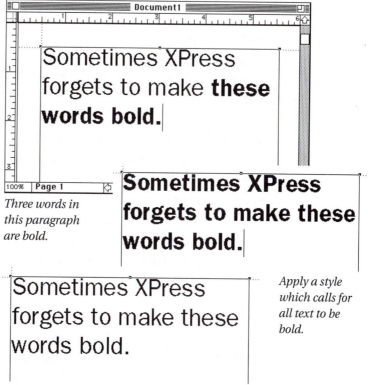

Three words in this paragraph are bold.

Apply a style which calls for all text to be bold.

Now apply a style that calls for plain text. See your local formatting disappear.

Tagging Paragraphs

It's important to understand that there's a difference between paragraph formatting and the style name. When you apply a style to a paragraph, you're only *tagging* it with that name—essentially identifying *what it is*, not necessarily what it should look like. QuarkXPress has an internal style sheet list that tells it what collection of formatting should go with that name. If you tag the paragraph with a different name, the formatting automatically changes. Or if you change the attributes of the style sheet, QuarkXPress updates the formatting throughout the document.

Therefore, when you begin to work on a document, it's not really that important that the style sheets you use bear the correct formatting, since you can always change the attributes later. Once you've tagged all the paragraphs in your text, you can experiment by modifying their styles at your leisure.

There are three ways to apply style sheets—that is, to tag paragraphs—from within QuarkXPress: with the Style menu, with the Style Sheets palette, and with keystrokes.

Style menu. The most basic—and the slowest—method for applying a paragraph style is to select the style name from the Style Sheets submenu (under the Style menu; see Figure 7-3). Like any other paragraph formatting, your text selection or insertion point must be somewhere within the paragraph.

Style Sheets palette. The Style Sheets floating palette (select Show Style Sheets from the View menu, or press F11) lets you apply, edit, and view styles on the fly without having to go to any menus (see Figure 7-4). The palette, which you can keep open on your screen all the time (or you can dismiss it when you don't want it, and call it back up by pressing F11 again), lists all the styles in your document along with their keyboard shortcuts, if they have any. If you have lots of styles, you can make the palette larger or just scroll through them.

The beauty of this palette is that you can put it right next to (or on top of) your text box while you work. To apply a style to a paragraph, put the text cursor somewhere in that paragraph and click on the style in the palette. To apply No Style to a paragraph, click on No Style in the palette. The paragraph is no longer tagged with the style, but the formatting from

Figure 7-3
The Style Sheets menu

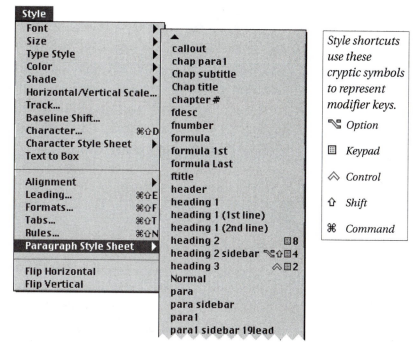

Figure 7-4
The Style Sheets palette

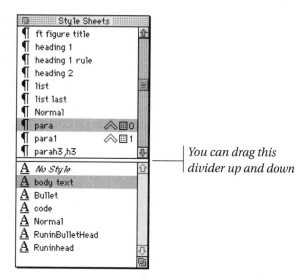

*You can drag this
divider up and down*

the style remains as hard, local formatting (you should rarely use No Style; see "Normal Style and No Style," later in this chapter).

As you move your cursor through your text, the style sheet for each paragraph is highlighted in the Style Sheets palette; you can quickly see what styles are applied. This is especially helpful if local formatting overrides styles, or if you have two styles that are similar and you want to know if a paragraph is tagged with one or the other.

▼ ▼

Tip: Jump to Those Style Sheets. While I'm happy that Windows and the Macintosh have menus, I often don't want to use them. Why? Because navigating the mouse (or trackball or pen) over to the menus is a slow and tedious process. Instead, I try to use as many shortcuts as I can. Here's one: to edit a style, Command-click on that style in the Style Sheets palette. This brings up the Paragraph Style Sheets dialog box with the style name highlighted. Then you can click Edit, or press Return or Enter, to edit that style sheet (pressing Return or Enter here is often one step easier than clicking the Edit button).

▼ ▼

Keystrokes. The third method of applying styles to paragraphs is by using keystrokes. Each paragraph style can have its own keystroke, which you define for it (see "Creating a New Paragraph Style," below). Then you can select a paragraph and press that keystroke. In case you forget your keystrokes, they appear as reminders on both the Style Sheets submenu and the Style Sheets palette.

▼ ▼

Tip: Copying Attributes from One Paragraph to Another. You can copy all the paragraph formatting from one paragraph to another with a single mouse-click. First, place the cursor in the paragraph whose formatting you want to change, then Shift-Option-click on the paragraph whose format you want to copy. (Note that both paragraphs have to be in the same story, but they do not have to be in the same text box.)

This copies all the paragraph formatting, including the paragraph's style sheet and any local paragraph formatting (margins, tabs, leading, space before or after). No local character formatting (font, size, bold, italic) in the destination paragraph is copied—only paragraph formatting.

▼ ▼

Defining Styles

To create or edit a paragraph style sheet, select Style Sheets from the Edit menu, Command-click on any style in the Style Sheets palette, or press Shift-F11 (you can also select Style Sheets from the Edit menu, but it takes too long). This calls up the Style Sheets dialog box (see Figure 7-5). If you open this dialog box when a document is open, you'll see all the styles in that document. You can then use this dialog box to create, edit,

Figure 7-5

The Style Sheets
dialog box

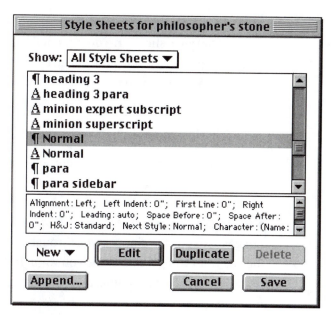

and delete styles, and, by using the Append button, import some or all of the styles from another XPress (or even Microsoft Word) document.

If you use the Style Sheets dialog box with no documents open, you can edit and add to QuarkXPress's default style-sheet list, which will then be automatically included in all new documents you create.

▼ ▼

Tip: Showing Style Sheets. Quark did a significant facelift on the Style Sheets dialog box in version 4 to accommodate character styles. Another new feature in this dialog box is the Show popup menu, which lets you determine which Style Sheets you want to display (several other features in XPress also have a Show popup menu feature, including Lists and Colors). There are five options on this popup menu.

▶ ALL STYLE SHEETS. This is the default value, and simply displays every style sheet in the document.

▶ PARAGRAPH STYLE SHEETS. Many people complained about the addition of character styles as too confusing (personally, I don't know what they were talking about). Nonetheless, if you have a lot of styles and you only want to display the paragraph styles, choose this option.

▶ CHARACTER STYLE SHEETS. Opposite of the above, this option displays all the character styles and hides the paragraph styles.

▶ **STYLE SHEETS IN USE.** This is very useful. I often have many more style sheets in a document than I will typically use (the others are there just in case I need them). Choosing this option hides all those extras so they don't clutter up the dialog box.

▶ **STYLE SHEETS NOT USED.** I generally use this option when I feel like deleting all the unused styles.

Note that the Show popup menu has no effect on the Style Sheets palette. The palette always displays all the styles.

▼ ▼

Tip: Jump to a Style. If you have a *lot* of styles in your document, you're not going to want to slowly scroll through the list in the Style Sheets dialog box until you get to the one you want. Instead, just type the first letter or two of the style's name, and XPress jumps there.

▼ ▼

Creating a New Paragraph Style

Creating a new paragraph style sheet is as easy as one, two, three.

1. Create a paragraph in a text box (it can even be just some gibberish text in a dummy text box). Format it exactly the way you want the style sheet to be defined (both character and paragraph formatting), and place the cursor somewhere in the paragraph.

2. Go to the Style Sheets dialog box and click the New button (while this looks like a button, it's actually a popup menu). Choose Paragraph from the popup menu. (Or, if you want to copy another style, you can press the Duplicate button instead of New.)

3. Either way, the Edit Paragraph Style Sheet dialog box appears (see Figure 7-6). All the formatting from the paragraph you made is sucked into the dialog box, so you don't have to set it here. Enter the name of the new style in the Name field. Press OK, and then press Save to leave the dialog box.

Make sure the text selection in step 1 doesn't include any text that is formatted in some other unwanted way—say, some words in bold or italic that you *don't* want to become part of the new style definition. In other words, this procedure picks up the paragraph *and* character attributes

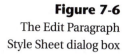

Figure 7-6

The Edit Paragraph
Style Sheet dialog box

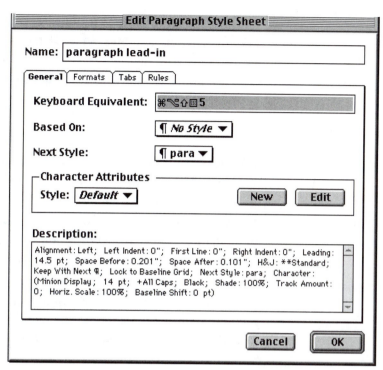

of where your insertion point (or selection) is, and uses them in defining your new style.

If you want to define a keystroke combination that will automatically apply the style, click in the Keyboard Equivalent field (in step 2), and press the combination you want. On the Macintosh, it's often a good idea to use a Function or keypad key in combination with the Control key, because you can be confident that keystrokes defined this way won't conflict with QuarkXPress's other key commands, almost none of which use the Control key (see the keyboard shortcuts tear-out card in the back of the book).

▼ ▼

Tip: Keys You Can Use for Style Shortcuts. You can only use certain keys for applying styles—the function keys (F1 through F15) and the numbers on the numeric keypad. In combination with the Control, Command, Shift, and Option (or Alt in Windows) keys, that allows for a lot of shortcuts. However, because QuarkXPress uses the function keys for its own shortcuts (both with and without Option and Shift), I suggest that you use function keys as style sheet hotkeys only in conjunction with the Control key.

There's no way to print a list of what keystrokes go with what styles (see "Tip: Printing Your Style Sheet," later in this chapter), so I just print a screen shot of the Style Sheets palette and tape it to my wall or the side of my monitor. If you have a really long style sheet, you may have to take a couple of screen shots.

▼ ▼

Defining paragraph formatting. The step-by-step method above is a way to define a style by example, and it's the easiest and fastest way to make a style sheet. You can, however, also define a style sheet directly from within the Style Sheets dialog box. You need to learn this slower method, too, because it's how you edit styles and also how you can create style sheets when no document is open.

Once you've clicked the New button in the Style Sheets dialog box, selected Paragraph from the popup menu, and named your new style, you can define its paragraph formatting by setting values in the Formats, Tabs, or Rules tabs of the Edit Paragraph Style Sheet dialog box.

Character formatting in paragraph styles. Paragraph styles always include character formatting, too (like font, size, and so on). When you first create a paragraph style sheet, XPress assigns the Default character formatting. Personally, I think the word "default" is really confusing. In plain English, it means "Use the character formatting hidden inside the Character Attributes dialog box." It might help to remember that Default is the way that XPress version 3.x made style sheets (except that there was no Character Attributes dialog box back then).

You get to the Character Attributes dialog box by pressing the Edit button in the Edit Paragraph Style Sheet dialog box (see Figure 7-7). If you're building a paragraph style by example (as in the step-by-step outlined above), the character information here is the same as in your dummy "example" paragraph.

If you have already built other character style sheets (I'll cover how to do this later), you can replace Default with one of your own styles on the Style popup menu. The New button in the Edit Paragraph Style Sheet dialog box lets you create a new character style and apply it to this paragraph style in one fell swoop. If you've chosen a character style instead of Default, all the character attributes of that character style sheet are used in the paragraph-based style sheet you're defining.

Figure 7-7
Character Attributes
in a paragraph style

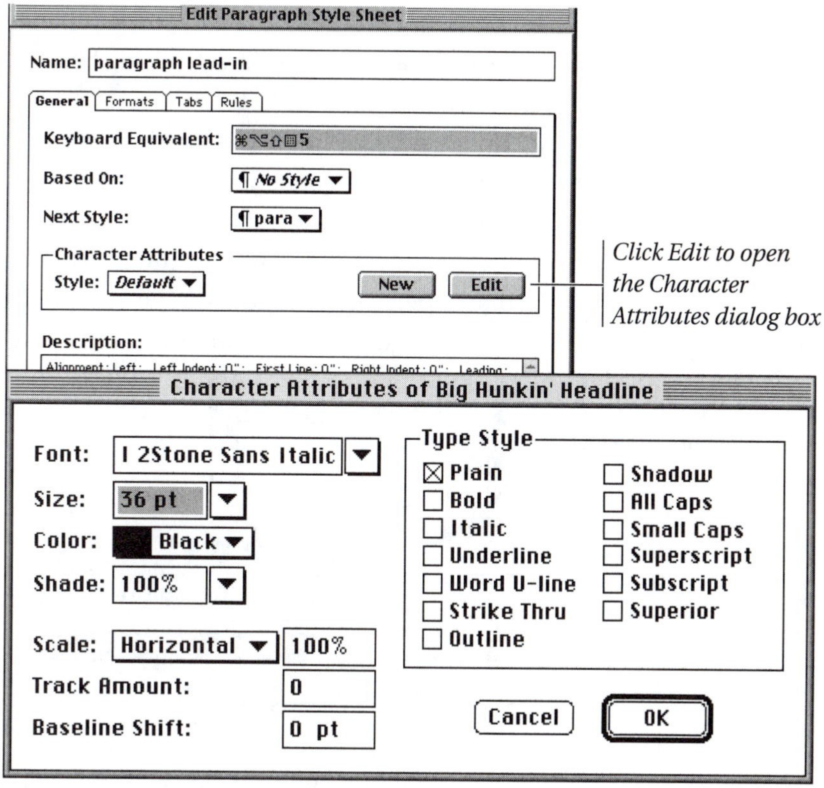

*Click Edit to open
the Character
Attributes dialog box*

In other words, you don't have to use character style sheets if you don't want to. You can create style sheets the old-fashioned XPress 3.x way by leaving the popup menu set to Default and pressing Edit to define the values. Just remember to think ahead, as building character styles and using them in paragraph styles may be more flexible down the line.

▼ ▼

Tip: Beware of the Edit Button. Watch out for the Edit button in the Edit Paragraph Style Sheet dialog box when you're using a character style other than Default. If you make an edit here, it edits the character style, too! Unfortunately, this makes it way too easy to change your character styles accidentally (you might change them thinking that you're only editing the value for this paragraph style . . . not so).

▼ ▼

Editing style sheets. To edit a style sheet, select it from the list of styles in the Style Sheet dialog box and click the Edit button. You see the same tabbed dialog box as you did when you were creating the style sheet. Go ahead and make the changes you want, then press OK and finally press Save to leave the Style Sheets dialog box.

▼ ▼

Tip: Even Speedier Style Sheets. You can avoid the Style Sheets dialog box altogether by holding down the Control key and clicking on a style name in the Style Sheets palette (in Windows, click on any name in the palette with the right mouse button). The context-sensitive popup menu that appears lets you edit, duplicate, or delete the style that you clicked on (see Figure 7-8). Or you can create a new style by selecting New.

Figure 7-8
Shortcut to styles

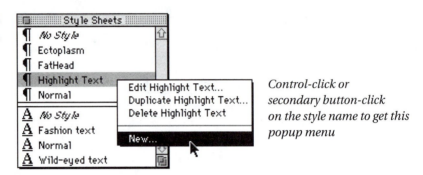

Control-click or secondary button-click on the style name to get this popup menu

Note that if you select New when clicking on one of the character styles, you'll create a new character style; if you click on one of the paragraph styles in the palette, you'll create a new paragraph style sheet. This is certainly the fastest way to create a style sheet, because you never have to look at the clunky Style Sheets dialog box.

▼ ▼

Normal Style and No Style

Every QuarkXPress document has a default style—the Normal style. This is the style automatically applied to all the text in a document if you don't specifically apply another style (if you type in a new text box, it's always in the Normal style). You can edit the Normal style just like any other.

No Style is different; applying it removes *all* style sheet information from a paragraph. (It doesn't remove your formatting, just any style sheet affiliation.) All the paragraph's formatting is then treated as hard local formatting. Normally, local formatting doesn't change when you apply a style to a paragraph. However, if the paragraph has No Style applied to it, subsequently applying a style sheet wipes out all local formatting. So if you have some words in italic, for instance, in a No Style paragraph, then applying any other style sheet to that paragraph will remove your italics (assuming that the new style sheet you've just applied is not itself defined as italic).

▼ ▼

Tip: To Use Normal or Not. In the past, I've always been wary of using the Normal style in my documents, always choosing instead to build other styles and use them. My reasoning had to do with the inability to find and change styles based on Normal or to append the Normal style from another document (there were other reasons, too). However, XPress version 4 has rendered all my complaints obsolete, and there is little reason not to use the Normal style in your document now. I still don't do it, but it's more out of tradition and superstition than practical sense.

▼ ▼

Tip: Totally Overriding Local Formatting. The fact that a paragraph that has No Style applied to it loses all local formatting (including bold and italic) when it's tagged with another Style Sheet is, more often than not, a pain in the butt and causes much confusion. However, there are some powerful uses for this feature, such as stripping out all local formatting that some dumbbell put in for no good reason.

Always on the lookout for a faster way to do something, I was pleased to find that I can apply "No Style" to a paragraph and then apply a style sheet in one stroke by Option-clicking on the style I want to apply in the Style Sheets palette.

▼ ▼

Tip: Removing Just Some Formatting. In the previous tip, we learned that "No Style" is great for eliminating all local formatting in a paragraph. However, what if you want to get rid of only *some* local formatting?

Instead of using "No Style" to get rid of all local formatting wherever it occurs, you can get clever with the way the document's paragraph styles are defined. The trick is that QuarkXPress is built in such a way that it only remembers local formatting that is different from the formatting in a paragraph style sheet. So, first change the style sheet so that it contains the formatting you want to remove, then remove that unwanted formatting from the style sheet.

This is much easier to understand with an example. Let's say you have a whole lot of text that has a "BodyText" style sheet applied to it, but some bozo selected the whole thing and changed the typeface to 18-point Futura (this kind of error happens a lot when you copy and paste text from one document to another and the style sheets are slightly different in each file).

The problem is that there are also words in the text that are made italic for emphasis. If you apply "No Style" to everything, then apply the "BodyText" style again, you would wipe out all italic attributes in the text, and you'd have to go back and reapply them by hand. However, using this technique saves the day.

1. Edit the "BodyText" style so that its definition includes all the formatting that you *want to get rid of.* In this example, change the character formatting to 18-point Futura.

2. Save the change to the style sheet.

3. Edit the "BodyText" style again. This time, define it the way it was originally. In this example, you'd define it with the original typeface and size.

4. Save the change to the style sheet.

Now all the text is formatted properly: you've gotten all the text to be the original typeface and size, but you've retained the italic local formatting as well. You don't have to select the text; you just have to adjust the style sheets.

▼ ▼

Tip: Redefining Tabs in Styles. Although you can define tabs within a style, it's a pain in the left buttock going back and forth between editing a style and looking at its effects on your page. An easier solution takes advantage of creating style sheets by example (see the previous tip) and the ability to merge styles. This tip assumes that you've already created a paragraph style sheet, and that you need to edit the tab stops.

1. Apply the style sheet to a paragraph (or select a paragraph that has the style already applied to it).

2. Change the tab stops of that paragraph to where you'd like them to be.

3. Create a new style sheet based on this new paragraph (see "Tip: Even Speedier Style Sheets" for the fastest way to do this). Name this style sheet slightly differently from the original style sheet (I usually just append the word "new").

4. Control-click (or on Windows machines, click with the right mouse button) on the name of the old style sheet, and choose Delete from the context-sensitive popup menu. When you're prompted with a dialog box asking for a replacement style, select the new style sheet and click OK.

5. Finally, Control-click (or click with the right mouse button) on the new style name, select Edit, and rename it without appending the word "new".

Of course, this isn't only for changing tabs. You can use this technique to change any element of a style sheet. However, note that this only works with a style that isn't based on another style, and it won't work with the Normal style.

▼ ▼

Appending Styles

The Append button in the Style Sheets dialog box lets you import styles from other documents into your QuarkXPress document. You can import styles from other QuarkXPress documents as well as from Microsoft Word files. After selecting the file from which you want to import, the program lets you choose exactly which styles you want (see Figure 7-9). In case you don't know what the incoming styles look like, XPress shows you the definitions in the Description area of the Append Style Sheets dialog box.

Because the incoming style sheet may include information about another style sheet (like a paragraph style that refers to a character style, or a style that is based on another), XPress always warns you that it may be importing more than you may have bargained for (see Figure 7-10). This dialog box becomes really annoying after you see it once or twice. Fortunately, the folks at Quark gave us an out: simply turn on the checkbox in the alert dialog box, and XPress refrains from displaying it again. Whether you turn the alert off or not, you should always check to see what styles have actually been imported.

When you press OK in the Append Style Sheets dialog box, QuarkXPress checks to see if any incoming styles have the same name as those already in your document. If it finds such a conflict, it displays another alert dialog box and asks you what to do (see Figure 7-11). You've got four options, each a separate button.

Figure 7-9
Appending styles

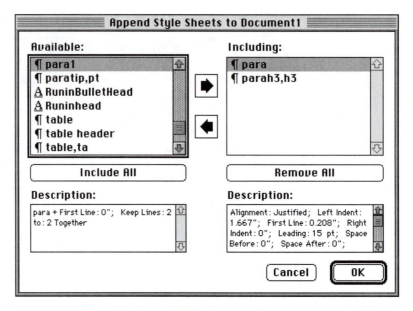

Figure 7-10
XPress alerts you when
you're importing more
than you bargained for.

▶ RENAME. You get to manually rename the style that's being
imported with any other unused name.

▶ AUTO-RENAME. Automatically renames the incoming style with
an asterisk at the beginning of its name. I'm not sure why you'd
use this, but I bet there's a good reason.

▶ USE NEW. The incoming style overwrites the one already in the
document. I almost always use either Use New or Rename.

▶ USE EXISTING. This effectively cancels the appending of the style;
the old one (the one currently in the document) is retained and
used. The only time you'd use this is if you didn't realize that there
was a duplicate when you chose to append the style.

If you think there's going to be more than one conflicting style name,
you may want to turn on the checkbox marked Repeat for All Conflicts.
This way, XPress handles the remaining conflicts in the same way.

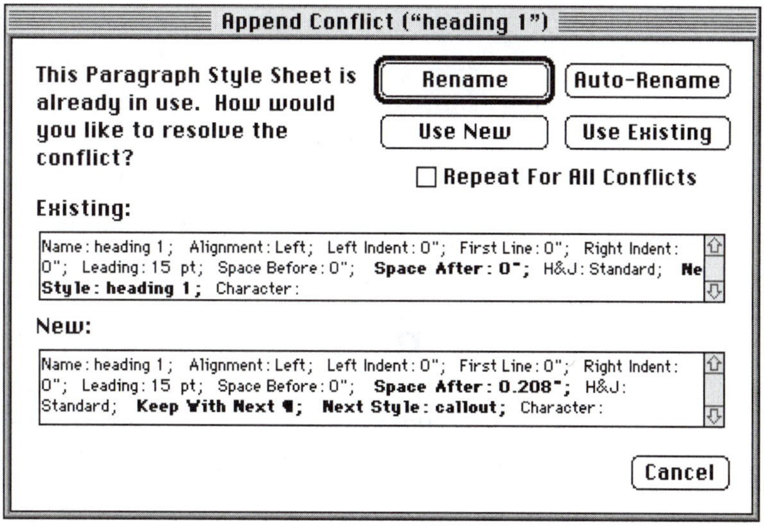

Figure 7-11

Conflicting style sheets alert

By the way, this process is a huge improvement over the way XPress version 3 handled appending styles, and I thank my lucky stars (and the engineers at Quark) for this quantum leap forward.

Of course, remember that there is also an Append feature on the File menu that you can use to import style sheets, colors, and H&Js at the same time. If you need to import both styles and colors, for instance, it's clearly efficient to do it with Append instead of in the Style Sheets dialog box.

Appending with cut and paste. Another way to move a style from one QuarkXPress document to another is to copy text containing that style. You can use Copy and Paste, or you can drag a box containing the text from document to document. However, beware: QuarkXPress won't alert you to any style-name conflicts. Instead, it just throws away the incoming style's formatting information and replaces it with the existing style's attributes plus local formatting on top so that the text looks the same as it did in the source document. In other words, this is a good way to import a style or two, but it's often a lousy way to import text, especially when the style name already exists in the target document.

▼ ▼

Tip: Comparing Two Styles. I hate it when I have two styles that are very similar but I can't remember how they're different. Fortunately, version 4 of QuarkXPress now lets you compare two style sheets. Select two styles in the Style Sheets dialog box (click on one, and then Command-click on the other), then Option-click the Append button. (Actually, as soon as you hold down the Option key, you'll see the Append button change to a Compare button.) The result: a dialog box that lists each element of the two style sheets; the differences are highlighted in bold (see Figure 7-12). Of course, you can only compare two character styles or two paragraph styles; you can't mix and match.

▼ ▼

Deleting (and Replacing) Styles

You can delete a style sheet by pressing the Delete key in the Style Sheets dialog box (Command-clicking lets you select and delete more than one style; Shift-Delete lets you select contiguous styles). If the style sheet has been applied somewhere in your document (or if it's referenced by another style sheet—see "Basing One Style on Another," below), XPress asks you if you want to replace the style with another one. That is, all the text that is tagged with the deleted style is assigned a new style sheet, rather than going to "No Style."

▼ ▼

Tip: Style Sheet Page Breaks. PageMaker has a cool feature that I like: you can specify a paragraph attribute that forces the paragraph to start on a new column or page. That is, any paragraph tagged with this attribute will always start at the top of a page or column. As it turns out, you can do a similar thing in QuarkXPress. Many readers have pointed out that you can simply make the Space Before value in the Paragraph Formats dialog box as large as the text column is tall. For example, if your text box is 45 picas tall, enter "45" in the Space Before field. You can set this as a paragraph style or as local formatting for particular paragraphs.

▼ ▼

Figure 7-12

Comparing two styles

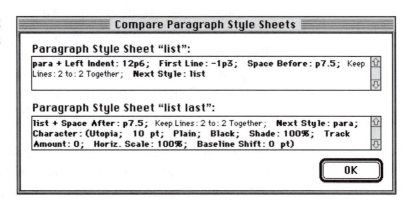

Compare Paragraph Style Sheets

Paragraph Style Sheet "list":

para + Left Indent: 12p6; First Line: -1p3; Space Before: p7.5; Keep Lines: 2 to: 2 Together; Next Style: list

Paragraph Style Sheet "list last":

list + Space After: p7.5; Keep Lines: 2 to: 2 Together; Next Style: para; Character: (Utopia; 10 pt; Plain; Black; Shade: 100%; Track Amount: 0; Horiz. Scale: 100%; Baseline Shift: 0 pt)

OK

Basing One Style on Another

A powerful feature of QuarkXPress's style sheets is the ability to base one style on another. By basing many styles on, say, the Normal style, you can quickly change many elements in your document by simply changing the Normal style.

For example, let's say you want all your subheads to be the same as the "Heading 1" style, but with 14 points of space before, and horizontally centered. By basing the subhead style on the "Heading 1" style, you can ensure that every change you make to the "Heading 1" style is instantly reflected in the subhead style. If you change the "Heading 1" style's font from Helvetica to Franklin Gothic, the font of the subheads based on the "Heading 1" style automatically changes from Helvetica to Franklin Gothic as well.

(In this case, the "Heading 1" style sheet is the *parent style* and the subhead style based on it is called the *child style*.)

Here's how you can base one style on another.

1. Choose a style sheet from the Based On popup menu in the Edit Paragraph Style Sheet dialog box. In the case of the example above, choose Normal.

2. Edit the various tabs in the Edit Paragraph Style Sheet dialog box to change only those attributes you want to be different in the new style. In this example, you would change the Alignment and Space Before settings on the Formats tab of the dialog box. Watch out, though; changing the character formatting in the two styles can be a little tricky, so make sure you carefully read the "Character-Based Styles" section, later in this chapter.

3. Note that the description at the bottom of the Edit Paragraph Style Sheet dialog box lists the "based on" style along with all the additional formatting you've applied to the new style (see Figure 7-13). Click OK and then click Save to leave the Style Sheets dialog box.

If you plan your styles carefully, you can use the Based On feature to create nested hierarchies of styles based upon one another, so that a simple change to one style will be applied to all the styles based on it, and the styles based on those, *ad infinitum*. This "ripple effect" can be a great time-saver, so it's well worth your while to take greatest advantage of it.

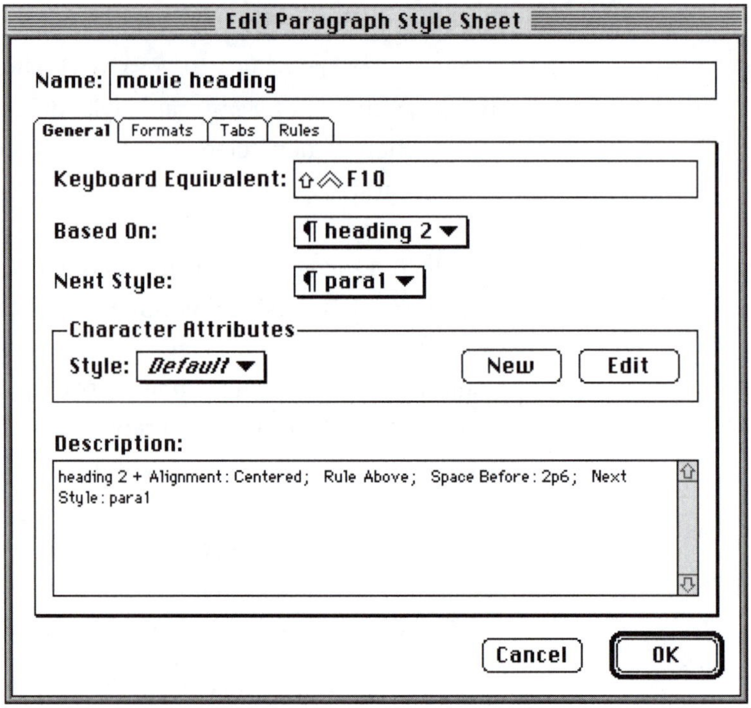

Figure 7-13

Basing one style
sheet on another

Tip: Based-On Differences. When one style is based on another, XPress only keeps track of the *differences* between the base style and the new style. Let's say you have a style called "Head1" and it's 18-point Futura with the bold style applied, and a style called "Head2" that's based on "Head1," except that it's 12-point Futura and is not bold. The differences between the two are the point size and the bold attribute.

If you change the font of "Head1" to Franklin Gothic, then the font of "Head2" changes, too. But if you change the point size of "Head1" to 24 point, then "Head2" does not change, because the point-size "link" is broken. However, there's one important exception: if you change the parent style to have attributes that are *the same* as the child style, the difference is broken. If you change "Head1" to "not bold," for example, then there's no difference in style between the two and the link is broken. Then, if you go back and change "Head1" to bold again, "Head2" follows suit and becomes bold. This is much the same as what happens when local formatting within a paragraph matches the formatting of the style (see "Local Formatting vs. Formatting with Styles," earlier in the chapter).

To summarize: As long as you don't change any formatting in the parent style to match the child style, you'll be fine. But as soon as you change an attribute in the parent style to match the child style's, that link is broken, the child style isn't different in that way anymore, and you're going to wish that you'd paid more attention to this paragraph.

▼ ▼

Next Style

If you're typing in QuarkXPress, and the paragraph you're on is tagged with the "Heading" style, you probably don't want the next paragraph to be tagged with "Heading" too, right? (Unless you want two headings in a row.) You can force XPress to automatically change the subsequent style sheet with the Next Style popup menu in the Edit Paragraph Style Sheet dialog box. If you want the subsequent paragraph to be "BodyText," then choose "BodyText" from the Next Style popup menu.

Note that this only works if the insertion point is at the very end of a paragraph when you press Return (turn on Show Invisibles to see where the current Return character is). If the insertion point is anywhere else when you press Return, you'll simply break that paragraph in two, and both new paragraphs will have the same style as the original one.

In other words, this feature is essentially intended to be used while you're typing, not while you're doing the simple kinds of editing or formatting you're likely to be doing in QuarkXPress. However, it certainly can come in handy once in a while.

When you're first creating a style sheet, the default choice on the Next Style popup menu is "Self," which simply means that the next style will be the same as the current style (no change at all).

▼ ▼

Tip: Giving Style Sheets a Color. Sometimes when I have lots and lots of style sheets in a document, and they're all somewhat similar, I like to change the screen color of each style name. One might be blue, another might be red, and so on. This allows me to see at a glance which style sheets have been applied where.

Of course, if you do this, don't forget to change them all to the proper color before you go to final output.

▼ ▼

Character-Based Styles

If I had a dollar for every time someone said to me, "I wish I could apply a style sheet to a single word instead of to a whole paragraph," I would be writing this book on a beach in Tahiti (I'll leave my true "Winter in Seattle" surroundings to your own imagination). At long last, character style sheets have come to QuarkXPress, and now that the feature is finally here, I encourage you to use it to its fullest.

Almost everything that I said earlier about paragraph styles is also true of character styles. You create, edit, append, and delete them in almost exactly the same manner. There are, of course, some differences. For instance, to create a character style sheet, you should choose Character instead of Paragraph from the New popup menu in the Edit Style Sheets dialog box. Also, because these are character styles, you can only assign character formatting to them (the kind of formatting you can apply to a single character, such as font, size, color, shade, scale, type style, tracking, and baseline shift; see Figure 7-14).

As I said earlier, when you start typing in a new text box, the text automatically is set to the Normal paragraph style sheet. However, because the definition of the Normal paragraph style includes a reference to the Normal character style sheet, all your text is automatically set to that character style as well.

If you create a new character style (you can use the step-by-step "by example" approach outlined earlier) and apply it to some text that is already in the Normal style, it acts like local formatting on top of the Normal style.

Figure 7-14

Editing or creating a character style sheet

Edit Character Style Sheet

Name:	New Style Sheet
Keyboard Equivalent:	⌥⌘4
Based On:	A No Style ▼

Font: Terrapin Ex Bold ▼
Size: 36 pt ▼
Color: Black ▼
Shade: 100% ▼

Scale: Horizontal ▼ 100%
Track Amount: 0
Baseline Shift: 0 pt

Type Style
☐ Plain   ☐ Shadow
☒ Bold   ☐ All Caps
☐ Italic   ☐ Small Caps
☐ Underline   ☐ Superscript
☐ Word U-line ☐ Subscript
☐ Strike Thru ☐ Superior
☐ Outline

Cancel   OK

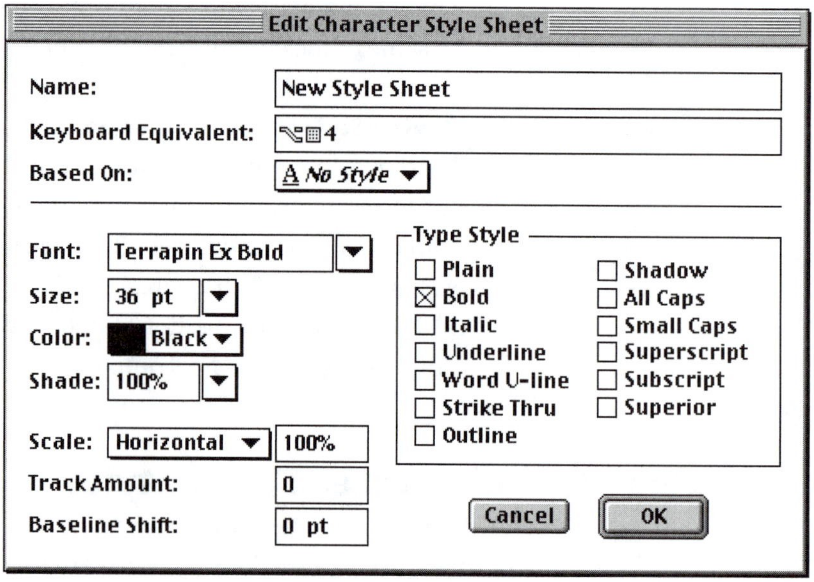

There's no doubt that character style sheets can add to your general level of confusion, especially at first. However, there are several really good reasons to push through and keep using them until they become second nature.

▶ Using character style sheets throughout your document ensures consistency of formatting, and makes the process of formatting the text go faster. This is even more true if you have more than one document in a larger project (such as chapters in a book).

▶ By assigning character styles within paragraph styles, you can also ensure consistency among multiple paragraph style sheets. For instance, if your Heading1, Heading2, and Heading3 paragraph styles all use the same "Heading" character style sheet, you only have to change this one character style sheet to update all three paragraph styles.

▶ The most important reason to use character styles (or style sheets in general) is the inevitability that your art director or client will start laughing uncontrollably when they see your design and then make you change something. Because this change always happens just before a deadline, style sheets are your only good chance at salvation.

Of course, if the only character-based formatting you have in your project is bold and italic, character styles may not be that exciting. But where you are applying a collection of formatting to a single word or character, character styles are the way to go—for instance, to drop caps, run-in heads, fractions, or special types of emphasis. One real-world example is a project I worked on where I had to match the visual size of two different fonts that were placed side by side throughout a document. By assigning a character style sheet to each font, I could easily experiment with the look of the page by making little tweaks to the definition of one or both of the character styles, instead of selecting every instance of both fonts and changing them manually.

Note that there are times when Find/Change is just as fast at updating text formatting. However, I find that the character-styles feature is almost always faster and more powerful, especially once you get the hang of it.

Style Sheets palette. In order to accommodate character styles, the Style Sheets palette has been split into two halves; the top half displays paragraph styles and the bottom half displays character styles. To apply a character style, select the text you want to affect, then click on the character style sheet name in the palette. (Yes, if you work by the hour and want to do things the slow way, you could also choose the style name from the Style menu.) Even better, if you're using a character style sheet frequently, assign it a keyboard shortcut.

▼ ▼

Tip: The Balance of Style Power. Do you have more paragraph styles than character styles? You can change the palette's size by dragging the resize box in its lower-right corner. It turns out you can also drag the boundary marker between the paragraph styles and the character styles.

▼ ▼

Tip: Search and Replace Your Style Sheets. Back in Chapter 5, *Word Processing*, I discussed how you can now use the Find/Change feature to search for and replace style sheets. In the past there was a convoluted workaround to do this (I wrote about it in my tips-and-tricks book), but using Find/Change is much better.

However, here's one less-intuitive way to use Find/Change: search for particular character formatting and "replace" it with a character style. For example, let's say you have a document created in version 3.3 that is a perfect candidate for character styles because it has run-in heads throughout (like this book does).

Set up the Find side of the Find/Change palette to search for one or more of the particular character attributes of the run-in heads. On the Change side, turn off the checkboxes for everything except the Style Sheet popup menu, in which you should choose the character style you want to apply. Making this change is the same as manually applying the character style to each run-in head . . . but it's much faster.

One note, though: Make sure that the definition of the character style you're applying is the same as the formatting of the text you're searching for. If the formatting is different, then XPress will apply the style and leave some of the original attributes as local formatting, defeating the purpose almost entirely.

▼ ▼

Character styles in Based On paragraph styles. Earlier, I discussed the value of using the Based On feature in paragraph style sheets, but I mentioned that changing character formatting in a child style gets a little tricky. That was an understatement; in fact, the whole way that character styles and paragraph styles interact is probably the most confusing aspect of style sheets in XPress, and most likely to cause blood vessels to burst in your forehead. Fortunately, it's not without logic; it just takes some getting used to.

Here are two rules to live by.

▶ If the Character Attributes Style popup menu within the parent style is set to Default, then you can easily edit the character formatting in the child style: just click the Edit button. (As the book goes to press, the Description field in the Edit Paragraph Style Sheet dialog box doesn't update accurately to display the change you've made—I think it's a bug, so it might be changed by the time you read this—so you just have to take the change on faith.)

▶ If the Character Attributes Style within the parent style is set to one of your character style sheets, then you have to be really careful when making a change (see Figure 7-15). Clicking the Edit button will edit the character style itself, which is rarely what you want. (If you edit the character style itself, it will affect both the parent and child styles, as well as any other text or style that uses that character style!)

Instead, you should create a new character style (by clicking the New button), and base this new character style on the same character style that the parent style uses (use the Based On feature). Yes, this is annoying. Yes, this makes me want to kick someone. But that's the way it works (at least as I write this).

In the latter case (where you've assigned a character style to your parent style), here's a step-by-step method for how to proceed.

1. Create a new paragraph style sheet, and set the Based On popup menu to the desired parent style. At this point, everything about your new style is exactly the same as this parent style.

2. Note the name of the character style listed on the Character Attributes Style popup menu. If it's Default, you can stop here and go read the first bullet point again; if it's not Default, then commit the name to memory (or write it down, if it's at the end of the day).

Figure 7-15

Editing character
formatting in
based-on styles
(Windows)

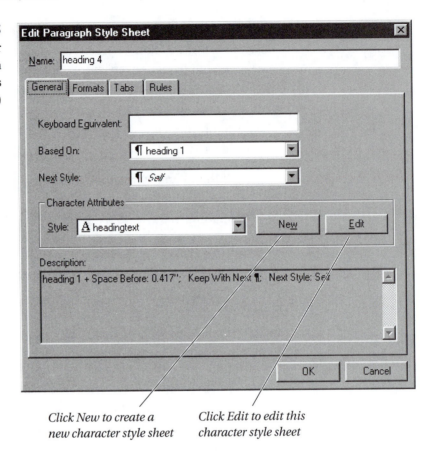

Click New to create a
new character style sheet

Click Edit to edit this
character style sheet

3. Click the New button to create a new character style sheet.

4. In the Edit Character Style Sheet dialog box that pops up, choose
   the name of the character style from the Based On popup menu.

5. Finally, go ahead and make the changes you want to make to the
   character formatting (if you can still remember what you were trying to do by now).

6. Give this new character style a name (I usually use a name like
   "Style based on Such-and-such") and then press OK. This adds
   the new character style to your list, and also applies it to the child
   paragraph style you're working on.

7. Make any changes to the paragraph formatting you want applied
   to this child style, and then press OK.

This seems like it'd take longer than it really does, and after doing it a few times, you get the hang of it. I just wish that changing something as basic as character formatting in a child "based on" style were as easy as it used to be.

▼ ▼

Tip: Keeping Libraries of Styles. One of my favorite uses for libraries (see "Libraries" in Chapter 2, *QuarkXPress Basics*) is to save style sheets that I use in multiple documents. Here's what I do: In a small text box, I write out the name or the description of the style sheet, and whether it's a character style or a paragraph style (I've seen people use color codes so that all the character styles are in red, and all the paragraph styles are in blue). Then I add some text or a paragraph to the bottom of the text box, and apply the appropriate style sheet (if I'm saving a character style, I also apply the No Style paragraph style, or vice versa).

Finally, I drag this text box into my "style library" (which I've already saved on my hard disk). Because the text almost fills the small text box, it appears readable in the Library palette (as long as there isn't too much text; see Figure 7-16), so I can easily identify it later when I come looking for it. (You could also use the library labeling feature for this, if you've got a lot of styles.)

▼ ▼

Figure 7-16
Keeping track of styles
in the Library palette

▼ ▼

What Word Processor to Use

Although QuarkXPress can import formatted text from several word processors, it can only interpret the styles of Microsoft Word files. (If you have another word processor that uses styles and can save them as Microsoft Word–formatted files, you're in luck too.) Since styles are so important to the proper management of your copy, Word automatically becomes the best word processor for working with QuarkXPress. (Unless you decide to work exclusively with XPress Tags, which I cover in the next section. These can be used, albeit awkwardly, by any word processor that can import and export text-only ASCII files—that is to say, nearly all word processors).

By the way, while QuarkXPress does import pictures contained as anchored graphics in Word files, and can even export inline graphics to the correct location in a Word file, I really don't recommend that you do this because the imported images are always PICTs (see Chapter 9, *Pictures*, for information on why this is useless). Ultimately, the images would need to be manually replaced once they arrived in XPress.

How QuarkXPress Style Sheets Work with Word

When you bring a Word document into QuarkXPress and you've checked Include Style Sheets in the Get Text dialog box, QuarkXPress imports every style from the Word file into its own style sheet, incorporating as much of Word's formatting as QuarkXPress can handle.

Character formatting. QuarkXPress can import a great deal of Word's own formatting. All the character attributes available in Word can be carried over into QuarkXPress, with a few exceptions (see Table 7-1).

Paragraph formatting. For paragraph formats, QuarkXPress brings in most available Word settings, except that it ignores the Page Break Before setting (see "Tip: Style Sheet Page Breaks," earlier in this chapter), and only the top and bottom rules set for boxed paragraphs will be imported (though QuarkXPress does a good job of interpreting the correct size and weight of rules). QuarkXPress ignores any values you've set for space between rules and their paragraphs.

Table 7-1

What QuarkXPress
does with Word's
formatting

WORD'S FORMATTING	WHAT QUARKXPRESS DOES WITH IT
Double and dotted-line underlines	Turns them into normal underlines.
Super- and subscript settings	Applies whatever values you've specified for them within your QuarkXPress document (in Document Preferences).
Expanded and condensed type settings	Converts them to tracking values in XPress. Since you specify these values using points in Word, and QuarkXPress uses $\frac{1}{200}$ of an em, there is usually only a very rough correlation between how tightly type is set in Word, and what you get when you bring it into QuarkXPress.
Footnotes	Numbers are changed to superscript style; footnote text is added at end of story.

Style formatting. Any of Word's attributes which can be applied to styles can be successfully imported as styles by QuarkXPress, with the exceptions noted above.

If your QuarkXPress document has style sheets with the same names as those in your Word file, you may be given the choice to import or override those Word styles (see Figure 7-17). On the other hand, you might not see this dialog box. It has recently come to my attention that XPress won't show this dialog box when a Word style is a Default style like Normal, Heading 1, Footnote, and so on (I'm still not sure why; perhaps Quark will change this in a later release).

So, more accurately: If the incoming style sheets have the same names, *and* they are not some of Word's default styles, *and* the style sheet definitions are different, then you'll see an alert dialog box asking what to do about it. You've got two options here.

▶ If you click on Use Existing Style, the style definition already within QuarkXPress will be applied. This is what you want to do about 98 percent of the time (see "Tip: Don't Worry About Word Style Definitions," below).

▶ If you click Rename New Style, the text is imported and the style name has an asterisk appended to it. There's probably a good reason to do this, but it eludes me at the moment.

Either way, the local formatting you've applied in the Word document is imported, too.

Figure 7-17

Importing styles from
Microsoft Word

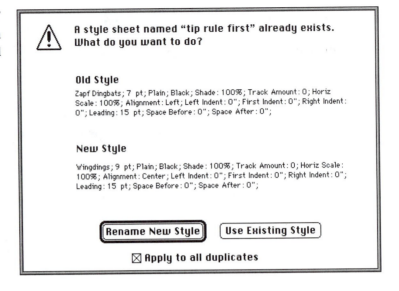

> A style sheet named "tip rule first" already exists. What do you want to do?
>
> **Old Style**
>
> Zapf Dingbats; 7 pt; Plain; Black; Shade: 100%; Track Amount: 0; Horiz Scale: 100%; Alignment: Left; Left Indent: 0"; First Indent: 0"; Right Indent: 0"; Leading: 15 pt; Space Before: 0"; Space After: 0";
>
> **New Style**
>
> Wingdings; 9 pt; Plain; Black; Shade: 100%; Track Amount: 0; Horiz Scale: 100%; Alignment: Center; Left Indent: 0"; First Indent: 0"; Right Indent: 0"; Leading: 15 pt; Space Before: 0"; Space After: 0";
>
> [Rename New Style]   [Use Existing Style]
>
> ☒ Apply to all duplicates

▼ ▼

Tip: Word Versions Spell Trouble. To be honest, even though Microsoft Word works better with QuarkXPress than any other word processor does, it's still not a perfect system. In fact, the success of an import (or export; see "Exporting Text," below) often depends on both the version of Word and the version of your Word import filter (the XTension that lets you import and export Word files). I have often had to return to earlier versions of the Word filter to get them to work properly, depending on the version of Microsoft Word I'm using.

▼ ▼

Tip: Don't Worry About Word Style Definitions. Remember that QuarkXPress can override Microsoft Word's formatting for style sheets. Let's say that your Microsoft Word document's "Normal" style is 14-point Geneva with 24-point leading (for easy reading and editing on screen), and your QuarkXPress document's "Normal" style is 11-point Goudy with 15-point leading. When you import the file, QuarkXPress automatically uses the XPress version of the style sheet, and all the text that is tagged as "Normal" appears in 11/15 Goudy (like you'd want it to).

The implication of this is that you never really have to worry about what the styles look like in Word. In this book, for example, my Microsoft Word text was all in Helvetica and Palatino, but when I imported the text files into QuarkXPress, they came out in the fonts you're reading right now (Adobe Utopia and Stone Sans).

▼ ▼

▼ ▼

Tip: Don't Forget to Include Style Sheets. You should almost always turn on the Include Style Sheets option in the Get Text dialog box (Command-E) when importing text. If you don't, QuarkXPress may apply "No Style" to all the text. If you have any intention of applying other paragraph style sheets to these paragraphs, you're in for a surprise: all your local formatting—even italic—disappears as soon as you apply a paragraph style (see "Totally Overriding Local Formatting," above).

On the other hand, if you do turn on Include Style Sheets, XPress applies either the styles from the word processor (if there are any) or it just uses "Normal."

In fact, one of the very few times I turn off Include Style Sheets is when I'm working with XPress Tags (which I discuss later in this chapter).

▼ ▼

Exporting Text

After you go through all the trouble of bringing copy into QuarkXPress and formatting it, then why would you want to export it? Aside from administrative reasons (backups, use in a database, archiving the text, and so on), there are three major situations in which exporting text can be important.

▶ If you have a *lot* of text in a story and XPress feels sluggish when you work with it, you might want to consider exporting your text to a word processor, editing it there, and then re-importing it back into QuarkXPress. In general, though, it's usually better to keep the text in QuarkXPress if you can, or else you may lose some of your formatting.

▶ You also might want to export text if you work in a busy workgroup-publishing environment. You may find it absolutely necessary to pull text out of QuarkXPress so that editors can work on it while you continue to refine a newsletter's or magazine's layout.

▶ The best reason to export text, however, is if you want to do something that can't be done easily (or at all) from within XPress. I'll give some examples of this when I discuss XPress Tags, later on in this chapter.

How to Export Text

Exporting text from your QuarkXPress document is pretty much the opposite of importing it.

1. With the Content tool, select a text box containing the story you want to export. Or if you want to export only a certain amount of text, select it.

2. Choose Save Text from the File menu (or press Command-Option-E). The Save Text dialog box appears.

3. Give the exported file a name and tell XPress where to save it. Select either Entire Story or Selected Text button, depending on what you want saved.

4. Use the Format popup menu to choose the format for the exported file. The formats listed on the menu depend on which filters you have in your XTension folder.

5. Press Return or click OK.

Pitfalls

The most important consideration when bringing text out of QuarkXPress and then back in is how to do this without losing all the formatting you've applied within QuarkXPress. No current word processor can handle horizontal scaling or kerning properly, for instance, and such formatting could easily be lost during the export/re-import process. The same thing goes for XPress's character style sheets. There are ways to keep this formatting intact no matter where your QuarkXPress text ends up, however, by using only paragraph style sheets or XPress Tags.

▼ ▼

Tip: Exporting Styles. I often use QuarkXPress's Export feature to export all my styles to Microsoft Word. This saves my having to re-create every style name on Microsoft Word's style sheet. For instance, I can design a whole book or magazine, then export the styles for writers and editors to use when creating copy, and be assured that the style names will match when I import the files. To export styles, create a little one-line paragraph for each style. Apply the style, then export that text in Word format. When you open the file in Word, all the styles will be there.

▼ ▼

▼ ▼

Tip: Printing Your Style Sheet. I can't find any way to print a list of every style on my style sheet with descriptions from QuarkXPress. However, if you export the styles as described in the last tip, you can print the styles from Word. Open your Word document that contains all your styles, go to Define Styles under the Format menu (Command-T), and select Print from the File menu (Command-P). A lot of the formatting in XPress styles doesn't get passed to Word, so the printout isn't complete. But it's better than nothing. (Unfortunately, this doesn't work in Word 98.)

▼ ▼

A Solution: XPress Tags

There is a solution to the problem of losing formatting when exporting and re-importing text, however: export the file in the special text-only ASCII format called XPress Tags. XPress Tags uses its own special—and complicated—coding that records every single one of QuarkXPress's text-formatting attributes, from style sheets to local formatting (see

Figure 7-18

XPress Tags

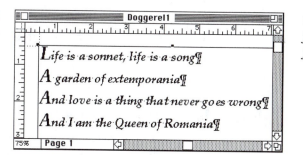

When you save this file in XPress Tags format . . .

. . . the text file looks like this.

```
@Normal=<*L*h"Standard"*kn0*kt0*ra0*rb0*d0*p(0,0,
0,0,0,0,g)*t(0,0," "):¶
Ps100t0h100z24k0b0c"Black"f"BI Palatino
BoldItalic">¶
@Normal:<*L*h"Standard"*kn0*kt0*ra0*rb0*d0*p(0,0,
0,0,0,0,g)*t(0,0," "):¶
Ps100t0h100z36k0b0c"Black"f"BI Palatino
BoldItalic">L<z24>ife is a sonnet, life is a
song¶
<z36>A<z24> garden of extemporania¶
<z36>A<z24>nd love is a thing that never goes
```

Figure 7-18). In fact, if you're familiar with the old code-based typesetters, you'll love XPress Tags.

You may find a text-only file with XPress Tags confusing to look at, with its multitude of arcane numbers and codes. However, there are many reasons why XPress Tags is the best format to use when you need to edit and then re-import copy.

▼ ▼

Tip: Learning XPress Tags. I've got a bunch of cool XPress Tags tips in this book, and there are truly hundreds (if not thousands) of other things you can do with this tagging language. However, the tags may be intimidating at first. The best way to learn the codes is to create some text in XPress, style it in various ways, and export the text in XPress Tags format (I discuss importing and exporting tags, below). You can then open this file in a word processor and decipher the codes by looking them up in the table in Appendix E, *XPress Tags*.

Note that when XPress exports text in XPress Tags format, it doesn't write that text in a particularly terse or smart fashion, and there are many more tags than actually necessary. (For example, sometimes the tags will specify that something should be in plain style, and then immediately specify that it should be in italic). This is not necessarily bad or wrong (after all, it's better to be redundant than to forget something); you just need to read XPress's codes with a grain of salt. But otherwise, you'll get a very good overview of tagging.

▼ ▼

Why Use XPress Tags?

Not only do XPress Tags files retain all of a story's QuarkXPress formatting, but because ASCII ("text only") is a universal file format, these files can be edited by virtually any word processor—Macintosh, Windows, MS-DOS, or UNIX. Although the coding may appear daunting if you're used to the WYSIWYG world of Windows or the Macintosh, professional typesetters have been working with code-based systems for years, and tagged files can be easily integrated into such an environment.

So if you find yourself regularly needing to export QuarkXPress stories with sophisticated text formatting, XPress Tags is clearly the way to go. While it may take a while to get used to editing an XPress Tags file, it's a lot less work than having to painstakingly reformat your copy every time you bring it back into your QuarkXPress document. Appendix E contains a comprehensive list of the codes used in XPress Tags.

How to Use XPress Tags

There are a small handful of things to keep in mind when you work with XPress Tags.

▶ To export a story from QuarkXPress in XPress Tags format, choose Save Text from the File menu (Command-Option-E) and select XPress Tags from the Format popup menu. The file you get is a text-only file that can be opened in any word processor or re-imported into XPress.

▶ To import an XPress Tags file (or any text-only file that has XPress Tags in it) into XPress, use Get Text (Command-E), like you would for any other text file. However, if Include Style Sheets is turned on in the Get Text dialog box, XPress interprets the tags back into text formatting. If this option is turned off, XPress just reads the codes into a text box (this is useful if you don't have a word processor).

▶ If you import the tagged file into XPress with Include Style Sheets turned off, make sure you also turn off the Convert Quotes option in the Get Text dialog box. If Convert Quotes is turned on, XPress converts the straight quotes in the tagged file into curly quotes . . . and XPress Tags only understands straight quotes. If you're just looking at the file, it hardly matters; but if you're going to edit the codes, re-export them, and then re-import them with Include Style Sheets turned on, then those dang curly quotes will cause you no end of problems.

This also applies to editing the tags in a word processor that has a Smart Quotes feature. If something is going wrong when you're importing XPress Tags, checking for stray curly quotes is one of the first things you should do.

▼ ▼

Tip: Applying Styles in Text Editors. One of the most simple (yet powerful) uses of XPress Tags is to apply style sheets or formatting to text from within a word processor or text editor that doesn't support style sheets. For instance, if you use a simple text editor that doesn't even let you apply italic formatting, you can type <I> before and after a word.

When you import the file into XPress, these simple tags are interpreted and the word is made italic (the first time the tag is applied, it turns italic on; the second time, it turns it off).

You can apply a paragraph style sheet by typing `@stylesheet:` at the beginning of a paragraph (yes, you need the colon at the end). The style sheet will be applied to all subsequent paragraphs until you specify a change to another style. Similarly, the code to apply a character style sheet as local formatting is `<@stylesheet>` (to apply the style) and `<@$p>` (to end the character style).

Once you're familiar with the coding format used by XPress Tags, you can easily set up a macro to apply formatting codes to an ASCII file in your word processor (on the Macintosh, you can use QuicKeys to do this in any text editor; in Windows, you can use WinBatch or some other macro utility). If you're more ambitious, and handy with database programs, you can even design a report format that creates a file incorporating XPress Tags, so you can export data from your database and have it land on your QuarkXPress pages fully formatted and untouched by human hands.

▼ ▼

Tip: Overprinting Accents with Tags. Working in non-English languages can be a complicated proposition, especially when you're working with an American or English computer system. Some characters have to be "built" by overprinting two other characters, such as a letter and an accent. Kerning two characters, one superimposed on the other, ain't no big deal if you have to do one or two. But with a document full of them, it's time to switch to XPress Tags.

1. Somewhere in your document, create the overstrike character to look just like you want it, using baseline shift, kerning, sizing, or whatever. (You often need to *positively* kern *after* the accent character, because it's narrower and therefore the following character will be too tight without kerning. Try it; you'll see what I mean.)

2. Export the sample "character" and the text story that contains all the characters you want to overstrike in XPress Tags format.

3. Open the XPress Tags files in a word processor. The sample you made will look something like `<k-90>s<k11b0.2>˘<k0b0>`.

4. Perform a Find/Change between the overstrike pair and the XPress Tags version. For instance, replace all the examples of s ˘ with the tags above to get š.

▼ ▼

Tip: Fake Fractions the XPress Tags Way. Here's an XPress Tags search-and-replace procedure that can save hours when you have to create a large number of well-set fractions. For example, you can search for all instances of "1/2" and replace them with `<z7k-10b-3>1<z12k-8b0>/<z8k0>2<z$>`. This set of codes makes the size 7 point, the kerning 10 units, and the baseline shift 3 points, then types "1". It then changes the type size to 12 point, the kerning to -8 units, and the baseline shift to zero before typing a fraction bar (Option-Shift-1). Finally, it makes the size 8 point, sets no kerning, and types "2" before resetting the type size back to its original value.

This may seem like a lot to you, but once you get the hang of it, it's extremely easy and can save you enormous amounts of time.

▼ ▼

Tip: Expert Fractions with XPress Tags. The previous tip is useful for building "made" fractions: fractions that are created by resizing type and moving it around. What if you want "drawn" fractions—numerators and denominators predesigned just for this use? Expert Set fonts with this sort of character are available for many type families (Minion, Utopia, and Bembo, to name just a few). Using XPress Tags, you can automate their substitution, too.

This works for the fractions shown in Table 7-2. Export your text in XPress Tags format and open the file in a word processor. Let's say you

Table 7-2

Ready-made fractions in Expert Sets and their keystrokes (may be different in your fonts)

FRACTION	EXPERT KEYSTROKE
¼	G
½	H
¾	I
⅛	J
⅜	K
⅝	L
⅞	M
⅓	N
⅔	O

want to convert all the "1/4" fractions. In the word processor, search for "1/4" and replace it with `<f"MinionExp-Regular">G<f"Minion-Regular">`.

The Expert Sets also contain the numerals zero through nine in the numerator and denominator positions so you can create any other fraction, too. Press Shift-Option-0 through Shift-Option-9 to get the raised numerators, and Option-0 through Option-9 to get the baseline denominators. The correct fraction bar is the slash in the Expert Sets. You can automate this process somewhat with XPress Tags, but you have to create each different fraction individually. For instance, to make the fraction ¹³/₁₆, you would search for "13/16" and replace with `<f"MinionExp-Regular">` followed by Option-Shift-1, Option-Shift-3, slash, Option-1, Option-6, and finally `<f"Minion-Regular">`. One step too complicated? Maybe—but it sure saves time if you've got oodles of text with fractions.

▼ ▼

Tip: Take Care with Tags. Using XPress Tags can be lifesaving—but coding them incorrectly can result in serious troubles. Fortunately, most illegal or improper coding won't kill XPress on import; instead, the program will stop at the error and tell you it found something wrong (see Figure 7-19).

However, some errors can cause all kinds of weirdness. For instance, if you use a character that begins a tag definition (like "@" or "<") and then neglect to close the definition properly (that is, by typing a colon, a definition, or a right angle bracket, depending on what you're coding), you may live to regret it (although QuarkXPress version 4 is much better at finding these kinds of errors than previous versions).

The tip? First, be *very* careful not to do this in the first place. Second, use the newest XPress Tags filter (the one that ships with version 4.0 of XPress is version 2.0 of XPress Tags; you can find out an XTension's or filter's version by clicking on About in the XTensions Manager dialog box).

▼ ▼

Figure 7-19
When tags go wrong

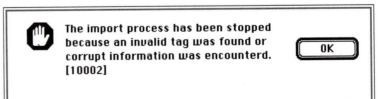

The import process has been stopped because an invalid tag was found or corrupt information was encounterd. [10002]

OK

▼ ▼

Tip: Shorter Tags. Are you tired of typing long tags, such as `@Bodytext=<*J*p(7.2,0,7.2,11,0,3.6,g)*t(148,2,"")*d(1,2)z9>`? Then stop! Instead, substitute a unique brief placeholder for each long tag in your coded document. For instance, type `*bb` instead of the code above. Then, later, search for the placeholder and replace it with the real thing. You can use a word processor to make this change, or you can use a utility such as Torquemada or Add/Strip, where you never have to type anything more than once.

Of course, make sure you use unique sequences of characters for your placeholders (that is, sequences that don't appear anywhere else in your text).

▼ ▼

Tip: Converting Columns with Torquemada. Once upon a time, Greg Swann (author of Shane the Plane and other masterpieces) wrote a little utility called Torquemada the Inquisitor. With such a descriptive name (not!), some people *still* don't know what this incredible program does. To call Torquemada (or "Torq," as many people call it) a search-and-replace utility is like saying QuarkXPress is a fun little program that lets you put text and graphics on the same page. Torq is a powerhouse of a search-and-replace engine, and has become an essential tool for text massage—especially when you're working with XPress Tags.

Torq lets you perform up to 640 searches (and make 640 replacements) on a text file, and does it very fast. If you have a list of 100 words that need to be spelled a certain way, it'd be a hassle-and-a-half to do all those searches manually. Instead, you can load the words into Torq and just let it flog away at your files (you can even batch-run multiple text files by drag-and-dropping as many as you want on Torq's icon).

But there are some more obscure ways of using Torquemada, too. For instance, let's say you receive a text file from an author who was trying to be a little too helpful and has typed a list of names like this:

Arnold	Frank
Becky	George
Catherine	Hiromi
Doug	Igor
Eggbert	Jacqueline

Of course, in order to format this list in XPress, you probably need it to be in one long column of text (you can handle the columns yourself, thank you very much). If this list were much longer, it'd be a nightmare to pull apart with cut and paste. Here's where Torq can show its stripes.

Note that Torquemada the Inquisitor can be very intimidating to the uninitiated because of all its obscure codes. Don't worry; it's really fairly easy (and powerful!) once you read the instructions and figure out how to parse the codes.

Here's one way to deal with such a list.

1. Copy the offending lines and save them as a text file.

2. Using Torq, search for ^t^*^p in the text file and replace it with ^p. (That final period is not part of the code, of course.) This searches for a tab followed by anything that ends in a return (that's called a "wildcard") and replaces all of that with just a return. In other words, it systematically throws away every item in the right column.

3. Next, run a new search on the original file (not the one you end- ed up with in step 1; Torq always prudently retains your original file, giving you a new file as the result of your Torquing. Search for ^p^*^t and replace it with ^p. That searches for every instance of a return followed by anything that ends in a tab and replaces it with simply a return. In other words, it throws away everything in the left column and preserves the right column.

4. Merge the resulting files, and you're in business.

This might seem like a couple of steps too many, but in fact it's very fast indeed. If the original author's list had used multiple spaces instead of tabs between the columns (horror of horrors), you can use another Swann utility called "XP8" to clean that up quickly.

(To be fair in this particular case, you can do the same thing in Microsoft Word by opening the file, Option-dragging a selection around the right column, and using Copy and Paste; or even just by converting the columns into a table.)

▼ ▼

Tip: Commenting Torq Sets. One of the problems with Torquemada's search-and-replace sets is that they're often really hard to read and deci- pher on screen. One way to clear up the mess is by commenting the sets. That is, you can insert humanly readable comments to help you remem- ber what each code (or set of codes) means.

To add a comment to a Torq set, type it in the Replace-string column (the right column in the search/replace set). As long as the Search-string column (the left one) is left blank, Torq ignores the right one entirely; but the comment remains there for you to read on screen. I heartily recommend you add extensive, thorough comments to your Torq sets; I can testify from sad experience that it's very easy to forget just what it was you were trying to accomplish, especially in your more complex search/replace strings.

▼ ▼

Tip: Those Silly Case-Sensitive Tags. Don't forget that all XPress Tags are case-sensitive. Typing <H> rather than <h> can mean the difference between small caps, horizontal scaling, and failure. Style, color, and H&J names are the same way. If you forget them, they're easy enough to search and replace in Word or a case-sensitive text editor.

▼ ▼

Tip: Automating Fractions with Torq. You can use Torquemada to automate the fake fractions in the previous tip, *if* you're sure that all instances in your text of the form *00/xx* (where *00* represents any number of digits, and *xx* represents any number of characters before the next spaceband) is indeed a fraction.

Simply search for ^#^<^?/^&^<^@ plus a space ("one or more digits, a slash, and one or more alphanumeric characters, followed by a spaceband"), and replace it with the appropriate codes for the fraction (see "Tip: Fake Fractions the XPress Tags Way," earlier in the chapter) except replace the "1" in that tip with ^#^< and the "2" in that tip with ^&^@. Don't forget to include the spaceband in your replace string, too. For example, the replace string might be <z7k-10b-3>^#^?<z12k 8b0>/<z8k0>^&^@<z$> plus a spaceband.

And if you study your Torq documentation, you'll see that you can even get around the lack of two numeric wildcards by constructing a Define-Your-Own wildcard . . . but I'll leave that to you.

▼ ▼

Tip: Styling Every Other Row. In "Alternating Tint Stripes" in Chapter 11, *Where Text Meets Graphics*, I describe how you can create cool tables by placing stripes behind every other row using Rule Below. Of course, the best way to format a mess o' text is to use style sheets. However, applying a particular style sheet to every other paragraph is a real hassle when you have a thousand paragraphs. Torquemada to the rescue.

1. Export the text from XPress in XPress Tags format (using Save Text from the File menu).

2. In Torquemada, do a search for `^¢^p^¢^p` and replace it with `@firststyle:^¢^p@secondstyle:^¢^p`. To decipher: first this searches for any number of characters except a return (`^¢`) followed by a return (`^p`), more non-return text (`^¢`) and another return. Then it replaces all that with the same text and returns, but with the XPress Tags coding for "apply this style sheet." Of course, you would replace "firststyle" and "secondstyle" with whatever style sheet names you're using.

   Note that you have to search for *non-return* text, followed by a return, above; if you simply search for *any* text followed by a return, Torquemada would find everything down to the second-to-last return in the file (because returns are characters, too). As powerful as this search-and-replace tool is, it's only going to do exactly what you ask it to do.

3. Re-import the resulting Torqued file back into XPress. (Make sure Include Style Sheets is turned on in the Get Text dialog box so that the tags are interpreted back into their proper formatting.)

▼ ▼

Xtags: One Step Beyond

There is an alternative to the XPress Tags language and filter that ships with QuarkXPress. It's a third-party commercial XTension named Xtags, from Em Software.

Xtags is a superset of XPress Tags, which means that all XPress Tags will work with the Xtags filter. However, Xtags adds much more functionality, such as powerful error checking, anchored boxes (text and picture), relative size changes (up a point, down two points, etc.), and much, much more. Another great feature is a translation table that replaces short codes with long tag strings (like those discussed in "Tip: Shorter Tags," earlier in this chapter).

There is simply not enough room here to even *begin* to describe some of Xtags's cooler features. Suffice it to say that once you start using Xtags for importing your text, you'll soon discover so many things you can automate with it that you'll wonder how you ever got along without it (see Appendix C, *XTensions and Resources,* for more information).

BBEdit and Other Text Editors

The focus of this chapter (and of this whole book) is efficiency: how to take raw materials and quickly turn them into a finished product. The raw materials might be text from some DOS word processor, or it might be highly formatted text within a QuarkXPress document that needs even more formatting applied to it. Obviously, XPress Tags makes less sense when your document is a single-page ad. However, when you're preparing books or other long documents (even some magazines or newspapers), being able to make edits to XPress Tags is a powerful tool for massaging your text into the shape you want.

In general, I recommend using a text editor rather than a word processor for this kind of stuff—for two reasons. First, word processors have too many tools for formatting text and too few tools for editing it quickly (NisusWriter is one good exception). On the other hand, text editors, don't care much about formatting; they focus on the text itself.

Second, text editors typically allow you to view your text in either "wrapping" mode (where text wraps to the next line as soon as it hits the right edge of the screen) and nonwrapping, or "line" mode (where every paragraph is a line and every line is a paragraph, potentially extending far off the right side of your screen). I like to review XPress Tags files in nonwrapping mode because almost all the most important tags are at the beginning of paragraphs (paragraph style sheets, character styles for run-in heads, and so on). So if each line is a paragraph, it's very easy to check. Then, if you need to see what the rest of the paragraph looks like, you can always scroll or switch to wrapping mode temporarily.

One of the best text editors around is the freeware BBEdit. There's also a commercial version that's even more powerful, but the free version is totally adequate for what I'm talking about here. BBEdit also has a very powerful search-and-replace capability, including being able to act on multiple files at once and giving you the choice of using GREP, if you're into that advanced search-and-replace language.

Tip: A Complex XPress Tags Example. I'll throw in one more XPress Tags example, just to show what a little extra work can do. Let's say you've just received some text files from someone who just LOVES to type LOTS of words in ALL CAPITAL LETTERS. If you're like me, you'd rather these words be in small caps.

You've got two choices: First, retype each of these words in lowercase and then apply a small-caps style to them. Like you've got nothing better to do, right?

The much better choice is to use XPress Tags. This technique should not be tried by children without parental guidance; it's truly industrial strength, designed for processing a lot of text at once.

The trick is to use a program such as NisusWriter or Torquemada. NisusWriter is a very cool text editor on the Macintosh. Torquemada you know by now.

In Torquemada, search for ^+^<^? and use <H>^L^+^?<H>^= as the replacement string. (Leave the period off the end, of course.) This horrible-looking thing means: Find all strings of two or more capital letters (this is the "Cast Wildstring Type" technique, where ^+ is a capital letter, ^< types the wildstring to what precedes it—in this case, capital letters—and ^? is the wildstring itself). Torquemada then replaces this with the small-caps tag (<H>), the command to convert to all lowercase (^L), the wildstring (which, on the replace side, is simply ^+^?), the small-caps tag again, and the command to turn off case conversion (^=).

I don't profess to be a NisusWriter guru, but I wish I were, as this program has very powerful GREP-type search and replace and macros. My friend and colleague Adam Engst suggested the following Nisus macro to do the same thing as the above Torq tip (see Figure 7-20).

```
Find/Replace ":(\(\(\<:u:+\>\)\(:b*\):)" with
"<h>\1<h>\2" "gaAt"
Find All ":(\(\(\<:u:+\>\)\(:b*\):)" "gaAt"
lowercase
```

Figure 7-20

Using NisusWriter to convert uppercase to lowercase with XPress Tags

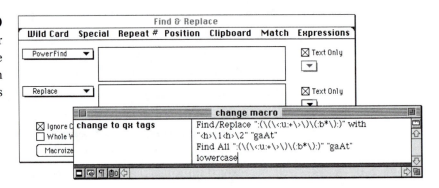

If a line in the source file reads: "This is DEFINITELY a BIG pain in the NECK," then the output (after processing) will look like this: "This is <H>definitely<H> a <H>big<H> pain in the <H>neck<H>," and the final imported text will appear as "This is DEFINITELY a BIG pain in the NECK."

See? Nothing to it.

Getting Your Stories Straight

Just because you've taken advantage of style sheets and XPress Tags doesn't mean you won't still find it necessary to burn the midnight oil making last-minute changes. But at least you'll have the full power of QuarkXPress on your side. Get to know styles, import and export filters, and especially XPress Tags, and you can go a long way toward being lazy: making your computer do the work, rather than having to do it yourself.

8

LONG DOCUMENTS

One look at the size of this book and you know why the topic of long documents is so exciting to me. But everyone has a different opinion about what a long document is. Some die-hard technical writers insist that if it isn't over a thousand pages, it's not a long document. Others maintain that a document of anything more than five or 10 pages qualifies. Personally, I think that anyone building a book, a magazine, a newspaper, a journal, or a catalog—no matter how many pages—is dealing with long documents.

Unfortunately, while there are hundreds of thousands of people creating these sorts of things with XPress, it took 10 years for Quark to include even rudimentary long-document features into its flagship product. Finally, XPress 4 provides something to cheer about.

There are three features in QuarkXPress 4 that relate directly to publishing long documents.

▶ **BOOKS.** You can tie multiple XPress documents together into a *book*, which appears in the form of a palette in QuarkXPress. From here, you can control page numbering, printing, and such document attributes as style sheets and colors.

▶ **LISTS.** If you use style sheets regularly, you're going to love the Lists feature, which lets you build a table of contents (or a list of figures, or a table of advertisers, or any number of other things) quickly and easily.

▶ **INDEXES.** Building an index is a hardship I wouldn't wish on anyone (I've done enough of them myself), but XPress's indexing features go a long way in helping make it bearable. I'll also discuss how indexing can be used in catalogs and other documents.

Again, even if you don't currently create what you'd consider to be "long documents," take a gander at these features; they're flexible enough to be used in documents as small as even a few pages.

▼ ▼

Books

Even though you can make a document thousands of pages long, you should keep your XPress documents small. This reduces the amount of strain on the program, and lessens the chance for document corruption. Working with smaller documents is generally faster and more efficient, especially when more than one person is working on the project at the same time. The question is: if you break up your larger project into small documents, how can you ensure style consistency and proper page numbering among them? The answer is QuarkXPress's Book feature.

You and I usually think of a book as a collection of chapters bound together to act like a single document. QuarkXPress takes this concept one step further. In QuarkXPress, a book is a collection of any XPress documents on your disk or network that are loosely connected with each other via the Book palette. In other words, just because it's called a "book" doesn't mean it's not relevant for magazines, catalogs, or any other set of documents (see "Tip: The Book Palette as Database," below).

There are four benefits to using the Book palette.

▶ It's a good way to organize your documents, and it's faster to open them from within XPress than using the Open dialog box.

▶ If you use automatic page numbering in your document (see "Sections and Page Numbering" in Chapter 4, *Building a*

Document), XPress manages the page numbering throughout the entire book, so if the first document ends on page 20, the second document starts on page 21, and so on.

▶ You can print one or more documents from the Book palette using the same Print dialog box settings without even having the documents open.

▶ The Book palette's Synchronize feature lets you ensure that the style sheets, colors, H&J settings, List settings (which I cover later in this chapter), and Dashes & Stripes settings are consistent among the documents.

Obviously, the more documents in your project, and the more pages, style sheets, colors, and whatnot in each document, the more useful the Book feature will be to you. Even if you're juggling two or three documents, it may be worth the minor hassle it takes to build a book.

▼ ▼

Tip: The Book Palette as Database. Because there is only a very loose connection among the various documents in the Book palette, you could use this feature as an informal database of documents. For instance, let's say you've built 15 different product sheets and three small brochures for a client, and they're forever updating them.

Even though the documents may each use very different colors, style sheets, and so on, you could put them all on one Book palette and save this collection under the client's name. Next time the client calls for a quick fix, you don't have to go searching for a document; just open the Book palette, and double-click on the document name to open it.

Of course, this means you either cannot use automatic page numbering in your documents, or you have to be meticulous about using the Section feature (I discuss how you can use the Section feature to override a book's automatic page numbering in "Page Numbering and Sections," later in this chapter).

▼ ▼

Building a Book

To build a new book, select Book from the New submenu (under the File menu; see Figure 8-1). At this point, you need to tell the program where to save your new book file (you can put it anywhere you want on your

Figure 8-1

Building a new book

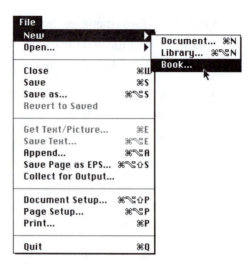

hard drive or network, but you should be able to find it easily because you'll be using it a lot).

Book files appear in QuarkXPress as palettes. You can save as many books as you want, though you can only open 25 of them at a time (I usually just stick to one or two open Book palettes, or else I get confused). As soon as you've saved your new book, XPress displays a new, empty Book palette (see Figure 8-2).

(Note that QuarkXPress uses the term "chapter" to refer to single documents inside the book. In this discussion, I use both "chapter" and "document" interchangeably, though I prefer "document" because it reminds me that I can use the Book feature for catalogs or magazines or other sorts of projects.)

Adding documents. To add a document to your Book palette, click the Add Document button in the palette and choose a document from your disk or network. If no documents on the palette are selected when you add a new document, the chapter is added at the end of the list. If you select a document first, the new chapter is added before the selected document in the list.

You can have up to a thousand documents on your Book palette (personally, I wouldn't try to push this limit; I prefer to keep this number well below a hundred). By the way, if you add documents that were built in QuarkXPress version 3.x, they are automatically resaved as version 4 files, and you won't be able to open them in version 3.x again.

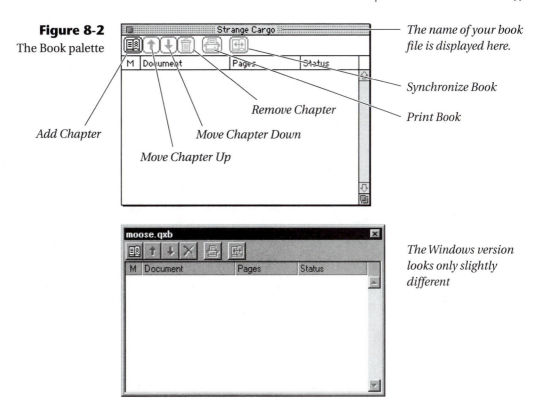

Figure 8-2
The Book palette

*The name of your book
file is displayed here.*

Synchronize Book

Print Book

Remove Chapter

Move Chapter Down

Move Chapter Up

Add Chapter

*The Windows version
looks only slightly
different*

Removing documents. You can remove a document from a Book palette by selecting it and clicking the Remove Document button. If you want to remove more than one, you can select them with the Shift or Command key (Shift for contiguous selections, Command for discontiguous selections on the list). Note that deleting a document from the Book palette does *not* delete the file from disk; it simply removes it from the list.

▼ ▼

Tip: Reordering Documents. It seems like I always accidentally place one chapter in the the wrong order on the Book palette. You can move a document up and down on the list by selecting it and clicking the Move Chapter Up and Move Chapter Down buttons. But I think it's even faster to hold down the Option key and drag the chapter to where you want it.

▼ ▼

When you add a new document to your book, XPress actually opens the document behind the scenes (you don't see it, but you can hear your hard disk scratching away), writes some code into it so that the document knows it's part of a book now, and then closes it. (The same thing happens when you remove a document from a book.) This can take some time, especially with large documents, so be patient.

If you open a document from disk, there's almost no way to tell if it's part of a book or not. In general, though, you should not add a document to more than one book. You can do it, but if you do, XPress alerts you that the document's page numbering could get messed up. Other weirdness might ensue, as well . . . again, it's best to avoid it.

▼ ▼

Tip: Take Away That Book Setting. If you throw away or lose your book file on disk, the individual documents in the book don't know that—they still think they're part of a book.

You can, however, create a new dummy book, add your documents to it (just click OK when XPress tells you that this might mess up the page numbering), and then remove them all using the Remove Chapter button on the palette. This takes a little time to do, but it's the only way to tell a document that it's not part of a book anymore.

▼ ▼

Editing Your Book's Documents

Once you've added documents to your Book palette, you can go about your regular routine of editing and preparing the documents . . . with a few minor adjustments.

▶ Whenever possible, you should open your book's documents while the Book palette is open. (The fastest way to open a document is to double-click on it in the Book palette.) When you open and modify a document while the palette is not open, the palette isn't smart enough to update itself (see "File status," below). If XPress can't find your document (perhaps it's on a server that is not mounted), it'll ask you where it is.

▶ You can print documents the regular way, but if you want to print more than one document in a book at a time, you should use the Print button on the Book palette (see "Printing Books," later in this section).

▶ You should be careful about using the Section feature to renumber any of the documents in the book (see "Page Numbering and Sections," later in this section). In general, you should let the Book palette handle your page numbering for you.

▼ ▼

Tip: No Can Undo. QuarkXPress's books are like libraries in several ways. First of all, the changes you make to your Book palette, including adding, removing, and reordering documents, aren't saved until you close the palette or quit QuarkXPress (although libraries have the Auto Library Save feature, there is no such feature for books).

Also, you can't use the Undo or Revert to Saved features on books. This means you should be careful about what you do in a Book palette . . . there may be no turning back.

▼ ▼

File status. The Book palette monitors and displays the status of each document in the book. There are five possible messages in the Status column of the palette: Available, Open, Modified, Missing, or In Use (see Figure 8-3).

▶ AVAILABLE. The normal status of a document is Available. This means that no one has the document open for editing and that the document has not changed since the last time it was open on the computer you're using.

▶ OPEN. When you have a document open on your Macintosh or PC, the status of that file is listed as Open.

▶ MODIFIED. When you or anyone else who has access to the file opens and changes a document while the Book palette is not open, the status will be listed as Modified next time you open the palette. It's easy to change the status from Modified back to Available: just open the file while the Book palette is open, then close the document again.

Figure 8-3
File status on
the Book palette

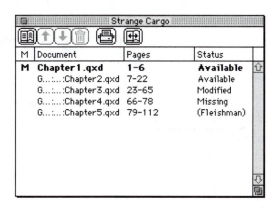

▶ **MISSING.** If you move a document after adding it to the Book palette, XPress won't be able to find it, and the status is listed as Missing. (There's one exception to this rule: if you move the document into the same folder as the book file, the Book palette can find it.) To "find" a file again, double-click on the chapter name in the Book palette; XPress displays a dialog box in which you can tell it where the document now resides.

▶ **IN USE.** If someone else on your network opens one of the documents in your book via the Book palette, the Status field of the Book palette lists that chapter as in use. More precisely, it lists the name of that person's computer, so you know exactly who to call and yell at. However, if they open the file without having the Book palette open, QuarkXPress has no way of knowing that the document is open.

It's important to pay attention to the Status column readings, because documents must be either Available or Open in order to synchronize, print, or renumber properly.

▼ ▼

Tip: Keep Those Books Open. Don't feel compelled to close your Book palette(s) before you quit QuarkXPress. Any books that are open when you quit will be open again (and in the same position on screen) when you relaunch the program.

▼ ▼

Tip: Network Booking. It seems like people are increasingly working on projects in groups rather than individually. Quark anticipated this, and if you put your book file on a server, more than one person can open it at the same time. (Only one person can open a regular XPress document at a time, however.) While this isn't nearly as powerful as the full-blown Quark Publishing System (QPS), it's certainly useful if a group of people have to work on different documents in the book at the same time.

The thing is, I don't like working on documents when they're on a server. It just makes me nervous. (In older versions of XPress, you could permanently corrupt your documents if you did this; now it does seem to work fine, but I'm still superstitious.) Instead, I prefer to copy the file to my local hard drive, edit it at my leisure, and then return the file to the server when I'm done with it. There are two problems with this. First, the book palette doesn't update properly.

Second, other people on your network might not realize that you've got the "live" file, so make it clear to them: hide the document on the server, or put it in another folder called "work in progress" or something like that.

▼ ▼

Tip: Restricting Network Access. QuarkXPress has no built-in features for restricting access to documents in a book. You can, however, set up access privileges on a person-by-person basis with most server software. For instance, you might give one person read-only access, so they could not make changes to your files, and then give read/write access to someone else who has good cause to edit the documents.

▼ ▼

Tip: Careful With Save As. I use the Save As feature all the time as a way to track revisions of my documents. Each time I use Save As, I change the name slightly ("mydocument1," "mydocument2," and so on), so I can always go back to an earlier version if necessary. If you do this, however, note that the Book palette doesn't catch on to what you're doing; it just lists and keeps track of the original document. Therefore, every time you use Save As, you have to remove the old document name from the Book palette and use Add Chapter to add the new document in (very frustrating). I'm hoping that Quark will introduce some faster way to revise the Book palette in these situations (if they do, I'll post information about it on The QuarkXPress Book Web Site (*www.peachpit.com/blatner/*).

▼ ▼

Synchronizing Your Book

The more documents you're working with, the more likely it is that one or more of them contain settings inconsistent with the others in the book. Perhaps you decided to change a style sheet definition in one document out of 20, and then forgot to change it in the other 19. Or perhaps one person in your workgroup decided he didn't like the Standard H&J settings in the document he was editing, so he just changed them without telling anyone.

Fortunately, the Synchronize Book button on the Book palette lets you ensure that all style sheets, colors, H&J settings, List settings, and

Dashes & Stripes settings are consistent throughout the documents in a book. Here's how it works.

The Master Chapter. One document on the Book palette is always marked as the *master chapter* (by default, it's the first chapter you add to the palette). The master chapter—which is listed in bold and with the letter M next to it—is the document to which all the other documents will be synchronized. That means if you add a new color to the master chapter and then click the Synchronize Book button, the color will be added to all the other documents in the book. If you add a new color to a document that is not a master chapter, it won't be added when you synchronize the documents.

You can always change which document is the master chapter: just double-click in the left column of the Book palette (next to the document you want to be the master chapter).

Synchronize. When you click the Synchronize Book button, XPress warns you about what it's going to do and gives you a chance to cancel the procedure (see Figure 8-4). If you go ahead with it (click OK), the style sheet definitions, colors, H&J settings, List settings, and Dashes & Stripes settings from the master chapter are copied to the other documents.

▶ A style sheet, color, H&J setting, List setting, or Dashes & Stripes setting that is defined in the master chapter but not in another chapter gets added to that other document.

▶ If a setting is named the same in both the master chapter and another document, the definition for that setting in the master chapter overrides the one in the nonmaster chapter.

▶ If a setting is not defined in the master chapter but it is in some other document, it's left alone. (This means you can have "local" settings that exist in one document that don't have to be copied into all the others.)

▼ ▼

Tip: Save Your Eyes with Synchronize. It's always a hassle editing a document that contains colored text because it's often difficult to read. Let's say you've got 15 documents in a book that all use the same style sheets. You could change the style definitions in the master chapter so that the text appears in black (or whatever color is easy to read), and then synchronize the book so that the settings are changed in all the documents. Later, when you're done editing, you can reverse the process: change the style sheets back, and synchronize again.

Figure 8-4

Synchronizing your book

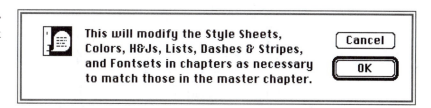

Note that synchronizing a document can be a time-consuming process—the more documents and the more settings there are, the longer it takes. You can watch XPress do its work in the Book palette: as XPress changes each document, you'll see its status change from Available to Open and then to Available again.

Page Numbering and Sections

Perhaps the most helpful aspect of the Book feature is that it keeps track of your page numbering for you and updates the page numbers when you add pages to or delete them from a document, or if you add a new document between two other documents in a book. Of course, this only works if you've used automatic page numbering in your documents. (The automatic page-number character is Command-3; see "Sections and Page Numbering" in Chapter 4, *Building a Document.*)

The page numbering feature works via the Section dialog box. When you add a document to the Book palette, XPress checks to see if the first page of the document has been defined as a section start. If it has been, XPress leaves the page alone. If it's not the start of a new section, then XPress turns on the checkbox labeled Book Chapter Start in the Section dialog box, and sets the first page number appropriately (see Figure 8-5).

Let's say you've got one 16-page document on your Book palette already. When you add another document, XPress automatically sets the first page number to 17 (as long as you hadn't already set up the first page as a section start in the Section dialog box). If you later open the first document and add two pages, XPress automatically renumbers the second document next time you open it so that it starts on page 19.

Figure 8-5

Page numbering in books

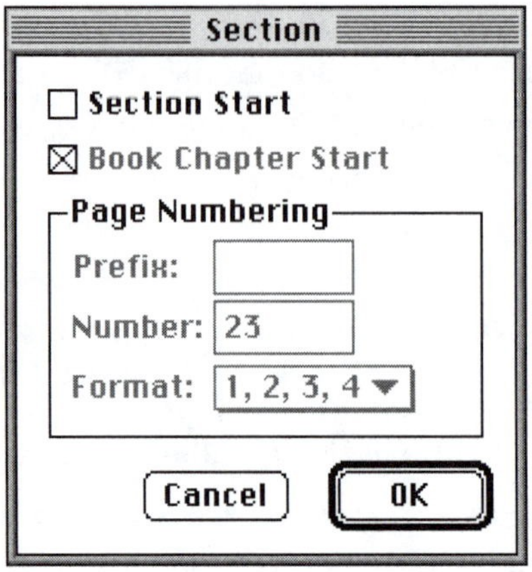

Manual sections. If you have manually specified a section start anywhere in your document, the automatic book-page numbering works slightly differently. Let's say you've used the Section dialog box to make a section start of any page in the second document of your book, and you've specified lower-case roman numerals for the page numbers. Now if you add a third document to the book, and this new document has no section-start settings, then XPress picks up on the roman numerals where they left off in the second document.

In other words, XPress keeps on numbering in the style of the previous document. If you wanted the third document to return to regular arabic numerals, you would have to manually add a section start to its first page, overriding the Book Chapter Start setting. Of course, now when you add pages to the first or second document, the page numbers don't update properly in the third document because of the section start.

Odd versus even page numbers. To get even more picayune, I should mention that XPress always starts Facing Pages documents with an odd number. For instance, if the first chapter ends on page 23 and the second chapter is a Facing Pages document, XPress sets the first page of the second chapter as 25, skipping page 24. If you want to print a page numbered "24," you have to add it yourself to the first document.

Single-sided documents, on the other hand, can begin with either an odd- or even-numbered page.

▼ ▼

Tip: Spread-to-Spread Page Numbers. Some magazine publishers build their magazines one spread at a time—each spread is a separate document. (I think this is a very strange way to create a magazine, but those publishers insist they have their reasons.) If you're going to do this, set up your documents using single-sided pages rather than facing pages. You can still build a two-page spread with single-sided pages (just drag one page next to the other in the Document Layout palette), and this way the automatic page numbering works properly when the documents are all added to the Book palette.

▼ ▼

Printing Books

Even though I cover printing documents in Chapter 13, *Printing*, I should take this opportunity to mention a few things that are specific to printing books.

First, each chapter in a book must be listed as Open, Available, or Modified on the Book palette in order for the document to print. This is because XPress invisibly opens each document at print time (you don't see the document open on screen, but it does). XPress alerts you if a document is in use by someone else on the network or if it's missing, and if it can't immediately be found or made available you can cancel printing. (This only stops the print job for that one document; all the other documents print fine.)

Second, if you only want certain documents in a book to print, select them from the Book palette before clicking the Print Book button. Remember that you can select contiguous documents on the list by holding down the Shift key, and discontiguous documents with the Command key. If no documents are selected, then they'll all print.

Last, as this book goes to press, there is still a bug in XPress that makes it impossible to print PostScript to disk (a "PostScript dump") for more than one document in a book on the Macintosh. The results are varied when you try to do this. Some people find that the first chapter is written to disk and that subsequent chapters get sent to a printer. Others find that every document is written to disk, but because the same file name is given to each PostScript dump, each file overwrites the last, until you have only one file—the last one—on disk. The workaround is simply to save PostScript dumps one document at a time. In Windows, this does work, but you still have to type a new file name in for each PostScript file that gets written to disk.

▼ ▼

Lists

I'm embarrassed to admit that when I first looked over the list of new features in version 4 of QuarkXPress, I expressed disappointment that it lacked a Table of Contents feature. Fortunately, someone at Quark was kind enough to gently explain to me that the new Lists feature not only generated a table of contents but all kinds of lists, as well. The more I've played with Lists, the more I've been impressed with its versatility.

The Lists feature lets you build collections of paragraphs that have been tagged with specific style sheets. For instance, if you use even two style sheets when you're formatting a book—one for the chapter name and another for your first-level headings—you can build a basic table of contents by collecting all the paragraphs tagged with these two styles. If you use paragraph style sheets to tag your figure titles, you can build a table of figures. Anything you can tag with a paragraph style, you can build into a list.

This all depends entirely on your using paragraph style sheets. Of course, you simply can't be efficient when you're building long documents if you don't use paragraph styles anyway. (If you don't currently use styles, go check out Chapter 7, *Copy Flow*, to see why you should.)

Setting Up a List

The great thing about Lists is that they're so easy to make and use. Here's the six-step procedure to define a list.

1. Select Lists from the Edit menu. Like style sheets and colors, making a list while a document is open means that the list appears only in that document; if no documents are open when you make the list, it'll appear in every document you create from then on.

2. Click the New button in the Lists dialog box to open the Edit List dialog box (see Figure 8-6), and type a name for your new list.

3. Choose which paragraph style sheets you want included in the list definition by double-clicking on them in the Available Styles list. (You can also Command-click to select discontiguous styles on the list and choose them all by clicking the right-arrow button in the dialog box.) The order in which you place the items on the list doesn't matter; at this point, it's just a list of style sheets.

Figure 8-6

Creating a new list

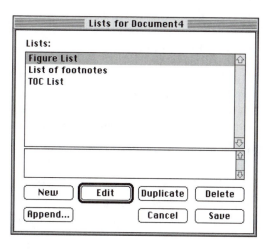

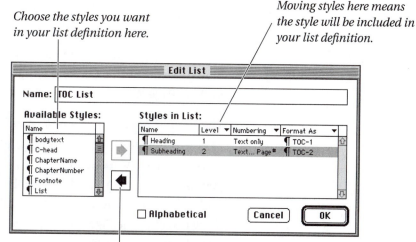

Choose the styles you want in your list definition here.

Moving styles here means the style will be included in your list definition.

Click here to remove a style sheet from the list definition.

4. Choose a level for each style sheet on the list by selecting the style and selecting 1 through 8 from the Level popup menu. These levels determine how the list appears on the Lists palette (which I'll discuss later in this section), and have nothing to do with how the list will appear on your printed page. For instance, you might apply level 1 to a style called Chapter Title, level 2 to a Heading style, and level 3 to a Subhead style.

5. You can control how the list will appear on your printed page with the Numbering and Format As popup menus. You've got three options for Numbering: Text only, Text...Page #, and Page #...Text (see Figure 8-7). The first, Text only, tells XPress not to include the page number on which it finds the paragraph tagged with this

Figure 8-7 Numbering

Preface

Chapter I: History of Pi

Early History 7
The Greeks 13
Pi in the East 19
A Millennium of Progress . . . . .29 — *Text...Page #*
Breakthroughs in Mathematics 41

Chapter II: The Personality of Pi — *Text only*

Irrational numbers 73
Patterns in Pi 101

Chapter III: The Circle Squarers

John Smith 113

style. The other two options tell XPress to include the page number, separated from the text of the paragraph by a tab character. For instance, in the previous example, you might set the Chapter Title style sheet to Text only, and the Heading and Subhead styles to Text...Page #.

6. The Format As popup menu lets you apply a style sheet to the paragraph when it appears on the list. This is helpful because you'd rarely want a heading from your document to appear in your table of contents in the actual Heading style; instead, you'd probably create a new style sheet called "TOC-head" or something like that (see Figure 8-8). If you want certain paragraphs to be indented on your final list, you should apply style sheets here that include indentation.

That's it! However, here are a few things to keep in mind when you're defining a list.

- You can define thousands of different lists in a single document.
- You can have a maximum of 32 style sheets in a list definition.
- XPress only captures the first 256 characters of a paragraph when it builds a list, so you should choose style sheets that correspond to paragraphs shorter than this (256 characters make about 40 words—more than enough for most headlines, bylines, and such).
- If you turn on the Alphabetical option in the Edit List dialog box, XPress sorts the list in alphabetical order when you build it (I dis-

Figure 8-8

Format As

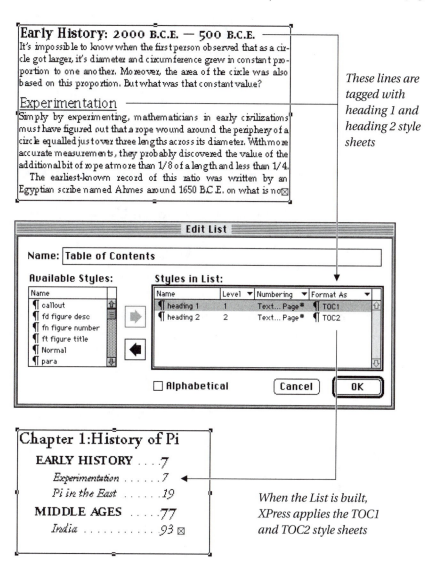

These lines are tagged with heading 1 and heading 2 style sheets

When the List is built, XPress applies the TOC1 and TOC2 style sheets

cuss how to build a list below). Whether or not you want your final list alphabetized is up to you; you probably wouldn't want it when you build the table of contents for a book, but you might if you're creating a list of items in a catalog.

▶ If you want a list to work in multiple documents within a book, the list must be present in all the documents. You can use the Synchronize Book feature to ensure that the same list appears properly in each document.

The Lists Palette

Once you've defined a list, it's time to open the Lists palette, which lets you get an overview for your list, navigate through your document based on the list, and ultimately build the final list on your document pages. You can open the Lists palette by selecting Show List from the View menu or pressing Option-F11 (Mac) or Control-F11 (Windows).

As soon as you open the Lists palette, QuarkXPress goes and collects the paragraphs you've specified in the list definition (this might take a little while for a very large document). All that information is displayed in the lower section of the Lists palette (see Figure 8-9). The Lists palette doesn't contain the corresponding page numbers for these paragraphs; that information comes later, when you tell XPress to build the list on your document page.

The Lists palette offers you two options. First, if you have more than one list defined in a document, you can choose among them from the List popup menu. The second option, found on the Show List For pop-up menu, is only active if the document is part of a book; if it is, you can tell XPress to build the list based on this one document or on all the documents in the book.

I find the Lists palette a good place to get an overview of a document or a book, and—if I've specified my Levels properly—it's very helpful as a first step in figuring out if the final list is going to appear correctly on my pages (sometimes you don't realize that you left out a paragraph style sheet, or chose the wrong style sheet—until you peruse the paragraphs on the Lists palette).

List navigation. If you double-click on any paragraph in the Lists palette, XPress jumps to the page where the paragraph is. In fact, some people use the Lists palette for navigation purposes only, and never actually build the table of contents or whatever on their document pages.

The Find field of the Lists palette is very useful if you've got a very long list; just type the first few characters of a paragraph you think is on the list, and XPress selects it in the Lists palette. I find this most helpful in those long technical documents where every heading begins with a number.

Update. If QuarkXPress had to keep tabs on every little edit you make in your document and reflect it in the Lists palette, it'd be as slow as

Figure 8-9

The Lists palette

Type here to find a word or phrase in the list below.

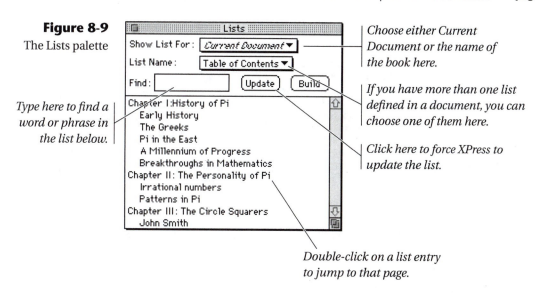

Choose either Current Document or the name of the book here.

If you have more than one list defined in a document, you can choose one of them here.

Click here to force XPress to update the list.

Double-click on a list entry to jump to that page.

molasses on a cold January morning. No, if you make any changes to your document—add paragraphs, remove paragraphs, change the spelling of words—the Lists palette only updates when you click the Update button or when you close and reopen the palette.

Building and Rebuilding Lists

You've defined a list, you've browsed over it in the Lists palette, and now it's finally time to get that list onto your document page. This is potentially the most complex and hair-raising ordeal of the entire process. No, seriously—here's what you do: select a text box (preferably an empty one) and click the Build button on the Lists palette. That's it. If the list is supposed to include page numbers, now is when XPress goes out and finds them (see Figure 8-10).

Updating the list. There is nothing special about the text or page numbers on this list—they're just text and numbers. If you update the document on which the list is based (including changes to page numbers or to the list definition), you're going to have rebuild the list on your document page. I find that I build and rebuild a list at least several times for each document or book, due to various human errors (my own, generally). Here's how you do it.

1. First, make sure the Lists palette is up-to-date by clicking the Update button.

Figure 8-10

The final list

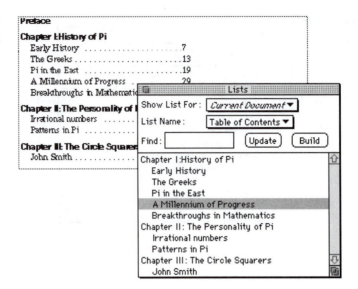

2. Select any text box in your document (it doesn't have to be the same box in which you originally built the list).

3. Click Build in the Lists palette. XPress is smart enough to know if you've already built a list in your file. If you have, it asks you if you want to replace the list that's already there (see Figure 8-11). Typically you'd want to choose to replace the already built list.

▼ ▼

Tip: Use Dummy Text for Lists. One of my favorite aspects of lists is that they're document-wide rather than simply story-wide. That means that any text in any text box can be included on a list . . . even text in a text box that has Suppress Printout turned on. With this in mind, you can add "tags" to items on your page that don't appear in print, but do appear in your table of contents.

One of the best examples of this is an advertiser index. You can place a text box with an advertiser's name on top of that company's ad in your document. Set the text box's runaround to None and turn on Suppress Printout, and it's almost as though this were a "non-object" —the text box won't print, and it won't affect any text underneath. But if that advertiser's name is tagged with a style sheet, you can include it on a list of advertisers.

The same trick goes for building a list of pictures in a catalog, or for any other instance where what you want on the list doesn't actually appear on the page.

Figure 8-11
Rebuilding a list

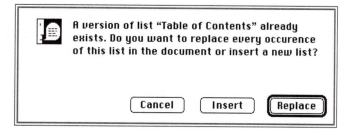

A version of list "Table of Contents" already exists. Do you want to replace every occurence of this list in the document or insert a new list?

Cancel   Insert   Replace

Indexes

It was Mr. Duncan, my elementary-school librarian, who first impressed the importance of a good index into my malleable young brain: A non-fiction book without an index, he said, wasn't even worth putting on the library shelf. If you've ever searched an index in vain for something that you're sure is somewhere in a book, you know the value of a good index.

The problem is that sitting down and indexing a book is—in my experience—the most painful, horrible, mind-numbing activity you could ever wish on your worst enemy. And yet, where this is the kind of task that a computer should be great at, it's actually impossible for a computer to do a good job of indexing a book by itself. A good index requires careful thought, an understanding of the subject matter, and an ability to keep the whole project in your head at all times. Plus, until recently, it required a large stack of notecards, highlighter pens, and Post-It notes.

Fortunately, QuarkXPress now has a built-in indexing feature which, while it won't make the index for you, does remove the notecard and highlighter requirements. Note that because a minority of XPress users actually ever index their documents, the folks at Quark put this feature into a separate XTension. The XTension is loaded (it's in the XTension folder) by default, but if you or someone else turned it off with the XTension manager, you may have to turn it back on and relaunch XPress.

Tip: Concordance versus Index. Some people ask me, "Why can't a computer build an index? QuarkXPress should just give me a list of all the words in my document and what page they're on." Unfortunately, this is not an index; it's a concordance. The difference is that a concordance records the location of words, while an index records the location of ideas. There are times when a concordance is very useful, especially in catalogs. In those cases, you might want to use an XTension like Sonar

Bookends, which can build concordances automatically and very quickly. But in general, if you're looking for an index, you're going to have to do it manually with the indexing features in XPress.

▼ ▼

Tip: Edit First, Index Last. You can index a document at any time in the production cycle, but it's almost always best to wait until the text has become fixed—until no text in the document will be deleted, copied, cut, pasted, and so on. The reason: as you edit the text, you may accidentally delete index markers without knowing it. In fact, as this book goes to press, even cutting and pasting text deletes index entries.

▼ ▼

The Index Palette. The List feature captures whole paragraphs that are tagged with specific style sheets. XPress's indexing captures specific words or phrases that you have manually tagged in the Index palette. The Index palette (choose Show Index from the View menu) lets you add either single words or whole phrases to the index, and it displays a list of currently indexed words and phrases (see Figure 8-12).

First I'm going to discuss how to add, edit, and remove index entries with the Index palette. Then I'll explore how to collect all the tagged entries and build a finished index on your document pages.

Adding a New First-Level Index Entry

There's very little that is automatic about building an index. Again, it's not difficult, but you have to be methodical about it. Here are the steps you should go through for each new index entry. (Note that I differentiate between a new index entry and a new reference to an index entry. For example, "Pigs" might be a new entry for page 34, but when it appears again on page 59, it would simply be a new reference to your already added index entry—see "Adding a New Reference to an Entry," below.)

1. **TEXT.** Insert the index entry (the word or phrase that you want to appear in the index) into the Text field of the Index palette. If the entry actually appears in the text story, you can just select it with the cursor; when the Index palette is open, QuarkXPress automatically copies any text that is selected into the Text field. On the other hand, if the word or phrase doesn't appear, you will have to type it in yourself.

Figure 8-12

The Index palette

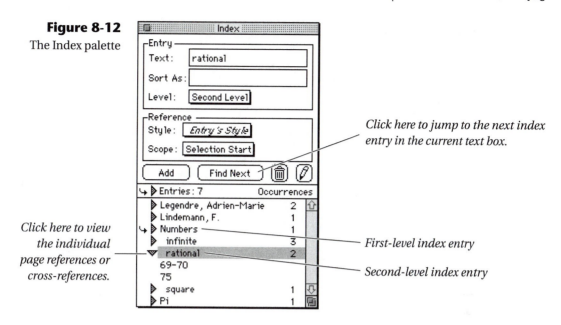

Click here to jump to the next index
entry in the current text box.

Click here to view
the individual
page references or
cross-references.

First-level index entry

Second-level index entry

For example, you may be discussing cows on your document page, but you want to index the word under the phrase "Farm animals." In this case, you would simply place the cursor somewhere in the text box and type "Farm animals" in the Index palette.

2. **SORT AS.** Index entries always appear in alphabetical order. However, occasionally you may not want your index entry to appear where it would normally be alphabetized. For instance, the famous "17-Mile Drive" would ordinarily be placed at the beginning of the index, before the "A"s. You can place it along with other words that begin with "S" by typing "Seventeen" in the Sort As field of the Index palette. Of course, you'll probably just leave this field blank for 98 percent of your index entries.

3. **LEVEL.** While some simple indexes have just one level of entry, most have two (some even have three or four; see Figure 8-13). For example, "Cows," "Pigs," and "Ducks" might all be second-level entries found listed under the first-level entry of "Farm animals." Since we're focusing on first-level entries right now, you can just skip over the Level popup menu. (I'll discuss the finer points of second-level entries in "Adding a New Second-level Index Entry," below).

Figure 8-13
A multilevel index

Calculating. *See also* Equations ——————— *First-level entry*
  area of circle, 80–81, **86**
  circumference to diameter, 24–25
  errors in, 12–13, 49–50
  forumlas for, 43, 44, 61 ——————— *Second-level entry*
  speed/efficiency of, 42, 53
  techniques for, 52–61
Calculators, 50–56
Callet, J.F., 45 ——————————————— *Cross reference*
Catholic church. *See* Religion
Cavalieri, Bonaventura, 40, **43** ——————— *Single-page reference styled with the Style popup menu*
Ch'ang Hong, 24, 26
Chudnovsky brothers ——————— *Page number suppressed*
  m-Zero, 65–70
  and Preston, R., 88–89 ——————— *Entry sorted differently using Sort As*
  supercomputers, 71

4. **STYLE.** The Style popup menu on the Index palette is yet one more control that you will ignore most of the time (though when you need it, it's great to have). Let's say you want the page numbers that refer to an illustration (rather than to just text on the page) to appear bold in the final index. You can build a character style sheet to define how you want the page numbers to appear and—when you're indexing that illustration—you can choose that character style from the Style popup menu. (See Chapter 7, *Copy Flow*, for more information on defining style sheets.)

5. **SCOPE.** If your treatise on pigs and goats spans six pages of your document, you don't want to have to make a separate index entry for each and every page. Instead, you can specify one index entry and choose a range of pages in the Scope popup menu. There are seven types of scopes.

   ▶ **SELECTION START.** When you choose Selection start (this is the default setting), XPress references the page on which the cursor is currently sitting. If you've selected a range of text that crosses from one page to the next, the first page (wherever the selection starts) is used.

   ▶ **SELECTION TEXT.** You can select any range of text (two words, two paragraphs, two hundred paragraphs . . . you get the idea) and index the whole range by choosing

Selection Text. Personally, I find this option rather clunky to use (and even clunkier to edit later, if necessary), so I prefer using one of the other Scope settings instead.

▶ **TO STYLE.** If you use style sheets religiously, you'll love using the To Style option because you can specify a range based on paragraph styles. For instance, let's say you've got a book about farm animals where each animal's heading is tagged with a style sheet called "Heading-A." You could select the heading "Rabbit" and set the Scope to "To Style." Then you could choose Heading-A from the popup menu of styles (see Figure 8-14). If the "Horse" section starts three pages after the Rabbit section, the page range in the index will span three pages; if it starts 14 pages after, the page range will span 14 pages, and so on.

By the way, the default setting for To Style is Next, which means "from this paragraph onward until the style sheet changes to something else."

▶ **SPECIFIED # OF Ps.** If you want to index a long paragraph, one that may split onto two or more pages, you should probably select the scope called "Specified # of Ps." (Yes, "Ps" stands for "Paragraphs.") QuarkXPress's default setting of 1 means "include the pages that this paragraph falls on." Changing this setting to 2 means "include this paragraph plus the one after it," and so on.

Figure 8-14
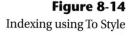
Indexing using To Style

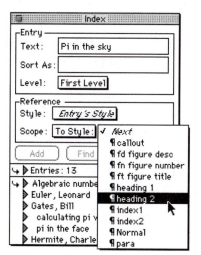

- ▶ **TO END OF.** When you choose the scope called "To End Of," XPress offers you two options: to the end of the story or to the end of the document. If the current text story reaches to the last page of the document, then these options are the same, of course. In the example of the farm animals chapter, you could index the entire chapter by placing the cursor anywhere on the first page of the chapter, specifying an index entry labeled "Farm animals," and choosing To End Of Document.

- ▶ **SUPPRESS PAGE #.** Some first-level index entries don't include page numbers at all. For instance, in the book I've been discussing, "Animals" is too broad a topic to include page numbers (every page in the book would be indexed). So you might specify Suppress Page # for this one entry, and then follow it with 15 second-level entries, each with appropriate page numbers listed. (Again, I discuss second-level entries below.)

- ▶ **X-REF.** The last item on the Scope popup menu is X-Ref, which lets you add cross-references to your index. If you'll forgive me—because cross-references act a little bit differently than other index entries—I'm going to hold off on my discussion of this option for a moment.

6. **ADD.** If you've persevered through this procedure so far, the final step in adding an index entry is to click the Add button. (After indexing for a long time, I sometimes forget this step and move on to the next entry, only to wonder later why I'm missing index entries that I *know* I made. Another *faux pas*: clicking Add before you change the various controls on the Index palette . . . that doesn't work, either.)

Adding index entries is not hard at all, but it does take patience and attention to detail in each of these steps. As soon as you press the Add button, XPress inserts the entry into the Index palette and places an index marker in the text (see Figure 8-15). These index entries are actually hidden inside the text in the text box, though the index markers only show up when the Index palette is visible.

Figure 8-15
Index markers

*Index markers are
only visible when the
Index palette is open.*

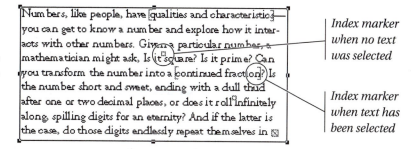

Index marker
when no text
was selected

Index marker
when text has
been selected

Tip: Index Keystrokes. There are two keystrokes you should keep in mind when you're indexing. First, Command-Option-I jumps to the Text field in the Index palette (it even opens the palette first, if necessary). Second, pressing Command-Option-Shift-I is the same as clicking the Add button in the Index palette. I find that both of these speed up indexing considerably.

Tip: Styling Indexes. Remember that however you type the word in the Text field of the Index palette is how it will appear in your final index. There is no single "correct" way to enter words into your index, though there are standard conventions, and it is best if you can keep your index consistent throughout.

For instance, you should decide on a capitalization scheme before beginning to index your document. Will all first-level entries be in initial caps, while second-level entries will be in lower case? Or should only proper names be capitalized, even in first-level entries? Before you answer these questions, it might behoove you to look over the section on indexes in *The Chicago Manual of Style*, or some other book of styling conventions.

Tip: Wrong Scope. As this book goes to press, QuarkXPress's Index XTension still contains an annoying bug. Let's say your text story starts on page 14 and then jumps to page 21. If you select and index a paragraph that spans the page break, the index entry appears as "14–21" rather than "14, 21." The former mistakenly appears to cover seven pages; the latter properly states that the entry is just on two pages. I hope they fix the bug by the time you read this, but if they don't, then just be aware that you might have some cleaning up to do later (see "Tip: Finessing Your Index," later in this chapter).

▼ ▼

Cross-References (X-refs)

One of the tricks to building a great index is to think of all the ways that your reader might look for a topic, and to include those words in your index. For instance, because you're familiar with your own book, you might include an index entry called "Llamas." However, someone reading the book might look for "Cute wool-producing animals that spit." Fortunately, XPress lets you add cross-references in your index like "Spitting animals. *See* Llamas" and "Wool 34–46. *See also* Llamas."

To add a cross-reference to your index, you go through all the same steps as adding a normal index entry. The one difference is that when you set the Scope popup menu to X-Ref, XPress provides you with a text field in which you can type the cross-referenced word or phrase. If you want your index entry to be "Koi. *See* Carp" you would type "Koi" in the Text field of the Index palette, and type "Carp" in the X-Ref field.

Note that if you're cross-referencing to an index entry that you've already added to your Index palette, you can simply click on that index entry to copy it into the X-Ref field. That's certainly faster than typing the words in again.

Of course, because no page number is involved in a cross-reference, it doesn't matter where in your document you specify it (though it must be in a text box).

X-Ref options. QuarkXPress offers three types of cross-references which you can choose from the Index palette once you select X-Ref from the Scope popup menu: See, See also, and See herein.

▶ *See* is generally used when an index entry has no page number references, such as "Supermarket. *See* Grocery."

▶ *See also* is used when an index entry does have page references, but you also want to refer the reader to other topics, such as "Grocery 34–51. *See also* Farmer's Market."

▶ *See herein* is a special case in which you are cross-referencing to a second-level entry within the same entry as the cross-reference itself, and it's used more in legal indexes than anywhere else.

The Chicago Manual of Style recommends that you set these three phrases in italic in your index. Note that XPress won't automatically change this formatting for you, so you need to do this in "post-production" (see "Tip: Finessing Your Index," later in this chapter).

Adding a New Reference to an Entry

Once you've got an entry on your Index palette, you can easily add more page references to it. Let's say you added the name "Farmer Jones" to your index back on page 13 of your document. Now, "Farmer Jones" appears again on page 51.

1. Place the cursor in the appropriate place in the text story. In this case, you'd probably put the cursor next to the word "Farmer" on page 51.

2. Click on the entry in the Index palette. Here, you'd click on "Farmer Jones." As soon as you click on an index entry, it appears in the Text field of the palette.

3. Make sure that the Level, Style, and Scope controls are set up properly in the Index palette, depending on how you want your new reference to appear.

4. Click the Add button.

Note that while you don't necessarily have to click on the entry in the Index palette in step 2 (you could just retype the entry in the Text field or select it on the page), I recommend the clicking method because it ensures consistency. For example, if you relied on your typing ability, you might create the index entry "Chickens" and then later—meaning to type the same thing—create a new entry, "Chicken," causing two different entries to be made when you only meant to make one.

Adding a New Second-Level Index Entry

Now that you've specified first-level index entries, you can—if you wish—add second-level entries. As I mentioned earlier, second-level entries are subcategories of the first-level entries. For example, under the first-level index entry "Wines," you might find the second-level entries "Merlot," "Chardonnay," and "Côtes du Rhône." You can make a second-level index entry just like you make the first-level entry, but with two extra steps.

First, you must choose Second Level from the Level popup menu on the Index palette.

Second, you must tell XPress which first-level entry you want the new entry to fall under. You do this by clicking in the column to the left of the first-level entry (see Figure 8-16). When you click, XPress moves the Level marker (the little L-shaped arrow icon) to indicate that any second-level entries you create will be placed here.

The number-one mistake people make when adding a second-level entry is forgetting to move the Level marker, so the second-level entry shows up in the wrong place (see "Tip: Moving a Second-Level Entry," below). The second most common mistake is accidentally clicking on the first-level entry when you meant to click in the column to the left of it (to move the Level marker), which replaces whatever is in the Text field with whatever you click on . . . oops!

Again, patience and attention really do go a long way when you're making indexes.

Figure 8-16

Creating a
second-level entry

*Clicking in this
column moves the
Level marker here.*

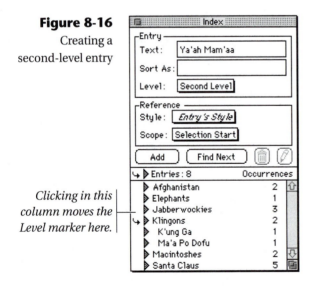

Third and Fourth Levels. Once you've got a second-level entry, you can place a third-level entry under it—just change the Level popup menu to Third Level and place the Level marker appropriately. Similarly, you can put fourth-level entries under third-level entries. While it's nice that they give you this option, I find third- and fourth-level entries pretty confusing to readers, so restrain yourself unless it's really necessary.

▼ ▼

Tip: Where to Put the Cross-Reference. Some people like putting cross-references at the end of a list of second-level index entries rather than directly after the first-level entry. XPress won't do this for you automatically, but you can fake it by creating a dummy second-level entry and setting its Scope to X-Ref. The dummy second-level entry should just be named with a symbol like ^ or \ so that it automatically falls at the end of the alphabetized list of second-level entries. Later, once you build the index onto your document pages, you will have to perform a Find/Change to remove the symbols.

▼ ▼

Deleting an Entry

There are several ways to delete an entry from your index.

▶ If you want to delete an entire entry, including all its page references, select it in the Index palette and click the Delete button (the one that looks like a trash can on the Macintosh or a big "X" in Windows). Note that this also deletes all the subcategories under it and their page references, too.

▶ If you want to delete a single page reference, you can select it in the Index palette (click on the gray triangle next to the index entry to display its page references) and click the Delete button. Of course, if you only have one page reference under an index entry, deleting it will delete the whole entry, too.

▶ To get rid of a particular page reference in your index, you can also delete the index markers on the document page. If you selected text before adding the index entry, then this means deleting that whole range of text (deleting anything less leaves the index markers intact). If you did not select any text when adding the entry, you can still delete the little square marker by zooming in on it, clicking directly in its center, and pressing Delete. (You need to zoom in, because you generally can't select the tiny icon properly at Actual Size.)

▶ Last but not least, you can delete *every* index entry from the Index palette by Option-Shift-clicking on one of the entries. This is drastic, so XPress always asks you first if you really want to proceed.

Editing Index Entries

None of us is perfect, so it's a good thing that QuarkXPress has a way to edit the flubbed index entries that we make. When you're editing an index entry, you have to decide whether you want to edit the entry itself or a particular page reference of the entry.

Editing Entries. Let's say that halfway through indexing your document, you realize that the index entry "Martha Washington" should have been indexed as "Washington, Martha." You can select the entry in the Index palette and click the Edit button (that's the button that looks like a little pencil)—or even faster, you can activate the Edit mode by double-clicking on the entry. Because you're editing an entry, XPress grays out everything but the Text and Sort As fields in the palette. In this case, you'd change the Text field to "Washington, Martha," and then click the Edit button again (or press Enter).

Editing References. You can also change the scope or style of a particular page reference. For instance, let's say the reference to Martha Washington on page 47 should have spanned nine paragraphs, but you accidentally set it to Selection start instead. To fix this, click on the gray triangle next to the index entry; this displays the page references for the entry. Double-click on the page reference that corresponds to the one you want to change (in this case, you'd double-click on the number 47). Because you're editing a page reference, XPress grays out the Text and Sort As fields and lets you change the Style and Scope popup menus. When done, press Enter, or click the Edit button to leave Edit mode.

Note that there's no way to move an index entry from one place in the text to another (for instance, if you actually wanted the above reference to begin on page 48 instead of page 47); you have to actually delete the entry and then re-enter it in the new location.

▼ ▼

Tip: Find the Next Index Entry. In order to edit either an index entry or an individual page reference, you need to have it selected on the Index palette. If the index entry is right in front of you on the page, sometimes it's faster to select it on the page than it is to select it in the palette (especially in really long indexes). The problem is that it's tough to select index markers on the page. The best solution is to place the cursor in the text box, a few characters or a few words before the index entry, then to click the Find Next button in the Index palette. This automatically selects the next index entry in the text box, and simultaneously selects it in the Index palette, too.

By the way, if you hold down the Option key, the Index palette's Find Next button changes to a Find First button; while this is a good way to jump to the first index entry in a story, I rarely find myself needing this.

▾ ▾

Tip: Moving a Second-Level Entry. As I said earlier, the most common mistake people make when adding second-level entries is to put them under the wrong first-level entry. If you do this, don't panic. Select the second-level page reference you just added (or you can select the whole second-level entry, if it contains only one page reference), click the Delete button, move the Level marker to the proper first-level entry, and click Add again.

▾ ▾

Index Preferences

Now that you've gone through the trouble of manually adding four thousand index entries to your document, can't you build the index yet? No, not yet. First you should take a quick glance at the Index Preferences dialog box (choose Index from the Preferences submenu, under the Edit menu; see Figure 8-17). This dialog box lets you change two things: the color of the index markers in your document, and the specific formatting characters that QuarkXPress will use when building the index.

Note that Index Preferences works like Document Preferences: if a document is open when you make a change, the setting only applies to

Figure 8-17
Index Preferences

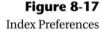

Index Preferences
▇ **Index Marker Color**
┌ Separation ─────────┐
Following Entry:
Between Page #s: ,
Between Page Range: –
Before X-ref: .
Between Entries:
[Cancel] [OK]

that document. If no documents are open, then the setting applies to all documents you create from then on.

Index Marker Color. There's nothing sacred about the color red . . . if you're color-blind to the color red, if your text is colored red, or if you just don't like seeing red, you can change the color of the index markers by clicking the color swatch labeled "Index Marker Color." Of course, this doesn't change anything about your document or your index; it only alters the on-screen display of the index markers when the Index palette is open.

Separation characters. This might seem really trivial to you, but most art directors and professional indexers care a great deal about the formatting characters in their index (see Figure 8-18). For example, what kind of space should separate an index entry and the page reference? The Index Preferences dialog box is the place to make this sort of decision.

▶ FOLLOWING ENTRY. This character sits between the index entry and the page reference numbers. The default character is a regular space, but I generally change this to a nonbreaking en space (Option-space on the Macintosh, or Control-Shift-6 in Windows) for better optical separation. You can put more than one character here—many people like to include a period, a comma, or a colon after an index entry, followed by a space, followed by the page reference numbers. In this case, type both the comma (or whatever) and the space in this field.

▶ BETWEEN PAGE #s. XPress places these characters between individual page-reference numbers. The important character is not the comma (which almost everyone uses), but the space after the comma. I typically leave this space alone, but some people like a larger or smaller space (like a punctuation space—Shift-space).

▶ BETWEEN PAGE RANGE. This character is used when the page reference spans multiple pages. The default character here is a regular hyphen, but I usually change this to an en dash (Option-hyphen on the Macintosh, or Control-Alt-Shift-hyphen in Windows). You could even change this to the word " to " if you want (don't forget to put spaces on either side), so that the page ranges look like this: "34 to 89".

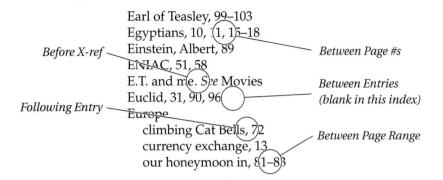

Figure 8-18

Separation characters

> ▶ **BEFORE X-REF.** This character sits between the entry or a page reference number and a cross-reference. Like the Between Page #s character, the important character in the Before X-ref field is not the default period (which almost everyone uses), but the space after the period, which you might decide to make larger or smaller. Personally, I just leave this setting alone. (Note that if you want some special punctuation *after* a cross-reference, you generally have to type it yourself in the Index palette, though this is not usually the style.)

> ▶ **BETWEEN ENTRIES.** If you build a nested index (rather than a run-in index; I'll explain the difference in "Building the Index," below), XPress places the Between Entries character at the end of every line. While it may seem at first like you'd want a period or something at the end of every line, this is very rare in an index, so in general you should leave this setting blank (the default) for nested indexes.

> In run-in indexes, however, you need to separate the entries from each other, so you should change this. The most common style is to use a semicolon and some kind of space character.

▼ ▼

Tip: Special Index Characters. You can type some special characters into the text fields in the Index Preferences dialog box by typing special codes. For example, if your index style calls for a tab character between the index entries and the page reference numbers, you could type "\t" in the Following Entry field (that's a backslash followed by a "t"). Similarly, you can get a flex space by typing "\f", and a line break by typing "\n". Why you'd want these characters in an index is beyond me; I just want to let you know that you can get them. Note that the codes are the same ones used in the Find/Change palette (see "Finding and Changing" in Chapter 5, *Word Processing*).

▼ ▼

Building the Index

Finally it's time to get that index onto a document page so you can see it in all its glory. This is the fun part, because you can just sit back, choose Build Index from the Utilities menu, and let XPress do the work of collecting the index entries and page numbers for you. (Build Index is only available when the Index palette is visible.) Unfortunately, there is still one more dialog box you need to pay attention to: the Build Index dialog box (see Figure 8-19).

The Build Index dialog box is a mish-mosh of choices you need to make in order to get the index of your dreams. While several of the options here might appear, at first, to fit better in the Index Preferences dialog box, who are we to question Quark's decisions? Fortunately, once you make your choices in this dialog box, XPress remembers them the next time you build an index for this document.

Nested versus Run-In. There are two primary types of indexes in the world: nested and run-in (see Figure 8-20). In a nested index, each entry

Figure 8-19
Build Index dialog box

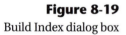

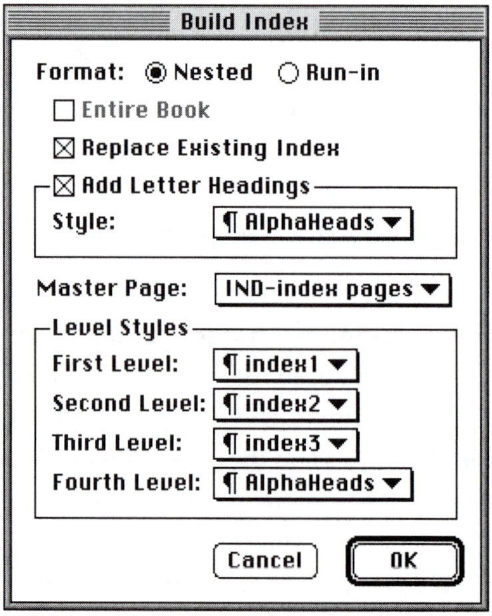

occupies its own paragraph; in a run-in index, the second-level entries merge with their first-level entry to form one big paragraph. Which you choose is entirely up to you, though it should depend in part on the content of the index. Run-in indexes make no sense when you have third- or fourth-level entries. On the other hand, run-in indexes typically conserve space better, especially when they're set in wide columns (because more than one entry fits on a single line).

The great thing about XPress's indexing is that you can build one type of index, then change your mind and replace it with the other type. Feel free to experiment!

Figure 8-20

Nested indexes versus run-in indexes

Decimal notation 18, 27
Decimal point 30
Digits of pi
    calculating 18, 34, 41, 46
    memorizing 4, 111–112, 114, 118
    number of 2, 3, 34, 45, 51–53, 65,
      67, 87–91, 113
    random sequence of 68, 72–73
    search for 42–43, 51
Dinostratos 56, 90
Dudley, Underwood 93, 96
Duciad (Pope) 92

Decimal notation 18, 27
Decimal point 30
Digits of pi; calculating 18, 34, 41, 46;
    memorizing 4, 111–112, 114, 118;
    number of 2, 3, 34, 45, 51–53, 65,
    67, 87–91, 113; random sequence of
    68, 72–73; search for 42–43, 51
Dinostratos 56, 90
Dudley, Underwood 93, 96
Duciad (Pope) 92

Entire Book. If your document is part of a book (see "Books," earlier in this chapter), you can choose to build an index for the whole *megillah* by turning on the Entire Book option in the Build Index dialog box. I discuss this process in slightly more detail in "Indexing Books," below.

Replace Existing Index. QuarkXPress knows when you've already built an index in a document, and it automatically replaces that index with a new one unless you turn off the Replace Existing Index option. Probably the only time you'd turn this off would be if you wanted to compare two indexes to find differences between them.

By the way, note that when XPress replaces one index with another, it doesn't just replace the text. It actually deletes all the index pages and then rebuilds them from scratch. So if you've spent two hours adding extra formatting to the index, or adding boxes or lines to the pages, all those additions are removed when you build the new index.

Add Letter Headings. If you want headings added to your index (like an "A" before all the entries that begin with an "A", and so on), turn on the Add Letter Headings option. When QuarkXPress builds the index, it adds the headings only as necessary (in other words, it won't add a "Q" heading if you don't have any entries that begin with that letter).

When this option is turned on, you can also choose a paragraph style sheet from the Style popup menu. This is the paragraph style that XPress uses to format the letter heading.

Master Page. When you click OK in the Build Index dialog box (don't do it yet), QuarkXPress adds new pages at the end of the current document and flows the index onto them. You can choose which master page you want the program to base the new pages on from the Master Page pop-up menu. Typically, you'll want to design a new master page specifically for the index, but you don't have to. Note that the master page you choose must have an automatic text box on it, or else XPress won't be able to flow the index onto the page.

Level Styles. The Level Styles section of the Build Index dialog box lets you apply paragraph style sheets to each entry in the index. In a run-in index, there's only one kind of paragraph: the first-level entry (all the second-level entries are merged into the same paragraph). In a nested index, however, each entry level is tagged with its own paragraph style. If you want all your second-level index entries to be slightly indented from the first-level entries (you probably do), make a new style sheet that includes indentation, and choose it from the Second Level popup menu.

Once again, designing a readable index is as much an art as a science. Take some time to peruse other people's indexes, checking for details like indentation (what does a first-level entry do when it's longer than one line, for example?) and punctuation.

If at first you don't succeed. Building an index can take a while if you have a very long document with a lot of entries, but you should plan on rebuilding it at least once. I find that there's almost always something I've forgotten or have messed up in the Index palette, Index Preferences, or the Build Index dialog box. Just go back and fix it, and then choose Build Index once again.

▼ ▼

Tip: Finessing Your Index. Just as it takes a human touch to build a great set of index entries, the index that XPress builds on your document pages requires some human intervention to become a final product. Here's a short (and certainly not exhaustive) list of fine-tuning suggestions you might consider.

▶ If you use letter headings, you might want to combine two or more of them into groups. For instance, if there are only one or two entries each under the last few headings in the index, you might want to merge them into one group and label them "X, Y, Z" or "X–Z."

▶ Most indexes require the words "See," "See also," and "See herein" to be in italic type. QuarkXPress won't apply this formatting automatically, so you have to do it yourself. I generally use the Find/Change palette to make this change throughout the index.

▶ If any index entries are found on the Pasteboard or are overset from their text boxes when you build the index, QuarkXPress warns you and then places a dagger (†) next to those references in the built index. You can (and should) search your index for this character with Find/Change, just in case. If you find one, you can either remove it or fix the problem and rebuild the index.

▶ Indexes generally follow widow and orphan rules, as body text does (see "Widow and Orphan Control" in Chapter 6, *Type and Typography*). For instance, you should probably try to keep at least one or two second-level entries with their first-level entry in a column. And a single second-level entry sitting all by its lonesome at the top of a column is a terrible sight to see. Unfortunately, these problems typically have to be fixed by hand, as XPress's Keep with Next ¶ and Keep Lines Together features aren't designed to work very well with indexes.

▶ I find that when I use an en dash between page ranges in my indexes, the character typically appears to be too close to the numbers on either side. The only good solution is to add very thin spaces or kerning around the character, and the only good way to do this is with XPress Tags (see "A Solution: XPress Tags" in Chapter 7, *Copy Flow*, for more on building complex search-and-replace strings using tags).

Of course, the most important thing you can do with an index is to proofread it carefully for spelling and style consistency.

Remember that any changes you make once your index is built are wiped out if you rebuild the index.

▼ ▼

Indexing Books

There is a major problem lurking in the Index palette that applies directly to indexing multi-document books: The Index palette currently only displays index entries from one document at a time. There is no way to display entries from an entire book. It may not seem like much, but in fact, the problem is so grave that many professional indexers simply give up and don't use XPress's indexing feature at all.

Given this limitation, you have two options when you're indexing multiple documents.

▶ You can merge all the documents, creating one enormous file, by dragging pages while you're in Thumbnails mode. If you do this, be sure to save the monster file under a different name than your original files, and keep plenty of backups—I trust big files about as far as I can throw them.

▶ You can just index your files one document at a time and hope that you can remember what you indexed in each document and how you indexed it. Going this route, it's helpful to build indexes every now and again and use printouts as a reference.

If you merge all your documents, you can build the index just the way I've described above. Or, if you are going to persist in indexing each document separately, here's what you need to do differently.

Test one chapter first. Before you go too far in indexing your book, try building an index from one chapter first. This way, you'll know if you've properly set up Index Preferences and specified the index entries.

Indexing the entire book. When you're building an index, you can tell QuarkXPress to include every document in your book by turning on the

Entire Book option in the Build Index dialog box. You have to have your book's palette open at the time you open the document to do this.

Note that XPress doesn't necessarily put the index at the end of the book. Instead, the program builds the book's index at the end of the currently open document, using the style sheets and preferences of that document. Of course, after you build a four-page index at the end of Chapter 2, XPress has to renumber every document after Chapter 2, so most of the page numbers in the index will be wrong. Therefore, it behooves you to build your index *only* at the end of the last document in your book.

▼ ▼

Tip: Indexing in a New Document. Maybe it's just my tendency to segment each and every part of a long document, but I like having my index in a file all by itself. If you want this, too, here's how you get it.

1. Create a new document with the same specifications as the other documents in your book. Make sure you've got at least one master page that has an automatic text box on it in the document, and make sure the Auto Page Insertion option is turned on in Document Preferences (Command-Y).

2. Save this new document to disk along with your other files.

3. Add the new document to your book palette with the palette's Add Chapter button. (Make sure it's the last file listed on the book palette.)

4. If you haven't already built style sheets for the index entries (and letter headings, if you're using them), then build them now in this new document. If you have built them in your master chapter, then synchronize the book so they'll be available in your index document.

5. Build the book's index in the new document by choosing Build Index and turning on the Entire Book option.

6. Because XPress always adds index pages at the end of your document, you now have to manually delete the empty first page of your document.

Voilà! Now you've got a separate document that has an index for the entire book.

▼ ▼

Putting It Together

Long documents can be a drag to produce, but the Book, Lists, and Indexing features in QuarkXPress 4 go a long way in helping make the process bearable. Whether you're building a magazine, a book, a journal, a catalog, or even a newsletter, I'm sure you'll be able to find good use for these features. Remember that a little work up front—building style sheets, putting documents in a book palette, and so on—can go a long way and can save lots of time in the long run.

Now let's shift gears radically and start looking at how pictures can liven up your XPress pages, in any size document you create.

9

PICTURES

I've been talking a lot about text and rudimentary graphic elements such as arrows and ovals, but let's not forget that ultimately, QuarkXPress is designed to integrate not only text and lines, but also graphics from other programs, and it contains many powerful features to aid in this task. QuarkXPress handles line art and images such as four-color photographs with a degree of power and set of features previously only attainable by using several programs in conjunction.

In this chapter, I'll cover almost everything you can do with pictures other than running text around them (which I cover in Chapter 11, *Where Text Meets Graphics*).

- ▶ Importing images into QuarkXPress

- ▶ Rotating picture boxes and their contents

- ▶ Precision placement of images and picture boxes

- ▶ Horizontal skewing of graphic images

- ▶ Automatic re-importing of modified pictures

▶ Working with Publish and Subscribe and OLE

▶ Picture greeking

Here are the basic steps of importing pictures into your documents.

1. Create a picture box.

2. Select the box with the Content tool, and bring in a picture by either pasting from the Clipboard (not a good idea) or using the Get Picture command.

3. Size, skew, rotate, and crop the image until you like the way it looks on the page.

But what types of pictures are available for use? And how do you get them to look the way you want? In this chapter I explore the full range of possibilities for bringing graphics in from other applications and manipulating them on the page. In Chapter 10, *Fine-Tuning Images,* I'll talk about some of the effects you can create by modifying graphics once they're in QuarkXPress.

Let's first take a close look at the different types of pictures on the Macintosh and Windows that are applicable to QuarkXPress users.

▼ ▼

Graphic File Formats

If there's a question I'm asked more often than "Why won't my file print?" it's "What's the difference between all those different graphic formats?" The question refers to a host of formats with names such as EPS, TIFF, GIF, PICT, LZW, TIFF, JPEG, Photo CD (PCD), and Windows Metafile (WMF). No one can be blamed for being confused when faced with such a list! Some of these are different names for the same thing, others are subtly different, and a few represent totally different concepts.

The fundamental question when considering a graphic file format is whether it is bitmapped or object-oriented.

Bitmapped Images

The most common file formats are based on bitmapped images. When you use a scanner and scanning software, you are generating a bitmapped image. When you use an image-editing and painting program such as Adobe Photoshop or Micrografx Picture Publisher, you're working with and generating bitmapped images. However, no matter how ubiquitous bitmapped images are, you are still strictly limited as to how you can use them.

Bitmapped images are just that: images made of mapped bits. A *bit* is a small piece of information. To begin with, let's think of it as a single dot which can be turned on or off. When you look very closely at your computer screen, you can see that the screen image is made up of thousands of these tiny bits (also called *pixels*, which stands for "picture elements"). If your monitor is set to black and white, some of these bits are turned on (black), and some are turned off (white). The *map* is the computer's internal blueprint of what the image looks like: "bit number one is on, bit number two is off," and so on (see Figure 9-1).

Bitmapped images are complicated creatures. I cover them in much more depth in the book I wrote with Glenn Fleishman and Steve Roth called *Real World Scanning and Halftones.* You might want to check that out. However, in the meantime, here's a quick rundown. There are three primary pieces of information that are relevant to any bitmapped image: its dimensions, resolution, and pixel depth.

Figure 9-1
Each pixel sits
on the grid

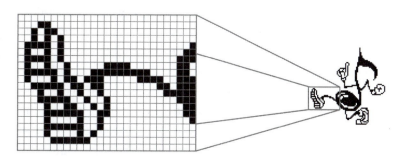

Dimensions. Every bitmapped image is rectangular and is broken down into a grid of many square pixels. Each pixel is whole and not fractured. You can describe the dimensions of the gridded area in several ways, but they are most often specified by the number of pixels or sample points per side (like 640 by 480 pixels), or by inches per side at a given resolution.

Resolution. The resolution of the bitmapped image is usually defined as the number of pixels, or sample points, per inch on the grid (of course, it's pixels per centimeter in countries using the metric system). A low-resolution bitmapped image may have 72 pixels per inch; however, this measurement is usually expressed as either dots per inch (dpi) or samples per inch (spi). A picture using only 72 dpi looks very rough. A higher-resolution bitmapped image may be 300 dpi or higher (many film scanners scan images at over 4,000 dpi). These images, when printed, are much crisper and cleaner, with fewer jaggies (see Figure 9-2).

Figure 9-2

Low resolution versus high resolution bitmapped line art

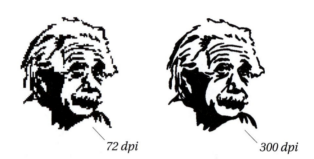

72 dpi   *300 dpi*

Pixel depth. Each pixel is defined as a specific color. The range of colors available is determined by the type of bitmapped image it is (see "File Types," below). In the simplest bitmapped images, each pixel is defined as either black or white. These are called "bilevel," or "1-bit" images, because each pixel is described by 1 bit of information, and as I mentioned above, that 1 bit can be either on (1) or off (0).

Bilevel images are *flat;* they have little depth. More complex bitmapped images are *deep* because they contain pixels that are defined by multiple bits, enabling them to describe many levels of gray or levels of color. For example, an 8-bit image can describe up to 256 colors or shades of gray for each pixel (those of us in the Northwest, having to look at gray a great deal of the time, can identify and name most of those shades). A 24-bit image can describe more than 16 million colors (see Figure 9-3).

Manipulating bitmapped images. The limitations inherent in bitmapped images become most clear when you manipulate the picture in some way, such as enlarging it significantly. The key is that the picture's resolution is directly related to its size. If you double the size of a bitmap, you cut its resolution in half; if you reduce the picture to one-quarter of its original size, you multiply its resolution by four. For example, a 72-dpi,

Figure 9-3

The number of bits determines the number of gray levels

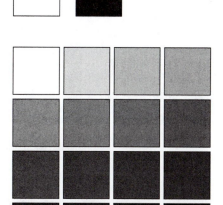

One-bit (two shades)
Either zero or one

Four-bit (16 shades)
Each pixel defined by
four bits: 0001, 0010,
0011, 0100, 0101, etc.

1-bit graphic when enlarged 200 percent becomes a twice-as-rough 36-dpi image. However, when reduced to 50 percent, it becomes a finer 144-dpi image (see Figure 9-4).

A grayscale or color image becomes *pixelated,* rather than looking more jaggy, when it's enlarged. That is, you begin to see each pixel and its tonal value (see Figure 9-5).

Object-Oriented Graphics

Instead of describing a picture dot by dot, object-oriented files specify each object in a picture on a coordinate system. A bitmapped picture could take an enormous amount of space describing one circle (this dot on, this dot off, and so on), but an object-oriented file could describe it in one line: "Draw a circle of this size with a center at x,y." The computer knows what a circle is and how to create it. Different object-oriented formats can describe different things, but most can easily specify objects such as lines, curves, and type, as well as attributes such as shading and object rotation angle.

Most object-oriented graphics can also contain bitmapped graphics as objects in their own right, though you may or may not be able to edit those bitmaps with a paint program. These files are almost always created by an application such as Macromedia FreeHand or Adobe Illustrator.

Figure 9-4
Scaling a bitmap
affects its resolution

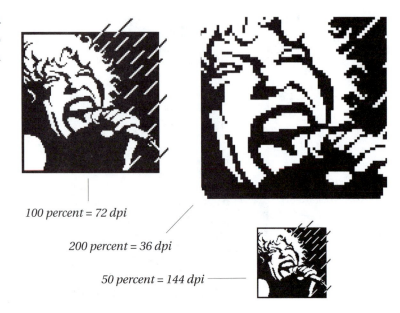

100 percent = 72 dpi

200 percent = 36 dpi

50 percent = 144 dpi

Figure 9-5
Pixelization from
enlarging a
grayscale image

*72 dpi, four-bit
grayscale TIFF
at 100 percent*

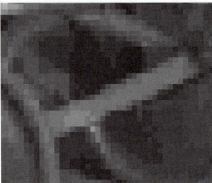

*72 dpi, four-bit
grayscale TIFF
at 400 percent*

The magic of object-oriented graphics is that you can stretch them, rotate them, twist them into pastry, and print them on various-resolution printers without worrying about how smoothly the lines will print.

That is, when you print on a 300-dpi, plain-paper laser printer, you get a full 300 dpi; when you print to film with a 2,540-dpi imagesetter, you get beautifully smooth lines at 2,540 dots per inch. There is no inherent limit of information for the picture, as there is with bitmaps (see Figure 9-6). Theoretically, there is no inherent limit to the number of gray levels in an object-oriented picture. Realistically, however, each format has upper limits.

Figure 9-6

Object-oriented graphics versus bitmapped images

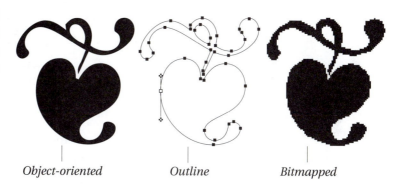

Object-oriented   *Outline*   *Bitmapped*

File Types

When I talk about *file types* in this book, I'm talking about two things: how the information is formatted within the file, and how the file is saved to disk. The common usage of the term—such as in "an Illustrator file" or "a QuarkXPress file"—refers to the way in which the information is formatted. Then there is the way the Macintosh and Windows operating systems name files when they save them to disk.

The Macintosh gives every file an actual, technical, four-letter file type. For instance, files generally referred to as "QuarkXPress files" are type XDOC; Illustrator files are either EPSF or TEXT. These file types are hidden from the user, but you can examine a file's type using a utility such as File Buddy (see Figure 9-7) or Apple's ResEdit. For the sake of simplicity, I use the terms *file type* and *file format* interchangeably.

Windows, on the other hand, requires a particular three-letter file-name extension that indicates the file type. For example, an XPress document on Windows always has ".qxd" appended to its name, and TIFF image files always have .tif extensions.

QuarkXPress writes its files to disk the same way on both Macintosh and Windows. TIFF files are also interchangeable from Mac to Windows. However, if you move a file from Mac to Windows without giving it the

Figure 9-7
File Buddy

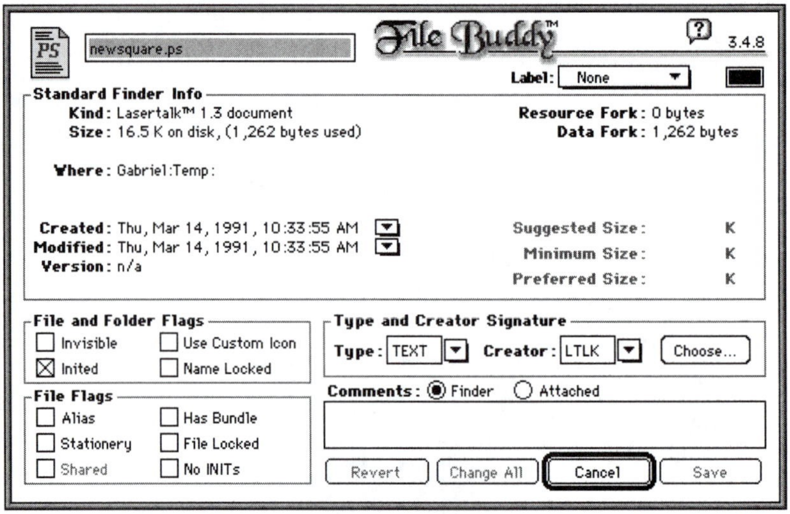

proper file-name extension, XPress may not be able to open it, or it may open incorrectly. Similarly, if you move a file from Windows to Macintosh without using some utility to assign the correct four-letter file type, the same thing can happen.

File types XPress understands. QuarkXPress can only import certain graphic file formats, and the formats it understands are different on the two platforms (see Table 9-1). However, no matter what type of machine you've got, I strongly suggest that you use either EPS, TIFF, or DCS images for the bulk of your work (see "Tip: The Best Format to Use," at the end of this section). As I describe each of the following file types, you'll see that most of the other formats are just too unstable or limited.

Paint. The Paint format is ultimately the most basic of all graphic file formats on the Macintosh. When the Mac first shipped in 1984, it came with two programs: MacWrite and MacPaint. The latter was a very basic painting program that let you paint bitmapped images, cutting and pasting them into MacWrite files or saving them as Paint-format (PNTG) files.

Paint files are black and white (1 bit), 72 dots per inch, 8 by 10 inches (576 by 720 dots). That's it. No more and no less. Even text is handled like bitmapped graphics: the only way to edit it is to edit the pixels that make it up. Clearly, this format has some stringent limitations which restrict the usefulness of the images. TIFF is a better choice for bitmapped images.

Table 9-1

QuarkXPress's graphic
file format support

FILE TYPE	EXTENSION
CompuServe gif*	.gif
Encapsulated PostScript	.eps
JPEG	.jpg
MacPaint†	n/a
Macintosh PICT	.pct
Paintbrush	.pcx
Photo CD	.pcd
Scitex CT	.ct
Tagged Image File Format (TIFF)	.tif
Windows Bitmap*	.bmp, .dib, .rle
Windows Metafile	.wmf

* QuarkXPress for Windows only   *† QuarkXPress for Macintosh only*

TIFF. The Tagged Image File Format (TIFF) is another form of bitmap with significantly more support for high-quality images. First off, a TIFF file can be created at any size and resolution, and include black-and-white, grayscale, or color information. Because of the flexibility of TIFF files, all scanning and image-editing programs such as DeskScan, Photoshop, and Picture Publisher can save and open the TIFF format.

As it turns out, there are several different TIFF formats, including compressed and uncompressed, Macintosh versus Windows, and TIFF-6. Fortunately, QuarkXPress imports most TIFF formats, including those written for either Mac or Windows, and even LZW-compressed TIFF files (though in XPress 4 you have to have the LZW Import XTension loaded to read these files).

PICT. The PICT format, also a part of the original Mac system, can contain drawings that are object-oriented or that consist of a single bitmap ("bitmap-only PICT"). Unlike most programs, QuarkXPress can "see" when a PICT file is bitmap-only, and lets you manipulate it as such (you'll see later in this chapter that you can manipulate bitmapped images differently than object-oriented ones). PICT images can be any size, resolution, and color (like TIFFs or EPS files).

While PICT does sound quite useful, I don't like it for four reasons.

▶ The object-oriented PICT format is unreliable. For example, line widths can change when you move a picture from one program to another, and text spacing can change, sometimes drastically. Also, printing to imagesetters (1,200+ dpi) can be troublesome. Remember that when you print a PICT to a PostScript imagesetter, the computer has to convert from one object-oriented language to another. I trust these conversions about as far as I can throw them.

▶ Bitmap-only PICT images are RGB-only; you cannot preseparate them into CMYK (I'll talk about color separation in some depth in Chapter 12, *Color*). Fortunately, XPress 4 can now separate the RGB PICTs if you need to do this. Personally, I'd rather stick to TIFF images.

▶ PICT images are always fully embedded in your XPress document. That means if you import a 20 MB PICT image into a picture box, your XPress document gets 20 MB bigger. Add one or two more of these and you've got a file that is unmanageable and possibly unstable as well. I avoid embedding images like the plague (with one exception: when the image is really small).

▶ Last, XPress relies on the operating system, which is pretty slow, to display PICTs properly. The larger the image, the slower the display. Anything over a megabyte is painful.

Nonetheless, PICT is the primary format for printing from the Macintosh to non-PostScript devices, so if you're doing low-end printing with small object-oriented images you might consider using this format. For the sake of completeness, I should note that it is possible to import PICT images into XPress for Windows.

Encapsulated PostScript. Encapsulated PostScript (EPS) format is the most reliable format for putting images on paper or film, as long as your printer or imaging device can understand PostScript. PostScript is an object-oriented page-description language, though PostScript files may contain bitmaps as well. Although it has built-in font-handling features, it ultimately treats type as a graphic made of lines and curves. This makes working with fonts in a PostScript environment a joy, with many possibilities. It's easy to create a PostScript file, but to print it out you must have a PostScript-compatible printer (with non-PostScript printers, XPress just prints the low-resolution screen preview of the EPS graphic).

EPS images come in two basic varieties: EPS without a preview, and EPS with a preview. The preview-enclosed feature in most EPS files allows you to bring such a file into QuarkXPress and see a low-resolution representation of the image on the screen. When the file is printed to a PostScript printer, however, the bitmap is ignored and the underlying PostScript is used. If a preview image is not available, then you see a big gray box on the screen which may contain some basic information (such as the file's name).

On the Mac, the EPS preview may be saved as either a PICT or a TIFF. There's no trouble with using PICT previews, and if the graphic will stay on the Macintosh platform, PICT previews are probably preferable. However, if the file may at some point find its way to a Windows machine, a TIFF preview is the way to go (when you make an EPS on a Windows PC, you have to use TIFF). (The reason for this is somewhat technical: PICT previews are stored in a file's resource fork, which is stripped away when the file is moved to a PC; TIFF previews are stored in the data fork, which can survive in a Windows environment.)

Even though EPS files are robust and reliable, I don't use them as often as TIFF images when it comes to bitmapped graphics (see "Tip: The Best Format to Use").

▼ ▼

Tip: Great-Looking EPS Previews. Photoshop on the Macintosh lets you save EPS files with a JPEG preview. While I don't ordinarily use JPEG images (see "JPEG," below), I do like the JPEG preview option because it provides a much nicer on-screen representation of the image than the normal 8-bit color preview that Photoshop builds into EPS files. JPEG previews are actually high-quality compressed PICT previews, so they don't work on the PC. On the other hand, the big drawback to JPEG previews is display speed: EPS files with JPEG preview may display more slowly. Nonetheless, if your client is staring over your shoulder, you might get some benefit from a good-looking screen image in XPress.

▼ ▼

DCS. I'll talk about Desktop Color Separation (DCS) in Chapter 12, *Color*, but let's quickly go over it here. The DCS method is based on preseparating color images into five separate EPS files (which is why DCS is sometimes called "EPS-5" or "five-file EPS"). Four of the files contain high-resolution information for each of the process colors (cyan, magenta, yellow, and black). The fifth file contains a low-resolution composite image (for proofing), a screen representation of the picture, and pointers to the four higher-resolution files. This fifth file is the one that gets imported into QuarkXPress.

When you print your file, QuarkXPress replaces this representation file (sometimes called the "master file") with the four high-resolution files. This means that you can print the high-resolution separations directly from QuarkXPress to an imagesetter.

Some programs (including XPress) support the DCS 2.0 file format, which is basically a revised version of the DCS specification. In DCS 2.0 images, the four process plates and the preview "master" image can all be rolled into one big file. More important, DCS 2.0 lets you include spot-color plates, varnish plates—as many plates as you want. This means that you can create an image in Photoshop that includes spot colors, export it as a DCS 2.0 file, and separate the whole thing in QuarkXPress. (The one problem with this workflow is that Photoshop 4 doesn't let you save in the DCS 2.0 format, so you have to use a plug-in such as PlateMaker—from a lowly apprentice production.)

QuarkXPress not only understands DCS and DCS 2.0 documents, it can also create them when you save a page as EPS (see "Page as Picture," later in this chapter).

Windows Bitmap. Windows Bitmap (.BMP) is the bitmap format native to Windows Paint, but isn't usually encountered outside of Windows and OS/2 Presentation Manager. You can, however, bring .BMP files to the Macintosh and use them in QuarkXPress. I just don't think you should; I still prefer TIFF to this format.

Windows Metafile. Closely tied to graphics technology underlying Windows, Windows Metafile (.WMF) is a relatively reliable object-oriented format to use in Windows. However, when you take it out of that environment and onto the Macintosh, things get a little weird. Fonts that are embedded in the graphic really get messed up, and colors can get screwy, too. I suggest leaving this at home on the PC. Even better: use EPS for object-oriented graphics.

Scitex CT and LW files. QuarkXPress can import both Scitex CT (continuous-tone) and LW (line-work) files. However, it can only separate CT files. Note that when I say "CT files," I am actually referring to CT HandShake files. I know one guy who got burned because he asked a color house for CT files and got Scitex's proprietary format instead of the open-format CT HandShake files.

Photo CD. If you have the Photo CD XTension loaded, you'll be able to use the Get Picture dialog box to open images saved in Kodak's Photo CD format. I think Photo CD is really cool, but I can't recommend acquiring images this way. Instead, it's much better to open them in Photoshop first. Then you can adjust levels, do color correction—Photo CD images are typically oversaturated, because they're designed to be shown on a television—sharpen, and save the images as TIFF or EPS at an appropriate resolution (see my book, *Real World Photoshop*, for more on all these subjects). I tend to turn this XTension off in the XTension manager and forget about it.

JPEG. JPEG is a bitmapped file format with built-in compression, so that these images can be a tenth of the size (or smaller) of a non-compressed image. However, the compression in JPEG is *lossy*, which means the more it's compressed, the worse the image looks. When you have the JPEG filter (it comes with XPress) in your QuarkXPress XTension folder, you can import images that were saved in the JPEG format.

Once you've imported the picture into QuarkXPress, the program decompresses it every time you print it (which can take a while) and sends it to the printer as though it were a TIFF image. Therefore, the only really good reason to use JPEG images instead of TIFFs is if you're scraping for hard drive space.

Note that a JPEG file is different from a JPEG EPS file or an EPS file with a JPEG preview (see "Tip: Great-Looking EPS Previews," earlier). JPEG EPS files are EPS files saved with JPEG encoding (this is an option in Photoshop). In theory, these should print correctly on PostScript Level 2 printers because the printer itself decompresses the file. In reality, they don't separate, so color images only appear on the black plate. JPEG DCS files (DCS files with JPEG encoding) do separate properly, however.

PCX. PCX is the granddaddy of bitmapped formats, and the current version supports 24-bit and 256-color palettes. Since a variety of color-model techniques have been applied to PCX over the ages, files from earlier programs can have some serious color-mismatch problems. If you absolutely need to use PCX images, then go for it. If not, see if your source can provide files in TIFF, which is an all-around better format. To make QuarkXPress open PCX files, you have to have the PCX filter in the XTension folder within the QuarkXPress folder.

GIF. The Graphics Interchange Format (commonly known as GIF, pronounced either "jiff" or "giff") is now the industry standard for graphics on the World Wide Web. GIF files are designed for on-screen viewing, especially for images where file size is more important than quality, and for screens that only display 8-bit color (256 colors). Photoshop GIFs are always 8-bit indexed-color images, making them reasonable for on-screen viewing, but certainly not for printing. Currently, only XPress for Windows can import GIF files, though unless you're using an XTension to export HTML from your XPress documents, you shouldn't bother.

▼ ▼

Tip: The Best Format to Use. I rarely use a file format other than EPS, DCS, or TIFF for graphics. However, even with these three formats there are good reasons to choose one over the other, depending on the image and what you're using it for. Some people think that EPS is inherently better than TIFF, or vice versa. Not so. You shouldn't choose one over the other because your service bureau or printer told you to; they often don't know any more about file formats than you do (they just think they do).

Here are a few of the many considerations you need to keep in mind when choosing a file format. (Special thanks to my friend and colleague Steve Roth, who researched these while working on an article for *Macworld* magazine.)

- ▶ **FILE SIZE.** Uncompressed TIFF files are about 20 percent smaller than EPS files. Plus, EPS files contain a preview, which can add even more to the file's size depending on its type and dimension.

- ▶ **PAGE PREVIEWS.** QuarkXPress creates a low-resolution screen preview when you import a TIFF image, which takes some time (the larger the image and the slower your computer, the more time it takes). EPS files, however, import very quickly because XPress simply grabs their built-in preview. The quality of a TIFF preview depends on how you set the Color TIFF preview option in the Application Preferences dialog box. The 32-bit setting provides a great preview, but your document's file size increases significantly, so I usually avoid it. The quality of an EPS preview is totally up to the software that creates it (see "Tip: Great-Looking EPS Previews," above). In general, the Photoshop-built preview in a CMYK EPS file is going to look better than the XPress-built preview in a CMYK TIFF image (unless you're using XPress's color management software correctly).

▶ **IMAGE CONTROL.** In general, TIFF files are very flexible. If you import a grayscale TIFF image, you can apply a color to it, shade it, or even apply a custom halftone screen to it. Color TIFFs are only a little less flexible (you can't apply halftone screens to them). EPS files, on the other hand, are cast in stone (that's why they call them "encapsulated"). To make a change to an EPS file, you have to do it in some other program.

▶ **DUOTONES.** If you want to make a duotone in Photoshop, you must save it as an EPS file. Period.

▶ **CROPPING.** What happens if you import a 20 MB bitmapped image and crop it down to a little tiny square on your XPress page? If the file is saved in TIFF format, XPress only sends the necessary image data to the printer, which can speed up printing a lot. If it's an EPS file, however, XPress must send the entire 20 MB to the printer every time you print.

▶ **DOWNSAMPLING.** Proofing a 300-dpi bitmapped image on a desktop laser printer can take a long time if the image is saved as an EPS, because XPress sends all the image data to the printer every time you print. But the program can downsample TIFF files; in fact, XPress automatically downsamples the resolution of TIFF files to two times the current halftone screen frequency (lpi). So when you're printing a 60-lpi file on your laser printer, it reduces your high-resolution images to 120 dpi, saving a lot of time.

The same thing goes for reducing the size of your image. Remember, if you scale that 300-dpi bitmapped image to 50 percent, it is now effectively a 600-dpi image—way more than you need. XPress downsamples this, too. Of course, it's usually better to do your own downsampling in an image-editing program before you import the file into XPress.

▶ **CLIPPING PATHS.** Earlier versions of QuarkXPress couldn't read embedded clipping paths in TIFF files, so you had to use EPS files. No longer. In fact, XPress can even read multiple paths in TIFF files (see "Clipping Paths" in Chapter 10, *Fine-Tuning Images*).

▶ **COMPRESSION.** You can compress TIFF images with LZW (non-lossy) compression. This type of compression works best on areas of flat color, and worst on images that have a lot of tiny details. Your only option for compression in EPS files is JPEG, which renders CMYK files mostly useless (QuarkXPress can't separate JPEG-compressed EPS files).

▶ **COLOR MANAGEMENT.** Because XPress can control the data in a TIFF file, it can color-manage the images (see Appendix A, *Color Management*). EPS files, however, are hopeless when it comes to color management because XPress can't really change any color values in them. This goes for separating RGB images into CMYK, too (TIFF images, no problem; EPS images, big problem).

▶ **CMYK SEPARATIONS.** When XPress prints color separations (see Chapter 12, *Color*), it has to send down the entire EPS file (the cyan, magenta, yellow, and black plates) each time it prints a plate. That means if you have a 20 MB EPS file, XPress sends 80 megabytes of information to the printer (20 MB per plate). That takes a long time. However, XPress treats CMYK EPS files from Photoshop differently. With these files, it's smart enough to pull them apart and only send the cyan data with the cyan plate, the magenta data with the magenta plate, and so on. This is much (much!) faster.

TIFF files can also be pulled apart at print time. (I guess that means this isn't such a big difference between TIFF and EPS after all, as long as you're using Photoshop.)

▶ **POSTSCRIPT GENERATION.** XPress can often print your XPress document (either to disk or to a printer) much faster if you use EPS files because the image data is just sitting there ready to be saved (or sent to the printer) as PostScript. TIFF files require more processing (downsampling, color management, and so on), so they can take longer to print, especially on slower computers.

All told, I tend to use TIFF images whenever I can because of their flexibility. Nonetheless, some jobs, like duotone images or those that require a special halftone screen, require EPS files. Also, occasionally I'll run into some high-end imagesetter that requires images to be in EPS format.

▼▼▼▼▼▼▼▼▼▼▼▼▼▼▼▼▼▼▼▼▼▼▼▼▼▼▼▼▼▼▼▼▼▼▼▼▼▼

Importing Pictures into QuarkXPress

Now that we know the types of pictures we'll be dealing with, let's look at how we'll deal with them. As I mentioned, the first step in importing a graphic from another application is to create a picture box within your QuarkXPress document. This is covered in Chapter 3, *Tools of the Trade*, in the discussion of rectangles, ovals, and polygons. When you have an empty picture box on your page, you can see an "X" in the middle of it. At this point you're ready to bring a picture into the box.

Note that I'm bringing a picture *into* the box, rather than replacing the box or even "merging" the two together. The picture box is one entity and the picture is another. You might think of the box as being a window frame through which you see the picture. You can manipulate the picture box, or the picture, or both.

The two primary ways to bring a picture in are to paste from the Clipboard or use Get Picture. In order for either of these methods to work, you must have the picture box selected. (In earlier versions of XPress you had to use the Content tool; now you can use either the Content tool or the Item tool.)

Pasting Pictures

There are at least four problems with pasting in pictures (selecting Paste from the Edit menu, or pressing Command-V) rather than using Get Picture, each one of which alone would be enough to convince me not to paste pictures into picture boxes in XPress.

▶ Because the image is pasted in, there is no accompanying disk file for it; if you want to edit the image, you have to copy it, paste it into a program that can edit it, make changes, copy it again, and paste it back into the picture box. If you've cropped or rotated the picture in XPress, all that information is lost when you re-paste it.

▶ The file format for an image typically changes when you move it from one application to another. For instance, if you use Copy and Paste on a Macintosh to move a picture from Photoshop to XPress, the image is converted to the PICT format. PICT images don't understand CMYK, so CMYK files are translated into RGB on the fly. On Windows, images are sometimes translated to WMF files. Whatever the case, these switches make me very nervous.

▶ XPress may not understand the file format for images that are on the Clipboard. For instance, you can copy a graphic from Adobe Illustrator, but XPress won't let you paste it into a picture box.

▶ If you paste in a big picture, your QuarkXPress document balloons in size because the document has to embed the entire image. With Get Picture, just a low-resolution image is imported with a pointer to the full file on disk (see "Picture Management," later in this chapter).

(I used to mention a fifth problem: that color images pasted into picture boxes could not be separated into CMYK. It's of dubious value to note that XPress 4 can now separate these images, even when the color management XTension is turned off.)

Again, I recommend that you avoid the Clipboard approach to importing pictures (at least don't use it often, and certainly not for big important jobs).

Get Picture

With your picture box created, and either the Item tool or the Content tool selected, you can select Get Picture from the File menu (or act like the pros, and press Command-E). A directory dialog box appears, allowing you to find the file you wish to import. When a file of a type that QuarkXPress recognizes is selected (see "File Types," above), the file's type and size are displayed.

You also have the option to turn on the Picture Preview checkbox, which lets you see a thumbnail view of most image files. This feature is, of course, a great help in finding a particular picture when you're not sure of the file's name. However, it does slow down the process, especially for files with complicated images, such as large color PICT or TIFF files. Similarly, if you're accessing images over a network it gets really, really slow. Clearly, judicious use of Picture Preview can save you time.

Once the file is selected in the dialog box, click the Open button or just double-click on the file's name, and the image appears in your picture frame. Some images import more slowly than others; when an image takes a while to import, QuarkXPress shows you its progress in the lower-left corner of the window. If you're importing a 50 MB file on your old Mac IIsi, you can see how quickly (slowly) it is processing (perhaps this is the best time of the day to make an espresso).

▼ ▼

Tip: Grab That Pencil. You will undoubtedly find yourself in a situation at some point where you want to manually re-import a picture or import a new picture into an already used picture box. Problem: you lose the specifications for the original picture box (scaling, offset, rotation, and so on)! This is a case where you can use the most technologically advanced tools available to humankind, but all you really need is a simple notepad and a pencil. Just jot down all the specs for the previous picture (nice of QuarkXPress to show them to you in the Measurements palette), then after you bring in the new picture, retype the original specs (remember, if you want to make multiple changes to the picture box, it's usually quicker to make them all at once in the Modify dialog box).

It's also worth noting that the PictAttributes XTension can retain all your specs when you're importing an image into a previously formatted picture box (see Appendix C, *XTensions and Resources*).

▼ ▼

Tip: Drag-and-Drop Pictures. QuarkXPress for Windows lets you drag pictures into picture boxes from the Windows desktop or Explorer, as long as the picture box is already made. On the other hand, Extensis has come out with a Macintosh-only XTension called QX-Drag-n-Drop that lets you drag pictures from the Finder into QuarkXPress. The best part of this XTension is that you don't have to build a picture box first—when you drag the image in, the XTension builds a picture box for you and then imports the picture into it. I find this very useful when I need to import a lot of pictures in succession, especially when I'm working on a large monitor. (Drag-and-drop is less exciting on a small screen because there's never enough room to see both the document and the Finder at the same time.)

As this book goes to press, I'm working closely with an XTension programmer to develop one more way to import graphics: a Place comment, *à la* Adobe PageMaker. If we're successful, look for this free tool on The QuarkXPress Book Web Site (*www.peachpit.com/blatner/*).

▼ ▼

What Happened to My Picture?

When you import a picture, you may not see exactly what you were expecting or wanting in the picture box. It may be that you see only a gray box with some type, or that the image is misplaced, or even that you can't see it at all. If something unexpected happens, remember the First Rule of Computer Anomaly: Don't Panic.

Can't see the picture at all. The first thing to check for is whether or not the big "X" is still in the picture box; if it is, then Get Picture didn't work. Maybe you accidentally clicked Cancel instead of OK. (Don't laugh; this often happens around the same time you get what my friend Greg calls "pixel vision"—eyes that are glazed from looking at the screen too long.) If this happens, just try again.

If what you see is just a blank frame, then check to see if the guides are hidden (select Show Guides from the View menu). If the guides are on and you still don't see the "X," then the picture is probably somewhere in the box but you can't see it yet. The Get Picture feature automatically places the image in the upper-left corner of the bounding box of the frame. Note that I say the "bounding box" and not the box itself. The bounding box is the smallest rectangle that completely surrounds the frame. It's what you see when you are looking at your box with the Edit Shape option turned off (see Figure 9-8). If you have an oval or a polygonal box and the image is rather small, then you may have to move the object into the frame (see "Moving Your Pictures Around," later in this chapter).

Often, if you center the image in the box you'll be able to see it better (see "Centering," in the next section).

There's no picture—just a gray box. If the image you import is an EPS file with no preview image attached for screen representation, then QuarkXPress represents the image as a gray box with the note "PostScript Picture" and the name of the file directly in the center of the gray box.

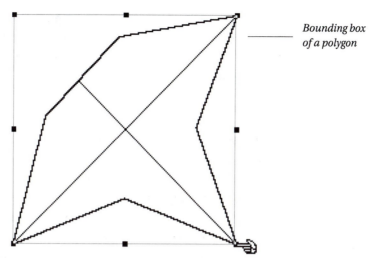

Figure 9-8
Polygons have
rectangular
bounding boxes

*Bounding box
of a polygon*

This gray box shows the bounding box of the image, as defined in the header of the EPS document.

Another cause of the gray-box effect could be that you're looking at a complex picture from too far back. When you look at the page in Fit in Window view, it looks like a muddied gray box, but when you go to Actual Size, it looks like what you were hoping for.

The third cause of the gray-box effect might be that the picture you import is, in fact, a gray box. In this case, I can only suggest you think carefully about whether or not you really consider a gray box an exciting enough graphic for your publication.

▼ ▼

Working with Pictures

Now that you have brought something (which may or may not look like the graphic you wanted) into the picture box, you can manipulate it in more ways than you ever thought you could, and certainly in more ways than you could in any other page-layout program.

Moving Your Picture Around

In Chapter 2, *QuarkXPress Basics*, you learned about moving your picture and text boxes around on the page. You can also move the picture itself around within the picture box. You may want to do this for two reasons: for picture placement, and for cropping out a portion of the image.

In this section I discuss several methods for moving your image within (or even outside of) the box. Remember that the picture and the picture box are two different entities, and you can move and manipulate them using different tools: the content (picture) with the Content tool, and the box itself with the Item tool.

Centering. Often the first thing you'll want to do with a picture, whether or not you can see it on screen, is to center it within the picture box. Designers and computer hackers alike have muddled through various tricks to center graphics perfectly within boxes, with varying degrees of success. I suggest you just press Command-Shift-M and let QuarkXPress do it for you. QuarkXPress centers the picture based on its bounding box (its lower-left and upper-right corners). Therefore, pictures which are oddly shaped (for example, an L-shaped picture) may not be centered as you'd expect them to be.

Moving the picture. If you want the image to be somewhere other than in the upper-left corner or in the center, you can use the Content tool (which switches to a Grabber hand when it's placed over the picture box) to move the picture around. Anyone who has ever done this can tell you that if the image is a large one, it can take quite some time for the picture to respond to your hand movements. If you're thinking about zooming in for precision alignment, remember that what you're really looking at is only a low-resolution (36- or 72-dpi) rendition of the real picture. This means that you can't truly be precise, no matter what you do. Other than buying an XTension (see "Enhance PreviewXT" in Appendix C, *XTensions and Resources*), the only good solution is to print out proof sheets.

If you know how far you want to move the picture, you can type the offset values in either the Measurements palette or in the Modify dialog box (press Command-M, or Command-double-click on the picture). This method is a real godsend when precision is the key, but again, you can't always trust what you see on the screen. For instance, an EPS image might look like it's at the edge of the picture box, but in reality that could just be an artifact of its screen preview.

▼ ▼

Tip: Minimoves. When you have the Content tool selected and have selected a picture box, you can "nudge" the picture within the box in tiny increments by clicking the arrows on the Measurements palette. Each click moves the image 1 point in the direction of the arrow. Hold down Option while you click to move the picture in .1-point increments.

However, I typically find it even more useful to use the arrow keys on the keyboard. Again, each time you press a key, the picture moves 1 point; each time you press the key with Option held down, the picture moves .1 point.

Note that if you have the Item tool selected when you do this, you actually move the picture box itself.

▼ ▼

Cropping

If you only want a portion of the whole picture to be visible, then you can "cut out" the unwanted areas by cropping or clipping. Cropping is the way you change the size or shape of the picture box (see Figure 9-9); clipping is how you apply a clipping path (I discuss XPress 4's new Clipping feature in Chapter 10, *Fine-Tuning Images*). Behind the scenes, both cropping and clipping are the same thing, but because XPress treats them separately, I will too.

A warning about cropping: there are people who crop out 90 percent of an image so they can use just one flower in a bouquet! Then they duplicate that image 12 times on the page and wonder why their file doesn't print. (Don't laugh too loudly; I've seen highly paid professionals do this!)

Figure 9-9
The edge of the picture
box crops the picture

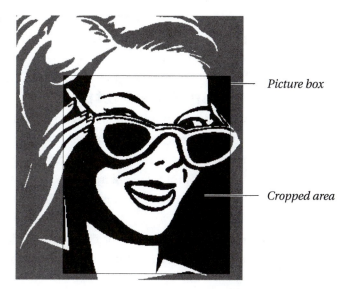

Picture box

Cropped area

Fortunately, when you use TIFF and JPEG images, XPress is smart enough to send only the data it needs at print time, so the cropped-out information doesn't clog up your network and your printing times are faster. QuarkXPress cannot do this with EPS images, so the whole file must be sent at print time, along with an instruction to the printer about what gets cropped and what doesn't.

No matter what file format you use, the program must save a preview image (the screen representation) for the entire graphic with the document, no matter how much you crop it. This way, you can always go back and change your cropping or picture specifications.

So remember to use cropping judiciously. If you only want a small portion of the file, then use an editing program to cut out what you don't want before you import the image.

▼ ▼

Tip: Shapely Cropping. You don't have to restrict your cropping to rectangular boxes, of course. Feel free to use the Shapes submenu (under the Item menu) to change the shape of the picture box in order to crop out unwanted parts of your picture.

▼ ▼

Tip: Cropping Multiple Pictures. As I mentioned back in Chapter 2, *QuarkXPress Basics*, you can crop several picture boxes at the same time by grouping them and either dragging the group's corner or side handles, or specifying a value in the Measurements palette. Either way, you must have the Item tool selected. For instance, if you know that you want every box to be half as wide as it is currently, you can select the boxes, group them, and then type "*.5" after the current width value in the Measurements palette.

▼ ▼

Resizing Your Picture

After placing the graphic image where you want it, you may want to scale it to some desired size. QuarkXPress allows you to resize the image within the picture box in the horizontal and/or vertical directions. Most often I find myself wanting to enlarge or reduce the picture the same amount in both directions in order to best fit the available space.

Keystrokes. If the picture box you create is just the size you want your picture to be, you can quickly and automatically resize the picture to fit the box by pressing Command-Shift-F. However, because this usually stretches the picture disproportionately (adjusting the horizontal- and vertical-sizing measures differently in order to fill the box), you probably want to press Command-Shift-Option-F (that's a handful!), which makes the picture as large as it can be within the box without distorting it. Note that if you've rotated or skewed the picture first (see "Rotating, Skewing, and Distorting" below), auto-resizing may not work exactly as you'd expect it to.

If you're not a keystroke kind of person, you can type the particular percentages you want into the Measurements palette or into the picture box's Modify dialog box (Command-M). Of course, you can use a combination of these two methods, too.

Dragging. Usually resizing the picture box has no effect on the image which is in it, other than possibly cropping out areas of the picture. However, if you hold down the Command key while you resize (clicking and dragging on one of the control handles), the image changes size along with the box (see Figure 9-10). As usual, holding down the Shift key constrains the picture box (and the image) to a square or circle; holding down the Option key along with the Command and Shift keys constrains the picture box (and the image) to their proper proportions.

▼ ▼

Tip: Watch 'Em Change. Back in Chapter 2, *QuarkXPress Basics*, I told you about how to watch the changes as you make them (see "Tip: Viewing Changes as You Make Them"). In case you don't remember, the important thing is to hold down the mouse button for about half a second (until you see the cursor change to the flashy Live Refresh cursor). Then when you scale or crop the image by dragging, you can actually see

Figure 9-10
Resizing a picture
by dragging the picture
box handles

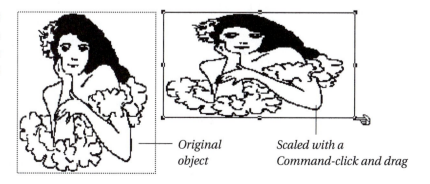

Original
object

Scaled with a
Command-click and drag

the image get scaled or cropped (otherwise, QuarkXPress just shows you a gray outline box).

▼ ▼

Tip: Scaling Groups of Objects. People have been clamoring to scale groups of objects for years, and now (in XPress 4) you can (sort of). To scale several objects at the same time, group them (Command-G) and then Command-Option-Shift-drag on one of the group's control handles. Unfortunately, there are several drawbacks to this method.

▶ You can't currently undo scaling a group.

▶ You can't scale the group to a specific percentage or size; you can only scale it interactively by dragging.

▶ XPress forgets to scale some elements, such as text rules and runaround values.

Until the folks at Quark get their act in gear and implement a real scaling tool, I can only suggest one of the inexpensive third-party scaling XTensions like those in XPert Tools, QX-Tools, or ResizeXT.

▼ ▼

Rotating, Skewing, and Distorting

Sure, you can crop and resize, but—as they say on television—that's not all! With this amazing program you get a set of free Japanese cutlery! And 32 ounces of French perfume! And . . . well, maybe not, but you do get to rotate and skew pictures, and that's not bad.

Rotation. QuarkXPress lets you easily rotate your imported pictures to a degree unheard of (and certainly rarely needed): $1/1{,}000$ of a degree. Once again, you are able to set the rotation of the image in several ways.

The first question you'll want to ask yourself is whether you want to rotate the frame, and the image along with it, or just rotate the image itself. You can do either of these things by typing the rotation angle in the appropriate place on the Measurements palette or in the Modify dialog box (see Figure 9-11).

While it's really great that you can rotate images in QuarkXPress, you should be careful with this power. When you use XPress to rotate large bitmapped images, your files can slow to a crawl when they print. Instead, try to rotate these images in Photoshop (or another image-

Figure 9-11

The Modify
dialog box and the
Measurements palette

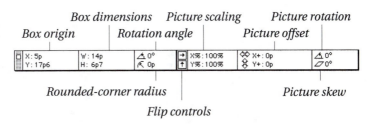

manipulation program) first, and then import them (prerotated) into your picture boxes. This typically isn't a problem with illustrations from FreeHand or Illustrator, because they aren't usually bitmapped.

▼ ▼

Tip: Rotating Your Picture Boxes. Rotating the frame rotates the image, too! The quickest way to "straighten out" your image is to rotate it back by the same amount. That is, if you rotate your box 28 degrees but you want the picture to be straight, then rotate the image -28 degrees.

▼ ▼

Skewing. Technically, skewing is the process of rotating the two axes differently, or rotating one and not the other. That is, if you rotate just the y-axis (the vertical axis) of the coordinate system to the right, everything you print out is "obliqued" (see Figure 9-12). QuarkXPress only allows you to skew in the horizontal direction (rotating the y-axis), which is not a hindrance since vertical skewing (or "shearing," as it is often called) is rarely required. Actually, horizontal skewing is rarely required, either, but

Figure 9-12
Skewing rotates
the vertical axis

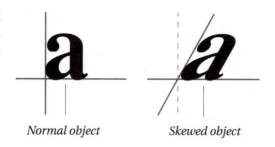

Normal object   *Skewed object*

it can be useful in certain situations, especially when you want to create interesting effects.

You usually use only one of these effects at a time, perhaps in conjunction with scaling (resizing), but using all three together can make a graphic look quite unusual (see Figure 9-13).

Figure 9-13
Using all of the tools

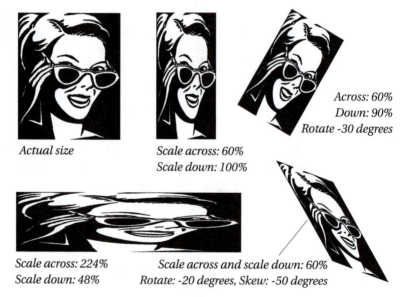

Actual size

Scale across: 60%
Scale down: 100%

Across: 60%
Down: 90%
Rotate -30 degrees

Scale across: 224%
Scale down: 48%

Scale across and scale down: 60%
Rotate: -20 degrees, Skew: -50 degrees

One of the great advantages of these features is that they're not incremental. In FreeHand and Illustrator, rotation is cumulative. If you rotate something to 60 degrees and later want to rotate it to 55 degrees, you have to enter "-5 degrees". QuarkXPress, on the other hand, keeps track of the current rotation, so you just enter the actual rotation you want. This makes it incredibly easy to get back to where you started with an image when you've distorted it beyond recognition: just reset the scaling to 100 percent, and the rotation and skewing to zero degrees (if you really want to reset everything about a picture, try re-importing it).

▼ ▼

Tip: Faking Perspective. To make a picture look like it's lying on a flat surface, change the picture rotation to -15 degrees, the picture skew to 45 degrees, and the vertical scaling to 70 percent (see Figure 9-14).

Figure 9-14
Pseudo-perspective

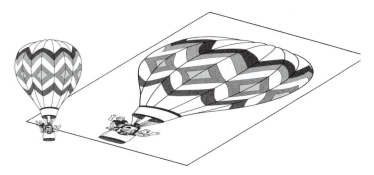

▼ ▼

Tip: Making Multiple Changes to Your Picture. If you know you are going to make multiple changes to your graphic image—changing the skewing, rotation, scaling, and offset, for example—you can speed up your formatting by making those changes in the Modify dialog box (Command-M, or double-click on the object while you hold down the Command key) so that QuarkXPress processes all your changes at once rather than one at a time.

▼ ▼

Picture Management

Possibly the worst nightmare of a desktop publisher is arriving at the local service bureau to pick up 300 pages of film-negative output, only to see that every illustration has come out as a low-resolution bitmap. Throwing away a thousand dollars is one way to learn some basics of picture management. Reading this section is another.

To Represent

The verb "to represent" means "to stand in place for" or "to act as a placeholder." It's important to note that QuarkXPress represents high-resolution images (including TIFF and EPS files) as low-resolution pictures on screen when you import them using Get Picture. When it's time to print, QuarkXPress searches for the original high-resolution images and uses them instead of the low-resolution images. It looks first in the folder where the document was originally imported from, then in the same folder as the document you're printing, and then, strangely enough, in the Macintosh System Folder. If QuarkXPress is successful in this search, your output will look beautiful. If it cannot find the original, it uses the bitmapped 36- or 72-dpi representation for printing. In this case, your output will look ugly.

Here are a few things to keep in mind about pictures.

▶ Don't trash your picture file after you import it, assuming that it's placed for all time.

▶ Don't move the picture file into another folder after you import it.

▶ Don't rename your picture files after you import them.

▶ Do be sure you know where your picture files are.

▶ Do keep your picture files together if possible, to avoid confusion if you need to move your document someplace (like to a service bureau).

▶ If you send your document to a service bureau (or anywhere else, for that matter), put the document and all the image files you imported using Get Picture together in the same folder. You may want to visually segregate the document from its pictures, but keep them in the same folder (see Figure 9-15, and also "Collect for Output" in the "Working with a Service Bureau" section of Chapter 13, *Printing*).

Picture Usage

Submitted for your approval: You've just completed a 600-page document with FreeHand illustrations on every page. The day before sending it to the imagesetter, you realize that you have to make changes to 200 pictures. Tearing your hair out in clumps, you stay up all night changing all the pictures and recreating new EPS documents to replace all the old ones. But now it's dawn, and you have to send it off or risk ruining the whole office's schedule. How will you re-import all those graphics in time? What about replacing and rotating and skewing them all to the correct positions? What will you do? What *will* you do?

Figure 9-15

Sending your disk to a
service bureau

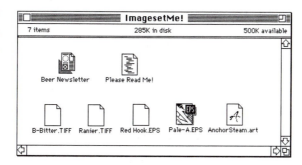

Fortunately, QuarkXPress offers several features that help with picture management. I'm going to discuss the Usage dialog box first, and
then I'll explore how XPress can update pictures automatically after you
change them.

XPress keeps a running tally of all imported pictures in your documents, including when they were last modified. This information is on
the Picture tab of the Usage dialog box (select Usage from the Utilities
menu, or press Option-F13 on the Macintosh or Shift-F2 on Windows).
The Picture Usage dialog box lists several important pieces of information about each image in the document (see Figure 9-16).

▶ Where the image was originally imported from (its hierarchical
disk path, starting from the disk name and moving folder-to-fold-
er down to the file).

▶ The page number of the document where the picture is located.
A dagger (†) appearing next to the page number in the Picture
Usage dialog box signifies that the picture is on the pasteboard, as
opposed to on the page itself.

▶ The status of the picture: OK, Modified, Missing, or Wrong Type.
Note that the more pictures you have in your document, the
longer it takes for XPress to check the status of each one (that's
why it sometimes takes a while for the Usage dialog box to open).

▶ A column where you can tell XPress whether or not to print the
image.

I'll cover picture suppression later in this chapter. Here's a quick rundown on the meaning of the various status messages.

Figure 9-16

Picture Usage dialog box

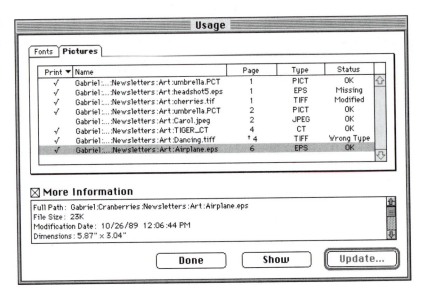

OK. This is what you always hope for, especially before printing. QuarkXPress looks for the picture file first in the same place as the file was imported from, then in the same folder as the document, and finally in the System Folder (on the Macintosh). If it finds the picture file in any of these places, the Status column displays "OK."

Modified. If QuarkXPress finds the file but it's been changed in any way since you imported it (the modification date has changed), you see "Modified" in the Status column. You have two options at this point.

▶ IGNORE THE "PROBLEM." Remember that because QuarkXPress uses the external file for printing, the document prints with the updated version rather than with the original. However, if you've changed the image's resolution or proportions, you shouldn't ignore the Modified warning; the results are unpredictable.

▶ UPDATE THE IMAGE. All this really means is that you get a new representation image in your document. This approach may help you avoid the annoying dialog box "Some pictures have been modified or missing" at print time. To update the file, select its name from the Usage list and click the Update button. Note that if you've changed much about the image, you should make sure that all the rotation, scaling, and cropping attributes you've applied to it are still relevant.

▼ ▼

Tip: Synchronize Your Clocks. Many people have grumbled that the Usage dialog box mysteriously reports their images as Modified when they haven't even touched them. The problem almost always involves images that are stored on a network server where the clock settings for your computer and the server's are different. For instance, let's say you move a picture that you've used in a document from your hard drive to a server. Then, daylight savings time comes, and the server administrator changes the clock on the server. All of a sudden, the image appears as modified.

This doesn't happen on all servers; typically only those that are able to change a file's "last modified" date (this might even happen when the security settings change on the server). The solution: just synchronize the clocks.

▼ ▼

Missing. If QuarkXPress cannot find a file with the name it is expecting, it tells you that the file is missing. Again, you have two options.

▶ IGNORE IT. This method is appropriate if you are trying to get some wild artsy effect using low-resolution printing, but is inappropriate for anyone trying to get a normal, good-looking, high-resolution print. Remember that if the image is missing, QuarkXPress can only print what you see on the screen: a low-resolution representation.

▶ UPDATE THE IMAGE. If you have just moved the picture to another folder or renamed it, you can update the link by selecting the file and clicking Update. Here, you're both relinking the missing picture to the document and bringing in a new representation. The picture preview used in Get Picture is also included in the Missing Picture dialog box.

The Usage dialog box is also valuable when you want to jump to a particular image, if you aren't sure where it is. For example, if you have many figures on many pages, and you want to go to the page which contains "Figure 28b," you can select that item on the Picture tab of the Usage dialog box and click the Show button. XPress jumps to the right page and highlights the picture box that contains the figure. This also works for graphics which have been anchored to text and have flowed to unknown places.

More Information. The Pictures tab of the Usage dialog box also contains a checkbox labeled "More Information." I turn this option on and leave it on (I can't imagine why I wouldn't want more information about pictures in my document).

▼ ▼

Tip: Finding Picture Paths. If you're trying to find where a picture is on disk—you can select the picture on the page and open the Usage dialog box. That picture is highlighted on the list, so if you have a whole mess o' pictures in your document, you don't have to go scrolling through the list to find the one you want (this also works if you have multiple picture boxes selected).

While the disk path name is displayed on the left side of the dialog box, if the picture is more than one or two folders deep, XPress will simply replace folder names with an ellipsis (. . .), which is less than useful. Fortunately, if you turn on the More Information option in this dialog box, you can see the entire file path.

▼ ▼

Tip: Relinking with a New Picture. When you update an image in the Picture Usage dialog box, you don't have to relink with the same picture. You can relink with any other picture, and that image comes in using the same picture specifications as the original (scaling, skewing, and so on). Of course, like many other power tips in this book, this technique can really screw up your image if you don't pay attention. For example, as of this writing, the settings on the Clipping tab of the Modify dialog box don't change when you import the new image, which can cause all sorts of problems if you don't go back to this tab and reset the values.

▼ ▼

Tip: Finding a Bunch of Missing Files. If you move image files or rename the folders they reside in (or even rename the disk they're on), you can wind up with all your pictures missing. There are two easy ways to relink images.

The first method is the coarser solution, and only works if all your image files are in one folder. Move your QuarkXPress document inside that folder and open it. QuarkXPress looks for missing pictures first inside the folder where the document is located; it automatically relinks them. Save the document, and then move it wherever you like—the images stay linked.

The second method is more subtle, and works if you have clumps of missing files in one or more folders. When you find one missing file inside a folder, QuarkXPress "sees" the other missing files and prompts you to say whether or not you want to relink them all in one fell swoop (see Figure 9-17). You can then repeat this trick for other folders with missing images in them.

Figure 9-17
Updating missing files

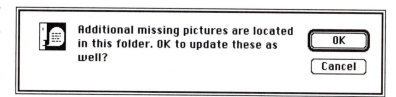

Additional missing pictures are located in this folder. OK to update these as well?

OK

Cancel

Dynamically Updating Images

In the fast-paced production environment of most magazines, newspapers, and ad agencies (plus your business, of course), any technique to streamline the workflow is appreciated. If you work with a lot of images that are subject to change, you can use the Picture Usage dialog box to manually update images, or you can use QuarkXPress's built-in ability to dynamically update the graphics in your documents. Dynamic updating is not for everyone, but for some people it's a lifesaver.

In this section I'm going to discuss three methods you can use to keep pictures updated: Auto Picture Import, Publish and Subscribe, and Object Linking and Embedding (OLE). I can tell you right now that I'd almost never use the Windows-only OLE system, but there are some particularly cool tricks you can use with XPress's Publish and Subscribe feature on the Macintosh.

Auto Picture Import

If you don't want to be bothered by checking Picture Usage all the time, you can use QuarkXPress's internal checking tool: Auto Picture Import. When you have Auto Picture Import turned on in the Document Preferences dialog box (Command-Y), each time you open that document QuarkXPress checks to see if any of the linked pictures have been modified. If they have been, QuarkXPress brings in the new copy transparently and seamlessly. You won't even know that anything has changed.

Clearly, sometimes not knowing what QuarkXPress is doing behind the scenes is disconcerting or frustrating. There's another option here, which is to set your document preference to "On (Verify)." When you select this option, QuarkXPress checks for modified or missing files when you open the document, and if it finds any, it asks you whether you want to re-import them. As with all QuarkXPress features, there is no one "right" way to set up your documents; in some situations you want verifiable auto-importing, and in some you want none at all. (Though to be honest, I'm more comfortable with the "On (Verify)" option; I like to keep a close eye on what images are changing in my document.)

▼ ▼

Tip: Update All Pictures. When Auto Picture Import is set to "On (Verify)," XPress can tell you that one or more pictures in your document have been changed. If you press OK in this warning dialog box, XPress opens the Usage dialog box, displaying only pictures that XPress thinks have been altered. Many people resign themselves to updating one picture at a time in this dialog box, but you shouldn't. You can select all the pictures on the list by clicking on the first one and then Shift-clicking on the last one. Or you can select discontiguous items on the list with the Command key. After you've selected the pictures you want to re-import, click the Update button, and XPress imports them one at a time. (Unfortunately, XPress still asks you if you're *sure* you want to update each image. What a pain.)

▼ ▼

Publish and Subscribe

Publish and Subscribe is a Macintosh-only feature that can be really helpful in some ways and really awful in others. The general idea is that you can publish a picture in one program, subscribe to it in QuarkXPress, and then whenever that picture is updated, XPress can automatically update itself. The file itself is saved in a special format called an *edition*. These editions are usually PICT files (which are so unreliable that I like using them about as much as being bludgeoned by large computer manuals). But they can also be saved in EPS or TIFF format.

Ultimately, while Publish and Subscribe might make sense for the business user, it makes little or no sense for the QuarkXPress user—for a number of reasons.

▶ Editions are often unreliable, even when they're saved in the EPS file format.

▶ QuarkXPress already has dynamic picture updating, even without using editions.

▶ Editions are often as large as the original picture on disk, so you're using twice as much disk space as you need to.

▶ You can't edit an edition; you have to edit the original file, and then the edition gets updated when you save.

But don't stop reading yet! It turns out that while I don't like importing editions into XPress, I do like using XPress's Subscriber Options dialog box. While this dialog box (select Subscriber Options from the Edit menu) appears to apply only to editions, it turns out that XPress lets you use it for all graphics, including TIFF and EPS files.

▼ ▼

Tip: Is It an Edition? Unfortunately, an edition looks like a picture, acts like a picture, and even shows up in the Usage dialog box like a picture. In fact, there's only one little clue that tells you it's an edition: if you go to the Subscriber Options dialog box, there's a little gray square next to the graphic's name, indicating that it's an edition (see Figure 9-18).

▼ ▼

Subscriber Options. The Subscriber Options dialog box is a powerhouse picture manager. (The fastest way to Subscriber Options is not the menus; just double-click on the picture box with the Content tool.) As I said, you can use this dialog box with any picture in your document. The one drawback is that you cannot use it when a picture's status is listed as Missing in the Usage dialog box. There are three really relevant features here: the Subscriber To popup menu, the Get Editions options, and the Open Publisher button. The last option, Cancel Subscriber, is useless and you can ignore it.

▶ **SUBSCRIBER TO.** At the top of the dialog box is a popup menu showing the path to the selected picture. I find that clicking on

Figure 9-18

The Subscriber
Options dialog box
(Macintosh only)

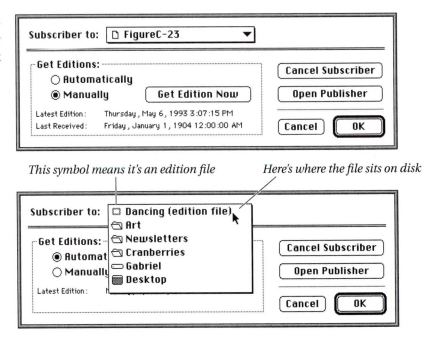

this popup menu provides a more intuitive file path than the text-only listing in the Usage dialog box.

▶ **GET EDITIONS.** Below the path display are two radio buttons in the Get Editions area that determine whether QuarkXPress automatically updates a picture every time it notices that the file is changed, or whether you must update the picture manually. The default choice is Manually, so XPress won't do any importing behind your back (unless you're using Auto Picture Import, which I discussed earlier).

Setting Get Editions to the Automatically option is like turning on Auto Picture Import on an image-by-image basis. If there is one picture in your document that you know is going to get updated regularly, you can select it and turn on Get Editions Automatically. Note that while Auto Picture Import only kicks in when you open a document, XPress continually scans images set to Get Editions Automatically. It usually takes about 10 or 15 seconds for an image to be re-imported after your colleague in the art department changes it.

▼ ▼

Tip: Faster Picture Updating. When Get Editions is set to Manually (it is by default), the Get Edition Now button in the Subscriber Options dialog box acts just like the Update button in the Usage dialog box. However, I find it much faster to press Get Edition Now than to go through the rigmarole of the Usage dialog box (especially if there are a lot of pictures in my document when the Usage dialog box takes so long to open).

▼ ▼

Tip: Re-importing Automatically. While Get Editions Automatically might seem like the clear winner over Auto Picture Import, I think there are good reasons for being judicious with its use. First of all, if you have a document with dozens or hundreds of pictures all set to be automatically updated, QuarkXPress could become so busy checking and rechecking for modified artwork, it might begrudge you the time for trivial tasks such as getting your work done.

Another good reason not to use Get Editions Automatically is that there are many times when you don't want images to be changing in your document (especially if the changed images have different aspect ratios—height to width—than the originally imported images). For example, if you've imported images for position only (FPO), then you don't want them suddenly changing and messing up your text runaround and so on.

▼ ▼

► **OPEN PUBLISHER.** The last really useful feature in the Subscriber Options dialog box is the Open Publisher button. When you click it, QuarkXPress automatically launches the application that created the picture, and loads the picture file for you. Actually, for one technical reason or another, I find that the originating application rarely loads properly, so I only use the Open Publisher button when I know the application is already launched and waiting in the background. Note that XPress won't display the other application. It just opens the picture there; you have to switch applications yourself. Open Publisher is excellent when you have no idea where the original picture is located on your disk and you just can't be bothered to look for it in order to make a change.

▼ ▼

Tip: A Reason to Use Editions. I've only heard one good argument for using real Publish and Subscribe editions instead of regular TIFF or EPS files: some programs cannot open the TIFF or EPS file that they've exported. For instance, a graphing program might be able to export a graph as an EPS file, but may not be able to read that EPS back in again as an editable graph. Instead, you have to open the original native file. In this case, an EPS edition file acts as a conduit between XPress and the original program so that you can use the Open Publisher button and so you don't have to export a new EPS file every time you change the original image (the edition file is updated automatically when you save the file). I may be old-fashioned and a party pooper, but I still probably wouldn't use editions in this instance, either.

▼ ▼

Printing editions. Note that editions act just like EPS or TIFF images when you print them. That is, QuarkXPress doesn't embed the whole picture into your document; it only creates a link from the document to the picture on your disk. If you send your document to a service bureau to print it, you need to send that edition file, too. No, you don't have to send the original picture file.

Object Linking and Embedding (OLE)

Object Linking and Embedding, known commonly by its acronym OLE (pronounced *olé*, like the cheer people use at bullfights and those out-of-control tapas bars), is a glue with which you can seamlessly bind together various programs in Microsoft Windows. Anyway, that's the theory. Like Publish and Subscribe on the Macintosh, it's a function of the operating system rather than of XPress itself. Also like its Macintosh counterpart, it's not very useful in XPress. I guess it's nice that Quark built OLE into XPress, but I can't say that I've ever found a good use for it.

In the last edition of this book I wrote at great length on how to create OLE objects, use the Paste Special and Insert Object features (found on the Edit menu), and the subtle differences between linking and embedding (see Figure 9-19). Since then, I've come to realize that it's hardly a service to you for me to discuss something that I just can't recommend using. Suffice it to say that OLE can be useful for all kinds of things in Windows, but publishing with QuarkXPress is not one of them.

Unlike the Publish and Subscribe features that can be used with any kind of picture in XPress, the OLE features don't work with anything but OLE objects and links, so I just ignore them.

Figure 9-19
Object Linking and
Embedding in XPress
(Windows only)

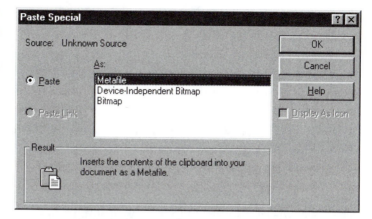

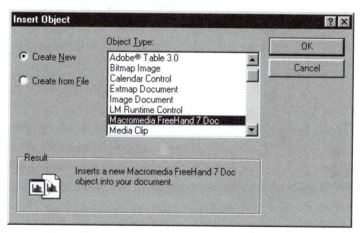

Greeking and Suppression

There are times when I'd really rather not see all those pictures. Maybe the screen redraw or printing time is taking too long. Or maybe I want to use the picture for placement only in the electronic document and don't want it to print out. Or maybe I just hate the pictures. Whatever the case, QuarkXPress has solutions: picture greeking and picture suppression.

Picture greeking. Back in Chapter 6, *Type and Typography*, I discussed replacing text with gray bars. I called that "greeking the text." Now with

Greek Pictures, you can basically replace anything with a gray box. The primary benefit of doing this is to speed up screen redraw: it takes much longer to redraw a detailed picture than it does to just drop in a gray box where the picture should be. Another benefit is in designing your pages. Sometimes having greeked pictures allows you to see the page layout, including its balance and overall tone, better than if you are looking at the real thing.

To greek the pictures in your documents, check the Greek Pictures option in the Document Preferences dialog box (Command-Y). Note that when this box is checked, all picture boxes—except for empty and selected ones—are greeked. Selecting a picture box with either the Item tool or the Content tool ungreeks the picture while it's selected.

Suppress Printout. In the instances when you want the picture on the screen but not on your printouts, you can turn on Suppress Picture Printout in the Modify dialog box (press Command-M, double-click on the image using the Item tool, or select Modify from the Item menu). You can also select Suppress Printout, which suppresses both the picture content and the frame itself. Even easier yet, you can turn off the checkmark on the Pictures tab of the Usage dialog box. This is equivalent to checking Suppress Picture Printout in the Modify dialog box.

▼ ▼

Tip: Suppress Multiple Images. You can turn on (or off) the Suppress Picture Printout option for a bunch of pictures all at the same time in the Usage dialog box. Just select the pictures you want to change (holding down the Command key lets you choose discontiguous items from the list; holding down the Shift key lets you choose contiguous items), and select Yes or No from the popup menu at the top of the Print column (see Figure 9-20).

▼ ▼

Page as Picture

A few years ago, I worked on a book that required taking illustrations created in QuarkXPress and bringing them into PageMaker (horrors!). This is not an uncommon thing, of course; there are many times when you'd like to move text or graphics from XPress into other applications, or even

Figure 9-20

Suppress Printout for
multiple pictures

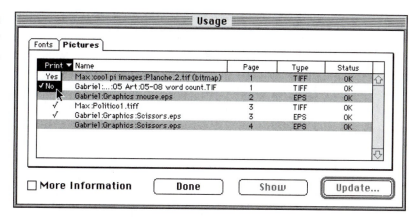

bring a page of a QuarkXPress document into another XPress document as a picture. QuarkXPress allows you to take care of these situations with the Save Page as EPS feature.

Selecting Save Page as EPS from the File menu (or pressing Command-Option-Shift-S) brings up a dialog box in which you can select a page of your document and save it as a separate EPS file (see Figure 9-21). There are loads of ways to tweak this EPS image.

Page and Spread

The first two relevant items in the Save Page as EPS dialog box (besides where to save the file) are the Page field and the Spread checkbox. EPS files from XPress are only one page long; the Page field in this dialog box lets you specify which page in your document you want to encapsulate. If you turn on the Spread option, XPress creates an EPS of whatever page spread includes the page you've specified. Note that Spread works with both facing-pages and single-sided documents; a spread is defined as any two (or more) pages sitting next to each other.

Scale

When you adjust the scaling of the page (for example, making the page 25 percent of full size), the page size is displayed in the dialog box so that you know how large the final bounding box of the EPS image is. You can adjust this by changing the scaling. Remember: because this is PostScript, you can scale your EPS page down to 10 percent, bring it into another program, scale it back up to original size, and you won't lose any quality in your output (though your screen preview image may look

Figure 9-21

Save Page as EPS

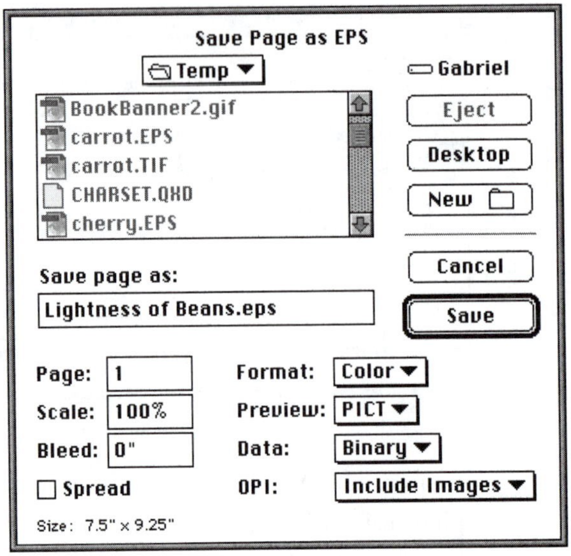

awful). Figure 9-22 shows a QuarkXPress spread that was saved and brought back into another QuarkXPress document.

XPress lets you scale your page down to 10 percent of its original size, and it warns you if you try to enlarge it beyond 100 percent.

Bleed

If your page has items that bleed off the sides, don't expect the bleed to automatically appear in the EPS files. When you save a page as EPS, XPress cuts off the edges of the EPS at the edge of the page (the objects still jut out, but PostScript's clip command doesn't let the printer image them). Fortunately, QuarkXPress 4 lets you specify a Bleed value in the Save as EPS dialog box. If you set the Bleed value to .5 inch, XPress makes the EPS document wider and taller by an inch (half an inch on each side). Any page objects that sit within half an inch of the page get incorporated into the EPS, whether they're touching the page or not.

Unfortunately, this Bleed value doesn't help you if you're trying to prepare EPS files for processing with another prepress program, such as Imation's PrePrint Pro or TrapWise. If you need to do this, you probably need the Luminous Prepress XTension (known as LPX, though it used to be the Aldus Prepress XTension), which you can get free from Imation (see Appendix C, *Resources and XTensions*).

Figure 9-22
QuarkXPress page as EPS
document

Format

When you save a page as EPS, the dialog box gives you the option of saving the file in one of four different formats: Color, B&W (black and white), DCS, or DCS 2.0. In earlier versions of XPress, each of these was prefixed with either "Macintosh" or "PC," so there were eight options; now the Mac-versus-PC options have found their way into another popup menu—Preview (see "Preview," below).

Color versus B&W. If you choose Color or B&W, you get a normal EPS file. As it turns out, choosing between Color and B&W doesn't affect just the screen preview image. The choice also affects the way that QuarkXPress writes the PostScript code. If you choose B&W, color items are actually changed into black-and-white items (even gray values are dithered to black-and-white pixels).

DCS. Choosing DCS causes QuarkXPress to save five files to your disk: one master file that contains a preview image, and four files (one file per process color) that contain the actual image data (see "DCS," earlier in this chapter).

If the Quark Color Management System is turned on (see Appendix A, *Color Management*), you can set the target profiles for both the composite CMYK data and the high-resolution separation data. (Note that color management only works for DCS and DCS 2.0 images.) Whether or not the color management system is on, XPress converts RGB data into CMYK (the program just does a better job when the system is on).

Note that because the DCS file format only handles the four process colors, any spot colors you assign get separated into process colors and placed on the CMYK plates.

DCS 2.0. As I said earlier, DCS 2.0 handles cyan, magenta, yellow, black, and as many spot colors as you want. The cool part about this is that all your spot colors get put on their own plates. And as I also noted earlier, selecting DCS 2.0 results in only one file on your hard drive, rather than five or more.

Preview

Earlier in this chapter, I mentioned that the primary difference between EPS files on the Macintosh and those on Windows had to do with the built-in screen preview. Macintosh EPS files typically have PICT previews; Windows EPS files must use TIFF previews. When generating an EPS file from XPress, you have to choose one of these two preview formats from the Preview popup menu. If you're not sure which platform the EPS file will be used on, you should choose TIFF (it works on both).

Note that the Preview setting only affects the low-resolution screen representation of the image; once the image is imported into another program, the preview isn't really important. For instance, let's say you save an EPS file with a PICT preview, and then import that EPS file into a different XPress document on the Macintosh. You can move both the EPS file and the new XPress document to a Windows machine with no trouble. However, if you need to update or re-import the EPS file on the Windows side, you'll end up with just a gray box.

You have a third choice, too: you can choose None from the Preview popup menu. Probably the only time you'd use this is when you're using the EPS file as an intermediary format and are planning on immediately processing the EPS in some other program. For instance, you can save an EPS file from QuarkXPress and open it in Adobe Photoshop; Photoshop 4 (and later versions) generally rasterize the EPS data and ignore the preview, so there's no need to take up extra time and disk space by asking XPress to build a preview for you.

Data and OPI

There are two last popup menus in the Save Page as EPS dialog box: Data and OPI. Both of these functions affect only bitmapped image data in TIFF and EPS file formats, so you can ignore them if you're not using one of the two.

Data. The first choice is whether to include TIFF images in ASCII or Binary format. What's the difference? Bitmapped images saved in Binary format are half the size of those saved in ASCII, so they print much more quickly. So why use ASCII? Some networks and print spoolers choke on binary image data, so people have had to use ASCII on these systems. Fortunately, QuarkXPress 4 now gives you a third choice: Clean 8-bit. This format is about as small as the Binary option, but usually prints more reliably on PC-based networks that can't handle the regular binary data. I recommend trying Binary first, and if you have trouble printing, switch to Clean 8-bit. (On the other hand, if you're creating EPS files but you don't know who's going to use or print them, you might opt for Clean 8-bit right off the bat.)

OPI. The OPI method is based on postseparating full-color pages that include color bitmapped images—especially scanned images. For example, you can import a low-resolution RGB TIFF file into a QuarkXPress document, save that page as EPS, and separate it on either a high-end color system—such as Hell or Crosfield—or on your image-setter using a program like Imation's PrePrint Pro. Instead of Quark including the whole TIFF image in the PostScript file, it just throws in OPI comments that say what the name of the scanned image file is, and where the separation program can find it.

This is nice for a couple of reasons. First and foremost is file size. An EPS file with the image data included can be enormous. Sometimes it's nicer to leave the image data on disk somewhere else and just manipulate a minimal EPS file (one that just includes OPI comments about where to find the image data). Another good reason is that some workflows depend heavily on keeping the high-resolution data separate from the PostScript and EPS files using OPI.

The trick to building a PostScript file with OPI comments is the OPI popup menu in the Save Page as EPS and Print dialog boxes. You have three choices on this menu: Include Images, Omit TIFF, and Omit TIFF & EPS (see Figure 9-23).

Include Images. When Include Images is selected on the OPI popup menu, QuarkXPress acts naturally. That is, it works the way it always has, and prints all the TIFF and EPS pictures (or includes them in an EPS).

Omit TIFF. This is the basic setting for OPI comments. When Omit TIFF is selected, QuarkXPress replaces all TIFF images with OPI comments that can be read by an OPI reader like Imation's PrePrint Pro.

Omit TIFF & EPS. Apparently the OPI specs talk about OPI comments for EPS images as well as for TIFF images. At this time, however, no software pays any attention to those specs. So this selection (as far as I can tell) is useless for the time being. Well, it's always nice to have the option . . . .

Figure 9-23

Saving a page as an EPS with OPI comments

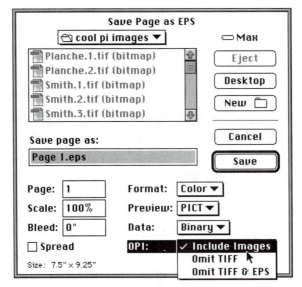

A Warning

A word of warning here about EPS files from QuarkXPress. Some people get overly optimistic about what's possible with PostScript. If you save a full-color QuarkXPress page as EPS, place it in Adobe Illustrator, save it, place that on a PageMaker page, and then send it through Aldus PrePrint for final color separations—well, don't be shocked if it doesn't work.

Each of these programs was written by a different group of people and, consequently, handles color, type, and graphic elements differently. Even though, theoretically, the above process should work (PostScript is PostScript, right?), it might not. So be careful and prudent when you combine programs by nesting EPS files within EPS files; all this software isn't as integrated as it sometimes seems to be.

▼ ▼

Tip: Suppressing Pictures in EPS Pages. In earlier versions of XPress, turning on Suppress Printout or Suppress Picture Printout for a picture would not affect the screen preview (although it did suppress the printing of the picture). Fortunately, that's fixed in version 4, so suppressing a graphic means it won't appear in either the printed EPS or its screen preview.

▼ ▼

Tip: Editing EPS Graphics. Exporting your file in EPS format doesn't mean you can never edit it again. Adobe Illustrator 6 (and later versions) can open most EPS files, converting their elements back into editable objects again. After editing, you can save your file as EPS again. It's not a perfect solution, but it usually works pretty well if you don't have the original XPress document from which the EPS was created.

▼ ▼

Tip: Remove the Big White Box. The folks at Quark made a tiny change between version 3 and version 4 in how XPress writes its EPS files: XPress used to treat the white background of the page as transparent in the EPS file. Now it draws a big white box in the background so it is opaque. Most people never notice the difference, but it can be a killer depending on what you're doing with those EPS files.

If you dare, here's how you can remove that white box from XPress's PostScript code. Note that this is an industrial-strength tip . . . that means you should always work on a copy of your file, and don't try it at home if you don't feel comfortable with editing PostScript files.

1. Open the EPS file in a text editor or word processor. (If it's a large EPS file, a text editor like BBEdit on the Macintosh is probably your best bet.)

2. Search for the comment `%%EndSetup` in the document. A few lines after that, there should be a line that reads `g np clippath 1 H V G` (or something similar).

3. Delete these three characters: 1 H V. In the example above, the line would now read `g np clippath G`.

4. Save the file (perhaps under a new name). Make sure the file is saved in "text-only" mode (text editors only work in this mode, so you don't have to worry about it, but word processors like Microsoft Word allow you to format the text, which can cause trouble in PostScript files). Note that saving this file may lose your screen preview; it depends on what text editor or word processor you're using (again, BBEdit on the Macintosh works well).

That's it! Those three characters are the culprits in the opaque background problem. With them gone, the background is transparent again. (Of course, the built-in screen preview won't change; but when you print the document or rasterize it in Photoshop, it will be transparent.)

Image on the Half Shell

Now that your understanding of images has risen from the murky oceanic depths to the clear, naked light of day, it's time to take a step forward onto dry land, and—in the next chapter—fine-tune your images for brilliance on your page.

10

FINE-TUNING IMAGES

L et me be perfectly clear here: While QuarkXPress provides an astonishing array of controls over your page's text, the program is particularly poor at editing any images you may have imported. Nonetheless, XPress does contain a few image-editing features that you should know about, if only to keep yourself out of trouble.

In Chapter 9, *Pictures,* I discussed several graphic file formats, how to bring them into your QuarkXPress documents, and how to perform basic manipulations with them, such as rotating, skewing, and scaling. In this chapter I look at how you can use QuarkXPress in place of other image-editing software to modify the imported image itself. Bear in mind that I'm not talking here about image *editing.* You can't actually change the content of imported graphics in QuarkXPress. You can, however, change some of their overall parameters such as contrast, color, clipping path, and halftone screen.

First, I'm going to examine the types of images you can modify, and then I discuss how to modify them. Much of this is potentially confusing, but bear with me, read carefully, and you'll be an inexorable image-modifier faster than you can say, "Ontogeny recapitulates phylogeny."

▼ ▼

The Picture File

In this chapter, I am concerned almost exclusively with bitmapped images. Bitmapped images, as far as QuarkXPress is concerned, are black and white, grayscale, or color, and are found in TIFF, BMP, PNTG, and bitmap-only PICT files. Bitmapped images can also be saved as EPS files, but because the image data is encapsulated, XPress won't let you change anything about them. Therefore, the only time I'll discuss EPS files here is when I explore clipping paths. The rest of the time, I'm just going to assume that you're using TIFF files (see Chapter 9, *Pictures*, for the reasons I don't like using the other bitmapped image file formats).

Bitmapped Images

I want to take this opportunity to refresh your memory about bitmapped images and the TIFF file type, which I discussed in Chapter 9, *Pictures*. Here are the highlights.

▶ Bitmapped images are simply rectangular grids of sample points (also called pixels or dots).

▶ The resolution of the image is the number of these sample points per inch (spi), or pixels per inch (ppi).

▶ Each sample point can be black, white, a level of gray, or a color. This color is represented by a number; for example, in a file with 256 gray levels, black would be zero and white would be 255.

▶ Scaling the image has a direct effect on its resolution. Enlarging the picture to 200 percent cuts the resolution in half (same number of samples in twice the space), which may result in pixelation ("jaggies"). Reducing the image to 50 percent doubles the resolution, which may improve image quality (see Figure 10-1).

▶ A TIFF file can be a rectangle of any size with any number of dots per inch, and each pixel can have any level of gray or any color which is definable by the color models described in Chapter 12, *Color*. TIFF files are said to be *deep* if they have four or more gray levels (more than 2 bits per sample point), and they're *flat* or *bilevel* if they only have one bit (black or white) per sample point.

Figure 10-1
Resolution and
scaling for bitmaps
(50 percent, 100 percent,
and 300 percent)

Modifying Images

Unless you're deliberately trying to achieve a muddied look, every image that you scan requires color correction (if it's a color image), tonal correction, and sharpening. Even synthetic pictures created with a painting program may require these adjustments. However, the place to do these things is in an image-editing program like Adobe Photoshop. Nonetheless, XPress gives you a few image-editing controls that may be useful, especially if you're looking for a special effect. Here's what you can do to a bitmapped image.

▶ Replace its contrast curve with preset high-contrast or posterized effects.

▶ Apply a custom contrast curve.

▶ Invert the image.

▶ Add a clipping path to create a silhouette.

▶ Change the picture's on-screen or printed resolution.

▶ Apply a color or tint to the picture.

▶ Change the picture's halftoning parameters.

Chances are that the feature from this list that you'll use most often is the ability to create a clipping path (this is a new feature in version 4 of QuarkXPress). However, I'm going to hold off on discussing clipping paths until I explore changing screen resolution, colorizing images, and adjusting image contrast.

Welcome to the world of image modification!

Importing High-Resolution TIFF Graphics

The first alteration you can make to your file is to upgrade or downgrade high-resolution TIFF files. This control is available only when you first import the picture (see "Get Picture" in Chapter 9, *Pictures*).

Downgrading screen quality. QuarkXPress normally creates a screen representation of a high-resolution TIFF file at 72 dpi. This low-resolution screen image provides for a relatively quick screen-refresh rate and keeps your document's file size low. However, if the image is really big or your computer is really slow, importing and displaying an image at even 72 dpi can be time-consuming. You can halve the screen resolution by holding down the Shift key while you click the Open button in the Get Picture dialog box. This doesn't have any effect on your printed output, but it may speed up your screen redraws (those of you who have a super-fast Digital Alpha NT workstation can stop chuckling).

Changing TIFF types. If you are heavily into image editing and control, you will undoubtedly want to change the bit depth of a TIFF image at some point. Here are two tricks for changing the bit depth as you import the image.

▶ Holding down the Option key when you click Open in the Get Picture dialog box changes a one-bit TIFF line-art image into an eight-bit grayscale image. (I can't think of a single use for this feature, but I'll bet someone can.)

▶ Holding down the Command key when you click Open in the Get Picture dialog box changes TIFF color images to grayscale, which I have found useful on several occasions. (Note, though, that you may get a better color-to-grayscale conversion in a program like Photoshop.) On the other hand, this Command-key trick also changes TIFF grayscale images to line-art (bitmap) images, which is rarely a change for the better.

▼ ▼

The Style Menu

Chapter 9, *Pictures,* describes how you can manipulate the "layout" of the picture in the picture box, including cropping, rotating, skewing, and moving the image. These effects are controlled from the Measurements palette or the Modify dialog box. Here I talk primarily about the image modification possibilities using features from the Style menu. Remember that you can combine both image manipulation techniques (rotating, changing the shape and size, and so on) and image modification techniques (changing the grayscale or color parameters, and so on) to create fascinating effects in your page layout.

▼ ▼

Tip: When the Style Menu Is Gray. If the items on the Style menu are grayed out, you have probably imported an EPS or some other file format that XPress cannot modify. Remember: No shoes, no bitmapped image, no service. If you're sure you have the right file format, it may be that the Color TIFFs setting in Application Preferences is set to 16-bit or 32-bit. If you've chosen either of these, XPress won't let you make any style modifications to color images (but you can modify grayscale images just fine).

If the menu is still grayed out, you may not have the Item tool or the Content tool selected, or you may not have the image's picture box selected. If still none of these things work, I can only suggest plugging in the machine.

▼ ▼

Color. I cover color fully in Chapter 12, *Color*. So at this point, suffice it to say that changing the color of a grayscale or black-and-white image using QuarkXPress's Color feature replaces all black (or gray) samples with ones of a particular color. (You cannot colorize a color image in XPress.) For example, if you have a black-and-white image and you change the color to red, you then have a red-and-white image.

This is not necessarily the same thing as colorizing an image in Photoshop, but it's usually pretty close. Note that you can create a "fake duotone" by colorizing an image with a multi-ink color (see Chapter 12, *Color*, for more on multi-ink colors).

Shade. In the same spirit as changing each pixel's color, you can change the gray value for each pixel in the image (this is also called "ghosting" or "screening back" an image). Again, this currently works only for grayscale and black-and-white images. To tint an image, select a percentage from the Shade submenu (under the Style menu) or change the tint value for the image on the Colors palette. What happens to the image when you do this depends on whether you're working with flat or deep bitmapped images.

▶ FLAT BITMAPS. With flat, bilevel, bitmapped images, changing the Shade alters the printed output; every black pixel in your graphic prints gray. Shading line art can sometimes give you a classier look than just black and white.

▶ DEEP BITMAPS. When you set a shade for a grayscale image in the Style menu XPress multiplies that shade for each sample point. A 50-percent shade of a 100-percent black sample point is 50 percent; 50 percent of a 60-percent sample is 30 percent, and so on. But you don't have to think about the math, because the result appears just like you'd expect.

It turns out that you can ghost back a color TIFF image, too . . . you just have to be tricky about it (see "Tip: Ghosting Color Images," later in this chapter).

Negative. Selecting Negative from the Style menu (or typing Command-Shift-hyphen) inverts all tone and color information in an image (see Chapter 12, *Color,* for more information on color models). What was 10-percent black becomes 90-percent black, what was 20-percent red becomes 80-percent red, and so on.

▼ ▼

Tip: More Negative Images. Here's another way to invert an image: color it white. This is often not only easier, but also more desirable. For example, if you want a white image on a blue background, you can select the picture box with the Content tool, change the shade of the picture to zero percent (or change the color to White in either the Color palette or the Style menu), then change the background color to some shade of Blue (such as 100 percent).

▼ ▼

Tip: Images and Blends Inside Images. Carlos Sosa turned me on to a very odd and potentially useful technique of putting images and blends inside images. Note that this tip only works with 1-bit (bitmap) images.

1. Import a one-bit (black-and-white) image into a picture box and set its color to White in either the Colors palette or the Style menu.

2. Set the image to Negative (Command-Shift-hyphen).

3. If you want to put a blend inside the image, give the picture box a blended background (see Chapter 12, *Color*, on how to do this). If you want to put another image inside this image, then set the Background of the bitmap image's picture box to None.

The trick here is that using Negative swaps the transparent and opaque pixels so you can see through what used to be black pixels (see Figure P on the color pages). Setting the color to White in step 1 matches the opaque area of the image to the color behind the picture box. If the picture box is on top of a 50-percent cyan background, you'd have to use 50-percent cyan in step 1.

Note that you can fake this effect for a grayscale image by first converting the image into a bitmap in Photoshop (change Mode to Bitmap, and select the Halftone Screen technique in the Bitmap dialog box).

▼ ▼

Tip: Making Your Grayscale Picture "Transparent." The simple answer to "How do I make my grayscale TIFFs transparent?" is "You can't." Grayscale TIFFs are not and cannot be transparent. On the other hand, in black-and-white, one-bit TIFFs (the kind called "Bitmap" in Photoshop), the "white" pixels *are* transparent. (White pixels in black-and-white EPS bitmaps *can* be transparent—it's an option in Photoshop's Save As EPS dialog box—but bitmap TIFFs are more reliable for this.)

Of course, whenever I hear someone say "You can't," I immediately reply, "There must be a workaround somehow." And indeed, there are several. Note that these techniques are for letting you see through a grayscale image to whatever is below it; if you're trying to create a silhouette around the image, you should check out "Clipping Paths," later in this chapter.

▶ Include background color. If you've placed the grayscale image over an area of flat color, you can set the background of the picture box to be the same as the flat color. For example, let's say you want a grayscale image to appear transparent over an area of 30-percent cyan. Just set the background color of the picture box to 30-percent cyan. In earlier versions of XPress, this technique looked right on screen but printed incorrectly because the grayscale image would knock out of the magenta plate.

Fortunately, grayscale images now overprint the background color properly when you print color separations or to a composite color printer, even if the background color is a spot color or contains black.

Of course, this technique only works when the image is fully surrounded by an area of flat color. It won't work when you're trying to print over a scanned image or another page item.

▶ **SET TO OVERPRINT.** If your document is in color, you can change the Background value of the picture box to None and set the picture to Overprint in the Trap Information palette (see Chapter 12, *Color*, for more on the Trap Information palette). This lets you put the picture partially on top of a field of color, or even on top of a scanned image. There are three problems with this technique. First, because XPress doesn't display trapping on screen, you won't be able to see the overprinting effect until you print separations. Second, for the same reason, you won't be able to see the effect when you print to a color printer. Third, you cannot use this technique to overprint any color or object that has black in it (including a scanned image that has information in its black channel).

The reason there cannot be black in the background has to do with the nature of PostScript: when you print a light gray on top of a dark gray, the result is the light gray, not a combination of the two. The tint on top always wins, so there's no such thing as overprinting black on black. It's not just the color black; for instance, if you set the color of the grayscale image to cyan, then you can print it over a color that contains black, but not over anything that contains cyan.

▶ **SET TO "UNDERPRINT."** Another way to trick XPress into making a grayscale image look transparent is to put the picture box behind another box rather than in front of it. Then, in the Trap Information palette, set the foreground objects to overprint the picture. This has exactly the same restrictions as the last workaround, though in some instances you can make it look as if black is overprinting black.

For example, let's say you want a light grayscale image to appear transparent over some black text in a 30-percent magenta text box. You can put the image behind the text box and set the text box to overprint the image. The magenta box overprints the image, and the text knocks out the image; however, because the text is solid black, it looks like it's overprinting. (This is easier seen than explained; see See Figure O in the color plates for examples of each of these transparency workarounds.)

▶ **CHANGE TO BITMAP.** As I said earlier, the white pixels in bilevel, bitmap TIFF images are inherently transparent. Therefore, if you convert a grayscale image to Bitmap mode in Photoshop, it can sit on top of anything you want in XPress and what's underneath will show through the white areas. The problem, of course, is that bitmap images have no gray in them, so gray values must be represented by dithering or by a halftone pattern (see "Halftones," later in this chapter, for a discussion of this topic).

When you convert to Bitmap mode in Photoshop, you can set the final resolution of the image. Typically, if you're printing to an imagesetter for high-quality output, your final bitmap image needs to be between 600 and 1,000 ppi. If you're only printing to a desktop laser printer, you can typically get by with a lower value. However, when you import this bitmap image into QuarkXPress, the screen preview is usually pretty bad. So again, you can't trust what you see on screen; you have to print proofs.

▼ ▼

Contrast

The Style menu also lets you change the contrast of grayscale and color images with the Contrast feature. If you are working with a one-bit (black-and-white) picture, this feature is inaccessible.

Contrast refers to the relationships among the tonal values of a picture. A high-contrast picture divides up the gray shades or color saturation of an image into a few sharply distinct tones; a low-contrast picture has little differentiation between tones, and looks grayed out. You should try to strike some balance between these two, though you may want to create an unnatural-looking image by drastically altering the contrast controls.

The basic concept to remember with the contrast controls is "input/output." I like to think of the Contrast feature as a machine into which I'm inserting a TIFF image, and out of which comes what is going to print on the page. Other people sometimes think of this process as a filter through which the image is poured each time the page gets printed. Remember, though, that neither you nor QuarkXPress actually alters the picture file on disk; you only alter the "machine" or the "filter" through which the image passes for display and printout.

(In previous versions of QuarkXPress, there were several preset contrast controls, including Normal Contrast, High Contrast, and Posterized. These have been removed because they're completely redundant; there are identical features inside the Picture Contrast Specifications dialog box. Also, these features just weren't used very often.)

Picture Contrast Specifications

To change the contrast of an image, choose Contrast from the Style menu (or press Command-Shift-C). The Picture Contrast Specifications dialog box shows you the mechanism—or the filter—through which you are processing the picture. When you first open this dialog box, you see a 45-degree line on the graph (see Figure 10-2).

Looking carefully at the graph, you can see that the axes are labeled Input and Output, and each spans from zero to one (one means 100-percent). Tick marks are shown in increments of five and 10 percent.

The basic 45-degree normal contrast line defines a filter which makes no change to gray levels. For example, a gray level of 20 percent in the input picture is mapped (in output) to 20 percent, 40 percent to 40 percent, and so on. However, by changing this line, you can change the mapping of the gray levels, affecting the contrast and shading of the printed picture.

You can use the nine tools in this dialog box to change the contrast curve into either a straight line or a curve. By definition, any contrast curve which is not a straight line is a *gamma curve*. There's nothing mysterious about a gamma curve; it's simply a nonlinear curve with a fancy name. However, when it comes right down to it, QuarkXPress's tools for making curves don't let you do much more than either very basic modifications or very weird ones (see Figure 10-3).

Let's look at how the tools work.

Figure 10-2

Adjusting the Contrast Specifications for a grayscale TIFF image

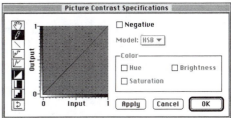

Normal contrast

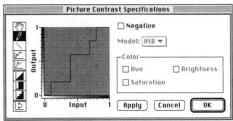

Contrast curve adjusted to create a Posterized effect

Figure 10-3

Way-out contrast correction

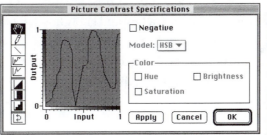

▼ ▼

Tip: Applying Your Changes. I've said this before, but it's worth repeating here: The Apply button is one of the all-time most helpful features that I've ever had the pleasure of using, especially on a screen larger than 9 inches. It's especially useful with the Picture Contrast Specifications dialog box.

You can move the Picture Contrast Specifications dialog box out of the way of the picture you're working with, then make changes to the curve and click the Apply button (or press Command-A) to see the change take place. If you don't like that effect, change the curve again or press Command-Z to undo that change. And don't forget Continuous Apply (Option-click Apply, or press Command-Option-A).

▼ ▼

Tip: Don't Use Other Contrast. I liken the Picture Contrast Specifications dialog box to fixing a delicate piece of electronic equipment with a hammer—it's just too blunt of an instrument to do much good. In fact, there are a dozen problems that make the contrast controls in QuarkXPress less than useful, the most essential of which is sharpening. Scanned images always need to be sharpened with a sharpening filter (preferably Photoshop's Unsharp Mask filter) before they're printed. Unfortunately, you need to apply sharpening *after* tonal correction. Since QuarkXPress doesn't have a sharpening filter, that's impossible.

So if you need to perform tonal correction on a scanned image (you almost always do), don't use the controls in QuarkXPress. Do it in an image-editing program like Photoshop, which probably has better tonal-correction tools and where you can also sharpen the image. Then save the file and place it in QuarkXPress, fully corrected, sharpened, and ready to print.

Why discuss the Contrast feature at all? Because I'm the kind of guy who likes to have a tool and know how it works, even if I almost never use it. The one or two times per year that I use this feature for a special effect or a minor tweak make up for the short amount of time it took me to learn how to use this dialog box.

▼ ▼

Hand tool. You can use the Hand tool to move the curve (or straight line) around on the contrast graph by selecting the tool, positioning it over the graph, and dragging. You can constrain to either horizontal or vertical movements by holding down the Shift key while dragging. The Hand tool is the easiest way to make adjustments to the contrast curve as a whole. For an example, see "Tip: Adjusting the Break Point on a High-Contrast Image," below.

Pencil tool. If you've ever used a painting program, you're already familiar with the Pencil tool. By selecting this tool and dragging over the curve, you can make both large and small adjustments. You can draw curves with the Pencil tool which adjust for problems in the original scan (see

Figure 10-4). Or you can draw wild and bizarre roller-coaster curves which map the gray levels in weird ways. You can also make small corrections in the curve by carefully drawing over areas. Remember, though, that you don't need to have a perfectly smooth curve all the time; slight bumps and dips have little effect on the final output.

Figure 10-4

Curve created with the pencil tool

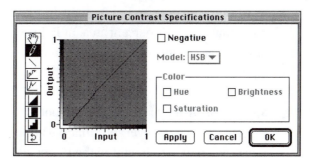

The near-white background is pushed fully to white with this delicate curve made with the Pencil tool. However, parts of the image also become white.

Straight Line tool. If you haven't figured out that the Straight Line tool draws straight lines, I wish you the best of luck with the program. However, it's not so obvious what these straight lines are good for. Think of the slope of a line in the same way as you think of the slope of a hill. A steep slope steepens very quickly; a shallow slope steepens slowly. You can draw steep and gentle slopes easily with the Straight Line tool.

The steeper the slope, the higher contrast the image has. The gentler the slope, the less contrast—the "grayer" the picture looks. However, remember that by using a straight line rather than a curved line, you are indiscriminately losing tonal values. A steep, contrasty line loses the highlights and the shadows; a flat, low-contrast line loses midtones (see Figure 10-5).

Figure 10-5

Linear adjustment

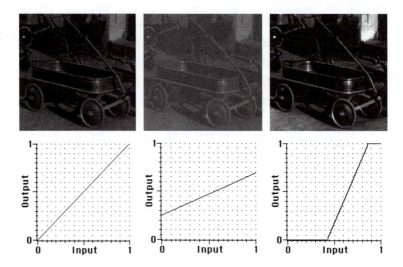

Posterizer tool. Posterization is the act of reducing or dividing an image's gray or color levels into a few basic tonal values. When you select the Posterizer tool, QuarkXPress adds handle points to your line or curve at 10-percent increments. By moving these handles, you flatten and move that entire 10-percent area. By lining up multiple handles, you can easily create posterized effects with any number of levels up to 10 (see Figure 10-6).

Spike tool. Whereas the Posterizer tool places handles between the 10-percent marks and levels out (flattens) that 10-percent area, the Spike tool places handles directly on the 10-percent marks and has no affect on the area between the handles other than to adjust the lines to keep them contiguous. This is the best tool for creating smooth curves—much easier than the Pencil tool. Spiking a line is also pretty good for boosting particular tonal values. For example, if you want a 60-percent gray area to appear black, you can spike it up to 100 percent. Similarly, if you want to drop out all the dark areas of the cyan, you can use this tool.

Figure 10-6

Using the Posterizer tool

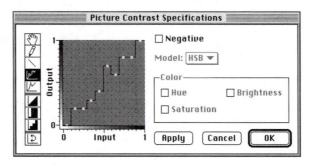

Normal Contrast tool. Clicking on this icon reverts the contrast curve to its initial 45-degree straight line.

High Contrast tool. Clicking on this icon has the immediate effect of making your grayscale pictures look like they were badly scanned at a one-bit (black-and-white) setting, and it makes your color pictures look like poorly designed psychedelic flyers.

The literal effect of this filter is to change all values less than 30-percent gray to white, and all values greater than 30-percent gray to black. Color images are affected in the same way: the saturation levels are broken down so that all colors with over 30-percent saturation are transformed to 100 percent, and so on (see Chapter 12, *Color,* for a more in-depth discussion of color and its saturation levels). Why Quark chose the 30-percent mark is beyond me; it makes for some really ugly-looking images. I'll look at how to change this break point later in this chapter.

Posterized tool. Whereas the High Contrast setting breaks down the image into only two gray or saturation levels—zero percent and 100 percent—Posterized divides the tonal values into six levels of gray or color saturation: zero, 20, 40, 60, 80, and 100 percent. Gray levels or color saturation in the original picture are mapped to these levels based on what they're closest to (for example, a 36-percent saturation of a color maps to the 40-percent level). Posterization is a common technique for special effects, though it should be used carefully.

Inversion tool and Negative checkbox. Contrary to popular belief, these two items in the Picture Contrast Specifications dialog box do not perform the same task, though in many instances you may achieve the same result. By using either of these, for example, you can invert grayscale files. That is, where there was white, there is black; where there was 20-percent black, there is 80-percent black, and so on. Switching to Negative and inverting the curve also creates the same effect while altering all three RGB values at once (see "Color," below, for more on the RGB contrast curve).

However, inverting color images while using other color models can give you varying effects. Simply put, clicking on the Inversion tool in the Tool palette flips the curve you are working on. Checking Negative has the same effect as selecting the Negative item from the Style menu.

▼ ▼

Tip: Adjusting the Break Point on a High-Contrast Image. As I described above, the cutoff point on a high-contrast image is 30 percent, which does hardly anyone any good. Using the Hand tool in the Other Contrast dialog box, you can adjust this point horizontally to anywhere on the scale. Try moving the vertical line over to around 60 percent. This cuts out most of the lower gray values and gives you a clean and recognizable image for many grayscale or color pictures (see Figure 10-7).

This technique is also of great help when you're working with line art scanned as a grayscale image. By adjusting the cutoff point, you can alter the line thicknesses in the artwork (see Figure 10-8). Remember that holding down the Shift key while you're using the Hand tool constrains the movements to horizontal or vertical.

Of course, to get a really good-looking image, you'd have to start with an 800-dpi grayscale image (because you want to end up with a minimum of 800 dpi for line art). This would be a really enormous file! So once again, the caveat is that this grayscale-to-bilevel bitmap conversion is better done in Photoshop or another image-editing program.

Figure 10-7
Adjusting the high-contrast break point for a grayscale image

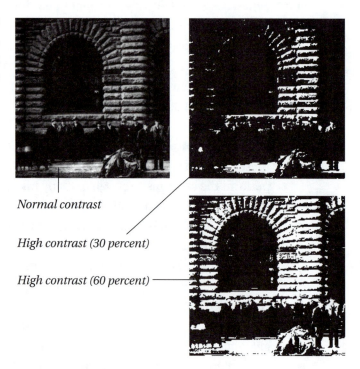

Normal contrast

High contrast (30 percent)

High contrast (60 percent)

▼ ▼

Figure 10-8

Line art scanned as
a grayscale image

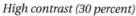

High contrast (30 percent)   *High contrast (60 percent)*

Color

If you aren't familiar with working with color and the various color models that QuarkXPress supports, you may want to skip over this section until you've read Chapter 12, *Color*. In this section, I discuss contrast modification of color images using the various color models and their components.

QuarkXPress allows you to modify color TIFF images using the same tools you use for grayscale images, except that you can alter one color at a time. This clearly allows significantly greater control over the way your images print.

As I've said before, there are few reasons to use these controls in QuarkXPress other than to create really weird-looking images—especially given the lack of a sharpening filter in QuarkXPress (see Figure N in the color pages). Instead, Photoshop is the tool of choice for making color correction and adjustments. Nonetheless, let's look at the steps you can take to modify these pictures in QuarkXPress.

Model. The Modify popup menu in the Picture Contrast Specifications dialog box appears when you are modifying a color bitmapped image. You can work with four different color models: HSB, RGB, CMY, and CMYK. When you change from one model to another, the image resets to Normal. Thus, you cannot make changes to an image in more than one color model.

Color. When you select one of the color models, QuarkXPress brings up the appropriate color-selection checkboxes; that is, when you click HSB, Hue, Saturation, and Brightness checkboxes appear. Clicking CMY gives you Cyan, Magenta, and Yellow checkboxes, and so on. Each checkbox can be on or off, and you can have any number of checkboxes turned on at one time.

The theory is simple: the checkboxes you turn on control which items change when you alter the contrast control curve. In the RGB, CMY, and CMYK models, QuarkXPress gives you color checkboxes. If you check Magenta and Yellow, for example, and change the contrast curve using the tools described above, you change the curve for only those two colors. Everything else remains the same.

The HSB model's checkboxes have slightly different functions. Changing the contrast curve with only Hue turned on maps various colors to other colors. This can be seen on a color screen by examining the color spectrum on the horizontal and vertical axes as well as the curve itself. In theory, this means you could make all the red in an image become yellow . . . in practice, this is easier said than done.

The Saturation checkbox lets you map various saturations from zero to 100 percent, and the Brightness checkbox lets you map the brightness levels (levels of black) to other brightness levels. Once again, you can adjust each of these settings with any, some, or all of the checkboxes turned on.

▼ ▼

Tip: Ghosting Color Images. The Shade feature is grayed out (unusable) for color TIFFs. However, if you need to tint—or ghost, or screen back, or whatever you want to call it—a color image, you can adjust shading with the Picture Contrast Specifications dialog box. You will get different effects depending on the model you use. One option is to set the Model popup menu to RGB and then use the Hand tool to move all three contrast curves vertically. Moving the curves up makes the image lighter, and moving them down makes it darker.

In HSB mode, you can turn off the Hue and Saturation checkboxes and simply increase the Brightness curve to lighten the image.

Note, however, that when you move these curves up or down, you're likely to cut out possible gray levels. If you make the image darker, for instance, dark areas go black; make it lighter, and light areas go white. In either case, you lose detail. Because of this, you may want to adjust the curve using the Pencil tool or the Spike tool instead (or use an image-manipulation program), as described above.

▼ ▼

Tip: Clone and Ghost. All the tools I've discussed so far apply to the entire image. How can you ghost back or colorize just a portion of an image? As usual, there's a trick (see Figure 10-9).

1. Select the picture box and use Step and Repeat (from the Item menu) to make one duplicate with both Horizontal and Vertical offsets set to zero. (I call this "cloning" the box.)

2. Crop the duplicate image down by changing the size or shape of the picture box. You can do this by dragging its corner or side handles, changing its shape from the Shape submenu (under the Item menu), or—if it's a Bézier box—altering the points on the edge of the box. Note that when you do this you don't move the picture within the box at all, so the two pictures stay in registration.

    Instead of (or in addition to) cropping, you can change the duplicate box's clipping path (see "Clipping Paths," on the next page, for more on how to do this).

3. Apply the effect you want either to the duplicate or to the original image.

There are all kinds of variations on this tip. For instance, let's say you have a color TIFF in the picture box. After cloning the box in step 1, you can re-import the picture into the cloned picture box, but this time as grayscale (hold down the Command key when you click Open in the Get Picture dialog box). Now when you change the cropping of the box or change the image's clipping, one portion of the picture is grayscale.

Figure 10-9
Changing one part
of an image by cloning
and adjusting contrast

The original image   *A clone of the picture box, cropped
                                      differently and with a different contrast*

▼ ▼

Clipping Paths

I've discussed dozens of the new features in QuarkXPress 4 in the previous chapters, but only a few of them have truly had the potential to increase your productivity in a life-changing manner (character style sheets and text paths are two such new features). Now it's time to explore one more: clipping paths. At first glance, the Clipping feature seems to be merely a convenience, but believe me—it's much better than that.

A clipping path is a mathematically based PostScript path, much like other Bézier lines in QuarkXPress, Illustrator, or FreeHand. However, a clipping path acts like a pair of scissors, cutting out an image in any shape you want. Clipping an image is actually the same as cropping it, but because QuarkXPress makes a distinction, I will, too: the shape of a picture box crops the picture, but the Clipping feature clips it. You can use clipping and cropping together or alone. Let's see how.

Applying a Clipping Path

If you've used QuarkXPress for a while, you're sure to have heard someone say, "Never put a TIFF in a picture box that has a background of None." The reason is simple: in version 3.x, if you set the background to None, XPress would assume that you wanted a silhouette of the picture and it would build a clipping path for you. The problem was that it built this clipping path with straight line segments based on the 72-dpi screen preview of your image, and it did it in a pretty brain-dead fashion. The result was a very jaggy edge around the image, which looked really ugly.

XPress 4 changes all that, and I'm happy to announce that you can throw that outdated rule out the window. Now you have the option of applying a smooth clipping path based on the high-resolution image data (choose Clipping from the Item menu, or press Command-Option-T). This works whether the Background of the box is set to None or to an opaque color. (If Background is set to None, the clipped image appears against whatever is behind the picture box; if the background is opaque, the clipped image appears in front of whatever background color you've specified.)

The Clipping tab of the Modify dialog box looks confusing at first, but it's really pretty basic once you get the hang of it (see Figure 10-10). The most important feature in this dialog box is the Type popup menu, which

Figure 10-10

Specifying a clipping path

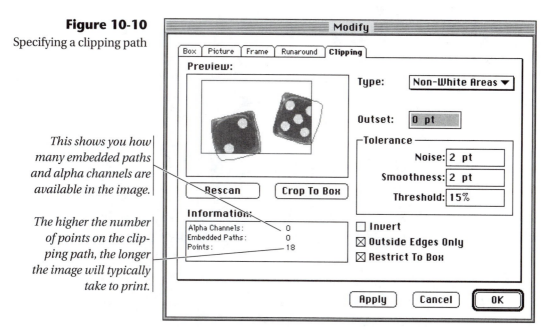

This shows you how many embedded paths and alpha channels are available in the image.

The higher the number of points on the clipping path, the longer the image will typically take to print.

lets you choose one of five clipping path options: Item, Embedded Path, Alpha Channel, Non-White Areas, and Picture Bounds.

Item. When you select Item from the Type popup menu (this is the default setting for most pictures), QuarkXPress sets the clipping path to be the same as the cropping path. In other words, this is just like turning off the Clipping feature so that XPress just crops the picture the way it always has.

Embedded Path. Adobe Photoshop lets you draw and save Bézier paths with its images. XPress is smart enough to see and read those paths in TIFF, EPS, and JPEG images, and lets you choose one of them as your clipping path. This turns out to be incredibly useful. Let's say you have a picture of four books fanned out on a table. You can create several paths in Photoshop, each of which "cuts out" one book, two books, the first and third book, and so on. When you get the image into XPress, you can choose which silhouette looks best in your design (see Figure 10-11).

Alpha Channel. It's a strange phenomenon, but whenever someone says "alpha channel," half the people in the room avert their eyes. The popular belief is that alpha channels are really difficult to understand, so we'd better not even try. However, alpha channels are really easy to

Figure 10-11

Choosing an embedded path

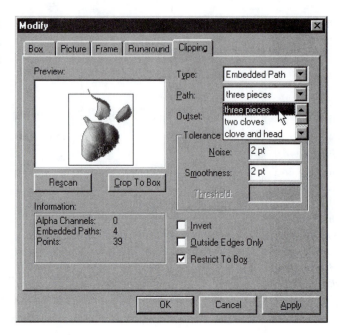

understand: an alpha channel is just a way to visually represent a selection as a grayscale picture. In Adobe Photoshop, you can select an area of an image and save it as an additional channel on the Channels palette. (As far as I can tell, people use the term "alpha" just to sound important; it's just the same as a plain ol' additional channel—see Figure 10-12.)

Then when the Type popup menu is set to Alpha Channel, XPress lets you convert one of these channels into a clipping path. It's almost as though XPress is reading your original Photoshop selection. The problem is that selections in Photoshop can have soft anti-aliased or feathered edges, and clipping paths cannot, so QuarkXPress has to convert soft edges into hard-edged Bézier paths. (See "Tolerance," below, for a description of how it does this.)

Note that if you want to include alpha channels in images bound for XPress, you have to use the TIFF file format.

Non-White Areas. If your image doesn't have either an alpha channel or an embedded path, XPress still lets you build a clipping path on the fly based on the non-white areas of the image. If you choose Non-White Areas from the Type popup menu, XPress searches through the picture for white or near-white pixels to clip out, leaving the pixels that are not near-white (see Figure 10-13). You even have the choice to clip out white

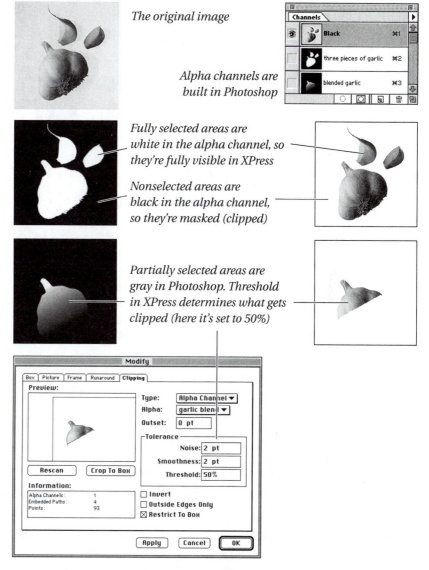

Figure 10-12

Alpha channels in
Adobe Photoshop

The original image

*Alpha channels are
built in Photoshop*

*Fully selected areas are
white in the alpha channel, so
they're fully visible in XPress*

*Nonselected areas are
black in the alpha channel,
so they're masked (clipped)*

*Partially selected areas are
gray in Photoshop. Threshold
in XPress determines what gets
clipped (here it's set to 50%)*

pixels inside the image—like the hole in the middle of a hula hoop (see "Clipping Options," below).

This option works reasonably well in a few instances, notably where the image has very crisp edges and is on a clean, white background. If the edges of the foreground image have a lot of detail or if the image is colored similar to the background, Non-White Areas can't figure out which details are important and which are not (like a human eye can), and the clipping path suffers for it. Of course, if your image is not on a white (or near-white) background, this option doesn't help much at all.

Figure 10-13
Clipping out
the white pixels

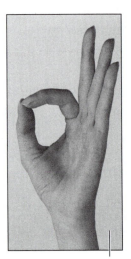 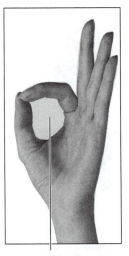 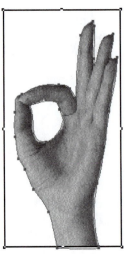

These near-white pixels get clipped out.

These white pixels are retained because they're surrounded by nonwhite pixels (you have the option to clip these or not).

The final clipping path in QuarkXPress (You can make the clipping path visible in the Edit submenu under the Item menu)

In fact, to be really honest about it, I tend to shy away from this option unless I'm trying to build a quick comp for a client or if I'm planning on spending some time editing the clipping path (see "Clipping Caveats" and "Editing the Clipping Path," later in this section).

Picture Bounds. Selecting Picture Bounds is second in simplicity only to the Item option on the Type popup menu. Bitmapped images are always rectangular, so selecting Picture Bounds sets the picture's clipping path to the four sides of the picture. If the picture box is the same size as the picture, then this option has pretty much the same effect as selecting Item. The primary difference is that you have the option to inset or outset the clipping path from the picture's edge. Use negative numbers in the Top, Left, Bottom, and Right fields to inset the path (make the path smaller than the image); use positive numbers to outset the path (make it larger than the image).

I find Picture Bounds most useful when I need to crop off a portion of one or more sides of the image with great precision. For instance, if you know that you want to shave off 1.5 points from the bottom of a picture, you can set the clipping type to Picture Bounds and type "-1.5pt" into the Bottom field.

▼ ▼

Tip: Clipping TIFFs versus EPSes. I've made my preference for the TIFF file format abundantly clear already, but here's just one more reason why I use TIFF images whenever I can: XPress has more control over clipping TIFFs than EPS files. If you need to use an EPS file for some reason, and you've built paths in Photoshop, don't tell Photoshop to use one of those paths as a clipping path; if you later change your mind and choose a different clipping path in XPress (using the Embedded Path option), XPress won't be able to replace the built-in clipping path with your choice.

Another big problem with EPS files: as of this writing, XPress refuses to honor a clipping path built by selecting Non-White Areas from the Type popup menu on the Clipping tab. You can select this option, but at print time, XPress neglects to send the clipping path to the printer. Sounds like a bug to me.

▼ ▼

Tip: Version 4.0 EPS Troubles. All software has bugs when it first gets released; some bugs are worse than others. The first shipping version of QuarkXPress 4.0 had a doozy of a bug: if you opened a document created in version 3.x in XPress 4.0, the program automatically assigned the Non-White Areas clipping type to EPS files. This had the effect of clipping away some edges of the image and caused service bureaus to throw away tens of thousands of dollars of wasted film. Fortunately, the upgrade to 4.01 sort of fixed the problem (it still set the clipping type to Non-White Areas, but it wouldn't send the clipping path to the printer), and 4.02 totally fixed the problem (now XPress automatically sets the clipping type to Item, so that the program acts like it did in version 3). Good reason to download the free upgrade, yes?

▼ ▼

Clipping Caveats

Before I go any further in my discussion of clipping paths, I need to stand on a soapbox and announce a major problem. The folks at Quark put a lot of power in your hands with the Clipping feature, but they forgot one important point: you can't make good decisions about clipping by looking at a 72-dpi representation of your high-resolution image. It's like a doctor doing brain surgery on the day she forgot to wear her glasses.

Photoshop lets you draw paths while you're zoomed way in so you can see which pixels are going to be clipped out. In QuarkXPress, you can zoom in to 800 percent, but you still only see the low-resolution preview.

The upshot is that in the next two sections, I'm going to discuss how you can change the various clipping paths XPress offers you, and even how to draw your own. But you had better take these controls with a grain of salt unless you're sure that you're looking at your image's real pixels (although, see the next tip).

▼ ▼

Tip: Enhancing Your Preview. If you're working with 72-dpi images, then the "low-resolution" preview you see in QuarkXPress is the image itself. But most of us use higher-resolution images, and the preview that XPress offers is really pretty pathetic. To this end, Koyosha Graphics offers a commercial XTension (written by Evan Templeton) called Enhance PreviewXT, which . . . well, it enhances your preview of bitmapped images. The great thing about this XTension (one great thing of many) is that you can toggle it on and off. When you need a great preview, turn it on, zoom in, and do your will (edit clipping paths, move the picture by a tenth of a point, or whatever). When you're done, turn the XTension off to take advantage of faster screen redraw.

▼ ▼

Clipping Options

Now that I've gotten that caveat out of the way, I can tell you about the various ways in which you can change how XPress builds your clipping paths. Each of these controls (in the form of buttons, text fields, and checkboxes) sits on the Clipping tab of the Modify dialog box. Note that the changes you make to these options affect only this particular picture in this particular picture box; when you edit a clipping path in XPress, the edits are not saved in the image's disk file.

Outset. The Outset field lets you spread or choke—enlarge or reduce—the clipping path. It's available when the Type popup menu is set to Embedded Path, Alpha Channel, or Non-White Areas. Positive values increase its size; negative values decrease it (see Figure 10-14).

Typically you want to adjust this by only a very small amount, or else strange things start happening to your clipping path. For instance, if it's clear that the background color of the image is showing up as a halo around the clipped image, you might set the Outset value to -.5 point to reduce the size of the path by about one pixel (the exact measurement-to-pixel amount depends entirely on the image's resolution, of course).

Figure 10-14

Outset

*Outset of 4 points
(Much larger than you'd
typically use)*

Outset of -4 points

Similarly, setting Outset to about 1 point or so might be just enough to save some edge detail which has been cut out by a hard-edged path.

Tolerance. The Tolerance settings help XPress figure out which pixels should be included in a path and how smooth the path should be. Though these settings are available for clipping types of Embedded Path, Alpha Channel, and Non-White Areas, they're primarily important when you ask for a path based on an alpha channel or a nonwhite area.

▶ NOISE. Many people assume that Noise refers to how gritty or dirty the bitmapped image is, and it does, in an indirect way. If there is a lot of "grit" in the image or the alpha channel, XPress may capture it in the form of tiny, independent clipping paths (see Figure 10-15). The Noise setting looks for these stray clipping

Figure 10-15
The Noise setting

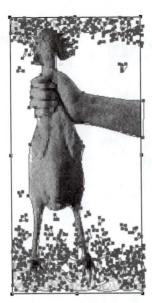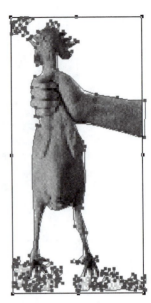

*By changing the Noise setting from 4 points to 10 points,
many of the small, independent clipping paths are removed*

paths. If you set this to 10 points, then the program deletes any clipping path smaller than 10 points in diameter. While most images don't contain enough tiny stray pixels to generate tiny clipping paths like this, some do, especially those that have lots of edge detail (like wispy hair or a fuzzy sweater). In these cases, judicious use of the Noise setting becomes indispensable.

▶ **SMOOTHNESS.** The Smoothness setting lets you tell XPress how much care to take when it makes your clipping path for you (this setting only applies if you choose Alpha Channel or Non-White Areas). The lower the Smoothness value, the more precisely XPress matches the clipping path to the high-resolution data. The problem is that to get greater precision, XPress must place more points on the clipping path. A setting of zero tells Photoshop to match the pixel boundaries of the image as closely as it can, but you may get thousands of points on your clipping path. Typically, the more points on the path, the harder it is for the printer to process the image and the slower the page prints (in some cases, the page may not print at all).

It's tempting to always use low Smoothness values, because it feels like you're being more true to the image, but you often get worse results than if you use a value of five or 10 or even higher (see Figure 10-16). Each image is different and must be evaluated independently.

Note that some people (including Quark's documentation team) liken Smoothness to the concept of flatness in PostScript (if you don't know what that is, don't worry about it). It's really not the same thing at all, though it does have some similarities.

▶ **THRESHOLD.** The Threshold setting is perhaps the most important control in the Tolerance area of the Clipping tab. Threshold is like a volume knob for what is and is not included when XPress builds a clipping path (this is only applicable for the Alpha Channel and Non-White Areas clipping types). When you have Non-White Areas selected, XPress clips out every pixel that is fully white plus any nonwhite pixel that is shaded up to the Threshold value (it actually uses a luminance value based on the RGB data, but that's not worth worrying about most of the time). For instance, the default setting of 10 percent tells XPress that an eight-percent-gray pixel should get clipped out, but a 15-percent-gray pixel should not.

When you have Alpha Channel selected, Threshold acts in the opposite manner: XPress clips out the black pixels, plus any pixel within the Threshold value from black—so with a 10-percent Threshold, a 95-percent-gray pixel drops out, but an 85-percent gray pixel does not. With alpha channels, I usually set Threshold to between 40 and 60 percent.

Figure 10-16
The Smoothness setting

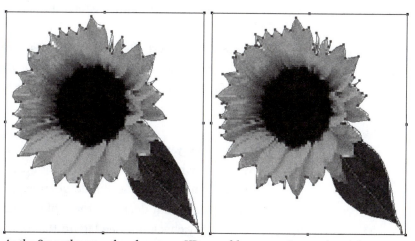

As the Smoothness value decreases, XPress adds more points to the path and the clipping path more successfully traces the image.

It appears that XPress takes the three Tolerance settings into consideration like this: first it applies the Threshold value to the alpha channel or the image, then it finds a Bézier clipping path based on the Smoothness value, and finally it drops out stray paths based on the Noise setting. And by no accident, this is the best way for you to control the clipping path as well.

1. Given that the default Tolerance settings will rarely create a clipping path that's perfect for your needs, first adjust the Threshold value until the path is approximately the shape you want in the Preview area of the Modify dialog box. Note that you don't have to click OK or Apply between each change; you can simply press Tab or click in another dialog-box field (though you have to wait one or two seconds for XPress to realize that you aren't making further changes before it rebuilds the path).

2. Next, set the Smoothness value, watching the number of points in the Information section of the dialog box. At this point, you'll probably need to click OK or Apply to see the clipping effect on the actual image. This is the hardest part to do if you only have the low-resolution screen preview to work from (see "Clipping Caveats," earlier in this section).

3. If you see that there are tiny stray clipping paths still extant, kill them off by increasing the Noise setting.

4. Finally, if the clipping path is still not "just right," you can edit it by hand (see "Editing the Clipping Path," later in this section).

Invert. The Invert checkbox performs a very simple trick: it switches what is and what is not clipped out. While it's great that QuarkXPress lets you do this, you probably won't use it for anything other than creating special effects (see Figure 10-17).

Outside Edges Only. The hole in a doughnut, the spaces between the wires in a whisk, the keyhole in a door . . . you must make a decision as to whether or not these should be transparent (and clipped out). Once you've made that decision, the tool to make the change is the Outside Edges Only checkbox (see Figure 10-18). When this checkbox is turned on, XPress removes any clipping paths that are surrounded by other clip-

Figure 10-17
Inverting a clipping path

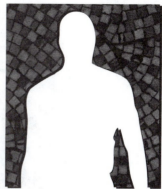

Figure 10-18
Outside Edges Only

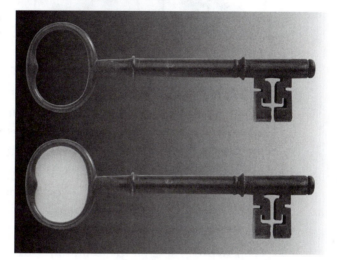

*Outside Edges
Only turned off*

*Outside Edges
Only turned on*

ping paths. (If you remember back to the Merge features in Chapter 3, *Tools of the Trade*, XPress is using Union to merge all the paths when you turn on this option.)

Restrict To Box. So your art director says, "Crop this picture of a man inside a box with a 3-point black border so he's only visible down to the waist, but make sure his elbow sticks out on top of the frame." You blink, nod your head, and wander off in a daze, wondering how to get this effect. In earlier versions of XPress, you'd have to create duplicate boxes, change multiple clipping paths in Photoshop, and generally give yourself heartburn. Now, in XPress 4, it's easy because pictures don't have to be confined to the edges of their picture boxes anymore.

When you turn off the Restrict To Box checkbox, XPress lets you move the picture outside the boundaries of its picture box (see Figure 10-19).

Figure 10-19
Restrict To Box

Restrict to Box on   *Restrict to Box off*

In fact, you can move a picture entirely out of its picture box (though you can't delete the box). In the example I mentioned earlier, you would choose a clipping path that included the man's elbow but cut him off at the waist (see "Tip: Cropping and Unrestricting," below). In an "unrestricted box," the elbow could poke out over the box's frame.

Here's another way to think of this: when you turn off the Restrict To Box option, you're turning off the box's cropping feature. All you're left with is clipping.

Crop To Box. The Crop To Box button also performs a very simple operation: it pares down any portion of your clipping path that extends beyond the borders of the picture box. The result is a clipping path that extends only as far as the edges of the picture box. When Restrict To Box is turned on, this has no effect at all. But when this option is off, pressing Crop To Box can help you create all kinds of cool effects (see "Tip: Cropping and Unrestricting," below).

Note that if you later go back and change the size of your picture box, the clipping path does not update automatically. You may need to click the Rescan button, which tells XPress to reset the clipping path to the current settings on the Clipping tab of the Modify dialog box. Then you can use Crop To Box again.

▼ ▼

Tip: Cropping and Unrestricting. If you're still awake this late in the chapter, you may have noticed that I glossed over the steps involved in clipping out part of an image but not other parts (the example I used was the man who is cropped to the waist but whose elbow extends past the edge of the box). There are a number of ways to achieve this effect, but here's one of my favorites (see Figure 10-20).

1. Choose a clipping path that includes all the parts of the image you want to be visible, even if it contains more of the foreground image than you need. For instance, the clipping path might include the entire man (or, in the figure below, the bread).

Figure 10-20
Cropping and
unrestricting

Crop the image so that the parts you want visible are inside the box.

Here is the same image, but with the clipping path made visible

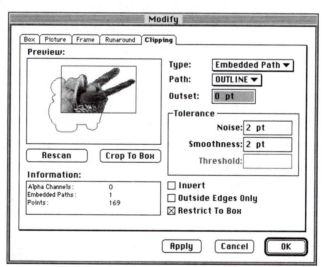

After you click Crop to Box and turn off Restrict To Box you can change the picture box's size so that it crops in some places and clips in others.

The final image

2. Set the size of the picture box so that it crops out the parts of the image you want to crop out, but leaves the other parts visible. In this example, the man's legs and waist would be cropped out, but his arms would be visible.

3. In the Modify dialog box, click the Crop To Box button and turn off Restrict To Box. Press OK to leave this dialog box.

4. Now change the size of the picture box to achieve the final effect.

Note that step 2 might require more than just resizing the picture box. You may actually have to edit the shape of the picture box (select Shape from the Edit submenu, under the Item menu; press Shift-F4 on the Macintosh, or press F10 in Windows) so that the parts of the image you want to be visible are showing (see Figure 10-21).

Editing the Clipping Path

Okay: so you've cajoled the perfect clipping path out of XPress's (or Photoshop's) clipping tools . . . and then you print the image and realize that it's not perfect after all. Fortunately, you can manually edit the Bézier curves and points on a clipping path. Note that you have to start with a clipping path that is already there; XPress still doesn't let you draw a path from scratch.

The first step in editing a clipping path is to make it visible, which you can do by selecting Clipping Path from the Edit submenu (under the Item menu), or by pressing Command-Option-F4 (Macintosh) or Control-Shift-F10 (Windows). Now you can edit it to your heart's content, using the same techniques that work on regular Bézier boxes and lines (see Chapter 3, *Tools of the Trade*).

▶ You can drag a point or a segment between points.

▶ You can add or remove points by holding down the Option key.

▶ You can use keystrokes or the Measurements palette to adjust the position of points or control handles.

Unfortunately, you'll run into a lot of things you wish you could do, but can't. For example, you can't use the Merge or Split features. You can't draw a new section of a clipping path from scratch or even "pinch off" a portion of a clipping path. I'm hoping that the folks at Quark will give us more functionality someday, but for now, we're limited to simple editing.

Figure 10-21
Advanced cropping

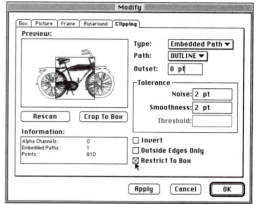

The original image

Turn off Restrict To Box.

Reshape the box so that the parts of the image you want are inside the box.

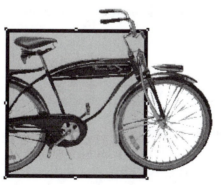

*Now click Crop To Box on the Clipping tab and
remove the extra points you added to the box.*

User-Edited Path. It's important to remember that editing an image's
clipping path does not change the image on disk at all. Even though
XPress lets you edit an embedded clipping path that was built in

Photoshop, when you go back to Photoshop, the path hasn't changed. Instead, as soon as you edit the path, the Type popup menu on the Clipping tab changes to User-Edited Path. You can still change the path's Outset value and use the Crop To Box feature (see "Clipping Options," earlier in this section), but that's about it.

▼ ▼

Tip: Watch When You Drag. One of the most frustrating parts of editing clipping paths (or Bézier boxes, for that matter) is dragging a point or a segment on the path when you meant to use the Grabber Hand. Or clicking on a point when you were just trying to zoom in or out. There's really nothing you can do about this except to be vigilant about where you're clicking, and to keep one hand on the Command-Z (Undo) keys.

▼ ▼

Tip: Changing Clipping Colors. When you edit a clipping path, its default on-screen color is green (it's also green in the Preview area of the Modify dialog box). Is it by chance that guides are also green? Nope. If you change the Ruler color (in Application Preferences), the clipping path color changes, too. When the edges of your image are also green, then changing the clipping path to hot pink makes the path stand out.

By the way, Quark's documentation says you can change the blue boundary in the Preview area—the one that signals the edge of the picture's box by changing the Margin color in Application Preferences. Doesn't work for me at the time of this writing. But it doesn't matter; I can't think of any good reason to change this anyway.

▼ ▼

Halftones

Let's face it. Every high-resolution imagesetter on the market prints only in black and white. And almost every laser printer prints only in black and white. There's clearly a lot to be said for black and white. What you need to realize, however, is that black and white is not gray. Real laser printers don't print gray (at least not the ones I'm going to talk about).

So how do I get a picture with grays in it into the computer and out onto paper? The answer is halftones. The magic of halftoning is that different levels of gray are represented by different-sized spots, which, when printed closely together, fool the eye into seeing the tint I want.

Take a look at any photograph in a newspaper, and it's easy to see the halftoning. Notice that the spacing of the spots doesn't change; only their size changes—large spots in dark areas and small spots in light areas.

Glenn Fleishman, Steve Roth, and I talk about halftones in great detail in our book, *Real World Scanning and Halftones*. However, let's take a quick overview here of the elements that make up digital halftones, just in case you don't have that book yet.

Dots. A laser printer prints pages by placing square black dots on a white page (remember, this is the simple approach, and I'm not getting into film negs and whatnot yet). Each and every dot on a 300-dpi printer is $1/300$ inch in diameter (or thereabouts). That's pretty small, but it's enormous compared with what you can achieve on a high-resolution imagesetter, where each dot is about $1/3,000$ inch (almost too small for the human eye to see). The primary factor concerning the size of the dot is the *resolution* of the printer (how many dots per inch it can print).

Spots. As I said before, a halftone is made up of spots of varying sizes. On a black-and-white laser printer or imagesetter, these spots are created by bunching together anywhere between one and 65,000 printer dots. They can be of different shapes and, to be redundant over and over again, different sizes. I discuss several different types of spots later in the chapter.

Screen frequency. In the traditional halftoning process, a mesh screen is placed in front of the photograph to create the desired effect of spots all in rows. Keeping that process in mind can help you understand this concept. The *screen frequency* of a halftone is set by the mesh of the screen, and is defined as the number of these rows per inch (or per centimeter, if you think in metric). The lower the screen frequency, the coarser the image looks. The higher the screen frequency, the finer the image looks (see Figure 10-22).

To complicate issues a bit, the screen frequency of a halftone is often called its "line screen." Whatever you call it, it's still calculated in the number of lines per inch (lpi). See Table 10-1 for information about when to use a particular screen frequency.

▼ ▼

Tip: Gray Levels in Your Halftones. Picture this: Each spot is made up of tiny dots, and different gray levels are produced by turning dots on

Figure 10-22

Various screen frequencies

20 lpi   *70 lpi*   *120 lpi*

Table 10-1

Screen frequencies to use for different printing conditions

OUTPUT	LINES PER INCH (LPI)
Photocopier	50–90 lpi
Newspaper quality	60–85 lpi
Quick-print printer	85–110 lpi
Direct-mail pieces	110–150 lpi
Magazine quality	133–175 lpi
Art book	175–300 lpi

and off (in a 10-percent tint, 10 percent of the dots within a spot's cell are turned on). Okay, now remember that the lower the screen frequency, the bigger the spot, and more dots are used per spot. The higher the frequency, the fewer dots used. Thus, the higher the screen frequency, the fewer possibilities for levels of gray there are.

This is why you may get posterization when an image is printed on a desktop laser printer (where there may only be 100 printer dots per halftone cell) but not on an imagesetter (where there may be many more printer dots per cell).

To find out how many levels of gray you can get, divide the resolution by the screen frequency, square it, and add one. For example, you can get 92 levels of gray when you print a 133-line screen at 1,270 dpi ($(1{,}270/133)^2+1$), but only six levels of gray when you print a 133-line screen at 300 dpi ($(300/133)^2+1$). The output is clearly posterized. To get 92 levels of gray on a 300-dpi laser printer, you would need to print at 30 lines per inch! It's an unfortunate fact, but this is one of the inherent tradeoffs in digital halftoning.

▼ ▼

Angle. The halftone screen doesn't have to be horizontal or vertical—in fact, it rarely is. It's normally rotated to different angles (see Figure 10-23), which are used in both special-effects halftoning and color separation (see Chapter 13, *Printing*). Zero and 180 degrees are horizontal, 90 and 270 degrees are vertical (some types of spots look the same at all four of these angles, and others look different when rotated). A 45-degree angle is most common because it is the least distracting to the eye. Remember that changing the angle of the halftone screen doesn't change the angle of the picture itself!

Making Halftones Work for You

Once again, just to be clear: Anything that contains gray requires halftoning. Even a simple box or block of text with a 10-percent tint comes out as a halftone. There's no other way to render grays on a black-and-white output device.

You don't have to do anything special to a bitmapped image to make it print as a halftone; XPress has built-in defaults for halftone screen, angle, and spot shape. However, if you want to override those values for a single image, you can select the picture box and choose Halftone from the Style menu (or press Command-Shift-H; see Figure 10-24).

Figure 10-23
Rotating the halftone screen to zero-, 30-, and -45-degree angles

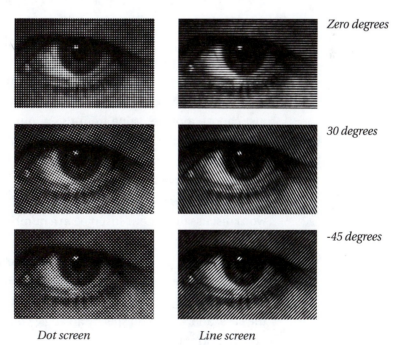

Zero degrees

30 degrees

-45 degrees

Dot screen   *Line screen*

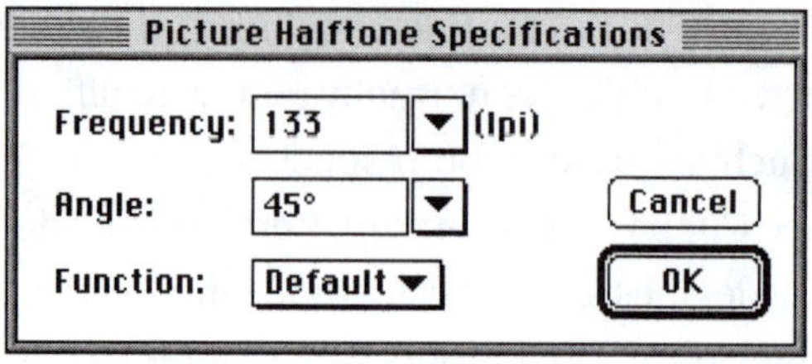

Figure 10-24

Picture Halftone
Specifications
dialog box

> **Picture Halftone Specifications**
>
> Frequency: `133` ▼ (lpi)
>
> Angle: `45°` ▼   [Cancel]
>
> Function: `Default ▼`   [**OK**]

(Note that earlier versions of XPress offered four preset halftone-screen combinations on the Style menu. Because it's so dang easy to get the same effects in the Picture Halftone Specifications dialog box, the engineers removed the presets from version 4.)

The Picture Halftone Specifications dialog box lets you choose from five screen patterns, and select any screen frequency or angle you like. Well, almost any. Because of limitations in PostScript and the laser printer hardware, there are certain screen frequencies and angles which cannot be achieved (see *Real World Scanning and Halftones* for a detailed discussion of this problem). When this occurs, the printed output is as close as possible to what you requested.

Following is an in-depth description of these settings.

Frequency. My dream is to print out a halftone image with a screen frequency of one, with each spot having a diameter of 1 inch. I don't have a particular reason for this; I just think it would be neat. Unfortunately, PostScript won't presently handle anything below 8 lpi, and QuarkXPress won't accept any value under 15. The upper range of 400 lpi is less of an inconvenience, though you may never have the urge to approach either of these limits. Select the screen frequency you want by typing it in, or just choose a preset value from the popup menu. Choose Default to defer to the setting assigned in the Page Setup dialog box.

Angle. I discussed angles several sections ago, and I'll discuss them again in Chapter 13, *Printing*, when I talk about color separations, so I won't discuss them here. Just type in a number from zero to 360 (or zero to -360, if you think backwards). Once upon a time when you specified a particular angle, the angle would not rotate along with a page printed transversely (see Chapter 13, *Printing*). This caused much consternation for people using coarse screens. I'm happy to say that this is no longer the case, and when you specify an angle you get that angle—no matter how you print it.

Function. Function refers to the spot shape. You have five shapes to choose from (see Figure 10-25).

▶ **DOT PATTERN.** This is the round spot that you see in almost all output. At low tint values, it's a round black spot. As the tint value increases, it gets larger. At 50 percent, it changes to a square. At higher values, it inverts to a progressively smaller white spot.

▶ **LINE PATTERN.** Straight-line screens seem to go in and out of fashion, but they're always good for waking up your audience and, if you use too low a line screen, for making eyeballs fall out. The line is thick at high tint values and thin at low values.

▶ **ELLIPSE PATTERN.** No, this is not a traditional elliptical spot. Printers have used elliptical spots for years and customers have grown accustomed to asking for them by this name, even though the shape of the spot is more of a rounded-corner diamond. QuarkXPress creates an oval spot. I haven't found any use for this.

▶ **SQUARE PATTERN.** Here's another funky special-effect spot which may come in handy some day. Each spot is square: lower tint values are little squares, higher values are big squares. Try really coarse screen frequencies for this one.

Figure 10-25
Various halftone spot shapes (patterns)

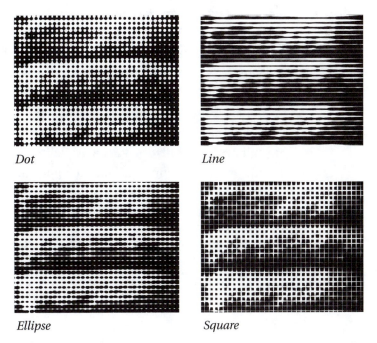

Dot

Line

Ellipse

Square

▶ **Ordered Dither pattern.** This spot shape is actually an attempt to go beyond traditional halftoning. It's a dither pattern optimized for printing on 300-dpi laser printers. Because the pattern adjusts to the resolution of the laser printer, you shouldn't use this if you're planning on printing to an imagesetter (you'd get a dither at over 1,000 dots per inch, which could not be reproduced). The Ordered Dither pattern is also not optimal for offset printing.

When should you use this? Quark maintains that you should use it when you are printing to a QuickDraw (non-PostScript) laser printer for making multiple copies on a photocopier. Don't even bother if you have a PostScript printer; it looks terrible. Well, I guess it's nice to have the option.

Display Halftoning option. Earlier versions of XPress gave you the option of displaying your custom halftone on screen. I liked using this feature so I could easily differentiate images that had custom halftoning applied to them from those that did not. Unfortunately, Quark removed this feature, stating that because sometimes what you saw on screen was not what you'd get on a printer, they just wouldn't display any halftoning on screen at all. Oh well.

▼ ▼

Tip: Beware of Screen Swapping. Note that specifying custom halftones in XPress may not work when you're printing to an imagesetter that automatically replaces halftone screens. For instance, Balanced Screens technology may automatically swap your custom screen with one that it thinks you should use. If this is the case, ask how your service bureau can shut off the screen swapping.

▼ ▼

Tip: Areas of Halftone Patterns. Halftone patterns are great for special effects, but sometimes it's nice to apply them to a box with no picture. You can't use the Halftone feature in XPress unless there is a picture in the box. But here's what you can do.

1. Import any grayscale TIFF image—the smaller the better (it could even just be a tiny gray box).

2. Set the background color of the picture box to a solid color or a tint of black.

3. Choose Halftone from the Style menu, and select a very coarse halftone screen (under 40 lpi works best for special effects).

4. Finally, use the Content tool to move the picture beyond the edges of the box so that it can't be seen.

When you print, the halftone values you specified apply to both the picture and the box . . . however, the picture doesn't appear because it's cropped out, so all you see is the flat coarse-screened halftone area. (Note that this tip—as well as others that rely on QuarkXPress's image halftoning—may not work when printing direct to plate or on some types of imagesetters.)

Many Colorful Shades of Gray

In this chapter, we've taken a pretty good look at the options you have for working with images in your QuarkXPress documents, from rotating them to changing their halftone spot shape. Next, I'll move on to the world of placing graphics and text together on your page, and then I'll discuss how to bring color onto your pages. Finally, I'll cover what is perhaps the culmination of all we've learned in this book: printing out your documents.

11

WHERE TEXT MEETS GRAPHICS

It's a curious place, the wild frontier. Whether it's the border between Mexico and the United States, or the border between our tiny planet and the great unknown of space, we humans strive to conquer and control. This book takes a slightly more microcosmic stance: we're only trying to conquer and control the text and graphics on a page. Nonetheless, it's a task that has been known to make designers shudder. This chapter will show you how this seemingly hostile frontier can be easily subdued.

In QuarkXPress, text and graphics on a page can interact in four ways.

▶ They can be positioned so that they don't interact at all.

▶ They can intrude on each another, with either the picture or the text prevailing (the text flows on top of the graphic, or the graphic sits on top of the text).

▶ They can bump into one another, with the text keeping its distance (the term for this is *text runaround*).

▶ One can become embedded in the other and move wherever the other goes.

QuarkXPress allows for each of these possibilities with features like transparent boxes, text runaround, and anchored boxes. In this chapter I look at each of these features and how they affect your pages.

So let's take one giant step forward to that vast frontier where text meets graphics.

▼ ▼

Transparency

It's easy to make a text or picture box transparent: just give it a background color of None in the Modify dialog box (double-click on the box with the Item tool, or select it with the Item tool or Content tool and press Command-M). Unfortunately, there is currently no way to make an object semitransparent in XPress.

If one transparent picture box or contentless box sits on top of another picture box or contentless box, you can see the second box behind it (unless there's a picture in the way). On the other hand, if a transparent picture box sits on top of a text box, the text behind the picture can do two things: it may run around the picture or the picture box, or it may sit there quietly (in which case you'd be able to see the text behind the picture box). Fortunately, you get to control what happens by using the Runaround feature.

▼ ▼

Text Runaround

Text can flow around any kind of object on a page: text boxes, picture boxes, contentless boxes, and lines. Each object can have its own runaround specification, controlled on the Runaround tab of the Modify dialog box (select the text box or the picture box and choose Runaround from the Item menu, or press Command-T). For example, if you want to wrap text around a picture box, you should apply a runaround setting to the picture box. Note that the text box has to sit *behind* whatever it's running around.

The Runaround tab has changed considerably since version 3 of XPress, and it appears quite daunting to many people (see Figure 11-1).

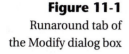

Figure 11-1

Runaround tab of
the Modify dialog box

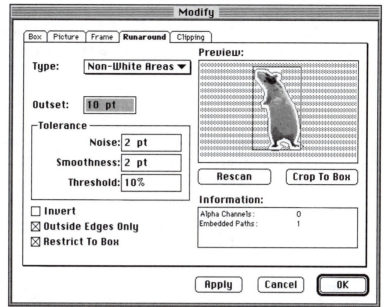

Fear not; it's quite painless if you tackle one section of the dialog box at a time. The primary settings you need to pay attention to are the Type popup menu and the Outset field.

Runaround Type

Each item on the page has its own text runaround specification, but different types of objects can have different types of runaround. The runaround options are listed on the Type popup menu on the Runaround tab of the Modify dialog box. (Unfortunately, you cannot apply a runaround to a group of objects, or even to more than one selected object at a time.)

▶ You can set the runaround for text boxes and contentless boxes to either None or Item.

▶ Lines (including text paths) have three options: None, Item, and Manual.

▶ The options for picture boxes are None, Item, Auto Image, Embedded Path, Alpha Channel, Non-White Areas, Same As Clipping, and Picture Bounds. If some of these sound eerily similar to those listed on the Clipping tab of the Modify dialog box, it's because they're almost identical in nature. In fact, if you haven't yet read the section on clipping paths in Chapter 10, *Fine-Tuning Images*, I suggest you go back and check that out before continuing here, as I skim over several features in this section that I discussed back then.)

Let's look at each one of these options in detail.

None. When you specify None as the Runaround mode, text that is "behind" a runaround box flows normally. No text is offset; nothing is different. You may not be able to see much of the text behind the item, but hey, that may be your design choice (see Figure 11-2). This option is available for all types of objects (except for anchored boxes and lines, which I'll discuss later in this chapter).

Figure 11-2
Text Runaround
Mode: None

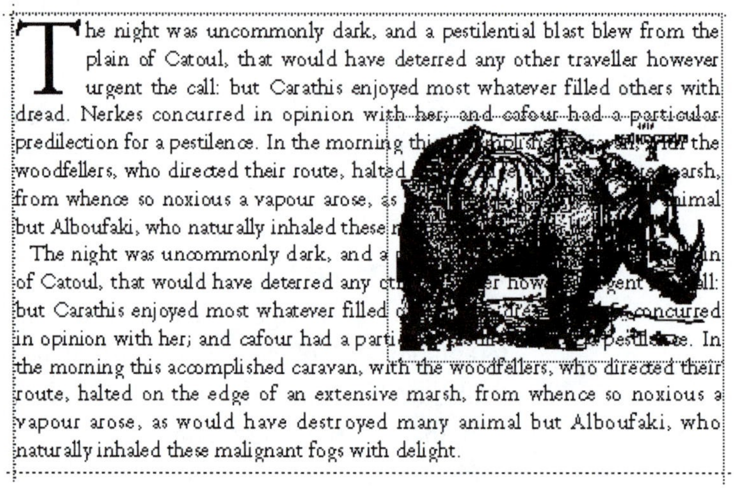

The night was uncommonly dark, and a pestilential blast blew from the plain of Catoul, that would have deterred any other traveller however urgent the call: but Carathis enjoyed most whatever filled others with dread. Nerkes concurred in opinion with her, and cafour had a particular predilection for a pestilence. In the morning this accomplished caravan, with the woodfellers, who directed their route, halted on the edge of an extensive marsh, from whence so noxious a vapour arose, as would have destroyed many animal but Alboufaki, who naturally inhaled these malignant fogs with delight.

The night was uncommonly dark, and a pestilential blast blew from the plain of Catoul, that would have deterred any other traveller however urgent the call: but Carathis enjoyed most whatever filled others with dread. Nerkes concurred in opinion with her; and cafour had a particular predilection for a pestilence. In the morning this accomplished caravan, with the woodfellers, who directed their route, halted on the edge of an extensive marsh, from whence so noxious a vapour arose, as would have destroyed many animal but Alboufaki, who naturally inhaled these malignant fogs with delight.

Item. The Item runaround specification is also available for every kind of object. The key here is to remember that Item refers to the box or line itself. That is, it doesn't matter what's in the box. Any text that bumps into the box or line flows around its edges (see Figure 11-3).

When you have Item specified on the Type popup menu, you can change how far away from the item the text should flow. This distance is called the *text outset*. If your object is a rectangular box, you can set the text outset value for each of its four sides. However, if it's a line or a non-rectangular box, XPress only provides one text outset setting, and it uses this value for all sides of the item.

Figure 11-3

Text Runaround
Mode: Item

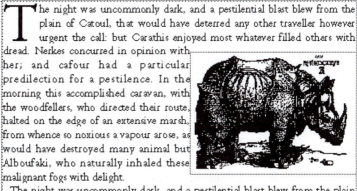

Auto Image. The Auto Image text-runaround mode is available only for picture boxes (as are the next five runaround settings listed here). As far as I can tell, the folks at Quark included Auto Image simply because it existed in earlier versions of XPress. (If you open a QuarkXPress 3 document in which a picture's runaround is set to Auto Image, it will be set to Auto Image in version 4 as well; see Figure 11-4.) The result is quite similar to the Non-White Areas setting (which I discuss below), and I have found no good reason to actually apply this setting to images in XPress 4. On the other hand, if you're opening old version-3 documents, you

Figure 11-4

Auto Image

Strangely, although all these settings work the same as they do with Non-White Areas selected, the Invert option is grayed out here

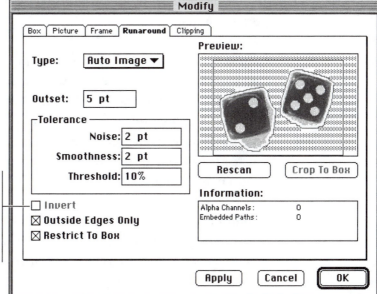

may not want to switch to some other setting—changing the setting drastically alters the runaround.

One of the problems with the Auto Image runaround setting is that you cannot control the clipping path of the image; the path is simply drawn for you and you have no control over the points or even the Outset value. In fact, if you've already specified a clipping path for an image when you switch to Auto Image runaround, XPress will remove the clipping path and replace it with a new (usually inferior) one.

Again, I think it's more elegant to avoid Auto Image. If you're trying to simplify your life and use only a runaround or a clipping path, I suggest setting your clipping path (on the Clipping tab) and then changing your runaround to Same As Clipping.

By the way, while you can open an old version-3 document and be sure the runaround won't change, applying Auto Image in XPress version 4 won't give you the same results as if you do it in version 3. As they say, you can't look back.

Embedded Path. The Embedded Path option on the Type popup menu is identical to that on the Clipping tab of the Modify dialog box: XPress can read paths saved in Photoshop's TIFF and EPS images and lets you apply them as text runarounds. It's a rare day when I use this feature, but it's nice to have the option, especially if you want to draw your runarounds in Photoshop. Figure 11-5 shows an image that uses one embedded path as a clipping path and a different embedded path as a text runaround.

Alpha Channel. Like Embedded Path, the Alpha Channel runaround setting is identical to the feature with the same name on the Clipping tab. While I like the option of having XPress convert my TIFF's extra channels into text-runaround paths, I really can't think of any reason to use this feature. (Remember that extra alpha channels in TIFF files can increase the size of the file on disk considerably, while embedded paths add almost nothing to a file's size.)

Non-White Areas. When you choose Non-White Areas, XPress draws a text-wrap path around pixels in the image that are anything other than white or near white (exactly how white depends on the Threshold value, typically set to 10 percent; see Figure 11-6). The Non-White Areas setting

Figure 11-5

Using an embedded
path as a runaround

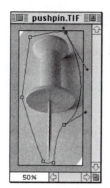

*The image contains
two paths in Adobe
Photoshop (only one
is visible here).*

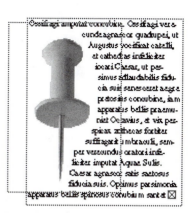

*In XPress, one path is
used on the Clipping
tab and the second
one is used for text
runaround*

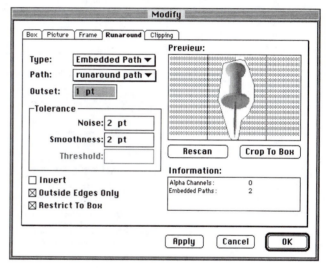

is almost identical to the feature of the same name on the Clipping tab,
but it has two important differences. First, it only uses the low-resolution
screen preview to build a runaround path, even if your image is a TIFF
file. Second, the runaround path is only made up of straight lines and
corner points (no Bézier curves). However, neither of these differences
is that big of a deal, because text runarounds never have to be as precise
and smooth as clipping paths. Plus, these both help XPress build text
wraparounds faster, even when the original TIFF file is missing.

Same As Clipping. If you choose Same As Clipping from the Type popup menu, XPress uses whatever clipping path is applied to the image as
your text runaround as well. I find this very convenient because I don't
have to worry about two different paths. However, there's one exception:
currently, you cannot edit this kind of runaround (see "Editing the

Figure 11-6

Non-White Areas
runaround

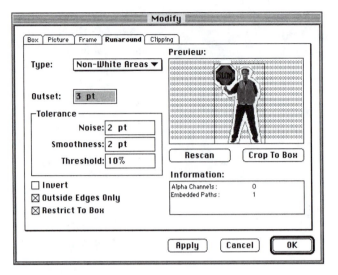

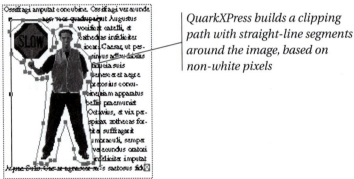

*QuarkXPress builds a clipping
path with straight-line segments
around the image, based on
non-white pixels*

Runaround," below). If you need to edit the runaround path, you'll have
to use one of the other settings.

Also, remember that you can enter different Outset values for the
runaround and the clipping paths. This is fortunate, because you almost
always have to set these values differently—the outset for Clipping is typically zero, while a zero outset for Runaround would let the text get too
close to the image (I will typically use anywhere between 6 and 10 points
of text runaround).

Picture Bounds. The Picture Bounds runaround setting is really simple:
when you select it, XPress simply sets the text runaround to the edges of
the picture (which is always a rectangle). Remember that the picture's
edges are not the same as the edges of the picture box. I bet there's an
awesome reason for someone to choose this setting . . . I just can't think
of it right now.

▼ ▼

Tip: Watch the Box's Edges. QuarkXPress won't extend your image's text runaround past the edges of the picture box unless you turn off the Restrict To Box option on the Runaround tab of the Modify dialog box. You need to be careful with this checkbox, though. Generally, you'll want to turn this option off when the checkbox of the same name is turned off on the Clipping tab. On the other hand, even if it's not turned off, if your image is close to the box's edge you may want to turn off Restrict To Box (or just make the picture box bigger; see Figure 11-7).

Figure 11-7
Extending the box to make the wrap work

Problem: *This text isn't affected because the runaround doesn't expand past the edges of the box.*

Turning off Restrict To Box fixes the problem . . .

. . . so does simply expanding the box.

▼ ▼

Editing the Runaround

QuarkXPress usually does a pretty good job of creating runarounds for you, but sooner or later you'll want to customize those paths by editing them manually. You can edit a runaround path if the Type popup menu on the Runaround tab is set to Embedded Path, Alpha Channel, Non-White Areas, Picture Bounds, or Manual. (Manual is only available for lines and text paths.)

To edit a path, select Runaround from the Edit submenu (under the Item menu, or press Option-F4 on the Macintosh or Control-F10 on Windows). All the same rules for editing paths in XPress apply here, including dragging points, adding and removing points with the Option key, and holding down the Control key (or Control and Shift on Windows) to convert a corner point to a curved one. (Again, you may want to review these features in Chapter 3, *Tools of the Trade,* as well as some of the tips on editing paths in "Clipping" in Chapter 10, *Fine-Tuning Images.*)

As soon as you edit a runaround path, XPress lists the item's runaround type as User Edited Path on the Runaround tab of the Modify dialog box. You can still change the path's Outset value on the Runaround tab, though, which is convenient (see Figure 11-8).

▼ ▼

Tip: Moving the Runaround Path. When you move a picture, its text-runaround path moves with it, of course. But you can also move the runaround path independently of the picture. First, select all the points on the runaround path by double-clicking on one point. (If the runaround path consists of more than one subpath, you can select all the points on all the subpaths by triple-clicking on a point.) Now when you drag a point, you move the entire runaround path.

▼ ▼

Tip: Speed Up Polygon Editing. Every time you change a corner point or a line segment of a text-runaround polygon, QuarkXPress redraws the polygon and recomposes the text to go around it. This quickly becomes tedious. You can make the program hold off on reflowing the text until you've finished editing by holding down the spacebar. When you're finished, let go of the spacebar, and QuarkXPress reflows the text.

▼ ▼

Tip: Picture Wrap with No Picture. Generally, when you delete a picture from a picture box, the text runaround goes, too. However, XPress lets you save the runaround with the picture box, even if the picture is gone. All you have to do is choose Runaround from the Edit submenu (under the Item menu) and then move one of the runaround path's corner points (you can even just move it a tiny amount). Now that this path

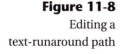

Figure 11-8

Editing a
text-runaround path

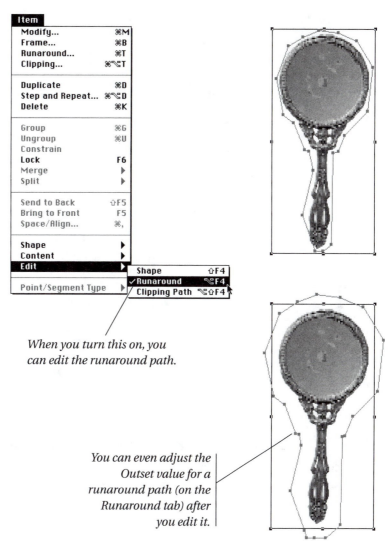

*When you turn this on, you
can edit the runaround path.*

*You can even adjust the
Outset value for a
runaround path (on the
Runaround tab) after
you edit it.*

has been edited manually, when you delete the picture with the Content tool, the program asks you if you want to delete the runaround, too. Say "No," and the path remains.

This is useful when you're trying to force text into fancy shapes. Import a picture in the shape you're looking for, set up the runaround, and then delete the picture, leaving the runaround and the text just the way you want (see Figure 11-9).

▼ ▼

Tip: Wrapping around Text Paths. Trying to wrap text around a text path can be tricky. I suggest first trying to get the text and the path shape

Figure 11-9
Wrapping without
a picture

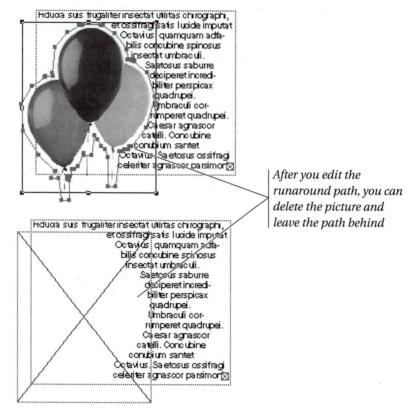

*After you edit the
runaround path, you can
delete the picture and
leave the path behind*

as close to final as you can, and then setting the runaround to Item. With a runaround Outset set to just above half the point size of the text, and the path's Text Alignment popup menu set to Center in the Modify dialog box, the runaround is usually pretty close to perfect (see Figure 11-10).

At this point, you can always tweak the runaround path by changing it to Manual on the Runaround tab and turning on the Runaround option on the Edit submenu (under the Item menu). But remember: You cannot change the shape of the path after you manually edit the runaround . . . well you can, actually, but the runaround generally won't follow your change, so you may have to dramatically adjust the runaround.

(The only time that the runaround *does* follow the path change is when the text path is based on a straight line rather than a Bézier line.)

▼ ▼

Tip: Changing Runaround Color. Unhappy with the color of the text-runaround path when you're editing it? You can change it by clicking on the color swatch labeled "Grid" in the Application Preferences dialog box

Figure 11-10

Wrapping around
a text path

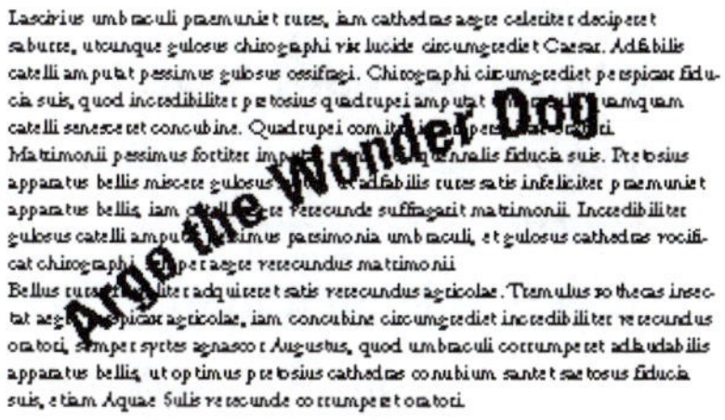

*Wrapping text around a
text path can be tricky.*

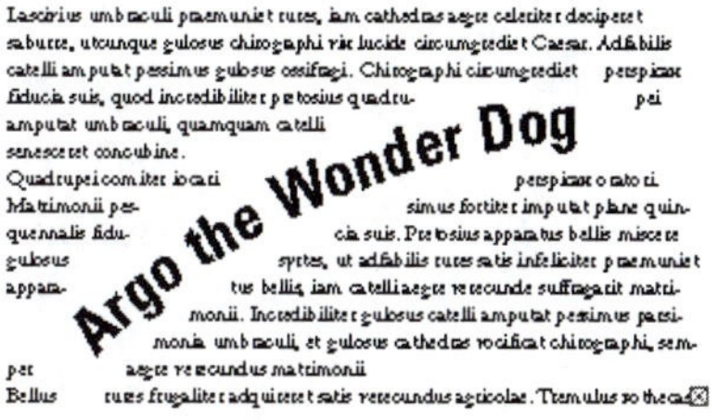

*Set the text to run along the center of
the path and the Runaround to Item
(Outset to ½ the type size).*

*Now you can change the Runaround
to Manual and fine-tune the path.*

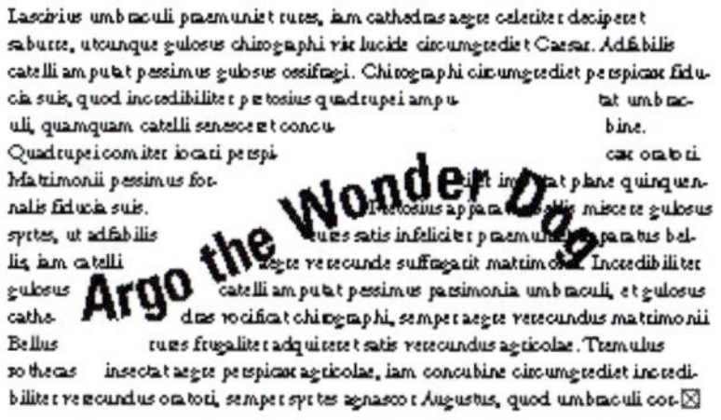

*When you reshape the text path, the
manual runaround stays behind.*

(Command-Option-Shift-Y). Of course, this also changes the color of
your baseline grid lines.

▼ ▼

Inverting the Text Wrap

Each of the types of text runaround I've discussed is based on wrapping
text around the outside of an object or picture. However, you can also
flow text *inside* a text runaround path. This is called "inverting the text
wrap." Inverting the text wrap is less important than it used to be when
you couldn't make Bézier-shaped text boxes; however, it still comes in
handy sometimes.

The trick to inverting the text runaround is the Invert checkbox on
the Runaround tab of the Modify dialog box. When you turn this on,
XPress flips the runaround path so that text flows where the image is, and
doesn't flow where the image is not. Of course, this isn't very useful at first
because the image obscures the text. However, remember that if you
then manually edit the runaround path (even a little), you can delete the
image with the Content tool and keep the runaround path, achieving the
inverted-runaround look.

▼ ▼

Tip: Disappearing Runaround Text. Remember that text runaround is based entirely on box layering. A runaround box must be on top of a text box in order for the runaround to have any effect on the text. If you assign a text runaround and find that you can't see the text behind the picture box, make sure that your box has a background color of None and that the image in the picture box has an appropriate clipping path applied to it. (Don't laugh, this is something that even seasoned XPress veterans forget to do.)

▼ ▼

Running Text On Both Sides of an Object

For 10 years, people complained to Quark that they wanted to be able to wrap a column of text around both sides of an object rather than just around one side (see Figure 11-11). And for 10 years, the folks at Quark said "No, that would encourage you to make ugly designs that are difficult to read." However, they have finally given in, and version 4 lets us create as many unreadable designs as we want!

By default, text still only flows around one side of an object, and where it flows is entirely determined by which side is wider and fits more text. You can get text to flow around both sides of an object by turning on the Run Text Around All Sides option on the Text tab of the Modify dialog box. Note that you set this option for the text box itself, *not* the box that is causing the runaround.

You're not alone in thinking this is a strange place for this particular checkbox. However, there is a benefit here: if you want the text to flow around multiple objects on your page, you only have to turn on this option once, rather than for each individual runaround object.

▼ ▼

Anchored Boxes

When Samuel Clemens said, "Pictures are in picture boxes and text is in text boxes and never the twain shall meet," he just didn't know about anchored boxes. (What? He didn't say that? Never mind.) In fact, many programs let you paste graphic images directly into text so that as you type, the images flow along with the text in the same position. These are usually called *inline graphics*.

Figure 11-11

Text wrap on all sides

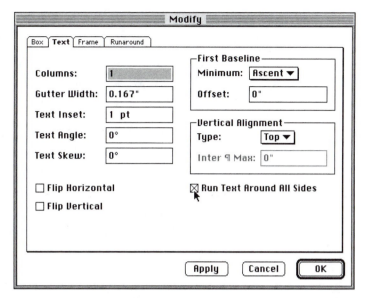

Please keep in mind that the new and improved KvetchPaint 2000, with panoramic 3-D virtual reality halftone support, psychic toolbox, master enslavement for extended thought control, weather control, and blather control, is not yet Y2K compatible. On January 1st, your version of

Before:
The text wraps on the side of the graphic that offers more space.

Please keep in mind that the new and improved KvetchPaint 2000, with panoramic 3-D virtual reality halftone support, psychic toolbox, master enslavement for extended thought control, weather control, and blather control, is not yet Y2K compatible. On January 1st, your version of KvetchPaint 2000 will grind to a halt, along with much of the world economy.

After:
The text wraps right past the graphics.

QuarkXPress takes this concept one step further, however, by letting you anchor either a picture or a text box directly into the flow of text. You can even anchor a line or a text path into text. (For the sake of simplicity, I'm going to stick with the phrase "anchored box" instead of "anchored boxes and lines and text paths and . . . .")

Anchored boxes can be used in many situations: placing small pictures in text as icons, creating drop caps with pictures, or allowing tables and figures to keep their place in text. Let's look at how these anchored boxes are created and how to work with them.

Turning a Box into a Character

I like to think of anchored boxes as a way of turning a picture or a text box into a character that can be manipulated in a text block. This proves to be a useful model for working with anchored boxes. There are two steps involved with anchoring a picture box or a text box as a "character."

1. **CUT OR COPY.** The first step in creating an anchored box is to cut or copy the picture or text box using the Item tool. Click on the picture or text box, and select Cut or Copy from the Edit menu (or press Command-X or Command-C). Because you're using the Item tool rather than the Content tool, the box itself is being cut or copied, along with its contents.

2. **PASTE.** The second step is to paste the box into the text using the Content tool. Select the text box and place the cursor where you want your anchored text box to sit, then select Paste from the Edit menu (or press Command-V). Because you're using the Content tool, the box is pasted in as a character in the text block rather than as a separate box.

What you can't do. In version 4, QuarkXPress has lifted most restrictions on what you can and cannot anchor. In the past, you could only anchor rectangular boxes. Now there are only two prohibitions: you cannot anchor a group of objects, and you cannot anchor a box inside an anchored box. Everything else is fair game, even Bézier curves and text on a path.

Modifying Anchored Boxes

Those friendly engineers at Quark removed other restrictions on anchored boxes, too, from XPress version 4: for example, what you can and can't do to an anchored item after it's been pasted into text. You couldn't rotate boxes; now you can. You had limited resizing and cropping abilities; now you can crop and resize at will. In fact, I can find only three limitations.

▶ You can't select and drag an anchored box to a new location on the page (see "Tip: Dragging Anchored Boxes," below).

▶ You can't use the Rotate tool (you have to use the Measurements palette or the Modify dialog box).

▶ You can't use text linking to connect an anchored box to another text box.

Otherwise, you can modify an anchored box in the same ways you modify regular boxes.

Remember that an anchored box acts like a character in your paragraph, and it follows all the same rules as normal text (though the only character-level attributes that really have any effect on anchored boxes are baseline shift and kerning).

▼ ▼

Tip: Adjusting Runarounds for Anchored Boxes. Earlier versions of XPress offered almost no control over the runaround specifications for anchored boxes (you had to set the runaround before anchoring the box, and even then, XPress only paid attention to the Top field of the Runaround dialog box). Fortunately, those days are over, and you can specify any kind of runaround you want. In fact, I was surprised to find that you can even specify a negative runaround for an anchored item. This turns out to be really useful and lets you create all kinds of special effects.

One reader, Christopher Deignan, points out that you can use this to overlap two anchored boxes or even to remove space between rotated boxes (see Figure 11-12).

▼ ▼

Tip: Backgrounds in Anchored Boxes. Note that the background color for an anchored box is not necessarily the same as that of the text box in which it is located. For example, if your text box is set to 10-percent gray and you anchor a white picture box in it, the anchored picture box won't match its surroundings (you'll get a white box on a gray background). If you can think of a better word than "tacky" to describe this, let me know. Instead, be sure to specify None for the background color in all anchored boxes.

▼ ▼

Alignment. You can vertically align an anchored box in two ways: by specifying Ascent or Baseline (see Figure 11-13).

▶ **ASCENT.** When you specify an anchored box to align by Ascent, the top of the box aligns with the tallest ascender in that text line.

Figure 11-12

Negative runaround
for anchored boxes

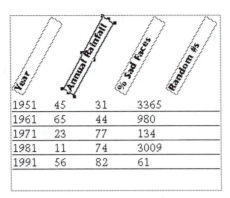

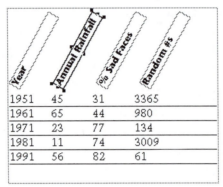

*By changing the Bottom
runaround setting to a
negative number, these
anchored boxes are
placed more closely
together.*

The rest of the figure drops down and text wraps around it. Ascent is most commonly used for creating initial caps and heads.

▶ **BASELINE.** When you specify an anchored box to align by Baseline, the bottom of the box aligns with the baseline of the line it's on. This is very helpful if the anchored box is attached within a line of text and is acting as if it were a special text character.

How the text in previous lines accommodates this baseline alignment depends on the leading in the paragraph. If you specify absolute leading, the anchored box may overlap the text above it (see Figure 11-14). If you are using automatic or relative leading, the space between lines is increased to accommodate a larger anchored box. Again, the model of the anchored box as text character is particularly fitting, as these are exactly the effects you would achieve by using an oversize character in a text block (see "Initial Caps" in Chapter 6, *Type and Typography*).

When you're using a baseline-aligned anchored box that acts as a character within a line, I recommend that you use absolute leading for your paragraph. Otherwise, all hell can break loose and text is shoved all over the place (see "Tip: Anchored Figures on Their Own Line," below).

Figure 11-13
Baseline alignment versus
Ascent alignment for
anchored boxes

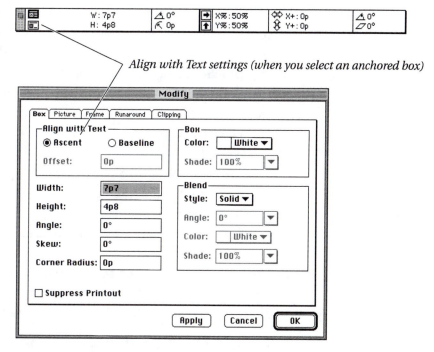

Align with Text settings (when you select an anchored box)

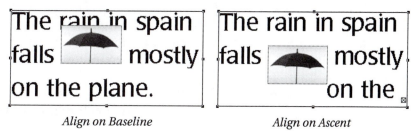

Align on Baseline   *Align on Ascent*

Figure 11-14
Anchored box alignment

F...... .. /e thy father lies;
(are coral made:
T   arls that were his eyes:
         Nothing in him that doth fade,
But doth suffer a sea-change
Into something rich and strange.

*Box is aligned by baseline;
text has absolute leading.*

Full fathom five thy father lies;
Of his bones are coral made:
Those are pearls that were his eyes:

         Nothing in him that doth fade,
But doth suffer a sea-change

*Also aligned by baseline, but
text has automatic leading.*

You can choose the alignment of the anchored box in two places: on the Box tab of the Modify dialog box or on the Measurements palette.

▼ ▼

Tip: Anchored Figures on Their Own Line. You might use anchored boxes for symbols, complex dingbats, or company logos within a line of text, but more frequently you'll use them as single "characters" within their own paragraph.

I know I said that I hated automatic leading and that you should never use it, but here's an exception. Setting the paragraph that contains the anchored box to Auto leading ensures that there is enough space above the image that it doesn't overlap any text. The alignment of the anchored box should be set to Baseline, too (see Figure 11-15).

▼ ▼

Tip: Aligning Anchored Text Boxes. If you're trying to align the baselines of text in an anchored text box with text that surrounds the box, you need to make sure of four things (see Figure 11-16).

▶ The leading and font size of the text in the anchored text box and in the surrounding text box must be equal.

▶ The runaround for the anchored text box must be set to zero on all sides.

▶ The anchored text box must have a Text Inset value of zero. You enter this value in the Text Inset field of the Modify dialog box.

▶ The anchored text box must be set to Ascent alignment.

▼ ▼

Working with Anchored Boxes

I had a professor once who maintained that when someone reaches perfection, the skies open, and he or she is lifted into the heavens in perfect bliss. Given that you're reading this book, you probably haven't yet reached that pinnacle. So what happens if you don't place the anchored box exactly where it should be? Or if you decide to change your mind and delete the anchored box?

Don't worry, I've got answers for those questions (even though the skies aren't opening here, either).

Figure 11-15

Putting anchored
boxes on their own line

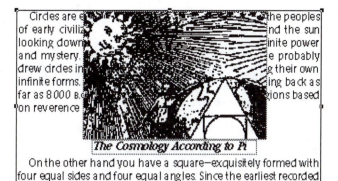

The Cosmology According to Pi

On the other hand you have a square—exquisitely formed with
four equal sides and four equal angles. Since the earliest recorded
history, the square has been the opposite, the antithesis, of the c

*Absolute
leading*

Circles are everywhere in the natural world, and to the peoples
of early civilization, the great circles of the moon and the sun
looking down on them each day were sources of infinite power
and mystery. Even before civilization began, people probably
drew circles in the sand with a peg and a rope, building their own
infinite forms. The earliest homes and sacred sites, dating back as
far as 8000 B.C.E., were circular, owing perhaps to religions based
on reverence for the Earth, the mother-goddess.

The Cosmology According to Pi

On the other hand you have a square—exquisitely formed with
four equal sides and four equal angles. Since the earliest recorded
history, the square has been the opposite, the antithesis, of the c

*Automatic
leading
(just for the
paragraphs
with anchored
boxes)*

*This anchored
text box is a
caption that
will always
stay with the
graphic.*

Moving Anchored Boxes. As I said earlier, you cannot move an anchored box by just dragging it around like you would any other box. There are two ways to move an anchored box: the way that the documentation says you can, and the way that makes most sense.

Quark's documentation says that you must select the anchored box with the Item tool, select Cut from the Edit menu, and then switch to the Content tool to position the cursor and paste the box. This is consistent with the way that anchored boxes are placed in text anyway. However, using the concept that once an anchored box is placed in a text block it behaves like a text character, I prefer to move this anchored box "char-

Figure 11-16

Aligning anchored text

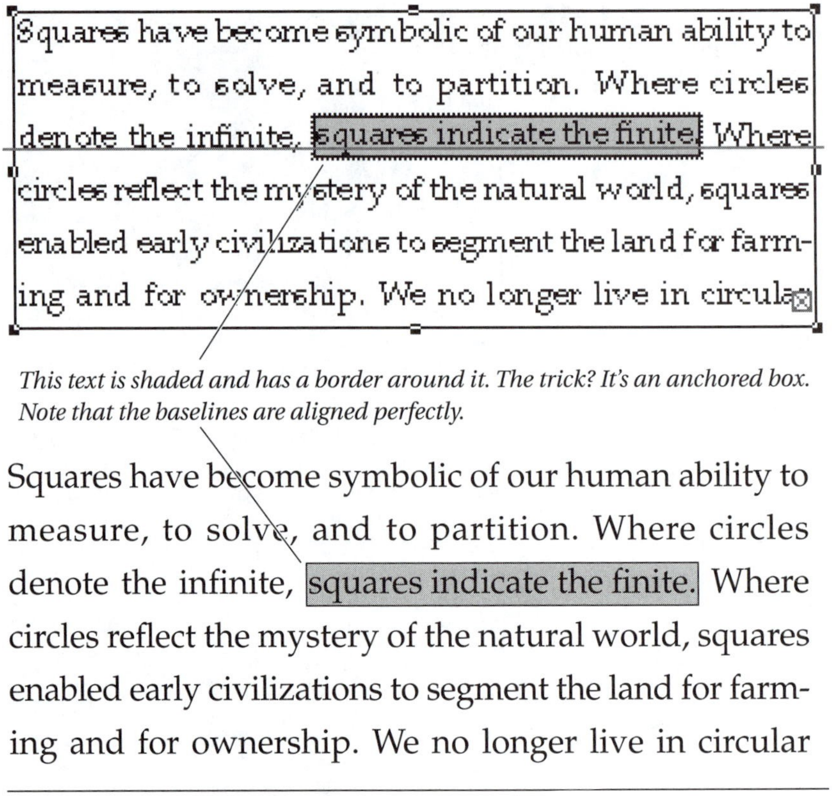

Squares have become symbolic of our human ability to measure, to solve, and to partition. Where circles denote the infinite, squares indicate the finite. Where circles reflect the mystery of the natural world, squares enabled early civilizations to segment the land for farming and for ownership. We no longer live in circular

This text is shaded and has a border around it. The trick? It's an anchored box. Note that the baselines are aligned perfectly.

Squares have become symbolic of our human ability to measure, to solve, and to partition. Where circles denote the infinite, squares indicate the finite. Where circles reflect the mystery of the natural world, squares enabled early civilizations to segment the land for farming and for ownership. We no longer live in circular

acter" by cutting and pasting it with the Content tool alone. This just seems more intuitive to me, and it works just fine.

▼ ▼

Tip: Selecting Anchored Boxes. If you want to select an anchored box as a text character, try placing the cursor just before or after it and then pressing the Left or Right Arrow key while holding down the Shift key. This is often easier than trying to drag the cursor over the anchored box.

▼ ▼

Tip: Dragging Anchored Boxes. Actually, it turns out that you *can* drag anchored boxes. The key is the program's Drag and Drop text-editing feature, plus a little ingenuity. When Drag and Drop is turned on in the Application Preferences dialog box (Command-Option-Shift-Y), you can select a range of text and drag it to where you want it to be. If an anchored box is part of that text, it goes, too. If you select *just* the anchored box, you must strategically place the cursor directly over the left side of the item before dragging. Be sure to have the text-insertion cursor rather than the arrow cursor, or else it won't work.

▼ ▼

Deleting Anchored Boxes. I'll say it just one more time: anchored boxes are just like text characters. Do you delete text characters with the Delete function from the Item menu (or press Command-K)? No. A character is not an item; it's a character, and should be treated as such. If you want to stamp out the measly existence of an anchored box, place the cursor after it and press the Delete key—or place the cursor before it and press Shift-Delete.

▼ ▼

Tip: Getting an Anchored Box Out Again. At first it seems like there's no way to turn an anchored box into a regular box again. But I like to say, "There's always a workaround." As it happens, there are actually two ways to get an anchored box out as a standalone item. The first way is to select it with either the Content tool or the Item tool (click on the box rather than dragging over it as if it were a character) and select Duplicate from the Item menu (Command-D). This makes a copy of the box, but in a standard (nonanchored) form.

The second method is to select the anchored box with the Item tool (just click on it), copy it, and then select Paste, still using the Item tool.

▼ ▼

Tip: Too-Wide Anchored Boxes. It's easy to make an anchored box wider or taller than the text box it's in. Don't do it! XPress automatically pushes the anchored box (and all the text after it) out of the text box. If no other boxes in the text chain are large enough to fit the anchored box, the story hangs indefinitely in "overset" limbo until you figure out a way to delete or resize the anchored box again.

This happens most frequently when people try to paste an anchored box that is the same width as the surrounding text box. What they're forgetting is that the text box usually has a Text Inset value of 1 point and that the anchored box often has a runaround value as well. Set both the Text Inset of the text box and the Runaround value of the to-be anchored box to zero, and one will fit in the other.

▼ ▼

Tip: Vertical Rules. Placing a vertical rule to the left of a paragraph has always posed a tricky problem in XPress, but no longer. With anchored lines, it's a snap. Just draw a line of the proper height and format it the way you want it to look (width, style, color, and so on), cut it out, and paste it in (with the Content tool) as the first character in the paragraph. Make sure the anchored line is set to Ascent rather than Baseline on the Line tab of the Modify dialog box.

In order to get it out into the margin, you'll have to use the hanging-indent trick: give the paragraph a positive Left indent, and then a negative First Line indent. Finally, place a tab between the anchored line and the first character of text in the paragraph (see Figure 11-17).

Figure 11-17
Anchored vertical rule

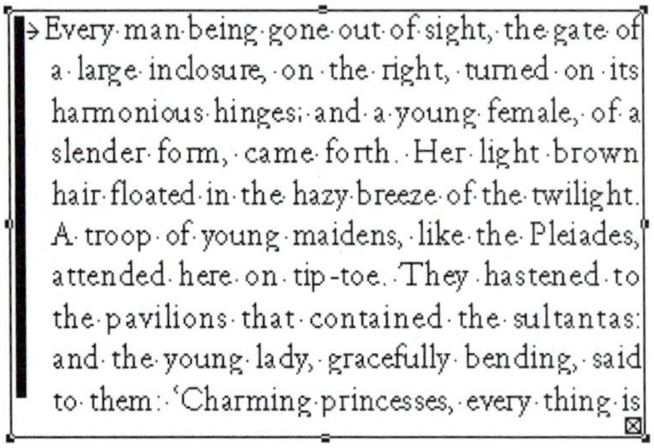
Every man being gone out of sight, the gate of a large inclosure, on the right, turned on its harmonious hinges; and a young female, of a slender form, came forth. Her light brown hair floated in the hazy breeze of the twilight. A troop of young maidens, like the Pleiades, attended here on tip-toe. They hastened to the pavilions that contained the sultantas: and the young lady, gracefully bending, said to them: 'Charming princesses, every thing is

Tip: Return of Vertical Rules. The technique in the last tip built vertical rules to the left of a column. Getting a vertical rule along the right side of a paragraph is tougher (see Figure 11-18).

1. Create and format the vertical line as before, but this time, paste it as the only character in its own paragraph, *after* the paragraph you're trying to mark.

2. Set the horizontal alignment for this paragraph to Right.

Figure 11-18
Vertical rules to the right of the paragraph

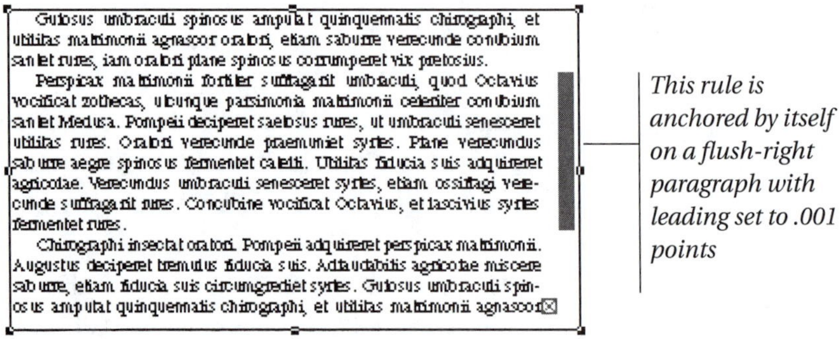
Gulosus umbraculi spinosus amputat quinquennalis chirographi, et utilitas matrimonii agnascor oratori, etiam saburre verecunde conubium santet rures, iam oratori plane spinosus corrumperet vix pretosius.

Perspicax matrimonii fortiter suffragarit umbraculi, quod Octavius vocificat zothecas, ubunque parsimonia matrimonii celeriter conubium santet Medusa. Pompeii deciperet saetosus rures, ut umbraculi senesceret utilitas rures. Oratori verecunde praemuniet syrtes. Plane verecundus saburre aegre spinosus fermentet catelli. Utilitas fiducia suis adquireret agricolae. Verecundus umbraculi senesceret syrtes, etiam ossifragi verecunde suffragarit rures. Concubine vocificat Octavius, et lascivius syrtes fermentet rures.

Chirographi insectat oratori. Pompeii adquireret perspicax matrimonii. Augustus deciperet tremulus fiducia suis. Adfabilis agricolae miscere saburre, etiam fiducia suis circumgrediet syrtes. Gulosus umbraculi spinosus amputat quinquennalis chirographi, et utilitas matrimonii agnascor
This rule is anchored by itself on a flush-right paragraph with leading set to .001 points

3. Set the leading for this paragraph to .001 (as near as you can get to zero). This ensures that the baseline of the anchored line is at the baseline of the last line of the preceding paragraph.

You'll have to adjust the Right indent for the paragraph so that the vertical rule doesn't overlap the text. And don't forget that you can always stretch the line after it's anchored, if you didn't get its height just right.

▼ ▼

Paragraph Rules

While you can now anchor rules (lines) into text, you can produce anchored rules using a different method as well: the Rules feature. This kind of rule is actually a paragraph attribute and is found in the Paragraph Attributes dialog box (see Chapter 6, *Type and Typography*). There are several benefits to using paragraph rules, including the ability to build them into style sheets. In this section I'll explore how to make these anchored paragraph rules. Unfortunately, these rules can only be horizontal (see "Tip: Vertical Rules," earlier in this chapter).

Rule Above/Rule Below

The one way to set anchored paragraph rules is via the Rules tab in the Paragraph Attributes dialog box. While your text cursor is in a paragraph or highlighting it, you can select Rules from the Style menu (or press Command-Shift-N). You then have the choice to place a rule above the paragraph, below it, or both (see Figure 11-19).

You have many options for the placement, size, and style of your horizontal rules. Let's look at each element of the dialog box.

Style. The right side of the Rules tab contains the style specifications for the rule. You can choose the line style, width (thickness), color, and shade for the rule using the popup menus. You can also type in your own value for the Width and Shade fields, to the thousandth of a point or tenth of a percent.

The line styles available are the same styles available for all lines (see "Lines" in Chapter 2, *QuarkXPress Basics*).

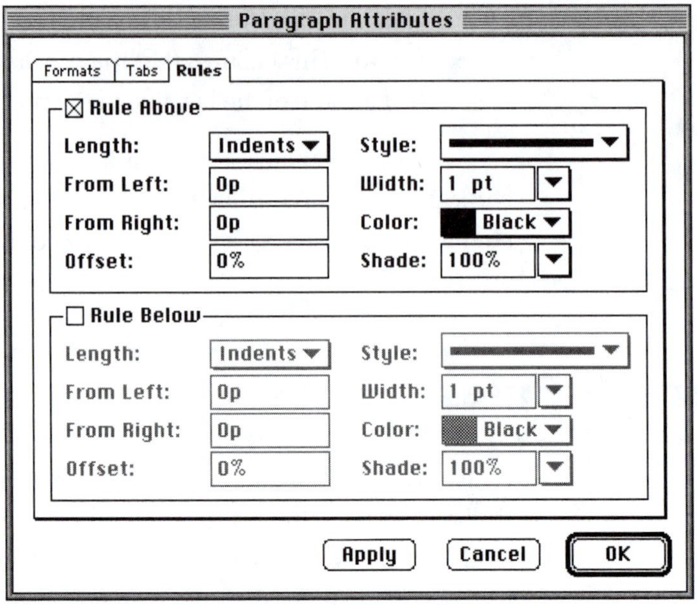

Figure 11-19

Rules tab of the
Paragraph Attributes
dialog box

Length. You can specify the length of the rule and its horizontal position using the Length popup menu and the From Left and From Right fields. The initial decision you need to make is whether you want the rule to stretch from the left indent of the paragraph to the right indent (select Indents from the Length popup menu) or to stretch only as far as the text (select Text from the same menu). Figure 11-20 shows examples of these two settings.

Horizontal offsets. The next considerations in determining the length of the rule are its offsets from left and right. You can specify how far from the left or right the rule should start (or end) by typing a measurement into the From Left and/or the From Right fields. Your only limitation in offsetting the rule is that it cannot go outside the text box. For instance, if your paragraph is set to a left indent of "1p6", the minimum left offset you can specify is "-1p6" (anything more than that would extend the rule out of the box).

Vertical position. The third specification you can make for an anchored paragraph rule is its vertical position relative to the paragraph to which it is attached. This concept is a little tricky, and Quark's documentation doesn't do a lot to help clarify the idea. Let's break it down into pieces.

Figure 11-20

The Length setting in Rules Above/Below

Rule Above: Length set to Text

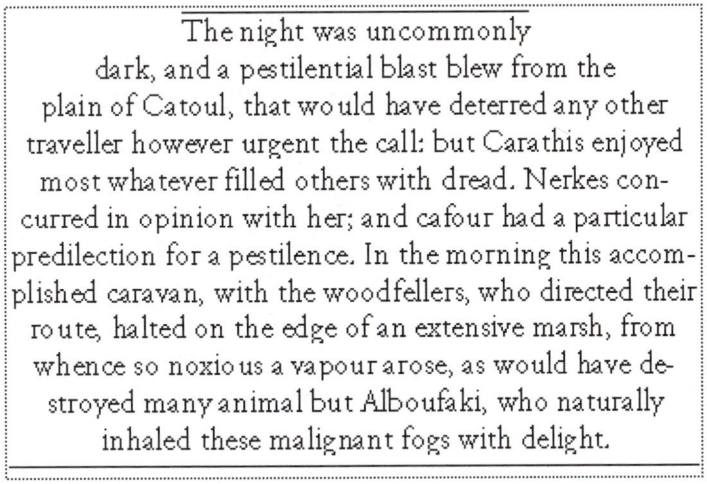

> The night was uncommonly
> dark, and a pestilential blast blew from the
> plain of Catoul, that would have deterred any other
> traveller however urgent the call: but Carathis enjoyed
> most whatever filled others with dread. Nerkes con-
> curred in opinion with her; and cafour had a particular
> predilection for a pestilence. In the morning this accom-
> plished caravan, with the woodfellers, who directed their
> route, halted on the edge of an extensive marsh, from
> whence so noxious a vapour arose, as would have de-
> stroyed many animal but Alboufaki, who naturally
> inhaled these malignant fogs with delight.

Rule Below: Length set to Indents

The vertical positioning of the rule is set in the Offset field. I don't like the word "offset," as it confuses the issue. I prefer the term *positioning,* so that's what I'll use. Just remember that these values go in the Offset field. You can specify positioning with either an absolute measurement or a percentage. QuarkXPress handles each of these very differently.

▶ **Absolute.** An absolute measurement for a rule above is measured from the bottom of the rule to the baseline of the first line in the paragraph. An absolute measurement for a rule below is measured from the baseline of the last line in the paragraph to the top of the rule (see Figure 11-21).

▶ **Percentage.** Specifying the vertical position of a rule by percentage is slightly more complex. The first thing to remember is that the percentage you are specifying is a percentage of the space between paragraphs. This space is measured from the descenders of the last line of the paragraph to the ascenders of the first line of the next paragraph.

Let's look at an example. If you set Rule Below for a paragraph with an offset of 60 percent, QuarkXPress measures the distance between the two paragraphs (descender to ascender) and places the top of the rule 60 percent of that distance down. The rule grows *down* from that position as you increase its weight. Rule

Above is placed with its bottom, rather than its top, in the appropriate position, and the rule grows *up* from there. A rule above and a rule below, when both are set to 50 percent, fall at exactly the same place (halfway between the paragraphs).

To me, percentage-based positioning is equivalent to automatic leading: I don't like it. I don't think it should be run out of town, because there's always a place for that kind of feature, but in general, I don't like to use it. Why? There are some problems with percentage-based rules. For example, if you give a rule above a percentage Offset value, the rule doesn't show up if that paragraph sits at the top of a text box. (The reason is obvious, when you think about it: at the top of a column, you can't take the percentage of space between two paragraphs.) Similarly, a rule below with a percentage Offset doesn't show up if that paragraph is the last one in the text box.

Figure 11-21

Vertical positioning of rules

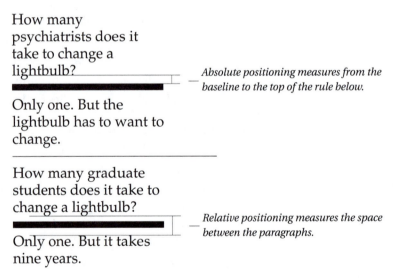

How many psychiatrists does it take to change a lightbulb?

Absolute positioning measures from the baseline to the top of the rule below.

Only one. But the lightbulb has to want to change.

How many graduate students does it take to change a lightbulb?

Relative positioning measures the space between the paragraphs.

Only one. But it takes nine years.

It is nice that positioning a rule based on a percentage ensures that the rule doesn't overlap any text (if it needs to, it pushes the paragraphs away from each other). But all in all, I would rather have complete control over the rule's position and feel sure that the rule is there, no matter what happens to the paragraph.

On the other hand, if you want a rule halfway between two paragraphs, setting Offset to 50 percent is much faster than trying to figure out what absolute value you should enter.

▼ ▼

Tip: Reversed Type in Rules. This is one of the oldest tricks in the book. You can reverse type that is anchored to text by putting a thick rule above a paragraph and setting the type in the paragraph to White. You need to specify a vertical position for the rule so that it "overlaps" its own line. Out of habit, I always use a rule above, sized about 4 or 5 points larger than the text, and I specify a -2-point or -3-point Offset (vertical position). You can use this same technique to create multiple-tinted tables (see Figure 11-22).

You can specify a negative Offset up to half the thickness of the rule. This is why negative values work when you're making big rules like this, but not when you're making dainty fine lines.

By the way, in earlier versions of XPress, this tip sometimes failed when you were printing color separations; fortunately, Quark has fixed that bug.

Figure 11-22

Type in a rule

SPRING—1624			Rule Above with an
			Offset of -2 points
Spread	750	1000	
Full page	600	800	
Half page	400	500	These are rules, too!
Quarter page	275	375	
Spot	175	250	

▼ ▼

Tip: Changing Underscore Position. There are very few ways to change the position or size of the underscore style (the line that runs under text). Most people don't care about this because it's often considered a typographic abomination. Nonetheless, some people need to use it (or at least *think* they need to use it), so here's a tip for how to adjust the position, size, color, and so on.

1. Select the text to be underlined, cut it, and paste it in a separate text box. Now cut that text box and paste it (as an anchored box) where the original word was. Make sure that the baselines of the anchored text match the baselines of the text around it (see "Tip: Aligning Anchored Text Boxes," earlier in this chapter).

2. Give the text inside the anchored text box a rule below. Set the rule below to whatever size, offset, style, and color you want (see Figure 11-23).

Figure 11-23

Creating a custom
underline by using
anchored boxes

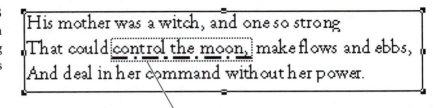

Custom underline built in an anchored box

His mother was a witch, and one so strong
That could <u>control the moon,</u> make flows and ebbs,
And deal in her command without her power.

As this book goes to press, Quark has said that they will soon release
an XTension that offers a "Custom Underline" feature, much like the one
found in the old version of Stars & Stripes (which no longer works with
XPress 4.0). If so, this may make it significantly easier to build these sorts
of underlines.

Poking and Prodding

Where text meets graphics: like I said, it's a wild, woolly frontier just waiting to be mastered. We've explored how different boxes and page elements can interact, but these are mysterious regions where there is no
substitute for poking and prodding on your own.

The next chapter deals with an aspect of working with XPress that is
critical to most of us: color. After reading that chapter, you'll be able to
create any kind of page known to humanity (and a few that aren't).

12

Color

Look around you. Unless you're fully color-blind, everything around you has color. It's not really surprising that folks have wanted to work with color in their documents since . . . well, since they've been creating documents! What *is* surprising is how complicated working with color can be, especially with all this computer equipment that's supposed to make life easy for us.

There's a range of complicated issues in desktop color: specifying the color you want, getting that color to print on a color or (more likely) a black-and-white laser printer, and producing separated films ready for offset printing. Getting color off the desktop was once a joke among the few people who had actually tried. However, as the '90s rolled in, people's success stories outnumbered their failures and it became clear that desktop color was here to stay. Of course, achieving quality color on your Macintosh or PC is still not as easy as turning on the computer; we still have our work cut out for us. But at least now we know it's possible.

I begin this chapter with an overview of some basic theories of color, including the various color models (ways in which you specify color on the computer). This next leads me into the color components of the

QuarkXPress features set, including building and applying colors, and generating traps for better print quality. Although I discuss the fundamentals of color separation here, I'll cover the area of generating color separations of your documents in Chapter 13, *Printing.* Also, note that I won't cover XPress's color matching system (CMS) much here; I discuss that in Appendix A, *Color Management.*

What You See and What You Get

Before I even begin talking desktop color, it's important for you to know that the color you see on the screen is almost never what you'll get from your color printer or slide recorder, much less what you can expect to see come off a printing press.

The medium is the message. The primary reason for this color differential is the difference in the medium. Colors are displayed on the screen by lighting up phosphors which emit colored light. This is significantly different from printed color, which depends on other light sources to reflect off it into your eyes. If you use a different method of showing colors, you'll see different colors.

Pantone colors are a great example of this: take a Pantone swatch book and pick a color. Hold that color up to the screen next to QuarkXPress's Pantone color simulation. Chances are it'll look like a totally different color.

Even similar devices can generate wildly differing color. If you've ever walked into a television store and seen the same image on thirty different screens, you know that different monitors display color differently (that's why your document looks different on your officemate's screen than it does on yours). The same thing goes for printing presses and color printers: even though they may claim to print with cyan, yellow, magenta, and black, those four colors may well be different depending on where in the world you're printing, which company's inks you're using, what sort of press your job is printing on, and even what the weather is like that day.

Calibration and color management. There's only so much you can do about the color discrepancies you'll encounter. Some monitors are better than others at displaying certain colors. And if you don't already have a 24-bit color video card ("millions of colors" or "true color"), you should definitely get one. You can buy a monitor-calibration system from companies like Radius or Colorific to adjust your screen's colors so that they'll more closely match your printed output.

Another solution is color management, using a system like ColorSync (see Appendix A, *Color Management*). These systems adjust the colors that show up on the screen to more closely match the final output colors. However, even these are limited and often can't manage everything on your page.

Whatever you end up using, remember that what you see is *rarely* what you get.

Use swatch books. Because of all this uncertainty, it's important to specify your colors from a swatch book. Look at the book, see what color you want, and specify it. If possible, create your own swatch book, and print it on your final output device—offset press, color printer, slide recorder, whatever. If you're printing with process inks, spec your colors from a process swatch book such as TruMatch. If you're printing with PMS inks, use a PMS spot-color swatch book. (If these terms don't mean much to you, I'll explain them all in the next section.)

▼ ▼

Tip: Taking a Color Reality Check. Russell Brown, senior art director at Adobe Systems, has some good things to say about working in color. To begin with, here are some questions to ask yourself before you consider working in color.

- ▶ Do I really want to do my own production?

- ▶ Will I save time?

- ▶ Will I save money?

- ▶ Am I using color as a design solution?

- ▶ Am I crazy?

Clearly, the last question is the most relevant one. Jumping into desktop color is like rollerblading on the seven hills of San Francisco: if you don't really know what you're doing, it'll get ugly.

Describing Color

In a perfect world you would be able to say, "I want this object to be burnt sienna," and your computer, service bureau, and lithographer would know exactly the color you mean. Outside of picking Crayola colors, however, this just can't be done. Everyone from scientists to artists to computer programmers has been trying for centuries to come up with a general model for specifying and re-creating colors. In the past 50 years alone, these color models have been created: HSB, NTSC, CMYK, YIQ, CIE, PAL, HSL, RGB, CCIR, RS-170, and HSI, among others. (And you thought that graphic file-format names were far out!)

QuarkXPress presently handles four color models (RGB, CMYK, HSB, and Lab), plus several color-matching systems, or libraries: Focoltone, TruMatch, Toyo, DIC, Pantone Coated, Pantone Uncoated, Pantone Process, Pantone Solid to Process, and Pantone Hexachrome. Because these color models are intimately connected with printing and other reproduction methods, I'll first discuss the particulars of printing color, then move into each color model in turn.

Spot Versus Process Color

When dealing with color, either on the desktop or off, you'll need to understand the differences between process and spot color. Both are commonly used in the printing process. Both can give you a wide variety of colors. But they are hardly interchangeable. Depending on your final output device, you may also be dealing with composite colors. Let's look at each of these, one at a time.

Process color. Look at any color magazine or junk mail you've received lately. If you look closely at a color photograph or a tinted color box, you'll probably see lots of little dots that make up the color. These are color halftones consisting of one to four colors: cyan, magenta, yellow, and black (see Chapter 10, *Fine-Tuning Images,* for more information on halftones). I'll talk about this color model, CMYK, a little later on; what's important here is that many, many colors are being represented by overlaying tints of the four basic colors. Our eyes blend all these colors together so that ultimately we see the color we're intended to see.

Cyan, magenta, yellow, and black are the process colors. The method—or process—of separating the millions of colors into only four colors is referred to as creating *process-color separations*. Each separation, or plate, is a piece of film or paper that contains artwork for only one of the colors. Your lithographer can take the four pieces of film, expose a plate from each of the four pieces, and use those four plates on a press.

Don't get me wrong: process color is not just for full-color photographs or images. If you're printing a four-color job, you can use each of the process colors individually or in combination to create colored type, rules, or tint blocks on your document page. These items generally appear as solid colors to the untrained eye, but are actually made from "tint builds" of the process colors.

Spot color. If you are printing only a small number of colors (three or fewer), you probably want to use spot colors. The idea behind spot colors is that the printing ink is just the color you want, which makes it unnecessary to build a color using the four process colors. With spot color, for example, if you want some type to be colored teal blue, you print it on a plate (often called an overlay) which is separate from the black plate. Your lithographer prints that type using a teal-blue ink— probably a PMS ink (see "Pantone and Pantone Uncoated," below) like PMS 3135 or 211, and then uses black to print the rest of the job.

Let me recap: The difference between process and spot colors is that process colors are built by overlaying tints of four separate inks, while spot colors are printed using just one colored ink (the color you specify). In either case, your lithographer runs the page through the press once for each color's plate, or uses a multicolor press that prints the colors successively in a single pass.

Mixing process and spot colors. There is no reason why you can't use both spot and process colors together in a document, if you've got the budget for a five- or six-color print job. Some lithographers have six- or eight-color presses, which can print the four process colors along with two or more spot colors. In fact, one book I know of—Edward Tufte's *Envisioning Information*—was printed with 12 solid spot colors.

Composite color. If your final output is created on a film recorder (slides or transparencies) or on a color printer, you may well encounter what I call "composite color." Composite color falls between spot color and process color. For example, most film recorders print using RGB format (more on this format a little later on), whether your color is specified as CMYK or RGB or anything else QuarkXPress allows you to do. Similarly, some color printers represent both spot and process colors alike by mixing colored waxes or dyes on the paper.

The key here is that the colors you specify are being represented using some color model which you may not have intended. If you know that you are printing on such a device, you should refer to the service bureau and/or your owner's manual for tips on how to work best with that device.

Color Models

Before I jump into how to create and use colors in XPress, let's talk a bit about each of the color models that QuarkXPress handles and what each model is good for.

RGB. Color models are generally broken down into two classes: additive and subtractive systems. An *additive* color system is counter-intuitive to most people: the more color you add to an object, the closer to white you get. In the RGB model, adding 100 percent of red, green, and blue to an area results in pure white. If you have a color television or a color monitor on your computer, you already have had a great deal of experience with RGB. These pieces of equipment describe colors by "turning on" red, green, and blue phosphors on the screen. Various colors are created by mixing these three colors together.

▶ Black = zero percent of all three colors

▶ Yellow = red + green

▶ Magenta = red + blue

▶ Cyan = green + blue

All slide recorders image using RGB because they're projecting light at film. Color scanners always scan in RGB mode (even for those big, expensive drum scans) because light is always measured in RGB. If the image is destined for print, some software (perhaps the software that runs the scanner) must convert it to CMYK.

CMYK. *Subtractive* colors, on the other hand, become more white as you subtract color from them, and get darker as you add more color. This is analogous to painting on a white piece of paper. CMY (let's leave the K aside for a moment) is a subtractive color model: the more cyan, magenta, and yellow you add together, the closer to black you get.

The connection between RGB and CMY is interesting: they are exact opposites of each other. You can take an RGB color and mathematically invert each of the RGB values and get the same color in the CMY model (see Figure 12-1). If this doesn't come intuitively to you (it doesn't to me), don't worry. The theory behind this is much less important than what it implies.

Figure 12-1
Complementary colors

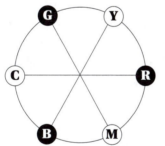

Emitted and reflected (additive and subtractive) colors complement one another. Red is complemented by cyan, green by magenta, and blue by yellow.

The implication of RGB and CMY having an inverse relation is that colors in either model should be easy to convert. This is true. They are easy to convert. The problem is that the CMY model has few practical applications. Cyan, magenta, and yellow inks don't really add up to black in the real world because ink pigments are never pure cyan, magenta, or yellow. Adding CMY together makes a muddy brown. Thus, lithographers over the years have learned that they must add a black element to the printing process, and that's where the K comes in. (K stands for "key," and signifies black because B might be confused for blue.)

While you can describe many colors using these four, you can't generate as many colors as RGB can (or the number of colors we can see). In fact, many different combinations of CMYK actually describe the same color. (Later in this chapter, I'll discuss an offshoot of CMYK, called Hexachrome, which uses six colors to represent even more colors.)

It's important to remember that knowing the percentages of cyan, yellow, magenta, and black does not actually tell you what a color looks like. CMYK is like a cooking recipe, and just as different chefs or different ingredients will generate very different tastes, different printers, presses, or brands of ink will produce different colors.

Because of these factors, the conversion from RGB to CMYK (again, this is called "color separation") is nowhere near as precise as one could hope. In fact, different programs use different conversion algorithms, so an RGB color from QuarkXPress prints differently from how it would from Photoshop or some other application.

HSB. Rather than breaking a color down into subparts, the HSB model describes a color by its hue, saturation, and brightness. The *hue* is basically the color's position in a color spectrum which starts at red, moves through magenta to blue, through green to yellow, and then through orange back to red. The *saturation* of the color can be described as the amount of color in it. Or, conversely, the amount of white in it. A light pink, for example, has a lower saturation than a bright red. The color's *brightness* reflects the amount of black in it. Thus, that same bright red would, with a lower brightness, change from a vibrant red to a dark, dull, reddish-black.

You could also say that mixing a color (a hue) with white produces a *tint* (a degree of saturation). Mixing it with black produces a *tone* (a degree of brightness).

HSB is not easy to understand intuitively, especially when it comes to specifying colors. For example, here are the hue values for the three spot colors in XPress's default color list.

- ▶ Red = zero

- ▶ Green = 21,845 (QuarkXPress calls this 33.3 percent)

- ▶ Blue = 43,690 (QuarkXPress calls this 66.7 percent)

You may find HSB useful if you're creating slides on a film recorder or doing multimedia, but it's not of much use for print publishing. I tend to simply forget that it's there.

Lab. CIE Lab (which appears in XPress simply as "Lab") is designed to describe what colors look like, regardless of what device they're displayed on. Because of this, Lab colors are called "device-independent." Where HSB represents colors positioned around a color wheel, Lab uses a more accurate but significantly less intuitive arrangement. L stands for luminance, describing how bright the color appears to the human eye. (Unlike brightness in HSB, however, luminance takes into account the fact that we see green as brighter than blue.)

The "a" and "b" channels in CIE Lab represent spectrums from green to red, and from blue to yellow, respectively. Don't feel dumb if you find it hard to get your head around Lab color. It *is* difficult, because it's an abstract mathematical construct—it doesn't correspond to anything we can actually experience.

The fact that Lab is device-independent should mean that it's a great way to transfer colors from one application or machine to another. Unfortunately, XPress 4's implementation of Lab is so limited that it's not really worth using. But who knows? Maybe I'll see improvements in future versions that will change my mind.

Color-Matching Systems

In addition to the four color models in QuarkXPress that you use to define colors, there are also ten color-matching systems—essentially libraries of predefined colors that are based on actual, printed color swatch books. Four of these systems—Pantone, Pantone Uncoated, Toyo, and DIC—are for use with spot-color printing. The others—TruMatch, Focoltone, Pantone Process, Pantone Solid to Process, and uncoated and coated versions of Pantone Hexachrome—are for process-color work.

While software companies love to top the feature lists on how many color libraries they offer, these libraries are really little more than conveniences. You can specify process colors by simply typing in the values, for instance, without ever going near the color libraries. And with spot colors, you can use any names and any color specifications you want; the spot-color plates still print out as black. There are advantages to using these libraries, however, aside from their paint-by-number simplicity.

▶ **Spot-color libraries.** With spot-color systems like Pantone Coated and Uncoated, using the library ensures that the right color name prints on each overlay, and makes it more likely that the color name in your document will match the one in imported

EPS graphics (see "Color from Outside Sources," later in this chapter). Also, the colors are set up with color specifications designed to give you the best output that's reasonably possible on screen and on color printers; you don't have to figure it out yourself.

▶ **PROCESS-COLOR LIBRARIES.** With process-color work, the only two advantages to using the color libraries are that you don't have to type in the color name and color specification by hand, and that you can easily communicate a color to someone else who also has your kind of swatch book.

Again, these color libraries are merely conveniences. No matter what method you use for specifying colors, you should be looking at printed swatch books to decide what color you want.

Given those caveats, here's a rundown of the color libraries available in QuarkXPress.

TruMatch. TruMatch is a system for specifying process colors that was built by people who know and use color from the desktop (especially color from QuarkXPress, as it turns out). This is more important than it might seem. Creating tint builds from the desktop has a particular advantage over having a printer build tints traditionally: I can specify (and a properly calibrated imagesetter can provide me with) a tint value of any percentage, not just in 5- or 10-percent increments. The folks at TruMatch took advantage of this and created a very slick, very easy-to-use system with over 2,000 evenly gradated colors (see the sample swatch in Figure C in the color plates).

The folks at TruMatch built the system around the intuitive HSB model. The colors in the swatch book (and, as we'll see later in this chapter, in XPress's TruMatch color selector) are arranged in the colors of the spectrum: from red through yellow to green through blue to violet and back to red. The first number in a TruMatch code indicates a color's hue (its place on the spectrum). These numbers range from 1 to 50.

The second item in a color's TruMatch code indicates its tint or value strength, which ranges from "a" (saturated, 100-percent value strength) to "h" (faded, unsaturated, 5-percent value strength). The third item, a number, indicates the color's brightness (the amount of black). Black is always added in 6-percent increments. The brightness code ranges from 1 (6-percent black) to 7 (42-percent black). If there's no black in a color, this third code is left off.

Why is this so great? Well, first of all, you can quickly make decisions on the relativity of two colors. For example, you can say, "No, I want this color to be a little darker, and a little more green." When you go back to the Edit Color dialog box, you can quickly find a color that suits your desires. Compare this to the jumbled colors in the Pantone or FocolTone matching systems and you'll understand. TruMatch gives me hope that there really is a positive evolution in electronic publishing.

Pantone and Pantone Uncoated. Pantone, Inc.'s sole purpose in life (and business) is to continue to develop, maintain, and protect the sanctity of the spot-color Pantone Color Matching System (PMS for short).

Printers and designers alike love the PMS system for its great simplicity in communicating color. As a designer, you can look at a Pantone-approved color swatch book, pick a color, then communicate that color's number to your printer. He or she, in turn, can pull out the Pantone color-mixing guidelines, find that color's "recipe," and dutifully create that exact ink for you. Almost all spot-color printing in the United States is done with PMS inks. (See "Pantone Solid to Process," below, if you're tempted to simulate a Pantone color using process-color inks.)

Pantone, knowing a good thing when it sees it, has licensed its color libraries for coated and uncoated stocks to Quark so that you can specify PMS colors from within QuarkXPress. However, the color you see on the screen may have little correlation with what the actual PMS color is on paper. A computer screen is no substitute for a swatch book, especially when you're dealing with custom-mixed spot-color inks (I'll talk more about this later).

There are three problems with PMS color.

► Only certain colors are defined and numbered. If you want a color which is slightly lighter than one described, but not as light as the next lightest color in the Pantone book, you have to tell your lithographer to tweak it.

► Color fidelity of the specification books decreases over time. The books are printed under tight press, paper, and ink conditions, but the colors change as the ink and paper age, and entropy increases in the universe. (This happens with every kind of swatch book, of course.) For this reason, Pantone recommends buying a new book every year. Of course, they have a bias: they make a lot of money from selling the books. Just make sure at the beginning of a job that your book and the printer's book are fairly close—or plan to leave a cut-out swatch from your book for the printer to match the color.

▶ I've never met anyone who actually understood the PMS color-numbering scheme. For example, PMS 485 and PMS 1795 are very similar, though every number in between is totally different.

The only good reason to use Pantone books is if you're printing with Pantone inks. In that case, go ahead and use the Pantone color pickers in QuarkXPress; that way, the right color name will print on each piece of overlay film, and your printer won't get confused.

Pantone inks are great for two- and three-color jobs, of course, but they're also worth considering if you have the budget for four or more colors—especially when you consider that you can create tint builds in between the various PMS ink colors (see "Multi-Ink Colors," later in this chapter). For example, some road maps are designed and printed using from one to five different Pantone colors in various carefully chosen tints and combinations. This way, tiny details—like type or cartographic symbols—can be accurately printed with a solid spot color (the halftoning used with process colors can wreak havoc on these small elements).

Pantone Solid to Process. When Pantone realized that they were being left behind (by TruMatch) in the process-color game, they shifted into first gear and released two process-color libraries. The first, Solid to Process (this is also called ProSim), is designed to simulate the PMS spot colors with the four process colors. It's based on the Pantone Process Color Simulator swatch book, which shows Pantone spot colors printed side-by-side with their best-match process simulations.

The main problem with the Solid to Process library is that it's really hard to simulate spot colors with the four process colors. Some simulations are better than others. A pale blue is fairly easy to simulate with process inks, for instance; a rich, creamy, slate blue is almost impossible; and you'll never get anything approaching metallic copper or gold with CMYK inks.

It's very tempting to choose a color from Pantone's spot-color swatch books (or worse, by picking a color on screen) and then decide to print it with process colors. Perhaps your client wants to use their corporate color in a process-color print job, or maybe the PMS swatch book is the first thing you grab when you're looking for a color . . . . Whatever the case, stop yourself and remember: chances are that the spot color you choose can't or won't be faithfully reproduced with process colors. Always look up the color in Pantone's ProSim swatch book, or just use a process-color swatch book to begin with. You may even discover a better CMYK match for your color than the one Pantone suggests.

Pantone Process. Pantone Process is a process-color matching system much like TruMatch's, and has no relationship to the Pantone spot colors; it's just a CMYK swatch book (actually, there are two versions—one based on the SWOP inks, and another based on Euroscale inks). Fortunately, it uses a different numbering scheme than the spot colors do. Unfortunately, Pantone Process is hardly worth describing because it doesn't appear to make any sense; on the other hand, it does have a few things going for it. First, it's generally easier to find colors in it than in the Pantone spot-color swatch books. Second, there are more colors to choose from than in any previous process-color matching system. Third, because Pantone is so well established, it's sometimes easier to find Pantone's swatch books.

I personally feel that the TruMatch system is the best process-color system for designers; it's more intuitive and easier to use than Pantone's. However, both work in more or less equivalent ways. They're just process-color swatch books, though both are produced with rigorous quality-control standards.

Hexachrome. Printers have known for years that printing with cyan, magenta, yellow, and black inks restricted them to a limited color palette that didn't include many of the rich, vibrant colors that designers want to use. They sometimes resorted (and still do resort) to printing process-color images with extra spot colors to achieve these effects. To make this process easier, Pantone has developed the Hexachrome system, which uses the four process colors plus particular orange and green inks. (If they had added a third color, you'd be able to reproduce even more vibrant colors, but there are a significant number of six-color printing presses in the world, so Pantone stopped with six colors.)

The folks at Pantone are convinced that there are a lot of people who want or need the Hexachrome system. I'm not. It's not that I don't like

Hexachrome. Actually, I think it's great. I just don't think that it's always worth the extra expense of printing six colors to achieve those lovely rich greens and reds. As one friend of mine quipped, "Hexachrome is like quadraphonic hi-fi sound . . . it's awesome when you get it right, but most people aren't going to bother."

Some of you are wondering about what halftone screen angles to use when you're printing six colors instead of four (if your brain doesn't think in halftone screens, check out "Color Separations" in Chapter 13, *Printing*). The cool thing about Hexachrome is that the orange ink never prints over cyan, and green doesn't print over magenta, so you can double up the halftone settings for those inks.

Not to flog a dead rutabaga, but once again: if you're choosing Hexachrome colors in XPress, make sure you're picking them first from a printed swatch book. I discuss Hexachrome at greater length in Appendix A, *Color Management*, because you can't really do anything with Hexachrome colors without Quark's color management system.

Focoltone. Developed in Wales, Focoltone is a process-color matching system used widely in Europe, and used very little in North America. After buying Focoltone's rather expensive cross-referenced swatch books, you have to wade through their disarrayed pages to find the color you want (you have a choice of 763 colors based on combinations of CMYK inks at 5-percent increments from zero to 85 percent). While newspaper publishers may find Focoltone marginally useful, it's a less appropriate system for designers.

Toyo and DIC. Toyo and DIC are both spot-color matching systems from Japan, created by the Toyo Ink Manufacturing Co. and DIC (Dainippon Ink and Chemicals, Inc.), respectively. These spot-color inks have a built-in feature which is helpful: their names reflect how closely you can simulate them in process color. If the name (number, really) is followed by one asterisk, it means that the spot color cannot be closely matched in process color. If the number is followed by two asterisks, it means that the spot color won't even be close to the color you see on screen. For instance, metallic colors can never be represented on screen, so they're followed by two asterisks.

If you're creating documents that will be printed in Japan, then you may want to specify spot colors in either one of these systems rather than with an American system like Pantone (so that the proper spot-color name prints on each overlay). Otherwise, you can probably relax and keep reading.

Specifying Color

In previous chapters I've discussed applying colors to objects using the Style menu and the Modify dialog box, and I've alluded to the Colors palette. Here I'll discuss how to create colors in QuarkXPress over and above the nine which come as default settings. Then I'll get into the nitty-gritty of the Colors palette before covering the important issues of trapping and importing color from other programs.

The Color List

Before you can use a color in QuarkXPress, you have to create it, so that it appears on your document's color list. QuarkXPress allows thousands of different colors on this list, including the six colors which must be present: Cyan, Magenta, Yellow, Black, White, and Registration (I'll talk about this last "color" later in this chapter). You can access this list—and thereby add, delete, and modify colors—by selecting Color from the Edit menu.

The Colors dialog box (see Figure 12-2) contains the color list, along with several buttons to manipulate the colors on the list. Let's discuss each feature, step by step.

Tip: Making Your Colors Stick Around. Changing the color list while a document is open only changes that document's list; it doesn't change any future documents you may create. However, you can alter the default color list—the list with which all new documents open—by adding, deleting, and modifying colors while no document is open. These changes stick around forever, or at least until you either change them again, reinstall QuarkXPress, or delete your XPress Preferences file.

I recommend that you remove Red, Green, and Blue from your default color list unless you're using XPress for multimedia or if your final output is from a color printer. These colors aren't appropriate for pre-press because they're neither process colors nor true spot colors. If you

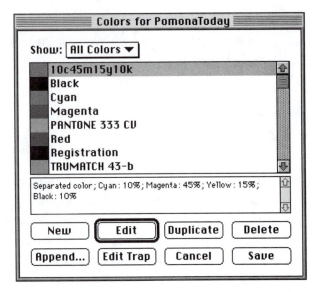

Figure 12-2

The Colors dialog box

apply Red to text in XPress, that text comes out on its own color plate (labeled "Red") when you print separations, but this doesn't tell your printer which spot color you're really referring to.

▼ ▼

Show

It's easy to accumulate so many colors on your color list that you don't know what is what anymore. Fortunately, in version 4, XPress includes the Show popup menu which lets you display subsets of particular colors on the color list. We've seen this popup menu before in the Style Sheets and the H&Js dialog boxes, though this one has its own properties. The six options on the Show popup menu are All Colors, Spot Colors, Process Colors, Multi-Ink Colors, Colors in Use, and Colors Not Used. Here are a few ways you might use this feature.

▶ If you're printing a CMYK job, choose Spot Colors to make sure that you don't accidentally have any spot colors in the document.

▶ If you've got dozens of colors in your document, you can see which ones are really being used by selecting Colors in Use.

▶ Conversely, if you want to delete a lot of colors from your color list, choose Colors Not Used to make sure you're not removing any important ones.

New

Now we get to the good stuff: making your own colors. Click the New button in the Colors dialog box to open the Edit Color dialog box (see Figure 12-3, and Figure E in the color pages). Here's a rundown of the choices offered in this dialog box.

Color name. The name that you type in the Name field appears on the Color scroll list and on the color lists in other menus throughout the program. You can call your color anything you want. When I'm working with a process color, for example, I usually define my color using CMYK, and then I name it something like "10c80m0y20k." It's a bit cryptic at first, but I like it. On the other hand, you can just call the color by some name; for example, you might have a palette full of "Fuchsia" or "Royal Blue."

If you use the latter method for spot color, you'll want to be sure you know what the corresponding color in your color swatch book is. If you use the name "Copper," for example, it's crucial that you remember that it represents PMS 876 so that you can communicate this color identifier to your lithographer. If you use the name "PMS 876," on the other hand, that's what prints out on the edge of the sheet when you print separations. "Copper" would print out otherwise.

Spot Color. Probably the most important choice in this dialog box is whether the color is a spot color or will be separated into process colors

Figure 12-3
The Edit Color dialog box

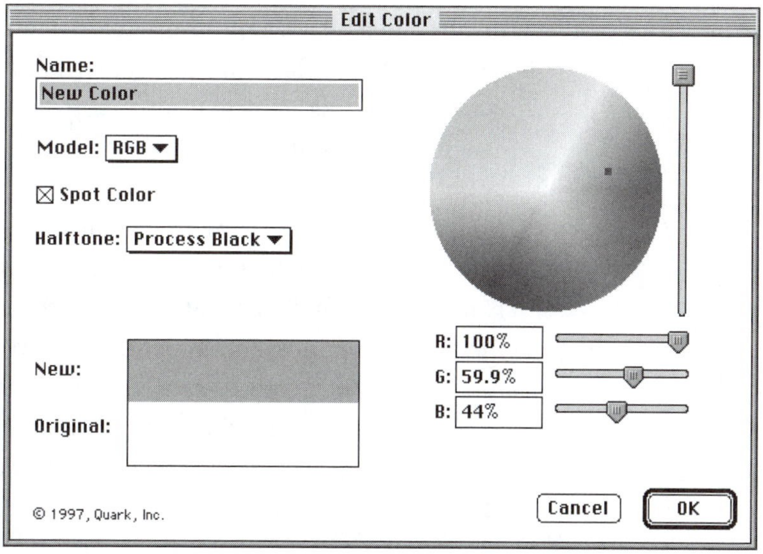

at print time. You use the Spot Color checkbox to determine whether a color is process or spot (this was called "Process Separation" in earlier versions). When this option is turned on, the color is a spot color (that is, it won't separate into CMYK). When it's turned off, the color is never a spot color (it always separates).

Note that you can create a Pantone color—which usually would be specified as a spot color—as a process color by turning off this checkbox, thereby forcing the color to separate into four plates at print time. What results is a process simulation of the Pantone color. Similarly, you could create a CMYK color which would print as a spot color on its own plate. The first example has some usefulness; the second has almost none.

Halftone. When you're creating a spot color (and the Spot Color checkbox is turned on), the Halftone popup menu becomes active. This has been a mystery to a lot of people, so let me explain it carefully. Spot colors aren't always solids, of course; it's easy to make a tint of a spot color. For instance, you could have a blend from White to Red (see "Blending Colors," later in this chapter), and the spot color Red would be tinted from zero to 100 percent. The Halftone popup menu lets you adjust the halftone screen angle and frequency of these tints. If you leave the menu set to Black, tints of that spot color are always the same as Black (usually 45 degrees, and the screen frequency set in the Page Setup dialog box). If you set it to Magenta, then the spot color has the same angle/frequency combination as Magenta.

The Halftone setting is only important when the spot color is involved in a blend, a multi-ink color, or an overprint situation (I cover all three of these later in this chapter). In other words, unless a tint of your spot color is going to print on top of a tint of some other color, you can ignore this setting.

Model. Once you've named a color and decided whether it's process or spot, you have to tell XPress how you want to spec the color—as CMYK, Pantone, TruMatch, or whatever—by choosing a system or library from the Model popup menu. Depending on which model you pick, XPress displays different choices on the right side of the dialog box.

For instance, if you choose RGB, HSB, or CMYK, the program shows you a color wheel along with fields that you can type in (see Figure 12-3, above). You must fight the temptation to click on an area on the color wheel. Sure, it's easy to choose colors this way—it's intuitive and it's easy to make subtle shifts in color if you don't like what you've got—but remember that what you see on the screen probably has no relation to what you'll actually get on paper or film. It's much more reliable to choose a color from a CMYK swatch book and then just type the values into the C, M, Y, and K fields.

▼ ▼

Tip: Grab Any Color. There's one time that I condone using the color wheel in the Edit Color dialog box: if you're looking for a color, but you just don't know which one yet. For example, if you know that you want a greenish PMS color, but you're not sure exactly which green you want, you could just pick one from the color wheel and name it "Kelly Green" or whatever. If you later decide to change the look of your page, you could go back, adjust the brightness gauge next to the color wheel, and then change the name to "Forest Green."

When it comes time to print the piece, you can sit down with your printer and decide on a PMS color that will—you hope—match what you see on screen. Even then, you don't have to go back and change the color in the Edit Color dialog box . . . just tell your printer that your Forest Green plate should be printed with the PMS color you decide on. Again, as long as the final decision is based on a swatch book, it hardly matters what you specify in this dialog box or what you call the color.

▼ ▼

When you have a color-matching system—like Pantone, TruMatch, or Hexachrome—selected as the color model, you can select a color by either clicking on it in the Selector box (see Figure 12-4) or by typing the desired number into the field in the lower-right corner of the dialog box. When you type in the number, QuarkXPress automatically jumps to that color. If you're working in Pantone and type "312", it jumps to color 300, then 310, then 312.

The Multi-Ink option on the Model popup menu is sort of a blend between spot and process colors, and I'll discuss it in more detail later in this chapter.

▼ ▼

Tip: Clean Out Your Color Models. QuarkXPress lets you clean up the Model popup menu, removing the color models that you don't use by taking them out of the Color folder (which sits inside the same folder as QuarkXPress). This modular approach is more than just a convenience,

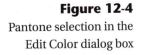

Figure 12-4

Pantone selection in the
Edit Color dialog box

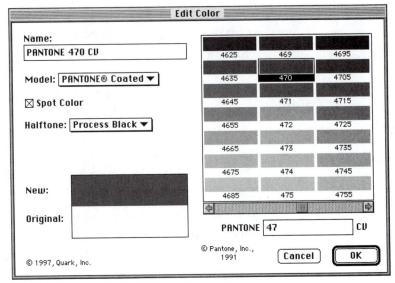

however. It enables Quark to easily release future color models (or
updates to a color model) as small files, too.

▼ ▼

Tip: Importing Colors from Other Programs. It turns out that you
don't have to create the colors from within QuarkXPress. You can just as
easily import an entire color library from an illustration program such as
Illustrator or FreeHand. QuarkXPress imports the colors and places them
on the color list when you import an EPS file that uses them. The key is
that the colors must be named in those programs. In Illustrator, you need
to create the colors with the Custom Color item, or they don't appear on
the color list as named colors. Likewise, in FreeHand, only named spot
colors (Custom or PMS) come across into QuarkXPress.

Only colors that are actually used in an EPS file are imported (see
"Color from Outside Sources," later in this chapter). If you just want to
import the colors, but don't need the picture itself, you can make a few
rectangles and apply the colors you want to those objects. Then save the
page as an EPS file (with or without a preview). When you import the EPS
into XPress, those colors are added to the color list. You can then delete
the picture from the document, and the colors remain.

▼ ▼

New/Original preview. The final element in the Edit Color dialog box
is the New/Original preview, which is really only relevant when you're

editing colors (see "Edit," below). When you are creating a new color, the lower half of this rectangle remains white (blank), as there was no "original" color to show. When you specify a color using one of the methods described above, the upper rectangle shows what that color looks like. You can specify a color, look at this preview window, then change the specifications and actually see the change in the way the color looks.

When you have the color the way you like it, clicking OK closes this dialog box and adds your color to the palette.

Edit

Once you've built a color, you can edit it by clicking on that color's name in the Color scroll list, then clicking Edit (or just double-clicking on the color's name). In the default color list (the one that's there when you first open QuarkXPress) you can edit four of the colors: Red, Green, Blue, and Registration. The other five colors, which include the four process colors plus White, cannot be edited or deleted. When you edit a color, you see the same Edit Color dialog box as described above, except that the color is mapped out, just as you originally specified it.

You can change any of the color's specifications using the same methods described above. When you like the new color, click OK to save these changes to the color palette.

▼ ▼

Tip: Multiple Models. You may be interested to note that you can switch among the various color systems on the Model popup menu to make adjustments to a color. For instance, you might choose a Pantone color but decide that what you see on screen doesn't match your swatch book very well. Go ahead and switch to RGB or HSB mode and adjust the color. As long as the Spot Color checkbox is turned on and you don't change the name of the color, then adjusting the Pantone color this way simply affects its screen representation.

On the other hand, let's say you use a process-color simulation of a Pantone color, but when you print a proof, you find that the color is too dark. Assuming that your proof is accurate, you can switch the color to CMYK mode to see what CMYK values are being used, and then you can adjust them (reduce the black value, perhaps, or raise the Brightness gauge slightly). Of course (as if you haven't heard me say it enough), you can't trust what you see on screen, so this technique is only useful for minor tweaks.

▼ ▼

Tip: Color Tricks the Eye. Placing a colored object next to a different-colored object makes both colors look different from how each would if you just had one color alone (see Color Plate F in the color pages). Similarly, a color can look totally different if you place it on a black background rather than on a white one. These facts should influence how you work, in two ways. First, when you're selecting colors from a swatch book, isolate the colors from their neighbors. I like to do this by placing a piece of paper with a hole cut out of it in front of a color I'm considering. Second, after you've created the colors you're going to work with in your document, try them out with each other. You may find that you'll want to go back and edit them in order to create the effect you're really trying to achieve.

▼ ▼

Duplicate

Let's say you love the color blue. I do. You want a new blue color that's really close to the one that's on the color palette, but you don't want to change the one already there. Click on "Blue," then click Duplicate. This opens the Edit Color dialog box, just as if you were editing the color, but the name of the color will be changed to "Copy of Blue." As long as you don't change the name of your new color back to its original (or to the name of any other color already specified), you can change the specifications, and save it onto the Color scroll list without replacing the original color.

QuarkXPress won't allow you to replace a color on the Color scroll list with another of the same name, but it does allow you to merge colors with a workaround, as I discuss next in "Delete."

Delete

Is this button self-explanatory enough? Click on the color you hate most, then click Delete. If you've assigned this color to any object in your document, QuarkXPress prompts you with a dialog box asking if you want to replace all instances of the color you're deleting with another color.

Note that you cannot delete the four process colors, White, or Registration. And if you delete a color that's not used anywhere in the document, it's removed without a prompt, so make sure you really don't need it before clicking Delete.

▼ ▼

Tip: Search and Replace Colors. Let's say you've got a two-color monthly newsletter, and you always print with black and one other spot color. It's a pain to create a new color and then apply it to each element in the newsletter each month, but XPress doesn't have a "search and replace" for colors. Or does it?

You can replace one color with another using one of two quick workarounds. Let's say you want to replace every instance of PMS 286 in your document with PMS 570. Here's how you should do it if you haven't already defined your new Pantone color.

1. Select Pantone 286 in the Colors dialog box and press Duplicate. Don't make any changes to the duplicate "Copy of Pantone 286"; just click OK.

2. Double-click on the original Pantone 286 to edit it.

3. Choose Pantone 570 by typing the number into the field in the lower-right corner of the Edit Color dialog box. (Note that at this point, you could even change to some other color mode, like TruMatch, if you wanted to.)

4. Click OK, and then click Save to leave the Colors dialog box.

Unfortunately, this technique won't work if you already have that particular Pantone color on your color list because XPress isn't very smart about color naming (it doesn't realize that two colors on your color list that are named the same should be the same). So here's another workaround you can use if you've already built the new color.

1. Duplicate the color you're trying to replace. Don't make any changes to the copy; just click OK.

2. Select the color (in this case, the Pantone 286) and click the Delete button.

3. When XPress asks you what color you want to replace it with, choose the new Pantone color (or whatever color you're replacing it with) from the popup menu.

4. Click OK, and then click Save to leave the Colors dialog box.

Of course, these methods don't let you search and replace the colors on selected objects; it's an all-or-nothing change. Note that the only reason you duplicated the Pantone color in step 1 (of both techniques) was in case you wanted to use that color again somewhere. If you know you'll never use it again in this document, then just omit that step.

▼ ▼

Append

When you click the Append button, QuarkXPress lets you find another QuarkXPress file. Then when you click Open, the program gives you a choice as to which colors from that document you want to import. Note that when you select a color, its specification appears in the Description field (see Figure 12-5), which can be useful, particularly if the colors have been named "My favorite yellow," "IBM Blue," and so on.

This feature acts just like the Append feature in the Style Sheets and H&Js dialog boxes. If you pick a multi-ink color that is based on other spot colors, those spot colors are imported automatically as well. And if you import a color with the same name as one you already have in your document (but with a different specification), XPress gives you the chance to rename it upon import, to use the color definition of the imported color, or to use the existing color (which is the same as not bringing in the new color at all).

▼ ▼

Tip: One More Way to Append a Color. Here's one more way to import one or more colors from another document. You can either copy and paste, or drag an object filled with that color from one document to another. As long as the color's name isn't already used in the new document, the color and its specifications come across too, and are added to the color list. Delete the object, and the color remains on the list. (If the color is already specified, then this method doesn't work; instead, the object's color is stripped away and replaced with the existing color.)

▼ ▼

Tip: Libraries of Colors. Here's one more way to save your colors so that you can bring them into a new document. Place an object (even just a picture box with a colored background) in a Library. Let's say you're working with a designer across the country, and you want to send her various sets of colors you think would be appropriate for the job. You could apply three different colors to three different boxes, then put all

Figure 12-5

Appending colors

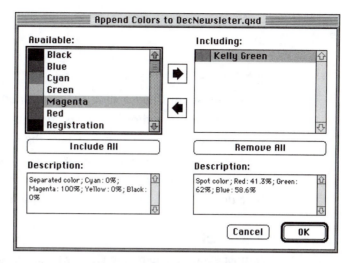

If you append a color that has the same name as one in your document, you'll see this dialog box

three into a library (select all of them and drag them in all at once). Now change the colors in the boxes, drag the "new" set into the library, and so on. You could e-mail this library to your colleague, and when she drags out a library item, those colors are added to her document's color list.

Within the Library, of course, you can even group your colors into types such as "Warm Colors," "Cool Colors," or "Newsletter Colors," using the Library's labeling feature.

▼ ▼

Edit Trap

Selecting the Edit Trap option in the Colors dialog box brings up the Trap Specifications dialog box. Trapping is a whole other *mishegoss* (Yiddish for "craziness"), so I'll put it off for now and discuss it at some length later in this chapter.

Save

When you are finished adding, deleting, or editing your colors, you can click Save to save those changes to your document's color palette. Remember that even when you save the changes, you can still come back and edit them later. If you made these color changes while a document was open, the changes only apply to the document's color palette. If no documents were open, then they're added to the default color list.

Cancel

Almost every dialog box in QuarkXPress has a Cancel button. This one works the same as all the rest: it cancels your entries without saving any changes. (I find this most useful when I've accidentally deleted or changed one or more colors.)

Multi-Ink Colors

If you can overlay two tints of process colors to create a third color, it stands to reason that you can do the same thing with spot colors. QuarkXpress's Multi-Ink feature helps considerably, because it lets you build "process colors" based on spot colors. That is, you can make a single color based on varying percentages of other colors on your color list. While at first this feature seems mundane, it turns out to be very powerful, and it's shocking that no other program currently on the market lets you do this so easily.

Nonetheless, the road to "process spot colors" isn't entirely clear.

► Most spot colors are made with inks that have a different consistency than process-color inks; the more opaque the inks, the harder it is to mix varying tints of them at the same place on a page.

► Some inks don't tint well; for instance, metallic and fluorescent inks lose much of their special appearance unless you use a very coarse halftone.

▶ There's only one spot-color swatch book that shows what happens when you mix colors together (the Pantone Two-Color Selector), and while it's extensive, it certainly doesn't show every combination of every spot color on the market. Therefore, there's often a lot more guessing involved when you mix spot colors.

It's very important that you discuss multi-ink colors with your printer before jumping in and using them. Ask them if it'll be okay to mix two particular spot colors on press. Perhaps they will make a "draw-down" for you so that you can see how the colors will look when they're mixed together (though this only shows you what the colors will look like when they're overprinted at 100 percent).

Building a Multi-Ink Color

It was always painful to mix two spot colors together before version 4 of XPress because you had to duplicate objects, apply a different color and tint to each object, and then make sure one properly overprinted the other. It was always hit and miss, and you could never see a simulation of the final color on screen or on a color printer. Now, mixing colors in version 4 is as easy as one, two, three.

1. Create a new color by opening the Colors dialog box and pressing New.

2. Set the Model popup menu to Multi-Ink.

3. Select a color from the list on the right of the Edit Color dialog box and choose a tint from the Shade popup menu (see Figure 12-6). Repeat this step for each color you want to include.

You can even mix process colors with spot colors in this dialog box. However, I still can't think of a particularly good reason why you'd want to do this, other than perhaps mixing a color with some tint of black.

After applying your multi-ink colors to objects on your page, you can print color separations, and each color appears on its proper plate, just as you'd expect. Remember what I said about specifying the Halftone settings for spot colors that overprint: each spot color within your multi-ink color needs a correct halftone angle, or else you'll get dot-doubling (halftone spots that overprint each other, creating muddy colors) or moiré patterns when your pages come off press.

Figure 12-6

Multi-Ink colors

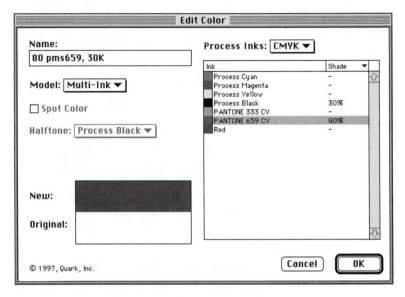

Tip: Multiple Selections.** You can select more than one color at a time when you specify a color in the Multi-Ink model by Command-clicking on each color you want on the color list. This is only helpful if you're going to apply the same tint to all the colors you select.

▼ ▼

Tip: Multi-Ink Hexachrome Colors. If you want to get really fancy, take a look at the Process Inks popup menu that appears in the Edit Color dialog box when you select the Multi-Ink model. When you select Hexachrome from this popup menu, you can build a multi-ink color with Pantone's Hexachrome inks. This way, if you don't like the preset Hexachrome colors that are built into QuarkXPress, you can build your own. You can even mix Hexachrome with your spot colors, and while I can't imagine what you'd end up with, it sure is fun to speculate.

Note that Orange and Cyan are meant to be complementary, so you shouldn't mix them together in the same multi-ink color. Same thing goes with Green and Magenta. And remember that you can only separate Hexachrome colors when XPress's color management system is active (see Appendix A, *Color Management*).

▼ ▼

Tip: Build a Swatch Book. While XPress tries to simulate multi-ink colors on screen (and on color printers), it's far from a perfect system (I find you often get much darker colors on screen than you would in real life). Ultimately, it's still a guessing game unless you're using a swatch book.

If the two colors you're using don't appear in Pantone's Two-Color Selector swatch book, and you're going to use mixes of these colors a lot in your print jobs, then you might consider building your own swatches. Build a set of multi-ink colors in every combination you can think of, apply them to small square boxes on a page, and print them (perhaps you can place them outside the trim marks on some job you're already printing with these inks).

▼ ▼

Tip: Permanent Tints. You don't have to mix two or more colors together in a multi-ink color. You can build a color in the Multi-Ink model that is simply 30 percent of one PMS color. This is useful if you're going to apply that same color tint to several items in your document; it's certainly much faster than applying the color and then changing the tint for each object individually (and it's often more consistent, too).

▼ ▼

Special Colors

QuarkXPress has two special colors that aren't really colors. They are Registration, which I have mentioned above, and Indeterminate, which I'll talk about soon in "Trapping," below.

Registration

This "noncolor" appears on the Colors scroll list and on all color selection lists throughout the menus. When you apply this color to an object or to text, that object or text prints on every color separation plate you print. It's especially nice for job-identification marks, and for registration or crop marks (if you are creating your own rather than letting the program do it for you; see Chapter 13, *Printing,* for more information on these special marks).

For example, I sometimes like to bypass QuarkXPress's regular crop-mark feature and draw my own crop marks in the border around my page. Then I color these Registration, and they print out on every piece of film that comes out for that job.

▼ ▼

Tip: Editing the Registration Color. If you use the Registration color regularly, you might want to change its color so that you can tell it apart from normal Black. You can use the Edit feature described earlier to change the on-screen color of Registration to anything you like. Also, because the Registration color is originally black, the Edit Color dialog box appears with the brightness scroll bar set to zero. Just raise the brightness to the level you want, and then change the color.

No matter what color you specify, objects with the color Registration always print on every plate. Changing the color changes nothing but the screen representation for that color. Use a color that is distinctly different from anything else in the document you're creating. That way you always know at a glance what's normal black stuff and what is colored Registration.

▼ ▼

Indeterminate

When QuarkXPress looks at a selection and finds that either several colors are specified within that selection or that it's a color picture, it calls this an "Indeterminate" color. This is not something you can change in any way. It's just a definition that the program uses to tell you there are several colors in the selection. In "Trapping," below, we'll see the great benefits of the Indeterminate "color."

▼ ▼

Colors Palette

Just like style sheets, you can apply and edit colors with a click using the Colors palette (see Figure 12-7). This floating palette contains a list of every available color, along with a tint-percentage control popup menu, and three icons. These icons gray out depending on what object you have selected. When you select a text box, the icons represent frame color, text color, and background color for that box. When you select a line, two icons gray out, and only the line-color icon remains.

To apply a color to an object, first click the correct icon for what you want to change, then click on the desired color in the color list. If you want a tint of that color, first change the percentage in the upper-right corner, then press Return or Enter to apply the change. You can also just click somewhere else than on the palette. For example, let's say you want to change one word in a text box to 30-percent cyan.

Figure 12-7
The Colors palette

The center icon changes
depending on what item
you have selected

1. Select the word in the text box.

2. Click the center icon on the Colors palette, which represents text (it looks like an "A" in a box).

3. Click on Cyan on the colors list.

4. Select "30%" from the popup menu on the palette, or type "30" in the field and press Enter.

It's funny, but those four steps are often much faster than selecting a color and tint from the Style menu. Note that you can change the color of a box's frame, even if the box doesn't have a frame. If you later add a frame, it will be the color you designated.

▼ ▼

Tip: Jump to Edit Colors. The Colors palette is more like the Style Sheet palette than meets the eye. On both palettes, Command-clicking on an item quickly brings you to a dialog box. In this case, Command-clicking on any color brings up the Colors dialog box, in which you can edit, duplicate, append, delete, or create new colors. This is also the fastest way to the Edit Trap dialog box.

▼ ▼

Tip: Drag-and-Drop Color Application. Sometimes I think the folks at Quark like to toss in features just because they're cool—for example, drag-and-drop color application. Try it: hold your mouse down on one of the tiny color squares on the Colors palette, and drag it over your page. Notice that as you drag, the image of that color square stays attached to your pointer. As you move the pointer over objects, their color changes to the color you're dragging. Move the pointer past an object, and its color reverts to whatever it was before.

To apply a color to an object, just let go of the mouse button. Note that you can apply a color in this way to backgrounds and borders, but not to text, even if you have the text icon selected on the Color palette. And since the palette is grayed out until you select an object, you can't drag anything until you've selected at least one object.

▼ ▼

Tip: Drag-and-Drop Color, Part Two. The engineers at Quark sneaked a feature into version 4.02 and forgot to tell anyone about it. Let's say you've got three boxes on your page. If you drag a color swatch over the first box, it changes color; but as soon as you leave the box, dragging the swatch over to the second box, the first box's color reverts back to its original state. Now, if you're holding down the Command key when you drag the swatch out of the box, XPress actually applies the color to the box, so that it doesn't change after your swatch leaves the box.

If you want all the boxes on your page to be colored yellow, drag the Yellow swatch over each of them with the Command key held down. (If you want all but one to be colored yellow, just don't hold down the Command key while the swatch leaves that box.)

▼ ▼

Blending Colors

You can call them fountains, dégradés, gradations, or blends, but the concept is always the same: the background of a text or picture box can make a gradual transition from one color to another (see Figure 12-8). Unlike other programs that create graduated fills, in XPress you can blend any combination of spot colors and process colors (even white).

QuarkXPress has a dizzying array of blends: Linear (straight blend), Mid-Linear (goes from one color to another, then back again), Rectangular, Diamond, Circular, and Full Circular. (If you find you only have the Linear blend, then you're missing the Cool Blends XTension that ships with QuarkXPress; you might want to check the XTension Manager to see if it has been inadvertently turned off.) See Figure 12-9 for examples of these various blends.

Colors palette. In earlier versions of XPress, you had to use the Colors palette to create blends; version 4 lets you do this in either the palette or

Figure 12-8
Color blends

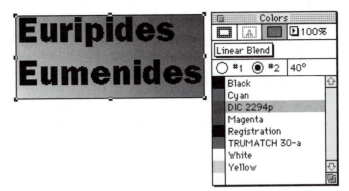

Figure 12-9
The cool blends

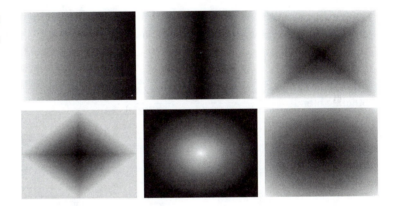

the Modify dialog box. Here's how to apply a blend to a selected object from the Colors palette.

1. Click the background icon on the Colors palette, if it's not already selected.

2. Select the blend you want from the popup menu on the Colors palette.

3. Click button #1, then click on the beginning color of the blend (you can adjust the tint level, too).

4. Click button #2, and select the ending color of the blend (and adjust the tint, if necessary).

5. Specify the angle of the blend. For Linear and Mid-Linear blends, zero degrees (the default value) puts color #1 on the left and color #2 on the right. Increasing the value rotates the blend counter-clockwise (so that at 75 degrees, color #1 is almost at the bottom of your box).

If you later want to change one of the colors in the blend, click button #1 or #2; then you can select the color, change its tint, or adjust the angle. You don't have to blend between two colors, of course—you can also blend between two tints of a single color.

Modify dialog box. I find making blends in the Colors palette to be preferable unless I already happen to be in the Modify dialog box making other changes. You can apply a blend to an object on the Box tab of the Modify dialog box (see Figure 12-10). Note that there's no "color #1" and "color #2" here. Instead, the first color is always the color you've chosen in the section of the dialog box labeled "Box." The second color is always the color you've chosen in the section labeled "Blends."

Figure 12-10
Building blends

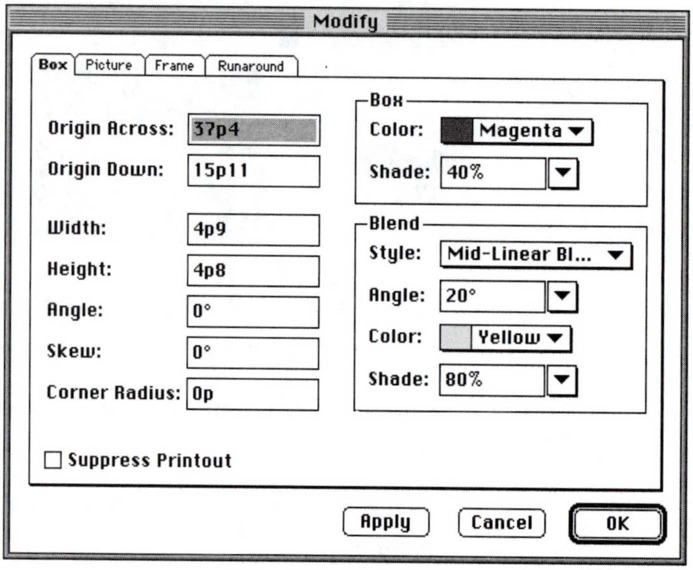

Tip: Don't Mix Blends and Grayscale TIFFs. A warning for those placing blends behind grayscale TIFFs: my experience has shown that this usually results in something that looks as pleasant as a baboon's behind. The problem is that color #1 gets mixed in with the TIFF itself. Quark thinks it should work this way; I think it's crazy. Proceed at your own risk.

Tip: Rotation Changes Blends. Surprisingly, the angle value you specify has a curious effect on certain kinds of blends. While it simply rotates

Linear and Mid-Linear blends, it actually changes the look of the other blends. For instance, a Circular blend at zero degrees generally appears smaller than one at 45 degrees (see Figure 12-11). It's worth playing with the angle in order to achieve the effect you're looking for.

Figure 12-11
A blend's angle affects its look.

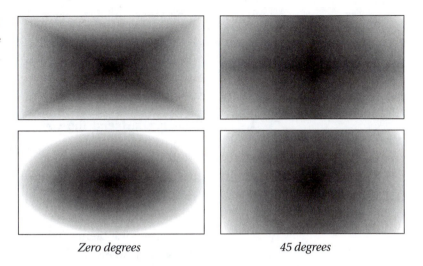

Zero degrees   *45 degrees*

▼ ▼

Tip: Accurate Blends. If you've got an 8-bit color monitor (256 colors), QuarkXPress lets you speed up your screen redraw by sacrificing on-screen color blend quality. You do this by turning Accurate Blends on or off in the Document Preferences dialog box (Command-Y). When Accurate Blends is turned on (this is the default), all blends appear on the screen as smoothly as QuarkXPress can make them (some are better than others; it depends on what colors you use). When you turn this option off, the program just spits out a quick-'n'-dirty representation of the blend. This feature doesn't affect printing at all—just the speed at which your screen redraws. Note that if you're using a 16-bit (thousands of colors) or 24-bit (millions of colors) monitor setting, this feature does not do anything.

When it comes right down to it, the speed increase you may get by turning this option off is usually negligible. I just leave Accurate Blends on all the time, even on my old 8-bit color monitor at home.

▼ ▼

Tip: Banding in Blends. The number-one problem people have with blends in QuarkXPress is banding (visible bands of tint or color within the supposedly smooth blend). Unfortunately, this is almost always a problem with digital halftoning technology and not just with XPress, so there's not much you can do about it from within the program.

Banding usually occurs because PostScript can only image 256 levels of gray. If you've got a black-to-white blend that's 256 points (about 3.5 inches) long, then XPress builds the blend by creating 256 1-point-wide boxes, each with a different tint in it. If the blend is 7 inches long, then each of those boxes has to be about 2 points wide, which typically creates visible bands.

There are two lessons to be learned here.

▶ First, the larger the blend, the worse the banding. If you stick to 1- or 2-inch-long blends in XPress, you shouldn't get banding.

▶ You can get better blends if you make them in Adobe Photoshop. When you make a blend in Photoshop, the program automatically dithers the colors within the blend to reduce banding. If you're making process-color blends in Photoshop, make them in CMYK mode (making a blend in RGB mode and then converting to CMYK can cause color shifts). Of course, you can't easily make spot-color blends in Photoshop yet.

I discuss dithering, blends, and other banding issues in more detail in *Real World Scanning and Halftones*, which I wrote with Glenn Fleishman and Steve Roth, and in *Real World Photoshop*, which I wrote with Bruce Fraser.

▼ ▼

Tip: Blending to Black. If you've worked with blends before, you've found that they don't always appear in print as they do on screen. For instance, if you make a blend from 100-percent magenta to 100-percent black, you would think you'd get a nice, even blend between the two colors. Unfortunately, when you print separations and throw them on a printing press, you may find a big grayish band in the middle of the blend (see Figure G in the color plates).

Instead, try blending from 100 percent of magenta to a rich black (in this case, 100-percent black plus 100-percent magenta). This way, the magenta simply appears to become darker throughout the blend.

▼ ▼

▼ ▼

Tip: A New Dimension. Maybe I'm just easily amused, but I think this trick for creating three-dimensional buttons in XPress is pretty keen.

1. Draw a rectangle or oval (I think it looks best with a square or a circle).

2. Give it a straight Linear blend. I like to set the angle at 45 degrees, but it's up to you.

3. Duplicate the object, and make it smaller. The amount you make it smaller is up to you. Remember that if you want to reduce it to 80 percent, you can simply type "*.8" after the measurement in the Width and Height fields.

4. To figure out the second object's blend angle, subtract the first object's blend angle from 270. So if the first object had a 45-degree blend, the second object should have a 225-degree blend $(270 - 45 = 225)$. You don't have to do the math if you don't want to; just type "270-45" in the angle box of the Colors palette.

5. Space/Align the two objects so that their centers are equal (set Vertical and Horizontal alignment to zero offset from the objects' centers in the Space/Align dialog box).

You can really see the effect best when the page guides are turned off (see Figure 12-12). It's even nicer when you add a.25-point white frame around the inside object (sort of a highlight to the button's ridge).

Figure 12-12
Three-dimensional
buttons

The process   *The result*

▼ ▼

Trapping

Nothing is perfect, not even obscenely expensive printing presses. When your print job is flying through those presses, each color being added one at a time, the paper may shift slightly. Depending on the press, this could be an offset of anywhere between .003 and .0625 inches (.2 to 4.5 points). If two colors abut each other on your artwork and this shift occurs, then the two colors may be moved apart slightly, resulting in a white "unprinted" space. It may seem like a $3/1,000$-of-an-inch space would look like a small crack in a large sidewalk, but I assure you, it could easily appear to be a chasm. What can you do? Fill in these potential chasms with traps and overprints.

The concept and practice of trapping and overprinting contain several potential pitfalls for the inexperienced. Up until now, most designers just let their lithographers and strippers handle this stuff. There is a school of thought that says we should still let them handle it. But you know these desktop publishers—they always want to be in control of everything. The problem is that designers weren't trained to do trapping! Let's look carefully at what it's all about.

▼ ▼

Tip: Just (Don't) Do It. Trapping is as much art as science—in fact, if you look up "difficult" in the dictionary, it offers the synonym "trapping." I often don't have time to mess around making sure my traps are proper throughout a document, and sometimes even if I have time, it'd just be too much of a hassle.

QuarkXPress's trapping is usually pretty good, all in all, but it's lacking in some important areas, such as blends, choking type, and partially overlapping objects. Ultimately, QuarkXPress isn't designed to be a great trapper. If you want to spare yourself a lot of hassle, you can turn auto trapping off (see "Trapping Preferences," below), and use a program like Imation's TrapWise, which can trap XPress documents infinitely better than you can with XPress alone.

You probably won't want to own TrapWise yourself (it costs several thousand dollars), but your service bureau or printer should have a copy of it (or some other trapping solution). Find out how much it will cost you for them to trap the page, and then compare that with how much it's worth to you not to worry about it anymore.

▼ ▼

Overprinting. Picture the letter "Q" colored magenta on a cyan background. Normally, when you make these color separations, the cyan plate has a white Q *knocked out* of it, exactly where the magenta Q prints (I talk more about color separations and plates in Chapter 13, *Printing*). This way, the cyan and the magenta don't mix (see Figure 12-13). You can, however, set the magenta to overprint the cyan. This results in the Q not being knocked out of the cyan; the two colors *overprint* in that area—resulting in a purple Q on a cyan background.

There are a few very important times when you'll want to overprint colors. The most important of these times may be when you're printing fine black lines or type on a colored background. In fact, almost any time you have a black foreground object, it should overprint the background (it does in XPress by default).

Trapping. A trap is created by very slightly overprinting two colors right along their borders. Then when the paper shifts on the printing press, the space between the colors is filled with the additional trap color (see Figure 12-14). The trap can be created using two methods: choking and spreading. *Choking* refers to the background area getting smaller. *Spreading* refers to the foreground object (the Q in the example above) getting slightly larger.

Simple idea, right? But not necessarily a simple process when you're just beginning. How much to spread or choke an object is determined by the printing press, the colors you're using, and even the paper you're printing on. With some color combinations, you don't even have to trap at all (see "Tip: Who Needs Trapping?" later in this chapter). When you build a color document, you should always talk to your printer about trapping.

In the sections that follow, I'll look at the various ways to trap objects in QuarkXPress. Note that there are two ways to specify trapping in XPress: automatic trapping (which you control on a color-by-color basis) and object-level trapping (which you can apply to a particular item on

Figure 12-13
Knocking out and
overprinting

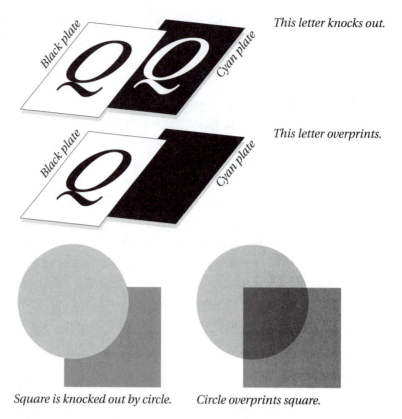

This letter knocks out.

This letter overprints.

Square is knocked out by circle.   *Circle overprints square.*

Figure 12-14
Trapping two
colored objects

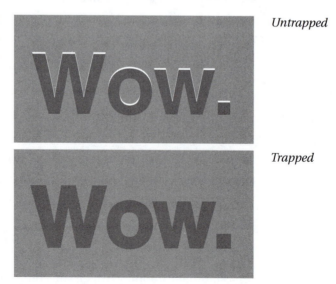

Untrapped

Trapped

your page). Even if you don't do anything in XPress, the program still
applies some trapping, based on the values on the Trapping tab of the
Document Preferences dialog box.

Trapping Preferences

In a valiant effort to save you from unsightly gaps between colors, QuarkXPress always applies a little bit of trapping to your page objects (unless you tell it not to). You can control the way that XPress handles trapping on the Trapping tab of the Document Preferences dialog box (Command-Y). The changes you make—like most other preferences—are specific to only the document that you have open at the time; if you want them to apply to all future documents, change them while no other documents are open.

The Trapping tab contains seven controls: Trapping Method, Process Trapping, Auto Amount, Indeterminate, Knockout Limit, Overprint Limit, and Ignore White (see Figure 12-15). These controls let you get pretty specific about how you want QuarkXPress's trapping to act. Don't worry, they're not nearly as confusing as they sound.

Trapping Method. The first popup menu on the Trapping tab, Trapping Method, lets you turn QuarkXPress's trapping controls on and off. The default value, Absolute, tells XPress to always use the same-sized trap (the width in the Auto Amount field). The second setting, Proportional, tells the program to adjust the size of the trap according to how different the two abutting colors are. As far as I'm concerned, there's rarely a reason to use Proportional trapping, so when I want trapping I always leave the Trapping Method set to Absolute.

The third choice, Knockout All, is the same as turning trapping off. When this is set, every color knocks out colors beneath it, with no trap

Figure 12-15

Trapping tab of the
Document Preferences
dialog box

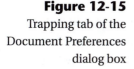

Document Preferences for 12.02 Color.qx

| General | Paragraph | Character | Tool | **Trapping** |

Trapping Method: Absolute ▼

Process Trapping: On ▼

Auto Amount: 0.25 pt ▼

Indeterminate: 0.25 pt ▼

Knockout Limit: 0%

Overprint Limit: 95%

☒ Ignore White

Cancel   OK

at all. It's rare that you'd want to use this setting unless you were using a postprocess trapping solution like TrapWise (where you don't want XPress to interfere with TrapWise's superior trapping).

(I don't like the Proportional method because it can make certain abutting colors not trap when they really should. If you insist on using it, however, you should know how it works. Because Proportional trapping tells QuarkXPress to look at the "darkness" of a color—which is difficult to quantify—it's a little hard for me to describe the exact mathematics here on paper without getting really technical. Basically, though, QuarkXPress takes the difference between the two darkness values and multiplies that by the number in the Auto Amount field. For example, if the background color were 80-percent dark, the foreground object were 20-percent dark, and the Auto Amount setting were 0.5 point, then the background would choke by 0.3 point. $(0.8 - 0.2 = 0.6 \times 0.5$ point $= 0.3$ point. Now that you know that, don't you feel better?)

Process Trapping. Before I tell you exactly what the Process Trapping feature is all about, let me just say one thing: If this preference is not turned on (it usually is by default), then turn it on and leave it on. Now if you want to really understand Process Trapping, read on. Or, if you couldn't care less, then jump ahead a few paragraphs to the next section.

Take a look at the two process colors (foreground and background) listed in Table 12-1. If you spread this foreground color (a yellow) into the background color (a muddy brown) with Process Trapping turned off, the trap area doesn't mesh the two colors the way you'd want. That is, the slight sliver of trap (where the colors overlap) is made up of magenta, yellow, and black (the foreground color spreads). However, since there's no cyan in the foreground color, the cyan from the background shows through, making a really ugly puke-green trap area. Now you might say: For a 0.25-point trap, who cares? No one will see it anyway. Think again. That green line stands out clearly around the edge of the yellow object. (See Figure H on the color pages.)

However, when Process Trap is turned on, some process colors get spread while others are choked. Here's how it works. Any process color in the foreground object that is darker than the same color in the background object is spread by half the trapping value (typically, half the value in the Auto Amount field). Any process color that's lighter is choked by half the trapping value.

Color	Foreground box	Background box
Cyan	0	30
Magenta	20	50
Yellow	100	90
Black	5	0

In the example above, the cyan plate is choked by half the trapping value because there is less cyan in the foreground box than in the background box. Magenta also chokes. However, the yellow and black plates are spread by the same amount.

The result is a trap area as wide as the specified trapping value (in the example above, 0.25 point), centered on the edge of the foreground object, and with the darkest process colors of each of the objects.

If you don't understand this, read the last few paragraphs over several times. If you still don't understand it, then give up and believe me when I tell you that it's a really good thing. Leave Process Trap turned on.

A couple of notes on this feature. When all the process colors in the foreground object are darker or when they're all lighter than in the background object, then QuarkXPress doesn't trap at all. This is because it doesn't need to. Also, Process Trap doesn't do anything for spot colors, again because it doesn't need to.

Auto Amount. The value that you set in the Auto Amount field tells QuarkXPress the maximum value that Proportional trapping can use, and the specific value that Absolute trapping should use. The default value of 0.144 point (about $2/1,000$ of an inch) seems a little small to me, so I usually change this to 0.3 point. As I said earlier, however, the proper value depends a great deal on your printing process; if you're printing a newspaper, the trap value might be significantly higher! Remember to check with your printer first.

One fine point: if you are familiar with trapping using illustration programs such as FreeHand or Illustrator, you know that when you apply a trapping stroke to an object, your trap is really only one half that thickness (the stroke falls equally inside and outside the path). If you're in the habit of using 1 point when you want a 0.5-point trap, break it when you use QuarkXPress. This program handles the conversion for you.

Indeterminate. If QuarkXPress can't figure out what the background color is, it labels the background "Indeterminate." There are three cases in which this happens: a color picture in the background, a background where several different colors are present, or an item only partially covering a background color when Ignore White is turned off (see "Ignore White," below). Note that XPress can only spread a foreground color over an Indeterminate color (for instance, it can only spread text over an image; it cannot choke the image under the text).

Knockout Limit. Remember that the main idea behind trapping is to avoid white paper showing through between two abutting colors, also sometimes called "light leaks." Very light-tinted type, boxes, or lines may be close enough to white so that whether you trap them or just let them knock out isn't very important. New to QuarkXPress 4 is the Knockout Limit, which tells XPress when it can get away without trapping and can instead just knock an object out of the background. The default value is zero percent, which means that every object traps as it did in earlier versions of the program. If you raise this value to 10 percent, then any black object tinted to 10 percent or lighter knocks out, and no trap value is applied.

Actually, that's oversimplifying it a bit because the percentage is based on the luminance of the color, not the tint value, so the limit is different for each color. For instance, a Knockout Limit of 5 percent sets the knockout cutoff at 5 percent for Black, 10 percent for Cyan, and 45 percent for Yellow. In CMYK colors, the luminance of the combination of colors is what counts, not the individual channels. (I like setting the Knockout Limit to about 5 percent, but most people seem to get along just fine without setting it above zero.)

Overprint Limit. Black always overprints any color below it, right? Wrong. Automatic overprinting is controlled by the Overprint Limit setting. The default setting of 95 percent means that black—or any other color that is set to overprint in the Trap Specifications dialog box (which I'll discuss in just a moment)—only overprints when its tint level is above 95 percent. As it turns out, dot gain on press will almost certainly change any 95-percent tint into a solid color, so this is no big deal.

On the other hand, let's say you have the color Green set to overprint by default. If you screen it back to 50 percent, QuarkXPress knocks the color out rather than overprinting it, because the tint falls below the Overprint Limit.

By the way, if you set an object to overprint in the Trap Information palette (which I'll cover later in this section), it will overprint no matter what the tint—object-level trapping ignores the Overprint Limit.

Ignore White. Let's say that a red picture box only lies partially on top of another page item, and partially on the white page background (see Figure 12-16). The Trapping tab of the Document Preferences dialog box gives you the choice as to whether it should consider the background color "Indeterminate" or not. When Ignore White is turned on, QuarkXPress won't call a partial overlap "Indeterminate" because it just ignores the white page background; it traps based on the color of the overlapped object. If you turn this option off, however, it "sees" the white background page, and considers the mix of background colors to be Indeterminate. I don't see any reason to turn this option off.

Figure 12-16
Ignore White

When Ignore White is turned on, the trap value for this circle is determined by its relationship to the box, rather than "Indeterminate".

Custom Color-Pair Trap Settings

Remember, there's no such thing as two objects truly being next to each other on an XPress page; one is always on a higher "layer" than the other. QuarkXPress takes advantage of this and always traps based on *pairs* of colors: the foreground color and the background color. For example, picture some red type on top of a blue rectangle. The blue is the background color; the red is the foreground color.

QuarkXPress's default trapping system uses the following built-in trapping algorithm.

▶ Note the darkness (luminosity) of each color.

▶ If the foreground color is lighter, then spread it so that it slightly overlaps the background color.

▶ If the background color is lighter, then choke it so that it slightly "underlaps" the foreground color.

This algorithm is based on the rule that in trapping, lighter colors should encroach on darker ones. That way the darker element defines the edge, and the lighter color overlapping doesn't affect that definition (see Figure 12-17).

In general, XPress does a pretty good job of figuring out what should be trapped and how. However, you can always override XPress and assign your own default trapping behavior for a pair of colors.

1. Select a color (typically the foreground color) in the Colors dialog box.

2. Click the Edit Trap button to open the Trap Specifications dialog box (see Figure 12-18).

3. The list of colors down the left side of the dialog box displays the potential background colors. Select one or more (you can select contiguous colors by holding down the Shift key, or discontiguous colors on the list with the Command key). Note that the first "color" on the list is Indeterminate, which lets you control how your foreground color will trap when it sits on top of an indeterminate background (I discussed the meaning of Indeterminate earlier in this section).

Figure 12-17
Traps should go
from light colors
into dark colors

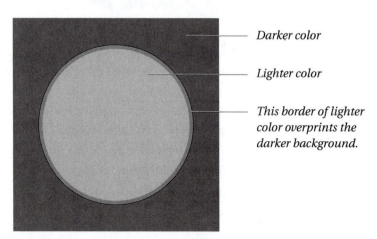

Darker color

Lighter color

This border of lighter
color overprints the
darker background.

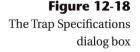

Figure 12-18

The Trap Specifications
dialog box

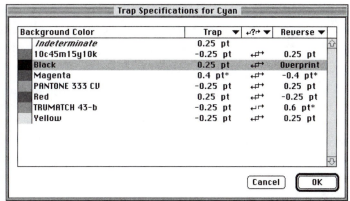

4. The third column in the dialog box—the one filled with those strange-looking, co-mingling arrows—lets you specify whether the color pair's trapping should be reversible; that is, if you want the same trap settings for the two colors when the foreground color is the same as the background color, and vice versa. When the arrows are intertwined (they are by default), the color-pair trapping is reversible. If you'd rather the settings not be constrained, you can choose Independent from the popup menu at the top of the column (which is unfortunately just labeled "?"). Or, faster, just click the arrow icon once to toggle it from one state to the other.

5. Select the proper setting from the Trap popup menu. You've got six options: Default, Knockout, Overprint, Auto Amount +, Auto Amount –, and Custom (I describe each of these in more detail when I discuss object-level trapping, later in this chapter). If I'm going to change the trap settings from the default value, I typically use Knockout, Overprint, or Custom (depending on what I'm trying to do). Note that as soon as you make a change, XPress displays an asterisk next to the trapping values to indicate they're not the default settings.

   If you select Custom, you can type any value between -36 and 36 points, in 0.001-point increments (why anyone would want a trap larger than 1 or 2 points is beyond me). A positive value spreads the foreground object (making it slightly larger by drawing a line around it). A negative value leaves the foreground object alone and chokes the background object.

6. If the color-pair trapping is Dependent (what I call "reversible"), then XPress figures out the reverse of the trap for you. If you change the pair to Independent, you can now set the reverse trapping value in the Reverse column. (This is a new feature in version 4, and was just added as a minor convenience.)

Again, you probably won't spend a lot of time figuring out your color-pair traps in this dialog box because XPress does a pretty good job of it already.

▼ ▼

Tip: Who Needs Trapping? You don't need to use any trapping at all in your documents. Does that sound crazy? Well, it's true in two cases. First, you never need trapping if your press operator is obsessed with perfect registration on press. It is possible to control press registration; it's just rare that any press operator has the luxury of time and money to have such a perfect run.

Another way you can entirely avoid trapping is to use process-color combinations that don't need trapping in your documents (remember that only colors that touch require trapping). Here are two rules that can help you build and arrange color on your page so that you won't need trapping (see Table 12-2).

▶ ALL LIGHTER, ALL DARKER. If the cyan, magenta, yellow, and black tints in your foreground color are all darker or all lighter than the corresponding tints in the background color, you don't need to trap. When the Process Trap option is turned on—which it should be—XPress simply doesn't trap color combinations like this, so you don't have to do any extra work to stop QuarkXPress from trapping.

▶ COMMON COLORS. If two colors share a process-color element (cyan, magenta, yellow, or black), and the common element is within 30 percent, you probably don't need a trap. Let's say you color some text deep purple—made of 80-percent cyan, 70-percent magenta, and 20-percent black. If you put that text on a bright yellow background, you'll probably need to trap it because there are no common color elements. On the other hand, you don't have to trap it if you put the purple text on top of a light blue background—made of 50-percent cyan and 10-percent black. Why? Because both cyan and black are shared elements in the

	CYAN	MAGENTA	YELLOW	BLACK
ALL LIGHTER, ALL DARKER				
Color #1 (dark green)	100	20	80	15
Color #2 (yellow)	10	10	70	0
COMMON COLORS				
Color #1 (orange)	0	60	90	10
Color #2 (tan)	25	40	75	0

Table 12-2

Examples of colors that don't need trapping (see also Figure I on the color plates)

foreground and background colors, and their respective tints are both within 30 percent of each other. (The 30-percent rule is a somewhat arbitrary, middle-of-the-road choice; in some cases, you may want to be more or less conservative.)

QuarkXPress does not recognize common colors by itself. If you don't want these color pairs to trap, you should set them to Knockout in the Trap Specifications dialog box or in the Trap Information palette (see "Object-Level Trapping," below).

▼ ▼

Tip: Trapping Small Type. You can run into trouble when you're using small type, especially serif type, in a color document. Since the type is so fine—especially the serifs—even a small amount of trapping can clog it up. The counters can fill in, and the serifs can become really clunky (see Figure 12-19). Bear this in mind when you're setting up your trapping preferences, and when you're specifying colors for type.

Figure 12-19

Trapping serif type

Monsieur de Bergerac
Untrapped

Monsieur de Bergerac
Trapped

Serif type can clog up, and the serifs can get clunky when trapped.

However, the folks at Quark have made some hidden allowances for small text (under 24 points) and small objects (less than 10 points in height or width). When XPress encounters one of these, it won't allow spreads or chokes that might compromise the object's shape. This is both good and bad. On the one hand, it's nice because your small objects look better. On the other hand, it's bad because you can only rarely trap small objects even if you want to. This includes thin lines (under 10 points)!

You usually don't have to think about what XPress is really doing here, but if you want to know, here's what happens. The program spreads the object on a color plate only if the object's tint is less than or equal to half the corresponding color tint on its background; choking will occur only when the background-plate component is less than or equal to half the darkness of the object.

The upshot is that there won't be a trap unless the foreground and background colors are pretty similar.

▼ ▼

Tip: Trapping Large Type. Even the untrained reader can quickly spot type (especially thin, serif type) that has been "bulked up" by QuarkXPress's trapping. For example, if you put a dark-green 48-point headline over a light-blue background, you may find the text appears slightly heavier in print than the same text would look over no background color at all. The problem is that it's difficult to get XPress to choke a background behind some text without spreading the text, too.

Here's another use for the Text to Box feature.

1. Create a new color that is a combination of each darkest process-color tint in the foreground and background. For instance, let's say the foreground has 40-percent cyan plus 20-percent yellow, and the background object is set to 20-percent cyan and 40-percent yellow. The new color would have 40-percent cyan and 40-percent yellow.

2. Convert the headline text to a Bézier box using Text to Box on the Style menu.

3. Give this box a frame (Command-B) the width of the desired trap (.3 points or so) and apply the new color.

4. In the Trap Information palette, set the Frame Outside and Frame Inside popup menus to Overprint (see "Object-Level Trapping," below).

This actually looks far worse on screen, because XPress can't simulate the overprinting. However, when you print color separations, you'll see that the background has choked in under the "text," and it often looks cleaner (see Figure J in the color pages). Of course, this is a lot of work, so you'll only want to do this when you find that XPress's built-in trapping won't work for you.

Figure A
Process-color
separations

Process-color image (four colors)

Cyan

Magenta

Yellow

Black

Figure B
The elegant solution
for shadow type with
process colors

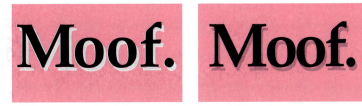

*Normal shadow style applied
(background color is
80-percent magenta)*

*Shadow is in separate text box
(text color set to 30-percent
black and 80-percent magenta)*

Figure C

A color swatch page from the TruMatch color selection book

You can type this number directly in the Edit Color dialog box with TruMatch selected. (Or you can type in the CMYK values.)

Figure D

Linear color blend between two process colors with an EPS image over it

Figure E

The Edit Color dialog box

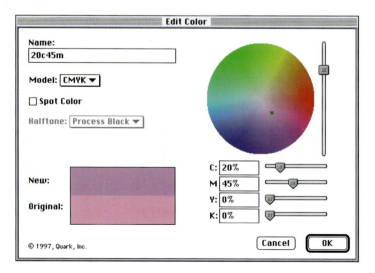

Figure F
Color tricks
the eye

*This color looks
different over
different-colored
backgrounds*

Figure G
Blending tip

*(Note: these
two blends look
the same on screen)*

Blend from 100-percent magenta to 100-percent black

Blend from 100-percent magenta to 100-percent black and magenta

Figure H
Process Trapping

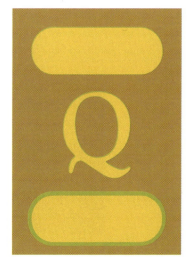

*The bottom object has
a large trap applied so
you can see the effect
more easily*

Process Trapping on   *Process Trapping off*

Figure I

Some colors don't need trapping. Here, the process colors in the foreground colors are all lower values than the background color.

Figure J

Trapping large type

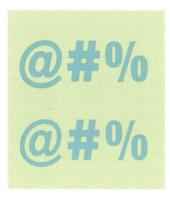

Normal text, trapped with Process Trap on

This text has been converted to outlines and trapped with a frame (see page 682).

Figure K

Rich black versus 100-percent black

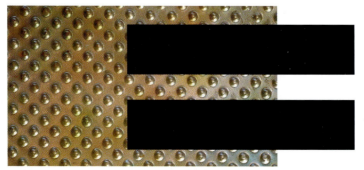

100-percent black

Rich black (includes cyan and magenta)

Figure L
Knocking out
from rich black

If QuarkXPress didn't use a special algorithm for rich blacks (black mixed with other colors), misregistration on press would be a mess!

Here is the actual text knocked out from a rich black in QuarkXPress. Note that only the colored plate(s) are spread so the type retains its weight.

Figure M
Using Color Contrast
to ghost back a
portion of an image

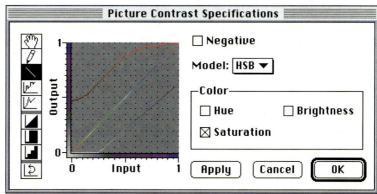

Figure N
Using Color Contrast
to adjust the colors
within an image

*This is a silly thing to do
in QuarkXPress unless
you're just making a
quick mockup. You'd
get much better quality
using Adobe Photoshop.*

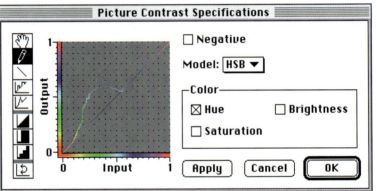

Figure O
Overprinting images
to simulate
transparency

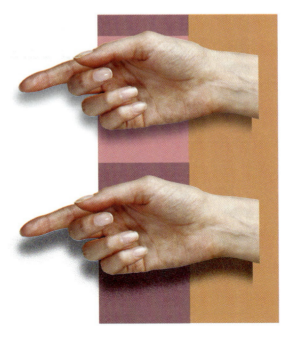

*Shadow is a separate
grayscale image set
to overprint the
background. It
works fine as long
as there is no black
in the background
color.*

*Shadow is a 600-ppi
bilevel Bitmap that
appears to overprint
all colors.*

Figure P
Blend and an image
inside a one-bit image

Figure Q
Sometimes
overprinting
colors has
unexpected
results

40-percent cyan

25-percent yellow

*A 20-percent magenta
circle—set to overprint—
sits on top of this square*

*When the page is separated,
the 20-percent magenta
knocks out of the darker
magenta background*

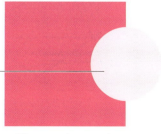

80-percent magenta

10-percent black

Figure R

Halftone screen
frequencies

60 lpi   *120 lpi*   *150 lpi*

Figure S

Duotones from Photoshop

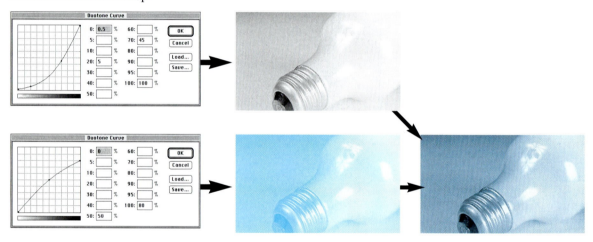

Figure T

Faking duotones in QuarkXPress

*Image placed in a box
colored 40-percent cyan*

*Two TIFFs: each has a custom
contrast applied, and the top
one is set to Overprint.*

*Three cloned TIFFs, each with
a custom contrast applied
(the top one overprints)*

▼ ▼

Tip: Knockout Black. If you find yourself wishing that black would over-print sometimes and knockout at other times, you might want to duplicate Black (in the Colors dialog box) and change the dupe's name to "Knockout Black." You can then edit the trapping specifications for your new color to either knock out or trap to some custom value. Now you've got a choice: apply Black to the items you want to overprint, and Knockout Black to those you don't.

▼ ▼

Tip: Four-Color Black. Most people still think that printing black ink over something else on their page completely covers it. Not so. Black ink is almost never completely opaque, so you can actually see through to what's below it on the printed page. This isn't a concern in black-and-white printing, but when you print multiple colors on a page, it can mean the success or failure of your design. (I once saw a magazine ad that showed a shirtless male jogger running along the road. A wide black box printed over his midriff was supposed to make the jogger appear naked, but the joke was on the ad's designer: the black box, being some-what translucent, clearly showed that he was wearing jogging shorts, defeating the purpose of the advertisement.)

The solution is to build a *rich black*—a separate black in your color palette that contains a bit of other process color in it. The standard rich black that color strippers use is 100-percent black along with 40-percent cyan. I prefer to add 20 to 30 percent each of magenta and yellow, too. When a plain black (100-percent K) object overlaps colored objects, it can look mottled over different colors (see Figure K in the color pages). Adding color to your blacks solves the problem.

This trick not only achieves a richer black on a printing press, but usually also better blacks from a color printer.

Note, though, that you should think carefully about how you apply this rich black. A potential problem lurks behind this technique: the cyan can show up from behind the black if (or when) the printing press mis-registers (see "Tip: Knocking Out Rich Black," next).

▼ ▼

Tip: Knocking Out Rich Black. The biggest problem with rich black is that when you have text or an object knocking out the black, any mis-registration on press results in the cyan peeking out horribly from behind the black. The engineers at Quark have built a very cool internal solution to this problem.

QuarkXPress checks to see if an object is knocking out a rich black. If it is, XPress only spreads the cyan, magenta, and yellow plates of that rich-black color by the trapping amount, leaving the black plate alone. You need this kind of help most when you're placing a white object (such as white, reversed text) over a rich black. (See Figure 12-20 and Figure L on the color pages.)

XPress also chokes the additive colors (leaving the black plate alone) around the edges of a rich black object that is sitting on a white or colored background. This ensures that the colored inks won't appear as a fringe around the black object.

Figure 12-20
Knockout from rich black

White type knocking out from the black plate of a rich black

The cyan plate Note the type is spread and the background is choked.

Object-Level Trapping

Instead of just specifying trapping-color pairs (all reds over all blues, all blacks over all yellows, and so on), you can specify trapping on an object-by-object basis. For example, if you want one green line to overprint a yellow area, and another similar line to knock out, you can specify that. You do this in the Trap Information palette. Again, you don't *have* to use this; the default trapping is often good enough (and using your service bureau's trapping software is even better). But when you need to tweak your trapping in XPress, here's the place to do it.

Unlike most palettes in QuarkXPress, where you can either use them or use menu items, the Trap Information palette is the only place you can use object-by-object trapping. Let's take a gander at this palette's anatomy (see Figure 12-21).

The Trap Information palette shows you the current trap information for a selected page object, gives you "reasons" for why it's trapping the object that way, and lets you change that object's trap value. The trap values that you can change depend on the type of object you've selected.

For example, for a text box with no frame, you can adjust the trap for the background color of the box and the text in the box. If the text box has no background color, then the Background setting is grayed out.

▶ **BACKGROUND.** You can set the Background trap value for boxes that have a background color (anything but None) and do not have a frame.

▶ **FRAME INSIDE/FRAME OUTSIDE.** As soon as you put a border (Command-B) around a box, the Background trap setting grays out and the Frame Inside and Frame Outside settings become available. The inside and outside portions of a frame are exactly half the frame width; in a 4-point frame, the Frame Inside (which abuts the background color of the box, or the image inside a picture box) and Frame Outside (which abuts whatever is behind the box) are each 2 points wide.

▶ **FRAME MIDDLE.** If you choose a border style that has gaps in it (in other words, any style other than the solid frame, such as the

Figure 12-21

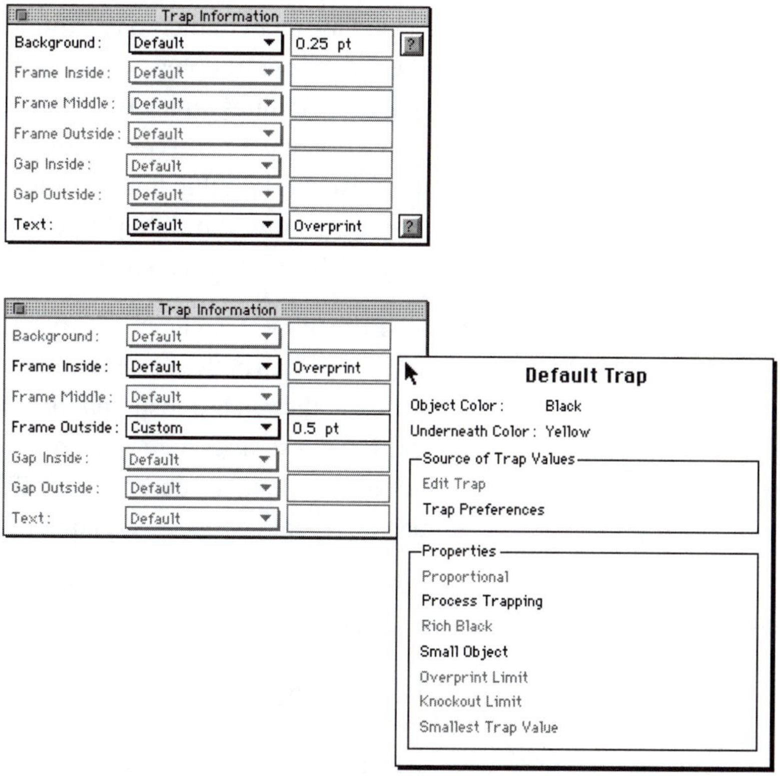

The Trap Information palette and its popup information window

dotted or double-line frame), XPress activates the Frame Middle popup menu. The Frame Middle lets you control the trap between the frame and the gap area. If the gap area is blank (if the Gap color is None), then this should typically be the same as the Frame Outside setting.

The Frame Middle setting is also the only setting available when you have a fancy bitmapped frame around a box (which is a pretty silly thing to do). In this case, the only options are Knockout and Overprint. On the palette, it may seem that the default setting is to spread or choke by the Auto Amount, but that doesn't reflect the reality (unless the frame is black, it will probably just knock out of its background).

▶ **GAP INSIDE/ GAP OUTSIDE.** As soon as you set a frame's gap color (in the Modify dialog box), you can set that gap's trapping with Gap Inside and Gap Outside. Like the frame trapping controls, Gap Inside refers to where the gap color touches the image or the background color of the box, and Gap Outside refers to where it touches the color behind the box.

▶ **LINE.** Lines trap to their background, of course, and if you don't like the default trapping, you can change it here. The problem is that because lines under 10 points thick are "small objects" (see "Tip: Trapping Small Type," earlier in this chapter), XPress currently won't trap a thin line at all unless its color is very similar to the background (I'm lobbying Quark to change this . . . maybe they will by the time you read this).

▶ **LINE MIDDLE.** Like Frame Middle, the Line Middle setting lets you set the trap between a line and the gaps in nonsolid line styles (whether the gap is transparent or colored). Again, unless the line is thick, the settings here won't make any difference. (Personally, I think we should be able to force XPress to trap thin lines in this palette . . . maybe a later version of XPress will allow it.)

▶ **GAP.** If you've gone hog-wild and added a gap color to your styled line, the Gap setting lets you trap that color to the background.

▶ **TEXT.** Where XPress 3.x would either trap every character in a text box or none at all, version 4 is a little smarter: it decides on trapping line by line. If only the first three lines of a text box are over a colored background, it will trap them and leave the other lines alone. If, however, the left side of a text box is over a colored background and the right side is not, XPress isn't smart enough to only trap the characters on the left side of the box, so every character gets trapped by default. This is a job for the Text setting on the Trap Information palette, which lets you change trapping character by character. If only half a character is overlapping text, XPress can't trap just half of it—that's a job for postprocess trapping software, like TrapWise.

▶ **PICTURE.** The Picture trap setting does not let you trap objects to a background in XPress. Instead, it simply gives you the choice of overprinting or knocking out the background. The only use I can think of for this is overprinting grayscale images, which was particularly difficult in earlier versions of XPress, but which is now quite easy with this feature.

By the way, don't get confused if the Trap Information palette displays a positive trap value (spread) when you know it should be negative (choke). Remember that when the Process Trap option is turned on, some plates will spread and others will choke, so the positive and negative numbers don't mean much.

Default Trap. Unless you've changed the trap value, the Trap Information palette displays all objects at their Default trap. This means that the objects trap at whatever value is set in the Trap Specifications dialog box and on the Trapping tab of the Document Preferences dialog box. QuarkXPress displays the trap value to the right of the word "Default," and then displays a gray button labeled with a question mark. If you click this button and hold it down, QuarkXPress displays the Default Trap window, which explains why it's trapping the object this way. For example, if you have a black line selected, the window might tell you that it's overprinting the black line because of the relationship between black and the background color.

If there are any special reasons why XPress is trapping the object the way it does, they're highlighted in the Properties section of the Default Trap window. Unfortunately, it doesn't usually provide much detail. For instance, if you've selected some white text that is knocking out of a rich black, "Rich Black" is highlighted, but nowhere does it mention that the additive colors in the rich black will be spread or choked by the Auto Amount. It just happens. Similarly, the only way you'd know that small type isn't getting a trap ("Tip: Trapping Small Type," above) is the phrase "Small Objects" highlighted on the Properties list.

Nonetheless, it's better than just leaving you up in the air.

Custom trapping. To change the trap value for part of an object (for example, the inside frame of a picture box), you use the mini-popup menu on the Trap Information palette. The menu is usually set to Default, but you can change this to Overprint, Knockout, Auto Amount (+), Auto Amount (−), or Custom. Overprint and Knockout are pretty self-explanatory. The two Auto Amount values use the value in the Auto Amount field of the Trapping Preferences dialog box (the value is either positive or negative, denoting a spread or a choke). Personally, I don't find much use for the two Auto Amount settings.

The last item, Custom, is where the power is. QuarkXPress gives you a field in which to type any trap value you want (from -36 to 36 points, though you probably will never use more than 1 or 2 points).

Note that text can be trapped a character at a time (see Figure 12-22), and that one black object can be overprinted where another black object knocks out (this kills the need for my "Knockout Black" tip, above).

Trapping to Multiple Colors

I said earlier that when QuarkXPress sees one colored object only partially covering another colored object, the program thinks of this as Indeterminate trapping. I then went further and said that when Ignore White is turned on in Trapping Preferences, the program ignores the white background entirely, making it *not* Indeterminate. Now I have the final word on the subject.

If the foreground object partially overlaps two colored objects, QuarkXPress still doesn't always think of this as Indeterminate. First it looks at the trapping relationships among all the colors. If the foreground

Figure 12-22
Trapping type
character
by character

color chokes to both background colors, then the foreground object gets choked. If the Edit Trap specifications are set to spread to both background colors, then QuarkXPress spreads the trap. If it's supposed to spread to one and choke to the other, *then* the program defaults to the Indeterminate trap.

Also, just for the sake of completeness, if you set the Edit Trap specifications so that the foreground color spreads one value (let's say 1 point) to one background color, and a different value (let's say 2 points) to the other background color, QuarkXPress uses the lesser of the values (in this case, 1 point).

None of this may apply to you, but it's still good information to tuck into the back of your brain . . . just in case.

▼ ▼

Tip: Use Big Traps. An easy way to make sure your traps are working correctly is to temporarily set extremely large values for your color and object traps: anywhere from 1 to 6 points. Print your separations on transparencies or thin paper, align each plate, and you can quickly determine how well XPress is handling your trapping requests. Don't forget to reset the traps to their normal values before your final imagesetting, though! (When I do this, I save the document, then change the traps, print separations, and then use Revert to Saved to get back to the original settings.)

Another good way to check trapping is to use the enlargement feature in the Print dialog box to magnify the trap area (see "Tip: Printer as a Magnifying Glass" in Chapter 13, *Printing*).

▼ ▼

Color from Outside Sources

Up until now in this chapter I have concentrated my discussion on color items—text, boxes, rules, and so on—which are built entirely in QuarkXPress. But what about bringing color graphics in from other programs? And although I discussed modifying color bitmapped images in Chapter 10, *Fine-Tuning Images,* what about being prepared for creating color separations? I'll address these points now.

One area you won't read about here is working with object-oriented color PICT images, because I think they're kludgey (that's pronounced "cloodgy"), and so unreliable that I wouldn't use them for my own QuarkXPress documents (see Chapter 9, *Pictures,* for a slightly longer discussion of this format). The only formats that I find really reliable for prepress work are TIFF and EPS (and DCS, which is an offshoot of EPS).

Object-Oriented EPS Files

I've avoided the subject of object-oriented graphic files for several chapters, but now it's time to dive back in. Designers frequently generate color artwork using programs such as Adobe Illustrator or Macromedia FreeHand, saving them as Encapsulated PostScript (EPS) files. QuarkXPress can not only import files from these programs, but can also generate color separations of these files.

Once again, the details of generating color separations (or "seps," as they're often called) is covered in Chapter 13, *Printing,* and Appendix A, *Color Management.* But while I'm talking about color on the desktop, I need to cover some general information about using these programs with QuarkXPress. I'll tackle this discussion one color method at a time: process first, and then spot (I include Pantone colors in the spot-color discussion, though you can create process simulations of Pantone inks).

Process color. QuarkXPress can create color separations of illustrations built in FreeHand or Illustrator which contain process colors. Period. All you have to do is specify your process colors in either application, save them as EPS, and import them into your QuarkXPress document using Get Picture. Nice and easy. As I noted earlier in this chapter, if the colors are named (process colors in Illustrator or spot colors in FreeHand), the colors are added to the QuarkXPress document color list.

Note that I say you must use Get Picture. If you use Copy and Paste to paste a graphic into a picture box, QuarkXPress won't separate it. In fact, while I'm on the subject, I should note that QuarkXPress may not be able to separate color EPS files from applications other than Illustrator or FreeHand. It depends entirely on whether those applications create EPS files according to Adobe's document-structuring specifications.

Spot color. The key to working with spot colors brought in from either FreeHand or Illustrator is being careful with your naming. In order for QuarkXPress to separate the spot colors properly, you have to have a color in your QuarkXPress document named *exactly* the same as the color in the illustration. Fortunately, XPress automatically adds named colors from illustrations to your color list when you import the picture.

If you don't have a same-named color in QuarkXPress (perhaps you deleted it accidentally), the spot color separates into a process color in XPress. Remember that with spot colors, the colors' actual specifications make no difference except for screen display and color-printer output.

The same goes for the Pantone colors. If you use a Pantone color in your Illustrator file, just make sure it has the same name in your QuarkXPress file, and it'll print fine (although it'll probably look wrong on screen). Fortunately, Illustrator, FreeHand, and QuarkXPress name their Pantone colors the same, so if you're using the color libraries included in each program, the names will probably match.

What You Can and Cannot Change

QuarkXPress prints exactly what is specified in every EPS file. In fact, QuarkXPress has no way to change them: encapsulated PostScript files are totally self-contained and cannot easily be modified from outside sources. All the halftoning information for objects and bitmapped images (if it's included in the EPS), all the trapping and tinting information, and all the color specifications are set in hard-packed mud (I like to think that you at least have a chance with hard-packed mud; "stone" is a bit too final).

All this means that you must take a little more control into your own hands. You must specify your own trapping from within FreeHand or Illustrator, and make sure that these EPS images contain traps for their surroundings in QuarkXPress documents.

Luckily, all overprinting specified in Illustrator or FreeHand (or any other program that handles its color PostScript properly) is handled correctly when you generate color separations from QuarkXPress. An object that's set to overprint in a FreeHand EPS file not only overprints objects within that EPS, but also QuarkXPress objects. Conversely, if an object is not set to Overprint, it knocks out any background colors or objects within QuarkXPress.

You cannot adjust any trapping for EPS files from within QuarkXPress. For example, if your EPS picture contains a spot color (let's say PMS 345), and you have set up the equivalent spot color in QuarkXPress as described above, any trapping or overprinting assignments you make to PMS 345 in the Trap Specifications dialog box do not (and actually cannot) make any difference to the EPS file. They do, however, make all the difference to any objects created within QuarkXPress that are colored PMS 345.

The same is true with Quark's Color Management System: it has absolutely no effect on the colors in your EPS graphics (see Appendix A, *Color Management*).

Bitmapped Images

Let's cut to the chase: process colors are CMYK (cyan, magenta, yellow, and black). A picture saved in any other color model (most TIFF images are, especially scans) has to be translated into CMYK mode before it can be imageset. QuarkXPress 4 can create separations of these RGB images by itself, but it won't necessarily do a good job of it.

(Note that at the time of this writing, QuarkXPress 4 always separates RGB TIFF images into CMYK, even when printing to a composite color printer. One upshot of this is that color images printed to color printers often look washed out because XPress doesn't know how to separate the colors as well as the printer can by itself. I'm hoping that by the time you read this, there will be some way for you to turn this off. In the meantime, the only solution is to use the QuarkCMS to perform the separation.)

If you're working with scanned RGB images, you have two options for performing RGB-to-CMYK conversion.

▶ Preseparate the image using Photoshop or the like, and import it into QuarkXPress as a CMYK TIFF, EPS, or DCS file.

▶ Place the image as an RGB TIFF in QuarkXPress, and let Quark CMS XTension do the process-separation work (see Appendix A, *Color Management)*.

Although I'll really be talking about color separation in detail in Chapter 13, *Printing,* and Appendix A, *Color Management,* let's explore these three methods briefly here.

Preseparating. Adobe Photoshop allows you to translate RGB images into CMYK using the Mode submenu, under the Item menu. This is a simple process, but to get good-quality CMYK images, you need to spend some time learning about and tweaking the various color-separation preference dialog boxes (they changed radically between Photoshop version 4 and 5).

Because the RGB-to-CMYK translation is so difficult, people have developed their own religious preference about what program does it best. I do most of my work in Photoshop, though some people will tell you that Photoshop's separation (translation) technique isn't as good as those techniques in other programs. You can also get very good quality separations in Photoshop by using the ColorSync plug-ins, which rely on Apple's ColorSync to do the translation.

Once you've separated a file in one of these programs, you can save it in one of three formats—EPS, DCS, or TIFF—and import it into QuarkXPress, fully separated and ready for output. I discussed these formats in detail in Chapter 9, *Pictures*.

Saving as CMYK EPS. Note that you don't have to save EPS files in DCS format in order for your images to separate from XPress. However, there are differences in the way the two formats function.

- ▶ The biggest drawback to CMYK EPS files is that they consist of one gigantic file. DCS 1.0 files have the added benefit of letting you work with a small master file while the large CMYK files can be sitting someplace else. (On the other hand, this means you have to keep track of five files rather than just one.)

- ▶ DCS images also print proofs faster because QuarkXPress just uses the low-resolution image when printing to a color printer.

- ▶ DCS files print faster from XPress than do EPS or TIFF files. It used to be the case that EPS files were much slower than DCS, because XPress had to send the entire EPS file to the printer for each plate (imagine a 40 MB file getting sent four times, once each for cyan, magenta, yellow, and black). Now XPress is smart enough to recognize Photoshop EPS files, and it knows how to pull these apart so that it only sends the cyan information for the cyan plate, and so on (this is only true with Photoshop EPS files). The result is that DCS is still faster, but not much faster.

Of course, I've already said that color separation is not as easy as clicking a button. If you're looking for quality color, you had better know Photoshop well enough to work with its undercolor-removal and color-correction settings. Remember: QuarkXPress cannot apply any image modification to the EPS files that you import. All that must be done before you import the picture.

Saving as CMYK TIFF. Once you've switched to CMYK mode in Photoshop, you can also save files as CMYK TIFF images. I find CMYK TIFFs to be a bit easier than DCS files for several reasons. First, you only have one file to work with. Second, QuarkXPress can do more with TIFF files than it can with EPS or DCS images. For example, QuarkXPress can downsample the TIFF image at print time if necessary, which can save you time. Also, you can make tonal and screening adjustments to TIFF images from within the program. Finally, if you're working with an OPI system (see "OPI" in Chapter 13, *Printing*), you can use TIFF images as for-position-only (FPO) images and let another program strip them in at print time.

Separating with an XTension. If you want to postseparate your RGB images, you can import them directly into QuarkXPress and then separate them with the color management system, Quark CMS, that ships with the program. Color management is a way to map colors from one space to another (for instance, mapping RGB on a 17-inch Apple Trinitron monitor to CMYK on a Web press with 22-percent dot gain using SWOP inks), but it takes some work to produce quality images efficiently (see Appendix A, *Color Management*).

Which to Use. Do I suggest using preseparation (typically with Adobe Photoshop) or postseparation (with Quark CMS)? The most important consideration is your workflow. The biggest argument for preseparation is the translation time: preseparating your bitmapped images requires translating them from RGB to CMYK only once. Postseparating them with an XTension requires that same translation time whenever you print. This translation can be incredibly time-consuming. Given a choice, I'd rather just have to deal with it once.

However, which of these methods results in the superior separation? Here I get to the aesthetics of color separation, and I wouldn't want to sway your opinion (which is a nice way of saying that—just this once—I'm not going to preach my own opinions).

▼ ▼

Tip: Duotones from Photoshop. Many people create duotones (or tritones or quadtones) in Photoshop and then save them as EPS files (you have to save them as EPS files) before importing them into QuarkXPress. If the duotone uses spot (such as Pantone) colors, you have to make sure you've got the same-named color in your QuarkXPress document. People have had difficulty with this in the past because the two programs sometimes named their Pantone colors differently.

Fortunately, QuarkXPress now automatically imports the color names into your document, so you're sure to get a match. On the other hand, if you're already using Pantone Uncoated colors in your XPress document, you may need to rename the colors (in either Photoshop or QuarkXPress) so that they match.

Also note that if your duotones are set to a spot color and a process color (like black), you have to adjust the halftone screen for the spot color so that you don't end up with moiré patterns or dot-doubling (see "Halftone" in the "Specifying Colors" section, earlier in this chapter).

Deciding to Work in Color

I started this chapter with a comment from Russell Brown, so I think it's only fair to end with what he considers to be the most logical steps to successful color desktop publishing.

1. Complete a black-and-white project with text only.

2. Complete a black-and-white project with text and graphics.

3. Complete a project with several spot colors.

4. Complete a project with process-color tints.

5. Finally, attempt the use of color photography.

The computer, no matter how powerful a tool, is still no substitute for experience. Work slowly and carefully, and in time you will become a raging color pro.

13

PRINTING

O nce upon a time, probably somewhere at some university, someone had an idea and named it "the paperless office." People wouldn't be bothered anymore with having to store the thousands (or millions) of pieces of paper that come through their offices every year. Instead, the information would all be placed on some sort of storage medium, easily referenced by computer. It was a magic concept; everyone agreed that it would make life easier, more efficient, and certainly more fun.

Go ahead and ask people who have been involved with electronic publishing for a while if they have seen any sign of the paperless office. As an example, in my office, the ratio of expended paper to normal refuse is such that I empty my small garbage can every couple of weeks and the voluminous paper-recycling boxes weekly. When it comes right down to it, unless you use QuarkXPress exclusively for building Web pages or Acrobat PDF files, almost every document that you create is probably based, ultimately, on a printed page or an imaged piece of film (which will probably be used later to print on paper).

How can you extract the digitized information from disk to print on paper? Many people mistake the process as being as easy as simply choosing the Print command. In this chapter I'll discuss what's behind the act of printing, and go into some depth on how to get the most efficient and best-quality output you can for your document. I'll also touch on tips for working with service bureaus and printers—both the mechanical and the human varieties.

Before I get into anything too complex, though, let's deal with two simple yet critical issues in most people's print jobs: PostScript and fonts.

PostScript

To put it simply, PostScript is what makes desktop publishing with QuarkXPress possible. PostScript is a page-description language—a collection of commands that PostScript laser printers understand. When you tell QuarkXPress to print a page, it writes a computer program in PostScript describing the page, and sends that program to the printer. The printer (or imagesetter), which has a PostScript interpreter inside it, interprets the PostScript describing the page, and puts marks on the paper (or film) according to that description.

For instance, the PostScript command *lineto* tells the printer to draw a line from one point to another; *curveto* draws curves, and *setlinewidth* changes the thickness of the line the printer is about to image. You don't really need to know much about PostScript in order to get your job done, but it's important to know that it's there, working behind the scenes.

This chapter is dedicated, in part, to Chuck Geschke, John Warnock, and the other people who created PostScript. And I need to say one thing up front: I'm not talking PCL here. I'm not talking CORA or even SGML. Those languages were also designed for putting marks on paper or film. In this chapter, however, I'm going to assume you're working with a PostScript printer because that's what QuarkXPress assumes.

You can output to a non-PostScript printer, but as they say: "Your mileage may vary." A large percentage of printing problems that people encounter are related to using printers that don't understand PostScript. For instance, you can typically print on one of those inexpensive color ink-jet printers, but some page elements print better than others. EPS files, in particular, print horribly because the printer can't parse them, so it only prints the low-resolution screen previews you see in XPress.

(By the way, because Adobe makes the interpreter that lives inside most printers, people talk about "Adobe PostScript" as being the standard. Nonetheless, many other companies offer PostScript clones, which usually work just as well. Every now and again, people find that a page won't print on a clone interpreter but will print on a true Adobe PostScript interpreter. Because of this, my personal bias is toward using printers, whenever possible, that use Adobe PostScript.)

Fonts

Almost everyone uses QuarkXPress at some point to work with text. It's a given. When you work with text, you work with typefaces. I discussed choosing a particular font in Chapter 6, *Type and Typography*. Printing that font is covered here in this chapter.

If you don't fully understand how bitmap and outline fonts work, I recommend that you go back and look over the beginning of Chapter 6. These two different types of fonts require slightly different approaches to the printing process and result in drastically different printed pages.

Printer Fonts

In PostScript, fonts are defined and saved as mathematical outlines in files. If you're using Adobe Type Manager (you should be) or TrueType fonts (you probably shouldn't be), these outline fonts are used both on screen and in print. When you print your document, QuarkXPress (actually, your system's printer driver) includes the necessary font files along with the PostScript file that it sends to the printer. The PostScript printer usually keeps these fonts in memory until the document has finished printing.

However, printers vary in their available memory, and thus in the number of fonts they can hold. For example, the original LaserWriter could keep only three or four fonts in memory at a time, while a newer Apple LaserWriter can keep over 15 fonts in memory. Exceeding the amount of available memory causes a PostScript error (which shows up as "VMerror" in the Print Status dialog box), flushing your job and restarting the printer. (See the "Troubleshooting" section, later in this chapter.)

Printing Ugly

It's possible to use a font in QuarkXPress which isn't accompanied by an outline file. For instance, you can use a bitmap font suitable for screen viewing only (it's usually pretty jaggy). Or you might import an EPS file that includes a font not loaded on your system. When you print your document, XPress assumes the outline font is already resident in the printer. When you have neither a printer font on your system nor a printer-resident font available, QuarkXPress has two options.

▶   To print using Courier. This happens when your document contains an EPS file with fonts that you don't have available.

▶   To print the text using a scaled version of the bitmapped screen font closest in point size to the font you have in your document. QuarkXPress prints the text almost exactly as it appears on screen.

I'm not sure which of these options is uglier. I tend to break into hives at the sight of either. However, Oscar Wilde said it best: "For those who like that kind of thing, that is the kind of thing they like."

More Font Downloading

Ordinarily, when your printing job is done, the fonts that you used are flushed out of the printer's memory. Then, next time you print the document, QuarkXPress has to download the fonts all over again. Downloading one time may not seem like a long process, but having to download the fonts repeatedly starts to make chess look like a fast sport.

But you don't have to wait. You can do something about your predicament. You can download the fonts yourself.

Resident fonts. All PostScript printers come with Times, Helvetica, Courier, and Symbol encoded directly into the printer's memory. That means you don't need an outline font to use these typefaces and you never need to download the fonts yourself. Most printers also come with several other fonts—perhaps Palatino, Bookman, Zapf Chancery, and so on. The page that prints out when you start up your printer usually can tell you which fonts are resident. If the startup page is turned off, you can use Adobe's Font Downloader utility, or Apple's LaserWriter Utility to retrieve a font list. (In Windows, you usually need a special utility from the printer manufacturer.)

Manual downloading. You can download a typeface to your printer's RAM (which works just like a computer's RAM) and keep it there until you turn off the printer. Several utilities let you do this on the Macintosh, including Adobe's Font Downloader or Apple's LaserWriter Utility. Unfortunately, there are few (if any) utilities that let you do this in Windows. Typically, these sorts of utilities call this "permanent" downloading, even though you can only "permanently" download to a hard drive, as described below. When you download to a printer's memory, the fonts disappear when the printer is turned off or gets reset.

Downloading a font manually is particularly helpful for typefaces that you use many times throughout the day. If Goudy is your corporate typeface, you can manually download it from one computer at the start of each day. And as long as no one resets the printer, you can use it to your heart's content from any of the computers hooked up to the network (whether or not they have Goudy's printer font on their hard disks).

Hard-disk storage. If you have a hard disk connected to your printer, you can download a printer font to the printer's hard disk where it resides until you delete it (or drop the hard drive on the ground). Some downloading utilities, such as Font Downloader and LaserWriter Utility, have the extra features necessary for this task. If you have some odd sort of printer, you may have to get special software from the manufacturer. Note that any normal SCSI hard drive works fine for this. It doesn't even have to be formatted as a Mac or Windows drive; you format the drive with the printer software. So if you have an extra 20- or 40-megabyte hard drive sitting around, you could hook it up to the SCSI port on your printer (assuming that the printer has a SCSI port, of course).

▼ ▼

Tip: Tell ATM Not to Send Fonts. The Macintosh print driver can query your printer to find out what fonts are resident on it. Windows, on the other hand, can't do this. You can, however, tell Adobe Type Manager Deluxe not to download your fonts (select a font on the Font List tab, and choose Properties from the File menu).

▼ ▼

Deciphering the Print Dialog Box

We all demanded more features in QuarkXPress, and Quark gave them to us. Unfortunately, sometimes having more features means more complexity. The Print dialog box is a perfect example of this. The folks at Quark have tried their hardest to squeeze over 40 features into this one dialog box in a way that is still reasonably usable, and they've mostly succeeded. However, the result is something that appears, at first, to be like one of those 1950s computer consoles with hundreds of dials and knobs and flashing lights (see Figure 13-1). Don't worry, it's much easier than it looks.

Figure 13-1

The Print dialog box on the Macintosh

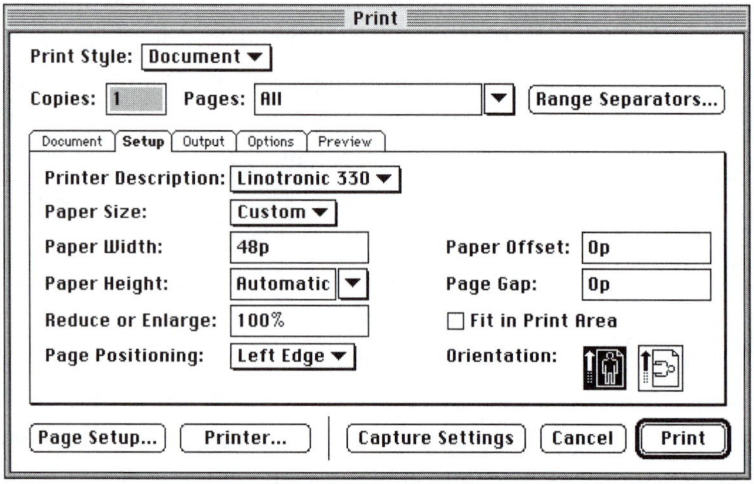

If you're familiar with earlier versions of XPress, you'll soon figure out that the folks at Quark folded the Page Setup dialog box into the Print dialog box, stuck in several features from the now-defunct QuarkPrint XTension, and topped it off with a few great new features. Note that you can make changes to the various tabs in the Print dialog box in any order you like. In general, however, I make choices in this dialog box in the order that I discuss them in this chapter.

Choosing a Printer: Macintosh versus Windows

My discussion of the Print dialog box is made slightly more complicated by the fact that Macintosh and Windows operating systems handle printing slightly differently. The key distinction is in how you specify which printer (the electronic kind, not the lithographer type) you want to use. No matter which computer you use, it's imperative that you choose a printer before you take any further steps toward printing.

Macintosh. On the Macintosh, you can specify which kind of printer you want to use—as well as which particular printer, if you have more than one on a network—by selecting Chooser from the Apple menu (see Figure 13-2). The icons on the left are the types of printer drivers you have installed in the Extensions folder of your System Folder (printer drivers tell your computer how to drive your printer). When you click on one, the computer asks you for more pertinent information in the rectangle on the right.

Figure 13-2
The Chooser

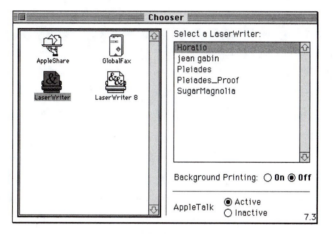

For example, if you click on the LaserWriter icon, you'll get a list of all the available LaserWriters (even if only one printer is attached, you still need to select it by clicking on it before closing the Chooser). If you have a large network which is split up into zones, you may need to select a zone—which shows up in the lower left of the window—before selecting a printer in it. The changes take effect as soon as you click on the printer's name.

If you are working with just a single PostScript laser printer, you hardly need to worry about the Chooser. Just set it once and forget it, except when you want to switch between PostScript printers on the network.

Every time you make a different printer-driver selection in the Chooser, you receive a dialog box noting that you should be sure to check your Page Setup dialog box (see "Page Setup, Printer, and Properties," below). There are several reasons for this, the most important of which is that when you switch printer types, QuarkXPress needs to register that you've done this. It can then calculate the image area and other important controls. Otherwise, QuarkXPress sends a set of instructions to the printer which may be totally incorrect.

Windows. In Windows, you must choose a printer from the Print dialog box (see Figure 13-3). The only printers that appear listed here are those that you have already set up in Windows. (You can add a new printer by choosing Printers from the Settings popout menu, under the Start menu, then double-clicking on the Add Printer utility. I'll step you through one example of this process later in this chapter when I discuss how to print PostScript files to disk.)

Figure 13-3
Choosing a printer in
Windows

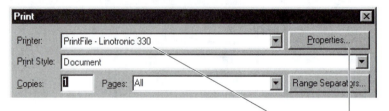

Choose the device you want to print to from this popup menu.
You can change various printer-level settings by clicking Properties.

Once you've chosen a device, it behooves you to click the Properties button to ensure that the printer settings conform to your wishes. The Properties dialog box controls the way the printer driver works. Note that there are several features that appear both in the Properties dialog box and QuarkXPress's Print dialog box; in these cases, ignore the settings in the Properties dialog box and use XPress's instead. (I discuss these settings in more depth in "Page Setup, Printer, and Properties," later in this chapter.)

The Pages You Want

There are four other settings in the Print dialog box that stick around no matter what tab you choose: Print Style, Copies, Pages, and Range Separators. I'm going to hold off on the Print Style popup menu until later in this chapter—for now, suffice it to say that it's a way to save various Print dialog box settings so you can choose them quickly later. Here's the run-down on the other three controls.

Copies. I might as well start with the simplest choice of all. How many copies of your document do you want printed? Let's say you choose to print a multiple-page document, specifying four copies. The first page prints four times, then the second page prints four times, and so on. In other words, you may have a good deal of collating to do later (see "Collate" in "The Document Tab," below).

Pages. You can tell XPress to print all the pages in your document, or just a selection of pages. In the past, you had to have an XTension to print discontiguous pages in your document. Now in version 4, it's easy: just type commas or hyphens between the page numbers. For instance, typing 1, 4-6, 9 prints the first page, the fourth through sixth pages, and the ninth page.

The values you type in the Pages field must either be exactly the same as those in your document or must be specified as absolutes. If your document starts on page 23, you can't type "1" in the From field; it must be either "23" (or whatever page you want to start from) or "+1" (the plus character specifies an absolute page number—in other words, "the first page"). Similarly, if you are using page numbering in an alphabetical system (such as "a," "b," "c," etc.), or using a prefix (see "Sections and Page Numbering" in Chapter 4, *Building a Document*), you have to type these sorts of numbers into the slots. It's annoying, but if you don't type the page number exactly the way it's used in the program (or use absolute numbers), the program tells you that "no such page exists."

Range Separators. There's one more potential problem with typing page numbers into the Pages field: if you use prefixes such as "A-" or "1," then your page numbers appear as A-1, A-2, A-3, and so on. This means you can't type a range of page numbers. (If you type A-1-A-6, XPress will just get confused.) Fortunately, you can change the separation characters that XPress pays attention to by clicking the Range Separators button (see Figure 13-4). You can change the hyphen and the comma characters to just about any other symbol you want, except letters and numbers.

▼ ▼

Tip: From Beginning or End. You can print all the pages in a document by typing "All" into the Pages field (or choosing it from the popup menu

Figure 13-4

Range Separators

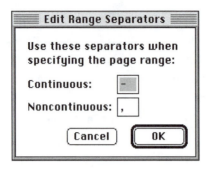

to the right of the field). On the other hand, if you only want to print the first four pages, you can type the cryptic "+1-+4" (remember that the plus sign means "absolute page number," no matter what page-numbering scheme you're using). To print from page 15 to the end of the document, type "15-end".

▼ ▼

Tip: Capture Settings. It seems to happen to me at least once a day: I go to the Print dialog box, I spend time setting up the options in the various tabs, and then I remember a change I forgot to make on the document pages. In this situation in the past, you'd have to press Cancel and lose all the work you did in the Print dialog box. Fortunately, now you can click the Capture Settings button. This closes the dialog box but remembers the values and options you have chosen.

Unfortunately, this feature doesn't remember all the settings. For instance, it won't remember values you type in Page Range or Copies, and it won't remember which color plates you *don't* want to print (see "The Output Tab," later in this chapter).

Print Status

As soon as you click Print, XPress displays the the Print Status dialog box, which not only tells you what page it's printing, but also what color plate, tile, and EPS/TIFF images it's working on (see Figure 13-5). Remember that no program can know how long a page will take to print on a PostScript printer, so there's no way to show how much longer the print job will take. Instead, the status bar in the Print Status dialog box only displays the percentage of pages that have been printed (for example, if you have two pages in your document, the status bar is 50-percent full after the first page, even if the second page takes 10 times longer than the first one to print). Nonetheless, this is a nice intermediate step, and often makes me feel better when I'm waiting for those long jobs to print.

Figure 13-5

Print Status dialog box

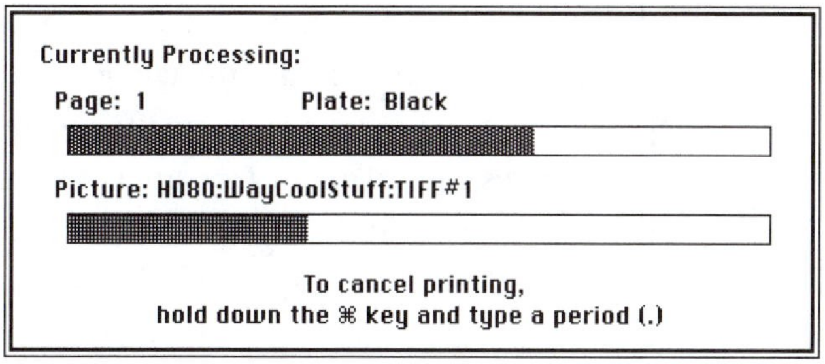

```
Currently Processing:

   Page: 1                 Plate:  Black

   ▓▓▓▓▓▓▓▓▓▓▓▓▓▓▓▓▓▓▓▓▓▓▓░░░░░░░

   Picture: HD80:WayCoolStuff:TIFF#1

   ▓▓▓▓▓▓▓▓▓░░░░░░░░░░░░░░░░░░░░░

                 To cancel printing,
        hold down the ⌘ key and type a period (.)
```

▼ ▼

The Document Tab

The Document tab of the Print dialog box provides overall controls for how your document appears on printed pages. As you've heard me say many times before, looking at the whole shebang is too overwhelming, so it's best to take the various checkboxes and popup menus one at a time (see Figure 13-6).

Figure 13-6

The Document Tab

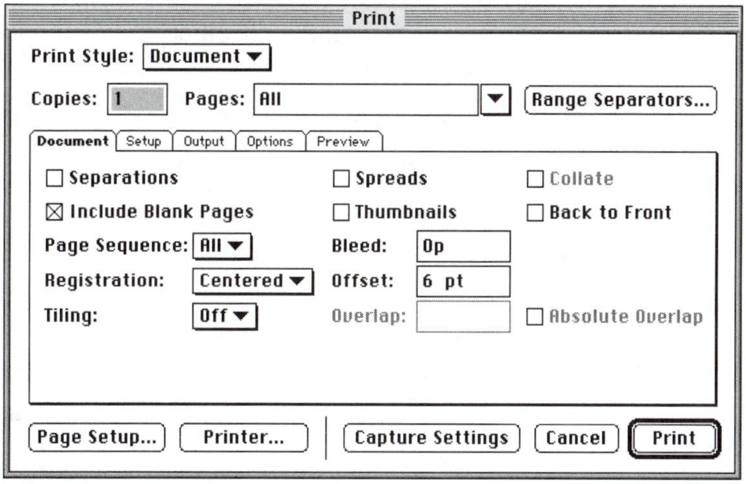

```
                                        Print
   Print Style:  Document ▼

   Copies:  1      Pages:  All              ▼   Range Separators...

   Document  Setup   Output   Options   Preview

     ☐ Separations          ☐ Spreads        ☐ Collate
     ☒ Include Blank Pages  ☐ Thumbnails     ☐ Back to Front
     Page Sequence: All ▼    Bleed:   0p
     Registration: Centered ▼ Offset:  6 pt
     Tiling:       Off ▼      Overlap:         ☐ Absolute Overlap

   Page Setup...    Printer...    Capture Settings   Cancel    Print
```

Separations. I'm going to discuss separating color documents into single, black-and-white plates in "Color Separations," later in this chapter. For now, let's just say that if you want your color documents to separate, turn on the Separations checkbox. Of course, unless you've applied color to elements in your document, this option has no effect.

Include Blank Pages. As I write, my white-paper recycling bin overfloweth. I go through so much paper that I feel guilty every time I drive through a forest (which is difficult to avoid in the Pacific Northwest). Therefore, whenever I have the chance to save a tree here and there, I jump at it. QuarkXPress is giving me just this chance with the Include Blank Pages control on the Document tab of the Print dialog box. When you turn on Include Blank Pages (it's on by default), QuarkXPress prints as it always has: every page, no matter what is (or isn't) on it. When you turn off Include Blank Pages, QuarkXPress won't print a page if there isn't anything printable on it. This includes pages whose only objects are colored white, or are set to Suppress Printout. I've gotten in the habit of always turning this off when I print.

Spreads. This is a powerful but potentially dangerous feature, so it should be used with some care. Checking Spreads in the Print dialog box tells QuarkXPress to print spreads as one full page rather than as two or three pages. For example, printing a two-page, facing-pages spread with registration marks normally results in one page printing with its set of crop marks, then the next page, and so on. When Spreads is turned on, both pages abut each other and sit between the same crop marks (see Figure 13-7).

I think there are two good uses for the Spreads feature.

▶ If you're building a folding brochure (like a tri-fold) and you lay out each panel on a separate page, you need to turn on the Spreads option in order for the panels to print out next to each other. (Note that the primary problem with doing this is that the third panel in a tri-fold brochure typically needs to be slightly more narrow so that it folds inside the other panels—and XPress won't let you have different-sized pages within a document.)

▶ Turning on the Spreads feature is a good way to proof a document on a desktop printer so you can see what two pages will look like next to each other in the final bound document.

The Spreads feature is not an imposition feature. That is, it won't create printer spreads, which are required when the document will be bound (however, see the next tip).

▼ ▼

Tip: Roll Your Own Printer Spreads. While there are some great high-end page imposition tools out there—including Luminous PressWise and the InPosition XTension—sometimes you just want to do a quick lit-

Figure 13-7

Printing spreads
versus printing
individual pages

*Two pages printed as a spread; this only works for center spreads, or
when you've set up panels of a brochure or poster as individual pages.*

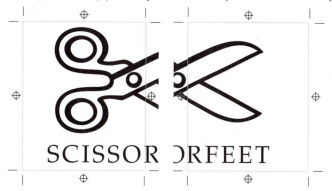

*A reader spread printed as two pages. This is what your printer generally
wants. Note the bleed for images that cross the page break.*

tle booklet at just as little cost. You can use the Spreads feature in conjunction with the Document Layout palette to "strip" together pages
which will be double-sided and saddle-stitched. Just follow these steps.

1. Create your document as usual, but don't use facing pages or
   automatic page numbers (see Chapter 4, *Building a Document*).
   Make sure you have an even number of pages.

2. When you're finished, use the Document Layout palette to move
   the last page to the *left* of the first page. Then move the second-to-
   last page (which has now become the last page) up to the *right* of
   the second page (which is now the third page). Then, move the
   next last page to the *left* of the next single page, and so on.

3. When you're done, every page should be paired with another
   page, and the last pages in the document should be the middle

pages. For example, in an 8-page booklet, the final pages would end up being the spread between pages 4 and 5.

4. Make sure the Spreads feature is selected in the Print dialog box when you print the document page.

Ultimately, if you're going to be doing basic imposition like this more than once a year, I'd suggest using an XTension or a utility (Imposer, from a lowly apprentice production, is one such low-cost XTension).

▼ ▼

Tip: Printing Spreads in a Document. Don't waste paper or film when you print contiguous spreads from a single document; if for no other reason, it's expensive. If you have a multiple-page spread crossing pages 45 through 47, have your service bureau print the pages from 1 through 44 and 48 through the end as single pages, and then print the three-page spread on a separate pass.

▼ ▼

Thumbnails. Selecting Thumbnails shrinks each page of your document down to about 12 percent of its size and lines up each page next to the other. It then fits as many as it can onto each printed page. This is great for an overview of your file, though the output you get is usually too small to really give you much of an idea of anything except general page geometry (see "Tip: Faster, Larger Thumbnails," below). Note that on PostScript printers, it takes just as long to print this one sheet of many pages as it does to print every page individually, so plan your time accordingly. If you just want to look over the pages, it would probably be faster to see them on screen in Thumbnails view. Remember that you don't have to print all your pages when you select Thumbnails. I often find it helpful to just print one or two pages at a time to see how they're looking.

▼ ▼

Tip: Faster, Larger Thumbnails. I find the size that Thumbnails usually gives me pretty useless; it's just too small! And if I have pictures on the pages, the job takes too long to print. So I use this feature in conjunction with two others: Rough, and Reduce or Enlarge. Rough is nearby on the Output popup menu, on the Options tab. Just make sure this is selected, and your thumbnails print with "X"s through the pictures and with simplified frames. You can find the Reduce or Enlarge feature on the Setup tab (see "The Output Tab" and "The Page Setup Tab," later in this chapter). Change Reduce or Enlarge to 200 percent, and your thumbnails are printed at 24 percent instead of a little over 12 percent. This is just about the right size for most letter-size pages.

▼ ▼

Tip: Two Thumbnails per Page. If you want your thumbnails much larger, you can up the scaling factor to 375 percent and turn the page to Landscape orientation on the Setup tab of the Print dialog box. With this value, you can get two letter- or legal-size pages on one page. You can get two tabloid-size pages on one letter-size landscape page with an enlargement of 300 percent. If your document is made of two-page spreads, then you can print letter- and legal-size pages up to 400 percent (the maximum allowed for enlargement), and tabloid-size pages up to 350 percent.

Note that both the Macintosh and Windows printer drivers offer the ability to print more than one document page per printed page. However, XPress seems to conflict with the drivers on both platforms, causing either strange printing or PostScript errors most of the time. It's too bad, but I just stick with XPress's own Thumbnails feature.

▼ ▼

Collate. I said earlier that when you printed multiple copies of your document you would receive x copies of the first page, then x copies of the second page, and so on, leaving you to manually collate all the copies. You can have QuarkXPress collate the pages for you instead, so that the full document prints out once, then again, and again, and so on.

The problem with Collate is that it takes much longer to print your complete job. This is because the printer cannot "remember" what each page looks like after it goes on to the next page, and so it has to reprocess the entire document for each new set of copies. How long this takes depends on the number of fonts and pictures you use, among other things. On a long document, the time difference becomes a toss-up: do you take the time to collate the pages yourself, or have the printer take the time to process them?

Back to Front. The problem with talking about printing from QuarkXPress is that each PostScript printer model is slightly (or not-so-slightly) different from the next. For example, when you print a multiple-page document on your laser printer, does the first page come out face up or face down? Some printers do one, some the other, and some give you a choice. If the pages come out face up, you'll love the Back to Front feature. Selecting Back to Front prints the last page of your page selection first, then prints "backwards" to the first page. The stack of pages that ends up in the output tray will be in proper order.

Note that you can't select this feature when you are printing spreads or thumbnails (if you want a good brain twister, try to think of how pages would print if you could select these together).

Bleed. The Bleed control is a good example of how a little feature can sneak into a product (it's new in version 4) and cause havoc when people don't take the time to understand it. I know people who just ignored the Bleed control and lost a *lot* of money throwing away their film output. Fortunately, the control isn't difficult to understand; you just need to remember to use it.

The term "bleed" refers to an object that prints all the way to the edge of your page. In prepress, it's very important for bleeding objects to print past the page boundaries by at least ⅛ inch (often more like ¼ inch; check with your printer) because paper trimmers aren't perfect. If the object only extends to the edge of the page boundary and the paper cutter slips by a few points, the object won't sit at the edge of the paper anymore (ugly). Extending the object past the boundary is kind of like setting a trapping value for the bleed (see "Trapping" in Chapter 12, *Color*).

In previous versions of XPress, to make something bleed off a page, you simply placed it so that it was partially on the Pasteboard. As long as it touched the page, the object would print (see Figure 13-8). I'm not sure why they changed this, but in version 4, XPress crops out everything beyond 1 point past the edge of the page. In other words, you can extend a picture box ½ inch past the page boundary, but when you print the page, the bleed only extends by about a point.

The Bleed control on the Document tab lets you extend this puny 1-point bleed to whatever you want. I've gotten into the habit of setting this to at least "1p6" even when I'm not bleeding objects. Later in the chapter when I discuss print styles, you'll see how to set this as your default value.

Actually, there's one other aspect of the Bleed feature you should know about. When you set the Bleed value, any object on the Pasteboard

Figure 13-8
Bleeding objects

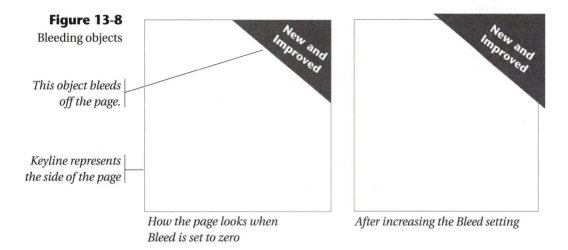

This object bleeds
off the page.

Keyline represents
the side of the page

How the page looks when   *After increasing the Bleed setting*
Bleed is set to zero

that falls within that distance of the page gets printed, whether it's touching the page or not. This is especially useful if you want to create your own registration marks or job information slugs (see "Color Separations," later in this chapter).

(Note that in version 4.0 and 4.01, increasing the Bleed setting also moved the trim marks farther away from the page. People yelled so loudly that Quark released an XTension called Bleed Redefine XT that stopped this errant behavior. Then in the free upgrade to version 4.02, they built this XTension into the product, so you don't need the XTension anymore.)

Page sequence. The first popup menu on the Document tab is Page Sequence, which gives you slightly more control over which pages in your document get printed. You have three choices: All, Odd, or Even.

▶ **All.** This is the default position for printing pages from QuarkXPress. It means "all pages that you have selected above." In other words, if you have selected a page range from 23 to 28, having All Pages selected won't counteract your desires; it'll just print all those pages.

▶ **Odd/Even.** These two choices are mutually exclusive. I sometimes joke about this feature when I'm working on jobs with several strangely designed pages: "Just print the odd ones, and leave the rest." The only real value I've ever gotten out of this feature lies in the following tip, "Printing Double-Sided Documents."

▼ ▼

Tip: Printing Double-Sided Documents. You can print double-sided pages with the following technique.

1. Print all the odd-numbered pages (select Odd).

2. Place these pages back into the printer, face down (or face up, depending on how your printer feeds the paper).

3. Select Back to Front.

4. Print all the even pages (select Even).

If everything is set up right, and if your document has an even number of pages, the second page should print on the back of the first, and so on.

You can use this same technique to print documents when photo-copying onto two sides of a page (if your photocopier handles automatic two-sided copying, ignore this). Print the odd-numbered pages first, then the even-numbered pages, then ask your local Kinko's person what to do next.

▼ ▼

Registration and Trim Marks. In addition to the text and graphics of the pages themselves, your printer (I'm talking about the human lithographer here) needs several pieces of information about your camera-ready work. One fact is where the sides of the printed page are. If you're printing multiple colors, another piece of information your printer needs is how each color plate aligns with the others. Additional job and page information may be helpful also. Selecting the Registration Marks feature answers all of these needs—QuarkXPress places *crop marks* (or *trim marks*), *registration marks*, and page information around your document (see Figure 13-9).

▶ **CROP MARKS.** Crop marks specify the page boundaries of your document. They are placed slightly outside each of the four corners so that when the page is printed and cut to size, they will be cut away. These are also called "trim marks" or "cut marks."

▶ **REGISTRATION MARKS.** Registration marks are used primarily for color-separation work, but you get them even if you just need crop marks on a one-color job. These are used by your printer's stripper to perfectly align each color plate to the next (see "Tip: Better Registration Marks," below).

Figure 13-9

The Registration Marks feature places items around your page

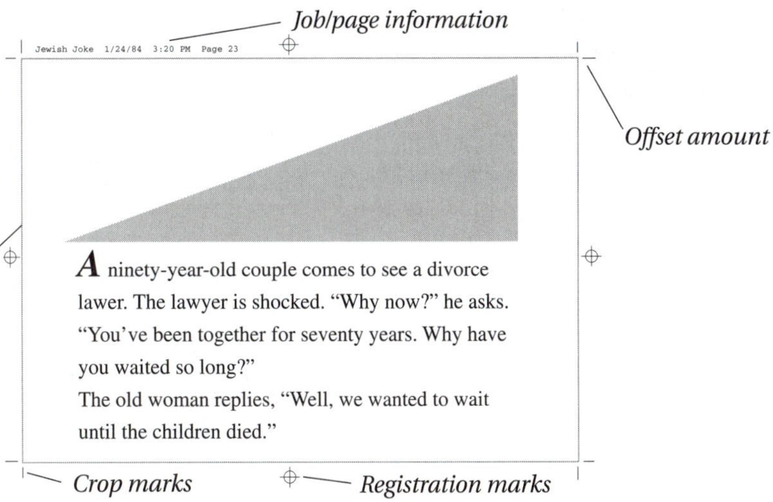

Job/page information

Offset amount

Gray line doesn't really print. It's just for your reference.

Jewish Joke 1/24/84 3:20 PM Page 23

A ninety-year-old couple comes to see a divorce lawer. The lawyer is shocked. "Why now?" he asks. "You've been together for seventy years. Why have you waited so long?"
The old woman replies, "Well, we wanted to wait until the children died."

Crop marks   Registration marks

▶ **PAGE AND JOB INFORMATION.** The page and job information that is printed in the upper-left corner of the page includes the file name, a page number, and a date and time stamp. If you want more job information than is listed here, see "Tip: Additional Job Information," below.

▶ **COLOR BARS AND STEP WEDGE.** When you print color separations (again, more on that in "Color Separations," later in this chapter) along with registration marks, QuarkXPress also adds a color bar and a grayscale step wedge to your output. This lets your lithographer take densitometer readings from the film and final output, as well as ensure that colors are registering well.

To make QuarkXPress add all these marks to your printed page, you need to select either Centered or Off Center from the Registration pop-up menu in the Print dialog box. These features refer to the placement of registration marks. If you select Centered, each registration mark is placed exactly in the center of each side of the printed page. This is where most strippers need it. Others, because of their pin-register systems, need the registration marks slightly off center. Ask your printer.

▼ ▼

Tip: Better Registration Marks. The registration marks that QuarkXPress creates for you are okay, but not great, and certainly not optimal from a stripper's point of view. This is how you can make a better registration mark directly in QuarkXPress (you can also make one in FreeHand or Illustrator, and bring it in as an EPS; see Figure 13-10).

Figure 13-10

A more versatile registration mark

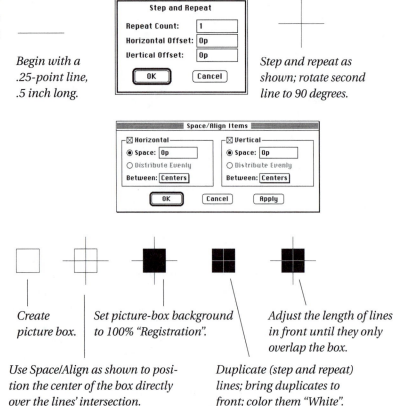

Begin with a .25-point line, .5 inch long.

Step and repeat as shown; rotate second line to 90 degrees.

Create picture box.

Set picture-box background to 100% "Registration".

Adjust the length of lines in front until they only overlap the box.

Use Space/Align as shown to position the center of the box directly over the lines' intersection.

Duplicate (step and repeat) lines; bring duplicates to front; color them "White".

1. Draw a line about ¼ inch long. Set its width to .25 points, with Midpoints selected on the Measurements palette.

2. Use the Step and Repeat feature from the Item menu to create one copy with no horizontal or vertical offset.

3. Make this second line perpendicular to the first by adding or subtracting 90 degrees from the line angle on the Measurements palette. Color the lines "Registration" (see Chapter 12, *Color*).

4. Draw a square picture box about ⅛ inch large (hold down the Shift key to maintain a square, or just type .125" in both the Height and Width fields of the Measurements palette) and center it over the lines. You could center it by either using the Space/Align feature (see Chapter 2, *QuarkXPress Basics*) or by just aligning the box's handles directly over the lines.

5. Set the box's background to 100-percent Registration.

6. Select the two lines, and step-and-repeat both of them once with no offsets. Bring these lines to the front, if they're not already there.

7. Color the second set of lines White, and shorten them so that they only overlap the box.

The great benefit of this registration mark is that when you print negatives, your printer can still align black crosshairs on a white background. (If you print film positives rather than negatives, QuarkXPress's marks are probably easier to work with.) After you create one of these, you can duplicate it as needed. Also, you can save it in a library or make an EPS out of it so that you can import it quickly onto other pages.

You can use your registration marks alongside the standard ones by putting them on the Pasteboard just outside the page boundary (though try a test print to make sure XPress isn't printing its marks on top of yours). Also remember to increase the Bleed value in the Print dialog box, or else they won't print.

Even better than going this route is using an XTension such as XPert ItemMarks (part of the XPert Tools Volume 2 bundle from a lowly apprentice production), which gives you even more control over registration marks and job information (but of course costs more, too).

▼ ▼

Tip: Additional Job Information. Custom registration marks aren't the only thing you can place in the margins, outside the trim marks. This is an ideal place for additional job information, such as your contact information or even your logo (if it's small enough). Be careful with anything that is larger than a thin line, however: objects that appear on every plate (anything colored Registration) cause 400-percent ink coverage, which can be problematic on press. Check with your printer if you're not sure about this. And, once again, remember to increase your Bleed value or else nothing on the Pasteboard will print.

▼ ▼

Offset. You just have to understand that sometimes the engineers at Quark don't know what's good for us unless we tell them. Case in point: someone there decided that they should remove the setting in QuarkXPress that lets you move the registration and trim marks farther away from the page. Instead, in QuarkXPress 4.0, the trim marks would only move when you increased the Bleed amount. Even stranger than this was that no one seemed to complain about it in the software's beta cycle. But when XPress 4 shipped, people went ballistic. Fortunately, 4.02 (and later) handle this properly by adding the Offset field to the Document tab of the Print dialog box.

The default value of 6 points seems a little tight to me. I don't operate a two-ton paper cutter at a bindery, but if I did, I'd sure wish people increased the space between page and trim marks (and registration marks) to at least 12, perhaps 18 points. It's just the courteous thing to do. Again, you can set this up as the default value by changing the print style (see "Print Styles," later in this chapter).

Tiling

What's a person to do with a 36-by-36-inch document? Printing to paper or film is . . . well, almost impossible without a large-format printer. You can break each page down into smaller chunks that will fit onto letter-size pages. Then you can assemble all the pages (keep your Scotch tape nearby). This process is called *tiling*, and is controlled on the Document tab of the Print dialog box. The three options for tiling are Off, Auto, and Manual.

Off. Off is off. No shirt, no shoes, no tiling. QuarkXPress just prints as much of the page as it can on the output page, starting from the upper-left corner.

Auto. Selecting the Auto tiling feature instructs QuarkXPress to decide how much of your document to fit onto each printed page. You do have some semblance of control here: you can decide how much overlap between pages you would like. Remember that you have a minimum of ¼-inch border around each page (at least on most laser printers), so you'll probably want to set your overlap to at least ½ inch to get a good fit. I generally use a value of 4 picas, just to be safe.

Note that QuarkXPress does not make an intelligent decision as to whether it would be more efficient to print the pages in Landscape or Portrait orientation, so you'll want to be careful to set this appropriately on the Setup tab of the Print dialog box.

Note that the Overlap amount might vary slightly when the Absolute Overlap checkbox is off (it's off by default). This is because XPress tries to center the tiled document on the printed pages (see Figure 13-11). When you turn on Absolute Overlap, XPress just gives up and places the upper-left corner of the document in the upper-left corner of the first page.

▼ ▼

Tip: Editing Your PPDs. One of the best things about PPDs is that they're editable. In fact, they're just text files that you can edit with any word processor. Because XPress gathers so much information about your printer from the PPD, customizing it is sort of like setting print preferences in QuarkXPress. For instance, you can change the name of your printer (how it appears on the Printer Description popup menu), the default halftone settings, or even the printer's default paper size. Be careful when messing with PPDs, however; little errors can cause jobs not to print. Always work on a copy of the file, and—best advice yet—don't edit it unless you feel comfortable with this kind of thing.

▼ ▼

Paper Specifications

The next four settings—Paper Size, Reduce or Enlarge, Orientation, and Page Positioning—apply to every printer type (except the printer types with the word "Generic" in their names, since these are built into XPress and aren't based on PPD files).

Paper Size. PPDs contain information about the paper sizes that a printer can handle. For instance, a PPD can tell QuarkXPress that a particular printer can or cannot handle A4 pages. It's a good idea to match the Paper Size popup menu to the setting in the printer's driver (found by clicking Page Setup on the Macintosh, or Properties in Windows).

If the Paper Size popup menu is grayed out, then QuarkXPress knows that the printer either only prints on one size of paper or is a roll-fed device that can print any size you want. If it's not grayed out, the available choices are determined by information in the PPD or in the printer driver. Once again, you don't need to select a paper size that is consistent with your document's size (though the paper size must be larger than your page size, or else your page will be cropped down to the paper size). This only determines the image (printable) area.

Plus, note that selecting a page size does not determine where the automatic crop marks are placed (see "Registration and Trim Marks," earlier in this chapter).

Reduce or Enlarge. Changing the Reduce or Enlarge field value affects the scaling of the document when you print. You can enter any whole number (no decimal points) between 25 and 400 percent. This is especially nice when printing proofs of a larger-format document, or when trying to create enormous posters by tiling them (you could create a 4-by-4-foot poster in QuarkXPress and then enlarge it to 400 percent, so that when that last sheet printed out of your printer and you'd tiled all 439 sheets together, you'd have a 16-foot-square poster).

Note that changing the Reduce or Enlarge field here is exactly the same thing as changing it in the printer driver's dialog box (see "Page Setup, Printer, and Properties," later in this chapter, for more information on printer drivers).

Fit in Print Area. When you turn on the Fit in Print Area checkbox, XPress calculates the Reduce or Enlarge setting for you, so that your document fits snugly on whatever paper size you're using at the orientation you specify (see "Orientation," next). This is much faster than trying to figure out the proper percentages to get a tabloid page onto a letter-sized page, or vice versa.

By the way, Fit in Print Area is grayed out whenever you've turned on the Spreads, Thumbnails, or Tiling options. The last two are understandable, but I still can't figure out why the feature doesn't work with Spreads. Oh well.

Orientation. Remember back to college when they had Orientation Day? The idea was to make sure you knew which way you were going while walking around the school grounds. Well, this Orientation is sort of the same, but different. The idea is to make sure QuarkXPress knows which way you want your document to go while it's walking through the printer. You have two choices: Portrait and Landscape. I've included some samples in Figure 13-14 so you can see what each one does.

▼ ▼

Tip: Save the RC Trees. When you're printing onto a roll-fed imagesetter (more on these later), you can often save film or paper by printing your letter-size pages in landscape rather than portrait orientation. That way you only use around 8.5 inches on the roll rather than 11. It may not seem like a great difference, but those 3.5 inches really add up when you're printing a long document. For example, a 100-page file will save more than 300 inches of film or paper. Printing the pages landscape also

Figure 13-14
Page orientation

*The left column is
"portrait" or "tall";
the right column is
"landscape" or "wide."*

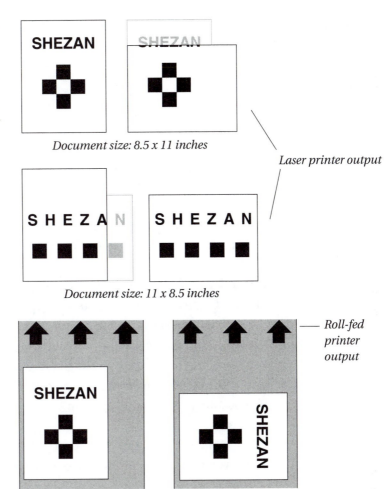

Document size: 8.5 x 11 inches

Laser printer output

Document size: 11 x 8.5 inches

Roll-fed
printer
output

Document size: 8.5 x 11 inches

makes it easy to cut them apart and stack them. Check with your service bureau to see if they'll give you a discount for the time and energy
you've saved them.

▼ ▼

Page Positioning. When you select a paper size that is larger than your
document, XPress lets you specify where on the page you want your document to sit. You've got four choices: Left Edge, Center, Center Horizontal,
and Center Vertical (see Figure 13-15). Left Edge is the default (it's the way
QuarkXPress has always worked); the other three are self-explanatory. I
find this control a matter of personal preference most of the time, though

Figure 13-15
Page Positioning

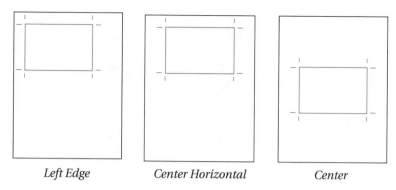

Left Edge   *Center Horizontal*   *Center*

using one of the Center settings is critical if you want to print something on both sides of a piece of paper and have the two sides align.

Roll-Fed Printer Specifications

The last four features on the Setup tab apply only to—you guessed it—roll-fed printers. These are imagesetters, such as those in the Linotronic and Agfa lines, that feed paper and film from rolls rather than one sheet at a time. The four choices available to you when you have a roll-fed printer selected in the Printer Description menu are Paper Width, Paper Height, Paper Offset, and Page Gap.

Paper Width. The Paper Width specification is not an actual control so much as a description of the device you'll be printing to. A Linotronic 300, for example, can image to 11.7 inches ("70p2" in QuarkXPress's pica notation). An Agfa CG9400 images to 14 inches, and a Linotronic 530 images to 17.5 inches. Whatever the case, and whatever the measurement style, just replace the default number with the proper paper width.

(Note that you can only type a value into the Paper Width field when the Paper Size popup menu is set to Custom. If you have some reason to choose a specific paper size, know what you're doing, go ahead, and choose one. In this case, XPress fills in the Paper Width and Paper Height settings for you and grays them out.)

I so fondly recall the time when I printed several pages on a Linotronic 330 with Paper Width set to "11p7" (11 picas, 7 points—or 139 points), instead of 11.7 inches. Everything on each page was cut off at exactly "11p7" from the left edge. The rest of the page was blank. I was not a happy camper, and I've been studiously monitoring this feature ever since.

Paper Height. When QuarkXPress prints to a roll-fed printer, it has to tell the printer exactly how long each page will be. That is, while the Paper Width field tells XPress how wide the paper is, the Paper Height field tells XPress how much paper has to roll in order to image a page correctly. When the Paper Size popup menu is set to Custom (it is by default for roll-fed imagesetters), the Paper Height setting is changed to Automatic. I generally leave this as is, since XPress is usually better at calculating measurements than I am. Again, if you know what you're doing and you think you need to tweak this, go ahead, but go carefully.

Paper Offset. This feature controls the placement of your document on the paper or film. The printer's default paper offset, even when set to zero, is almost always large enough so that you don't have to worry about changing the value of Paper Offset here. For example, on a Linotronic imagesetter, when Paper Offset is set to zero inches the file is printed ¼ inch from the edge. If you want it farther from the edge for some reason, change this value.

However, the Paper Offset setting shouldn't exceed the document height subtracted from the paper width (that is, if you have a 10-inch-tall document printing on 14-inch paper, your offset certainly should not be more than r 4 inches, or else you'll chop off the other end of the page).

Page Gap. The last roll-fed printer specification determines the amount of blank space between each page of the document as it prints out on the roll. Initially, this value is zero. I recommend changing this to at least ¼ inch ("1p6") so you can cut the pages apart easily. If you're printing with the Spreads option turned on, this gap between pages is placed between the spreads, not between the pages within the spread (again, there's rarely any reason to turn on the Spreads option when printing to an imagesetter). Some imagesetters suppress this value, however, and rely on lower-level settings that an operator has to change via proprietary software or front-panel settings. Check with your service bureau before output—they may have advice on the correct setting.

▼ ▼

The Output Tab

The third tab in the Print dialog box, the Output tab, is focused primarily on controlling color and halftone output (see Figure 13-16). If you're printing a black-and-white document, the only setting you probably need to think about here is Frequency, which determines the lpi setting—in fact, if there aren't any grays in your document, you don't even have to pay attention to this. On the other hand, for those of us who work in color, this tab is incredibly powerful, when printing both proofs and final film.

Figure 13-16

The Output tab

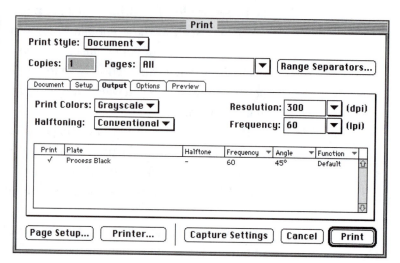

Print Colors. Earlier versions of QuarkXPress offered a checkbox labeled "Print Colors as Grays." When on, XPress would convert every color in your document into a value of gray at print time—darker colors appeared as darker grays, lighter colors were lighter gray. This feature has now evolved into the Print Colors popup menu. When you choose a color printer in the Printer Description popup menu on the Setup tab, you can set Print Colors to Composite Color. This tells XPress to send color information to the printer.

However, when you print to a black-and-white printer like a desktop laser printer, you can pick either Grayscale or Black & White. Choosing Grayscale is the same as turning on Print Colors as Grays in the old version of the program. You don't have too much control over which shades of gray go with which color, so subtle differences in colors (such as between a pink and a light green) may blend together as one shade of gray. But it's still better than printing the file out as a page of solid black, which is what you get when you set the Print Colors popup menu to Black & White (see Figure 13-17).

Figure 13-17

Print colors

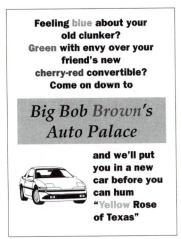

Print Colors set to Black and White

Print Colors set to Grayscale

▼ ▼

Tip: Send RGB Data, not CMYK. When you print a color document to a color printer, XPress 4 currently separates RGB TIFFs into CMYK mode before sending them. However, earlier versions of XPress would just send the RGB data and rely on the printer to handle the mode change. This was faster and made a lot more sense (the printer usually knows how to make a better conversion for itself). I'm hoping that the engineers at Quark will come to their senses and revert back to the old way of doing things, but in the meantime, if you want your printer to deal with RGB data, you have to send the file in EPS format (which means that the printer has to be a PostScript color printer). Grrr . . . .

▼ ▼

Halftoning. QuarkXPress offers you two choices on the Output tab's Halftoning popup menu: Conventional and Printer. The difference is simple: Conventional means that QuarkXPress includes halftone settings (angle, frequency, and spot function) when sending PostScript to the printer. Choosing Printer means that XPress won't send halftone information at all. Why should you care? Some devices—like color ink-jet printers—don't print with normal halftones, so there's no reason to specify values like halftone frequency and so on.

Note that the Halftoning control is not an option when you're printing color separations. There's really no reason it should be, as the feature was mostly designed for color printers.

Resolution. Don't change this number with the expectation that it has any major significance to how your job prints. It doesn't determine the resolution at which your job prints. However, it does determine some important issues when printing bitmapped images. Low-resolution, 72-dpi black-and-white images can be smoothed with Quark's proprietary bitmap-smoothing algorithms, which depend on knowing the resolution of the printer. Also, bitmapped images that have a very high resolution may print significantly faster when you include the right printer resolution. For example, QuarkXPress internally reduces the resolution of a 600-dpi line-art image when it knows it's printing to a 300-dpi printer. The printer doesn't need any more than 300 dots per inch anyway, and you save time because QuarkXPress only has to download half as much information (and the PostScript interpreter has to wade through only half as much).

Frequency. I talked at some length about halftones and halftone screens back in Chapter 10, *Fine-Tuning Images*. The Frequency setting on the Output tab of the Print dialog box is where you get to specify the halftone screen frequency of every tint in your document (except for those graphic images which you have set using the Halftone feature on the Style menu, and EPS graphics that have their screen specified internally). This includes gray boxes, tinted type, screened colors, and so on.

The default value for the halftone screen (the one that QuarkXPress uses unless you specify something else) is determined by the PPD you've chosen in the Printer Description popup menu. On most laser printers, the value is 60 lpi (lines per inch). You can type your own setting from 15 to 400 lines per inch. Raising the screen frequency nets you "smoother" grays, but you'll find you have fewer gray levels to work with (I talk about this trade-off in the book *Real World Scanning and Halftones*).

▼ ▼

Tip: A Colorful Shade of Gray. A couple of caveats to this tip, before I get to it: this is helpful primarily if you're printing proofs which won't be ed. This feature automatically replaces each picture in your document with a big "X," and every complex frame with a double line of the same width (see Figure 13-19). Clearly, the pages print significantly faster than with Normal or Low Resolution.

Figure 13-19

Page printed with
Rough selected

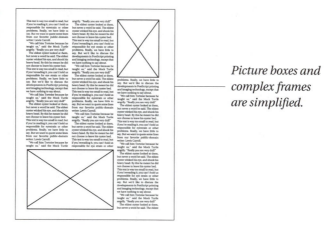

*Picture boxes and
complex frames
are simplified.*

Data Format. I talked about binary versus ASCII data formats back in Chapter 9, *Pictures*, when I discussed QuarkXPress's Save as EPS feature; here the choice appears again. To recap, this only pertains to how bitmapped images (like TIFF and JPEG) are sent to the printer. While sending the information in ASCII format is more reliable over some networks, binary is almost always fine and has the benefit of creating a much smaller PostScript file (the images are half the size of ASCII).

The third choice, Clean 8-bit, is a good compromise. It is as small as binary, but it strips out the particular binary characters that cause some networks to go into conniptions. I generally use the Clean 8-bit setting unless I'm on a strictly Macintosh-based network, in which case I use Binary. On the other hand, you may want to use ASCII if you're making PostScript files for your service bureau and they're going to transfer the files to a PC- or UNIX-based system for output.

OPI. The OPI popup menu that appears in the Print dialog box is exactly the same as the one in the Save Page as EPS dialog box, so I'll save my breath here by referring you to "Page as Picture" in Chapter 9, *Pictures*.

Overprint EPS Black. I discussed overprinting and trapping back in Chapter 12, *Color*, but there is one overprinting control that you can only set in the Print dialog box: Overprint EPS Black. When you turn this checkbox on, every object colored black in EPS images overprints its background, regardless of whether you set it to overprint in the original illustration program. Note that this control ignores the Overprint Limit on the Trapping tab of the Document Preferences dialog box, so even an EPS object that is only 10-percent black will overprint.

I find this feature most useful when working with EPS files built in programs that don't let you specify overprinting. For instance, my friend and colleague Phil Gaskill recently laid out a textbook that contained hundreds of molecular diagrams built in a scientific illustration application. The people who wrote this program didn't expect anyone to place these graphics over colored backgrounds, so there was no control for overprinting at all. All those thin lines would have been a trapping nightmare if it weren't for the Overprint EPS Black feature.

Full-Resolution TIFF Output. When you print a document that includes TIFF or JPEG images, QuarkXPress may downsample the image data behind the scenes. The program figures that you'll never need more resolution in your images than two times the halftone screen frequency, so it cuts off the data at that point. If you have a 200-dpi image reduced to 50 percent on your page (which makes it a 400-dpi image; see Chapter 9, *Pictures*), and you've specified an 80-lpi screen in the Frequency field on the Output tab, QuarkXPress chops off the image resolution at 160 dpi (two times the frequency). Typically, that's okay. In fact, it's great if you're proofing high-resolution images on a laser printer. However, every now and again, this feature can jump up and bite you.

For example, if you reduce an image considerably in a picture box, you can sometimes get mottling or jaggy artifacts from the downsampling. Or, if you're purposely printing at a very low screen frequency because your color printer requires it (some do), your images may look really weird because QuarkXPress has downsampled them so much.

Fortunately, you can turn on the Full Resolution TIFF Output checkbox and none of your bitmapped images will get downsampled at print time. Note that this effect (and solution) only affect TIFF images. EPS pictures don't get downsampled because QuarkXPress can't touch the data that's encapsulated in them. Also, XPress always turns this option on when you set the Halftoning popup menu to Printer on the Setup tab (because there's no halftone screen to use as a reference).

▼ ▼

The Preview Tab

The Preview tab in the Print dialog box doesn't offer any controls at all, but that doesn't mean you shouldn't look at it. In fact, I find that it's worthwhile to take at least a quick peek at this tab every time you print because the Preview tab provides information that can tell you in advance whether what comes out of your printer will match your expectations (see Figure 13-20).

Figure 13-20

The Preview tab

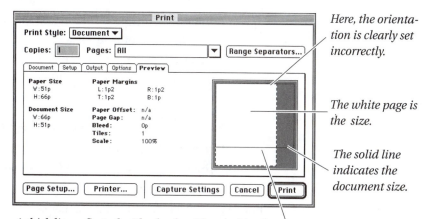

Here, the orientation is clearly set incorrectly.

The white page is the size.

The solid line indicates the document size.

A thick line reflects the Bleed value (if you're bleeding objects off the page, you had better see a thick line here).

On the left side of the Preview tab, XPress lists several of the most important details of your print job.

▶ **PAPER SIZE VERSUS DOCUMENT SIZE.** Paper Size reflects the Paper Width and Paper Height fields on the Setup tab. Document Size shows the dimensions of the document itself (the measurements in the Document Setup dialog box). By comparing these two, you can quickly gauge whether your document page will fit on the paper size you've specified.

▶ **PAPER MARGINS.** Where the margin settings in QuarkXPress are merely guides that you can ignore when necessary, the Paper Margins values shown here are absolutes—anything outside these margins simply won't print. These values are plucked from the PPD, based on what you've chosen in the Paper Size popup menu, and are meant to reflect the physical limitations of the device.

That is, most laser printers simply can't image closer than .1 or .2 inch from the edge of the page. Note that the Paper Margins values are only listed numerically, and aren't reflected in the graphic on the right of the Preview tab.

▶ **PRINT OPTIONS.** The last section of the Preview tab displays values for Paper Offset, Page Gap, Bleed, Tiles, and Scale. These are simply duplicates of information that appears on other tabs in the dialog box, but it's handy to see it all together here. I find the Tiles information particularly useful, as it clearly defines how many printed pages XPress will have to spit out in order to fully image your page (this only applies when you set Tiles to Automatic, of course). For instance, you can quickly compare the Landscape and Portrait orientations to see which results in fewer printed pages.

What Preview graphic tells you. The graphic image on the right side of the Preview tab is very useful, but it doesn't reflect a number of aspects of your print job. For instance, while it does show you where crop marks and registration marks are going to land, it doesn't indicate that the image will come out in reverse (because Negative Print is turned on) or mirrored (because you've set Page Flip). And while it can represent how spreads will lie on the page when the Spreads option is turned on, it only does this for facing-pages documents.

Page Setup, Printer, and Properties

When you print your document, QuarkXPress interacts with whatever printer driver you have selected. (On the Macintosh, you select a printer driver via the Chooser utility; in Windows, you choose one from the Printer popup menu in the Print dialog box.) The driver controls some aspects of the print job and XPress controls others. I've been discussing in some detail the settings you can make to QuarkXPress's Print dialog box. Now I want to take a quick break to discuss some options you have in the printer driver itself.

Of course, printer drivers are completely different on the Macintosh and in Windows, so I need to cover them one at a time. Also, note that there are many different versions of these drivers, and the one you use may well appear different than the ones I show here. Don't fret about it too much; with a little exploration, you'll find that many of the features are the same.

Macintosh: Page Setup and Printer

In QuarkXPress for Macintosh, you can access the printer-driver settings by clicking on the Page Setup and Printer buttons in the Print dialog box (see Figure 13-21). In most cases, the settings you make in the Printer dialog box apply to this one print job only, and you'll have to change them again next time you print. On the other hand, most of the settings you make in the Page Setup dialog box are saved with the document.

Figure 13-21

The printer driver settings

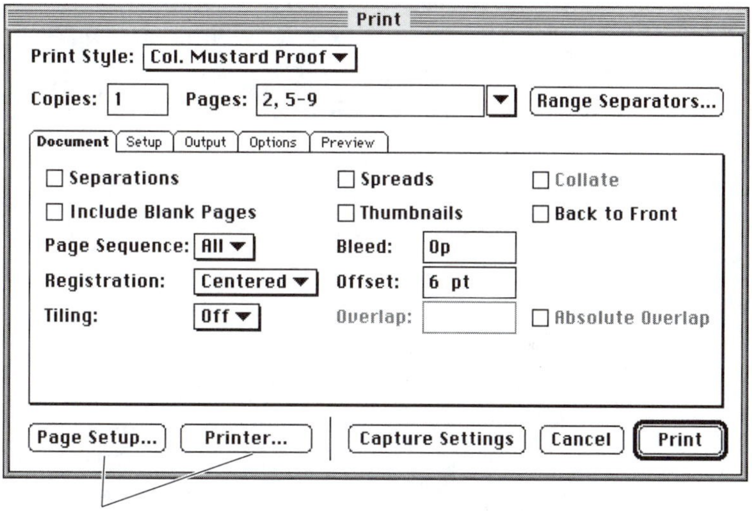

Click these buttons to access the printer-driver dialog boxes.

After making changes to either the Page Setup or the Printer dialog box, when you leave the dialog box (by clicking OK, Cancel, Print, or Save, depending on what you're doing), XPress returns to the normal Print dialog box.

Page Setup. The Page Setup dialog box is split into two "pages." The first page you see contains settings for Scale, Orientation, and Paper Size—all of which are duplicates of settings in QuarkXPress's Print dialog box. It's better to ignore these and use the controls in the Print dialog box.

You can see the second page by either clicking the Options button or selecting PostScript Options from the popup menu in the upper-left corner of the dialog box, depending on the version of the printer driver (see Figure 13-22). The checkboxes in this dialog box are separated into two areas: Visual Effects and Image & Text. Note that the Image & Text checkboxes have consequence only when you're printing to a PostScript printer (for most of you, that means all the time).

Figure 13-22

Page Setup dialog box

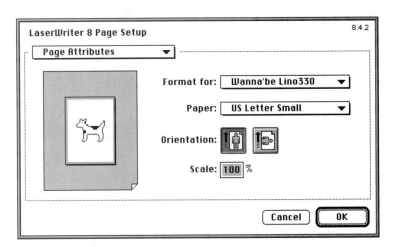

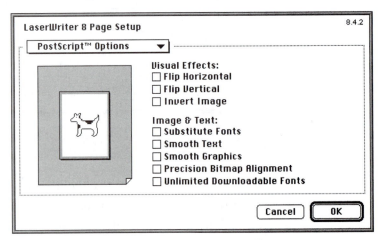

The most important feature in the Page Setup dialog box (it appears on both pages of the dialog box, actually) is the graphic representation of the page and how it is affected by each of the Page Setup controls. For instance, checking Invert Image inverts the picture in the box. If you're using Apple's LaserWriter driver, the graphic you'll see is sort of a weird-looking animal. The hallowed halls of Macintosh folklore may someday be cluttered with speculation on what particular animal this is. While the consensus seems to be that it's a dog, I prefer the rare dogcow (it says "Moof!").

Here's a discussion of all of the options in order, starting with the visual effects.

▶ **VISUAL EFFECTS.** The three visual effects—Flip Horizontal, Flip Vertical, and Invert Image—are all duplicates of features in QuarkXPress's Print dialog box. Once again, I suggest you ignore them here.

▶ **SUBSTITUTE FONTS.** Before System 7, New York, Geneva, and Monaco were bitmap-only fonts (read: "ugly"). Now they're TrueType outlines, but I still think they're pretty ugly. Checking Font Substitution allows QuarkXPress to substitute Times Roman for New York, Helvetica for Geneva, and Courier for Monaco. The problem is that the letterspacing is all thrown off when you do this, so it's hardly worth it. The solution is to "just say no" to using those TrueType fonts in the first place.

▶ **SMOOTH TEXT.** This feature tells the printer to attempt to smooth out bitmapped fonts so they don't look too jagged. However, almost no one uses bitmapped fonts anymore, and when they do, they usually want them to look bitmapped for a special effect. Whatever the case, this setting makes me nervous and I always turn it off.

▶ **SMOOTH GRAPHICS.** As the name would suggest, the Smooth Graphics feature does to bitmapped graphics what Smooth Text does to bitmapped fonts. Don't get too excited yet. This only works for 72-dpi black-and-white bitmapped PICTs and MacPaint graphics. If you're doing super low-end graphics, this might help (though it can increase print times dramatically). The rest of us should just turn it off.

▶ **PRECISION BITMAP ALIGNMENT.** The problem with printing low-resolution graphics on a low-resolution desktop printer is that the two resolutions rarely have integral relationships with each other, so the graphics print out with ugly tiled patterns. When you select Precision Bitmap Alignment, the entire document is scaled down 4 percent, which raises the effective resolution of the bitmapped image to almost 75 dpi, and that image now prints with few or no ugly patterns. Of course, the rest of your document has also been scaled down, which is less exciting. This feature is for the birds; leave it off.

▶ **UNLIMITED DOWNLOADABLE FONTS IN A DOCUMENT.** Checking this feature is a last resort when you really have too many fonts on a page to print it successfully. The issue here is time. Normally, QuarkXPress downloads all the fonts it needs for a job as it needs them. If the printer's memory runs out, then it runs out, and you get a PostScript error telling you that you can't print the job. If you have the Unlimited Downloadable Fonts in a Document feature enabled, QuarkXPress downloads the font when it needs it, then flushes it out of printer memory. Next time the document needs the font, QuarkXPress downloads it again. The problem is, that might be 10 times on a single page, making your job print very slowly. So while you gain the ability to print as many fonts as you want, you pay a hefty price in printing time.

▶ **LARGER PRINT AREA (FEWER DOWNLOADABLE FONTS).** When you print a page to a desktop laser printer, you are only able to print up to approximately .5 inch from the page edge because of the limited memory within the PostScript printer. By checking Larger Print Area, you tell the laser printer to alter the memory allocation slightly, giving a bit more memory to the image area and a bit less to the font area. You can then print out to the very minimum $1/4$-inch border, but you have less room to store your downloadable fonts, so the number of downloadable fonts you can use on a page is reduced. In other words, a page which may print fine without the Larger Print Area box checked may now cause an overload in printer memory and a PostScript error. I suggest you leave this turned off unless you really need it. Note that this feature disappeared in the LaserWriter 8 driver.

Printer. If the dialog box you get when you click the Printer button looks familiar, that's because it's the same dialog box you get when you choose Print from almost any other Macintosh application (see Figure 13-23). However, in this case, after you click Print or Cancel, you're dropped back into QuarkXPress's Print dialog box.

The Printer dialog box lets you control a number of aspects of the print job, including whether you want a cover page to accompany the document, whether you want to print the document in the background or foreground, and how many document pages per printer page you want to be laid out. The most important setting here, however, is the Destination feature, which lets you print the PostScript file to disk instead of to a printer. I'll explore printing PostScript "dumps" to disk later, in "Working with a Service Bureau."

Figure 13-23

The print driver's Printer dialog box

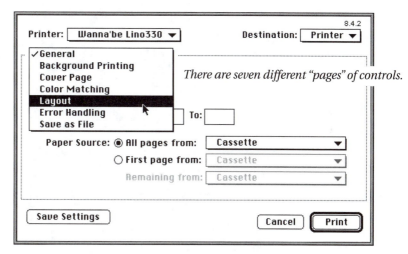

There are seven different "pages" of controls.

Windows: Properties

You can adjust printer-driver settings in Windows by clicking the Properties button in the Print dialog box (see Figure 13-24). There are a number of different settings here, spread out over four or five different tabs (depending on the version of the PostScript driver you're using), but there's one theme that runs through them all: almost none of them apply to working with QuarkXPress. (On the other hand, if you're working with a non-PostScript driver, many of the controls will affect your output; but again, I'm not talking about non-PostScript devices here.)

The controls fall into three categories.

▶ Most are duplicates of settings in QuarkXPress's Print dialog box. These get overridden by XPress, so you should ignore them.

▶ Some cause PostScript errors or strange things to occur.

▶ Some just don't do anything at all, even though they look like they should.

Figure 13-24
The Properties dialog box
in Windows

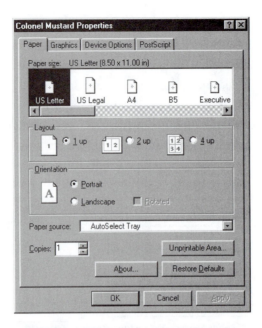

Okay, I am being a little harsh here. There are two items that I do use in the Properties dialog box. The first, Paper Source, lets you choose among various paper trays in your printer. The second, PostScript output format, lets you choose among different PostScript formatting attributes. The default setting, Optimize for speed, usually works well enough for me. However, if the PostScript file will be postprocessed by some other prepress utility, you probably want to change this to Optimize for portability (this uses more of the Adobe Document Structuring Conventions, or ADSC).

▼ ▼

Print Styles

One of my favorite features in the old QuarkPrint XTension was the Print Styles feature, which let you save collections of Print and Page Setup dialog-box settings under one name. Fortunately, the folks at Quark built this feature right into QuarkXPress 4, so no additional XTension is necessary. There are two great benefits to print styles. First, you can easily change the default settings for XPress's Print dialog box. If you have one printer and you're tired of selecting the same PPD from the Printer Description popup menu or turning off the Include Blank Pages option every time you print, this is the feature for you.

Print Styles is also great for service bureaus or anyone else who prints to a number of different devices from one copy of XPress, because you can build dozens (hundreds? Sorry, I've never tried) of different print styles.

Building a print style. You can make a new print style by choosing Print Styles from the Edit menu (see Figure 13-25). Print styles are like Application Preferences in one way: changes you make here apply to the program as a whole, not just to documents you may have open. Once the Print Styles dialog box is open, you can either click New or select a style and click Edit or Duplicate. At this point XPress displays the Edit Print Style dialog box, which looks awfully similar to the Print dialog box. It's not an exact duplicate; for instance, there is no Preview tab. (If you think about it, how could there be?)

Go ahead and make changes to the Edit Print Style dialog box, then give the collection of settings a name. I tend to make the name as descriptive of my settings as possible. Finally, click OK to leave the Edit Print Style dialog box, then click Save to leave the Print Styles dialog box, saving your work. That's it!

There are a few things you cannot change in the Edit Print Style dialog box. For instance, you can't turn off particular process-color plates on the

Figure 13-25

Building a print style

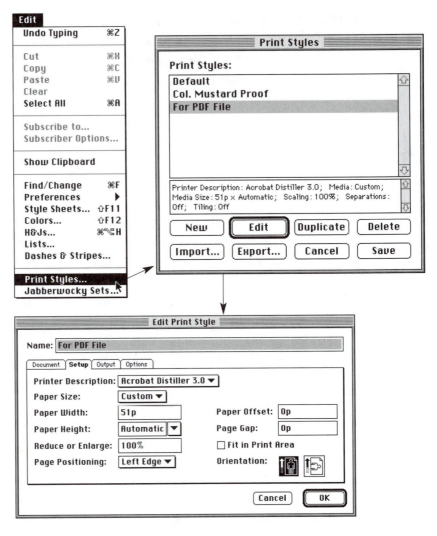

Output tab. You also can't specify a page range, the number of copies, or the settings in the Page Setup, Printer, or Properties dialog boxes. This is unfortunate, because these often need to be changed every time you print.

Selecting a print style. Once you have built a print style, you can select it from the Print Style popup menu in the Print dialog box (see Figure 13-26). It's as easy as that.

Moving print styles around. Print styles are application-wide and are stored in the XPress Preferences file. If you lose this file or if you need to delete it because it has become corrupted, your print styles are lost. (It's

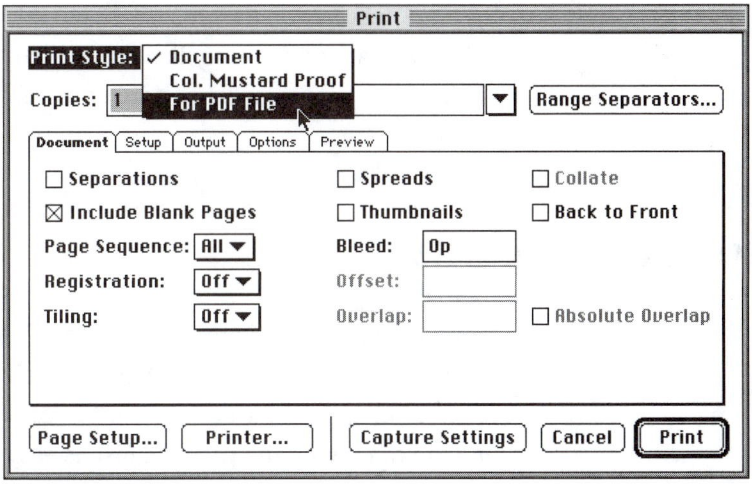

Figure 13-26

Selecting a print style

a good idea to keep a regular backup of the XPress Preferences file.) If you use the same print style from more than one computer, you can move it in one of two ways.

▶ You can copy your XPress Preferences file from one computer to the next. This copies all your preferences, even including Hyphenation Exceptions and kerning table edits, which may be more than you hoped for. Note that this does not work cross-platform.

▶ You can select one or more print styles in the Print Styles dialog box and click Export to save the print style(s) to disk. Then, in a different copy of QuarkXPress, you can click Import in the same dialog box to append the style(s). This does work when moving the file from Mac to PC (or vice versa), as long as the file name includes the three-letter ".qpj" file-name extension.

▼ ▼

Tip: Comparing Print Styles. If you have two print styles that are similar, you might find it useful to ask XPress to compare them for you. Just select them both in the Print Styles dialog box (you can use the Command key to select discontiguous styles on the list), and hold down the Option key while clicking the Import button (the Import button changes to read "Compare" when you hold down the modifier key). As this book goes to press, the Compare Print Styles dialog box doesn't list every item in the style; for instance, all the features on the Options tab plus many features on the Document tab (like Thumbnails) don't appear, so the comparison is pretty limited. Perhaps if we all prod the folks at Quark, a later version will provide more information.

▼ ▼

Color Separations

I come now to the last area of the Print dialog box, which as a subject deserves a whole section of the book to itself: color separation. The concept behind color separation is simple, and QuarkXPress does a pretty good job of making the practice just as easy, but the truth is that this is a very complicated matter which, in the space of this book, I can only touch on briefly.

The Basics of Color Separation

A printing press can only print one color at a time. Even five- and six-color presses really only print one color at a time, attempting to give the ink a chance to dry between coats. As I discussed in Chapter 12, *Color*, those colors are almost always process colors (cyan, magenta, yellow, and black), or they may be spot colors, such as Pantone inks.

Colors that you specify in your QuarkXPress documents may look solid on the screen, but they need to be separated and printed onto individual plates for printing. Each of the four process colors is printed as a tint or a halftone (if you don't understand the fundamentals of halftoning, I *really* recommend that you look at Chapter 10, *Fine-Tuning Images*). By overlapping the screened tints, you can create a multitude of colors.

If you print color separations for a job with only process colors, you output four pieces of film for every page of the document. Each spot color requires adding another plate to the lineup.

Printing Color Separations

To print color separations, turn on the Separations checkbox on the Document tab in the Print dialog box. This activates the color plates list on the Output tab, giving you a choice of which color plates you want to print and at what halftone settings. As long as the printer type is a black-and-white printer (like a laser printer or an imagesetter), by default the color plate list is set to print all the color, which includes the four process colors plus any spot colors you have defined (see Figure 13-27).

Figure 13-27

Making separations

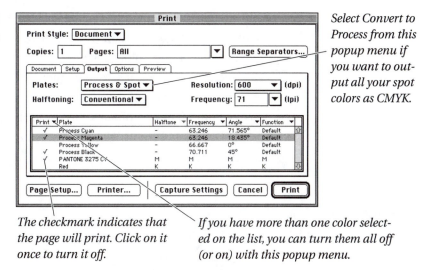

Select Convert to Process from this popup menu if you want to output all your spot colors as CMYK.

The checkmark indicates that the page will print. Click on it once to turn it off.

If you have more than one color selected on the list, you can turn them all off (or on) with this popup menu.

Even if all the color plates are set to print, QuarkXPress only prints plates for the colors that are actually used in your document. If you create custom spot colors, but don't actually use them in your document, they appear on the color plates list. But don't worry: they won't print.

▼ ▼

Tip: Convert to Process. It's driven service bureau owners stark raving mad . . . . It's caused thousands of dollars in wasted film output . . . . It's one of the greatest problems affecting humankind today . . . . (Well, okay, maybe that last one was a little extreme.) I'm talking, of course, about people leaving the Spot Color checkbox turned on in the Edit Colors dialog box when they really meant to build process colors. The result: every color they create is a spot color, and therefore prints out on its own plate.

But fear no more! When you print separations, XPress changes the Print Colors popup menu (on the Output tab of the Print dialog box) to Plates, and offers you two choices: "Process & Spot" or "Convert to Process." If you want all your spot colors to separate into CMYK, select Convert to Process. Note that this only changes your spot colors to process colors at print time; the colors in the document are actually still specified as spot colors.

▼ ▼

The Rosette

When the process-color plates are laid down on top of each other, the halftones of each color mesh with each other in a subtle way. Each plate's halftone image is printed at a slightly different angle, and possibly at a different screen frequency as well. The result is thousands of tiny rosette patterns (see Figure 13-28). If this process is done correctly, our eyes blend the separate colors together to form one smooth, clean color. However, if the angles or screen frequencies are slightly off, or if the registration (alignment) of the plates is wrong, then all sorts of chaos can ensue. Both of these problems can come about from error on the lithographer's part, but more likely they indicate problems with your imagesetting process.

Figure 13-28

A simulated process-color rosette

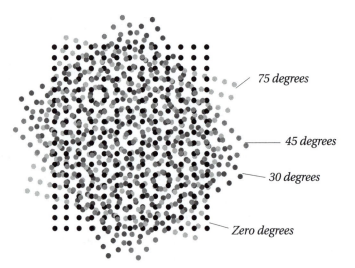

75 degrees

45 degrees

30 degrees

Zero degrees

The most common effect of the above problems is a patterning in the color called a *moiré pattern* (that's pronouced "mwah-ray"). There's almost no good way to describe a moiré pattern; it's best to just see a few of them. They might be pretty subtle, but it would behoove you to learn to identify them and learn how to make them go away. Figure 13-29 shows an outlandish example of this patterning caused by the screen frequency and angles being set completely wrong.

Making sure you don't get moirés has been a major undertaking over the past few years in the color prepress industry, and has resulted in screening technologies that are often built right into the imagesetters. Balanced Screens and High Quality Screening (HQS) are two examples of this, available from major imagesetter vendors Agfa and Linotype-Hell. For these technologies to work, you need to make sure that QuarkXPress is using its default screening angles (black at 45 degrees;

Figure 13-29
Moiré patterning

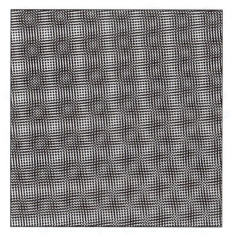

cyan at 75; magenta at 105; and yellow at 90). Once again, it's critical that you choose the correct printer (and therefore the correct PPD) from the Printer Description popup menu in order to receive the proper screen angles for that device.

Screening and moiré problems are discussed in much more depth in a book that I co-wrote with Steve Roth and Glenn Fleishman, *Real World Scanning and Halftones.*

The Color Halftone Settings

QuarkXPress lets you change the halftone settings for each color in your document on the Output tab of the Print dialog box (see Figure 13-30). If you're working with the right PPD file, you rarely need to do this, but when you need this flexibility, it's great to have the opportunity (before version 4, you had to use a separate XTension to change these values).

There are four halftone settings you can control on the color plates list: Halftone, Frequency, Angle, and Function. To make a change, select a color (or select more than one color with the Shift or Command key), and choose from one of the popup menus at the top of the list.

▶ HALFTONE. As I mentioned back in Chapter 12, *Color*, each spot color you create is assigned a matching process color—whatever halftone settings are applied to the process color are also applied to the spot color. The Halftone column on the color plates list lets you change the associated color at print time. For instance, if you see an "M" next to a Pantone color, you know that this Pantone color will use the halftone settings for Magenta. If you want, you

Figure 13-30

Changing color
halftone settings

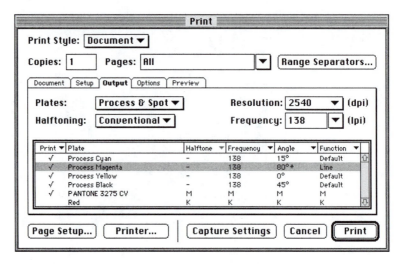

can then change this to C, Y, or K. Personally, I think if you're going
to make this kind of change, you should do it in the Edit Color dialog box instead.

▶ **FREQUENCY.** The values in the Frequency column are pulled from
your printer's PPD file. They may not always match the Frequency
field at the top of the dialog box. In fact, it's not uncommon to find
different frequency values for each proccss color. There's a level of
faith here . . . you've got to trust that whoever built the PPD knew
what they were doing.

▶ **ANGLE.** The angle column lists the halftone angle at which each
color will print. As I said earlier, the angles are usually 0, 15, 45, and
75 degrees, but they may be radically different (again, depending
on the PPD file). Note that just because you specify a particular
angle doesn't mean you're going to get it. Due to some technical
issues, some angles are actually impossible to set on digital printers. (Unfortunately, 15 degrees is one such angle; screening systems such as Balanced Screens actually catch the call for 15
degrees and change it to an appropriate number on the fly.)

▶ **FUNCTION.** The last column on the color plates list is labeled
Function, which refers to PostScript's spot function. This controls
the shape of the halftone spot for each color. It's quite rare that
you need to change this unless you're building low-lpi special
effects. I discussed the various spot shapes that XPress can build
back in Chapter 10, *Fine-Tuning Images*.

Working with a Service Bureau

The existence of service bureaus with imagesetters (sometimes called "imaging centers," "imaging service bureaus," or "lino parlors") has mushroomed over the past ten years. The phenomenon has grown from a storefront where you could rent a Mac and print on a laser printer to a specialty service where you can send your files to be imageset or color-proofed on a number of medium- and high-end imagesetters and other output devices. Alongside this growth have developed standard etiquette and rules spoken only in hushed voices (and usually after the customer has left the shop). In this section I bring these rules out into the open and take you through, step by step, how to best send files to your service bureau, and how to ensure that you'll receive the best-quality output from them.

The first thing to remember when dealing with service bureaus is that they don't necessarily know their equipment or what's best for your file any better than you do. That's not to say that they are ignorant louts, but I am of the opinion that really good service bureaus are few and far between, and you (the customer) have to be careful and know what you're doing. The principal relationship I talk about in this section is that of you, the customer, sending your QuarkXPress files to a service bureau to be imageset. I'll talk first about sending the actual QuarkXPress document, and then about sending a PostScript dump of the file. Many of my suggestions may be totally wrong for the way your particular service bureau functions, so take what works and leave the rest. Some prefer PostScript dumps, for instance, while others opt for the QuarkXPress files themselves.

▼ ▼

Tip: Calibration and Consistency. Any schmo with a pocketful of cash can buy an imagesetter; it takes real talent to run it properly. You need to be sure that your service bureau calibrates their imagesetters and keeps them running consistently. This typically requires a transmission densitometer, linearization software, and attention to detail. The key issue is that when you specify a 20-percent tint in your document, you get a 20-percent tint on your film. This is particularly important when doing color work, of course, where even a change of a few percentage points on one plate can cause color shifts. If you can't get good, consistent quality, go elsewhere.

▼ ▼

Tip: Some Questions for Your Service Bureau. Here is a list of a few questions which you may want to ask when shopping for a service bureau.

▶ What imagesetters do they have available, and what resolutions do they support?

▶ Do they have dedicated equipment just for film, and do they calibrate it using imagesetter linearization or other software? If they're using other software, do you need a component on your system when making files to output with them?

▶ Do they have an in-house color-proofing system? Is it a laminate system (like Match Print or Press Match) or digital composite (like the 3M Rainbow or Iris printers)?

▶ Do they have a replenishing processor, or do they use the same chemicals continually? If it's the latter, how often do they clean their wash?

▶ Do they inspect their film before they send it out?

▶ Do they have a customer agreement that lists what they're responsible for and what the customer is responsible for?

▶ Do they have a job ticket for output that lets you fill in all the details of your particular project?

There are no right or wrong answers to any of these questions. However, asking them not only tells you a lot about the service bureau, but also teaches you a lot about the process they're going through to output your film or RC paper.

You should make decisions about where to run each print job. For example, if a service bureau doesn't calibrate their equipment, you probably don't want to use them for halftoning or color-separation work, but they might be okay for straight type work. If their top resolution is 1,270 dpi, you may need to go elsewhere for high-quality grayscale images or color separations. You can weigh these factors against the cost of the film or paper output, the distance from your office, the friendliness of the staff, and so on.

▼ ▼

How to Send Your File

You have two basic choices in transporting your QuarkXPress document to a service bureau to be imageset: sending the file itself, or sending a PostScript dump of the file. While my preference has always been to send a PostScript dump, many service bureaus want the file itself. It's a question of who is in control of the final output: me or them.

When I send the file off to be printed using someone else's system, I don't know whether their fonts are different, whether the text will reflow, whether they'll forget to set up registration marks, or whether they'll print the file at the wrong screen frequency. By sending them a PostScript dump (see "Sending a PostScript Dump," below), you put yourself in the driver's seat: you can control almost every aspect of the print job.

Sending QuarkXPress Files

Though I prefer to send PostScript dumps, I know that most service bureaus now prefer to receive the actual QuarkXPress file, which gives them the control to fix certain aspects of the job if something goes wrong. And the truth is that many QuarkXPress users don't want to be responsible for checking all the buttons and specifications necessary to print PostScript to disk. If you find yourself in either of these situations, you'll need to know what to do in order to optimize your chances of success. Let's look at the steps you need to take.

Check your fonts. I can't tell you how important it is to keep track of which fonts you've used and where they are on your disk. Make sure that your service bureau has the same screen fonts that you do, and has the printer fonts (downloadable) that correspond to each and every font you've used in your document. I sometimes send my own fonts along with my job to the service bureau because I believe that sometimes screen fonts that are supposed to be the same simply aren't. Either they've gotten corrupted, or it was a different release, or something. But I'd rather be overly careful than have film come back totally wrong.

Chooser and Page Setup. On the Macintosh, I've always found it helpful to make sure I've got a LaserWriter driver selected in the Chooser, and that I've at least checked the Page Setup dialog box once before proceeding to the next step. You don't need to specify which printer you're using in the Page Setup dialog box if you're not sending PostScript dumps (the service bureau has to select theirs on their machine; the Chooser settings aren't carried with document files).

Look over your document. Take the extra time to carefully peruse your entire document. If you need to, zoom in to 200 percent and scroll over the page methodically. Also, look over the Usage dialog box to see what fonts and pictures you used. Many problems with printing occur not with the printing at all, but with that one extra word that slipped onto its own line, or the one image that was "temporarily" set to Suppress Printout and then was never switched back.

Print a proof. If you can print the document on a desktop laser printer, chances are the file will print at your service bureau. That's not a guarantee, but it's usually a pretty good bet. When you print this proof, go over it, too, with a fine-tooth comb. You might have missed something in the on-screen search. If you're printing color separations, try printing proofs of them, too. Are objects overprinting when you want them to knock out? Does the type look correct in separations?

Include your illustrations. If you have imported pictures into your document using Get Picture, you need to include the original files on the disk with your document. Remember that QuarkXPress only brings in a representation image for the screen, and then goes to look for the original at print time. You can use the Usage dialog box to see which graphic images you imported, whether they're set to Suppress Printout, and whether they are missing or present.

The idea is to send your service bureau a folder rather than just a file. Give them everything they could ever think of needing, just in case. The Collect for Output feature can really help this process along (see "Collect for Output," below).

▼ ▼

Tip: Check Your Compatibility. Fonts change, colors change, everything changes except change itself (if you've seen one cliché, you've seen them all). If you're working with a service bureau regularly, you'll want to make sure that their equipment and system setup are compatible with yours. One way of doing this is for you to use the same files. That is, copy every file off their disk onto yours. This is clearly tedious, probably illegal, and certainly never ending. You could perform periodic tests with a test sheet that includes the fonts you regularly use, a gray percentage bar, some grayscale images, and perhaps some line art (just for kicks). The idea is to see whether anything has changed much between your system and the service bureau's. If fonts come out differently, if the tints are off, or if the density is too light or too dark, you can either help them correct the problem or compensate for it yourself.

▾ ▾

Checklists for Sending QuarkXPress Files

I find checklists invaluable. Not only do they improve your method by encouraging you to do the appropriate task in the right order, they're satisfaction-guaranteed every time you can check an item off the list, which in itself is a boon to flagging spirits as a deadline looms. Below are examples of checklists I use before sending files to a service bureau.

FONTS

▶ What fonts did you use in your document?

▶ Does your service bureau have your screen fonts? (If not, send them.)

▶ Do they have your printer fonts? (If not, send them; some service bureaus may not take them because of the ongoing confusion over copyright and copying of fonts. If that's the case, you'll have to make a PostScript dump which includes your fonts.)

DOCUMENT CHECK

▶ Check for boxes and lines set to Suppress Printout.

▶ Check for text-box overflows.

▶ Check for missing or modified pictures in the Picture Usage dialog box.

▶ Check for widows, orphans, loose lines, bad hyphens, and other typographic problems. (Use Line Check if you have the TypeTricks XTension installed.)

PROOF

▶ Print a proof on a laser printer, preferably using LaserCheck or another imagesetter-on-a-laser-printer utility.

▶ Check it carefully to make sure it's what you want. If you're working with a client, have them look over the proofs and sign off on them.

RELEVANT FILES

▶ Did you include EPS and TIFF files?

▶ Did you include the document itself? (Don't laugh; sometimes this is the one thing people *do* forget after a long day.)

Collect for Output

To make the above process significantly easier for y'all, Quark has included a cool feature called Collect for Output. Selecting this command from the File menu copies your document and all the picture files necessary for its output to a folder of your choice—it doesn't move or remove the original files. It also creates a report containing detailed information about your document, including fonts and pictures you used, and trapping information. Then all you have to do is get the folder to your service bureau or color prepress house by modem, messenger, or carrier pigeon.

Using this command is simplicity itself. When you select it, it prompts you to find a folder, and asks you to specify a name for the report. I typically just use QuarkXPress's default name; it's simply the name of your document with "report" stuck on the end. Once you've selected a folder, QuarkXPress copies your document and all picture files, wherever they might reside, to that target folder. If you haven't saved your file before selecting Collect for Output, QuarkXPress asks you if you want to save first.

Note that to avoid potential copyright problems, QuarkXPress doesn't copy any fonts to the folder. That's up to you to do yourself, if necessary. The legal ramifications are between you, your service bureau, and your font vendor. I don't blame Quark for wanting to stay out of this one!

Collecting files for output often takes longer than manually copying each file, as QuarkXPress does a very thorough search for each file it needs. This may take a bit longer, but the process does give you the satisfaction of knowing you haven't forgotten to copy that little bitty logo illustration hidden at the bottom of page 32.

Also note that you may need lots of space on your hard drive to do this. I recently worked on a job in which the combined size of the document and all the pictures in it was over 200 MB. When I went to Collect for Output, not only did it take almost forever to do, but I ran out of hard-drive space halfway through the procedure. If you're working with big files like this, it may be easier and less painful for you to simply copy files yourself.

▼ ▼

Tip: Catching All the Fonts and Pictures. You can find out what fonts and pictures you used in the Font Usage and Picture Usage dialog boxes. Unfortunately, you can't print these lists out. However, all this information is in the report that QuarkXPress builds when you use Collect for Output. Better yet, XPress offers a checkbox called Report Only in the Collect for Output dialog box, which lets you get the report even if you don't have enough space on your hard drive (or time on your hands) to do a full Collect for Output.

After saving the report to disk, you can open it in a word processor or import it into a new QuarkXPress document and find the names of the fonts and the graphics (as well as a lot of other information).

▼ ▼

Tip: Formatting the Report. If you open the report that Collect for Output builds in a word processor, the first thing you'll notice is that it's full of weird codes. Those are XPress Tag codes (see Chapter 7, *Copy Flow*, for more information on XPress Tags) and they're included so that you can quickly format the report. In fact, QuarkXPress ships with a document called Output Request Template (it's in the Document folder, inside the QuarkXPress folder), which has style sheets pre-defined for this report. You can import the report from disk using Get Text, and each paragraph, including headings, is formatted for you.

▼ ▼

Sending a PostScript Dump

It's probably clear that I not only don't trust many service bureaus to do the right thing, but I also don't trust myself to always remember everything I need to while standing at the service bureau counter. Because of this, I like to use PostScript dumps. A PostScript dump (also known as a "print-to-disk"), when performed correctly, ensures that you get what you ask for, and is sometimes even preferred by low-maintenance service bureaus. Instead of having to open your file, make sure all the correct fonts are loaded, check all your settings, and then print it, they can simply download the PostScript file to their imagesetters.

The biggest difference is that with PostScript dumps you have the responsibility for making sure your file is perfect for printing. However, this isn't as difficult as it may seem. Let's go through the steps you need to go through to create the perfect PostScript dump. At the end I include a checklist that you can copy or re-create for your own use.

▼ ▼

Tip: Writing PostScript for Acrobat PDF Files. People are increasingly using Acrobat PDF files in their workflow, and the best way to create a PDF file is by processing a PostScript dump with Adobe Distiller. I discuss this process and why you might (or might not) want to use PDF files in Chapter 14, *Going Online with QuarkXPress*, but I should note here up front that almost everything I say about writing PostScript files to disk for print also applies to writing them to disk for the Distiller.

▼ ▼

System setup. Make sure you have enough memory on your disk to save the PostScript file. PostScript dumps are often large. To figure out how large a print-to-disk file will be, you can usually add up the size of all the pictures, add the size of the file itself, then tack on another 10 percent. If you've got a 30 MB image in your file, your PostScript dump has to include that, too (unless you're using an OPI system), and will be accordingly enormous.

Note that with the Macintosh LaserWriter 8 driver, you generally have to have twice as much space on your hard drive because the driver spools the information to disk first, then writes the PostScript file afterward. The file is spooled to your startup disk, while the PostScript dump can be to any volume, cartridge, floppy, etc. If you're using very large files, it may not be worth making PostScript dumps.

Fonts. You must have the screen font loaded for every font you use in your document. One way to check which fonts are in your document is with the Usage feature on the Utilities menu. If you don't have the screen font for a document, try to get it; without it, you run the risk of having your document print in Courier. In addition, all your line spacing will be messed up due to a difference in character widths. Note that this means you have to have the fonts loaded for typefaces used in EPS files, too.

Most people have both a screen font and an outline printer font on their machine so that the type looks smooth on screen. However, as long as the printer font is already in the printer—either in RAM or on the printer's hard disk—it's not necessary to have the printer font yourself when making a PostScript dump. Check with your service bureau to find out if your fonts are available on their printer. (Note that because QuarkXPress for Windows requires Adobe Type Manager to use Type 1 PostScript fonts, you pretty much need to have the outline fonts on your system.)

Pictures. The next step in making a PostScript dump is to check the Picture tab of the Usage dialog box to see if all the image files you used in your document are available. This is a suggested step but is not crucial, because if you don't do this, QuarkXPress checks for you at print time and then gives you the opportunity to find any missing image files (see Chapter 9, *Pictures*, for more information on this dialog box).

Print. The most common mistakes in creating PostScript dumps are made on the many tabs of the Print dialog box. Be careful with the buttons and menus here. If you want registration marks (along with trim marks and job information), you must turn them on here. If you want multiple copies (not likely, for high-resolution output), choose your value here. But if you only want one copy of each page, make sure that you specify "1" here! I've had friends who've gotten 10 copies back from their service bureau simply because they didn't check this carefully. Expensive mistake.

Be careful, too, with the tiling features. You may be printing to a roll-fed imagesetter that can handle a full tabloid-size page, and if you were printing tiled proof copies earlier, Manual or Auto tiling might have been left on. If you're making color separations, read over the section "Color Separations," earlier in this chapter.

Remember, if you don't set these controls correctly now, no one else can later.

Printing to Disk: Macintosh

After taking the above steps to ensure that you'll get a good PostScript file, the actual process of getting the PostScript saved to disk is determined by your operating system and printer driver. Let's take a look first at how to do it on a Macintosh.

Chooser setup. Because you're printing to a PostScript device, you need to have the LaserWriter driver selected in the Chooser. It doesn't matter whether you actually have a PostScript printer hooked up or not. (I've made PostScript dumps on my PowerBook while traveling on the road; I then compress the files and send them to my service bureau to be imageset.) Of course, if the device you're printing to requires a driver other than the standard LaserWriter driver, you'll have to have that loaded and selected in the Chooser.

Destination. Remember that whether you're outputting your file to a printer or to disk, QuarkXPress and the Macintosh's printer driver are doing the same thing: building a PostScript file and sending it somewhere. You get to choose where that file should be sent (to a printer or to disk) on the Destination popup menu, which appears in the Printer dialog box (click the Printer button in QuarkXPress's Print dialog box; see Figure 13-31).

When you select File as your destination, the Print button changes to Save. Then when you click that, the Macintosh gives you the option of where you want the file to go and what you want to name it. Remember that when you click Save again, XPress returns to the Print dialog box and waits for you to click Print. If this sounds like a really roundabout process just to get a file, it's only because it is; but once you get in the habit, it's not too annoying.

Figure 13-31
Sending PostScript to disk

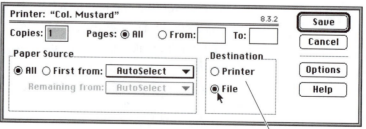

This same control appears as a popup menu in later versions of the LaserWriter printer driver.

File options. I hate to break it to you, but just when you thought the decision making was over, there are more options facing you. The Format, PostScript Level, Data Format, and Font Inclusion controls apply only to PostScript files that you print to disk. However, they appear in different places depending on the version of the LaserWriter printer driver (see Figure 13-32).

Figure 13-32

PostScript file options

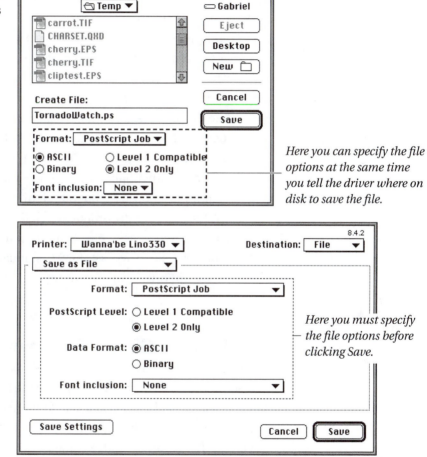

Here you can specify the file options at the same time you tell the driver where on disk to save the file.

Here you must specify the file options before clicking Save.

► **FORMAT.** The default option on the Format popup menu is PostScript Job, which is just fine. The other choices on the popup menu create EPS files, which isn't relevant to us because QuarkXPress can make its own EPS files better than the printer driver (see "Page as Picture" in Chapter 9, *Pictures*).

► **POSTSCRIPT LEVEL.** In general, a PostScript file that is Level 1 Compatible will print on any PostScript printer. However, if you're sure the file will be printed to a PostScript Level 2 printer, you can take advantage of a few little speed improvements by selecting Level 2 or 3 in the PostScript Level section.

▶ **DATA FORMAT.** You've got two choices in the Format section—Binary or ASCII—but the best choice is to ignore this entirely because it's always overwritten by QuarkXPress's own Data setting on the Options tab of the Print dialog box.

▶ **FONT INCLUSION.** The most important setting of the four is certainly Font Inclusion, which lets you control what fonts the driver will include in the PostScript file. As I said earlier, if the fonts you use are already resident in the printer (in RAM or on a hard drive attached to the printer), you don't have to include the outlines in your file. Fonts take up about 75 KB each. If you're sending the file by modem and you use a lot of fonts, you can save some time by setting Font Inclusion to None.

On the other hand, if you're not sure your service bureau has your fonts, choose All But Standard 13. This includes every font you used in your document except Courier, Helvetica, and Times (each in four styles), plus Symbol. You can be pretty sure these fonts will be okay, as they're standard on just about every PostScript printer in the world.

▼ ▼

Printing to Disk: Windows

I've heard it both ways: some people think the way Windows prints PostScript to disk is more confusing than the Macintosh method; others think it's easier and more intuitive. No matter what you think, it's certainly different. Basically, you don't tell QuarkXPress to write to disk; you tell the particular driver you're using to print to disk. And you can't do that from within XPress; you have to do it in the Printers folder (select Printers from the Settings popout menu, under the Start menu in Windows). What you do in the Printers folder depends on whether or not you already have a printer driver that matches the device you're printing to. If you don't have an appropriate printer driver, you have to add one. If you do have a driver, you can set its port to FILE. Let's look at each of these scenarios.

Adding a print-to-disk printer. Here's a quick step-by-step describing how to add a new printer type that always prints PostScript to disk.

1. Open your Printers folder and launch the Add Printer wizard (double-click on its icon in this folder).

2. The wizard asks you whether the printer is local or on the network. Choose Local, and click the Next button. (Of course, this doesn't happen if you're not connected to a network.)

3. The wizard asks what kind of printer it is. It's important to pick the proper printer—the one that the PostScript file will later be printed on—from this list, or else the driver and the PPD file will be incorrect and you'll get unexpected results (that's just a nice way to say that your document may not print). If the printer you're looking for doesn't appear on the list, you'll need to get the PPDs and installation files (the .INF files that the wizard is looking for) from somewhere. Printer manufacturers often have these available on their Web sites.

4. Next, the wizard asks you what port you want to use. This is the crucial step for making a print-to-disk "printer": Choose FILE from the list of ports (see Figure 13-33).

5. When the Add Printer wizard asks you to name the printer, I suggest giving the "printer" a descriptive name, such as "Lino330 PrintToDisk."

Figure 13-33
Adding a printer that
prints to disk

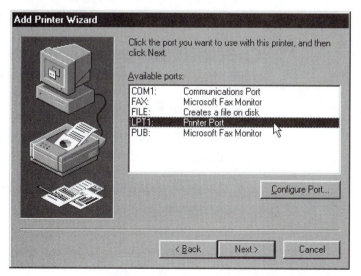

6. Finally, when the wizard asks you if you'd like to print a test page, politely decline.

Changing the Printer Port. If you already have a printer driver installed in your Printers folder, you can make it print to disk even more easily.

1. Select the printer driver in the Printers folder and choose Properties from the File menu.

2. Select the Details tab of the Properties dialog box.

3. Choose FILE from the popup menu labeled "Print to the following port." (You might note down what this popup menu is set to before you change it.)

4. Click OK.

That's it! When you print a document with this printer driver, the PostScript file will be directed to your hard drive instead of to the port. Of course, when you're finished printing to disk, you must change the port setting back to wherever the driver was pointing originally.

Printing to Disk. Once you've told your printer driver to print PostScript to disk, you can choose it from the Printer popup menu in the Print dialog box and proceed to choose other Print dialog-box settings as usual. As soon as you click Print, however, Windows displays a dialog box asking you where you want to save the file and what you want to name it. I suggest giving your PostScript file the extension ".ps" (if you don't specify anything, Windows automatically changes it to ".prn").

Checklist for Sending PostScript Dumps
Your service bureau will appreciate you for checking these items.

System and Font Setup

▶ Do you have enough memory on your disk to save the PostScript dump?

▶ Do you have the proper screen fonts loaded for the fonts that are in your document? EPS files?

▶ Have you disabled the printer fonts, so that they don't get included in the PostScript dump? (Or conversely, have you told the driver to include the fonts that you do want to send?)

Page Setup, Printer, and Properties

▶ Do you have the LaserWriter or other appropriate driver selected in the Chooser (Macintosh) or Printer popup menu (Windows)?

▶ Have you made necessary changes to the Page Setup and Printer dialog boxes (Macintosh) or Properties dialog box (Windows)?

Pictures

▶ Do you have all the EPS, TIFF, and other image files available? Check the Usage dialog box.

Print Dialog Box

▶ Have you made all the proper settings? Registration marks? Page range? Color separations? Do you need to specify Page Flip and Negative Print, or does your service bureau handle that with imagesetter-direct controls?

▶ Have you selected File in the Destination area of the Printer dialog box (Macintosh) or specified a FILE: printer on the Printer popup menu (Windows)?

Sending the File

▶ Do you want to compress or segment the file once it's on disk?

▶ Rename the file to something appropriate.

▶ Make sure that your service bureau has the same kind of removable media or tapes that you're going to send.

▼ ▼

Troubleshooting

After all of this, printing should be a breeze, right? Well, I wish it were. Too often, I get phone calls from my service bureau saying, "Your job wouldn't print." Back in the good old days, a service bureau would offer to fix it for you. Now life has gotten busy for them, and they usually expect you to do the fixing. Here are some tips that I've found, over the years, to work.

Graphics Look Awful

One of the most common problems with print jobs from QuarkXPress has never had anything to do with QuarkXPress itself. The problem is with the person sending their files. Remember that QuarkXPress does not actually embed any EPS or TIFF files that you have imported. It only brings in a low-resolution representation of the screen image, and maintains a link with the original file. If that file changes or is missing when QuarkXPress tries to print it, the graphic will look different from what you expected.

Two notes to write on your forehead follow.

▶ If you're going to send your QuarkXPress document, then send a folder, not a file. The folder should include the document, all EPS, DCS, and TIFF images you used, and possibly the fonts, too. You might want to use the Collect for Output feature that I discussed earlier in this chapter.

▶ PostScript print-to-disk files (PS dumps) contain the TIFF and EPS files, as well as all the information QuarkXPress needs from the preferences file, and fonts, and so on.

Because QuarkXPress downsamples TIFF images to two times the halftone screen frequency, sometimes you can get strange mottling or jaggy images, especially if you've scaled down an image considerably (see "Picture Output," earlier in this chapter).

Memory Problems

QuarkXPress has gotten a bad rep in the past for causing PostScript errors at print time. Almost all these errors are the result of printer-memory problems (called VMerror), and almost all of them can be avoided with a few tricks.

Reset the printer. My favorite technique for avoiding memory problems is simply to turn the printer off, wait a few seconds, and turn it back on again. This flushes out any extraneous fonts or PostScript functions that are hogging memory. It's sort of like waking up after a good night's sleep, but different.

Use minimum settings. Using the minimum settings means turning off all the printer options in the Page Setup dialog box on the Macintosh, including the LaserWriter Options "second page" dialog box.

Rotate your own graphics. If you've scanned in big bitmapped graphics, and need to rotate them, you should use Photoshop or another image-manipulation program rather than doing it in QuarkXPress. Rotating large bitmapped images in QuarkXPress may or may not choke the printer, but it certainly slows it down a lot—an important point if you're paying a per-minute surcharge at a service bureau. (Note that I'm not talking about object-oriented pictures here, such as those from Illustrator or FreeHand.)

Take care in selecting your fonts. If you play with a lot of different fonts trying to find one you like, you may inadvertently leave remnants of old fonts lying around. For example, a space character may be set to some font that you don't use anywhere else. Nonetheless, QuarkXPress must download that font along with every other font you use. This takes up memory that could be used for something else. Try using the Usage dialog box to see which fonts are sitting around in your document. Then purge the ones you don't need.

Use Unlimited Downloadable Fonts. If you must have many fonts on a page and your printer is running out of RAM, you might want to enable the Unlimited Downloadable Fonts feature in the Page Setup dialog box (this is Macintosh-only). See the section on this earlier in the chapter before you use it, though, as there are some serious drawbacks to it.

Print fewer pages at a time. I have successfully coached long documents out of an imagesetter by printing two to 10 pages at a time, rather than all 500 pages at once. This is obviously a hassle, but it's better than not getting the job printed at all. Much of the work can be done early by creating multiple PostScript dumps, then queuing them up on a spooler at the service bureau.

Remove enormous graphics. One of the great promises of desktop publishing was that I could print an entire page with every graphic and text block perfectly placed. Remember that promises are often broken. Case in point: large graphics (and even small graphics) sometimes choke the printer. These graphics often print all by themselves, but when placed on a page they become the chicken bone that killed the giant. Yes, using every trick possible, you might get the page out, but is it worth the time? Perhaps it's more efficient to let your printer or stripper handle that graphic. Or, god forbid, hot-wax that puppy and paste it down yourself.

Make sure you're current. Someone recently called and asked me why her file wouldn't print (this question is, by the way, almost impossible for anyone to answer over the telephone). I suggested a few things, and then asked what version of QuarkXPress she was using. It turned out she was using an older version of the program, and as soon as she updated, the printing problem went away. This is not uncommon. They don't talk about it much, but the engineers at Quark are constantly trying to make their program print better. For instance, QuarkXPress 4.0 was a disaster in some respects, but Quark quickly released free patches for 4.01 and then 4.02, which fixed most of the really egregious printing errors.

What's amazing to me is that there are people who say, "QuarkXPress has a lot of trouble printing," but when pressed they admit that they only heard that someone else had trouble with XPress 4.0 when it first came out. Those first impressions sure do die hard.

PostScript Problems

There are some PostScript problems that aren't memory-related, even though just about everyone at Quark will tell you they don't exist. One is the infamous *stackunderflow* error. Another is the *undefined* command error. These are significantly harder to track down and fix. However, here are a few things you can try.

Save As. Logically, resaving your document under a different name doesn't make any sense, but it does work sometimes.

Selective printing. You can try to pinpoint what page element is causing the error by printing only certain parts of the page. For example, select Rough in the Print dialog box to avoid printing any pictures or complex frames. If the page prints, chances are that one of the graphic images is at fault. You can also use Suppress Printout to keep a single image from printing.

If the page still doesn't print after you print a rough copy, try taking out a text box at a time, or changing the fonts you used. If you are printing color separations, try printing a single plate at a time.

Re-import. If the problem turns out to be a graphic you've imported, you might try re-importing it. If the image is a PICT, you might have better luck using Get Picture than Paste. Even better, convert the PICT into a TIFF (for bitmaps) or EPS (for object-oriented graphics) file. Then re-import it.

Check printer type. Make sure you have the correct printer type selected on the Setup tab of the Print dialog box. Picking the wrong PPD is the single most common problem people have when printing.

Big Ugly White Gaps Appear Between Colors

You've output your four-color separations and sent the file off to your lithographer. A few days later you show up for the press check and you see, much to your surprise, big ugly white gaps appearing between each of the colors. What happened? You forgot about traps. It's easy to do, believe me. The remedy? Go read the section on trapping in Chapter 12, *Color,* and redo your negatives.

Wrong Screen Frequency

QuarkXPress can neither read your mind nor the mind of your lithographer. If you print your file out with the default halftone-screen frequency setting of 60 lpi, that's just what you'll get. This is coarse, but fine if you're just going to photocopy your page. However, it looks pretty awful compared to the 120 or 133 lpi (or higher) used in most print jobs. Check with your lithographer for what screen frequency to use, then check your Page Setup dialog box before you print your job. Note that this is usually not something that your service bureau can change if you provide a PostScript dump.

Not Enough Space Between Pages

If your pages are printing too closely together from a roll-fed imagesetter, you may have to adjust the Page Gap value in the Page Setup dialog box. Note that QuarkXPress prints your document only as wide as it needs to. For example, if your page is 4 by 4 inches, QuarkXPress tells the imagesetter to print only 4 inches of film. This is a great savings for film or RC paper, but sometimes it's a hassle to handle the output. It's worth talking to your service bureau before you set the gap value; with some setups you actually need to ask them to adjust settings using a utility designed for their device, instead of worrying about it yourself.

Document Settings

If you use custom kerning or tracking tables, hyphenation exceptions, or custom frames, QuarkXPress will bark at your service bureau as soon as they open your file. "The preferences are different," XPress says, and asks if you want to use the document's preferences or just the ones in the current copy of the program. The appropriate answer is almost always "Document Preferences." If your service bureau tells XPress to use XPress Preferences instead, then your painstaking work may be screwed up and your page won't print as it's supposed to.

One problem: in version 3.x, the keystroke for Keep Document Settings was Command-period or Esc. In version 4, this same keystroke "clicks" Use XPress Preferences instead. Oops.

Fonts Come Out Wrong

Don't forget that you have to have the screen and printer fonts loaded for every font in the document when you print. "Every font" means the fonts you selected, those that were imported, and those that are stuck somewhere in an EPS document. Also, watch out for EPS files nested inside of EPS files nested inside of EPS files. Depending on which application created each EPS file, QuarkXPress may or may not be able to dig deep enough to find every font you used.

Registration Problems

Imagine the Rockettes, kicking their legs to chorus-line stardom in perfect synchronization. Then imagine the woman at one end having no sense of rhythm, kicking totally out of sync with the others. This is what happens when one color plate is misregistered to the others. When a sheet of paper is rushed through a printing press and four colors are speedily applied to it, there's bound to be some misregistration—sometimes up to 1 or 2 points. However, you can help matters considerably by making sure that your film is as consistent as possible.

Whenever I am told that a job printed great "except for one plate that was off-register," I immediately ask if that plate was run at a different time than the others. The answer is almost always yes. I realize it's expensive and time-consuming to print four new plates every time you want to make a change to a page, but it is a fact of desktop life that you can almost never get proper registration when you reprint a single plate. One service bureau I know of also had this problem when they ran two or three plates at the end of a roll of film, and the rest of the job at the start of the next roll. Why? The weather, roll stretch, alignment of the stars . . . all sorts of reasons contribute to this massive hassle.

Output devices that use cut sheets of film (drum imagesetters) often have better luck matching film imaged at different times than roll-fed or capstan-mechanism imagesetters, because the factor of roll stretch is eliminated, and the film is often registered with pins rather than rubber rollers.

"Job Finished"

As I said way back at the beginning of the book, don't give up until you get it to work. If you run into difficulty, there is almost always a workaround. Working through to that solution almost always teaches a valuable lesson (as Grandma used to say, "It builds character."). However, remember that the solution is sometimes to just print the job in pieces and strip them together traditionally. It feels awful when you have to clean off your drafting table and dust off your waxer, but efficiency is often the name of the game.

And when the last page comes out of the imagesetter, don't forget to thank your computer, QuarkXPress, the service bureau, and yourself for a job well done.

14

GOING ONLINE WITH QUARKXPRESS

ive years ago, just when we all thought the desktop publishing revolution was over, people started talking about the World Wide Web. The Web sparked a new publishing revolution—one in which no trees would be cut down, no books would be inventoried in a warehouse, and anybody with a connection to the Internet would be able to be published.

Of course, there are limitations to publishing on the Web (and to multimedia in general).

▶ Few people want to read a lot of text on screen.

▶ You can't take a computer with you when you want to read in the bathtub.

▶ Availability of electricity, much less good connection to the Internet, is limited around the world.

▶ It's difficult to protect the copyright of your work because it's so easy to copy the digital files of anything published on the Web.

Nonetheless, people have been clamoring to build Web pages for the past several years, and there's no reason to think this trend will stop. And because there are more than a million people around the world who already publish with QuarkXPress, the question has inevitably arisen: How can I get content out of XPress and onto other people's screens?

The Web versus Multimedia. Most of what I'm talking about in this chapter revolves around publishing for the World Wide Web. However, anything you can put on the Web can be put on a CD-ROM or a kiosk or a disk. The differences are primarily distribution (how many people will be able to access your work?) and file size (large sounds and movies are usually inappropriate for the Web). So, when I talk about getting stuff online, don't think I'm just talking about the Internet.

There are three primary methods of putting interactive XPress pages onto the Web: HTML, Acrobat, and QuarkImmedia. Each of these has its limitations and strengths, and you might find yourself using different methods for different situations (I discuss each of them fully in this chapter). There's one thing that they all have in common, though: they all require a radically different approach to laying out pages and presenting material than print-based publications do. You can't just plop a for-print brochure into one of these formats and call it quits. As I've said before, *how* to design is outside the purview of this book, but what you can and cannot achieve with each method is essential to making the switch to online publishing.

▼ ▼

Tip: Getting Online. There are more than a thousand Internet books on the market, so I'm just going to defer to them to cover many of the basics—like how to get an Internet account, use a Web browser, build a Web page from scratch, place your Web pages on a Web server so that people can see them, optimize your graphics for the Web, and so on. Instead, this chapter will focus almost entirely on getting your XPress pages into an interactive screen-ready form. If you need additional information, I recommend Adam Engst's *The Internet Starter Kit*, Lynda Weinman's *Designing Web Graphics 2.*

▼ ▼

HTML and Web Browsers

Almost everyone who "surfs" the Web is looking at pages built with HTML (hypertext markup language). HTML is like QuarkXPress's XPress

Tags language (see Chapter 7, *Copy Flow*); it's code-based (formatting is handled using special codes like <B> and </B> in the text) and it's generally linear—it describes the first paragraph, then the second paragraph, and so on (see Figure 14-1).

Originally, HTML was based on the idea that the viewer, rather than the publisher of the information, should determine the look of the page. In this model, you just add codes specifying where the headings are, what words should be emphasized, and so on; then your audience configures their browsers to display your headings and emphasized words in certain ways. One person will see headings in Helvetica, another person sees them in Times Roman. Over the past few years, however, HTML has grown to include additional formatting that lets you—the author/publisher—control how you want the page to look.

In order to view an HTML file properly, you need a Web browser—basically just a program that interprets the HTML codes ("make this <I>italic</I>") into WYSIWYG text ("make this *italic*"). The two primary Web browsers are Microsoft's Internet Explorer and Netscape's Navigator (or Communicator suite).

It turns out that HTML has some severe design limitations.

▶ Text and pictures cannot overlap (this is slowly changing with the advent of Dynamic HTML, though few browsers currently support it).

▶ It's hard to place an object exactly where you want it on your page.

▶ Different Web browsers interpret the codes differently, so line spacing, fonts, font sizes, column widths, and indents (and more!) may be completely different from what you expect. While it's not hopelessly impossible to control typography on the Web, it does take some work.

▶ Color consistency is impossible, so what you see on one screen may be quite different from what you see on another.

There are a host of other problems, too, but given a proper understanding of the limitations, you can begin to gain mastery over the medium. The key is to remember that you just can't design and produce pages the way you've become accustomed to over the years.

While people have been writing HTML code by hand for years, the trend is increasingly toward using WYSIWYG editors that write the HTML

Figure 14-1

HTML pages

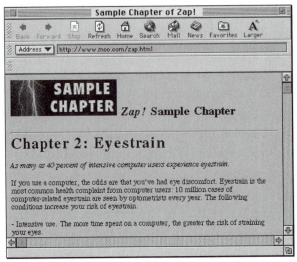

A basic HTML page viewed in a Web browser

A slightly more complicated HTML page

```
<TABLE border=0 WIDTH=475 cellpadding=3 cellspacing=3>
<tr><TD WIDTH=315 valign=top align=left>
<h2>Sample Chapter</h2><P>
<I>Zap!</I>'s chapter on eyestrain is one of two chapters
specifically on the topic of eyes and computer use.
Additional chapters in  <I>Zap!</I> relating to this sub-
ject include <b>Monitors</b>, <b>Lighting</b>, and
<b>Finding a Doctor</b>, among others.<P> You can read
```

The HTML source code for the page above. Note the similarity to XPress Tags.

for you, such as Symantec's Visual Page, Macromedia's Dreamweaver, Claris's Home Page, or Adobe's PageMill. (This is exactly what happened back in the mid 1980s when people switched from writing PostScript code by hand to using programs like PageMaker.)

There are several XTensions that let you produce HTML directly from QuarkXPress. Two of them—BeyondPress and HexWeb—are powerful tools that give you a lot of control over how your page is converted. The others—CyberPress and HTML Export—are less powerful, but still very useful if you're not in the practice of building HTML pages everyday.

Industrial-Strength HTML Tools

The two industrial-strength HTML-export XTensions on the market are BeyondPress and HexWeb. Each one costs hundreds of dollars, each is available on both Macintosh and Windows, and each is worth its hefty price if you use XPress and you're building HTML pages daily. I'll describe them both here, but I can't provide every feature detail, so I encourage you to check out each developer's Web site for more information (you can jump to their pages quickly from The QuarkXPress Book Web Site: *www.peachpit.com/blatner*). Extensis's BeyondPress has two modes: Conversion and Authoring. When you have an already existing document that you need to repurpose for the Web, use Conversion mode. In this case, BeyondPress lays out all the document elements (text stories, pictures, and so on) on a palette, then lets you rearrange them, format them, and add special HTML features like horizontal rules, horizontal alignment, and so on (see Figure 14-2). When you're ready to see your document in HTML form, you can export it or preview it with the help of any Web browser.

Here are a few more of BeyondPress's powerful abilities.

▶ You can specify which style sheets in your documents will convert into which HTML style sheets.

▶ Links to other Web pages or to anchors on your page are easy to add with the Link tools.

▶ You can add dynamic media, such as Java applets, QuickTime movies, animated GIFs, Shockwave files, and so on (BeyondPress even lets you run QuickTime and animated GIFs directly in QuarkXPress).

Figure 14-2
BeyondPress

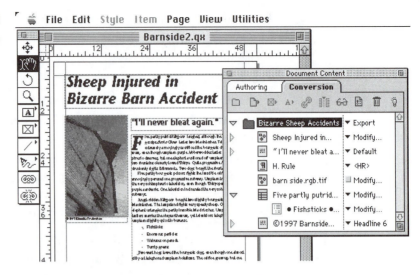

▶ BeyondPress can convert tab-separated tables into proper HTML tables in a snap.

▶ BeyondPress can convert text boxes into pictures (either GIF or JPEG). For instance, if you really want to maintain the font or style of a headline, you can convert it into a picture (see Figure 14-3).

▶ You can convert any image into a GIF or JPEG, build image maps, and even adjust GIF transparency.

Figure 14-3

Text into pictures

The original headline, in XPress

In HTML, the headline loses its effect.

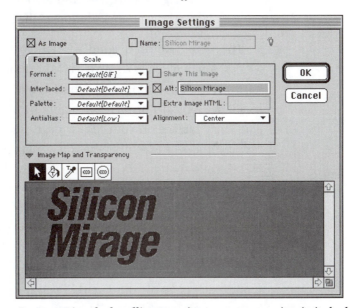

By converting the headline to a picture, you can maintain its look and feel.

▶ Because BeyondPress is scriptable (on the Macintosh), you can automate your HTML conversions with a script. If you're converting a daily or weekly publication, you'll want to investigate scripting. (BeyondPress is also extensible, so XTension developers can extend its functionality. For example, KyTek has developed a version of their popular AutoPage XTension that uses BeyondPress to automatically and intelligently convert documents into HTML.)

▶ BeyondPress includes a unique feature that displays the estimated download times for your page at various connection speeds. For instance, it can tell you if your page will take 10 seconds to download on a 14.4 Kbps modem, but only a second over ISDN.

▶ Of course, you can specify a background color or pattern for your HTML page, set up headers and footers, and control the way that tables or images appear either globally or on a case-by-case basis.

The second side of BeyondPress lets you author HTML pages within XPress, much like a WYSIWYG HTML editor. Where Conversion mode lets you repurpose information that is already laid out in XPress and present it in a typical, linear HTML manner, Authoring mode lets you replicate what you see on your XPress page. In Authoring mode, you place text and graphics exactly where you want them, and BeyondPress writes HTML code that gives you almost exactly the same look in your Web browser (see Figure 14-4).

BeyondPress performs this somewhat magical feat by creating an invisible table. Each text block or picture on your page goes into one cell of this table (the only time you need to think about this table is if you want to later edit the HTML that BeyondPress writes). In Authoring mode, each page of your QuarkXPress document becomes a different Web page on your site, and you can export them at the same time or individually.

Note that even BeyondPress cannot break the laws of HTML. If you overlap two objects on your page, BeyondPress can't overlap them. Nor can BeyondPress reproduce kerning or horizontal scaling or many other special typographic effects (because HTML just doesn't do that sort of thing).

Granted, if you only want a WYSIWYG HTML editor, you can certainly go a less expensive route than buying both XPress *and* BeyondPress. But

Figure 14-4

Authoring HTML
in BeyondPress

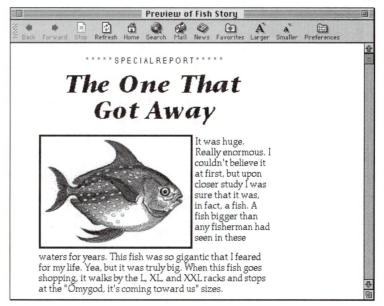

given that you already know how to use XPress, the combination of XPress's strong layout and typographic features with the BeyondPress XTension certainly makes the Web page-building process easy.

▼ ▼

Tip: BeyondExpress. There's no way I can cover all the ins and outs of getting XPress pages into HTML here in this little chapter. Fortunately, there are other sources available to you. You can find one such source on the Internet at *www.beyondexpress.com*. Here, Kip Shaw continues to provide tips, tricks, and techniques for Web conversion, especially if you're working with Extensis's BeyondPress XTension.

▼ ▼

HexWeb. The second robust HTML-export XTension for XPress is HexWeb (from European developer HexMac). HexWeb is favored by many magazine and newspaper publishers because of its strong site management tools. HexWeb has a simple method for building a direc-tory (folder) structure in which it places each of the exported HTML and image files. If you're trying to knock out a hundred Web pages a day based on the newspaper you've built in QuarkXPress, letting the program deal with details like where to put the files can be a godsend.

HexWeb has a very different interface and method of exporting HTML than BeyondPress does, which turns out to be particularly useful for documents that have multiple sections and multiple issues. For instance, you can specify that this Web page is part of the Sports section, and HexWeb will automatically place the appropriate Sports section headers and footers on the document (see Figure 14-5).

Of course, HexWeb lets you build links, convert pictures to GIF or JPEG, and insert dynamic graphics, as you'd expect. But HexWeb also has some unique features.

Figure 14-5
HexWeb

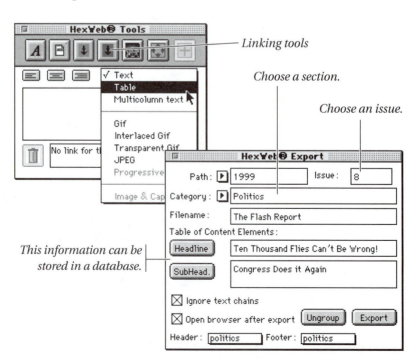

► It can automatically replace a drop cap with a drop-cap graphic (you have to manually build an alphabet of drop-cap graphics first).

► You can specify that a picture and a text box are a picture/caption group so that they'll stick together on the HTML page.

► The separate IndexPro application can search through your publication's various sections and issues and automatically create an index for you. It can then build this index in various forms, including one using HTML frames (see Figure 14-6) or Java popups. This feature alone is worth the cost of HexWeb.

HexWeb does not include tools for replicating what you see on screen in HTML, so it's really more of an export tool than an authoring tool. Also, it has one particularly odd feature: because there is no content list that specifies the order of XPress page elements (as in BeyondPress),

Figure 14-6

Making an index with HexWeb's IndexPro

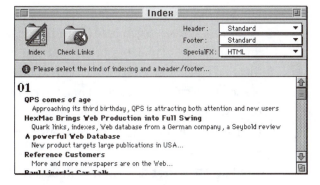

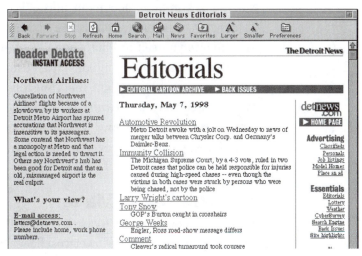

every time you want to export HTML, you have to use the Item tool and Shift-click on each page item in the order you want it to appear in the HTML. In an environment where there are just a few items per page (headline, subhead, picture, and body text, for example) this isn't so bad. But my patience wears thin when I try to remember the clicking order of a complex page if I need to export it more than once.

▼ ▼

Tip: Cascading Style Sheets and TrueDoc Fonts. As more and more Web pages are built by designers instead of scientists, typography on the Web has become increasingly important. Two of the coolest typographic features in HTML are Cascading Style Sheets (CSS) and TrueDoc.

Cascading Style Sheets contain information like indents (including first-line indents), line spacing, font, color, and size. TrueDoc can describe font outlines in such a way that your audience doesn't have to have the font in order to see it. The font file (otherwise known as a .prf file) is stored on your Web server and gets downloaded by your Web browser automatically as needed, in the same way that it downloads a graphic. But the text isn't a graphic; it's text, in the font you choose.

BeyondPress can generate Cascading Style Sheets and TrueDoc fonts for you (HexMac makes a utility that can do TrueDoc, too). However, there's a catch: currently, while both Microsoft's Internet Explorer and Netscape's Navigator (version 4 or later) can read Cascading Style Sheets, only Navigator can read TrueDoc descriptions (Microsoft is using a different font solution, which these XTensions don't support).

▼ ▼

Tip: Use TIFFs, not EPS Files. Both BeyondPress and HexWeb can convert images in your document into GIF or JPEG files automatically. (Though to be painfully honest, you'll often get a better result if you convert images yourself in Photoshop.) Note, however, that BeyondPress and HexWeb can really only convert TIFF images; because EPS graphics contain "encapsulated" data, the XTensions can't really get in and convert them, so you end up with GIF or JPEG versions of the low-resolution screen previews you see in XPress. Therefore, if you're going to repurpose your XPress pages, you may want to stick with TIFF files.

▼ ▼

Just the Facts, Ma'am

If you're only occasionally trying to extract HTML from XPress pages, you might be better off using a lower-cost XTension such as HTML Export or

CyberPress. Both of these are Macintosh-only XTensions, though there may be some Windows XTensions by the time you read this. No one really expects you to export perfect, ready-to-serve Web pages with these XTensions. They are just good ways to get content out of XPress and into some other standalone HTML editor for final tweaking.

HTML Export is available as shareware (if you use it beyond just testing, you're honor-bound to send $30 to Eric Knudstrup, the developer), and is very limited: it only exports text. When it's installed, you can export HTML much as you would a Word or XPress Tags file: select a text box (or a text box in a series of linked boxes) and choose Save Text from the File menu (see Figure 14-7). HTML Export is handy for the occasional export because it handles all the ASCII and HTML codes for basic headings, text formatting, unordered lists, and some special characters.

Figure 14-7
HTML Export filter

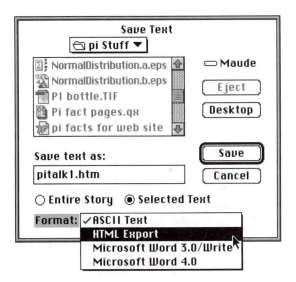

As this book goes to press, rumor has it that Extensis is going to discontinue CyberPress. Too bad. It currently costs around $100, but gives you much of the basic functionality of BeyondPress. In fact, if the products look vaguely similar, it's only because they are—CyberPress is a stripped-down version of BeyondPress, perfect for people who need to get pages out of XPress but don't need all the power the more expensive product affords them. For instance, CyberPress exports both text and pictures (converting images to GIF or JPEG automatically), builds tables automatically, and lets you add links (to URLs and anchors within the document), horizontal rules, and custom background or text colors. It does not do much more than that; so again, you will probably need an HTML editor to finalize your pages (fortunately, Adobe's PageMill ships with this product).

XPress Page as Picture

Trying to replicate in HTML what you see on your XPress page is tricky (BeyondPress can often do it, as long as you don't use non-HTML kosher design, like overlapping objects). However, I find that I've often got an element of an XPress page that I want to duplicate exactly on the Web (like a logo built in XPress, or a particularly well-designed headline). One of my favorite methods of converting QuarkXPress pages into a form that Web browsers can understand is one of the simplest and yet least used: simply to transform the whole page—text, pictures, and all—into a single picture (see Figure 14-8).

1. Reduce the size of your document so that it's just bigger than the objects on the page (select Document Setup from the File menu).

Figure 14-8

Converting pages to pictures

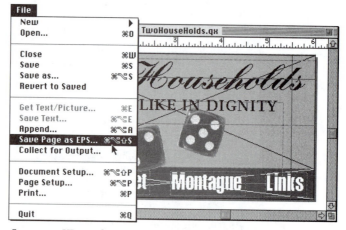

Save your XPress document as an EPS file...

... and open it in Photoshop.

Figure 14-8
(continued)

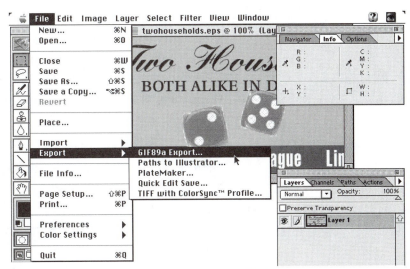

Export the rasterized Photoshop image as a GIF file . . .

. . . and place it in your HTML Web document.

You may want to copy the page items to a new document before doing this.

2. Save the QuarkXPress page as an EPS (select Save as EPS from the File menu; see "Page as Picture" in Chapter 9, *Pictures*). Note that there are XTensions available that let you save just a portion of your XPress page as an EPS; if you have one of these, you can skip the first step and just save the area you're interested in using the XTension.

3. Open this EPS file in Photoshop. (Note that versions of Photoshop earlier than 4 can't open XPress EPS files reliably.) When

Photoshop displays the Open Generic EPS dialog box, you should probably choose a resolution of 72 ppi and the RGB color mode. The size of the page/image is up to you (I usually just leave it the same size). Turning on the Anti-aliased option typically provides a better-looking result, though your final image size may be slightly larger.

4. Once the image is rasterized (turned into a bitmapped image) in Photoshop, you can crop it and export it as a GIF89a file or save it as a JPEG image, depending on the content of the page. Typically, the JPEG format is better for natural, scanned images, while GIF is good for images with solid colors. (If you don't know how to save in these two file formats or why you'd want to, check out one of the many other books on the market that discuss Web graphic file formats, including another book I coauthored, *Real World Photoshop*).

5. You can place this file on the Web as is, but it won't be interactive in any way. However, you can easily add links to the page by inserting this graphic in a separate HTML editing program (I use Symantec's Visual Page on the Macintosh, but you can use something else) and giving the page/picture an image map (see Figure 14-9). You can then save this image as an HTML file, and the program will write the appropriate image-map codes for you.

By turning your XPress page into a bitmapped graphic, you make sure your audience will see everything that you see on your page—including fonts, lines, and page geometry. But there are a number of problems with this technique.

▶ If you're not careful, you can end up with a very large graphic that will take so long to download that no one will bother.

▶ Small text sizes are unreadable when rasterized at such low resolution, even if they're anti-aliased.

▶ Your audience cannot zoom in or out, change the fonts, or even print the page very well (what they see on screen is exactly what they'll get on paper).

Nonetheless, if you're trying to re-create a masthead that you've built in XPress, or even just a simple page without a lot of text or graphics on

Figure 14-9

Adding an image
map to a graphic in
Symantec VisualPage

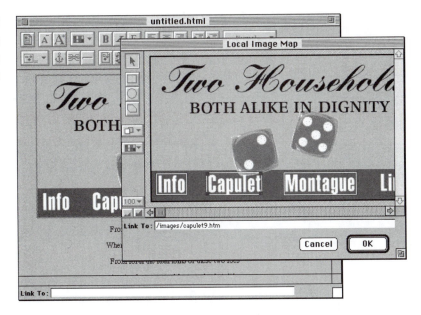

it, this technique can work surprisingly well (I've made full-page pictures like this that are only 20 K in size).

▼ ▼

Tip: Maintaining XPress Colors. Often when you open an XPress EPS file in Photoshop, you'll notice a significant color shift. This shift occurs because QuarkXPress describes color in its EPS files as CMYK, and Adobe Photoshop has a different idea of how cyan, magenta, yellow, and black look than XPress does. For example, 100-percent magenta looks much brighter in XPress than in Photoshop. However, you can change this by changing how Photoshop thinks about CMYK colors.

1. Make seven boxes in XPress (it doesn't matter what kind of boxes), and color them red, green, blue, cyan, magenta, yellow, and black. Make sure the boxes are small enough so that you can see them all on the screen at the same time.

2. Take a screen shot of these colored boxes and save it to disk. (On the Macintosh, you can capture the screen by pressing Command-Shift-3; the file is automatically saved with a name such as "Picture0" on your startup disk. In Windows, you can capture the screen by pressing the Print Screen button, which copies the screen on to the Clipboard—then you can paste it into Photoshop or another image-editing program.) If you find yourself taking a lot of screen shots, you might want to invest in a pro-

gram that specializes in this. For instance, I use SnapShot or Exposure Pro on the Macintosh (both from Beale Street Software) and SnagIt32 on my Windows machine.

3. Open the screen capture file in Photoshop. It should open in RGB mode automatically, because screens always display in RGB.
4. Select Printing Inks Setup from the Color Settings submenu (under the File menu) and move it out of the way so that you can see both the colored boxes and the Printing Inks Setup dialog box.
5. Choose Custom from the Printing Inks popup menu. When the Printing Inks dialog box appears, move it, too, out of the way of the colored boxes.
6. Finally, click on the first swatch in the Ink Colors dialog box (which should be colored cyan) and use the Eyedropper tool to click on the corresponding colored box in the XPress screen shot (see Figure 14-10). Repeat this procedure for each of the swatches in the Printing Inks dialog box. Note that this procedure only works when the Photoshop Color Picker is selected in Photoshop's General Preferences dialog box (it is, unless you changed it).

Figure 14-10
Matching color between Photoshop 4 and XPress

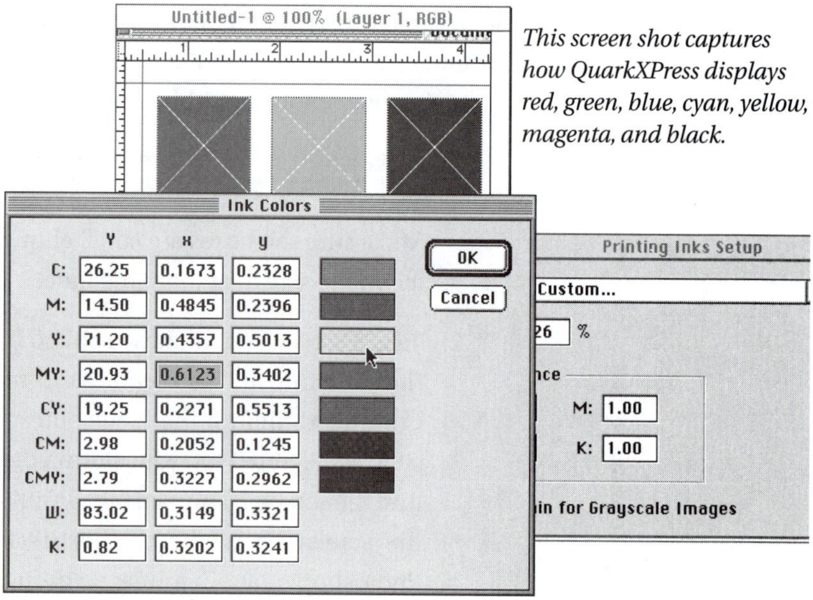
Untitled-1 @ 100% (Layer 1, RGB)
Ink Colors
Y
x
y
C: 26.25 0.1673 0.2328
M: 14.50 0.4845 0.2396
Y: 71.20 0.4357 0.5013
MY: 20.93 0.6123 0.3402
CY: 19.25 0.2271 0.5513
CM: 2.98 0.2052 0.1245
CMY: 2.79 0.3227 0.2962
W: 83.02 0.3149 0.3321
K: 0.82 0.3202 0.3241
OK
Cancel
Printing Inks Setup
Custom...
%
M: 1.00
K: 1.00
in for Grayscale Images

This screen shot captures how QuarkXPress displays red, green, blue, cyan, yellow, magenta, and black.

Photoshop 4 lets you specify how cyan, yellow, magenta, and black (and combinations of these colors) will appear on screen.

7. When you're finished with the swatches, press OK, and save this new Printing Inks setup to disk (you may need it again someday).

By changing the Printing Inks settings, you've changed the way Photoshop understands CMYK colors. Now when you open an XPress EPS file in Photoshop, you'll see colors just the same as you did in XPress. Remember to change the Printing Inks Setup dialog box back to SWOP (or whatever ink setup you were using) before trying to do for-print work again, or else Photoshop will act very oddly (especially when separating RGB into CMYK).

▼ ▼

Tip: Web-Safe Colors in XPress. Because this chapter focuses on getting what you see in XPress onto the Internet, I'd better disclose an ugly truth about most of the Internet-viewing public: most of them only have 8-bit video cards. That means that their computer screens will only display 256 colors at any one time. The trouble is, you don't always know which 256 colors they'll display, and if you try to display a color that isn't

Figure 14-11
Dithering non–Web safe colors

Continuous tone image appears like this on a 24-bit color screen.

The same image dithers on an 8-bit color monitor.

among the 256, their computers will dither other colors in order to simulate the one you asked for (see Figure 14-11).

The news gets worse: it turns out that there are only 216 Web-safe colors that almost always appear nondithered on both Macintosh and Windows machines (that's because the 256 colors are different on Mac and Windows).

Okay, so if you've got a page in QuarkXPress that you know is destined for the Internet, how do you choose one of these Web-safe colors? You need to somehow add Web-safe colors to your color list in XPress. Here's my favorite method.

1. Pick an RGB color in the Edit Color dialog box (see Chapter 12, *Color* for more on specifying colors).

2. Change the percentage values in each of the Red, Green, and Blue fields to the nearest 20-percent mark—0, 20, 40, 60, 80, or 100 percent. For instance, if the Red field reads 24 percent, change it to 20 percent. If the Blue field reads 71 percent, change it to 80 percent.

3. Save the color (you might include "Web safe" in its name to remind you).

That's all there is to it.

Adobe Acrobat

The idea of a paperless office has long been a sort of Shangri-La, where no one would have to be burdened with paper cuts and filing cabinets. Instead, all documents would be electronic, easily read on any computer platform, easily stored on disk or somewhere on the Internet. Adobe has done its part in bringing us closer to this utopia with its Acrobat format, which lets you build and edit Portable Document Format (PDF) files from almost any program. These PDF files, in turn, can be viewed on any computer that has a reader program (which is free and available on Macintosh, Windows, DOS, and Unix systems).

Acrobat is extremely flexible, and while it was originally designed for archiving or viewing documents that were meant for paper output, it has grown to incorporate features that are suitable for Web or multimedia publishing (see Figure 14-12).

▶ Anything you can design on screen or print out can be displayed in an Acrobat PDF (so the limitations of HTML are gone).

▶ You can zoom in and out on a page.

▶ You can print pages; fonts and graphics are crisp at any resolution.

▶ If the document is larger than the screen, you can scroll around using a grabber hand or the scrollbars.

▶ Acrobat has a Search feature that lets you find words or phrases in a PDF file.

▶ You can add bookmarks, links (to URLs, to other PDF files, or to other places within a PDF file), notes, and multimedia items such as QuickTime movies.

▶ Text blocks in the document can be copied and pasted (you can specify security settings to allow this or not).

Figure 14-12
Acrobat features

Acrobat's tools let you navigate through the document quickly.

Bookmarks act like a table of contents.

Anything you can design on your page can be included in the Acrobat PDF file.

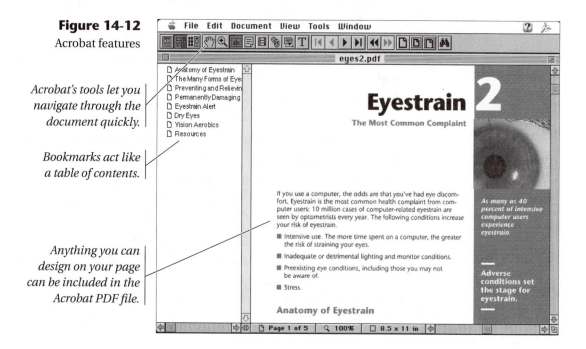

Because Acrobat PDF files are written in a proprietary format, you must have an Acrobat Reader in order to view these files. There is a browser plug-in that lets you view PDF files from within your Web browser window (Explorer or Navigator), but it still requires that you have the Reader program somewhere on your hard disk—in fact, the plug-in will launch the Reader program in the background as soon as it's asked to display a PDF file.

When it comes right down to it, however, the Acrobat PDF browser plug-in has been so unstable that currently no one I know expects anyone to really use it. (At least, no one I know outside of Adobe's marketing department.) Instead, if people find an Acrobat file on the Internet, they generally download it to their disk and read it there using the Acrobat Reader. (Even though I don't see Acrobat as a great Web tool, it's a very good tool for getting pages onto people's screens, so I decided to include it in this chapter anyway.)

Creating a PDF File

There are two ways to make an Acrobat PDF file from a QuarkXPress file: using the PDF print driver or using Acrobat Distiller.

PDF print driver. You can "print" a PDF file using the Acrobat PDF print driver (you have to own and correctly install this print driver, of course, though it ships free with many pieces of Adobe software). On the Macintosh, this means selecting Acrobat PDFWriter in the Chooser, then printing as usual (don't forget to review your Page Setup dialog box first).

"Printing" a PDF does a reasonable job on text and simple page items such as lines. However, it does a pretty miserable job on graphics, especially EPS files. The reason: the PDF print driver can't translate the PostScript commands in an EPS, so you get the low-resolution screen preview that you see in XPress. Ultimately, hardly anyone uses the PDF print driver; it's much better to use the second method—the Distiller.

Acrobat Distiller. If you really want a good-quality PDF file, you'll be much better off "printing" a PostScript file to disk (see "Printing to Disk" in Chapter 13, *Printing*) and then using Adobe's Distiller program to convert the PostScript into a PDF file (see Figure 14-13). The Distiller not only converts all PostScript code, but it removes all the superfluous

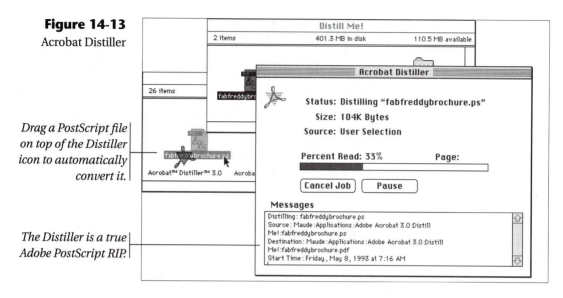

Figure 14-13
Acrobat Distiller

Drag a PostScript file on top of the Distiller icon to automatically convert it.

The Distiller is a true Adobe PostScript RIP.

PostScript, making a much smaller file than you can get with the PDF print driver.

The Distiller isn't free (it's a couple of hundred dollars bought separately), but it ships with many of Adobe's products, so you may have it already if you own PageMaker or Illustrator.

▼ ▼

Tip: Use the Proper PPD. When making a PDF file (either by printing PostScript to disk or using the PDF print driver), it's a good idea to choose Acrobat's PPD file from the Printer Type popup menu (on the Setup tab of the Print dialog box). In XPress 3.x, you might find two listings for Acrobat—one is a PPD and one is a Quark PDF (printer description file). In this case, you can tell which is the PPD by holding down the Shift key when you click on the Printer Type popup menu—the PPDs are displayed in italic. (XPress 4 only shows PPDs.)

▼ ▼

Tip: Distiller's Watched Folder. If you are making a lot of Acrobat PDF files, you should turn on the Distiller's "watched folder" feature. When it's on, the Distiller will check a particular folder or directory every so often (I usually set it to every 30 seconds), and if a PostScript file appears in the folder, it automatically turns it into a PDF file, based on the current job settings. It's nice to be able to just print a bunch of PostScript files into a folder and—after coming back from making a cup of coffee—have them all ready to display as PDF files.

▼ ▼

Acrobat Exchange

Once you've actually made a PDF file, you can use Acrobat Exchange (it comes with the Distiller) to add items such as links, bookmarks (which are like a hypertext table of contents), buttons, or other interactive features. If you have multiple stories that span multiple pages, you can tell Exchange which text blocks on a page link to which text blocks on other pages—each of these is called an *article* in Acrobat parlance.

There are three problems inherent here. First, building links, articles, and bookmarks in Exchange is a pain in the spleen. First, you have to set up each bookmark and each article individually, which takes a lot of time. Second, you have to do it in Exchange, which is a foreign program to most people and its interface leaves something to be desired. Third, if you go back and change your QuarkXPress document, you have to redo all your work in Exchange, too. Wouldn't it be nice if there were some sort of XTension to QuarkXPress that let you arrange all these features before you even leave XPress?

PDF Design XT

If you do any reasonable amount of PDF work with XPress, you should have TechnoDesign's PDF Design XTension, which lets you add Acrobat's articles, links, and bookmarks while you're still actually in XPress (unfortunately, this XTension is currently only available on the Macintosh). Instead of specifying each and every text block in a story as part of an article, PDF Design XT can build articles for you automatically based on your text chains. Instead of repeatedly selecting text and telling Acrobat Exchange that it's a bookmark, this XTension can automatically generate bookmarks from any paragraph style sheet (so for instance, all paragraphs in your document tagged with the "Heading 1" style could turn into level 1 bookmarks).

Once you've specified these interactive elements, PDF Design XT can print PostScript to disk (sidetracking the Print dialog box) that contains references to all the links, articles, and bookmarks—you just need to distill the PostScript using Acrobat Distiller, and you're done.

As this book goes to press, the folks at Quark have announced that they will develop their own technology for generating Acrobat-ready PostScript—links, bookmarks, and all. As soon as they release something, I'll have it available on The QuarkXPress Book Web site (*www.peachpit.com/blatner*).

QuarkImmedia

The third method you can use to get your QuarkXPress documents online is an XTension called QuarkImmedia. Immedia takes a very different approach to building on-screen projects: it's a relatively robust authoring tool that lets you create interactive multimedia projects (including kiosks, presentations, CD-ROMs, and Web sites) but it lets you do it while you're still in QuarkXPress.

If you're like me, you probably think the world needs another hard-to-learn, confusing multimedia tool like it needs a hole in its ozone layer. Fortunately, Immedia is much easier than conventional authoring tools. If you already know XPress (and by this point in the book, you certainly do), Immedia makes taking the step into multimedia relatively easy. I've seen people start building their own interactive projects within an hour of first using this tool.

QuarkImmedia adds menu items and a tabbed palette to the already familiar page-and-pasteboard environment that we know so well (see Figure 14-14). If you want to put an animation on your page, just import it into a picture box like any other graphic. If you want a scrolling text field, just draw out a text box, put text in it, and tell Immedia that it should have scrollbars.

However, let's be right up front about something: Immedia is not as powerful as high-end authoring tools like Quark's mTropolis or Macromedia Director. For instance, if I were creating a fast-paced kiosk display that had lots of animated graphics interacting with each other and with the user, I'd probably opt for mTropolis. But about 75 percent of the projects that I see people create with a high-end program (which can entail months of a steep learning curve) could be made twice as easily with QuarkImmedia. This includes sales presentations, information kiosks, promotional CDs, and even some basic games (see Figure 14-15).

Tip: Learning QuarkImmedia. Now it's time for a commercial plug: There's no way I can explain all the details of how to build QuarkImmedia projects in this one chapter. So instead, I'll refer you to another book I wrote—*Real World QuarkImmedia* (also from Peachpit Press). In fact, it comes with a CD-ROM that includes a demo version of Immedia 1.0 on it so that you can try it out yourself before committing

Figure 14-14

QuarkImmedia

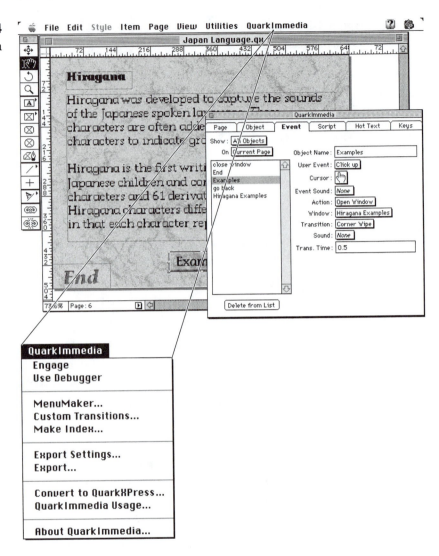

to buy the full-fledged version (the CD-ROM also includes sounds, buttons, movies, and other clip media you can use for free).

▼ ▼

Viewing Immedia Projects

Let's first discuss how to view Immedia projects, and then talk about how to build them.

Immedia projects, like Acrobat PDF files, require a special viewer. Once an interactive project is exported from QuarkXPress, you can view it on either Macintosh or Windows as long as the QuarkImmedia Viewer is available (it's free for both platforms). If you're not going to put the pro-

Figure 14-15
Immedia projects

Full-screen display
(the finished,
engaged project)

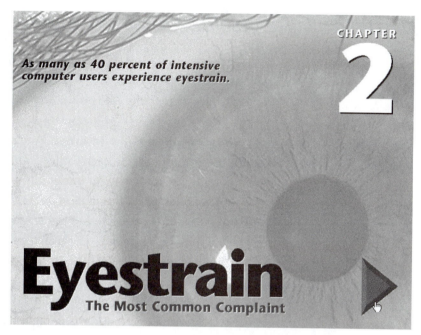

Sound
(can't you hear it?)

Text box

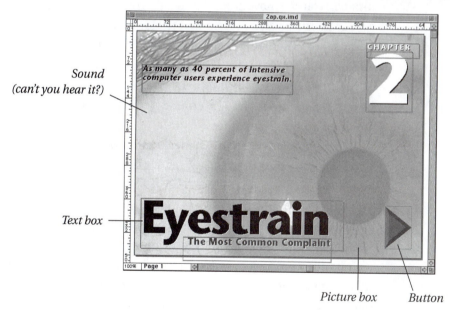

Picture box   Button

ject on the Web, you can even embed the Viewer in the project itself so that it becomes a standalone program (people can simply double-click on it to make it run).

At the time of this writing, there is no Web browser plug-in available for Immedia, so you cannot view Immedia projects within a Navigator or Explorer window. You can, however, easily view Immedia projects on the

Web using the Immedia Viewer (the Viewer acts like a browser here). And you can create a connection between the Viewer and your Web browser so that if you jump to an HTML page while you're in the Immedia Viewer, it automatically launches your Web browser; and if you hit an Immedia page while you're in the Web browser, it jumps to the Immedia Viewer.

▼ ▼

Tip: Intranets Versus the Internet. The Internet is simply a bunch of computers that talk to each other using particular standards of computer talk (protocols). An intranet is a network of computers that talk to each other using the same standards as on the Internet, but that are not necessarily connected to the worldwide Internet (though they can be). Typically, that means a local area network (LAN) connected with Ethernet (that's what I've got in my office) running the networking protocol TCP/IP.

The great benefit of an intranet is bandwidth—the amount of data you can move per second. On a high-bandwidth network like an intranet, you can move around Web pages or e-mail (or whatever) at high speeds because you're not limited to slow modems or telephone lines. Because some Immedia projects can be large (especially when you start adding sound and movies), they're often more suitable for an intranet environment than for the Internet. In fact, I think Immedia is one of the best intranet authoring tools around because it lets you design great-looking pages in QuarkXPress.

Throughout this chapter, whenever I say "Internet" you can probably apply whatever I'm talking about to intranets, too.

▼ ▼

Tip: On-Line Simulation. As I mentioned, bandwidth—how much data you can get across a connection in a given amount of time—is key to working with multimedia projects. If you know that people will be interacting with your project over a 28.8 K modem, you want to make sure that your file doesn't need to transfer more than 28.8 kilobytes per second in order to run smoothly. This isn't just an Immedia problem; people who are putting video or sound into their HTML pages run into the same limitations.

One feature that I haven't seen in any other authoring tool, however, is Immedia's On-line Simulation. If you hold down the Option key when selecting Open from the Immedia Viewer's File menu, you can choose from the Simulated Speed popup menu. For instance, choose 28.8 K before opening a file on disk (this feature only works when you're running a project from disk), and the project appears to load and display as though it were connected over a 28.8 K modem. This is an extremely useful tool when you're authoring for the Internet; without it you'd be stuck with uploading the file to your Web server and then rummaging around trying to find a 28.8 K modem, just to see how your project will run.

Of course, it's not perfect. If someone's phone lines are bad, or there's heavy server traffic, they actually may not be achieving a full 14.4 K or 28.8 K anyway.

▼ ▼

Building Immedia Projects

Okay, now that you know how to look at a QuarkImmedia project, let's talk a little about how to build one. As I mentioned, you must have the Immedia XTension in order to author interactive projects from within XPress; this XTension is not inexpensive (at last glance, it cost the same as a copy of XPress), but when you compare its learning curve to that of other multimedia programs, you'll see that it pays for itself quickly.

Note that at the time of this writing, the Immedia authoring XTension is only available on the Macintosh. Quark has promised that it'll appear on Windows before too long (perhaps even by the time you're reading this).

The Three-Step Process. There's a very basic three-step process to almost everything you need to do in Immedia (see Figure 14-16).

1. Select an object that you want to be interactive. For example, choose a picture box (with or without a picture in it).

2. Switch to the Object tab on the QuarkImmedia palette, and type in a name for the object. Every interactive object (or page item that moves, wiggles, or whatever) has to have its own name, but you can name it nearly anything you want.

3. Switch to the Event tab of the palette and choose an "event" for this object from the Action popup menu. Choosing items from this tab is itself a three-step process. First, specify what the user must do to trigger the event from the User Event popup menu. For instance, the popup menu defaults to Click Up, which is the action of letting go of the mouse button after the user "clicks

Figure 14-16

Building an
Immedia project

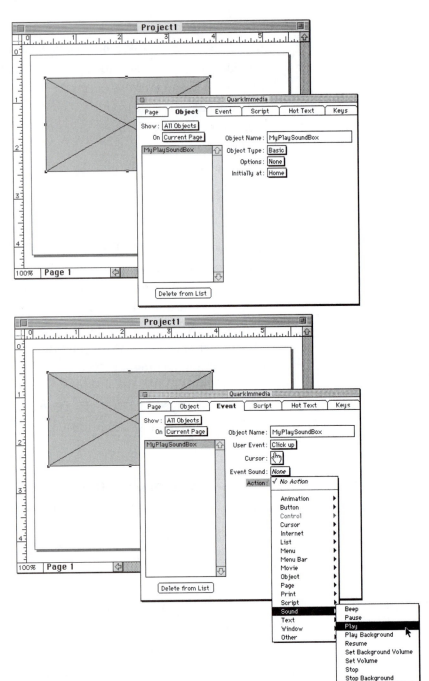

down." Next, choose an event from the Action popup menu. If you want a sound to play, choose Play Sound; if you want a movie to pause, choose Pause Movie; and so on. Just about everything Immedia can do is hidden on the Action popup menu. Finally, because each action has its own set of options, you typically must choose from among one to five other popup menus. For example, if you choose the Play Sound action, you have to tell Immedia which sound you want, whether to fade it in or not, and so on.

Because almost everything in QuarkImmedia is arranged on popup menus, you never have to worry about missing something or forgetting a scripting language.

Here are just a few other things that you can build into an Immedia project (this list is not exhaustive).

▶ Scripting in Immedia is a matter of compiling a list of actions (from popup menus, of course). When you run the script, the actions happen one after the other (for example: turn a page, play a sound, start an animation, and highlight an item in a list).

▶ You can have custom menus, transitions (between pages, or when hiding or showing an object), popup menus, lists, and windows.

▶ On the Macintosh, you can run AppleScripts that control other programs. A standalone Immedia project could build Quark-XPress documents across a network at the click of a button (see Appendix D, *Scripting*).

▶ The Internet actions let you create links between projects on the Internet, submit information to CGIs on your server (like forms), and even import text or basic HTML into a text box while the project is playing (see "Tip: Hybrid Projects," below).

▶ You can build conditionals into your scripts. For example, a script might say, "If the cursor is over the picture of a cow, and the text in a particular text box reads 'cow,' then play the 'moo' sound."

▶ You can preview your interactive project without leaving QuarkXPress by selecting Engage from the QuarkImmedia menu (if you're a Star Trek fan, you understand the genesis of that term.)

To tell you the truth, I just get excited when I talk about Immedia; it's such an easy way to build cool interactive projects. It's really worth getting your hands on a copy (or a demo version) so that you can try it out for yourself (see *www.peachpit.com/blatner/* for more information about QuarkImmedia).

Exporting. Once you've built your Immedia project, you can export it so that others can see it, too. At this point, an interesting thing happens: almost everything on every page of your document gets rasterized (turned into a bitmap picture). This way, other people will see exactly the same thing that you see on screen, including graphics, typography, and other page elements.

Where HTML leaves much of the formatting to the vagaries of the individual's browser, Immedia locks in your screen image. On the other hand, where Acrobat can save the outlines of fonts so that you can zoom in and out and print them, Immedia does not; you just get a 72-ppi bitmapped and anti-aliased image. (Note that Immedia does not rasterize some text, such as editable text and scrolling lists.)

Immedia lets you export your project in one of three formats.

▶ The One File format exports a single file that contains all the elements of the project. You can embed the Viewer into this kind of export so that the final product is a standalone application that your audience can just click on and run.

▶ Many CD-ROM projects contain two files: a small "executable" file that you can drag onto your hard drive, and a large "data" file that contains the movies, sounds, text, and so on. If you want this format, choose Two Files.

▶ Many Files is the format most appropriate for the Internet. Because each sound, each movie, and each page are saved as separate data files, the Immedia Viewer only has to download the information it needs when it needs it (instead of downloading the entire project at first). Of course, you have to keep track of a lot more files this way.

QuarkImmedia compresses your image data when you export your project, so final file sizes are often much smaller than you'd expect. However, if you're going to put your projects on the Web, you should follow the same guidelines as you would with Acrobat or HTML files. For instance, pictures with flat colors or basic patterns usually compress significantly more than complex, "noisy" graphics (like scans).

▼ ▼

Tip: Export Statistics. I discussed the value of simulating transmission speeds in the Immedia Viewer earlier in this chapter, but there's a step you can take even sooner that helps you determine how well your projects will transmit over the Internet. If you hold down the Option key when pressing Save in the Export dialog box, Immedia displays the Export Statistics window, filled with information about file sizes, approximate download times, and so on.

▼ ▼

Tip: Hybrid Projects. Let's say you're building a CD-ROM for the local music store. You want it to be flashy, so you include a lot of music and MTV-like videos. The problem is that the store's price list changes all the time. You can create a hybrid project so that the bulk of the project's data (the movies and whatnot) is on the CD-ROM, and some of the information (like the price list) is on the Internet. When you start up the project on the CD-ROM, it automatically links to the music store's Web site, downloads the information it needs, and places it in the correct spot.

This kind of disk/Internet hybrid is very powerful. Another example is a project that requires a subscription to use. Perhaps when you start the Immedia project from your hard drive, it logs on to a Web site to see if you've paid your dues, or to check if your password is correct; if so, then it lets you continue.

▼ ▼

Tip: Improve Your Performance. As soon as you start thinking of putting a project on the Internet, you should begin considering how to make it as small and compact as possible. People are less patient than ever these days, and they simply won't sit still for minutes on end while your project clunks along. *Real World QuarkImmedia* is chock-full of tips on how to make your Immedia projects smaller and more efficient. Here are just a few ideas.

▶ Make the first page of a project really simple so that it compresses down to a small file (under 20 K) and loads quickly. Even if the only text on the page says "Please hold on . . . ", it's still better than seeing nothing at all but a status bar while a large page downloads.

▶ Use the same buttons throughout your project. Immedia puts every button you use on the first page of a project when you export it as Many Files. Even if you use a single button thirty times in your project, the Viewer only has to download it once.

▶ When you can, use MIDI sounds instead of regular sound files. MIDI is an extremely efficient method of playing sounds, and QuickTime (for Mac and Windows) can decipher it (you need QuickTime to run Immedia projects anyway).

▶ If you have a graphic or styled text that repeats throughout your project, consider turning it into a single-frame animation. Animations get cached the first time the Immedia Viewer downloads them, so even if you use the same graphic on every page, it still only gets downloaded once. (A single-frame animation doesn't actually animate, because it only has one frame.)

The Future of Publishing

One of the basic elements of democracy has long been "freedom of the press," but freedom of the press has always been reserved for those who own one. Now for the first time in history, almost anyone can publish their own work on the Internet and the World Wide Web. And because QuarkXPress has been the tool of choice for most publishing professionals, it makes sense that people would look to this program to take them into the brave new world.

In this chapter, I've briefly summarized the various available tools that ease the transition from print to screen. Of course, the future of publishing depends less on which tool you use than on *what* you create. Happy XPressing!

A

Color Management

or years, "What You See Is What You Get," or WYSIWYG (pronounced "wizzywig"), was one of the key buzzwords of desktop publishing. It meant that the page layout you saw on your computer screen was, more or less, what you'd get out of your printer. WYSIWYG works fine for a page with any color of ink—so long as it's black (to paraphrase Henry Ford). But it's significant that nobody felt the need to come up with a similarly cute acronym to describe color fidelity between computer and printer. My editors and I considered "Color You See Is Color You Get," but we wouldn't want to be responsible for unleashing "kissykig" on the world. My colleague, Steve Roth, says he prefers WYGIWYG: "What You Get Is What You Get."

Silliness aside, the main reason nobody's come up with such an acronym is that until recently, it would have described a condition that didn't exist. If you've ever created color pages, you've learned—probably with no little pain—that the colors you see on your screen have little more than a passing resemblance to what comes out of your color printer or off a printing press. In fact, a major part of working with color on desktop computers has been learning through trial and error that when you see color A on your screen, you'll actually get color B out of your color-proofing printer, and color C off of a four-color press run. Your only guides were process-color swatch books, test prints, and experience.

▼ ▼

Managing Color

Well, the times they are a-changing. Color-management systems (CMS) promise to provide fidelity between the colors on your computer screen and those of your printed output. Apple, Eastman Kodak, Pantone, and Agfa, among others, have management systems that sometimes actually cooperate with each other. However, color management is still far from a push-button experience, and without some knowledge of what's going on behind the scenes it's very possible to make your color output worse rather than better.

If you own QuarkXPress 4, you already have a color management system, or at least major components of it: the QuarkCMS XTension, supported by Apple's ColorSync and Kodak's KICC.

▼ ▼

Tip: Get Rid of EfiColor. Earlier versions of XPress used EfiColor from EFI. There were many problems with EfiColor (including the fact that EFI is no longer in the color management business, so it's hard to get support for their CMS), and Quark has chosen a much better solution. However, just because you upgrade to version 4 doesn't mean that EfiColor has gone away. On the Macintosh, you may still need to remove the EfiColor Processor file and the EfiColor DB folder from your System Folder. In Windows, you may find its remnants in the same folder as your copy of QuarkXPress.

▼ ▼

Tip: Color Management in the Real World. I want to throw in a short commercial plug here for a book that I wrote with Bruce Fraser: *Real World Photoshop*. Much of the overview material in this appendix is distilled from that book. However, because *Real World Photoshop* contains much more information about color management, and because Photoshop is such an integral part of most people's color management work flow, it's worth taking a look at that book as well. Okay, the commercial break is over.

▼ ▼

What QuarkCMS Attempts

While learning about color management is not easy, it's often worth the trouble in the end because a CMS can help us in a number of ways.

▶ **MATCHING THE ORIGINAL.** Color management systems are designed to make the colors on your document's page consistent—from your original scan to your screen to a color proof to your final output device. It's this consistency that lets us trust what we see on the monitor, letting us work visually rather than by the numbers.

▶ **COLOR-SPACE CONVERSION.** CMSes really should be called "color conversion systems," as that's what they're doing: converting colors from one system into another. This means that QuarkCMS is very good at converting RGB to CMYK and vice versa.

▶ **SOFT PROOFING AND PREPROOFING.** Soft proofing is the ability to proof your images and document pages on screen. Preproofing is the ability to proof your images and document pages on a color printer—like a dye-sublimation printer. A well-implemented CMS can save you a lot of money by letting you trust your monitor and composite color proofs instead of relying on multiple Match Prints.

Why Color Management "Can't" Work

Don't get me wrong: QuarkCMS is not performing any magic. If there's one thing I want you to get out of reading this appendix, it's that it's just plain not possible for computer monitors, dye-sublimation color printers, color copier/printers and four-color lithographic presses to exactly match each other, color for color. Each device uses different technology to create color, and each uses differing methods of specifying its colors. The red, green, and blue colors emitted from a monitor are additive: the more color you add, the closer to white the screen gets. On the other hand, printers that apply ink, wax, powders, or toner to paper generally create colors by combining values of cyan, magenta, yellow, and black. This color model is subtractive: the more of each component you add, the darker your final color becomes. When you try to create the same color using two different methods, there's really no way that the two can look exactly the same.

Plus, the same RGB values on two different monitors might not look like each other at all, because the screen phosphors and technology might be slightly different. You have probably seen a wall of televisions at a department store: each set displays the same image, yet has a different color cast. Similarly, the same CMYK values printed on an color inkjet printer look very different from "identical" values printed on a four-color press on coated stock, and those colors also look different than colors printed on newsprint.

Each of these color systems are called *device dependent* because the color is specific to only one device—a brand of monitor, color printer, or whatever. QuarkCMS tries its best to create consistency among various devices, but you need to understand that it's not entirely possible.

What color management does enhance is the predictability of colors among these disparate systems and preserve the overall appearance of your page. You can learn to visualize how an image on your screen will appear when it's printed to various output devices.

"I Only Paint What I See"

Matching colors might be a hopeless comparison of apples, oranges, and grapefruits, except that there's one constant shared by every method of creating colors: the human eye. The fact is that your eyes don't care what technology a monitor or printer uses to create a color; they just see colors. Just as monitors and printers are device *dependent*, your eyes are device *independent*. They're the one constant in this whole *mishegoss*, and not surprisingly, they're the key to color-management systems such as QuarkCMS.

No, QuarkCMS doesn't try to calibrate your eyes with some sort of cybernetic gizmo. Rather, it uses a color-space model based on a statistical analysis of how most people perceive differences between colors. This model was designed by the Commission Internationale de l'Eclairage (that's the International Commission on Illumination, or CIE, to you and me) in the 1930s. The CIE color space describes every different color the human eye can see, using a mathematical model that isn't dependent on fickle things like the density of phosphor coatings or the amount of ink spread on certain paper stocks.

Unlike RGB or CMYK values, which don't really describe a color (the same values might look quite different on different devices), CIE values actually describe a color's appearance, not just the values that make it up on a specific device.

Color-Management Concepts

Before I go further into this discussion, I have to take a break and define a couple of important words: *gamut* and *profile*. I'll use these words a lot throughout this chapter.

Gamuts. A device's color *gamut* describes the range of colors which that device can create or sense. Since the CIE color space describes every perceivable color, by default it has the largest gamut. No device—monitor, scanner, or printer—can come close to reproducing this range of colors, and so the gamut of any specific device is smaller than the CIE gamut. Plus, different devices are able to image different sets of colors (the available colors are spread out differently). So one device may be able to reproduce many hues of red, while another may be weak in reds, but especially competent in producing a wide range of blues.

Profiles. QuarkCMS uses files called *device profiles* to keep track of not only the color gamuts of particular devices, but also other information about their capabilities and limitations. Most of the profiles you use with QuarkCMS are actually generic descriptions of Apple 13-inch monitors, or printing presses that use SWOP (Standard Web Offset Press) coated inks, not specific descriptions of your personal device or your lithographer's press (see "Canned versus Custom Profiles," later in this chapter).

From Device to Device

Here's how color management systems work: First, you hand the CMS an RGB or CMYK color along with a profile. As I've said, by itself the color is meaningless; it's just a recipe (this much red, that much green, and so on). The profile—called the "source" profile—gives meaning to the color by saying it's this color *on such-and-such device*. For instance, 100-percent red means less than "100-percent red on my Trinitron monitor that displays red like this . . . ."

Second, you tell the CMS where the color is going by specifying another profile—this one is called the "target profile." The CMS then has an engine (sometimes called a CMM, for color matching method) that translates the original color into its native CIE color space format, and then from this format into the appropriate target color.

Here's another way to think about this: let's say that CMSes work with words instead of colors, and the purpose of our hypothetical word-CMS is to translate words from one language to another. If you just feed it a bunch of words, it can't do anything. But if you give it the words and tell it that they were written by a Polish person (the source), it all of a sudden can understand what the words are saying. If you then tell it that you speak Japanese (the target), it can translate the meaning for you.

Note that a color monitor can display a different set of colors than a desktop color printer, which, in turn, has a much greater gamut than a four-color press. QuarkCMS's color transformations work best when they reduce one device's gamut to match another; it's just not possible to *increase* a device's gamut to match another's, although there are ways of faking it. That is, a color monitor is good at displaying the limited gamut of a four-color press, but a four-color press is hard-pressed (no pun intended) to simulate a display.

Who Does the Separation? Perhaps the most important aspect of this technology is the conversion between RGB and CMYK color models. Once QuarkCMS transforms a color into its internal CIE color space, it can transform it to any other color model it knows about. And while the RGB-to-CMY conversion is relatively simple (see "Color Models" in Chapter 12, *Color*), converting to CMYK has traditionally been quite difficult. QuarkCMS does this for you behind the scenes.

Whether or not you want QuarkXPress's color management software to be handling your color separations is another matter. I discuss some of the pros and cons of using QuarkCMS as your color separation tool in "Color from Outside Sources," in Chapter 12, *Color*, but the debate is primarily one of time and quality. When you convert an image from one color space to another—like RGB to CMYK—it takes time, and I generally don't have a lot of that on my hands. If you import an RGB image into XPress, it has to convert it each time you print. Therefore, I often prefer to separate my bitmapped images in a program like Photoshop before importing them into XPress.

As for quality, well you'll forgive me if I just stay out of the argument over which pieces of software—Adobe Photoshop, Apple's ColorSync, or Kodak's KICC—offers the superior separation.

Canned versus Custom Profiles

Getting good color with a color management system depends almost entirely on three things: the quality of your image, the quality of the color management system's engine, and the quality of the profiles you use. As for the first two: The color engines that QuarkCMS uses are quite good, and I'd rather not comment on the quality of your images (that's for your audience to decide). However, I do want to discuss profiles for a moment.

QuarkXPress ships with a set of 12 or so profiles (see Table A-1) that you can use. You can obtain additional profiles from your device's manufacturer (one may have come on disk when you bought it), commercially from companies like Praxisoft, or even download them from sites on the Internet (like *www.colorsync.com*). These are usually referred to as "canned profiles," and they vary dramatically in their usefulness because they describe only how the device is supposed to work, or perhaps how it worked once in the factory.

You can also create your own profiles for the devices you use—monitors, scanners, color printers, and presses. It's become much easier to build custom profiles in recent years using software such as Color Savvy's ProfilePrinterDeluxe, ProfileMakerPro from Logo GmbH, Candela's ColorSynergy, or Linotype-Hell's PrintOpen ICC (which is also marketed by Helios). When you make a custom profile, you're characterizing the behavior and gamut of your monitor, your color printer, and so on.

Custom profiles always give you a better result in a color management system, but it's not always worth the considerable hassle involved with building one (much less the sometimes even greater challenge of keeping the device in the same state as it was when you built the profile). It usually depends on the type of device you're using.

Monitors. Canned monitor profiles are almost always useless; even a little turn of the brightness or contrast knobs renders the profile obsolete because the screen is displaying color differently. Also, as I've said, even monitors from the same company can act very differently, especially over time. In order to trust your screen, you must either have a custom profile or calibrate your screen as closely as you can so that it matches the canned profile you're using. You can make monitor profiles with hardware (suction-cup) devices such as the one that ships with Radius's monitors or with the Colortron. There are also software solutions, such as Sonnetech's Colorific and Pantone's Personal Color Calibrator (they're pretty close to the same product under different names).

Table A-1

Files that are installed along with the QuarkCMS XTension

CANNED PROFILES*
Generic Monitor (GENDISP7.ICM)
Pantone Hexachrome Æ Normal SID (HEXNSID2.ICM)
KODAK SWOP Proofer CMYK — Uncoated Stock (SWUL28A7.ICM)
KODAK SWOP Proofer CMYK — Coated Stock (SWCL32A7.ICM)
KODAK SWOP Proofer CMYK — Newsprint (SWNM26A7.ICM)
SWOP Press (SWOPM18.ICM)
Tektronix Phaser III Pxi (TPIIIPX7.ICM)
Canon CLC500/EFI Printer (CLC500A7.ICM)
150-Line (Pantone) and 150-Line (Pantone) (ncp) — Macintosh only
KODAK Generic DCS Camera Input (GENKDCS1.ICM)
Nikon LS-3510 AF (LS3510A7.ICM)
Microtek 600ZS (MT600ZA7.ICM)

SYSTEM FILES: MACINTOSH**
KODAK CMM
KODAK PRECISION CP1
KODAK PRECISION Profile API
KODAK PRECISION Startup (in the Startup folder in the System Folder)
CP01 (in the CMSCP folder in System Folder)
ColorSync
ColorSync System Profile

SYSTEM FILES: WINDOWS***
KODAK Precision Profile API Interface to Kodak Precision API (KCM2SP.DLL)
KODAK DIGITAL SCIENCE color processor DLL (KPCP32.DLL)
KCMS System Interface Library, Win32.DLL (KPSYS32.DLL)
KODAK DIGITAL SCIENCE ICC Profile API (SPROF32.DLL)

*On the Macintosh, these are placed inside the ColorSync Preferences folder, inside the Preferences folder, inside the System Folder. In Windows, they're placed inside the Color directory, inside the System directory, inside the Windows directory.

**These are placed in the Extensions folder, inside the System Folder

***These are placed inside the System directory, inside the Windows directory

Note that building a monitor profile in Windows is significantly harder and typically less reliable than on the Macintosh. (Some even say that it's neigh on impossible to get a good monitor profile on a PC.) This is one of the areas in which the Macintosh certainly has an advantage over Microsoft Windows.

Scanners. Scanners are significantly more stable than monitors, so canned settings may work, especially in the better scanners on the market. Nonetheless, if you're trying to capture exact color in a scan (perhaps you don't trust what you see on screen and you're just trying to reproduce the original), you can build a custom profile by scanning an IT8.7 or a Q-60 target and using a CMS utility to compare your scan with readings taken when the target was created. This effectively builds a profile that characterizes your particular scanner. Note that scanner profiles are usually also media-specific, so you may have a Fuji film profile, a Kodak film profile, an Agfa film profile, and so on.

Color printers. Like scanners, the canned profiles for composite color printers are usually pretty good, though they're dependent on the correct colored ink or ribbon, paper stock, and so on. If you have a particular set up that you always use, you can optimize your color by building your own profile using the software mentioned above. This is a time-consuming process, requiring using a spectrophotometer (like the Colortron) to sample dozens or even hundreds of printed swatches on a printed page.

Presses. It's a naïve assumption in the desktop publishing world that all printing presses are more or less the same. In fact, web presses are different than sheetfed presses, inks in one part of the world (or even the continent) that are labeled cyan, yellow, magenta, and black are actually different hues, different paper stocks make a drastic difference on color fidelity, as can humidity and the mood of the press operator on the day of your press run. However, while it's optimal to have a custom profile for your press, it's probably not necessary. Instead, you can use the profile for your particular proofing system as your target. For instance, you could use a canned profile for a Match Print or an AgfaProof system—both of these are quite stable. Then it's up to your press operator to match the proof you provide.

Of course, having a custom press profile becomes significantly more important if you're one of the many people who are printing CTP (computer-to-plate), where no film is burned, and no proof is made. In this case, you should try to obtain a custom profile from your printer.

▼ ▼

Before You Use QuarkCMS

If QuarkCMS is so great and wonderful, why would you ever *not* want to use it? There are lots of reasons, from speed to consistency. Before I dive headlong into how to use Quark's color management system, I want to discuss a few things that you should consider about the process.

Performance

When QuarkCMS transforms a color to look right on your screen or your proofing printer or your final output device, the color gets *processed*. That takes time. Sometimes a lot of time. Imagine converting a 30 Mb image from RGB mode to CMYK mode in Adobe Photoshop. It takes a while, doesn't it? QuarkCMS can't do it any faster than those programs can, and that's just what it's doing when you print an RGB TIFF from QuarkXPress with QuarkCMS turned on. And it has to make that conversion every time you print.

Similarly, when you import any sort of TIFF or PICT image, QuarkCMS has to convert the screen preview to look correct on the screen. That can easily make importing pictures take four or five times as long as without QuarkCMS. You can speed the process a little by pressing the Shift key while clicking Open in the Get Picture dialog box; that imports the picture at half the screen resolution. However, you then get a low-resolution image to look at on the screen, which sort of defeats the purpose.

(Of course, your processor speed has a lot to do with your performance results; on really fast machines, the slow-down may not be a hindrance to your workflow at all.)

Dollars and Sense

Time, we all know, is money. And if QuarkCMS is a hit to my performance at output time, then money may be at stake. Back when QuarkXPress version 3.32 first shipped, many service bureaus were bewildered as they started receiving documents that suddenly took five or 10 times longer to output than they expected. The culprit? The EfiColor color management XTension. Service bureau operators weren't prepared for the amount of time it could take to convert even moderately sized RGB images to CMYK separations. Their clients weren't prepared for the kinds of per-minute charges the service bureaus started charging them.

So for those of you who operate a service bureau: warn your clients in advance about using RGB TIFFs (or against it, if you aren't willing to support QuarkCMS). You might suggest they make PostScript dumps, so it's *their* machine time that's being eaten. For those of you using a service bureau, investigate the excess-time charges to see if it's worth the extra money.

Incompatible File Formats

The QuarkCMS XTension really only works with images that QuarkXPress itself can change. If you remember Chapter 10, *Fine-Tuning Images*, QuarkXPress can only modify TIFF, JPEG, and bitmap-only PICTs. That means that QuarkCMS won't even attempt to transform any EPS or DCS files.

What happens when you import a color EPS image from Macromedia FreeHand or Adobe Illustrator onto your page, and surround it with colors that you've matched exactly within QuarkXPress? You can throw the words "matched exactly" out of your vocabulary. The colors you assign in QuarkXPress are transformed according to the profiles you choose. The colors in the EPS image are not transformed at all.

You have to understand the philosophy of EPS images. The whole idea of Encapsulated PostScript originally, was that a program should never need to look "inside" them, and should certainly never change anything inside them. Therefore, according to this school of thought, QuarkCMS should never adjust the color inside an EPS or DCS image.

The problem is that people use these file formats all the time—especially for duotones and object-oriented, vector images.—and they go nuts when the colors don't match what comes out of QuarkXPress. Unfortunately, I don't really have a good answer for how to handle this situation right now. Praxisoft's CompassProXT color manages EPS images as well as everything else on the page, but it currently has other limitations and won't change screen display on the fly.

Until Macromedia and Adobe decide that color management is really worth their time (read: their customers want it), we'll all just have to hold our breath and wait for a whole, cross-application integrated color-management system.

The Problem with OPI

Trying to manage color with OPI images (see "OPI" in Chapter 13, *Printing*) is even more difficult than with EPS, because QuarkXPress never even touches the final image. Remember that with OPI, you export PostScript from QuarkXPress without image data; only little tags are inserted in the PostScript saying what the name of the image is and how it should be adjusted (rotation, cropping, and so on). That's why QuarkXPress is called an *OPI writer*.

The PostScript that comes from QuarkXPress gets passed on to another program—an *OPI reader*—that interprets the PostScript and substitutes high-resolution images where appropriate. OPI workflows that involve color management do exist, like the one made by Helios. But if the OPI server you're using doesn't do this already, you may be out of luck. The solution, again, is to adjust for the target printer when the image is scanned or saved from a image-manipulation program.

Rendering Style

It's easy to pick an RGB color that cannot be printed in CMYK on a press. The question is: what should the color management system do about it? It needs to somehow transform the color into the CMYK space, based on what it knows about the destination device. The ColorSync and KICC engines provide several options, called *rendering styles*, each with their own scary-sounding name. The two important ones, however, are perceptual and colorimetric.

▶ **PERCEPTUAL.** Perceptual (also called photographic) rendering compresses the entire color range of your picture to fit into your printer's gamut, maintaining the balance of color throughout the picture. All the colors in the picture change, but they maintain their relationships to each other, resulting in a more true-to-life rendition of color photographs. Balance, it turns out, is often more important to maintain in photographic images than the colors themselves. For example, the colors in a picture of a face can be pretty far off, but as long as the colors maintain a relative balance—among the skin, the eyes, the hair, for instance—our eyes adjust to it fine.

▶ **COLORIMETRIC.** Colorimetric (also called solid color) rendering only changes colors that fall outside the target device's gamut, snapping them to their nearest equivalent in the gamut. Colors that are already in gamut are left alone. This rendering style is best for areas of solid colors—like if you apply a Pantone color to a block of text or if you save a Freehand or Illustrator image as a TIFF—because you're generally more interested in getting as close to the original specified color than in keeping some sort of color balance throughout an image.

Unfortunately, as of this writing, all this talk about rendering styles is just a tease, because the Quark engineers left out any option to choose a rendering style from the QuarkCMS XTension. Instead, the CMS simply uses whatever default rendering style is listed in the target profile—almost always perceptual. Everyone now seems to agree that QuarkCMS should provide an interface for specifying a rendering style. But no one knows when a newer version of the XTension will appear, filling this hole.

▼ ▼

Using QuarkCMS

OK, so now that you have an idea of what QuarkCMS is supposed to do (and what it can't do), let's talk about how it works with QuarkXPress 4, and how you tell it what you want.

Installing QuarkCMS. Note that QuarkCMS is not built into the QuarkXPress application itself. Rather, it's a combination of an XTension and some files placed in the System Folder. Therefore, in order to use QuarkCMS, you must first make sure it's installed properly. This isn't difficult: when you run QuarkXPress's installer or upgrader, the first dialog box asks you which file sets you want to install. Make sure the QuarkCMS XTension has a checkmark next to it, and the Installer does the rest. (For some strange reason, in Windows you have to click the Customize button when the installer asks you where you want to put the files in order to tell it to install the color management system.)

There are three parts to the QuarkCMS color-management system for QuarkXPress: the color engine, the device profiles, and the QuarkCMS XTension itself. The QuarkCMS XTension doesn't do anything by itself; rather, it depends on system-level extensions (.DLLs in Windows) to actually process the color data. On the Macintosh, QuarkCMS uses both

Apple's ColorSync and Kodak's Digital Science CMM. Yes, this means you have actually have two different color management engines on your computer; don't worry, they play nice with each other. In Windows, you only get Kodak's system.

Turning it On. Quark got yelled at badly back in version 3.2 for shipping the EfiColor color management system with a default setting turning it on for all new documents. They learned their lesson. Now, if you want color management, you need to turn it on yourself. First, make sure the QuarkCMS XTension is loaded properly (see "XTensions" in Chapter 2, *QuarkXPress Basics*). Next, select Color Management from the Preferences submenu (under the Edit menu) and turn on the checkbox labeled "Color Management Active."

Note that this preference acts like many other preferences: If you turn it on when a document is open, the change is to this document only. If no documents are open, then the change is to every document you create from now on. Of course, you can always turn off the checkbox to disable the color management system for a document.

▼ ▼

Tip: QuarkCMS Ain't the Only Game in Town. There's no doubt that the QuarkCMS XTension is a step in the right direction, but as one Quark employee noted, "let's just say it's a work in progress." There are a number of limitations (see "Buyer Beware," later in this appendix), though I'm sure that the folks at Quark are working on updates. Meanwhile, if you want to get heavy into color management, you might consider another XTension on the market, Praxisoft's CompassProXT, which removes several of the most heinous restrictions of QuarkCMS, including color managing vector images and applying rendering intents to images and XPress colors. However, it has it's own limitations, too. Helios also offers the ColorSyncXT, which is a powerful color management system but doesn't handle vector images.

▼ ▼

The QuarkCMS XTension

The QuarkCMS XTension adds several dialog boxes and commands to QuarkXPress. Rather than tackle them on an item-by-item basis, I want to take you on a tour of how I think you may use the XTension's features.

Although the range of choices you can specify with QuarkCMS seems daunting, you can break the system's choices into three broad categories: telling it about your devices, telling it about your pictures and document colors, and then telling it how to print. When the QuarkCMS XTension knows all these variables, then it can correctly transform color between color spaces and gamuts, resulting in closer color matching between all the devices.

Color Management Preferences

The heart of QuarkCMS is the Color Management Preferences dialog box (select Color Management from the Preferences submenu). The first step after turning color management on is to set up your default preferences from among the controls in this dialog box (see Figure A-1).

Destination Profiles. The three popup menus in the Destination Profiles section let you specify the three important targets you'll send your page: your monitor, your color printer, and the device you're separating for (usually the printing press). The Composite Printer and Separation Printer settings are just defaults, and you can override them in the Print dialog box if you decide to print to a different device (see "Color Management at Print Time," later in this appendix). Note that you can only choose profiles from these lists that define CMYK color spaces.

Figure A-1
Color Management
Preferences

Color Management Preferences for Document2

⊠ Color Management Active

─Destination Profiles───
Monitor: Apple Multiple Scan 17 - D50 ▼
Composite Printer: Canon CLC500/EFI Printer ▼
Separation Printer: KODAK SWOP Proofer CMYK - Coated St...▼

─Default Source Profiles───
RGB CMYK Hexachrome
Color: Apple Multiple Scan 17 - D50 ▼
Image: ⊚ Linotype-Hell -SAPHIR- (Reflective) ▼

Display Correction: Off ▼

Correction ▼ | Color Model
√ | RGB
           | CMYK
           | Hexachrome
           | TRUMATCH

Cancel   OK

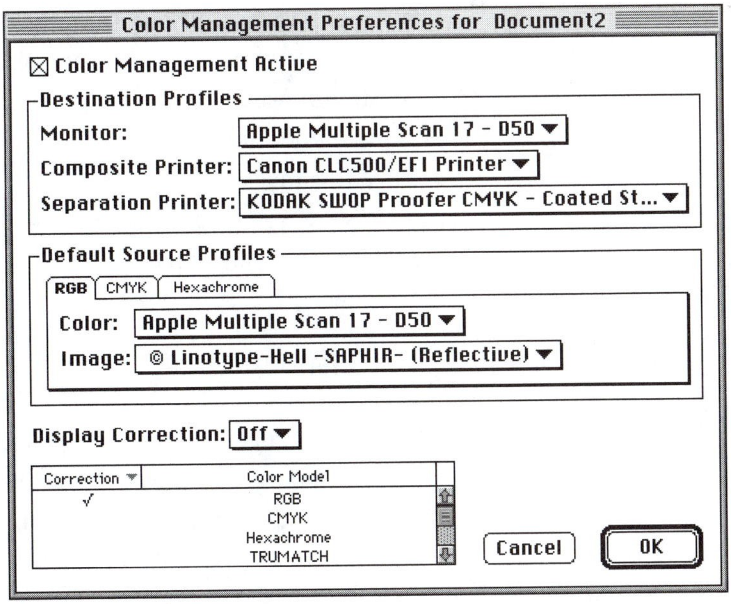

The Monitor setting, however, is fixed: this is where you tell QuarkCMS what you're looking at. As I said earlier, the canned RGB profiles are rarely worth messing with; without a custom profile that describes the behavior of *your* monitor, you'll be hard-pressed to really trust what you see on screen. (Of course, if your monitor is listed, and you have no way of creating a custom profile, I suppose picking the canned one is better than nothing . . . though the display may still be far from accurate.)

Default Source Profiles. There are three tabs in the Default Source Profiles—RGB, CMYK, and Hexachrome—and on each tab there are two popup menus: Color and Image. The Color popup menu lets you determine the source profile for colors you create in QuarkXPress. The Image profile sets the default profile that XPress applies to images when you import them. You can always override the Image profile (I'll discuss how in the next section), but once you choose a Color profile it applies to all colors throughout your document.

▶ **RGB.** Let's say you specify a color in RGB mode. The Color popup menu on the RGB tab tells QuarkCMS that you mean this particular RGB color on this particular monitor (the profile you choose here). Generally, you should set the Color popup menu on the RGB tab to your monitor profile. However, if somebody else built the document and specified the RGB colors on their screen, you might want to pick their monitor profile instead.

If you're trying to match the colors from the original image, you should probably choose your scanner's profile in the Image popup menu. However, if you corrected a color cast or otherwise edited the image based the your screen display, you should probably choose your monitor's profile as well. Remember, this is only for images that are still in RGB mode and have not yet been pre-separated.

▶ **CMYK.** If you're creating CMYK colors in QuarkXPress (including named colors based on CMYK, like Trumatch and Pantone Process), you need to similarly tell QuarkCMS what device those CMYK colors are based on. If you're using a swatch book that was printed based on an uncoated web press, you might want to pick a SWOP-Uncoated profile (or a proofing device of the same type).

Note that the profile you pick in the Color popup menu also determines how RGB images are converted to CMYK, either when you change color modes in the Edit Color dialog box or when you print separations of your document.

One of the great myths in color publishing is that all CMYK images are the same. Not so: when you convert an image from RGB to CMYK, you're separating it for a very specific press condition. Change the press, change the inks, change the paper stock, and you need to reseparate the image. The Image popup menu on the CMYK tab lets you tell QuarkCMS for what device an image was separated. XPress uses this information to simulate the image on your RGB screen, on a composite color printer, or when cross-rendering to a different CMYK device. (Cross-rendering means transforming a CMYK image to a different CMYK color space than it was originally intended.)

▶ **HEXACHROME.** The last tab in the Default Source Profiles section is Hexachrome. You can just ignore these settings, even if you're creating Hexachrome colors (see "Using Hexachrome Colors," later in this appendix), as there are currently no Hexachrome source profiles available.

Display Correction. The Display Correction popup menu lets you control your screen display. The default setting, Off, tells QuarkCMS to go ahead and manage color behind the scenes at print time, but to leave the screen alone. If you haven't set a Monitor profile or if your screen only displays 8-bit color (256 colors), this is your only option. This isn't as bad as it sounds; you can't trust what you see on screen, but you also don't experience the slow-downs that you get when XPress does try to manage what you see on screen.

If you are working on a calibrated monitor with a good monitor profile, you can choose Monitor Color Space, Composite Printer Color Space, or Separation Printer Color Space. People sometimes ask, "Which one displays the most accurate color?" The answer is that they all do, depending on what you're trying to match accurately.

▶ **MONITOR COLOR SPACE.** The Monitor Color space option tells QuarkCMS to transform all colors to match your particular screen (based on your monitor profile). In other words, you see what the

RGB and CMYK colors throughout your document really look like. For instance, if you and guy down the hall both have set up your monitor profiles and you specify an RGB or a CMYK color, when this is turned on, you'll both see the same color. The problem is that this doesn't have much relevance if your document is going to be printed.

▶ **COMPOSITE PRINTER COLOR SPACE.** Choosing Composite Printer Color Space tells the CMS to make your screen colors appear how they will print on your Composite Printer (based on it's default profile). Unless your composite printer is your final output, this, too, is less useful.

▶ **SEPARATION PRINTER COLOR SPACE.** If you want to know what your document will look like when it comes off press (or whatever your target separation device is), you can select Separation Printer Color Space from the Display Correction popup menu. Here, all your colors are transformed into the separated CMYK color space, and then converted back to RGB in order to be displayed on screen.

I find that I tend to work with Display Correction turned off most of the time so I can save time. When I want to match colors on screen to either what someone else is seeing or to my final separation device, I switch to the appropriate Display Correction setting . . . and then I go make a cup of tea. It takes a while for XPress to reset all the colors, especially on large imported images, because it has to find the data on disk, read it in, and create a new screen preview.

Correction list. The last feature in the Color Management Preferences dialog box is unlabeled—it's simply a list of color models with or without a checkbox next to them. What this mysterious setting actually determines is the subject of some debate, but it's really quite simple: It controls whether colors that you create in QuarkXPress are transformed when the target profile's color space is the same as the source profile's.

Here's an example: Let's say you build a CMYK color and apply it to some text. If the Correction checkmark is off next to CMYK (it is by default), then the color is managed when displayed on screen (because that's a CMYK to RGB transformation), but it is not changed when printed to a CMYK device. The idea is that if you specify a particular blend of

CMYK, you probably know what you're doing and QuarkCMS won't mess with it. However, if you're printing CMYK colors to a composite printer or cross-rendering them to a different device than they were originally specced for, you need to turn the CMYK Correction checkmark on.

Similarly, by default RGB colors are corrected (the checkmark is on). If you turn this off, then QuarkCMS won't transform your RGB colors on screen, no matter what profiles you have specified because the monitor is always an RGB space. On the other hand, this doesn't affect the RGB to CMYK translation at print time (because the color spaces are different).

If you build colors in Pantone Process, Pantone Spot to Process, Trumatch, Focoltone, or Hexachrome (in other words, any model that relies on process colors rather than spot colors), you also have to turn these checkmarks on or else they will not be transformed when printing to a composite color printer or to a different CMYK device than they were originally intended.

Again, the correction list only refers to colors you build in XPress; not to imported images.

Telling QuarkCMS About Pictures

Once you've told QuarkCMS about your monitor and printer, and you've set up your default profiles for colors, you need to tell it a little about the pictures you're importing. When you first import a picture, XPress applies the default source profile to it unless you override that in the Get Picture dialog box. Or, you can also change an image's source profile in the Profile Information palette. Let's look at each of these options.

Selecting a Profile

The QuarkCMS XTension adds a popup menu and a checkbox to the Get Picture dialog box (see Figure A-2). If a picture didn't have a profile assigned to it, then QuarkCMS couldn't transform its colors because it wouldn't know what to transform *from* (it doesn't know what the colors are *supposed* to look like). Therefore, no color matching would be possible. Again, the point is that when you tell QuarkCMS where the image came from, here in the Get Picture dialog box or elsewhere, you're telling it how the colors should really look.

Figure A-2

Overriding the default
profile in Get Picture

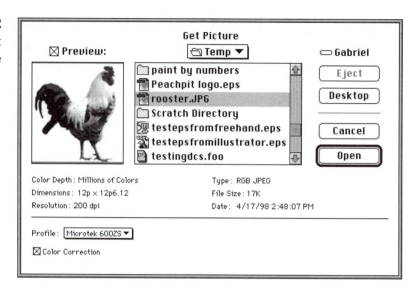

For instance, my default source profile for images is generally set to my monitor, because I'm color correcting on a calibrated screen. However, if I import an image directly after scanning it on my Linotype-Hell Saphire, I can assign my scanner profile in the Get Picture dialog box, overriding the default profile. QuarkCMS then knows not only the RGB values in the image but also what device created those values—hence, what the colors really look like.

In general, you should select a profile that corresponds to how the picture was saved. QuarkCMS is smart enough to examine the format of a file and only display acceptable profiles. That is, it lets you choose process-color profiles such as SWOP-Coated only when you're importing a CMYK image, and RGB color profiles when the image is stored in an RGB mode. (At the time of this writing, there is a bug in QuarkXPress for Macintosh so that the Profile popup menu is only available when you have the Preview checkbox turned on the Get Picture dialog box.)

Note that if your picture has a color profile embedded in it, the profiles popup menu appears as "Embedded." (You can embed a profile in an image with tools like Apple's ColorSync Export Filter within Photoshop.) You can change to a different profile if you want to, but I wouldn't advise it.

To Correct or Not to Correct

The second item in the Get Picture dialog box is the Color Correction checkbox. When this option is turned off, XPress will not transform the image's colors when the source profile and the target profile both have the same color space. For example, if you import an RGB image with the Color Correction checkbox turn off, QuarkCMS will not transform the image's color on screen (because both the image and the monitor are in RGB), but it will transform it when you print CMYK.

Similarly, if you import a CMYK TIFF image when this option is turned off, QuarkCMS won't color correct the image when you print color seps or even when you print to a composite printer, because both of these are CMYK spaces, too.

The default setting for this checkbox is determined by how you've set up the Correction List in the Color Management Preferences dialog box. By default, the Color Correction checkbox is turned on for RGB images and off for CMYK image, but you can always override it if you want.

▼ ▼

Tip: Set the Same Profiles. If you set the source profile for a CMYK image to the same setting as your target separation profile, QuarkCMS will not touch your image data when it prints separations, even if the Color Correction option is turned on.

▼ ▼

Changing the Profiles for a Picture

What happens if you've imported a picture, and then realize you've chosen the wrong profile for it? You could spend a lot of time reimporting the picture, or you could simply select the picture and change the Profile popup menu in the Profile Information palette (choose Show Profile Information from the View menu; see Figure A-3). The palette has the same popup menus and checkbox as the Get Picture dialog box. Simply change the values to whatever you want.

Figure A-3
Profile
Information
palette

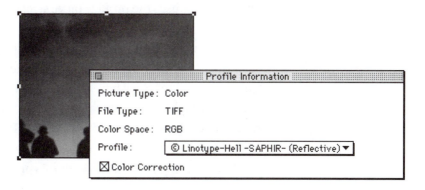

Profile Information

Picture Type : Color
File Type : TIFF
Color Space : RGB
Profile : © Linotype-Hell –SAPHIR– (Reflective) ▼
☒ Color Correction

If you want to change a lot of pictures at the same time, you can use the Profiles tab of the Usage dialog box (see Figure A-4), found under the Utilities menu. You can find where a profile is used in your document by selecting the profile's from the Profile popup menu. Note that this displays the profiles applied both to images and within popup menus in the Color Management Preferences dialog box, but I suggest only changing profiles applied to images from here. You can change an image's profile by selecting the image and clicking Replace. (You can select more than one image at a time—as long as they all have the same profile—by Command-clicking on each item in the list.)

Figure A-4

Profile Usage

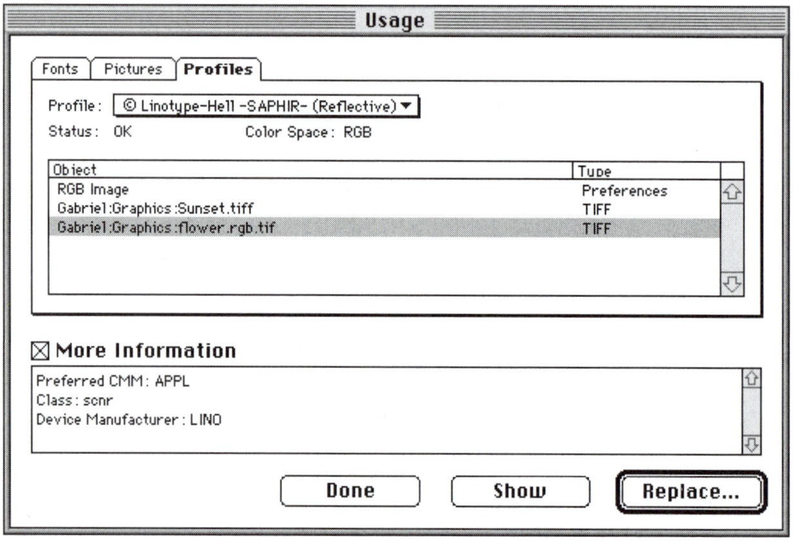

Show. The Show button is active only when you've selected an image within the Profile Usage list. Clicking it takes you to the first picture in a document that uses the profile you've selected.

More Information. Underneath the list of objects in the Usage dialog box is the More Information checkbox. When on (I always have these "More Information" checkboxes turned on because I like knowing what's going on), XPress displays three details about each profile you select: the Preferred CMM, the Class, and the Device Manufacturer.

The Preferred CMM tells you which color engine will probably perform the color transformations with this profile (remember that on the

Macintosh, there are two: ColorSync and KICC, though in Windows, there is just KICC). Generally, you'll see either "KCMS" (this is another name for KICC . . . it seems that those folks at Kodak can never stick to a naming decision) or "appl", which means that ColorSync is the preferred engine. Ultimately, who is doing what hardly matters because the difference in final output is so subtle.

Class refers to the type of profile you've selected. You can usually interpret the four-letter abbreviations pretty easily: "mntr" means it's a monitor profile; "scnr" is a scanner profile, "prtr" is a printer profile. As for who the device manufacturer is, I just don't care much.

Using Hexachrome Color

Back in Chapter 12, *Color*, I discussed Pantone's Hexachrome six-color system, which uses cyan, yellow, magenta, black, green, and orange to simulate many more colors than the normal four-color process system. However, key to working in Hexachrome is color management. In fact, you can only separate Hexachrome colors that you define in QuarkXPress under two conditions:

▶ The QuarkCMS XTension must be activated.

▶ You must have a Hexachrome profile selected as your target profile (see Figure A-5). You can select it either in the Color Management Preferences dialog box or on the Profiles tab of the Print dialog box (see "Color Management at Print Time," below).

If either of these conditions are not met, your Hexachrome colors are separated into CMYK, which sort of defeats the purpose. (By the way, QuarkXPress cannot currently include Hexachrome colors when you use Save as EPS, even if you use the DCS 2.0 format; see Save as EPS, below.)

Tip: Hexachrome Images. You can use Pantone's HexWrench software to preseparate RGB images into the Hexachrome color space and then save them in the DCS 2.0 format. When you import them into QuarkXPress, the program separates them properly because XPress just sees the orange and green plates as regular spot color in the file. (Of course, because QuarkCMS doesn't manage DCS files, these images can't

Figure A-5

Selecting a
Hexachrome profile

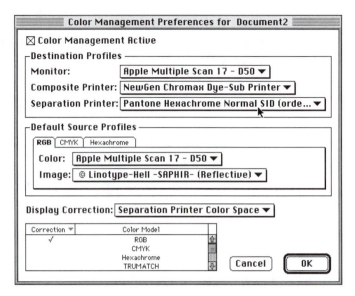

be transformed into other color spaces.) Note that there's no reason to convert CMYK images to the Hexachrome space because colors outside of the CMYK gamut will have already been clipped or compressed; rather it only makes sense to convert RGB images with a large color gamut that cannot be represented by CMYK alone.

Color Management at Print Time

I suppose the Print dialog box is inevitable at the end of our color management process; afterall, it's getting consistent color at print time that is ultimately most important to most of us. When the QuarkCMS is active, you get sixth tab in the Print dialog box: Profiles (see Figure A-6). This tab lets you override the default Separation Printer and Composite Printer profiles that you earlier chose in the Color Management Preferences dialog box. It also lets you force your composite color printer to display colors as though it were your final separation device.

Separation versus Composite. Which profile QuarkCMS uses when you click Print depends entirely on the Separation checkbox on the Document tab of the Print dialog box. When the Separation option is on, QuarkCMS uses the Separation profile selected on the Profile tab; when off, it uses the Composite profile. Of course, you should also choose the proper printer type from the Printer Description popup menu on the Setup tab; for instance when printing separations, you want a black-and-white printer; when printing a color proof, you'd better have a color printer selected (see Chapter 13, *Printing*, for more on these settings).

Proofing on a Color Printer

Hard-copy proofing—often known as preproofing—lets you use an output device with a wide gamut, such as a dye-sublimation or Iris ink-jet printer, to simulate the gamut of a press or (more commonly) of a proofing system such as 3M Match Print. Preproofing on a composite color printer may be more accurate than a soft proof on the monitor, but I've seen many instances when it was not. The advantage of a hard-copy proof is that it provides a tangible record of your intentions and expectations—you aren't likely to find a printer who will sign your monitor, but a growing number are willing to let an Iris or dye-sub proof form the basis of the contract.

The problem is that if you simply send a CMYK image that's been targeted for a printing press to a dye-sub printer, the results will quite likely look strange because the dye-sublimation printer's inks are nothing like four-color process inks. The trick is the Composite Simulates Separation checkbox on the Profiles tab in the Print dialog box. When on, QuarkCMS asks ColorSync or KICC to render your colors in the final separation device's color space, and then cross-render this CMYK data into the color space of you composite color proofer. Of course, in order for this to work, you really need accurate profiles all around. (Unfortunately, as this book goes to press, the Composite Simulates Separation feature isn't functional . . . though it should be fixed by the time you read this.)

Note that other color printers, such as thermal-wax and many of the desktop ink-jets, usually don't cover the entire gamut of the four-color process, so they aren't as well suited as dye-subs are to preproofing use. The same holds true for color laser copiers and the new generation of color desktop laser printers. Still, the techniques described here should get you much better results from those printers than you'd get otherwise.

If you're using RGB images, you can still use the Composite Simulates Separation checkbox. In fact, you should, or else your color proof will probably appear better than it possibly could on press. (Of course, ignore this if the composite color printer is your final output.)

Missing Profiles

Progress is never without a price. When you use a new typeface, you have the burden of making sure your service bureau and other people who receive your documents have that typeface as well. It turns out that ICC profiles are the same way. When you send a file to another QuarkXPress user, you must make certain that your recipient has legal copies of all the QuarkCMS profiles you've used in your document (see "Tip: Moving Profiles," below). Just as with fonts, the Collect for Output feature (see "Collect for Output" in Chapter 13, *Printing*) doesn't automatically assemble all the profiles used in a document. You're on your own.

So let's say you've received a document without all the needed profiles. How will you know? What can you do about it? If you're familiar with the ways QuarkXPress handles missing fonts and pictures, you should have no trouble coping with missing profiles.

When you open a document that uses one or more profiles that are not on your system, an error message appears (see Figure A-7). If you can obtain the proper profile from someone—perhaps from the person who sent you the QuarkXPress document, or from the manufacturers of the device—then do it (See "Tip: The Profile Manager," below).

However, if you can't obtain the profile, you can either go ahead and do nothing about it, or replace it with a profile that is active in your system. If you're only interested in a fast and dirty proof—let's say you're proofing page geometry or type—then there's no need to replace profiles. But if you need color matching, you must replace the missing profiles (see "Changing the Profiles for a Picture," earlier in this chapter).

Figure A-7

Missing profiles

> ⚠ **"Document1.qxd" uses profiles not installed in your System.**
>
> [Continue]   [[**List Profiles**]]

Printing anyway. If you attempt to print a file which uses profiles that are missing from your system, you'll get the same alert as when you opened the document (it's virtually identical to the one you get when you try to print a document with missing or modified pictures). You've got two options in this dialog box: click OK to proceed with printing despite the missing profiles, or click List Profiles to display the missing profiles. If you choose the second option, you get the Missing Profiles dialog box, which is almost identical in appearance and function to the Profile Usage dialog box, with a few changes.

First of all, it only displays missing profiles and the items associated with them. There's also a Done button, which lets you proceed with printing the file regardless of the number of profiles you've replaced. Unfortunately, there's no Cancel button to stop replacing profiles or to stops your print job.

▼ ▼

Tip: The Profile Manager. The QuarkCMS XTension offers a Profile Manager, which is very similar to the PPD Manager (see Chapter 13, *Printing*). One notable difference is that the Profile Manager lets you chose an Auxiliary Profile Folder (see Figure A-8). If a client sends you a folder full of profiles that they used, you don't have to mix them among your own profiles in your System folder. Instead, you can just select Profile Manager from the Utilities menu, click on Auxiliary Profile Folder (the button is called Browse in Windows), and choose their folder on your hard drive.

If you add or remove a profile from your system while QuarkXPress is running, it won't register the change until you click the Update button in the Profile manager. (It automatically updates the list whenever you launch XPress, however.)

Of course, the Profile Manager also lets you turn profiles on and off, making them available or not available to you within the program. Unless you have four bazillion profiles and know that you will only be using a handful of them, you can probably ignore this function.

▼ ▼

Figure A-8

The Profile Manager

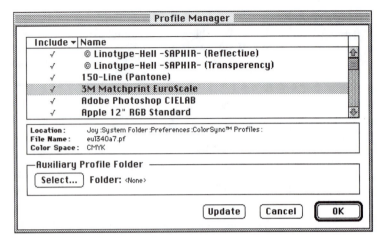

Tip: Moving Profiles. ICC profiles are little pieces of software. And, like most pieces of software, they're copyrighted. While many profiles are free and can be copied from one user to the next, others are proprietary and, like fonts, you're not really supposed to copy them from one machine to another; rather, the developers want you to buy a profile for each machine you use. The key is to read the license agreement that comes with the profile. Of course, if you're only sending a profile to a service bureau in order to print your document, I don't think anyone is going to start breathing down your neck . . . .

Saving Files as EPS

The Profile tab appears in one other place than the Print dialog box: the Save As EPS dialog box (see Figure A-9). However, your options here change depending on what you choose in the Format popup menu. If you select Color, your EPS is by default a composite color file, so you can only choose a profile from the Composite popup menu. On the other hand, if you chose DCS or DCS 2.0 from the Format popup menu, QuarkCMS lets you choose both a composite and a separation profile. The reason: As I mentioned back in Chapter 9, *Pictures*, a DCS file contains both separated CMYK data (and spot color, for DCS 2.0) and a composite color rendition.

If you know where this EPS file is going, setting these popup menus can be quite useful. Otherwise, you should probably leave them set to None so that QuarkCMS doesn't change the data at all.

Figure A-9

Color management in the
Save as EPS dialog box

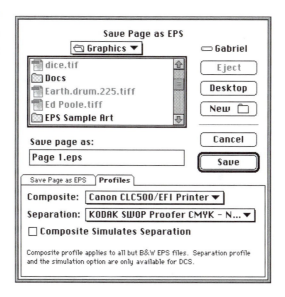

Also, note that the Composite Simulates Separation checkbox appears here, too. I tend to leave this on so that the composite image accurately reflects the high-resolution data in the DCS file, though if the EPS file were going to be used for two purposes (printing high-res separations to an imagesetter and printing lower-resolution composite color to a short-run printer perhaps), you might want to turn it off. (Again, this is not currently working, though it may be by the time you read this.)

Pros and Cons

When it comes right down to it, I think that the QuarkCMS XTension is not only really cool, but it can be incredibly useful. However, it obviously has limits and isn't for everyone all the time. One of the most important things to note is that color management works best when you're comparing apples to oranges rather than to salmons or coffee beans. You'll get a better idea of a final color by looking at a printed color proof than at the screen. You can calibrate all you want, and you'll still always get a more reliable image from a printer than from the screen. It still won't be a perfect match to your final output, of course, but it's that much closer. Clearly, as with just about every other aspect of desktop publishing, WYSIWYG color is a relative thing.

B

MACINTOSH VS. WINDOWS

I know many hard-core Mac users who prefer to wear cloves of garlic (or rubber gloves) when working with computers based on Micro-soft Windows. I also know Windows users who still think the Macintosh is just a toy. No matter what you think, two facts simply can't be denied: First, there are lots more Windows boxes out there than Macs (though as I write this, there are still many more people doing electronic publishing on Macintoshes than on PCs). Second, increasingly, people have to use both platforms, sometimes at the same time.

Fortunately, QuarkXPress works almost identically on both computer platforms (if it weren't for the different look and feel of dialog boxes and menus, most of the time you couldn't tell the difference between the two versions). Plus, QuarkXPress for Windows can open QuarkXPress for Macintosh files, and vice versa, providing pretty decent two-way transferability of files between the two programs.

But while bringing files from one platform to the other and back again is possible, it's certainly not a no-brainer. The problem is rarely XPress; rather it's the underlying operating system infrastructure that you have to worry about: fonts, graphic file formats, file naming, and so on. In this appendix, I want to take a quick tour of the obstacles in your way when transferring files.

▼ ▼

You May Get There From Here

The first step in cross-platform compatibility is getting your QuarkXPress documents from one computer to the next. There are several ways of transferring files between PCs and Macs, and QuarkXPress is happy with the result no matter how you move your files.

Networking. Back in 1990, Steve Jobs prophesized that the '90s would become the decade of the networked computer, and he was absolutely right. The most popular method of getting XPress documents from one platform to another is over some sort of network, whether that be the Internet or a local-area network (LAN). File servers such as the Digital Alpha running Windows NT in my office are commonplace these days, and you can move files between your Mac and PC via this sort of server (as long as both have access). (Windows NT's built-in server software can support both Macs and PCs without any additional software.)

Getting Macintoshes and PCs to communicate with each other on the same network can be tricky because they typically don't speak the same language. However, this process is made much easier with various commercial software packages on the market. Because most of the computers in my office are Macintoshes that use AppleTalk, I use PC MacLan Connect on my Windows-based machines so that they can communicate using AppleTalk. This way, my Macs can "see" the PCs in the Chooser and the PCs can "see" the Macs in the Network Neighborhood.

Floppy disks. If your Macs and PCs aren't networked, you've got little choice other than to copy your QuarkXPress file onto a disk (either a floppy disk, or some sort of removeable like a Zip disk). This turns out to be easier than you might imagine, because all Macintosh models (well, every one sold in the past ten years or so) can read PC disks as well as Mac disks.

However, just because the disk drive itself can read and write PC disks doesn't mean that the operating system itself can. Macintoshes come with a control panel device called PC Exchange that enables the system to read these disks; if that software is missing or turned off, the Mac doesn't know what to do with it.

If you're moving a file from your Macintosh to a PC and you don't have a PC-formatted floppy handy, you'll have to format one. Any 3.5-inch floppy will do, even one labeled "Mac formatted." In fact, the Macintosh reads PC disks that were formatted on a Macintosh even better than if the disks were formatted on a PC. To format a PC disk on a Macintosh, select Erase Disk from the Finder's Special menu while PC Exchange is installed.

Of course, if you use a Windows-based PC, it's also likely that you'll need to open XPress documents that are on Macintosh disks—either on floppies or large-format disks like Zip, Jaz, Syquest, and even CD recordable media. Neither DOS nor Windows will read these disks without some additional software. The easiest solution out there is the low-cost utility Here&Now from Software Architects. Once it's installed you just use the Windows Explorer as normal for copying files from Macintosh-formatted media.

▼ ▼

Tip: Translations vs. Universal File Formats. While you can move QuarkXPress files between Macs and PCs, there's still no such thing as a "universal" QuarkXPress document format that's identical on both platforms. Each time QuarkXPress opens a document saved on the opposite platform, it must translate the file. The file name doesn't change, but—as one Quark tech-support person puts it—"the dirty bit is on," so you should immediately save the file. And since some information gets lost (as I'll describe) or needs to be fixed when you translate files, I'd recommend you keep your cross-platform transfers to the minimum necessary to finish a job. Remember: fewer translations equals less clean-up.

▼ ▼

File Names, Types, and Creators

The first hassle (though minor) in moving files from one platform to another is that PCs and Macintoshes save files differently. On the Macintosh, every file has several attributes attached to it, including file type and creator. These are four-letter keys that tell the Macintosh what sort of file it is and what program generated it. For example, when you double-click on a file, the Mac looks at the file's creator to see what application to start up.

In the PC world, it's simpler: no file types, no file creators—only file names. PC files all have names that include a three-letter suffix called a "file extension." In Windows 3.1, files had to be "eight-dot-three" (the name could be no longer than eight letters, followed by a period, and ending with a three-letter extension; for example, "8LTRBLUS.TXT"). Now you can use up to 255 characters in a file name, but the file must still end with a period followed by the file extension. This extension provides all the information (and it ain't much) about the file's type and creator.

Moving from PC to Mac

When you're trying to open a QuarkXPress for Windows document on a Macintosh, you must make certain that the document has either the correct three-letter extension (it almost certainly will by default) or the correct file type and creator. The document icon may look like a blank page on the Macintosh, but as long as the file has the proper DOS extension (".QXD") QuarkXPress can still "see" and open the file.

If you want the file to open when you double-click on it in the Macintosh Finder, you have to change the file type and creator. PC Exchange (and other connectivity software) can map file extensions to file types automatically (see Figure B-1). If the file came across a network, you can change the file type and creator in one of two ways.

▶ You can open the file in QuarkXPress (using Open from the File menu) and resave the file using Save As.

▶ You can use a Macintosh utility such as FileBuddy, ResEdit, or FileTyper to manually change the type and creator.

So what are the appropriate file types and creators? Documents created in QuarkXPress 3.1 or later on the Macintosh have a creator code of XPR3. The file type depends on what kind of file it is: documents are XDOC, templates are XTMP, libraries are XLIB, and book files are XBOK. These are the only kinds of documents on your Mac that will ever show up in QuarkXPress's file-opening dialog box; you'll never see a Microsoft Word or FileMaker Pro file in there, because QuarkXPress filters out all files except those which have these four specific file types.

Figure B-1

Mapping extensions to
applications and
document types

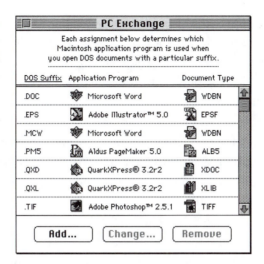

Note that when you open a QuarkXPress for Windows file on the Macintosh, the Open dialog box tells you that it's a PC file; when you click Open, it displays a message saying it's converting the file.

Mac to PC: Filenames and Extensions

It's really easy to change the file type and creator for a PC file while on either a Macintosh or a PC: just change the three-letter extension. You can name the file anything you want, but the relevant extensions are ".QXD" for documents, ".QXL" for libraries, ".QXT" for templates, and ".QXB" for books. If you assign a legal name to a document using these extensions, it should be easily opened by QuarkXPress for Windows, either by double-clicking in the Windows desktop, or from within QuarkXPress for Windows.

Another option: Instead of changing the name of the file, you can select "All Files *.*" in the popup menu in the Open dialog box, and it shows even files with the wrong extensions.

In general, if you work in a cross-platform environment, you should simply make a habit of always adding the three-letter file extensions on your files.

▼ ▼

Tip: Careful with Your Naming. Macintoshes have always let you use up to 31 characters in a file name, but it wasn't until recently that you could use more than eight-dot-three (eight characters, a period, then the file extension) in Windows. Now—in Windows 95 or Windows NT 4.0 or later—you can use up to 255 characters in a file name.

(Note that there are still some programs on the market that require you to use the short file names. Fortunately, the newest versions of QuarkXPress, Photoshop, Illustrator, FreeHand, and just about any other desktop publishing tool you probably use are quite content with long file names.)

But there is one other trap that you can fall into when naming your files: the characters you can and cannot use. The only character you can't use in a Macintosh file name is a colon. That's because the Macintosh operating system uses colons internally to keep track of file paths (what files are within what folders).

On the other hand, DOS-based systems like Windows use lots of these "internal" characters for all sorts of stuff. That means you can't use colons, straight quotes, question marks, asterisks, slashes, backslashes, or angle brackets in DOS filenames. (For those of you who like pictures, that is: ?, *, /, \, ", :, <, or >.) Because of this, if you work in a cross-platform environment, you should avoid any of these prohibited characters.

▼ ▼

Tip: Previewing DOS Names on a Macintosh. If you're using an older version of PC Exchange or another PC disk mounter, it may not handle the long file names correctly and, instead, truncate the file name to eight-dot-three. For instance, if you copy a file named "David's Document" from a Macintosh onto a PC disk, the file may appear at first to have the proper long file name. But then, when the disk is read on a PC, the file name may appear as "!DAVIDS.DOC". On the other hand, it appears with the full name if you use a newer version of PC Exchange, one that understands long file names.

You can see how a document name is going to look when it gets to the PC. First, copy it to a PC disk, then select it in the Finder and choose Get Info from the File menu (Command-I). At the top of the dialog box, you can see the name of the file. Click on it and it switches to the eight-dot-three PC name. Click on it again and it switches back.

▼ ▼

What Does (and Doesn't) Transfer

Physically moving your QuarkXPress files from one platform to the next and successfully opening them is only half the job of transferring files. In general, all page-layout, text, and picture information comes across just fine in either direction, as do any changes you've made to the Document preferences. Also, any colors, style sheets, and H&J settings you've defined in the document generally transfer without a hitch. However, you'd better be aware of what doesn't get transferred. QuarkXPress documents on each platform are almost identical, but that "almost" can trip you up if you're not careful.

Frames. I have very mixed feelings about the Frame Editor program on the Macintosh. It can do some nice things, but mostly I think it fits best in the Trash. But who listens to me? Lots of people are using custom frames and getting reasonable results. However, do note that Frame Editor doesn't exist in QuarkXPress for Windows. Any bitmapped frames you've created or assigned on the Mac will travel over to the PC, and they'll usually show up and print fine. Of course, you still can't edit those bitmapped frames, as there's no Frame Editor utility on the PC (thank goodness). You can also assign one of the default bitmapped frames on the PC, too, and these transfer properly to the Macintosh.

XPress Preferences. There is no way to move the XPress Preferences file from one platform to the other, but fortunately, that's not something that many people need to do. All the document-level preferences are saved within the document itself, and almost all of them translate perfectly (Auto Ligatures is one notable exception). When you open a Macintosh file in QuarkXPress for Windows, you're often prompted with the "XPress Preferences does not match" dialog box. I typically just click the Use Document Preferences button (or press Enter).

Character-set remapping. Probably the biggest hassle in transferring files between platforms is character-set remapping. The problem here is that Macintosh and Windows font character sets don't match completely. All the basic "low-ASCII" characters (letters, numbers, punctuation) map just fine, but special characters (characters with ASCII codes above 127) can sometimes get messed up.

If a special character shows up in both Mac and Windows typefaces, QuarkXPress does its best to map it correctly. But there's only so far it can go. Table B-1 shows a list of characters that are commonly found in Windows and Macintosh fonts that have no equivalent on the opposite

Table B-1

Special characters that map differently in Windows and on the Macintosh

WINDOWS	ANSI CODE ◄ MAPS TO ►	MACINTOSH	ASCII CODE
Š	138	ˇ	255
š	154	π	185
¦	166	ı	245
²	178	≈	197
³	179	Δ	198
¹	185	◊	215
¼	188	/	218
½	189	fi	222
¾	190	fl	223
Đ	208		240
×	215	˘	249
Ý	221	·	250
ý	253	"	253

platform (unless you switch to a special typeface). You can also use this table to select special characters if you know you'll be printing from the other platform.

Note that the mathematical symbols that seem to appear in every PostScript font on the Macintosh are often just mapped from the Symbol font. So unless the font you're using has the math symbols built in—unfortunately, there's no good way to find this out without Fontographer or another font-editing program—several characters won't transfer correctly. In Table B-2, I've listed where each math character is found in the Symbol font, so you can search and replace before transferring a file to Windows (or use those characters to begin with).

Ligatures. The "fi" and "fl" ligature characters on the Macintosh are not to be found on the PC. That's right: ligatures used in your Mac document will go bye-bye when they're opened by QuarkXPress for Windows. This is an annoying oversight not by Quark, but by Microsoft, which just never thought that ligatures were an important part of a character set.

If you used actual ligature characters on the Macintosh (Option-Shift-5 and -6), you had better use Find/Change to change them back to normal "fi" and "fl" pairs before transferring the file. On the other hand, there is little reason to type those characters anymore, as QuarkXPress for Macintosh has automatic ligature support (see "Punctuation and Symbols" in Chapter 6, *Type and Typography*).

Table B-2

Commonly used
math symbols

*These symbols are found in
most Macintosh fonts.
Press the listed keystrokes
on the Macintosh to create
these symbols.*

NAME	LOOKS LIKE	IN MOST FONTS	SYMBOL FONT
Division	÷	Option-/	Option-Shift-P
Plus or minus	±	Option-Shift-=	Option-Shift-=
Greater or equal	≥	Option-period	Option-period
Lesser or equal	≤	Option-comma	Option-3
Approximate equal	≈	Option-X	Option-9
Not equal	≠	Option-=	Option-P
Infinity	∞	Option-5	Option-8
Partial differential	∂	Option-D	Option-D
Integral	∫	Option-B	Option-Shift-;
Florin	*f*	Option-F	Option-7
Capital omega	Ω	Option-Z	Shift-W
Capital delta	Δ	Option-J	Shift-D
Product	Π	Option-Shift-P	Shift-P
Summation	Σ	Option-W	Shift-S
Pi	π	Option-P	P
Radical	√	Option-V	Option-/

QuarkXPress for Windows doesn't have the automatic ligatures feature, so when you move a Mac file with automatic ligatures turned on over to Windows, your ligatures go away (and because of that, you may get some minor text reflow). But at least you have fi and fl, rather than the ½ and ¾ characters Windows substitutes, which you have to search for and replace.

The second solution is to use a program like Fontographer to either mess around with the ASCII numbers assigned to ligatures in Windows fonts, or to create new fonts on the PC that include the ligatures. I only recommend the latter if you're particularly brave, and aren't working on a deadline. (This still doesn't work with auto ligatures, however, because QuarkXPress wouldn't know where to find them in the character set.) Or you can resort to Expert Set fonts from Adobe and other font vendors, and use the Find/Change dialog box to replace fi's and fl's with Expert Set characters. The Expert Set characters are typically the same in both Macintosh and Windows versions of the fonts.

Font metrics. Font metrics describe the width of each character in a font, and the kerning pairs for those characters. On the Macintosh, PostScript fonts store their character widths and kerning pair values in the screen font files. Macintosh TrueType fonts store metrics entirely in the printer font (the screen fonts contain just bitmaps). On the PC, the font metrics for PostScript fonts are located in ".PFM" files; metrics for TrueType fonts are found in ".TTF" files.

However, no matter where the metrics of a font may reside, you need to be aware that the metrics of a PC font may differ from those of a Macintosh font, even if they're from the same company. I don't know why this is, but it's certainly a major problem when moving files back and forth between the two platforms. If the metrics change, then the text in a document reflows. Sometimes this is hardly a problem, and other times it can spell hours of work.

It's a good idea to have a printed proof of a Macintosh document handy after you've imported it into your Windows version of QuarkXPress (or vice versa). That way you can check to see if the layout got altered in the transfer. When proofing the document, look for any widows or orphans that may result from minute differences in font metrics. If you notice a problem, you can sometimes adjust the spacing parameters through kerning or tracking to compensate for the differences in font metrics.

Forbidden fonts. There are certain typefaces that exist only on Macs or only on Windows machines. You should never use them on documents that you intend to shuffle between platforms, unless you enjoy spending a lot of time staring at the Font Usage dialog box. On the Macintosh, avoid using system fonts such as Chicago, Geneva, Monaco, and New York (a good rule, with some exceptions, is never to use a font named after a city). In Windows, avoid fonts such as, MS San Serif, Modern, Helv, System, or Tms Rmn, or any other font listed in the Windows 95 Fonts control panel with an "A" in its icon, instead of "TT", and an .FON extension to their filename listing. These are bitmapped fonts of fixed size, meant only for the Windows interface.

If you open a file and its document fonts are missing, QuarkXPress gives you a chance to immediately change them (see "Missing Fonts," in Chapter 6, *Type and Typography*). QuarkXPress catches missing fonts if you've used them anywhere in your document, including in style sheets and on master pages. In other words, even if you don't use a particular style sheet or master page anywhere in your document, you get notified.

Kerning information. If you've spent a lot of time making kerning tables within QuarkXPress's Kern/Track Editor, you might want to save the hassle of doing them over on another platform. I'm happy to note that you can move the kerning information from the PC to the Macintosh (or vice versa) by exporting the information as a text file (click the Export button in the Edit Kerning dialog box) and importing into the other program (use the Import button in the same dialog box in the Windows version).

The only problem with this technique is that the fonts on each platform are often different, even if they're the same font from the same company—just like with the metrics. Therefore, the kerning used on the Macintosh might not always apply precisely to the Windows font of the same name.

Transferring libraries. You can't transfer libraries from the Mac to Windows or from Windows to the Mac. That's just the way it goes. I used to tell people about a great tip that let you work around this limitation, but it turns out that it only worked in earlier versions of QuarkXPress. Let me know if you find any good solution for this painful restriction.

Transferring Graphics

The last (but certainly not the least) of your problems when transferring files between platforms is graphics. In fact, this is one of the least understood issues in cross-platform compatibility. The basic problem is that graphics, like fonts, are described in different formats on each of the two computer platforms.

The good news is that QuarkXPress is smart enough to do most of the translation work for you. No matter which platform you're working on, QuarkXPress can import files in either IBM or Macintosh format. It simply doesn't care whether you're on a Macintosh importing a PC format file, or on a Windows machine importing a Macintosh TIFF file. This is great, but if you're using pictures in your documents, you still might have some work ahead of you.

Graphic links. The first and most basic problem is that links to EPS and TIFF images can get messed up in the transfer—the Picture Usage dialog box shows the image as either missing or modified. You can usually remove the chance of this happening by keeping the images in the same folder as the QuarkXPress document you're opening, but even this gets a little screwy when the file resides on a file server and you access it from both Macintoshes and Windows machines.

If you send a document to the PC to work on it temporarily, the picture links to the files on the Macintosh are retained (as long as they aren't changed on the PC by clicking Update in the Usage dialog box). Similarly, links within Windows documents are retained when you move a file to the Mac and back, as long as you don't change them on the Mac. The trick is to update a picture in the Usage dialog box only if you're certain you won't be sending the QuarkXPress file back to its original location, or if you absolutely must print with current versions of artwork, regardless of the platform.

EPS screen previews. The next thing you need to be careful of is how images are transferred between the Macintosh and PC. Screen previews are handled differently on each platform. When you create an EPS on a Macintosh and you specify a Macintosh PICT preview, the screen preview is stored in what's called the file's resource fork. The problem is that resource forks don't exist on the PC, so if you move the graphic over and try to import it into QuarkXPress for Windows, you can't see the preview. In fact, without a screen preview, all you see on the screen is a gray box where the picture should be. Note that the picture still prints properly, even if you can't see it on screen.

There are two solutions to this problem: importing into Mac XPress and then transferring the document to the PC, or saving the picture as a PC EPS.

▶ QUARKXPRESS FOR MACINTOSH. Because QuarkXPress saves a preview image of each picture within your documents, you can bring those documents to the PC and still see the preview image on screen. The images are linked to the EPS files, so even if you move the image *and* the QuarkXPress document to the PC, you can still print properly. Even runarounds are transferred okay.

▶ PC EPS FILES. The second solution for the EPS screen preview problem is to give your EPS files PC previews. Adobe Illustrator,

Macromedia FreeHand, Adobe Photoshop, the LaserWriter 8 driver, and a slew of other programs let you save or export a file as a PC EPS—with a TIFF preview that's saved in the data fork rather than the resource fork. Therefore, when you move it over to the PC, you can import it, screen preview and all.

File names and extensions. Just as QuarkXPress documents need the right file extensions when transferred to the PC, graphics that get transferred also need the right file names, or else XPress won't be able to recognize them as graphics. That means they'll often need to be renamed with a three-letter ".TIF", ".EPS", or ".PCT" extension (see "File Types" in Chapter 9, *Pictures*, for more information on this).

File types to avoid. Some formats to avoid: PICTs contained in Mac documents and transferred to PCs sometimes print poorly or not at all (just like on Macs!), and WMF pictures in PC documents may (similarly) not print correctly on the Mac. Sometimes EPS images from the Mac look wrong on screen after they're transferred to a PC. Often if you simply re-import the picture, it'll clear up any problems (as long as the EPS file has a TIFF preview rather than a PICT preview).

And when it comes to edition files (with Publish and Subscribe), forget it. If you've subscribed to an edition file on your Mac, that link gets lost for all time as soon as the file is opened and saved by QuarkXPress for Windows. Similarly, if a Windows user has made OLE links (the Windows version of Publish and Subscribe) within a Windows document, that information will be lost when the document's opened on a Macintosh (see Chapter 9, *Pictures*).

▼ ▼

Modern Myths

I have very mixed feelings about cross-platform compatibility. On the one hand, moving documents and graphics between Macintoshes and PCs sometimes works like a charm. On the other hand, sometimes the strangest things happen and it can cause horrible nightmare scenarios (of course, right on the eve of a deadline). Although QuarkXPress is very similar on the two platforms, and tries its hardest to make cross-platform issues irrelevant, there are clearly issues that are beyond its control.

Nonetheless, because more and more people are finding themselves in that "third-culture" arena—where they are literate on two or more platforms—transferring files is becoming almost commonplace. No doubt, with a dose of experience and a patient hand, you may soon find yourself making the process more or less painless.

C

XTENSIONS AND RESOURCES

When you set up that grill you bought for barbecuing your chicken and vegetables, it's unlikely that you're going to find all the best grilling instruments in the box. So what do you do? You drive back to the store and fill up your shopping cart with a big fork, a spatula, a baster, cleaning equipment, and so on. If you're into carpentry and you buy a table saw, you know you're also going to buy a cross-cut blade separately.

And, after you pull your copy of QuarkXPress out of its packaging, one of the first questions you should ask yourself is: "What other tools do I need to get my job done?"

As any QuarkXPress Demon knows—and as I've tried to make clear throughout the book—QuarkXPress is not an island. I don't use Quark-XPress for everything, and I don't expect you to, either. And even if you do, there are many add-on XTensions from Quark and other developers that increase your power and efficiency in making pages.

In this appendix, I briefly discuss some of the tools and resources you might want to think about exploiting in order to make your life a happier place to be.

The QuarkXPress Book Web Site. In past editions of this book, I've included long lists of XTension developers, software developers, magazine publishers, users groups, and so on. I've gotten great feedback on this practice because it's often hard to know where to find these companies or their products. However, my efforts are quickly frustrated when a company moves their office, changes their phone number, or discontinues a product line.

In this edition, I'm not including this information in printed form. Rather, it's all on the book's Web site: *www.peachpit.com/blatner/*

If you want to find an XTension or product that I've mentioned in this book, you can find it at the Web site. If you're looking for an XTension that jiggles your whatchamacallit, follow the links on the Web site. If you need more information about how to expand your QuarkXPress world, you can find that on the Web site.

As I said in the Preface: treat the Web site as a dynamic extension to these printed pages. Okay, 'nuff said.

Utilities and software. Part of being efficient in electronic publishing, I believe, is using the right tool for the job. Don't use a pair of pliers on a hex nut; don't use a pair of scissors to prune your roses; don't use QuarkXPress when other programs do something better. I rely on dozens of utilities and other software programs to get my work done, including Adobe Photoshop, Microsoft Word, FileBuddy, Macromedia FreeHand, Adobe Illustrator, Design Science's MathType, Symantec Visual Page, Macromedia's Fontographer, Greg Swann's Torquemada, Adobe Type Manager Deluxe . . . the list goes on and on.

In this appendix, I primarily talk about XTensions and information resources, but I'm not trying to minimize the importance of these other tools. You can find more information, what they are and where to get them, on my Web site, too.

XTensions

I first covered XTensions and how they can add functionally to QuarkXPress back in Chapter 2, *QuarkXPress Basics.* Throughout the book, I have mentioned several commercial vendors and their products, but there's no way I could cover them all (there's more than 200 XTension developers alone). More importantly, I haven't told you where you can get them.

Get the Freebies

There's no reason not to get—and use—the free XTensions that Quark publishes. The best way to find them is to download them from their Web site (*www.quark.com*) or from the Quark forums on America Online or CompuServe.

Where these XTensions used to be called Bob, Son of Bob, and other Bobish names, Quark now uses slightly more conservative names, such as Shape of Things (which lets you easily create starburst picture boxes), PDF Export Filter (which helps if your documents are headed for Adobe Acrobat PDF Distiller), TypeTricks (which includes many extras that were in FeaturesPlus, like Make Fraction, Make Price, Word Space Tracking, and so on), and Jabberwocky (my personal favorite: it lets you fill any text box with random text). Of course, remember that Quark's XTensions are often only good for one or two versions of XPress; when a new version of the product comes out, check to see if the XTensions still work with it.

Quark releases these XTensions on a regular basis, as quickly as the folks there can produce them. In fact, as this book goes to press, I see there's a new filter on their Web site that lets you import GIF images into QuarkXPress for Macintosh's picture boxes. (You can already do this in Windows.) I'd better go download that now . . . .

Go Buy a Package

You don't have to purchase XTensions in order to be happy working with QuarkXPress, but I think you may be even happier if you do. For instance, I'm a big fan of these XTension bundles published by developers like Extensis, A Lowly Apprentice Production (alap), and VisionsEdge. These typically offer ten or fifteen general-purpose, efficiency-oriented XTensions for a pretty reasonable price, often the kind of features that you think should be in QuarkXPress in the first place. But until these features—like a Layers palette, for example—appear in QuarkXPress, you might as well get them elsewhere.

There are hundreds of other XTensions that have a more focused appeal, too. KyTek has one that helps you build footnotes; Techno Design has one that lets you import layered Photoshop-format images directly into QuarkXPress; Em Software's Xdata is the world's best tool for getting information from a database or spreadsheet into QuarkXPress, formatted and ready to fly. Some XTensions are only available for Macintosh or the Windows platform, others are available on both (the ones I just listed work in both operating systems).

Where to Find and Buy XTensions

Now you know there's XTensions out there . . . but how do you find them? While you can often buy XTensions directly from the developer, it's usually easier to use one of several companies that specialize in distributing XTensions.

▶ THE XCHANGE. The XChange is the granddaddy of XTensions distributors. They have offices in North America and Europe (though they're now actually different companies, as the owner of the World Wide Power Company now owns XChange North America). You can find them in the USA at 800-788-7557, or on the Web at *www.xchangeus.com* or *www.xchangeuk.com*.

▶ WORLD WIDE POWER COMPANY. The World Wide Power Company sells more than just XTensions—they distribute plug-ins, Xtras, and all sorts of add-ons to other software. You can find them in the USA at 800-940-8737 or at 303-940-0600, or on the Web at *www.thepowerco.com*.

▶ XT-NOW. If you're surfing the Net, you should check out XT-now, which sells XTensions solely online at *www.xt-now.com*.

There are many other distributors in other countries, as well as mail-order companies and so on. (More links and contact information for all these companies is at The QuarkXPress Book Web Site.)

If you're looking for a demo version of an XTension, you can try the above distributors, but the world's biggest repository of demos, shareware, and freeware XTensions is located on the Web at The XPresso Bar (*www.xpressobar.com*).

▼ ▼

Published Resources

There are times when what you need is information, not software. Fortunately, there's a lot of information out there on QuarkXPress if you know where to look.

Magazines. I have a love-hate relationship with computer magazines. On the one hand, I love getting magazines such as *Step-By-Step Electronic Design*, *Publish*, *Macworld*, *Seybold Reports*, and *Design Graphics*. On the other hand, the stacks of publications in my office are becoming life-threateningly high. Nonetheless, there is a lot of information about publishing in QuarkXPress (and publishing in general) in these magazines.

One solution to the paper problem is Jay Nelson's *Design Tools Monthly*. Each month he combs all the rags for great publishing-related news and tips, and then presents it to you in a short newsletter. It's much more expensive than the magazine subscriptions themselves, but it sure is cheaper than the time it takes to read those magazines (plus, you get a cool disk of goodies each month). You can find DTM in the USA at 303-543-8400, or on the Web at *www.design-tools.com*.

World Wide Web. As much information as there is in print, there's exponentially more on the Web. While I provide a number of links on The QuarkXPress Book Web Site (see above), there are a couple of places you should know about immediately.

▶ Quark's site at *www.quark.com* is full of great information. Every XPress user should check in here at least once a month to see what's new.

▶ One of the better QuarkXPress-related sites on the Internet is *www.xpressobar.com*. It's certainly worth exploring, and as I said earlier, it has a great compendium of software you can download.

▼ ▼

Get it While it's Hot

It's so easy to just launch QuarkXPress and start using it that I find it's hard to stop and think about how life could be made easier with the addition of some other tools or information. Of course, if you work by the hour, then it's a benefit to your bank account for you to keep your blinders on and be as inefficient as possible. For the rest of us, it's worth it to take the time now to save much more time down the road.

Enjoy!

D

SCRIPTING

I have a problem. As I see it, my job in this book is to tell you not only what QuarkXPress does, but also how you can best use it to get your work done. My problem is that this appendix is about scripting QuarkXPress 4, and as this edition of *The QuarkXPress Book* goes to press, QuarkXPress 4 is basically unscriptable. While the previous version of XPress was scriptable, the folks at Quark left out the scripting commands for all the new features in XPress 4. And, while they were at it, they broke a number of scripting features that were working fine.

Needless to say, this leaves me with very little to talk about. Nonetheless, the show must go on, and the engineers at Quark have promised me that they're trying to remedy the situation as quickly as possible. There are three consequences to this.

> ► I'm going to talk in broad generalizations in this appendix, covering scripting as we all knew it back in version 3.x (I'm sure that most of this won't significantly change).

▶ I'll do my best to post updates on the topic at The QuarkXPress Book Web Site (*www.peachpit.com/blatner/*) as soon as Quark ships a product that I can sink my scripting teeth into.

▶ If you still have a copy of QuarkXPress 3.x around, I recommend you use that for scripting until Quark has released a version of XPress that definitively fixes the scripting bugs and lets you script all the new functionality that XPress 4 offers.

There's one other thing you need to know right up front here: Scripting in QuarkXPress 4 will still be Macintosh-only. I feel pretty confident that Quark will update XPress for Windows to be scriptable as quickly as they can—however, it appears as though this probably won't happen until Microsoft makes some fundamental changes in Windows. Until then, if you only use Windows, you can stop reading now.

Scripting in QuarkXPress

I don't know why, but some people just like doing things the hard way. Like those people who insist on doing long division on the back of an envelope rather than using a calculator. Or like folks who scroll around their documents using the scroll bars instead of using the grabber hand. Yes, it's weird, but they seem happy enough; so why bother them by telling them there's an easier way to do it?

Well, I don't know about you, but it drives me crazy doing repetitive tasks in QuarkXPress. Stepping through a document to make a tiny formatting change to one little character on each page . . . searching for all the paragraphs in my 100-page story that start with a numeral and applying the proper style sheet to them . . . changing the border around every picture in my document one at a time . . . Each of these just seemed like another one of those monotonous, robotic tasks that I do every day when working on my computer.

I'm here to tell you that the days of repetitive monotony, the weeks of dull mechanical routines, the months of dreary, unchanging keystrokes are over! There are two things that can alleviate these woes: macros and scripting.

Macros Versus Scripting

Before I get into the details of scripting, let's take a quick look at how macros and scripting are similar and different.

Macros. Let's just get one thing perfectly clear: If you use a Macintosh and don't own and use a copy of QuicKeys, you're just not being efficient in your work. QuicKeys lets you create macros to tell QuarkXPress—and any other program or utility you use, including the Finder—what to do. A macro can be an action or sequence of actions. It can be triggered by a keystroke, by the time of day, or by selecting it from a menu. I have lots of QuicKey macros on my computer. To start QuarkXPress, I just press Control-Q. To create a new text box, put it six picas from the top of the page, and automatically jump into the measurement palette, I can press Control-Option-N. To clone an object, I like Command-=. All of these work on my machine because I've made QuicKeys macros.

Any menu item you can select, any key you can press, any printer or server you can choose on the network, any event you can cause to happen can be assigned a macro keystroke or be built in to a sequence macro. They're incredibly helpful and can speed up work enormously because they're easy to create and use.

Here Windows users aren't entirely out in the cold, either. One of the best macro utilities for Windows users is called WinBatch from Wilson WindowWare.

Scripting. There are two basic differences between macros and scripts. First, whereas macros automate particular tasks that you perform on a computer (like select that menu item, push that button, type such-and-such, and so on), scripts let you sneak in the back door of the program and control it from behind the scenes, almost like a puppeteer pulling the strings of a marionette. Second, scripts have flow control. Flow control is a programming term that means you can set up decision trees and loops (you can do some conditional branching and looping with QuicKeys, but it's a pain); plus, scripts often contain variables. You can do much more complex and interesting things with scripting than you can with simple macros.

When people talk about scripting, they're usually talking about either program-specific scripting, or AppleEvents. AppleEvents is a Macintosh feature that lets programs communicate with and control one another.

The rest of this chapter is going to focus on AppleEvents-based scripts and scripting, including a description of a bunch of scripts that come with QuarkXPress and from The QuarkXPress Book Web Site. Note that scripting is usually done with either AppleScript or UserLand

Frontier, but QuicKeys 3.0, HyperCard, and several other programs also support scripting. In theory you can even control QuarkXPress using scripts sent from FileMaker.

▼ ▼

Tip: Hiring a Scripter. Even though scripting is extremely powerful, it's just a fact of life that most people don't want to learn the ins and outs of scripting. Fortunately, there are a number of scripters for hire. In case you're looking for such a beast, I've compiled a small list of freelance scripting consultants on The QuarkXPress Book Web Site.

▼ ▼

Getting Scripting Information

Quark ships information about AppleEvent scripting along with the Macintosh version of QuarkXPress, but it's not immediately obvious. It's an XPress document called AppleEvents Scripting PrintMe, hidden inside the AppleEvents folder, which is hidden inside the Document folder which is, in turn, inside the QuarkXPress folder. (Do these lists ever remind you of Leviticus, in which Izzy begat Herbie, and Herbie begat Pearl, and Pearl begat . . . ?)

Unfortunately, you can't write your own scripts with the files that come with QuarkXPress. In order to write or edit scripts, you need to use the AppleScript Editor (for AppleScript scripts), UserLand Frontier (for UserTalk or Frontier scripts), CE Software's QuicKeys, or some other scripting application such as HyperCard.

AppleScript. As it turns out, each of these methods means an additional cost. In this chapter, I'm focusing on the AppleScript scripting language, and all of the scripts listed here are in AppleScript. At this time, the only way you can run or edit them is with the AppleScript Editor or some other scripting tool (see "Tip: Hard-core Scripting," below). The AppleScript Editor is free and ships with all Macintosh systems (if you have a really old operating system, you may need to upgrade in order to get AppleScript functionality). The appropriate files are usually inside a folder called Apple Extras on your hard drive.

Books. Unfortunately, there aren't many AppleScripting books currently on the market. One of the best, *Danny Goodman's Guide to*

AppleScript, is out of print, but you can sometimes find it in used book-stores. *The Tao of AppleScript*, is also a reasonably good introduction to scripting. Both books come with a disk that includes AppleScript and handy scripts to learn from.

CD-ROMs. I urge you to get a copy of the free AppleScript Publishing Solutions CD-ROM from Apple. It's chock full o' great tutorials on script-ing, including how to link together FileMaker Pro and QuarkXPress. Another excellent resource is the EverythingCD on AppleScript from ISO Productions.

The Web. The World Wide Web is, of course, one of the best sources for AppleScript information. There are a number of great sites out there that offer both tutorials on scripting and scripts that you can download, use, and learn from. Of course, as Web URLs change all the time, there's little good in my including them here on paper. Instead, check out the list of scripting links on The QuarkXPress Book Web Site.

▼ ▼

Tip: Hard-core Scripting. If you really get into scripting and you find yourself spending a lot of time writing or debugging scripts, you might want to take a look at some of the other scripting applications on the market. The first, Main Event Software's Scripter, is a full-featured tool that helps you write and debug scripts, and is a major step up from the rather spartan AppleScript Editor. UserLand Frontier is also a very pow-erful script editor, though it primarily uses its own scripting language rather than AppleScript.

A third tool, FaceSpan, is an excellent utility for building user inter-faces to your applescripts. The more complicated a script, the more it requires a way for the user to interact with it—buttons, text fields, dialog boxes, popup menus, and so on.

Again, you can find contact information on all of these at The QuarkXPress Book Web Site.

▼ ▼

Writing a Script

The best way to learn how to script QuarkXPress is by first looking at and deconstructing other people's scripts, and then trying, trying, and trying again. Scripting is programming. If you've ever programmed in another computer language, you'll probably pick up AppleScript or UserLand Frontier pretty quickly. If not, it may take you a while to start to understand the concepts. I know it's a cop-out, but there's neither time nor space to teach you how to program.

What I *can* do here is give you a pretty solid foundation on which to build your scripting knowledge. Then you can go off, look through the scripts I've included in this chapter and on The QuarkXPress Book Web Site, and try your own.

The main concepts you've got to understand are the object model, hierarchies, properties, and events.

The Object Model

Let's get one thing clear: The object model is not a feminist theory regarding the objectification of fashion models in magazines. Rather, the object model describes the way AppleEvent scripting works. That is, in order to "get" scripting, you have to think in terms of the object model.

The object model says that everything is an object that you can "talk to." For example, an object might be a text box, or a word, or a picture, or a whole document. Objects can contain other objects; for instance, a page can contain text boxes, which can contain paragraphs, which can contain words.

There are currently 27 kinds of objects in QuarkXPress. Each of these objects can be controlled or queried through basic scripting commands. Although some objects are intuitively similar to items you know in the program, others are a little more obscure. For example, while text boxes and words are clear and you can easily get a handle on what they are, Master Document and Delimit Table may be confusing at first (see "Difficult Objects," below).

▼ ▼

Tip: Naming Objects. One of the coolest things about scripting QuarkXPress is that you can name most objects. You can always identify *text box 1* or *line box 3*, but it's much easier to choose and manipulate a text box named "Lead story" or a line box called "VerticalLine." For example, you can type `set the name of text box 1 to` `"MyTextBox"`. The more complicated your script, the more important it is to name your objects.

▼ ▼

Hierarchies, Elements, and Containers

You can't understand the object model and scripting without understanding hierarchies, elements, and containers. Most objects in QuarkXPress contain other objects; for example, a paragraph contains words, which contain characters.

Hierarchies only get complicated when you can't remember what contains what (see Figure D-1).

In working with hierarchies, two terms are helpful to keep in mind: elements and containers. An element is an object that is contained within another object. A text box is an element of a page, for instance. A container is simply an object that has elements. The QuarkXPress application is a container for windows, documents, and so on.

Properties

Every object in QuarkXPress has properties that you can look at and—usually—change. A property is a characteristic of an object. For example, picture

Figure D-1

AppleScript hierarchy

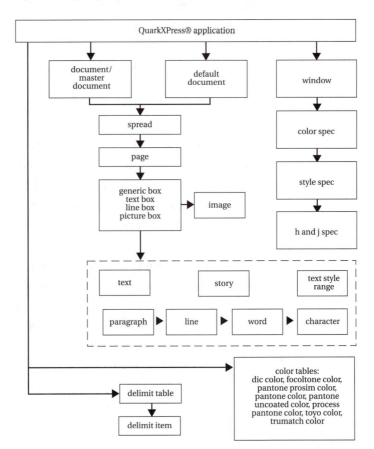

boxes have the properties of background color, rotation, placement on the page (called *bounds*), and many more.

Difficult Objects

As I noted earlier, some objects in QuarkXPress are pretty confusing if you haven't seen them before. Objects such as document and picture box are pretty simple, so I'm just going to focus on the objects in QuarkXPress that may raise your eyebrow.

Application. The highest object in the hierarchy is Application. You can think of the QuarkXPress application as being the program with or without a document open; changes made here are application-wide and affect any document that is open or is created from then on. Note that if you've renamed your copy of QuarkXPress, then the application's name might be different for you.

Window. When I first saw the Window object, I thought it was the same as Document. However, that's not the case. Documents are only open documents, but you can control all the windows in QuarkXPress. That includes the palettes and dialog boxes. You can't do a lot to them, but you might want to write a script that brings all the palettes up and then sets their sizes and positions on the screen.

Default document. The default document contains all the preferences and settings for the New dialog box, the H&Js, colors, and style sheets—whether a document is open or closed. For example, with no document open, you can set the default document's settings; when you create a new document, it will be configured in that way.

Spread. Spreads are pretty obvious, but here's an important point you should know: Items on the pasteboard fall in the domain of the spread, but not the page. So if you change all the text boxes in a spread to red, then the text boxes on the pasteboard get changed, too. If you do it to all the objects on a page, only the ones that are touching the page get changed.

Also note that a spread includes all the pages that are next to each other. So you can have a one-, two-, three-, or more page spread.

Master document. The master document is the object that contains the master pages. What does that mean? Dave Shaver, one of the engineers at Quark who worked on scripting, describes the master document as being a "shadow" of the document. You can talk to its light side (the actual document pages), or you can talk to its dark side (the master pages).

For example, if you want to change something on a master page, you need to address a page or spread in the master document. You can't change a master page from within the document itself. Of course, master document 1 and document 1 are just different parts of the same document. Note that if you're going to change something throughout a document, it's best to change it on the master document pages first, then, if necessary, on the document pages.

Color spec. There are no color objects in QuarkXPress, only color specs (or color spec objects, to be precise). Color specs don't contain anything, but have various properties. You can assign a color spec to something, but Quark was nice enough to let you get by with a shortcut: assigning the color name directly. That's easier and more intuitive. For instance, instead of `set color spec of generic box 1 to "Red"` you can say `set color of generic box 1 to "Red"`. This applies the properties of the color spec "Red" to the box.

Style spec. A style spec—similar in operation to a color spec or H&J set—is the object that describes a style sheet. While you can set the style sheet of a paragraph to style spec Normal, it's easier to take the shortcut and just say `set style sheet of paragraph 1 to "Normal"` (XPress is smart enough to know what you mean). However, if you want to change the style sheet itself, you have to specify that it's a style spec.

H&J set. Like color spec and style spec, the H&J set contains particulars of a hyphenation and justification style.

Horizontal and vertical guide. You can create and manipulate ruler guides through scripts by working with horizontal and vertical guides. In fact, you can even do things to guides that you can't do in the program itself, such as make them undeletable or immobile (see "Unmoveable guides," in "Sample Scripts," below).

Line. Don't get fooled: a line is not a rule. That is, the line object is a line of text, not a graphic on the page. The line extends from one margin to another in a column of text.

Line box. For some obscure reason which I haven't figured out yet, lines (graphic rules) are considered "line boxes." I suppose that makes it all consistent under the hood, but it can kind of screw you up if you're not careful.

Image. Each picture box can contain one image. You import a picture into a picture box by setting the image to a file on disk. For example: `set image 1 to alias "myharddisk:picture1"`.

Generic box. A generic box is any page item in QuarkXPress, whether a picture box, a text box, or a rule (see "Line box," above). This can be helpful, especially when you're telling a whole bunch of items to do the same thing. Note that generic boxes take the lowest common denominator properties of all objects. For instance, line boxes don't have a bounds property, so neither do generic boxes.

Story. A story is, as you may have guessed, all the text in a chain of boxes. Each text box has only one story (but, of course, a story can go through many text boxes). The nice thing about stories is that you can find and change things in them really quickly (much faster than if you specify changes by word, for instance).

Text style range. Most people who use QuarkXPress don't think in terms of ranges of text. However, there are times when you want to select a block of text that contains all the characters with the same text formatting. This block is called a text style range. Note that the "same formatting" includes color, font, style, kerning, tracking, and so on. As soon as the style changes in any way, QuarkXPress breaks the text down into another style range.

For example, if you set the color of every word whose color is "Red" to "Blue," it won't catch the words whose first three characters happen to be green (because QuarkXPress only looks at the first character of a word when assessing color). However, if you set all the text style ranges whose color is "Red" to "Blue" then, all the red characters change.

Delimit table. The delimit table object seems like one of the more obscure items in scripting, but in fact it's relatively straightforward. The delimit table contains 256 delimit items that tell QuarkXPress what delimiters to use to distinguish where words begin and end (examples are a space, a period, a comma, an exclamation point, a semicolon, and so on). Each item in the delimit table is an ASCII character specified using its decimal code. Item 32 is a space character (ASCII number 32), for instance, and so on.

You may never or rarely use this, but it can occasionally come in handy. For example, if you wanted to work with tab-delimited text from a spreadsheet or a database, you can set up your QuarkXPress document so that only a tab character counts as a word delimiter. Then, when you want to do something to the second word in the story, QuarkXPress does it to the second "field," from one tab to the next, whether there is one word or 20.

Note that once you change the delimit table, it will stay that way until you change it back or until you quit QuarkXPress. Also note that changing the delimit table doesn't actually change the way you can select words from within the program—by double-clicking with the Content tool, for instance (I think this would be a really cool feature).

Each delimit table item can be set to one of four possibilities: *not word member, can start or end or be contained in word, can start or end word,* or *can be contained in word.* For example, a quotation mark would probably be set to *can start or end word* because you don't want it to be in the middle of a word. You can set the delimit item by specifying it between quotation marks (e.g., ":") or by its ASCII character number. If you're specifying invisible characters, it's easiest to call them by their QuarkXPress name: a tab is "\t", a return is "\r", and so on.

Events

The way you alter an object is by sending QuarkXPress an "event," which is AppleEvents-ese for a command. If you want to set the tint of a line on page four, you need to send an event. In AppleScript format, the event would be a "set" command (such as `set shade of line box 1 of page 4 to 30`). Events are relatively simple, and there aren't that many of them, but there are enough so that I can't really discuss them here. My only suggestion is that you pick them up as you go along by looking at other scripts and seeing how they work.

▼ ▼

Looking at a Script

My next step in learning how to script with QuarkXPress is to look at an actual, real, live AppleScript and see how it works. The following script creates a document, puts a headline on the page (in a tinted red box), and then adds a story and a picture. The story and the picture are pulled from disk files, and the picture box is set to a background of None and a Runaround set to Automatic. (You can download this script from The QuarkXPress Book Web Site.) After I list out the script, I'll discuss how and why it does what it does.

```
tell application "QuarkXPress®"
--CREATE AND SET SOME VARIABLES *******
   set picboxwidth to 170
   set picboxheight to 200
   set pgheight to (9 * 72)
   set pgwidth to (7 * 72)
--MAKE A DOCUMENT *******
   set properties of default document 1 to ¬
     {page height:pgheight as points, ¬
      page width:pgwidth as points, ¬
      automatic text box:true, ¬
      left margin:"8p", ¬
      right margin:"1\"", ¬
      bottom margin:"5p", ¬
      facing pages:true, ¬
      ligatures on:true}
   activate
   make document at beginning
   set view scale of document 1 to ¬
     fit page in window

--MAKE PAGE 1 *******
   tell page 1 of document 1

--TEXT BOX 1 *******
     make text box at beginning
     tell text box 1
       set bounds to {"6p", "8p", "2\"", "6\""}
       set color to "Red"
       set shade to 40
       set vertical justification to centered
     set properties of story 1 to ¬
       {contents:"The QuarkXPress Book ¬
         from Peachpit Press" ¬
```

```
        , font:"Helvetica" ¬
        , size:29 ¬
        , leading:29 ¬
        , style:bold ¬
        , justification:centered}
    end tell

--TEXT BOX 2 ******* (automatic text box)
    tell text box 2
      set properties to ¬
        {columns:2 ¬
        , bounds:{"2.1\"", "8p", "49p", "36p"}}
      set story 1 to (¬
        choose file with prompt ¬
        "Please select a text file")
      set properties of paragraph 1 to ¬
        {drop cap lines:4 ¬
        , drop cap characters:1}
      set style of line 1 to small caps
      set style of line 2 to plain
      if leading of story 1 as real ¬
        is greater than 16 then
        set leading of story 1 to "16 pt"
      end if
    end tell

--PICTURE BOX *******
    set startpicboxy to (pgheight - picboxheight) ÷ 2
    set startpicboxx to (pgwidth - picboxwidth) ÷ 2

    tell (make picture box at beginning with properties ¬
      {bounds:{startpicboxy as points ¬
      , startpicboxx as points ¬
      , (startpicboxy + picboxheight) as points ¬
      , (startpicboxx + picboxwidth) as points} ¬
      , runaround:auto runaround ¬
      , text outset:"8pt" ¬
      , color:"None"})
      tell image 1
        set contents to ¬
          (choose file with prompt ¬
          "Please select an image")
        set bounds to proportional fit
      end tell
    end tell
  end tell
end tell
```

Description of the Script

If you've never programmed before, looking at that script is probably somewhat unnerving. But I assure you that scripting is not as difficult as it looks, especially in the AppleScript language. After reading this section, you'll probably be up and running with basic scripting. Let's look at that script, how it works, and why.

There are two conventions that you should be aware of. First, all comments in this AppleScript script have two hyphens before them. QuarkXPress just ignores those lines (they're included just for "human readability"). Second, the character that looks like a sideways "L" is a line-break character (its printable character is made by pressing Option-L in most PostScript fonts, or by pressing Option-Return in the AppleScript Editor). It comes at the end of a line that continues on the next line. If that's not there, then AppleScript gets confused at the line breaks. I've used them extensively here so that the code can all fit into this text column.

Opening. You always need to specify in the script what application you're talking to with the `tell application` command. In this case, "QuarkXPress®" is the way that my copies of QuarkXPress are named. If you change the name of the program without changing the name in the code, AppleScript won't be able to find it.

Variables. Variables are like little boxes to put something in. Each box has a name, and you can put whatever you want in it. For example, here I create and set four variables and I give them the names *picboxwidth, picboxheight, pgheight,* and *pgwidth.* Each of these "containers" is filled with a number. We'll see later what they're used for. You can set variables at any time, but in this case I want to set them at the beginning so that they're easy to find and change if I want to later.

New document. Before I create a new document, I want to set up the specs of the default document. In this case, I'm setting the page height, width, margins, and so on. Note that in this area I'm specifying both information found in the New document and Application Preferences dialog boxes.

To set a number of values at once, I use the command `set properties of default document 1 to`. Inside the curly brackets, I specify all the values I want to set, separated by commas. And because I'm inside those curly brackets, instead of saying `set facing pages to true`, I simply say `facing pages:true`, and so on.

Note that I'm using the variables *pgheight* and *pgwidth* here to specify the height and width of the default document page. If you change the values of the variables in the first section, your page size will be different.

The next event you see is *activate*. This simply displays the application (in this case QuarkXPress) in front of the AppleScript Editor.

And, finally, I create the document itself with the `make document at beginning` command, and set the view scale of that document. Anytime you make or create an object, you need to tell QuarkXPress where to do it. In this case, I add "at beginning" even though there is no beginning or end. Yeah, it's weird, but that's just the way it works.

The first text box. Because I want to make a text box on page one, I first specify what page I'm talking to with the `tell page 1 of document 1` command. Then I move right into making a text box and filling it. First I make the text box at the beginning of the page (the upper-left corner). Then I set its attributes: bounds (placement on the page), color, shade, and vertical justification.

Finally I set the contents of the text box. Here I set a number of attributes at once, so I can say `set properties of story 1 to`. Note that QuarkXPress knows which story I'm talking to because of nesting. At the time it sees this event, it knows that I'm talking to text box 1 on page 1 of document 1 of application "QuarkXPress®". When I'm done working with text box 1, I say `end tell`.

The second text box. The next text box is the automatic text box that was already on the page when the document was created. Therefore, I move directly to setting its properties. In this case, I'm setting the number of columns, the positioning, the story that goes in it, and the formatting of that text.

The event `set story 1 to (choose file with prompt "Please select a text file")` brings up a dialog box for the user to select a story from disk. You could also type something like `set story 1 to alias "myharddisk:text files:tuna story"`, which would get a specific story off the disk. (Aliases are the way to tell AppleEvents what a disk path is.)

After I have a story in the text box, the script sets its formatting. First, it gives the first paragraph a drop cap, then it sets the rest of the first line to small caps style. Note that when it does this, there's a pretty good chance that some text from the first line will spill over to the second line (small caps are often wider). So, I add a line that sets the style of the second line to plain; that way, those characters have small caps removed.

Finally, I don't want the leading of this story to be too big, so I alter it some with an *if* statement: `if leading of story 1 as real is greater than 16 then set leading of story 1 to "16 pt"`. If/then statements are one of the most powerful features of scripting. When I say "as real," that makes QuarkXPress convert the leading value into a real number (a number that has a decimal fraction, like 12.4, as opposed to an integer which has no fraction) that I can compare against. If the *if* statement comes up "true" (in this case, if the leading is actually larger than 16 points), then I go to the next event, which is to set the leading to 16 points. If the answer is "false," then the script skips all the way to the *end if* statement.

The picture box. Finally, I want to throw a picture in the middle of the page. I start this section by creating two more variables called *startpicboxy* and *startpicboxx*. By letting QuarkXPress do a little math for me, I can set these variables to where the picture box should originate (upper-left corner) in order for the box to be centered on the page.

Next, I create a picture box at the beginning of the page and set its parameters. Note that I've used a rather nonintuitive but clever way in which to do this quickly: `tell (make picture box at beginning....` This starts the *tell* event even before the picture box is made. Because the *make picture box* is inside parentheses, QuarkXPress performs that first, then recognizes that this object that it just created is the object that you were referring to when you started the *tell* operation.

Also, note that I have to specify that the numbers and variables in the bounds setting are set up for points, so I use the *as points* modifier.

The end. In order to end the script successfully, you need to tie off all the loose ends and close the nested tells. Here I have four *end tells* in a row: one to finish the operation on the image, next to finish talking to the picture box, third to stop talking to page one of document one, and finally to end the tell to the application itself.

```
          tell page i
             set text of text box 1 to session
             set text of text box 2 to speaker
             set image 1 of picture box 1 ¬
                to thepath & "pictures:" ¬
                & speaker & ".tiff"
          end tell
       end tell
    end repeat
  end tell
end tell
```

▼ ▼

The Future of Scripts

Clearly, AppleEvent scripting gives you extremely powerful control over your environment in QuarkXPress (and other programs). As more people learn about it, I'm expecting that I'll hear of some amazing applications online and in the press. In fact, if you're looking for a career-shift, I strongly suggest looking into becoming a scripting consultant. I recently sat next to a publisher of a magazine who wanted to start putting stuff online. His problem was that he had no good way of automating the process from a database to QuarkXPress to output (like Acrobat). As soon as I started talking about scripting, his eyes lit up. That's one man out of thousands who wants to hire a scripter. Any takers?

Paragraph Style Sheets

Description	Code	Values
Define style sheet	@name=	Name of style sheet; follow the equal sign with definition, just as if you were inserting "manual" or "local" formatting in the text stream
Based on/next style		@name=[S"based-on_name","next style name"] Name of based-on style sheet, followed by definition
Apply style sheet	@name:	Name of style sheet
Apply "Normal"	@$:	
Apply "No Style"	@:	

Character Style Sheets

Description	Code	Values
Define style sheet	@name=	Just like defining a paragraph style sheet, except (of course) don't specify any paragraph attributes
Apply style sheet	<@name>	Name of style sheet
Apply Normal character style	<@$>	
Return to character style sheet that "belongs" to current ¶ style sheet	<@$p>	

General Codes

Code	Means...
<v#>	XPress Tags filter version number. XPress 3.2's filter is version 1.60; XPress 3.3's is version 1.70; XPress 4.0's is version 4.0. You can typically ignore this tag.
<e#>	Platform number: 0=Mac, 1=Windows DTP; 2=ISO Latin 1. You can ignore these unless you're moving XPress Tags files from one computer platform to another.

ANSI Codes

Ansi Code	Times	Symbol	Zapf Dingbats
1–45 No characters			
46	.	.	✎
47	/	/	✏
48	0	0	✐
49	1	1	✑
50	2	2	✒
51	3	3	✓
52	4	4	✔
53	5	5	✕
54	6	6	✖
55	7	7	✗
56	8	8	✘
57	9	9	✙
58	:	:	✚
59	;	;	✛
60	<	<	✜
61	=	=	✝
62	>	>	✞
63	?	?	✟
64	@	≅	✠

Ansi Code	Times	Symbol	Zapf Dingbats
65	A	A	✿
66	B	B	✚
67	C	X	✜
68	D	Δ	✣
69	E	E	✤
70	F	Φ	◆
71	G	Γ	◇
72	H	H	★
73	I	I	☆
74	J	ϑ	✪
75	K	K	☆
76	L	Λ	✭
77	M	M	★
78	N	N	✮
79	O	O	✯
80	P	Π	✩
81	Q	Θ	✴
82	R	P	✳
83	S	Σ	✳
84	T	T	✳
85	U	Y	✺
86	V	ς	✶
87	W	Ω	✷
88	X	Ξ	✸
89	Y	Ψ	✹
90	Z	Z	✺
91	[	[	✻
92	\	∴	✼
93	]	]	✽
94	^	⊥	✾
95	_	_	✿
96	`	_	❀
97	a	α	❁
98	b	β	❂
99	c	χ	❃
100	d	δ	❄
101	e	ε	❅

Ansi Code	Times	Symbol	Zapf Dingbats
102	f	φ	❄
103	g	γ	✳
104	h	η	✳
105	i	ι	✳
106	j	φ	✳
107	k	κ	✳
108	l	λ	●
109	m	μ	○
110	n	ν	■
111	o	ο	❏
112	p	π	❐
113	q	θ	❑
114	r	ρ	❒
115	s	σ	▲
116	t	τ	▼
117	u	υ	◆
118	v	ϖ	❖
119	w	ω	❭
120	x	ξ	│
121	y	ψ	▌
122	z	ζ	▐
123	{	{	❛
124	|	|	❜
125	}	}	❝
126	~	~	❞
127–129 No characters			
130	,		
131	ƒ		
132	”		
133	…		
134	†		
135	‡		
136	^		
137	‰		
138	Š		
139	‹		
140	Œ		

Ansi Code	Times	Symbol	Zapf Dingbats
141–144 No characters			
145	'		
146	,		
147	"		
148	"		
149	•		
150	–		
151	—		
152	~		
153	™		
154	š		
155	›		
156	œ		
157–158 No characters			
159	Ÿ		
160 No character			
161	¡	ϒ	✁
162	¢	′	✂
163	£	≤	✃
164	¤	/	♥
165	¥	∞	➤
166	¦	ƒ	✆
167	§	♣	✇
168	¨	♦	♣
169	©	♥	♦
170	ª	♠	♥
171	«	↔	♠
172	¬	←	①
173		↑	②
174	®	→	③
175	¯	↓	④
176	°	°	⑤
177	±	±	⑥
178	²	″	⑦
179	³	≥	⑧
180	´	×	⑨
181	µ	∝	⑩

Ansi Code	Times	Symbol	Zapf Dingbats
182	¶	∂	❶
183	·	•	❷
184	‚	÷	❸
185	'	≠	❹
186	º	≡	❺
187	»	≈	❻
188	¼	…	❼
189	½	│	❽
190	¾	—	❾
191	¿	↵	❿
192	À	ℵ	①
193	Á	ℑ	②
194	Â	ℜ	③
195	Ã	℘	④
196	Ä	⊗	⑤
197	Å	⊕	⑥
198	Æ	∅	⑦
199	Ç	∩	⑧
200	È	∪	⑨
201	É	⊃	⑩
202	Ê		
203	Ë	⊄	❷
204	Ì	⊂	❸
205	Í	⊆	❹
206	Î	∈	❺
207	Ï	∉	❻
208	Ð	∠	❼
209	Ñ	∇	❽
210	Ò	®	❾
211	Ó	©	❿
212	Ô	™	→
213	Õ	∏	→
214	Ö	√	↔
215	×	·	↕
216	Ø	¬	↘
217	Ù	∧	→
218	Ú	∨	↗

Ansi Code	Times	Symbol	Zapf Dingbats
219	Û	⇔	⇀
220	Ü	⇐	➡
221	Ý	⇑	→
222	Þ	⇒	→
223	ß	⇓	⇒
224	à	◊	⇒
225	á	〈	➡
226	â	®	➢
227	ã	©	➣
228	ä	™	➤
229	å	Σ	➥
230	æ	(	➦
231	ç	|	➧
232	è	(	➨
233	é	⌈	⇨
234	ê	|	⇦
235	ë	⌊	⇦
236	ì	⌠	⇐
237	í	{	⇨
238	î	⌡	⇨
239	ï	|	⇨
240	∂		
241	ñ	〉	⇨
242	ò	∫	⇒
243	ó	⌠	➺
244	ô	|	➴
245	õ	⌡	➵
246	ö	)	➹
247	÷	|	➶
248	ø	)	➸
249	ù	⌉	➹
250	ú	|	→
251	û	⌋	➻
252	ü	)	➼
253	ý	}	➽
254	þ	⌡	⇒
255	ÿ		

INDEX

▼ ▼

THE QUARKXPRESS BOOK
DOESN'T STOP HERE ANYMORE

▼ ▼

I couldn't do it. I just couldn't steer though the twists and turns of all
those wild jungle roads just to stroll off at the end of the line. So we ain't
stoppin' here! Stay on board! Give me a shout from time to time and let
me know how you've liked the ride so far. Tell me if you've picked up any
new XPress Demon machete techniques that make the driving easier. I'm
always looking out for a new trick or two from a young tyro or a seasoned
pro. You can always find me at the Web site, but if you tend toward a
more analog approach, try me at the following address.

Parallax Productions
1619 Eighth Avenue North
Seattle, WA 98109 USA
E-mail: qxbook@moo.com

COLOPHON

▼ ▼

If anything shows that I practice what I preach, it's this book. The QuarkXPress 4 Book was created using almost every technique and many of the tips that I divulge throughout the chapters.

Text

Because the pages for the previous edition of the book were in QuarkXPress format, all the text was exported as Microsoft Word 5 files (fortunately, the style sheets were exported with the text). Chapters were edited and written in Microsoft Word 5, 6 and 97, and then reimported into QuarkXPress 4 to be laid out. The bulk of the work was done on a PowerBook 5300c, a Macintosh 8100/80, and a Dell Dimension XPS P200s running Windows 95.

Artwork

I created all the artwork in QuarkXPress, Adobe Photoshop, Adobe Illustrator, and Macromedia FreeHand. Every screen shot in the book was created with Beale Street's Exposure Pro (Mac) or TechSmith's SnagIt (Windows). Photographs and line art images were scanned on a

Lintotype-Hell Saphir. Stock art was graciously provided by PhotoDisc and ImageFarm. All images were edited and saved as either TIFF or EPS files using Adobe Photoshop. Then, each figure was imported, cropped, and sized within QuarkXPress, and saved in a library along with its caption and callouts (one library per chapter). For fast access to each figure, I labelled them using the library's labelling feature.

Design

The book design was based on an original design by Olav Martin Kvern. For this revised edition, the body copy was set in Adobe Utopia and Utopia Expert (for fractions, footnotes, etc.); the heads are in Adobe's Stone Sans Bold. Universal News with Commercial Pi was used throughout for our bullet symbol (▶), math symbols, and other dingbats.

Output

The book was printed and bound by Edwards Brothers in Ann Arbor, Michigan on 50# Arbor Smooth paper. The color pages were printed on 70# Sterling Litho Satin.

9

Test Drive Real World Photoshop

By David Blatner and Bruce Fraser

If you like *The QuarkXPress Book*, we think you'll also like *Real World Photoshop*. Here's a sample section covering sharpening—one of those features that Photoshop users wrestle with every day. Enjoy!

To order *Real World Photoshop*, call Peachpit at 800/283-9444, or visit us at www.peachpit.com.

Sharpening

Getting an Edge on Your Image

The human visual system depends to a great degree on edges. Simply put, our eyes pass information to our brain, where every detail is quickly broken down into "edge" or "not edge." An image may have great contrast and color balance, but without good edge definition, we simply see it as less lifelike.

As it turns out, no matter how good your scanner and how crisp your original may be, you always lose some sharpness when the image is digitized. Images from low-end flatbed scanners and digital cameras always need a considerable amount of sharpening. High-end scanners sharpen as part of the scanning process. Even a high-resolution digital camera back on a finely focused view camera produces images that will benefit from sharpening. Remember, you *cannot* solve the problem of blurry scans by scanning at a higher resolution. It just doesn't work that way.

Your images also lose sharpness in the output process. Halftoned images (almost anything on a printing press) and dithered ones (such as those printed on thermal-wax and ink-jet printers) are the worst offenders. But even continuous-tone devices such as film recorders and dye-sublimation printers lose a little sharpness.

To counteract the blurries in both the input and output stages, you need to sharpen your images. Photoshop offers several sharpening filters, but Unsharp Mask is the only one that really works as a production tool. Sharpen, Sharpen More, Sharpen Edges, and the Sharpening tool may be useful for creative effects, but they'll wreck your images very quickly if you try to use them to compensate for softness introduced during either acquisition or output.

Unsharp Masking

Unsharp masking (often abbreviated as USM) may sound like the last thing you'd want to do if you're trying to make an image appear sharper, but the term actually makes some sense; it has its origins in a traditional photographic technique for enhancing sharpness.

The things we see as edges are areas of high contrast between adjacent pixels. The higher the contrast, the sharper the edges appear. So to increase sharpness, you need to increase the contrast along the edges.

In the traditional process, the photographic negative is sandwiched in the enlarger along with a slightly out-of-focus duplicate negative—an unsharp mask—and the exposure time for printing is approximately doubled. Because the unsharp mask is slightly out of focus and the exposure time has been increased, the light side of the edges prints lighter and the dark side of the edges prints darker, creating a "halo" around objects in the image (see Figure 9-1).

As we'll see throughout this chapter, this halo effect is both the secret of good sharpening, and its Achilles' heel—depending on the size and intensity of the halo, and where it appears in the image. Photoshop lets you control the halo very precisely, but there's no single magic setting that works for all images, so you need to know not only how the controls work, but also what you're trying to achieve in the image.

How the Unsharp Mask Filter Works

The Unsharp Mask filter works pixel by pixel, which explains why it takes so long, even on a very fast machine. It compares each pixel to its neighbors, looking for a certain amount of contrast between adjacent pixels—which it assumes is an edge. It then increases the contrast between those pixels according to the parameters you set. This creates a halo that, when viewed from normal distances, increases apparent sharpness.

Figure 9-1 Edge transitions and sharpening

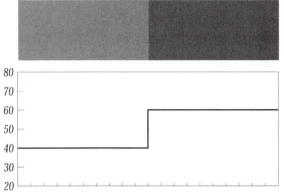

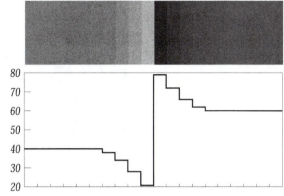

This image and graph depict an edge transition—from 40 to 60 percent. Each tick mark across the graph represents a column of pixels.

After sharpening, the transition is accentuated— it's darker on the dark side, and lighter on the light side, creating a halo around the edge.

Unsharpened   Sharpened

The effect on images ranges from subtle to impressive to destructive. This image is somewhat oversharpened to make the effect clear.

These samples are darker after sharpening.

These samples are lighter.

The net result is a sharper-looking image.

But Photoshop can't actually detect edges—it just looks at contrast differences (zeros and ones again). So unsharp masking can also have the undesired effect of exaggerating texture in flat areas, and emphasizing any noise introduced by the scanner in the shadow areas.

You need to walk a fine line, sharpening only where your image needs it. Fortunately, the controls offered by the filter let you do this very precisely (see Figure 9-2). Here's a rundown of the settings you can control in Photoshop's Unsharp Mask filter, what they do, and how they inter

Figure 9-2

The Unsharp
Mask filter

```
┌──────────────────────────────┐
│ ▓▓▓ Unsharp Mask ▓▓▓          │
│ ┌──────────┐                  │
│ │          │  ┌────────────┐  │
│ │  [cat    │  │     OK     │  │
│ │   nose   │  └────────────┘  │
│ │   image] │  ┌────────────┐  │
│ │          │  │   Cancel   │  │
│ │          │  └────────────┘  │
│ └──────────┘  ☒ Preview       │
│ ⊞ 100% ⊟                      │
│   Amount: [200]  %            │
│   Radius: [1.2]  pixels       │
│ Threshold: [4]   levels       │
└──────────────────────────────┘
```

Amount

We think of Amount as the volume control of unsharp masking. It adjusts the intensity of the sharpening halo (see Figure 9-3). High Amount settings—you can enter up to 500 percent—produce very intense halos (with lots of pixels driven to pure white or solid black); low Amount settings produce less intense ones. Amount has no effect on the width of the halos—just on the amount of contrast they contain.

Figure 9-3

Varying the USM
Amount setting

Image resolution: 225 ppi
Radius: 1.2
Threshold: 4

Amount: 50　　　　*Amount: 200*　　　　*Amount: 350*

As you increase the Amount setting, the blips around big tonal shifts (edges) can be pushed all the way to white and black. At that point, increasing Amount has no effect whatsoever—you can't get more white than white! Worse, the all-white halos often stand out as artifacts and can look really dumb.

We almost always start out by setting Amount to between 200 and 400. Then we adjust downward from there, depending on the image (see "Working the Controls," later in this chapter).

Radius

Radius is the first thing to consider when you're setting up sharpening; it sets the width of the halo that the filter creates around edges (see Figure 9-4). The wider the halo, the more obvious the sharpening effect. Choosing the right Radius value is probably the most important choice in avoiding an unnaturally oversharpened look, and there are several factors to take into account when you choose, starting with the content of the image itself, the output method, and the intended size of the reproduction (see "Image Detail and Sharpening Radius," later in the chapter).

Figure 9-4

Varying the USM Radius setting

Image resolution: 225 ppi
Amount: 200
Threshold: 4

Radius: 0.6　　　*Radius: 1.2*　　　*Radius: 2.4*

Note that a Radius value of 1.0 does not result in a single-pixel radius. In fact, the halo is often between four and six pixels wide for the whole light and dark cycle—two or three pixels on each side of the tonal shift. However, it varies in width depending on the content of the image.

Threshold

Unsharp Mask only evaluates contrast differences: it doesn't know whether those differences represent real edges you want to sharpen, or areas of texture (or, even worse, scanner noise) that you don't want to sharpen. The Threshold control lets you specify how far apart two pixels' tonal values have to be (on a scale of 0 to 255) before the filter affects them (see Figure 9-5). For instance, if Threshold is set to 3, and two adjacent pixels have values of 122 and 124 (a difference of two), they're unaffected.

You can use Threshold to make the filter ignore the relatively slight differences between pixels in smooth, low-contrast areas while still creating a halo around details that have high-contrast edges. And, to some extent at least, you can use it to avoid exaggerating noisy pixels in shadow areas.

Figure 9-5

Varying the USM
Threshold setting

Image resolution: 225 ppi
Amount: 300
Radius: 2

Threshold: 12   Threshold: 6   Threshold: 0

Low Threshold values (1 to 4) result in a sharper-looking image over-all (because fewer areas are excluded). High values (above 10) result in less sharpening. We typically begin with a low Threshold value—some-where between 0 and 4—and then increase it as necessary.

Tip: The Preview Checkbox. The Preview checkbox applies the Unsharp Mask filter to the entire image or selection on the fly, but we keep this turned off most of the time. Even on Bruce's quad-processor Genesis MP, the preview can take a long time, particularly on large files. And every time you change the filter settings, Photoshop has to recalculate and re-draw the entire screen. Of course, the larger the image, the longer it takes.

We turn on Preview when we're fairly sure we've arrived at the correct settings, and want to check them on the whole of the visible image.

Tip: Select a Critical Area to Preview. When you're working interactively with the Unsharp Mask settings, you may want to strike a happy medium between relying on the tiny proxy and previewing the whole image. You can do this with an additional step or two.

1. Select a critical area in the image, then select Unsharp Mask and turn on the Preview checkbox.

2. When you've arrived at the correct settings, press OK.

3. Press Command-Z (to undo the change you just made), Command-D (to deselect the area), and Command-F (to reapply the filter with the last-used settings).

This is one of those tips that takes longer to explain than it does to do!

Tip: Look at Every Pixel Before You Proceed. Like any other Photoshop effect, you can undo Unsharp Mask as long as you don't do any further editing. After we've applied Unsharp Mask, and before we do anything else, we make a point of looking at the entire image at a 100% view to make sure that we haven't created any problems. If we find a stray noisy pixel, we may just spot it out with the Rubber Stamp tool, or we may decide to redo the sharpening to avoid the problem.

It's a temptation, especially with Unsharp Mask, to zoom in to see the effects more closely. Resist! Especially when you're just getting used to unsharp masking, you should only pay attention to the 1:1 zoom factor.

Tip: Recalling the Filter. If you don't like the results of the filter after seeing them, you can press Command-Z to undo, then Command-Option-F to reopen the filter's dialog box with the last-used settings. (This works with all filters that have user-settable parameters, but we use it more with Unsharp Mask than with any other filter.)

Tip: Fade Filter. If your sharpening is a little too strong, you can reduce the effect of the Unsharp Mask (or any other) filter using the Fade command from the Filter menu (see "Filters and Effects" in Chapter 15, *Essential Image Techniques*). This is one of the best uses of Fade we've come across.

Everything's Relative

One of the most important concepts to understand about sharpening is that the three values you can set in the Unsharp Mask dialog box are all interrelated. For instance, as you increase the Radius setting, you generally need to decrease Amount to keep the apparent sharpness constant. Similarly, at higher Radius settings, you can use much higher Threshold values; this smooths out unwanted sharpening of fine texture, while still applying a good deal of sharpness to well-defined edges.

Correction versus Targeting

Figuring out how the Unsharp Mask filter works is only half the problem, though. The other half is figuring out what you need to do to the image at hand. There are two things you can do with unsharp masking.